Roots of the Republic

ROOTS OF THE REPUBLIC

American Founding Documents Interpreted

Stephen L. Schechter, Editor

Richard B. Bernstein and Donald S. Lutz, Contributing Editors

Published for
The New York State Commission on the
Bicentennial of the United States Constitution

In cooperation with
The Center for the Study of Federalism
Temple University
and
The Council for Citizenship Education
Russell Sage College

MADISON HOUSE

Madison   1990

LIBRARY OF CONGRESS CATALOGING-IN-PUBLICATION DATA

Roots of the Republic : American founding documents interpreted /
edited by Stephen L. Schechter, with the assistance of Richard B.
Bernstein. — 1st ed.
p.   cm.
"Published for the New York State Commission on the Bicentennial
of the United States Constitution with the support of the Center for
the Study of Federalism, Temple University."
Includes bibliographical references (p.   ) and index.
ISBN 0-945612-20-6 — ISBN 0-945612-19-2 (pbk.)
1. *United States—Politics and government—Colonial period, ca.
1600–1775*—Sources.   2. United States—Politics and government—
Revolution, 1775–1783—Sources.   3. United States—Politics and
government—1783–1809—Sources.   4. New York (State)—Poliitcs and
government—Colonial period, ca. 1600–1775—Sources.   5. New York
(State)—Politics and government—Revolution, 1775–1783—Sources.
I. Schechter, Stephen L., 1945–   . II. Bernstein, Richard B., 1956–   .
III. New York State Commission on the Bicentennial of the United States
Constitution.   IV. Temple University, Center for the
Study of Federalism.

E187.R66   1990   90-6396
973.2—dc20   CIP

ISBN 0-945612-20-6 (HC)
ISBN 0-945612-19-2 (PBK)

Designed by William Kasdorf

Typeset in Caslon and produced for Madison House
by Impressions, Inc., P.O. Box 3304, Madison, WI 53704

Published by Madison House Publishers, Inc.
Post Office Box 3100
Madison, Wisconsin 53704-0100

FIRST EDITION

Contents

Introduction   1

I. The Mayflower Compact, 1620   17
    Commentary by Donald S. Lutz

II. The Fundamental Orders of Connecticut, 1639   24
    Commentary by Donald S. Lutz

III. The Ten Farms Covenant, 1665   36
    Commentary by Stephen L. Schechter

IV. The New York Charter of Liberties, 1683 and 1691   47
    Commentary by John M. Murrin

V. The New York City Charter, 1686   83
    Commentary by Leo Hershkowitz

VI. The Albany Plan of Union, 1754   106
    Commentary by Thomas E. Burke

VII. John Adams's Thoughts on Government, 1776   118
    Commentary by Richard B. Bernstein

VIII. The Declaration of Independence, 1776   138
    Commentary by Donald S. Lutz

IX. The Virginia Declaration of Rights and Constitution, 1776   150
Commentary by Donald S. Lutz

X. The New York State Constitution, 1777   166
Commentary by Stephen L. Schechter

XI. The Massachusetts Constitution, 1780   188
Commentary by Richard B. Bernstein

XII. The Articles of Confederation, 1781   227
Commentary by Donald S. Lutz

XIII. The Northwest Ordinance, 1787   249
Commentary by Peter S. Onuf

XIV. The United States Constitution, 1787   266
Commentary by Donald S. Lutz

XV. *The Federalist* on Federalism, 1787–1788   291
Commentary by Stephen L. Schechter

XVI. *The Federalist* on Energetic Government, 1787–1788   335
Commentary by Richard B. Bernstein

XVII. Antifederalist Essays and Speeches, 1787–1788   381
Commentary by Ralph Ketcham

XVIII. The Bill of Rights, 1791   423
Commentary by John P. Kaminski and Richard B. Bernstein

Afterword
Thomas Jefferson's Letter to Roger D. Weightman, 1826   441
Commentary by Richard B. Bernstein

Appendix
Catalog of American Founding Documents   449
Compiled by Donald S. Lutz

Index   455

Contributors   463

Acknowledgments

This book has been a dream of mine for many years. It began to take shape at a teacher institute, "Classic Works of American Federal Democracy," held in Big Sky, Montana, in the summer of 1984, with the assistance of a grant from the National Endowment for the Humanities. Organized by the Center for the Study of Federalism at Temple University, the workshop provided various opportunities for collegial exchange on the value of teaching with documents and the need for a collection of founding documents planned for classroom use. Three workshop instructors and good friends—Daniel J. Elazar, Donald S. Lutz, and I—resolved to find some way to put together such a collection.

Several years later, I became executive director of the New York State Bicentennial Commission. At the Commission, Stephanie A. Thompson (the Commission's education coordinator) and I coordinated ten teacher courses in New York State as part of a national program, "The Constitution: Our Written Legacy," on the teaching of constitutional documents, administered by the National Constitution Center with a grant from the federal Commission on the Bicentennial of the United States Constitution. Working with New York teachers, we found the need for a documentary history which brought together the colonial and early constitutional documents of New York and the Union.

At about that time, Donald Lutz and I participated in a federalism colloquium for teachers co-sponsored by the Center for the Study of Federalism and Liberty Fund, in Bloomington, Indiana, where we met John J. Patrick of Indiana University. Donald and I spoke with John about our earlier commitment and resolved to begin preparing commentaries and documents for use in one of the courses that Stephanie and I were teaching. The sample documents and commentaries were well received, and we determined to organize a full collection.

As work progressed on the publication, my appreciation of two colleagues grew to awesome heights. One of the greatest pleasures of this project is the opportunity I have now to express my thanks to Richard B. Bernstein and Donald S. Lutz who wrote the lion's share of this book. Working with these two good friends and colleagues on this project has been a great joy. As research director of the Commission, Richard also was of immeasurable assistance at various levels in editing this manuscript.

I also owe a special debt to those at the Commission who helped in the preparation of this publication. Cynthia Shorts, Margaret Gordon-

Cooke, and Tracy Sinnott typed my commentaries and other parts of the manuscript, while Shirley A. Rice and Stephanie A. Thompson assisted in the copyediting of the entire manuscript. I also want to take this opportunity to thank the chairman of the New York State Bicentennial Commission, Chief Judge Sol Wachtler, for his inspiration and support for this project.

Dean John E. Sexton of New York University School of Law provided Richard Bernstein with the office support needed to work on this and other Commission publications. Richard and I both express our thanks to Dean Sexton, to his staff (Karen Stember, Eva M. Memon, April Holder, Rhonda Malvey, and Alessandra Messineo), and to the collegial advice offered to Richard by Professors John Phillip Reid and William E. Nelson, and by Dennis G. Combs.

After the manuscript was submitted to Madison House, my indebtedness grew, as did my gratitude. William E. Kasdorf, president of Madison House, has treated this manuscript with a special care rare among chief executive officers. His associate, Gregory M. Britton, has been of great help in the final editorial stages of the manuscript, as has John P. Kaminski, who has been a coach on this project from the beginning.

A final word of thanks to Russell Sage College which I rejoined midway through this project. I thank the administration for its support, my colleagues for their advice, and Victoria R. Burns and Wendy A. O'Dea for typing the Introduction.

Troy, New York   S.L.S.

Introduction

ONE HUNDRED YEARS AGO, PROFESSOR WOODROW WILSON addressed the Owl Club in Hartford, Connecticut, on the occasion of the centennial of the establishment of the national government. Wilson observed:

> Our democracy, plainly, was not a body of doctrine: it was a stage of development. Our democratic state was not a piece of developed theory, but a piece of developed habit. It was not created by mere aspirations or by new faith; it was built up by slow custom. Its process was experience, its basis old wont, its meaning national organic oneness and effective life. It came like manhood, as a fruit of youth.

Wilson's organic metaphor suggests one way of understanding the American constitutional experience—a model that naturally came to mind in an era preoccupied by Darwinian theories of the natural world and the social order. At about the same time, however, the great Liberal Prime Minister of Great Britain, William E. Gladstone, made his famous distinction between the English constitution as "the most subtle organism which has proceeded from progressive history" and the United States Constitution as "the most wonderful work ever struck off at a given time by the brain and purpose of man."[1]

---

[1] Woodrow Wilson, "Nature of Democracy in the United States," May 17, 1989, in Arthur S. Link, ed., *The Papers on Woodrow Wilson* (Princeton, N.J., 1969), 6: 229; William E. Gladstone, "Kin Beyond Sea," *North American Review* 127 (September 1878): 185. For

Then as now, our commemorations of the origins of the Constitution—and our arguments over how the Constitution should be interpreted—are dominated by the clash between the organic vision of the
Constitution as the product of centuries of growth, development, and interpretation, and the "intentionist" vision of the document emphasizing
the Founding Fathers' calculated, purposeful design of government *de
novo* based on fixed political principles.

The title of this collection, *Roots of the Republic: American Founding
Documents Interpreted*, embodies this conflict of interpretations. "Roots"
can convey an organic sense of the republic as a seed planted and taking
root. By contrast, the term "founding documents" suggests that, as a
matter of doctrine and institutional history, the American republic was
called into existence out of a blueprint of fixed principles by the far-
seeing deliberations of the Founders.

Neither view is complete or wholly satisfactory. The organic view
implies that one can somehow find special republican seeds and that republics can only grow if one plants those seeds in the right soil and tends
them as some sort of outside "gardener" removed from the actual process of growth and development. The organic view thus fails to recognize
the importance of human creativity in the invention and development of
government. On the other hand, although the intentionist or doctrinal
view does envision a central role for human beings in the human process
of framing, adopting, and administering government, it implies that
these governments sprang forth from carefully contrived plans as if the
participants knew exactly what they were doing and exactly what they
wanted their handiwork to accomplish. The doctrinal or intentionist
model thus affords little room for serendipity, compromise, or the other
unplanned consequences of human experiments in self-government.

As the following pages of text and interpretation make clear, the
contributors to this volume believe that it is best to understand American
founding documents as the product of the clashing and commingling of
habit and doctrine. The documents presented here span 170 years, from
the beginning of the seventeenth century to the end of the eighteenth
century. Some texts, such as the Ten Farms Covenant, leave the reader
with the distinct impression that their founders, knowing exactly what
they were doing, adopted and adapted a pre-configured template of community and polity. Other texts, notably the early attempts at constitution-making in 1776 and 1777 by the new states and the young Confeder-

---

a useful discussion of the organic and other metaphors of the Constitution, see Michael
Kammen, *A Machine That Would Go of Itself: The Constitution in American Culture* (New
York, 1986).

ation, convey a sense of experimentation and uncertainty; the template of polity and community in these instances was simultaneously developed and applied. Finally, the handiwork of the Founders of 1787–88 fits neither model exactly, yet has features in common with both. Such metaphors and models are too risky as comprehensive descriptions of this range of experience; nonetheless, if used with care and sensitivity, they enable the reader to appreciate the challenges inherent in founding a polity based on ideas of popular consent, limited government, and the rule of law.

This publication introduces the reader to the original texts of some of the basic documents of early American history. Our objective is twofold: to enable the reader to learn how to read those documents, and to catalyze an interest in reading other documents in order to comprehend the various types and meanings of founding documents. To these ends, a commentary preceding each document introduces the reader to the text, its historical context, and its original meanings, as well as suggesting how to read the text. With two noted exceptions, each text is presented in full and literal form, with all misspellings, extra verbiage, and inconsistencies.[2] Where a particular word, phrase, or provision of the documentary text needs explanation, we provide that additional information in the commentary or in a footnote to the text.

Why read founding documents? How should one read them? Why have we included certain documents and not others? And what can one learn from these documents? This introduction seeks to answer the first three questions; the reader can derive answers to the last from the body of this book.

Why Read Founding Documents?

Alexander Hamilton began *The Federalist* with this challenge:

> It has been frequently remarked, that it seems to have been reserved to the people of this country, by their conduct and example, to decide

---

[2] Except in the New York City Charter, certain vagaries of early American English (both written and printed) have been eliminated—for example, the thorn (ye), the tilde, superscript abbreviations, and the long and short "s." The seventeenth-century uses of "u" instead of "v" and of "i" instead of "j" also have been modernized. Unintelligible words and phrases are interpreted in brackets.

The only exceptions to the policy of presenting complete texts are that one or two brief passages are omitted from the Fundamental Orders of Connecticut and that extraneous points have been omitted from the reprinted speeches of Patrick Henry and Melancton Smith. All omissions are indicated by ellipsis marks.

the important question, whether societies of men are really capable or not, of establishing good government from reflection and choice, or whether they are forever destined to depend, for their political constitutions, on accident and force.[3]

Since the beginning of the seventeenth century, the Americans have founded and refounded their political societies, from small settlements and colonies to a large nation, by "reflection and choice" more than by "accident" or the natural growth and development of communities. American foundings reflect at least five profound influences: the colonial mission of a "covenantal people"; the Enlightenment ideal of rational choice; the republican principles of popular consent and limited government; the principle of the rule of law derived from the Anglo-American common-law tradition; and the federal principle of organizing polities by distributing and sharing power between general and constituent governments. The reader can trace these ideas in the two stages of the founding process brought together in this collection—namely, the foundations laid over the course of our colonial history and the constitutional foundings of the Revolutionary period.

As to Hamilton's third alternative, Americans have rarely used "force" in the traditional sense of founding empires by conquest and inclusion. In fact, many of the founding documents presented here are based on the idea of inclusion by voluntary compliance as expressed through such devices as the oath of allegiance. However, Americans have used force to exclude conquered or subjugated peoples—namely, Native Americans and African-Americans—from what the historian Henry Adams called the "political population."[4] Further, in critical times such as the American Revolution and the Civil War, loyalty oaths and disputes over citizenship were used as political weapons. This was especially true of the harsh measures taken by the new Revolutionary governments against both the Loyalists and those who sought to remain neutral during the Revolutionary War.[5]

---

[3] The Federalist No. 1 in Jacob E. Cooke, ed., The Federalist (Middletown, Conn., 1961), 3.

[4] For this phrase, see chapter one of Henry Adams, History of the United States during the Administrations of Thomas Jefferson and James Madison (1889–91; 1986).

[5] See generally James H. Kettner, The Development of American Citizenship, 1607–1870 (Chapel Hill, 1975); Kenneth Karst, Belonging to America (New Haven, 1989); David H. Mainwaring, Render Unto Caesar: The Flag Salute Cases (Chicago, 1962); Harold M. Hyman, Era of the Oath (Berkeley, 1954); and Harold M. Hyman, To Try Men's Souls: Loyalty Oaths in American History (Berkeley, 1960). On the Loyalists, see, e.g., Claude H. Van Tyne, The Loyalists in the American Revolution (1902; Gloucester, Mass., 1959); William H. Nelson, The American Tory (Boston, 1961); and Robert McC. Calhoon, The Loyalists in Revolutionary America (New York, 1971).

These documents provide important clues about how their drafters, self-conscious founders, faced the task of establishing civil societies along republican lines. John Adams captured the intellectual element of the founder's challenge, when he observed in the conclusion of his pamphlet *Thoughts on Government* (reprinted in this collection):

> You and I, my dear Friend, have been sent into life, at a time when the greatest law givers of antiquity would have wished to have lived.— How few of the human race have ever enjoyed an opportunity of making an election of government more than of air, soil, or climate, for themselves or their children.—When! Before the present epocha, had three millions of people full power and a fair opportunity to form and establish the wisest and happiest government that human wisdom can contrive?

Expressing the views of most Americans of the Revolutionary generation, Adams began *Thoughts on Government* by rejecting Alexander Pope's famous epigram:

> For forms of government let fools contest,
> That which is best administered is best.[6]

Adams countered, and his contemporaries agreed: "Nothing is more certain from the history of nations, and the nature of man, than that some forms of government are better fitted for being well administered than others."

What continuities of the founding experience cut across the generations from 1620 to 1790? What discontinuities, new circumstances, and changing conceptions of constitutional government distinguish the experiences of founding a new commonwealth at Plymouth, extending the Puritan empire into Connecticut and New Netherland, securing a charter of liberties from the Crown, declaring independence from the mother country, establishing independent state polities, framing a confederation of those polities, and reshaping that system into a stronger national union? How do the ideas and instruments of consent, choice, and constitution-making evolve over these generations? Toward what specific ends were these founding documents directed, and how well did the founders accomplish the ends sought? The answers to these questions provide some of the reasons for reading these documents.

[6] Alexander Pope, *An Essay on Man*, Epistle III, ll. 303–4.

How to Read Founding Documents

The first step in reading a document is to decide what type of document it is. Once we determine a document's type, it is easier to identify its purposes and parts.

The documents in this collection are of four basic types: agreements, charters, constitutions, and commentaries.[7] The simplest and most basic is the *agreement*, under which parties agree, whether by contract, compact, or covenant, to come together or combine for a specified purpose or purposes. Typically, the purposes of such an agreement are to create a new people, establish a new government, and set forth the basic values or principles shared by the people.

In reading an agreement, we can expect to find a statement of principles, an enumeration of purposes, language embodying the act of agreement (often following the words, "We, therefore, do . . . "), and a list of the parties (or signers) and witnesses. If God is enlisted as a major party or witness, or is implicated in a purpose, then the agreement is a *covenant*. For example, the Mayflower Compact and the Ten Farms Covenant are clearly covenantal agreements, while the Declaration of Independence is a national compact in that representatives of the states came together for the purpose of declaring the reasons for their separation from British rule.

A second type of founding document is a *charter*. This type of public document grants certain rights in the law (or exemptions from the law), or incorporates certain entities, or both; inasmuch as such an agreement is the formal instrument conveying a gift from the sovereign to an individual, a group of individuals, a community, or a colony, it is often called a "patent."[8] Typically, an agreement and a charter are alternative ways of creating a people and a government. The agreement is normally understood to subsist between co-equal parties or partners; the charter in colonial times took the form of a hierarchical grant from the Crown or its agent to its subjects, organized in a given form. The line between agreements and charters is blurred, but not erased, when an agreement is formed by an oligarchy or when a colonial charter is prepared by duly elected representatives of the people.

---

[7] The discussion in this section draws on Donald S. Lutz, *The Origins of American Constitutionalism* (Baton Rouge, La., 1988), 13–22, 35–38.

[8] Our modern understanding of the term "patent"—that is, a federal grant of exclusive rights to an invention or process for a specified term of years—is but one kind of "patent" under the English constitution and common law.

According to Donald S. Lutz, a colonial charter usually contains eight elements:[9]

> The identification of a grantor; the creation or identification of a grantee; a statement of the reasons for the grant; a statement of what was being granted; the license or exclusive use given by the grant; a statement of how the grant was to be administered; specific restrictions or limits on the grant; and the reciprocal duties owed the grantor by the grantee.

A third type of founding document is a *constitution*, in which parties agree to come together *and* to frame a government. It is an agreement *plus* a framework of government, or a charter *as* a framework of government. Hence, the Fundamental Orders of Connecticut (1638–39) is an agreement plus a constitution of the inhabitants and residents of three towns to "assotiate and conjoyne our selves to be as one Publike State or Commonwelthe . . ." By contrast, the New York Charter of Liberties (1683) is "granted by his Royall Highnesse to the Inhabitants of New Yorke . . . For better Establishing the Government of this province of New Yorke and that Justice and Right may be Equally done to all persons within the same [.] " Clearly, this is a charter as a constitution.

This collection contains three levels of constitutions. The first consists of constitution-like community agreements and city charters which founded civil communities; the second embraces colonial charters and state constitutions; and the third includes attempts to establish a union of those colonies (as in the proposed Albany Plan of Union), states (as in the Articles of Confederation, which was our first constitution), or peoples of the several states (as in the United States Constitution of 1787). Documents categorized at the third level are not necessarily more complex than those at the other levels. As we have just seen, the Fundamental Orders of Connecticut is a confederation of towns, while many state constitutions contain lengthy and often complex provisions regarding the organization (or incorporation) and powers of local governments. Regardless of the level, the reader should look for certain standard elements in a constitution:[10]

Creation of a people, including provisions on the nature of citizenship and how it is acquired, the rights and responsibilities of citizens, and the rights and responsibilities of other residents.

Creation of a government, including provisions for its name (or "style"), form (for example, confederation, federal republic, etc.), au-

---

[9] Lutz, *Origins*, 35.
[10] The first four elements are drawn from Donald Lutz's commentaries in this collection.

thority of the constitution (for example, popular sovereignty, as in "We the People . . . "), locus of sovereignty (typically residing in the constitutional authority), and constituting parties (that is, the parties represented by the framers, often symbolized by the framers' signatures).

Establishment of the principles of association, including statements of the ends of association and the operating principles of governance. (These statements are often contained in a preamble of the constitution, or in a declaration of intent which may be attached to the constitution.)

Framework of governmental institutions, including provisions for lawmaking, administration of the law, and adjudication of cases arising under the law. We might expect to find such frameworks reflecting the modern doctrine of separation of powers (as set forth in its most familiar form in Article XXX of the Declaration of Rights of the Massachusetts Constitution of 1780), this doctrine took its modern form only after a long and complex history.[11] Thus, most of the constitutions in this volume assign governmental functions in a variety of ways, often involving complex power-sharing arrangements, taking forms that seem confused and unfamiliar to our eyes. The modern reader may have to hunt for all the pieces of the allocation system. Whether or not that system is governed by strict separation of powers, its constitutional framework should contain the following elements:

Representation and consent, providing for voter eligibility, requirements for holding elective public office, electoral procedures, nature of the representational system (for example, proportional, single-member, and so forth), and the basis for reapportionment of legislative districts.

Arrangement of offices, setting out elected and appointed offices and establishing qualifications, duration, and other relevant characteristics of those offices.

Powers of government, including provisions for the powers and limits of those governmental institutions created by the constitution, the areas of competence or jurisdiction within which those powers may be exercised, and the process and organization through which those powers are wielded.

Relations with other governments, including a "supremacy" clause or, as in the Articles of Confederation, an "abide-by" clause; possibly provisions governing the creation and regulation of constituent governments (whether those be state or local); and perhaps procedures for incorporating and regulating public corporations.

---

[11] See generally William B. Gwyn, *The Meaning of the Separation of Powers*, Tulane Studies in Political Science, IX (1965), and M. J. C. Vile, *Constitutionalism and the Separation of Powers* (Oxford, England, 1967).

Ratification and amendment procedures, for bringing the constitution into effect and for its subsequent amendment. Amendment provisions were not commonplace until the 1780s.

If some of these elements are missing, the framers may have intended to leave the constitution incomplete. Indeed, in a federal system, composed of constituent and federal (or confederal) constitutions, both types of constitutions may well be incomplete because each type is intended to complement the other. Framers also omit elements of a constitution because they deem them irrelevant, inappropriate, or politically sensitive. Finally, it is possible that constitution-makers simply overlook the need to include certain elements.

Keeping these elements in mind as we read a constitution enables us to identify the various provisions of a given constitution and to compare constitutions. For example, the outline set forth in Figure 1 makes it possible to compare the structural similarities of the Articles of Confederation and the Constitution of 1787.

The fourth type of founding document is a *commentary*: a book, pamphlet, speech, or newspaper essay combining the functions of advocacy and interpretation. Included in this collection are such commentaries as essays from *The Federalist*, selected Antifederalist speeches and essays, and John Adams's *Thoughts on Government* (1776), which examines the nature of constitutions and governments.

Although varying in form, commentaries provide important clues into the founders' conceptions of civil society and of the principles and institutions upon which civil society is best founded. The concise yet illustrative commentaries on American constitutional government presented here are only the tip of the iceberg. In fact, the interested reader can turn to a variety of commentaries, legislative histories, correspondence, and other material for further insights into the reflections and choices of the Revolutionary generation that founded the American republic.

Why These Documents?

The American system was built by scores of documented acts of founding. These founding documents have become part of the American people's political and cultural heritage. Founding documents not only perform vital political functions; their drafters recognized the importance of addressing posterity as well. Donald S. Lutz has identified 170 American founding documents; his list, reprinted in the Appendix, includes 86 constitution-like documents written by American colonists

Figure 1
Comparative Outline of the Articles of Confederation
Cross-Referenced to the U.S. Constitution

Confederation Articles	Provisions	Constitution Articles
Preamble	Nature of Compact & Parties	Preamble
Article I	Name of Union	Preamble
Article II	Locus of Sovereignty	Preamble
Article III	Ends of Union	Preamble
Article IV	Interstate Relations	Article IV
Article V	Congress: Organization and Elections	Article I, 1–7
Article VI	State Limits	Article I, 10
Article VII	Raising Army; Appointing Officers	Article I, 8
Article VIII	Revenue; Appropriations	Article I, 8
Article IX	Congress: Powers	Article I, 8
Article IX	Congress: Limits	Article I, 9
Article IX	Judiciary	Article III
Article X	[Executive] Committee of the States	Article II
Article XI	Admission of Canada, New States	Article IV, 3
Article XII	Assumption of the Debt of Prior Congress	Article VI
Article XIII	"Abide-by" Supremacy Clause	Article VI
Article XIII	Amendment Procedure	Article V
Article XIII	Ratification Procedure Names of Signers	Article VII

before 1722, 42 constitution-like documents written in England for the colonists before 1735, 24 proposals for federating or uniting the colonies or the states, and 18 early state constitutions.

The documents reprinted in this volume are only a sampling of American founding documents, chosen for their *heuristic* or illustrative value as means to introduce the reader to the process of reading and interpreting founding documents. We hope that this collection will inspire further investigation of the much larger body of founding documents and commentaries on those basic texts of the American political tradition.

Where the "obligatory documents"—that is, those documents that virtually every student of American constitutional history would include—are insufficient in number or variety, we have added selected New York documents. Our choices have been guided by three reasons. First, this writer is a native New Yorker and most familiar with the New York founding experience. Second, this collection is published for the New York State Commission on the Bicentennial of the U.S. Constitution, which is sponsoring it in order to provide New Yorkers with a better understanding of their state's political tradition and of the American founding experience of which it was a part. Third, New York has been unjustly neglected by most constitutional historians, even though its political and constitutional tradition was a prototype of the United States Constitution of 1787 and the model of the commercial republic on which it was based.

As noted above, we have attempted to include all of the obligatory founding documents. The collection begins with the Mayflower Compact (1620) because it was the first covenant struck in the New World and because it provided a model and framework for the extension of the Puritan empire. The Fundamental Orders of Connecticut (1639) is the first written constitution in the New World and one of the instruments used in extending that empire.

Although the Ten Farms Covenant (1664) is hardly a landmark founding document, it nicely illustrates three important points: the use of a covenant to found a local civil community; the dilution or adaptation of covenantal principles in the second generation of the Puritan empire; and the meeting of Puritan and Dutch cultures on the eve of the English invasion of New Netherland. By contrast, the New York City Charter of 1686 shows how, twenty years later, another local community was refounded by a royal charter that was the result of complex negotiations between the city fathers and Royal Governor Thomas Dongan. At the same time, New York's provincial leaders proved less successful in obtaining a colonial charter of liberties both before and after the Glorious Revolution of 1688. Nonetheless, John M. Murrin's commentary on the New York Charter of Liberties provides an excellent case study of the constitutional expectations and politics of a pluralistic colonial society operating without a charter.

The Albany Plan of Union illustrates an important shift in focus from colonial foundings to intercolonial relations. This dimension of the American founding experience began not with the Albany Congress of 1754 but with the formation of the New England Confederation in 1643. The Albany proposals occurred midway through a list of approximately two dozen proposals for federating or uniting the colonies or states, even though they were developed over a century after the first. As Thomas E. Burke shows in his commentary, the importance of the Albany Congress is that its vote on a plan of union "represented the consensus of opinion of the most representative and politically capable and experienced body of colonials from the thirteen colonies to meet prior to the Stamp Act Congress of 1765." Moreover, addressing as it does both the means and the ends of union through federation as of 1754, the Albany Plan of Union is a useful reference point for considering subsequent plans of union through federation embodied in the Articles of Confederation, the Northwest Ordinance, and the United States Constitution.

John Adams's *Thoughts on Government* introduces the modern reader, as it did the reader of 1776, to the great challenge of constitution-making. Adams intended this commentary to serve as a constitution-maker's guide, and his intended readers so regarded it. The pamphlet aided constitutional drafters, and others of the Revolutionary generation, to think constitutionally about the impending necessity to refound the colonies as independent states. The sketch it presented of a model state constitution both served as a model for several states (including his own state of Massachusetts) and provided a basis for politicians in other states to attack more radical state constitutions (such as Benjamin Rush's strictures on the Pennsylvania Constitution of 1776).

Thoughts on Government was published not a moment too soon. Within a month of its first appearance, the Second Continental Congress adopted a resolution on May 10, 1776, which

> recommended to the respective Assemblies and Conventions of the
> United Colonies, where no Governments sufficient to the exigencies
> of their affairs has been hitherto established, to adopt such Govern-
> ment as shall in the opinion of the Representatives of the People best
> conduce to the happiness and safety of their Constituents in particular,
> and America in general.

Even before the adoption of this resolution, which authorized the colonists to supersede their royal charters, Americans began to frame constitutions and establish constitutional governments at an unparalleled rate. New Hampshire was the first, adopting a provisional constitution in January of 1776. Only two states did not write new constitutions; Rhode Island and Connecticut instead revised their old royal charters to remove all references to Great Britain. The ideological poles in the American state constitutions are represented by the Pennsylvania Constitution of 1776, which lodged the powers of government in a unicameral legislature and did not even create an independent executive, and the Massachusetts Constitution of 1780, which was the first to provide explicitly for a separation of powers among the legislative, executive, and judicial branches, and which served as a model for most of the state constitutions drafted in the late 1780s and afterward. This collection presents the state constitutions of Virginia, New York, and Massachusetts to illustrate the progression of constitutional thought in the states during the Revolutionary era.[12]

While state lawmakers were wrestling with the problems of constitution-making, the Second Continental Congress adopted the Declaration of Independence, debated and approved the Articles of Confederation, and submitted the Articles to the states for ratification. The Articles were then debated in the states at the same time that the processes of writing and implementing state constitutions continued. By 1781, therefore, this set of documents—the Declaration, the Articles, and the state constitutions—comprised the first American constitutional system. Each component of that system satisfied a distinctive yet complementary constitutional need. The Declaration created a people and set forth its goals and principles of government; the Articles of Confederation framed and authorized the general government; and the state constitutions framed and authorized the constituent governments. At the same time, these documents, in articulating the thinking of the American people about the constitutional principles and the politics of their day, were manifestations of an emerging American political culture.

The final set of documents in this collection illustrate the establishment of the second American constitutional system. This system, while replacing the first, did not overthrow it altogether. Rather, we can understand its establishment in retrospect as a reformulation of the first. For example, the Northwest Ordinance of 1787 was enacted by the Confederation Congress as the culmination of a prolonged debate over western lands. At the same time, this legislation established the framework of the American territorial system; when joined with Article IV of the United States Constitution of 1787, this ordinance made it possible to admit new states and to expand the American republic without risking the dangers of a new colonial system. Also, the United States Constitution of 1787 neatly replaced the Articles of Confedera-

---

[12] See generally Donald S. Lutz, *Popular Consent and Popular Control: Whig Political Theory and the State Constitutions* (Baton Rouge, La., 1980); Willi Paul Adams, *The First American Constitutions* (Chapel Hill, 1980); and Edward S. Corwin, "The Progress of Constitutional Theory between the Declaration of Independence and the Meeting of the Philadelphia Convention," *American Historical Review* 30 (1925): 511–36.

tion, fitting into place with the Declaration of Independence and the existing state constitutions. This second system was completed on December 15, 1791, when Virginia's ratification of the Bill of Rights added the first ten amendments to the federal Constitution.[13]

The reformulation of the American constitutional system took nearly five years, from the calling of the Federal Convention by the Confederation Congress in February of 1787 to Virginia's ratification of the Bill of Rights in December of 1791. Its evolution was the result both of constitutional design and of political compromise. The selections from *The Federalist* included in this volume present the most sophisticated and influential statement of the Framers' constitutional design of republican government. We present them in two groups. The first focuses on the traditional emphases of *Federalist* scholarship—limiting the power of government to preserve liberty. This group explains the virtues of the extended republic, the combination of national and federal elements needed to maintain liberty in a federal system, and the Constitution's use of doctrines of separation of powers and checks and balances to complement the delicate balance of federalism. The second group focuses on a vital feature of the Constitution and the Federalists' case for it overlooked in most modern examinations of "Publius"—the need for energetic government and, in particular, for a vigorous executive and a strong judiciary.

The Antifederalist commentaries presented here trace an alternative constitutional design of republican government. As Ralph Ketcham explains in his commentary, the Antifederalists not only opposed the Constitution, but they had "a positive vision of what the government of the United States should be—a republican vision which they thought was far closer to the principles and goals of the American Revolution than the political and commercial ambitions of the Federalists." For Ketcham, then, "[t]he ratification contest . . . was at bottom a debate over the future of the nation. Beneath the disputes about detailed clauses were deep differences over what fulfillment of the American Revolution meant."

Although there is no comprehensive Antifederalist commentary comparable to *The Federalist*, these Antifederalist speeches and essays

---

[13] Documents in this collection are dated by their ratification, except for the United States Constitution (which is most widely known by the date of September 17, 1787, when it was signed in Convention) and the New York Charters of Liberties of 1683 and 1691 (which were never approved). The only documents in this collection which were drafted and ratified in different calendar years are: the Articles of Confederation (1777/ 1781), the United States Constitution (1787/1788), and the United States Bill of Rights (1789/1791).

show how Antifederalist spokesmen countered arguments presented in *The Federalist* and in other pro-Constitution publications. For example, Patrick Henry's speeches challenged the arguments in *The Federalist No. 1* for a stronger union, while *Centinel No. 1*, questioning the value of diversity, disputed the argument of *The Federalist Nos. 10* and *51*. "Brutus" argued against the new conception of federalism presented by "Publius" in *The Federalist Nos. 37* and *39* and against the case for an independent judiciary offered in *The Federalist No. 78*, while Melancton Smith proposed a populist alternative to Alexander Hamilton's argument for a vigorous executive as the centerpiece of an energetic general government in *The Federalist No. 70*.

The Antifederalists' strongest argument against the Constitution was that it lacked a declaration of rights. Such Federalists as Alexander Hamilton (in *The Federalist No. 84*), James Madison, and James Wilson argued that a federal bill of rights not only was unnecessary, as the federal government had no power to injure rights, but could be dangerous, because it might omit some rights, leave other rights insufficient protection, and damage state declarations of rights. Despite these qualms, moderate Federalists recognized the demands of political necessity and agreed to work to amend the Constitution to add a bill of rights. The framing and adoption of the Bill of Rights marked the end of the first stage of the constitution-making of the founding period.

Conclusion

Our final selection is a valedictory—the last letter written by Thomas Jefferson. He wrote to Mayor Roger D. Weightman of Washington, D.C., on June 24, 1826, ten days before the fiftieth anniversary of the Declaration of Independence. In what started as a polite expression of regret that he could not attend the city's commemoration of the jubilee of the Declaration, Jefferson stressed the Declaration's larger significance, and the significance of the Revolution it inspired, for human history: "May it be to the world, what I believe it will be, (to some parts sooner, to others later, but finally to all,) the signal of arousing men to burst the chains under which monkish ignorance and superstition had persuaded them to bind themselves, and to assume the blessings and security of self-government." He continued:

> All eyes are opened, or opening, to the rights of man. The general
> spread of the light of science has already laid open to every view the
> palpable truth, that the mass of mankind has not been born with

saddles on their backs, nor a favored few booted and spurred, ready to ride them legitimately, by the grace of God. These are grounds of hope for others. For ourselves, let the annual return of this day [July Fourth] forever refresh our recollections of these rights, and an undiminished devotion to them.

Especially at the time this book appears, in the aftermath of what are already being called the "revolutions of '89" (revolutions that invoked the examples of the American and the French Revolutions),[14] no brighter light, no clearer meaning, no wider hope can be cast over the American founding experience.

[14] For a superb eyewitness account, see Timothy Garton Ash, *The Magic Lantern: The Revolution of '89 Witnessed in Warsaw, Budapest, Berlin and Prague* (New York, 1990), a sequel to Timothy Garton Ash, *The Uses of Adversity: Essays on the Fate of Central Europe* (New York, 1989). It is suggestive, in the context of the subject of the present volume, that the original British edition of *The Magic Lantern* was entitled *We the People* . . . (Cambridge, England, 1990).

I

The Mayflower Compact

1620

COMMENTARY BY DONALD S. LUTZ

THE DOCUMENT WE NOW KNOW as the "Mayflower Compact" originally did not have a title, but was known informally by the settlers as "The Plymouth Combination," or simply "The Combination." An historian from New York City published it in 1793, and not only did he give those outside of Plymouth a first look at the document, but he also named it the "Mayflower Compact."

The various names all imply the same thing. Those signing this document were agreeing to combine themselves into a new people, or, as they put it, into a new "civil body politick." No one ever referred to the document as a "contract," for this would have implied that their relationship was temporary or only partial. Instead, they were compacting a new people into a stable and lasting polity.

The forming of a tightly knit community was important to them for they were stepping into a hostile wilderness with no European neighbors, few tools, little food, and no hope of further help from England for at least six months. They understood that a few years earlier the first English colony at Roanoke, Virginia, had disappeared without a trace, and that the weather and terrain at Plymouth looked worse than at Roanoke. They would live or die together, as a group. This, their founding document, was an attempt to forge the kind of cooperative community that could survive through joint effort.

It is little wonder that the very first thing in their compact was a call upon God to witness the agreement. They were a religious people used to starting their documents in this way; but also, they surely felt that they needed all the help they could get. By calling upon God as a witness to the agreement, those signing it were bound by an oath much the same way as witnesses in courts today take an oath to tell the truth. Breaking the oath threatened eternal punishment. They were compacting themselves into an inseparable unit ordained and sanctioned by God.

While they hoped to become inseparable, they also hoped to preserve what we call freedom, and what they called liberty. They had come to America for religious liberty; and central to their notion of liberty was the ability to create and run their own churches independent of the Church of England. The Puritans, like many of the people who migrated to America during the 1600s, had a relatively democratic way of organizing their churches. First they would form a church by having all members sign a document known as a church covenant. Then they would elect a council of elders to run the church. Even the minister was elected, or hired, by the congregation. Church matters were often subjected to vote by the membership. All in all, members of the church had much to say about how things were run. When it came to forming political institutions, the Pilgrims borrowed the notion of liberty and the instrument of the covenant.

What is the difference between a Puritan and a Pilgrim? England during the 1600s witnessed the rise of many Protestant sects which sought to overcome the power of the Church of England. They wished to purify the Church by ridding it of what they considered false doctrines, pompous liturgy, the use of statues and idols, and an attempt to prohibit free exercise of religion. Above all, they wished to focus much more upon the Bible as the basis for religion. Because they wished to *purify* the Church of England, these various groups were together known as Puritans.

A few of the more radical sects wished to establish a Christian commonwealth—a political system run on the basis of the Bible. When it became clear that they would never accomplish this in England, they planned to establish a pure city in America based on God's word. Christians who traveled to Jerusalem were called pilgrims, and hence those sects seeking the New Jerusalem were dubbed Pilgrims. The Pilgrims who came to America on the *Mayflower* belonged to one of these more radical Puritan groups who wished to create a new city of God—a society run according to the dictates of the Bible. Most of those who came to America for religious freedom were not radical Pilgrims, but Congregationalists, Presbyterians, Baptists, Quakers, and a wide range of Puritans.

There were no lawyers on board the *Mayflower* but there were ministers. The one kind of document with which they were familiar was the church covenant. They literally took the form and language of the church covenant and substituted "civil body politick" for "church." In reading the Mayflower Compact, substitute "church," and the document turns once more into a church covenant.

The idea of covenant had been taken by Christians from Hebraic law in the Old Testament. A covenant had two important elements. First, it called upon God as a witness. Second, it rested upon each member consenting to be a member. This second ingredient meant that even though a new, indivisible group was formed, its members were still a free people who continued to act through their own consent. This is the basic idea of a covenant—to create a new entity that is indivisible but still preserves the freedom of those agreeing to it.

The Latin word for covenant is *fœdus*, and it is from this word that we get "federalism." It is clear that federalism as a principle of government was present from the very beginning of government in America. The Mayflower Compact was a covenant and therefore a federal document. The idea of federalism would later evolve into the notion of combining *communities* rather than of individuals, but in either case federalism means the same thing—the creation of a new, larger entity out of many smaller ones in a way that simultaneously makes the larger entity indivisible, yet preserves the freedom of the smaller units. In the case of the Mayflower Compact, the larger entity was the "civil body politick." The smaller units were the individuals signing the covenant. These individuals not only created the government through their own consent; they continued to run the government by consenting to their officers (leaders), laws, and constitutions.

During the 1600s, over 100 other founding documents similar to the Mayflower Compact would be written by American colonists. Some of these agreements would create single settlements, while others (such as the Fundamental Orders of Connecticut) would join several existing covenanted communities into a broader association. In each case the people created by the agreement would be identified by those who signed the document. It is a peculiarly American trait that founding documents like the Declaration of Independence and the United States Constitution have signatures at the end. This expectation is part of the legacy of early agreements like the Mayflower Compact; just as "We the People" is derived from "We the undersigned."

Some signed their name as "Mr." and others did not. This title usually implied a gentleman—a person of somewhat higher social status than a commoner, but not a member of the aristocracy. Since this title was not conferred by the king or anyone else, one could choose to use it or not as one wished. If others felt someone was claiming more prestige than was his due, he might be considered pretentious or a social climber for using it, although no one could be prevented from using this title. A minister, someone with a college degree, a professional, or someone with a modest amount of land might use the title as their due.

Note that there were no signatures of women. Under the practice of the day, women were considered to give their consent through their husband, father, brother, son, or some other male legally responsible for them. Women were not considered morally inferior and were even accorded membership in churches. Since it was impossible at that time for non-aristocratic women to be economically independent, however, they were unable to assert their moral, political, or social independence outside of the family. Children did not sign for another reason—they were not yet responsible adults. The practice of having someone sign for others who were dependent upon him was known as *virtual representation*. It was often the case in England that adult men who were tenant farmers, who did not own land and thus were not economically independent, or who for physical reasons could not support themselves were represented virtually by some other male.

However, in this instance, all of the adult males signed. Indeed, no man was allowed to leave the ship until he had signed. Records are not entirely clear, but it appears that almost half of the signers were not Pilgrims. Some came from less rigorous or fervent Puritan groups, and a few were not even religious, but the Pilgrims wanted to bind these men with an oath to the welfare of the Pilgrim community. These men had been needed to make up a full passenger list so the costs of the ship sailing to America could be covered. The *Mayflower* had languished for a time in Plymouth, England, because the Pilgrims could not at first find enough of their own community to go. Ironically, the signature requirement was extended to several indentured servants who normally would not have been considered able to consent on their own because they were dependent economically upon their masters.

Considered as a whole, the Mayflower Compact accomplished a number of important, interrelated things. First, it *created a new people*— of those "whose names are underwritten." Not everyone aboard the *Mayflower* was a Pilgrim, but once they or their representatives signed the compact they all became members of the new community of New Plymouth. An essential part of relationships in a federal system created by a political covenant is that new additions are just as much a part of the system as the first members. For this reason, newer states like Alaska entered the Union on an equal footing with Massachusetts and other original states. We take the political equality of its members for granted today, but it was an historically important innovation. With the Mayflower Compact we see its first expression.

Second, the Mayflower Compact also *created a government* when it combined them into a civil body politic. Put another way, the signers created a society, and then they created a government for that society. About seventy-five years later, John Locke published his *Second Treatise on Government* in which he described civil society resting upon the consent of its members as expressed in a compact. He used the word "compact," not contract. This compact created a society and then a government for that society. On the *Mayflower* we find the colonists doing essentially everything that Locke would later recommend. Since no other agreement in history had done this before, the Mayflower Compact, like the Declaration of Independence 150 years later, played out the design of Enlightenment theories of state.

Third, the Mayflower Compact *laid out the fundamental values and commitments of a people.* The Pilgrims were a religious people. They were a free people who based things on their own consent. They believed in justice and equality (at least for propertied white males), were law-abiding, and had a strong commitment to the community. Individualism had not yet supplanted community as a motivating ethic. Their statement of values evolved into the bills of rights contained in early state constitutions found elsewhere in this volume. There is a clear, direct lineage between the value statements in the early colonial political compacts and covenants and later bills of rights.

A modern constitution performs all three of these functions plus one more—*it describes the political institutions for making community decisions.* The Mayflower Compact does not describe any political institutions and thus is not really a constitution. The second document in this volume, the Fundamental Orders of Connecticut, accomplished all of these things and became the first true written constitution in the modern world.

For Further Reading

Andrew C. McLaughlin. *The Foundations of American Constitutionalism.* New York, 1932.

Clinton Rossiter. *Seedtime of the Republic: The Origin of the American Tradition of Political Liberty.* New York, 1953.

Samuel Eliot Morison. *Builders of the Bay Colony.* Boston, 1930.

[The Mayflower Compact]

[November 11, 1620]

In the Name of God Amen. We whose names are underwriten, the loyall subjects of our dread soveraigne Lord King James[1] by the grace of God, of great Britaine, Franc, and Ireland king, defender of the faith, &c.

Having undertaken, for the glorie of God,[2] and advancements of the Christian faith and honour of our king and countrie, a vouage to plant the first Colonie in the Northerne Parts of Virginia,[3] doe by these presents[4] solemnly & mutualy in the presence of God, and one of another, covenant & combine our selves togeather into a civil body

---

The original Mayflower Compact is no longer extant; the text survives only in the manuscript of Governor William Bradford's *History of Plimoth Plantations*. The text given above is reprinted by permission of the publisher from Samuel Eliot Morison's edition, *Of Plymouth Plantation, 1620–1647* by William Bradford (New York: Alfred A. Knopf, Inc., 1952), copyright © 1952 by Samuel Eliot Morison and renewed 1980 by Emily M. Beck. Following Morison, the only alterations made to the original text as Bradford reported it are silent renderings of "u" and "v" and "i" and "j" to modern spelling.

Capitalization was a common practice in the early 1600s. Similar to a language like German, a capital letter began many nouns or important words. They were not always consistent in this practice.

[1] The word "dread" was usually used to imply deep awe or reverence. The Pilgrims did not want to anger the king so they portrayed themselves as loyal subjects and used a polite form of address. They did not fear him; more likely they did not like him because of his religious convictions.

[2] God's glory is mentioned before the king's honor because as a religious people they saw this as most important, followed by spreading the Christian religion. The honor of king and country came third in this hierarchy.

[3] Virginia is mentioned because they were supposed to have gone to Virginia. The land in front of them did not yet have a name. In fact, they were not entirely certain where they were, except that they were too far north. "Northern parts of Virginia" seemed as good a name as any. Some historians argue that the Pilgrims landed north of Virginia on purpose in order to place themselves outside of the provisions of the Virginia charter and thereby to gain independence. Whether this is accurate or not, while the spot where they landed was outside of the officially chartered colony of Virginia, it was on land claimed by the king of England. Thus it was only a matter of time before they came under a similar charter. Massachusetts is a name derived from the name of the Indian tribe that inhabited the area they settled. Since the Indians had no alphabet, and since the English did not know how to translate the Indian name into English, a variety of spellings were used, including "Masatusenets." It was half a century before the modern spelling was officially adopted.

[4] Here "presents" means "formal statements."

politick; for our better ordering,[5] & preservation & furtherance of the ends aforesaid;[6] and by vertue hearof to enacte, constitute, and frame,[7] shuch just & equall lawes, ordinances,[8] Acts, constitutions, & offices, from time to time, as shall be thought most meete[9] & convenient for the generall good of the Colonie: unto which we promise all due submission and obedience.

In witnes whereof we have hereunto subscribed our names at Cap-Codd the * 11 * of November, in the year the raigne of our soveraigne Lord King James of England, France, & Ireland the eighteenth and of Scotland the fiftie fourth. Anno Dom. 1620.

Mr. John Carver

Mr. William Bradford	Mr. Samuel Fuller	
Mr. Edward Winslow	Mr. Christopher Martin	Edward Tilly
Mr. William Brewster	Mr. William Mullins	John Tilly
Isaac Allerton	Mr. William White	Francis Cooke
Myles Standish	Mr. Richard Warren	Thomas Rogers
John Alden	John Howland	Thomas Tinker
John Turner	Mr. Steven Hopkins	John Ridgdale
Francis Eaton	Digery Priest	Edward Fuller
James Chilton	Thomas Williams	Richard Clark
John Craxton	Gilbert Winslow	Richard Gardiner
John Billington	Edmund Margesson	Mr. John Allerton
Joses Fletcher	Peter Brown	Thomas English
John Goodman	Richard Britteridge	Edward Doten
	George Soule	Edward Liester

[5] "Better Ordering" means here to bring better law and order.

[6] "Ends aforesaid" refers to the ends or purposes mentioned earlier—advancement of the Christian faith, etc.

[7] They could not just say "enact" instead of "enact, constitute, and frame." Civil societies enact laws, constitute a form of government, and frame ordinances. They should also have said "elect" since one does not enact, frame, or constitute officers.

[8] "Frame ordinances" signifies what we today would term "codification," as in the creation of particular "codes" such as an education code or a building code. After a number of laws have been passed, they are often organized into a set of ordinances which brings all the laws on a given topic together in one place and puts them in a logical order. Otherwise they remain scattered through the records of the legislature. A logically ordered set of ordinances was often called a frame—sometimes a frame of government. The term ordinances was synonymous with statutes.

[9] "Meet" means "in conformity with our wishes."

II

The Fundamental Orders
of Connecticut

1639

COMMENTARY BY DONALD S. LUTZ

CONNECTICUT BEGAN AS TWO COLONIES—each a cluster of towns. The Colony of Connecticut was in the center of what is now the state and consisted in 1639 of three towns—Hartford, Windsor, and Wethersfield. To the south, along the coast, the Colony of New Haven was composed of the towns of New Haven, Guilford, Milford, Stamford, Branford, and Southold. The last town was across Long Island Sound and on Long Island, which is now part of the State of New York. Each town in these two colonies had its own government, based upon a document much like the Mayflower Compact. In 1639, the three towns in the Colony of Connecticut decided to form a common government while at the same time preserving each town government. When several independent governments agree to form a common government with certain powers binding on all of them, yet at the same time retain certain powers for exclusive use by the constituent governments upon which the common government is based, the relationship between general and local governments is one based upon the principle of federalism. We could examine any one of over 100 colonial documents to learn about the basic origins of American constitutionalism. The Fundamental Orders of Connecticut, however, is a good place to start because not only was it the first constitution in America; it also created the first federal political system of colony-wide proportions, thereby extending the principles set out a generation earlier in the Mayflower Compact.

In 1643, the Colony of New Haven also created a federal system. Both colonies grew, and by 1662 the Colony of Connecticut also included the towns of Saybrook, New London, Fairfield, and Norwalk as well as East Hampton and South Hampton on Long Island. This demonstrated one of the great advantages of federalism—it makes possible the addition of new parts as equal partners under the common government. When the United States Constitution was written in 1787, it too created a federal system which allowed the addition of new states to the original thirteen as equal partners. There was nothing in European political theory or practice from which these two central principles of American constitutionalism could have been derived—they were derived from colonial governments created by the colonists. The Fundamental Orders of Connecticut was only the first of many federal systems created by the colonists. Many of the original thirteen states were built from many towns or counties banding together in a federal structure.

On April 23, 1662, the king of England, Charles II, signed a new charter for the Colony of Connecticut. Under it, the colonies of Connecticut and New Haven merged. The charter preserved almost exactly the same government as the colonists had created with the Fundamental Orders. When the final town agreed to join under the charter in 1665, the Colony of Connecticut took the final shape known today as the State of Connecticut, and it was governed according to the system originally set out in the Fundamental Orders of Connecticut.

This form of government was so successful that when Connecticut became an independent state in 1776, it simply readopted the 1662 charter as its state constitution. The only changes made were to delete all references to the king and to change the title from Charter of 1662 to Constitution of 1776. This means that the Fundamental Orders of Connecticut passed in 1639 was now a true state constitution, one that would remain in effect until replaced by a new constitution in 1818. Thus, the Fundamental Orders of Connecticut provided a form of constitutional government for 179 years.

Rhode Island followed a similar pattern of creating a colony-wide government out of many towns, using its charter of 1663 to reaffirm the form of government created earlier, and then, in 1776, without even readopting it or changing its name, pretending as if its charter had been a constitution all along. Other states created new constitutions in 1776 or 1777, but these new constitutions were based heavily upon the institutions each state had developed as a colony, institutions that were usually federal in design and therefore preserved local government intact. It is no wonder, then, and hardly an accident that when the states formed a common government for the United States, it too would be federal in design and preserve much political power for exclusive use by state governments.

The Fundamental Orders is a compact much like the Mayflower Compact, although it is not a covenant since God is not called upon to witness the agreement. (1) It creates a new people—the people of Connecticut. (2) It creates a new government—the Commonwealth of Connecticut. (3) It lays out the basic values shared by the people who are religious, peaceful, orderly, liberty-loving, and committed to equality, majority rule, and the common good. (4) It also lays out the basic political institutions in addition to the above, and is thus also a constitution.

The document also follows the cycle of a legislative calendar which ascribes communal ritual to the polity. Consider the basic outline of the institutions and processes of government.

A. The legislature was called the General Court. The General Court met twice a year beginning on specified days in April and September, although it could be called into special session more often. It passed laws, but was also involved in elections.

B. Beginning on the second Thursday of September, the General Court first put together a list of candidates for governor and magistrates to be elected at the next session the following April. Each town was allowed to nominate two candidates for magistrate, and these names were brought to the General Court by the town's deputies. The General Court was allowed to add more names during the September session. Then it passed any needed laws.

C. Beginning on the second Thursday in April, the General Court met again, and its first item of business was to hold elections. Then it passed laws. The entire meeting, involving both activities, was called the Court of Election. A meeting of the General Court usually lasted for only a day or two—at least during the seventeenth century.

D. The General Court consisted of a governor, at least six magistrates, and four deputies from each town.
   1. The deputies were elected by the inhabitants of their town to represent the town in the legislature (General Court). This was a very broad suffrage since an eligible voter did not need to own property or even be a freeman. It was understood that the suffrage applied only to adult males, although the language logically includes adult females as well. To be eligible for nomination, one must have been a freeman in that town. The four names with the most votes won, and this was a plurality.

2. The deputies elected the magistrates from a list of candidates put together by the General Court at the previous fall session. A candidate for magistrate must have been a freeman. The result was a kind of bicameral legislature in which the lower house of deputies elected the upper house of magistrates. Majority rule was used to ratify the nominations unless six failed to muster majority support. In this case, the next highest vote-getters were elected using plurality rule.

3. The governor was also elected by the deputies from a list compiled at the previous fall session. The governor was viewed as the chief magistrate. To be eligible for governor one had to have been a magistrate and a member of an approved church. The governor was elected by a plurality vote.

E. All elected officials served one-year terms; magistrates and deputies could serve more than one year in a row; however, the governor could not serve two consecutive terms.

Beyond this basic overview of the institutions, several observations can be made about the system of government created by the Fundamental Orders.

First, the General Court included all three parts of the government which met together. Between meetings of the General Court, the governor managed the government, and the other magistrates met fairly often to advise and assist the governor. In the days before strict separation of powers, it was not uncommon for various parts of governmment to meet together as a legislative body.

Second, the towns continued to have their own governments. The town meetings, composed of its freemen, elected a mayor and a town council, often called a council of selectmen. The mayor functioned exactly like the governor on the local level, and the selectmen functioned locally exactly as the magistrates did at the colony level. Deputies stood in for the town freemen at the colony level through direct elections.

Next, the towns were linked in a common government, yet they retained a certain amount of local freedom. The colony-wide government rested upon the consent of the town inhabitants, as did the town governments. Freemen were simultaneously citizens of a town and of the colony. The result was a very modern federal system.

Fourth, the powers of the general government were specifically listed in Article 10 of the Fundamental Orders of Connecticut in a fashion similar to that found in the United States Constitution. Included were the powers to grant levies (the power to tax), to make laws for the common good and repeal those not in the common good, to settle land disputes between towns, and to punish crimes.

Fifth, there was a supremacy clause similar to that found in the United States Constitution. The Fundamental Orders said in Article 10: In which the General Courts *"shall consist the supreme power of the Commonwelth. . . ."* Article VI of the Constitution says: "This Constitution, and the Laws of the United States which shall be made in Pursuance thereof; and all the Treaties made, or which shall be made, under the Authority of the United States, shall be the supreme Law of the Land. . . ."

Unlike the Mayflower Compact, the Fundamental Orders of Connecticut used a system of representation; and, like the United State Constitution, it distinguished between representatives of local majorities and representatives who represent an entire people.

Finally, the entire government rested upon an operating commitment to popular sovereignty. The people had the right and ability, if the governor and magistrates did not call a session of the General Court, to assemble and constitute themselves. Ultimate political power rested with the people. This commitment to popular sovereignty was startling in the context of the times. First, there was nothing in English common law that resembled popular sovereignty. Instead, parliamentary sovereignty has been as far as Britain would go, even to this day. Also, there was not yet a good theory of popular sovereignty. John Locke would develop such a theory, but he was only seven years old in 1639. And yet American colonists were already using much of what would go into the United States Constitution 150 years later, including the most fundamental assumption of all—popular sovereignty.

For Further Reading

Charles McLean Andrews. *The Colonial Period of American History.* 4 vols. New Haven, 1936, 2: 94–113.

Mary Jeanne Anderson Jones. *Congregational Commonwealth: Connecticut, 1636–1662.* Middleton, Conn., 1968.

Perry Miller. *Errand into the Wilderness.* Cambridge, Mass., 1956.

Robert J. Taylor. *Colonial Connecticut: A History.* Millwood, N.Y., 1979.

[The Fundamental Orders of Connecticut]

[1639]

Forasmuch as it hath pleased the Allmighty God by the wise disposition of his divyne providence so to Order and dispose of things that we the Inhabitants and Residents of Windsor, Harteford and Wethersfield are now cohabiting and dwelling in and uppon [upon] the River of Conectecotte [Connecticut] and the Lands thereunto adjoyneing; And well knowing where a people are gathered together the word of God requires that to mayntayne the peace and union of such a people there should be an orderly and decent Government established according to God, to order and dispose of the affayres of the people at all seasons as occation [occasion] shall require; doe therefore assotiate [associate] and conjoyne our selves to be as one Publike State or Commonwe[a]lth; and doe, for our selves and our Successors and such as shall be adjoyned to us at any tyme hereafter, enter into Combination and Confederation togather, to mayntayne and presearve the liberty and purity of the gospell of our Lord Jesus which we now professe, as also the disciplyne of the Churches, which according to the truth of the said gospell is now practiced amongst us; As also in our Civell Affaires to be guided and governed according to such Lawes, Rules, Orders and decrees as shall be made, ordered & decreed, as followeth:—

1. It is Ordered, sentenced and decreed,[1] that there shall be yerely [yearly] two generall Assemblies or Courts,[2] the on[e] the second thursday in April, the other the second thursday in September, following;[3]

Reprinted from Francis Newton Thorpe, ed., *The Federal and State Constitutions, Colonial Charters, and Other Organic Laws ... of the United States,* 7 vols. (Washington, D.C., 1909), 1: 519–23. Some sections of the document have been omitted because of their length.

[1] "Ordered," "sentenced," and "decreed" essentially all meant "commanded," although in each case a different body was implied. Decisions promulgated by the executive were decrees, those by the judiciary were sentences, and those by the legislature were orders or laws. The formulation thus implies that all branches of government are in agreement with the decision and are bound by it.

[2] The legislature was called a "court," or the General Court. This should not be confused with a court of law with judge and jury.

[3] Read this to say "the following September."

the first shall be called the Courte of Election, wherein shall be yerely Chosen from tyme to tyme soe many Magestrats and other publike Officers as shall be found requisitte;[4] Whereof[5] one to be chosen Governour for the yeare ensueing and untill another be chosen, and no other Magestrat to be chosen for more than one yeare; provided allwayes there be six chosen besid[e]s the Governour; which being chosen and sworne according to an Oath recorded for that purpose[6] shall have power to administer justice according to the Lawes here established, and for want thereof according to the rule of the word of God;[7] which choise shall be made by all that are admitted freemen[8] and have taken the Oath of Fidellity, and doe cohabitte[9] within this Jurisdiction, (having beene admitted Inhabitants by the major part of the Towne wherein they live,)[10] or the major parte of such as shall be then present.[11]

[4] "Requisitte" means "needed" or "necessary." Examples of other officers later found to be needed were a treasurer, a keeper of records (called a coroner), a secretary for the legislature, peace officers, keepers of weights and measures, surveyors of highways, tax collectors, and many other officers we now associate with government. Note that today all of these other offices are usually appointed, whereas colonial Connecticut elected them just as they did the members of the legislature.

[5] "Whereof" usually meant "of whom," which in this context is not very enlightening. The governor should be one of the magistrates, not in the sense that he must be elected from one of the currently elected magistrates, but in the sense that he will be added to the magistrates if he is not already one. The magistrates, as we shall see, are elected one way, while the governor is elected in another and could well be someone who is not currently a magistrate, but upon his election becomes one. However, the governor must have been a magistrate in the past, if he is not now.

[6] The oath for the governor was "recorded" at the end of the Fundamental Orders. The United States Constitution also has an oath that the chief executive must take, providing another example of constitutional borrowing from an early colonial document where there was no equivalent in Europe or the English common law.

[7] In other words, if there is no law available to govern some matter that arises, the colonists will consult the Bible for guidance.

[8] A freeman was an adult male whom a town permitted to live, work, and own property within its boundaries. In effect, he was free to come and go as he pleased. This does not mean that the rest were slaves, but that they needed permission from the town to do certain things. A person was made a freeman by majority vote of the town freemen already living there. This was a way of controlling the actions of outsiders. After proving one's productivity and trustworthiness, a person would be made a freeman. The concept of granting all people rights regardless of their economic status, gender, race, or ethnicity is a relatively recent development in the history of constitution-making. To include women in this process, for example, would be out of the social context of 1639.

[9] "Cohabitte" meant "inhabit with the rest of the freemen."

[10] According to Thorpe, "This clause has been interlined in a different handwriting, and at a more recent period" (p. 520).

[11] "Major parte" means "majority."

2. It is Ordered, sentensed and decreed, that the Election of the aforesaid Magestrats shall be on this manner; every person present and quallified for choyse[12] shall bring in (to the persons deputed to receave them) one single paper with the name of him written in yt [it] whom he desires to have Governour, and he that hath the greatest number of papers shall be Governor for that yeare.[13] And the rest of the Magestrats or publike Officers to be chosen in this manner: The Secretary for the tyme being[14] shall first read the names of all that are to be put to choise and then shall severally nominate them distinctly, and every one that would have the person nominated to be chosen shall bring in one single paper written uppon, and he that would not have him chosen shall bring in a blanke: and every one that hath more written papers than blanks shall be a Magistrat for that yeare;[15] which papers shall be receaved and told[16] by one or more that shall be then chosen by the court and sworne to be faythfull therein; but in case there should not be sixe chosen as aforesaid, besid[e]s the Governor, out of those which are nominated, then he or they which have the most written papers shall be a Magestrat or Magestrats for the ensueing yeare, to make up the aforesaid number.[17]

3. It is Ordered, sentenced and decreed, that the Secretary shall not nominate any person, nor shall any person be chosen newly into the Magestracy which was not propownded [propounded][18] in some

[12] Read this to say "qualified to be chosen."

[13] To be elected governor one needed a plurality of votes, not a majority of the votes cast. Candidates for governor were nominated at the Court the previous September. Elections were held in April at the Court of Election, where each person brought a piece of paper with the name of his selection from among those nominated. No campaigning was permitted, even though voters had all winter to consider their choice. The nominee named on the most pieces of paper won the election.

[14] Read "The Secretary for the tyme being" to mean "The temporary secretary."

[15] Candidates for this position.

[16] One or more people present will be selected to read the pieces of paper, count the number of each with a given name, as well as the blanks, and "tell" who has won.

[17] Candidates for these positions were also nominated at the Court that met the previous September (this now being April). The secretary reads off the name of the first nominee. Everyone hands in a piece of paper. If the paper has the nominee's name written on it, it is a "yes" vote. If the paper is a blank, it is a "no" vote. If there are more "yes" votes than "no" votes, the candidate is elected a magistrate. In effect, the vote is whether or not a person is suited for the job, not whether he is better than another person. Then, the name of the second nominee is read. Everyone hands in a paper again. If he gets more "yes" votes than blank papers he becomes a magistrate. The process continues through all the nominees. Note that there can be more than six magistrates, but there must be at least six. If the secretary stops reading the names after six are elected, the place of one's name on the list is critical since those at the bottom will never be reached. Over time, this is what happened.

[18] Whose name was not put forth as a potential candidate.

Generall Courte before, to be nominated the next Election; and to that
end yt shall be lawfull for e[a]ch of the Townes aforesaid by their
deputyes to nominate any two whom they conceave fitte to be put to
election; and the Court may ad[d] so many more as they judge requisitt.

4. It is Ordered, sentenced and decreed that noe person be chosen
Governor above once in two yeares,[19] and that the Governor be always
a member of some approved congregation, and formerly of the Magestracy within this Jurisdiction; and all the Magestrats Freemen of this
Commonwelth. . . .[20]

5. It is Ordered, sentenced and decreed, that to the aforesaid Courte
of Election the severall Townes shall send their deputyes, and when
the Elections are ended they may proceed in any publike searvice as
at other Courts. Also the other Generall Courte in September shall be
for makeing of laws, and any other publike occasion, which conserns
the good of the Commonwelth.

6. It is Ordered, sentenced and decreed, that the Governor shall,
e[i]ther by himselfe or by the secretary, send out summons to the
Constables of every Towne for the cauleing [calling] of these two standing Courts, on[e] month at le[a]st before their severall tymes; And
also if the Governor and the gre[a]test parte of the Magestrats see
cause uppon any spetiall [special] occation to call a generall Courte,
they may give order to the secretary soe to doe within fowerteene
[fourteen] dayes warneing; and if urgent necessity so require, uppon
a shorter notice, giveing sufficient grownds for yt to the deputyes when
they meete, or els[e] be questioned for the same; And if the Governor
and Major parte of Magestrats shall e[i]ther neglect or refuse to call
the two Generall standing Courts or e[i]ther of them, as also at other
tymes when the occations of the Commonwelth require, the Freemen
thereof, or the Major parte of them, shall petition to them soe to doe:
if then yt be e[i]ther denied or neglected the said Freemen or the
Major parte of them shall have power to give order to the Constables
of the severall Townes to doe the same, and so may meete togather,
and chuse to themselves a Moderator, and may proceed to do any Acte
of power, which any other Generall Courte may.

[19] He can serve more than once, but must take off at least one year between each
term of office.

[20] Every governor had to be a former magistrate, and every magistrate had to be
a freeman in one of the towns. Each governor also had to be a member in good standing
of some recognized church. Jews and Catholics were not at first among the recognized
churches, nor were Quakers. Almost all other Protestant churches, including Baptists,
were recognized. By 1776 there were no specific restrictions on the few Catholics and
Jews in Connecticut, although their chances of being elected governor were still zero.

7. It is Ordered, sentenced and decreed that after there are warrents given out for any of the said Generall Courts, the Constable or Constables of e[a]ch Town shall forthwith give notice distinctly to the inhabitants of the same, in some Publike Assembly or by goeing and sending from howse to howse [house to house], that at a place and tyme by him or them lymited [limited] and sett, they meet and assemble them selves togather to elect and chuse certen [certain] deputyes to be att the Generall Courte then following to agitate[21] the afayres of the cmmonwelth; which said Deputyes shall be chosen by all that are admitted Inhabitants in the severall Townes and have taken the oath of fidellity; provided that non[e] be chosen a Deputy for any Generall Cour[t]e which is not a Freeman of this Commonwelth.

The a-foresaid deputyes shall be chosen in manner following: every person that is present and quallifed as before expressed, shall bring the names of such, written in severall papers, as they desire to have chosen for that Imployment, and these 3 or 4, more or lesse, being the number agreed on to be chosen for that tyme, that have greatest number of papers written for them shall be deputyes for that Courte; whose names shall be endorsed on the backe side of the warrant and returned into the Courte, which the Constable or Constables hand unto the same.[22]

8. It is Ordered, sentenced and decreed, that Wyndsor, Hartford and Wethersfield shall have power, e[a]ch Towne, to send fower [four] of their freemen as deputyes to every Generall Courte; and whatsoever other Townes shall be hereafter added to this Jurisdiction, they shall send so many deputyes as the Courte shall judge meete,[23] a re[a]sonable proportion to the number of Freemen that are in the said Townes being to be attended therein; which deputyes shall have the power of the whole Towne to give their voats [votes] and al[l]owance[24] to all such lawes and orders as may be for the publike good, and unto which the said Townes are to be bownd [bound].

9. It is ordered and decreed, that the deputyes thus chosen shall have power and liberty to appoynt a tyme and a place of meeting togather before any Generall Courte to advise and consult of all such things as may concerne the good of the publike, as also to examine their owne Elections, whether according to the order, and if they or the

[21] "Agitate" here means to "discuss."

[22] This means that the four nominees with the most votes become the deputies from that town. They may or may not have a majority of the votes cast. The constable then certifies the winners on a warrant or deposition which is delivered to the General Court by him or by his agent.

[23] Appropriate or reasonable.

[24] Votes and permission, or consent.

gre[a]test parte of them find any election to be illegall they may seclud [exclude] such for present from their meeting, and rethrn [return] the same and their re[a]sons to the Courte; and if yt prove true, the Court may fyne [fine] the party or partyes so intruding and the Towne, if they see cause, and give out a warrant to go to a newe election in a legall way, either *in whole or* in parte. Also the said deputyes shall have power to fyne any that shall be disorderly at their meetings, or for not coming in due tyme or place according to appoyntment; and they may returne the said fynes into the Courte if yt be refused to be paid, and the tre[a]surer to take notice of yt, and to estreet or levy the same as he doth other fynes.

10. It is Ordered, sentenced and decreed, that every Generall Courte, except such as through neglecte of the Governor and the greatest part of Magestrats the Freemen themselves doe call, shall consist of the Governor, or some one chosen to moderate the Court, and 4 other Magestrats at le[a]st, which the major parte of the deputyes of the severall Townes legally chosen[25] . . . *shall consist the supreme power of the Commonwelth*, and they only shall have power to make laws ore repeale them, to graunt [grant] levyes,[26] to admitt of Freemen, dispose of lands undisposed of, to severall Townes or persons, and also shall have power to call e[i]ther Courte or Magestrate or any other person whatsoever into question for any misdemeanour, and may for just causes displace or deale otherwise according to the nature of the offence; and also may deale in any other manner that concerns the good of this common welth, excepte election of Magestrats, which shall be done by the whole boddy of Freemen: In which Courte the Governour or Moderator shall have power to order the Courte to give liberty of spe[e]ch, and silence unceasonable [27] and disorderly speakeings, to put all things to voate, and in case the vote be equall to have the casting voice.[28] But non[e] of these Courts shall be adjo[u]rned or dissolved without the consent of the major parte of the Court.

[25] The General Court consists of the governor, the magistrates (of which there are at least six), and a majority of the deputies elected by the towns. Initially, the three towns each elected four deputies for a total of twelve. A majority of twelve is seven, which makes a minimum of fourteen out of the nineteen members who must be present for a General Court to be legal: one governor plus six magistrates plus seven deputies. The entire General Court meets only twice a year, unless called into special session, while the magistrates meet intermittently throughout the year to assist the governor as a privy or private council.

[26] To levy taxes.

[27] Speaking out of turn without being recognized by the moderator. "Unceasonable" means both "out of turn" as in violation of the expected cycle, and "inappropriately" in the sense of not in keeping with expected behavior.

[28] In tie votes, the governor will cast the deciding vote.

11. It is ordered, setenced and decreed, that when any Generall Courte upon the occations of the Commonwelth[29] have agreed uppon any summe or somes [sum or sums] of money to be levyed uppon the severall Townes within this Jurisdiction, that a Committee be chosen to sett out and appoynt[30] what shall be the proportion of every Towne to pay of the said levy, provided the Committees be made up of an equall number out of each Towne.

14th January, 1638, the 11 Orders abovesaid are voted.[31]

The Oath of the Governor, for the [Present]

I N.W.[32] being now chosen to be Governor within this Jurisdiction, for the yeare ensueing, and until a new be chosen, doe sweare by the greate and dreadfull[33] name of the everliveing God, to promote the publicke good and peace of the same, according to the best of my skill; as also will mayntayne all lawfull priviledges[34] of this Commonwelth; as also that all whol[e]some laws that are or shall be made by lawfull authority here established, be duly executed; and will further the execution of Justice according to the rule of Gods word; so helpe me God, in the name of the Lord Jesus Christ.

[A similar oath for the Magistrates which follows is omitted.]

[29] Read this as saying "when any General Court, based upon the needs of the Commonwealth, . . ."

[30] "To sett out and appoynt" means "to determine."

[31] The calendar in use at the time began the new year with the equinox in March so that January was the eleventh month of the year previous to that in our counting. Thus, using today's calendar system the Fundamental Orders were approved January 14, 1639, not 1638.

[32] The initials represent the places to insert the first and last name of whichever governor is taking the oath. These particular initials have no meaning.

[33] "Dreadfull" was then a word of respect that also implied something way above the ordinary. The word "awesome" might also have been used. Recall the reference to the "dread" King James in the Mayflower Compact, footnote 1.

[34] "Priviledges" was sometimes used as a synonym for "rights," and is being so used here.

III

The Ten Farms Covenant

1665

COMMENTARY BY STEPHEN L. SCHECHTER

ON JUNE 24, 1664, Thomas Pell granted a parcel of land in what is now Eastchester, New York, to ten families from Fairfield, Connecticut. The following year, those ten families were joined by sixteen other families from Fairfield, and together they entered into an unusually detailed covenant governing the internal organization of their new civil community. The historical circumstances and text of this rather obscure document affords some insights into the founding of the covenantal community and its role in the development of the American constitutional system.

The Context

As recounted by local histories, the tale is plain enough.[1] In 1654, Thomas Pell bought a tract of land called West-Chester from the Indian sachem Ann-Hoock in the border territory under dispute between Dutch New Netherland and the Connecticut (Hartford) Colony.

Revised with permission of the Center for the Study of Federalism, Temple University, from Stephen L. Schechter, "From Covenant to Constitution in American Political Thought," *Publius* 10, no. 4 (Fall 1980): 173–83.
[1] For example, see Frederick Shonnard and W. W. Spooner, *History of Westchester County, New York* (New York, 1900).

Thomas Pell had been a gentleman in the bedchamber of Charles I. After migrating to the New World, he briefly settled in Fairfield. Refusing to take the Connecticut oath, he moved on to the disputed lands in what is today Westchester County, New York, where he established himself as an unlicensed land agent. The Indian sachem from whom he purchased the land had previously assumed the name, Ann-Hoock, after his most famous victim, Anne Hutchinson, slain nine years earlier near the site of Pell's transaction.

Pell quickly granted the parcel of land closest to New Amsterdam to a group of Connecticut and Long Island settlers who named their settlement "Westchester." In 1662, the year that Charles II granted a royal charter to Connecticut, the General Court of Connecticut accepted the membership of the new town of Westchester along with the towns of Guilford, Stamford, and Greenwich, and instructed the newly admitted towns to send their delegates and petitions to Fairfield. In 1663, the General Court granted Pell a license, recognizing his earlier land purchase and authorizing his additional purchase of adjacent lands to the east.

On June 24, 1664, Pell granted part of his additional purchase to the aforementioned ten families from Fairfield. Less than two months later, the English fleet sailed into the harbor of New Amsterdam; and after the Dutch surrender, King Charles II granted the former Dutch possessions to his brother James, the duke of York. In November 1664, representatives of the Duke of York and the Colony of Connecticut fixed the border of the two colonies, placing the nascent Ten Farms community of Eastchester under the jurisdiction of New York. The following year, the Eastchester settlers, then numbering twenty-six families, signed a detailed civil (not church) covenant; and in 1666 those families received a royal charter, recognizing Eastchester as a mere "plantation" (or settlement) within the town and court of Westchester.

Why did the Fairfield settlers migrate to Eastchester? Why did they covenant at Eastchester? What impact did the covenant have on the subsequent development of Eastchester? Unfortunately, historical records offer no clear answers to those questions, but we can offer several conjectures.

Why did the settlers migrate to Eastchester? In 1654, Thomas Pell was not the only one to leave Fairfield. In that same year, Roger Ludlow returned to England. Ludlow had been one of the original founders of the Connecticut Colony. In 1630, he was elected as an assistant to the Massachusetts Bay Company, and shortly after arriving in the New World he helped found Dorchester, Massachusetts (now in Boston). In 1634, he was elected deputy-governor. In 1636, he presided at the first court in Connecticut at Windsor, and the following year he led a Windsor expedition against the Pequots. In 1639, he led a band of Windsor settlers to the site of his previous expedition, founding the town of Fairfield near Long Island Sound at the outermost reaches of the then-Hartford Colony. That same year, Roger Ludlow is believed to have been principally responsible for the final wording of the Fundamental Orders of Connecticut. As the colony's only trained lawyer, he was requested by the General Court in 1646 to draft a body of laws for the governance of the colony. The result was the Code of 1650, known as "Ludlow's Code."

In 1653, the New England Confederation began considering the possibility of invading New Netherland. It seems that both Ludlow and the town of Fairfield were at the forefront of the forces for invasion. However, in 1653, Massachusetts Bay voted against invasion and the plan seems to have been halted then and there. Receiving news of this setback, Governor Eaton informed the New Haven General Court on November 22 that he had received "a letter from Mr. Ludlow, informing of a meeting they have had at Fairfield, at which they have concluded to goe against the Dutch, and have chosen him for their cheife and he hath accepted it."[2] Shortly thereafter, Ludlow returned to England and Fairfield's planned invasion was scrapped.

Ten years later, just before the English invasion of New Netherland, Fairfield, the stronghold of invasion enthusiasts, sent ten families to establish a town in the heart of New Netherland. Could this new town have been founded as a "fifth column" or "cultural beachhead" in disputed Dutch territory? The attraction to Eastchester was considerable. Thomas Pell, a former townsman, had established himself as a land agent, and other settlers from southwestern Connecticut had previously settled in Westchester County and Long Island. While there is no evidence to suggest whether Anne Hutchinson's burial site held any symbolic value, it is clear that the site was of strategic value, buttressing the eastern border of West-Chester. There also seems to have been various reasons for leaving Fairfield at that time. The Half-Way Covenant had been recently adopted despite vociferous opposition to its key provision allowing church membership for the grandchildren of saints without requiring evidence of the conversion of their parents. Elsewhere in Connecticut, at Hartford, Windsor, and Wethersfield,

[2] *New Haven Records, 1653–1665*, 47–48, as discussed in R. V. Coleman, *Mr. Ludlow Goes for Old England* (Westport, Conn., 1935), 17–18. For a further account of Ludlow's participation in colonial affairs, see Roy V. Coleman, *A Note Concerning the Formulation of the Fundamental Orders . . .* (Westport, Conn., 1934).

those in opposition to the Half-Way Covenant had left their churches and formed new ones or moved to new towns. This or some other equally wrenching controversy probably came to Fairfield, for in February 1664 the town imposed a fine for disorderly conduct in town meetings. There also was a dispute between Fairfield and a neighboring town over conflicting land claims. Like other Puritan towns at mid-century, Fairfield had more town residents than town members and more town members than church members; and the "half-way" solution of control over purity was undoubtedly as heated an issue as the continuing need for expansion and cheap land.[3] There is, however, no evidence to suggest that the Eastchester settlers left Fairfield in opposition to the Half-Way Covenant.

The Covenant

What type of local community did the Eastchester settlers establish and what functions did their covenant serve? Between their land purchase and their petition for a royal charter, the newly arrived Eastchester settlers drafted and signed a local covenant in the form of twenty-seven articles of agreement. Those articles (except for the twenty-first, which no longer exists or never existed) are presented at the end of this commentary. We also have reorganized and modernized those articles in a second presentation.

Preamble

The Ten Farms Covenant begins with the location of the covenanters' tract, a statement of "first principles," and the establishment of operating rules. The association created is neither a church nor an incorporated town, but an unincorporated civil community. Though the variety of rules set out suggests a general frame of governance, this document clearly does not serve the constitutional function of setting out a framework of government.

The first principles of this association are to keep and maintain Christian love and civil honesty and to deal plainly with one another. In secular terms, the covenant joins its signers to behave in a neighborly and law-abiding manner. These principles and their straightforward, bourgeois tone of moderation suggest that the Eastchester covenanters

---

[3] Richard L. Bushman, *From Puritan to Yankee* (Cambridge, Mass., 1967), 148.

were not among the diehard Puritans fleeing the liberalism of the Half-Way Covenant.

These and other articles can be traced back to the Letters of Paul. Pauline references are included in the covenant where relevant. Compare the reiteration in the Ten Farms Covenant of Paul's instructions—to love one's neighbor and follow the law—with the first principles of perfectionism set out in the earlier town covenant of Dedham, Massachusetts, which begins: "We whose names ar[e] here unto subscribed doe, in the feare and Reverence of our Allmightie God, Mutually and generally promise amongst our selves and each to other to profess and practice one trueth according to that most perfect rule, the foundation whereof is Everlasting Love."[4]

At the same time, there is an affinity between these two statements that stands in comparison, say, to the nineteenth-century statements of perfectionism found in John Humphrey Noyes's Oneida community. More distant still, but nonetheless interesting in comparison, is the statement of "first principles" found in the quintessential "moralistic civil community" of the nineteenth century—namely, the temperance community. Consider the following statement from the temperance charter of Longemont, Colorado, settled by the Chicago-Colorado Company:

> Industry, Temperance, and Morality are the watch-words of the Chicago-Colorado Company. . . . The requirement that ardent spirits shall neither be sold or manufactured on the Colony grounds, brings together an organized and select body, the moral part of mankind, who hitherto have always lived disassociated . . . a new class of men, stronger by reason of accumulated intellect . . . come together and clasp hands.[5]

Conflict and Consensus

The idea that a community can be founded on moral principles is clearly one of the basic hallmarks of the covenantal community. An equally distinctive trait is the application of those principles to the task of social control, particularly as concerns the processes of consensus building and conflict resolution. It was toward the goal of social control that the Half-Way Covenant, for example, had sought to liberalize church membership. The Eastchester model of third-party mediation (Article 5), mutual

---

[4] Quoted in Frank Smith, *A History of Dedham, Massachusetts* (Dedham, Mass., 1936), 7.

[5] Quoted in Page Smith, *As a City Upon a Hill* (Cambridge, Mass., 1973), 29.

self-criticism (Article 3), and regular meetings (Article 19) can be found in one form or another not only in the seventeenth-century Puritan village but also in the planned communalistic societies of the nineteenth and twentieth century. In fact, the Eastchester model (of meeting every other week, for one hour, once everyone is settled) seems particularly relaxed in comparison with earlier and later communitarian experiments. By comparison, the Dedham town covenant of 1636, characteristic of first generation New England covenants, provided: "That we shall by all meanes Laboure to keepe off from us all such as ar[e] contrarye minded. And receave onely such unto us . . . as may be probably of one harte, with us. . . ."[6]

By the nineteenth century, covenantal control mechanisms seem to have been reduced to something of a science. On admission, Shaker neophytes were required to make a complete and honest confession, as one elder wrote, "of every improper transaction or sin that lies within the reach of their memory." And John Noyes describes the control mechanisms on admission to his perfectionist communities as follows:

> The measures relied upon for good government in these community families are, first, *daily evening meetings*, which all are expected to attend. In these meetings, religious, social, and business matters are freely discussed, and opportunity given for exhortation and reproof. Secondly, *the system of mutual criticism*. This system takes the place of backbiting in ordinary society, and is regarded as one of the greatest means of improvement and fellowship. All of the members are accustomed to voluntarily invite the benefit of this ordinance from time to time. Sometimes persons are criticised by the entire family; at other times by a committee. . . .[7]

Land and Community Affairs

The Eastchester settlers were not looking to invent a "patent office model of the good society," to borrow Arthur Bestor's term.[8] Rather, the Eastchester settlers seemed more concerned with securing an upright and working agricultural community along the lines to which they were accustomed and which necessity demanded. It is perhaps for this reason that the Eastchester covenant resembles more a cultural umbrella

---

[6] Quoted in Frank Smith, *A History of Dedham*, 7.

[7] Quoted in Charles Nordhoff, *The Communistic Societies of the United States* (New York, 1875), 289.

[8] Arthur Bestor, "Patent-Office Models of the Good Society," *American Historical Review 53* (April 1953): 505–26.

or "a framework of the good society" than the earlier model, in Dedham and elsewhere, of the town covenant as "a matrix of perfection." Provisions for educating children (Article 14), constructing and financing public works (Articles 13 and 27), regulating land distribution and transfers (Articles 7–12 and 26), scheduling the sowing and planting of fields (Article 18), building fences and securing homes (Articles 17 and 24), protecting cattle (Articles 16 and 25), rotating guard duty on the Sabbath (Article 23), regulating the hosting of strangers (Article 15), and turning out once a year to kill rattlesnakes (Article 22) are necessary concerns for new settlers in a foreign land.

But why did the Eastchester settlers choose to transmit their cultural traditions and practical improvisations in the form of a covenant? It was not as if those settlers were unaccustomed to traveling. Many of their parents, after all, made the trek from England to Boston, from Boston to Windsor or Wethersfield, and from there to Fairfield, over a period of ten years. Undoubtedly, the Eastchester settlers believed that they were operating under extraordinary circumstances that required extraordinary precautions, located, as they were, in disputed territory and near the temptations of New Amsterdam. Basically, however, the Eastchester settlers were a covenantal people who expected to conduct their civic life in a covenantal way following what they believed to be the instructions of their God. Along the way, this and countless other acts of founding covenental communities would provide useful practice for the challenge of establishing constitutional societies a century later.

For Further Reading

Patricia U. Bonomi. *A Factious People: Politics and Society in Colonial New York.* New York, 1971.
Richard L. Bushman. *From Puritan to Yankee.* Cambridge, Mass., 1967.
Michael Kammen. *Colonial New York: A History.* New York, 1975.
Robert C. Ritchie. *The Duke's Province: A Study of New York Politics and Society, 1664–1691.* Chapel Hill, 1977.
Frederick Shonnard and W. W. Spooner. *History of Westchester County, New York.* New York, 1900.
Langdon G. Wright. "In Search of Peace and Harmony: New York Communities in the Seventeenth Century." *New York History* (January 1980): 5–21.
Langdon G. Wright. "Local Government in Colonial New York, 1640–1710." Ph.D. dissertation: Cornell University, 1974.

[The Ten Farms Covenant]

[1665]

Artickells of Agrement betwext us whos names are under writen 1665

1. Imprimus that we by the grace of God sitt down on the track of land lieng betwext Huchessons [Hutchinson's] broock whear the hous was untell it com unto the river that runeth in at the head of the meados——

2. That we indeavor to keepe & maintayn Christian love and sivell honesty——

3. That we faithfully consoall [counsel] what may be of infermyti in any one of us——

4. Plainlie to dealle one with another in Christian love——

5. If any trespas be don the trespasd and the trespaser shall chuse tow [two] of this Company and they A thirde man if need be required to end the mater without any further trubell——

6. That all & every one of us or that shall be of us do paye unto the minester acording to his meados and estat——

7. That non exed the quantity of 15 ackers untill all have that quantity——

8. That every man hath that meado that is most conveaniant for him

9. That every man build & inhabit on his home lot befor the next winter——

10. That no man make salle of his lott befor he hath built & inhabited one year & then to tender it to the Company or to A man hom they approve——

11. That any man may sell part of his alotment to his neighbor

12. That noo man shall ingrosse to himself by buying his neighbours lott for his peculer interest but with respect to sell it If an aproved man com and that without much advantag so judged by the company

13. That all publicke affairs as bridges higways or mill be cared on joyntly acording to meados and estats

14. That provision be indavored for education of Chilldren and dew Encouragment be given unto any that shall tak pains according to our former way or rating—

15. That no man shall give intertainment to a sogernor who shall carey himsellfe obnotctious to the company except amendment be after warning given——

Reprinted from *Records of the Town of Eastchester* (Eastchester, N.Y., 1964), I: 74–75.

16. That all shal joyne in guarding of Cattell when the Company se it Conveniant

17. That every man make & maintain a good fenc about all his arabell lands & in due tim a man chosen to veyne [view] it if the company be good

18. That etch man sow his land when most of the Company do sow or plant in either feeld——

19. That we give some encouragment to Mr. Bruwster eatch other weecke to give us a word of exortation and that when we are settelled we mete togeather etch other weeke one hour to talke of the best things——

20. That one man either of himsellfe or by consent may give entertainment to strangers for mony——

22. That one day every Spring be improved for the destroing of rattellsnackes——

23. That some every Lords Day staye at home for securiti of our wifes and Chilldren

24. That every man gett and keepe a good locke to his doare as son as he can

25. That a Conveniant place be apointed for oxen if ned requir

26. If any man meado or upland be worse in qualiti that be considered in quantitie

27. That every man that hath taken up lottes shall paie to all publicke chardges equall with thos that goo now [got none] that all that hath or shall take up lots within this track of land mentioned in the primises shall subscribe to these artickells

Phillip Pinkney	The mark of	John Goding
Thomas Shute	Joseph Joans	The mark of
The mark of	The mark of	Henery Fowler
Nathaniel White	Samuel Goding	John Emery
The Mark of	Moses Hoit	John Jackson
Nathaniel Tompkins	The mark of	Moses Jackson
William Haidens	William Squires	John Clark
John Hoit	David Osburn	The mark of
The Mark of	The mark of	John Drake
John Gee	John Tompkins	The mark of
James Eustis	Richard Hedly	John
	Samewell Drake	

This is a true coppie according to the originall Transcribed by me Richard Shute This 25th of No 68 An agreement by voate for an adishon unto this Covenante in page the 2

Ten Farms Covenant, Eastchester, N.Y.

Articles of Agreement betwixt us whose names are underwritten, A.D. 1665.

PREAMBLE[1]

(1) Imprimis, that we, by the grace of God, set down on the tract of land lying betwixt Hutchinson's brook, where the house was, until it comes unto the river, that runneth in at the head of the meadow. (2) That we endeavor to keep and maintain Christian love and civil honesty (Romans 19$^{9\text{-}13^{14}}$). (4) Plainly to deal one with another in Christian love (I Corinthians 6$^{1\text{-}7}$).

CONFLICT AND CONSENSUS

(5) If any trespass be done, the trespassed and the trespasser shall choose two of this company, and they a third man if need be required, to end the matter, without any further trouble (I Cor. 6$^{1\text{-}7}$). (3) That we faithfully counsel what may be of infirmity in any one of us. (19) . . . and that when we are settled we meet together each other week, one hour, to talk of the best things (Gal. 6$^{1\text{-}2}$).

COMMUNAL AFFAIRS AND INTERNAL IMPROVEMENTS

(19) That we give some encouragement to Mr. Brewster each other week, to give us a word of exhortation. . . . (6) That all and every one of us, or that shall be of us, do pay unto the minister, according to his meadows and estate (II Cor. 9$^{7\text{-}12}$). (13) That all public affairs as bridges, highways, or mill, be carried on jointly, according to meadows and estates. (14) That provision be endeavored for education of children, and due encouragement be given unto any that shall take pains according to our former way of rating.

Revised with permission from Schechter, "From Covenant to Constitution," 182–83.
[1] The articles have been arranged by category, though the original numbers have been retained. References to Letters of Paul have been added for the readers' convenience.

Distribution and Transfer of Land and Charges

(7) That none exceed the quantity of fifteen acres, until all have that quantity. (8) That every man hath that meadow that is most convenient for him. (9) That every man build and inhabit on his home lot before the next winter. (10) That no man make sale of his lot before he hath built and inhabited one year, and then to tender it to the company, or to a man whom they approve. (11) That any man may sell part of his allotment to his neighbor. (12) That no man shall engross to himself by buying his neighbor's lot for his particular interest, but with respect to sell it if an approved man come, and that without much advantage, so judged by the company. (18) That each man sow his land when most of the company do sow or plant in either field. (26) If any man's meadow or upland be worse in quality, that be considered in quantity. (27) That every man that hath taken up lots shall pay to all public charges equal with those that got none.

Defense and Foreign Relations

(16) That all shall join in guarding of cattle when the company see it convenient. (25) That a convenient place be appointed for oxen if need require. (17) That every man make and maintain a good fence about all his arable land, and in due time a man chosen to view if the company be good. (22) That one day every spring be improved for the destroying of rattlesnakes. (21) *missing.* (23) That some, every Lord's day, stay at home for security of our wives and children. (24) That every man get a good lock to his door as soon as he can. (20) That one man, either of himself, or by consent, may give entertaintment to strangers for money. (15) That no man shall give entertaintment to a sojourner who shall carry himself obnoxious to the company except amendment be after warning given.

That all that hath or shall take up lots within this tract of land mentioned in the primises shall subscribe to these articles.

IV

The New York
Charter of Liberties

1683 and 1691

COMMENTARY BY JOHN M. MURRIN

FOR TWO BRIEF PERIODS, 1683 to 1685 and 1691 to 1697, colonial New York was governed under a constitutional system drafted by the provincial assembly and called, in 1683, "The Charter of Libertyes and priviledges." The 1691 version revived and amended the original text. The 1683 document has been intensely studied. Its 1691 counterpart is seldom even mentioned. Most historians have struggled to find a positive relationship between the two charters and Jacob Leisler's revolutionary regime of 1689–91, the New York counterpart of England's Glorious Revolution. However, except for the New England population of Long Island and Westchester, nobody who actively supported Leisler played a significant role in creating the 1683 charter. When Anti-Leislerians returned to power in 1691, two items headed their agenda. They murdered Leisler, and they reenacted the Charter of Liberties.

The troubled history of the charter makes sense only within a very broad context. The transatlantic dimension must be able to accommodate political changes in both England and The Netherlands in the age of Louis XIV (1642–1715). Within North America, the story involves New York's ethnic and religious differences, splits within New York's Dutch, English, and New England communities over constitutional principles, and New York's precarious ability to compete with its neighbors in New England, New Jersey, and Pennsylvania.

New York's Charter of Liberties took shape in an environment of intense intercolonial competition for new settlers. Founded as the Dutch colony of New Netherland, the province was just beginning to thrive under Director Peter Stuyvesant when the English conquered it in 1664. King Charles II (1660–85) had recently granted the area between the Connecticut and Delaware rivers to his brother James, duke of York. York dispatched a military expedition under Colonel Richard Nicolls, who persuaded New Amsterdam to surrender without serious resistance. In honor of the duke, he renamed the colony and its capital city New York, the fur-trading town of New Orange became Albany (another of the duke's titles), and the most English parts of New Netherland—Long Island (half of which he took from Connecticut) and what is now the Bronx and Westchester—were organized as a county called Yorkshire. He offered religious toleration to the highly diverse peoples of the colony. To English settlers on Long Island, nearly all of whom had supported the invasion fleet, he promised "equall (if not greater freedomes & Imumityes) than any of his Majesties Colonyes in new England" already possessed.[1] He could never satisfy the expectations that this promise aroused.

James's patent from the king made him lord proprietor of New York, which was very nearly the broadest grant of power that the Crown could make to anybody. Beginning with Maryland in the 1630s, lords proprietors exercised within their colonies almost every power claimed by the Crown within the kingdom of England. Other proprietary charters permitted a proprietor to make laws with the advice and consent of the settlers. New York's patent contained no such restriction. From the start, the duke probably intended to carry out in his colony what would have been an extremely dangerous policy in England for a man whose father, Charles I (1625–49), had been beheaded by the parliamentary opposition as recently as 1649. James had decided to create an absolutist government in his colony. He did not intend to make an elective assembly any part of his political system.

He did permit one temporary exception. Nicolls drafted a law code, culled mostly from New England sources and then modified in a more authoritarian direction. For example, town meetings would not govern towns. They would chose a board of overseers to do the job. Nicolls designed this code for the most English part of the colony, Yorkshire, and presented it to an assembly of representatives from those towns that met for ten days at Hempstead in 1665.

---

[1] Nicolls to Mr. John Howell and Capt. John Young, Dec. 1, 1664, Edmund Bailey O'Callaghan et al., eds., *Documents relative to the Colonial History of the State of New York* (Albany, 1853–87), 14: 561.

Many of the thirty-four delegates to that assembly were not pleased to learn that no other legislative body of its kind would meet again, that the duke would not even give them a continuing voice in levying taxes, and that their only functions were to accept the Duke's Laws, vote a permanent revenue, and submit their land titles to him for approval. All future amendments and all new laws would be drafted and implemented by the governor through his appointed court of assizes, which consisted of the provincial council, the city corporation of New York, and the justices of Yorkshire.

With more difficulty than the final vote of 32–0 with two abstentions would indicate, Nicolls got the delegates' assent. He boasted that he had laid "the foundations of Kingly Government in these parts," and that he had revised the New England codes in a way that would "revive the Memory of old England amongst us. For Democracy hath taken so deepe a Roote in these parts, that the very name of a Justice of the Peace is an Abomination."[2] New York's career as an interesting English experiment in overseas absolutism had begun.

So had the competition for settlers. Nicolls knew that the province could not remain secure as an English possession so long as most of the colonists were Dutch, even if "Dutch" really meant an extravagant mixture of diverse peoples—Flemings, Walloons, French Huguenots, Germans, Scandinavians, and, without including the New Englanders on Long Island, even a few Englishmen and Scots who had mingled closely and sometimes intermarried with their Dutch neighbors. Three of Manhattan's wealthiest men in 1664 were English.

Nicolls saw the area between the Hudson and Delaware rivers as the ideal place to plant new English settlements. To him, New York made no sense as a military and strategic entity unless it controlled that fertile and promising hinterland. The governor granted two patents for settlements in this area, which he called Albania. The Elizabethtown patent soon became Elizabethtown and Woodbridge. The Monmouth patent spawned Middletown and Shrewsbury. Unfortunately for Nicolls's plan, most of the settlers for these communities came from Long Island, not other parts of America. So far, Nicolls had merely succeeded in moving scarce Englishmen from one part of the duke's province to another.

Later in the year, he received the alarming news that, in a fit of princely generosity, James had granted the area between the Hudson and the Delaware to two loyal supporters, Sir George Carteret and John

[2] Nicolls to Lord Clarendon, April 1666, The New-York Historical Society *Collections* (1869), 118, 119.

Lord Berkeley. Although their patent only gave them title to the soil, they quickly asserted the prerogatives of other lords proprietors, assumed full powers of government, changed the name of their possession from Albania to New Jersey, and began advertising for settlers.

One of their devices was the Concessions and Agreements of February 1665, a document largely copied from one of the same name recently drafted by the Carolina Board of Proprietors, to which both Carteret and Berkeley belonged. The New Jersey Concessions matched New York's guarantee of religious toleration, offered generous terms for acquiring land, and promised a system of government that would include an elective assembly. These terms began to attract settlers from New England. One group of highly orthodox Puritans from New Haven Colony founded Newark, and another more moderate band from Massachusetts established the town of Piscataway. Nicolls, meanwhile, had no success recruiting for New York.

As early as 1666, a larger pattern was already becoming clear. New Jersey attracted Yankees; New York did not. It remained far more hospitable to Dutch colonists, who preferred to keep living among people they already knew and understood. On the eve of the English conquest, for example, the Dutch town of Bergen (also in New Jersey) had been the most rapidly growing community in New Netherland. As it became obvious that New Englanders were pouring into New Jersey by the hundreds, the Dutch flow to Bergen dried up. New Jersey tended to drain English settlers from New York and keep Dutch colonists there. The duke's province of New York was supposed to be a major addition to England's imperial power. Instead, it remained a painful and dangerous Dutch thorn in Britannia's body that no one knew how to extract.

This development had ominous implications for the security of the colony, as the third Anglo-Dutch war (1672–74) soon revealed. This conflict was largely a sideshow to a much more serious confrontation on the European mainland, where powerful Roman Catholic armies of King Louis XIV of France threatened to overwhelm the United Provinces of The Netherlands, a Protestant republic. At the beginning of this struggle, young William of Orange emerged to claim the military leadership of the republic through his family's hereditary office of *stadholder* (the nearest equivalent English phrase at the time was "captain general," a title given to every royal governor in the colonies), and William quickly became a potent symbol of beleaguered international Protestantism. To take command in a republic that had abolished the office of *stadholder* while he was a minor, he had to dislodge the civilian leadership of wealthy merchants under Jan De Witt. An angry Orange mob, unfairly suspecting De Witt and his brother Cornelius of pro-

French sympathies, murdered them in 1672, desecrated the bodies, and even cannibalized parts of them.[3]

As spokesmen for the oligarchic regent class that ruled Dutch cities, the De Witts had favored *de facto* religious toleration broad enough to include Catholics, provided they worshipped only in private and did not otherwise disturb the peace. William's supporters were strict Calvinist defenders of the Dutch Reformed Church and strong opponents of religious dissent, particularly from Catholics. Many regents feared that, if William's men ever got their way completely, they might turn the House of Orange into an authoritarian Protestant monarchy.

The Duke of York, who completed his conversion to Roman Catholicism in these years and would not even try to disguise his loyalties by the mid-1670s, became a symbol of a different kind. As heir to Charles II's throne (Queen Catherine had no children when she reached menopause), he raised the extremely emotional issue whether Protestant England would be able to accept rule by a Catholic king. An alarmed parliamentary opposition began to ask why England was on the wrong side in this war. They did not know that, in a secret clause of the Treaty of Dover (1670), Charles had promised Louis to return England to the Church of Rome after their joint victory over the Dutch republic.

In the summer of 1673, a Dutch fleet, after raiding Chesapeake Bay, sailed north toward Manhattan. No Dutch settler offered to fight to preserve the duke's rule, but some of them cheerfully assisted the invaders as they demanded the surrender of Fort James at the southern tip of the island. Like Stuyvesant in 1664, the English garrison yielded without significant resistance, and for the next fifteen months the colony became Dutch again. Fort James was renamed Fort William Henry (Willem Hendrik) after the Prince of Orange, while the province again became New Netherland, and its capital was called New Orange.

Dutch settlers put considerable energy into making the colony's defenses formidable, in case the English should attack again. Instead, the Dutch republic, eager to detach England from its alliance with Louis XIV, made peace with Charles II in 1674 and willingly gave New Netherland back in the process. The duke would have another chance to decide how to govern a province that had eloquently demonstrated its

---

[3] Technically, the United Provinces had no single military commander. Each province named its own *stadholder*, but until the 1650s, Holland, much the wealthiest province, chose the Prince of Orange, and the other six usually followed suit. In 1654, as the price of a peace treaty ending the first Anglo-Dutch War, England's Oliver Cromwell forced Holland to exclude William III, then a child, from the office. In 1667 Holland abolished the position itself.

disloyalty to him. He had no intention of retreating from his absolutist principles. His open Catholicism would not make his task any simpler.

The duke's new governor, Major Edmund Andros, soon learned what the history of the colony had taught his predecessors. Policies that might placate the Dutch could antagonize the English, and *vice versa*. Calvinism and constitutionalism had evolved differently in these two Protestant societies. In The Netherlands, the merchant oligarchy favored localism, decentralized rule, and broad toleration—a combination that apologists called "true liberty." Strict Calvinists usually rallied behind the prince of Orange and, unlike their English counterparts, had devised few means for the systematic limitation of *legitimate* power. (Like most other Calvinists, they did have experience in resisting and overthrowing an illegitimate ruler or tyrant.)

In England, the broadest push for complete toleration came from the monarchy, with its Catholic inclinations, and from such radical Protestant sects as the Society of Friends, or Quakers. As Anglicans, the parliamentary majority (soon to be called Tories) favored the suppression of both Catholics and Protestant dissenters and grew ever more suspicious of the court, though utterly unwilling to attack the monarchy directly or tamper with the succession. An emerging parliamentary opposition (called Whigs by about 1680 when they briefly gained control) favored toleration for Protestant dissenters, but not Catholics, and stronger constitutional constraints upon the monarchy. Many Whigs hoped to bar James from the succession to the throne.

These tendencies had their counterparts in North America, where Calvinist New Englanders harbored strong suspicions of arbitrary executive power and favored wide popular participation in government, at least among true believers. The English merchants moving into New York City resembled the Anglican majority in Parliament in their willingness to work with a Catholic executive provided they could obtain guarantees of constitutional liberty. The Dutch merchants who accepted office under Andros were rather like the regent class of The Netherlands. Long Island Yankees were New York's Whigs. Settlers devoted to the orthodoxy of the Dutch Reformed Church were a potential Orangist party.

Andros rapidly assumed command. He severely punished seven prominent Dutch merchants when they refused to swear an oath that might oblige them to bear arms against fellow Dutchmen. But having made the point that New York must remain English, he took quiet steps to protect and encourage direct trade between the colony and Amsterdam, even though the Navigation Acts of the 1660s were aimed primarily at excluding the Dutch from England's colonial trade. Like his predecessors, he also began appointing prominent Dutch settlers to office, including his council.

As before, the New England communities on Long Island made clear their desire for an elective assembly, but now they had allies who agreed that the question was becoming truly urgent. The small but growing community of English merchants in New York City threatened to leave the colony unless this and similar demands were met. Andros probably agreed with them, for he tried without success to persuade the duke to change his mind in 1675.

Once again New Jersey provided the catalyst. In 1674, Carteret and Berkeley divided their colony into Carteret's East Jersey and Berkeley's West Jersey. Berkeley promptly sold his province to a coalition of English Quakers who began to plan a large emigration in 1676–77. The terms they offered were embodied in the West Jersey Concessions and Agreements of 1677, the most radical constitutional system ever put into practice in an English colony before American independence. Drawing upon English Leveller ideas of the 1640s which were still considered quite subversive in England, they intended to place nearly all power in a large assembly of 100 deputies who would govern with a weaker plural executive of ten men. Within the court system, they gave juries power over both fact and law and left judges with almost no discretionary authority. As pacifists, they made no military demands on any settlers they might attract, and they promised complete religious toleration with no taxes for the support of any church. One of these promoters was William Penn, who by 1681 would have his own proprietary charter from Charles II and who spent much of the next two years drafting a Frame of Government for his province of Pennsylvania. His system was less radical than West Jersey's, but to potential newcomers it seemed far more attractive than anything New York could offer.

Andros recognized this danger and tried to contain it by reasserting political control over the Jerseys in the late 1670s. West Jersey Quakers were compelled to accept his authority for awhile, but by appealing to the attorney general of England they managed to implement much of the West Jersey Concessions anyway after 1680. Andros took direct action against East Jersey in 1679–80. He arrested Philip Carteret, the colony's proprietary governor, carried him off to New York, and tried him for infringing upon the duke's powers of government. To the embarrassment of Andros, his largely English court of assizes acquitted Carteret in May 1680. As an autocratic form of government, the duke's regime had little support among English settlers of any background, including its own officials. Yet Andros again crossed over to Elizabethtown in June, met with an assembly designed to replicate the function of the Hempstead Assembly of 1665, asked them to approve the Duke's Laws, and responded with exasperation when they demanded the right to sit once a year. His vague promise to call a future assembly sometime could not disguise the stalemate. He did not know that, at almost that moment, the duke—upon the advice of a Whig attorney general—was surrendering his claim to the customs duties of West Jersey, thus encouraging the Quakers to try for a much fuller implementation of the radical Concessions.

In January 1681, Andros returned to England to answer complaints that he had misappropriated the duke's revenues and had favored Dutch merchants over English. His autocratic regime promptly disintegrated throughout the region. Before leaving, he neglected to renew a revenue act that had just expired. In May 1681, English merchants in New York City organized a tax strike against the expired law. When the duke's collector tried to compel payment, the duke's own court of assizes, staffed by his own people and encouraged by a heavily English grand jury, arrested the man and tried him for treason. A largely English jury convicted the collector, but rather than hang him, the court shipped him back to England where, of course, the duke exonerated him. James wondered why Lieutenant Governor Anthony Brockholls and the council had not simply renewed the expiring revenue act. The duke never quite grasped how little support his absolutism had even among the officials who tried to implement it.

Public meetings among the English towns on Long Island called loudly for political reform. So did the court of assizes. With several prominent merchants already deserting the colony for the Delaware Valley, the matter had become pressing. This time James yielded. He had been driven into virtual exile in Scotland by the popular fury in England over the Popish Plot of 1678. (Most Englishmen believed that Jesuits were planning to assassinate the king and turn the nation over to the papists.) This opposition in turn led to the creation of the Whig party and a determined campaign to bar James from succession to the throne. Most Whigs favored William of Orange as the alternative to James, even though James had tried to secure his position with William and the English public by marrying his Protestant daughter Mary to William just before the Popish Plot exploded. James, in short, needed no new turmoil. He agreed to grant New York an elective assembly provided the assembly in turn gave him a permanent revenue adequate to meet the costs of the colony's government.

The Charter of Liberties grew out of this concession, and it came at a time when intercolonial competition in such matters had become fiercer than ever. When William Penn came to America, his settlers persuaded him to revise his Frame of Government into a simpler plan, the Second Frame, or the Pennsylvania Charter of Liberties, which went into effect in early 1683. Quakers, who were busy implementing their most radical constitution in West Jersey, had just recently gained control of East Jersey's proprietary as well, and in 1683 that colony adopted a complex document which was called the Fundamental Constitutions for the Province of East Jersey in America. East Jersey and the Delaware Valley had already cost New York City about a third of its import trade from England. Pennsylvania was cutting sharply into New York's exports to the West Indies. More merchants might leave New York unless something was done. The colony needed its own Charter of Liberties, and that document had to demonstrate that the colony was truly an English province with English liberties, not a Dutch outpost of Amsterdam's trade.

The colony's new governor, Colonel Thomas Dongan, was an Irish Catholic soldier who had risen in the duke's service. He issued election writs for an assembly scheduled to meet in New York City on Wednesday, October 17, 1683, but a quorum did not arrive until the following week. A majority of the eighteen delegates were English. Of the five known Dutch members, three were conspicuous anglicizers—that is, they fully accepted English rule and had learned to cooperate openly with the duke's government, including its Catholics. Almost completely excluded from the assembly were spokesmen for militant orthodoxy within the Dutch Reformed Church, although the delegate from Schenectady may have matched that description. In other words, any potential Orange party in New York had no role in the legislation of 1683. If anything, these people were its chief victims, that part of the population the reformers hoped to transform or overwhelm with newcomers.

The assembly proposed a drastic anglicization of New York's public life. English counties and courts (including trial by jury) replaced Dutch courts and law even where the Dutch were an overwhelming majority, as in Kings and the upper Hudson Valley. The first item in this program, indeed the first law passed by New York's first true legislative assembly, was the Charter of Liberties, signed by the governor on October 30. Its principal author may have been either Speaker Matthias Nicolls, who had had a role in drafting the Duke's Laws of 1665, or Thomas Rudyard, about whom little is known.

If Rudyard did play such a role, he deserves recognition as a major architect of colonial liberties. He made important contributions to Penn's First Frame. He served as secretary and acting governor of East Jersey in the spring of 1683 when that colony adopted its Fundamental Constitutions and a General Law, several clauses of which later appeared in the New York Charter of Liberties.[4] As New York's attorney general under Dongan, he would have been a logical choice for composing important bills. The 1691 assembly remarked in passing that it had been customary to request the attorney general to draft legislation. Such a practice had to have taken hold between 1683 and 1685, the only years before 1689 in which assemblies had met, but no evidence survives to prove whether it was in place for the first law of the first assembly.

New York's Charter of Liberties imposed an English constitutional system on a colony that was still mostly Dutch. It ended absolutist rule, at least for a few years. Nearly half of its articles defined the assembly and its functions. Another block of paragraphs dealt with the judicial system. Still others covered a range of subjects from the legal rights of women to the quartering of soldiers and religious freedom.

The charter gave the power to make laws to a general assembly, consisting of the governor, his appointive council, and an elective assembly. Only the assembly could vote taxes, and a session had to be summoned at least once every three years. Its members claimed an impressive list of parliamentary privileges to protect their right to debate. The charter also contained strong guarantees of trial by jury, which was not necessarily an attractive prospect for Dutch settlers, who had possessed the option of using juries in parts of the colony since the conquest but had almost never chosen to do so. The longest article in the charter proclaimed toleration for all Christians, permitted Long Island Yankees to tax themselves to support their ministers, and promised to make enforceable at law any contract entered into between any Christian congregation and its minister. If carried out, this policy would have permitted every Christian denomination to share the benefits of established churches elsewhere, provided its own members were willing to participate. Quakers believed that a "hireling ministry" in any form was an abomination and were not willing to pay taxes for this purpose. Except in the New England communities on Long Island, even Quakers would not have been forced to give tax money to any church under this law.

Except for religious toleration (in which New York outpaced New England), these reforms failed to match what the colony's English neigh-

---

[4] In the 1683 version of the Charter of Liberties, compare paragraphs 17 and 18 with clause XIII of East Jersey's General Law of March 1683, paragraph 19 with clause XVI, paragraph 23 with clause XVII, paragraph 24 with clause XIX, and paragraph 25 with clause XX. See Aaron Leaming and Jacob Spicer, eds., *The Grants, Concessions, and Original Constitutions of the Province of New Jersey*, 2nd edition (Somerville, N.J., 1881), 235–36. For Rudyard's contribution to William Penn's Frame of Government, see Mary Maples Dunn, Richard S. Dunn et al., eds., *The Papers of William Penn* (Philadelphia, 1981–86), 2: 138–40, 184–202.

bors were doing. Two severe differences stood out. The New England colonies, West Jersey, and Pennsylvania all provided annual elections (semi-annual in Connecticut). East Jersey had staggered triennial elections. The New York Charter of Liberties demanded only a *session* of the assembly at least once every three years. It said nothing about how often new elections would have to be held. Dongan called a second session of the first assembly in October 1684, and new elections were held for the 1685 assembly, doubtless because the death of Charles II had intervened and thus terminated the life of all legislative bodies. No contemporary statement informs us whether Dongan planned frequent elections, or whether he intended to rule with the same assembly throughout his entire administration or perhaps the entire reign of the monarch, as was the tradition in Ireland. Second, the 1683 assembly voted a permanent revenue to the duke and a generous gift to Dongan. Together these grants made New York a more heavily taxed society than any neighboring colony. The drain of people to the Delaware Valley probably slowed or even stopped, but New York failed to attract newcomers, as Dongan admitted in 1687. The policy of accelerated anglicization may have angered more Dutch settlers than it placated newcomers. Several Dutchmen complained vocally about the new taxes.

Calvinists also worried about the growing Jesuit influence in New York City, where one priest had opened a school. They soon found much graver reasons for alarm. In 1685, Louis XIV revoked the Edict of Nantes of 1598, which had given legal toleration to French Protestants, or Huguenots. This action was carried out with a ruthlessness that drove at least 160,000 Huguenots into exile, the largest forced migration in the history of early modern Europe. Some headed toward England and New York. Although James's own commitment to toleration was firm and had been a consistent policy of his since 1660, he tried to suppress reports of Huguenot sufferings in France and thus destroyed any prospect he ever had that English Protestants would trust his motives when he insisted on toleration for Catholics in England. Against the background of Louis's ferocious persecution, the wavering of James had to seem sinister and ominous.

In New York, the most active merchant to take up the cause of Huguenot exiles was Jacob Leisler, a descendant of sixteenth-century refugee Huguenots who had been raised in the German city of Frankfort. The son of a Calvinist minister, he moved to Amsterdam as a young man and then sailed to New Netherland as a soldier with the rank of captain in 1660. In the 1670s, he had taken a vigorous part in the restored Dutch regime of New Orange. A few years later, he actively supported Dutch Calvinist orthodoxy over meddling by Andros in the appointment of a heterodox minister in Albany, and in the mid-1680s he dropped out of the Dutch Reformed Church when it chose as its new minister Henricus Selyns, a man whose Calvinist convictions were suspect. Leisler, who spoke Dutch, German, French, and English, joined the Huguenot Church instead, although his family remained with the Dutch Reformed congregation. Leisler seemed willing to work with and tolerate Catholics so long as they did not menace Protestant liberties. He accepted a militia captaincy under Dongan and even married one of his daughters to a Dongan stalwart. In all probability, Louis's persecution of the Huguenots and James's equivocal reaction then began to drive Leisler in a strongly Orangist direction. He could no longer trust men he had once accepted.

In England, the duke approved the Charter of Liberties, but before he notified the colony of this decision, Charles died, and the duke became King James II (1685-88). As king he began to perceive other possibilities for America. English New Yorkers had asked to be as free as their neighbors. James found a different way to fulfill that desire. With his accession to the throne, New York had become a royal colony because the province's lord proprietor had become king. As king, James II now disallowed the Charter of Liberties but approved of the permanent revenue act that the assembly had passed in exchange for the charter. Between 1686 and 1688, he also deprived all of New York's rivals except Pennsylvania of their special charter privileges, including the right to an elective assembly. Beginning with Massachusetts, he created a new province, called the Dominion of New England, to which New Hampshire, Plymouth, Rhode Island, and Connecticut were added by 1687, and New York and the Jerseys in 1688. The new governor was Sir Edmund Andros, the man who had tried to organize New York and the Delaware Valley as an absolutist regime after 1674. Andros made Boston his capital. James sent another soldier, Captain Francis Nicholson, to New York as lieutenant governor.

With the birth of a son—and Catholic heir to the throne—in the summer of 1688, events in England came to a crisis. In November 1688, at the secret invitation of Whig and Tory leaders, William of Orange invaded England with a small Protestant army and promised, rather vaguely, to liberate the kingdom from popery and tyranny. James sent his much larger army against him, but nearly all of it defected to William. In late December, James fled his kingdom to take refuge in France, William took possession of London, and a month later Parliament declared him and his princess joint sovereigns as King William III (1689-1702) and Queen Mary II (1689-94). It passed a Declaration of Rights that banned Catholics from the throne, helped ensure that Parliament would become a permanent part of the governing process (it has met every year since 1689), and banned such practices as the king's power to suspend a law or dispense an individual from its requirements. Parliament also granted toleration to Protestant dissenters but denied it to Catholics.

In America on April 18–19, 1689, after news arrived that William had landed in England but before the resisters knew whether James or William had won, the town of Boston took a day-and-a-half to dismantle the Andros regime and imprison its leading officials. From there, resistance spread to the New England population of eastern Long Island and soon reached New York City. As men who owed their public careers to James, Andros and Nicholson both tried to suppress all news of William's landing. At first they no doubt expected James to win, much as he had vanquished the rebellion of the duke of Monmouth in 1685. Because William was still *stadholder* of The Netherlands, they also expected a fourth Anglo-Dutch war. But by March Nicholson learned that London had embraced William and that James had tried to flee to France, as eventually he succeeded in doing. William's triumph thus meant war between England and France instead, and it compelled Nicholson to decide to whom or what he was loyal—to King James as his sovereign and patron, or to the English state. In April he clearly chose the English state, as his surviving correspondence demonstrates, but many colonists did not believe him. To most settlers, the refusal of Andros or Nicholson to make any public statement on behalf of William raised the inevitable suspicion that both intended to turn their colonies over to Louis XIV. But Nicholson did not know whether William had become king or perhaps had only been named regent to rule in James's name or on behalf of the infant Prince of Wales. He was not willing to jeopardize his whole career by proclaiming the wrong person.

Control of the fort in Manhattan Harbor symbolized this larger struggle. It had been named and renamed for the two men contesting for the throne of England. It had also housed the assembly that passed the Charter of Liberties.

Nicholson put together an expanded council or committee of officeholders to help him preserve order, and Leisler, a militia captain, served on this body. As always after a prolonged era of peace, New York's defenses were in miserable condition, and Nicholson tried to demonstrate his loyalty to England by speeding their repair. Then, much as in 1681, some merchants objected to paying import duties under the permanent revenue act. Sometime in May, Leisler also refused to pay the duties, not because the revenue had been granted only in exchange for the Charter of Liberties which had been rescinded unfairly (Article

II was also ambiguous enough to sustain an argument that James had surrendered the power of disallowance before becoming king), but because the collector, Matthew Plowman, was a "papist." Nicholson tried to placate opponents by agreeing that all moneys collected by Plowman were to be used to repair fortifications at Fort James, and for a time this strategy worked. Yet the youthful Nicholson's control deteriorated as suspicions increased about the Catholics in his garrison of redcoats, and especially when, in a rash moment of extremely bad temper, he threatened to burn the city down unless the militia ceased adding to its many demands upon him. Greatly alarmed by this outburst, the city militia took direct control of the fort on May 31. Leisler was the highest ranking officer willing to assume command. He still demanded Plowman's removal, but the other captains refused to act without direct orders from England. Poor Plowman wailed that the office was rightly his because he had bought it—at considerable cost.

In England, the events of 1688 became "glorious" because Whigs and moderate Tories were able to cooperate long enough to drive out James without significant violence. Apart from a brief anti-Catholic riot on "Irish night," London had no popular violence of the kind associated with an aroused Orange party in The Netherlands. New York, by contrast, had thousands of angry Orangists. They terrified New York City's equivalent of England's moderate Tories, the English merchants who had organized the tax strike of 1681 and demanded the Charter of Liberties. These men had always seen the ethnic Dutch as the main barriers to their own prosperity and growth. They had also recognized that they needed the support of the House of Stuart and its provincial officials to hold power in the colony. They did not dare repudiate James until certain beyond any question that he had lost and that they could work with William. To them the Leislerian triumph looked disturbingly like the Dutch reconquest of 1673—from within. The English, warned one observer, "had been greatly provoked by their losing the fort a second time."[5]

Leisler's rule of nearly two years sharply polarized Dutch Calvinist principles and English notions of constitutionalism. Within the city, his opponents were nearly all moderate Anglicans or moderate Dutch Protestants (in technical theological terms, Arminians or "Cocceians" as against strict Calvinist "Voetians"). In June and July, he had a strong majority with him as he moved to dislodge opponents from positions

[5] Rudolphus Varick to the classis of Amsterdam, April 9, 1693, Hugh Hastings and E. T. Corwin, eds., *Ecclesiastical Records of the State of New York* (New York, 1901–16), 2: 1050.

of power, mostly by encouraging new local elections and by asking the various constituencies to choose delegates to sit on his extemporized committee of safety. So long as the legitimacy of his own position seemed precarious, he recognized a need to diffuse responsibility for the revolution as broadly as possible. Elections met this need, and the support he received encouraged him to act as *de facto* governor, although he probably thought of himself more as a *stadholder* for New York, a military commander entitled to override local resistance, if necessary. In December, he accepted a letter from the king addressed to the lieutenant governor or whomever "for the time being take care for Preserving the Peace" of the province.[6] He now insisted that he be accepted as the legitimate lieutenant governor until the Crown sent a successor, and his regime became more arbitrary, at least in the eyes of its opponents.

Early in their revolution, the Leislerians had condemned the revenue act passed under the Dominion of New England because no elective assembly had ever consented to it, but that objection did not apply to Dongan's revenue act of 1683. In mid-December, Leisler proclaimed it still in force because he needed money to fight the French and Indians. His opponents ripped down his message at the customs house and replaced it with a manifesto that quoted from Magna Carta and other venerable statements of traditional English liberties before condemning the revived revenue act as a menace to "the Rights Libertyes and priviledges of their Majestyes good subjects." Leisler condemned this act of resistance and quoted Article One of the Charter of Liberties in vindication of the tax. It declared, he reminded his opponents, that government in New York must be by governor, council, and elective assembly, and his government believed that the revenue act met that test. His opponents replied that the tax had been approved only in exchange for the Charter of Liberties, which James had disallowed, and therefore both were now invalid.[7]

Over the next year these men worked hard to stigmatize Leisler and his regime as systematic despoilers of English liberties. Partly because the Leislerians never devised any comprehensive response to this criticism, it began to stick, even though Leisler's basic constitutional preferences did not differ strikingly from his enemies'. He probably

[6] Letter of William III, July 30, 1689, O'Callaghan, ed., *Documents relative to the Colonial History of the State of New York*, 3: 606.

[7] "By the English Freemen of the province of New York," December 19, 1689, C.O. 5/1081/203, British Public Record Office, London; Edmund Bailey O'Callaghan, ed., *Documentary History of the State of New York* (Albany, 1849–51), 2: 163. My thanks to David William Voorhees for providing a copy of the PRO manuscript.

was not terribly well informed on the subject. Although Leisler showed interest in petitioning the Crown to give New York a set of liberties comparable to New England's, for example, he also admitted that he did not know what those privileges were, and he and his followers never displayed any interest in reviving or reenacting the Charter of Liberties. He held elections in 1689 to dislodge his enemies from the government of New York City, but although his own city corporation met several times after the formal records cease in December 1689, apparently no elections were held in 1690, though required by the city charter. In the bitter struggles of 1689–91, the Charter of Liberties slowly became an explicitly Anti-Leislerian text. Men who had refused to proclaim William and Mary were among those most likely to appeal to it.

Leisler did summon an assembly in 1690 to raise money for the war against New France, but his predominantly Dutch followers apparently did not respond to his February call for elections. His most committed supporters came from Continental Protestant backgrounds and had almost no experience with an English legislative system. New writs had to be issued in April. They established a process of indirect elections similar to the one used to create the 1683 assembly, not the general vote of all freeholders and freemen required by the Charter of Liberties.

Apart from fighting the war against France and rendering his own regime internally secure, Leisler had no legislative agenda. In the assembly's April session, he approved a revenue act and a bill ending New York City's monopoly of bolting flour. In the second session, he obtained another tax, a law punishing anyone who refused to accept office under him, and a few other measures. He prorogued the first session as soon as the delegates began to discuss English liberties, a sensitive question so long as he held many of his enemies in prison without trial. The delegates at the second session raised this issue at the outset before granting a new tax. Leisler finally yielded most of what they demanded and after two weeks of strife got his revenue. As one opponent complained, "we have good cause to judge he [Leisler] is little acquainted" with the "Laws and Liberties of the English Nation."[8] This claim was much exaggerated, but Leisler became ever more vulnerable to such charges. People believed them.

Leisler did know what a *stadholder* could do. He was determined to maintain military control of the province against the threat of a French conquest, but the measures that he took to implement that policy began to antagonize more people than they placated. His first tax provoked

---

[8] Nicholas Bayard, *A Modest and Impartial Narrative* . . . (London, 1690), in Charles M. Andrews, ed., *Narratives of the Insurrections, 1675–1690* (New York, 1915), 329.

a major riot in New York City in the summer of 1690, and his second led to widespread armed resistance in Queens before the end of the year.

In the course of 1690–91, Leisler thus alienated much of the support of New England Calvinists he had relied upon in 1689, the only part of his coalition that had played an important role in winning the Charter of Liberties. Numerous settlers in Queens expressed outrage against his method of collecting taxes and accused his followers of sheer plunder. Suffolk County drifted quietly out of his coalition, sending two delegates to the first assembly session but apparently none to the second. After an intercolonial assault on Canada became an utter fiasco, Leisler outraged the government of Connecticut by arresting its commanding general, Fitz-John Winthrop. As Connecticut's secretary angrily told him in September 1690, "a prison is not a catholicon for al State Maladyes, though so much used by you, nor could you in any one action have more disobliged al New England."[9]

Leisler's base was growing ever narrower. What began as a Dutch Calvinist and New England Puritan protest against popery and tyranny on behalf of the Prince of Orange was becoming a popular Orange party explosion in the narrow sense of that term. The movement had lost most of its constitutional content along the way because war with France always seemed more important to Leisler. Sadly for him, William's English government also undercut him. His first attempt to justify his actions to London went awry when the French captured the vessel containing his communications. His opponents, not he, won the attention of the English government and secured the appointment of a governor favorable to them, Colonel Henry Sloughter, who carried orders to install a solid slate of Anti-Leislerians on his council. Because the Orangist government in New York found no way to get through to William of Orange as king of England, Leisler and his English son-in-law, Jacob Milborne, lost their lives shortly after surrendering the fort to Sloughter. The new governor arrested them, tried them for treason, denied them an opportunity to appeal to England, and finally hanged them both in May 1691.

This alignment of factions explains the later history of the Charter of Liberties. Sloughter summoned an assembly shortly after taking charge, and it was utterly dominated by Anti-Leislerians. While encouraging the execution of Leisler and Milborne, the delegates also reenacted the Charter of Liberties with a few modifications. The 1691 version demanded annual meetings of the assembly instead of one every

---

[9] O'Callaghan, ed., *Documentary History of the State of New York*, 2: 163.

three years, but it still included no clause about the frequency of elections. It explicitly recognized the royal disallowance, a point left ambiguous in the earlier text. It omitted an article about the property rights of widows, banned Catholics from office, denied them any claim to religious toleration, and said nothing about the public support of Christian clergymen. The government of William III, whose approval had made the Anti-Leislerian triumph possible, added a final irony to the story. In 1697 it disallowed the new Charter of Liberties, just as James II had repudiated the first version.

When the Leislerians returned to power for several years at the turn of the century under a sympathetic royal governor (Richard Coote, earl of Bellomont), they proved far more able to defend themselves in the language of English constitutionalism. They were learning, but they made no attempt to draft a Charter of Liberties of their own. New York entered the eighteenth century with no formal protection of this kind.

Yet the two charters and the Leislerian struggles of which they became a part did have a long-term impact. The upheaval of 1689 ended forever James II's experiment in absolutism in North America. Government by consent became the norm in New York as in all of the English colonies. English law, including trial by jury, became a routine part of the judicial system, and Dutch legal customs slowly wilted away. But if no governor of New York could invoke absolutist principles again, that office in New York remained uniquely powerful within the mainland colonies. The continuing animosity between Leislerians and Anti-Leislerians gave all governors unusual leverage. At least until 1704, the party supported by the governor won general elections. Until the 1740s, most governors found ways to win a majority within the assembly, and those majorities in turn showed their gratitude by helping to convert the office into the single most lucrative patronage position in British North America. Several governors kept one assembly in being from 1716 to 1726 and another assembly from 1728 to 1737 without calling new elections. This problem was not resolved until the 1740s when the assembly finally won approval for a Septennial Act, which required general elections at least once every seven years. No other mainland colony faced comparable problems after 1700.

Absolutism had been defeated between 1664 and 1691. The struggle to tame royal prerogative would take much longer. New York's failure to trim executive power as successfully as other colonies managed to do undoubtedly gave some encouragement to the acceptance of a fairly strong governor in the state Constitution of 1777. The model of that executive soon contributed to the creation of another—the presidency of the United States. Though many stages removed from the Leislerian struggles by then, New York's failures became, in a perverse sort of way, America's success.

For Further Reading

Stephen B. Baxter. *William III and the Defense of European Liberty, 1650–1702.* New York, 1966.

Jon Butler. *The Huguenots in America: A Refugee People in New World Society.* Cambridge, Mass., 1983.

J. R. Jones. *The Revolution of 1688 in England.* New York, 1972.

Michael Kammen. *Colonial New York: A History.* New York, 1975.

E. H. Kossman. *In Praise of the Dutch Republic: Some Seventeenth-Century Attitudes.* London, 1963.

Douglas R. Lacey. *Dissent and Parliamentary Politics in England, 1661–1689: A Study in the Perpetuation and Tempering of Parliamentarianism.* New Brunswick, N. J., 1969.

David S. Lovejoy. "Equality and Empire: The New York Charter of Libertyes, 1683," *William and Mary Quarterly,* 3d ser., (1964).

David S. Lovejoy. *The Glorious Revolution in America.* New York, 1972.

John M. Murrin. "English Rights as Ethnic Aggression: The English Conquest, the Charter of Liberties of 1683, and Leisler's Rebellion in New York," in William Pencak and Conrad Edick Wright, eds., *Authority and Resistance in Early New York.* New York, 1988.

Robert C. Ritchie. *The Duke's Province: A Study of New York Politics and Society, 1664–1691.* Chapel Hill, 1977.

Herbert H. Rowen. and John de Witt. *Grand Pensionary of Holland, 1625–1672.* Princeton, 1978.

Simon Schama. *The Embarrassment of Riches: An Interpretation of Dutch Culture in the Golden Age.* New York, 1987.

Lois G. Schwoerer. *The Declaration of Rights, 1689.* Baltimore, 1981.

David William Voorhees. " 'In Behalf of the True Protestant Religion': The Glorious Revolution in New York." Ph.D. dissertation: New York University, 1988.

J. R. Western. *Monarchy and Revolution: The English State in the 1680's.* London, 1972.

[The New York Charter of Liberties]

[1683]

FIRST GENERAL ASSEMBLY HELD AT
FORT JAMES IN THE CITY OF NEW YORK

THE CHARTER of Libertyes and priviledges granted by his Royall Highnesse to the Inhabitants of New Yorke and its Dependencyes.

[Passed, October 30, 1683]

For better Establishing the Government of this province of New Yorke and that Justice and Right may be Equally done to all persons within the same

BEE It Enacted by the Governour Councell and Representatives now in Generall Assembly mett and assembled and by the authority of the same.

1. THAT The Supreme Legislative Authority under his Majesty and Royall Highnesse James Duke of Yorke Albany &c Lord proprietor of the said province shall forever be and reside in a Governour, Councell, and the people mett in Generall Assembly.

2. THAT The Exercise of the Cheife Magistracy and Administracon of the Government over the said province shall bee in the said Governour assisted by a Councell with whose advice and Consent or with at least four of them he is to rule and Governe the same according to the Lawes thereof.[1]

3. THAT in Case the Governour shall dye or be absent out of the province and that there be noe person within the said province Comissionated by his Royal Highnesse his heires or Successours to be Governour or Comander in Cheife there That then the Councell for the time being or Soe many of them as are in the Said province doe take upon them the Administracon of the Governour and the Execucon of

---

To facilitate comparisons between the 1683 and 1691 versions of the Charter of Liberties, the 1691 text has been divided into paragraphs, and the paragraphs of both versions have been numbered. In Article 6 of the 1683 Charter, two paragraphs of the original have been merged into one. Source: Charles Z. Lincoln, ed., *The Colonial Laws of New York from the Year 1664 to the Revolution* (Albany, 1894), 1: 111–16, 244–48.

[1] Although the Charter of Liberties never makes the point explicit, the clear understanding at the time was that members of the council would, as before, be appointed by the duke, who in turn usually accepted the recommendations of his governor.

the Lawes thereof and powers and authorityes belonging to the Governour and Councell the first in nominacon in which Councell is to preside untill the said Governour shall returne and arrive in the said province againe, or the pleasure of his Royall Highnesse his heires or Successours Shall be further knowne.[2]

4. THAT According to the usage Custome and practice of the Realme of England a sessions of a Generall Assembly be held in this province once in three yeares at least.[3]

5. THAT Every Freeholder within this province and Freeman in any Corporacon Shall have his free Choise and Vote in the Electing of the Representatives without any manner of constraint or Imposicon. [A]nd that in all Eleccons the Majority of Voices shall carry itt and by freeholders is understood every one who is Soe understood according to the Lawes of England.[4]

6. THAT the persons to be Elected to sitt as representatives in the Generall Assembly from time to time for the severall Cittyes townes Countyes Shires or Divisions of this province and all places within the same shall be according to the proporcon and number hereafter Expressed[,] that is to say for the Citty and County of New Yorke four, for the County of Suffolke two, for Queens County two, for Kings County two, for the County of Richmond two[,] for the County of West Chester two[,] for the County of Ulster two[,] for the County of Albany two[,] and for Schenectade within the said County one[,] for Dukes County two, for the County of Cornwall two[,] and as many more as his Royall highnesse shall think fitt to Establish.[5]

[2] Nothing in this clause would prevent the duke from commissioning a lieutenant governor to preside over the province in the absence of the governor. The councillor first in nomination was the one with the oldest commission.

[3] This clause only required a session of the assembly to be held every three years. It said nothing about the frequency of elections. In England, the Cavalier Parliament was elected in 1661 and not dissolved until 1678. In Ireland, parliaments routinely sat for the entire reign of the monarch.

[4] A freeholder was a man who owned his own land. To vote in England, a freeholder's land had to be worth an annual rental value of 40 shillings. Nearly all New York farms would have met this requirement. By "corporation" the charter meant city, specifically New York City and Albany, both of which would receive formal charters of incorporation from Governor Thomas Dongan in 1686. A resident became a freeman by paying a small fee. This requirement was somewhat more restrictive than the freehold limitation for farmers, but the electorate became quite broad anyway.

[5] Shire was an older word for county. It was relevant in New York because, from 1665 to 1683, Long Island and Westchester were organized as a judicial unit called "Yorkshire," which was subdivided into three divisions or "ridings" within which justices of the peace rode circuit. In 1683, the West Riding became Kings County, the North Riding was divided into Queens and Westchester counties, and the East Riding became

7. THAT all persons Chosen and Assembled in manner aforesaid or the Major part of them shall be deemed and accounted the Representatives of this province which said Representatives together with the Governour and his Councell Shall forever be the Supreame and only Legislative power under his Royall Highnesse of the said province.[6]

8. THAT The said Representatives may appoint their owne Times of meeting dureing their sessions and may adjourne their house from time to time to such time as to them shall seeme meet and convenient.[7]

9. THAT The said Representatives are the sole Judges of the Qualificacons of their owne members, and likewise of all undue Eleccons and may from time to time purge their house as they shall see occasion dureing the said sessions.[8]

10. THAT noe member of the general Assembly or their servants dureing the time of their Sessions and whilest they shall be goeing to and returning from the said Assembly shall be arrested sued imprisoned or any wayes molested or troubled nor be compelled to make answere to any suite, Bill, plaint, Declaracon or otherwise, (Cases of High Treason and felony only Excepted) provided the number of the said servants shall not Exceed three.[9]

Suffolk. Of the other jurisdictions mentioned here, Dukes County (Martha's Vineyard) and Cornwall (eastern Maine) were governed by the Duke of York in the 1680s but given to Massachusetts in its new royal charter of 1691. Note that the duke, not the assembly, had the power to create new constituencies.

[6] This clause clearly was intended to deprive the governor and council of the power to make laws, a function they had routinely exercised since the English conquest of 1664. In all probability, the charter was not denying the power of Parliament to control the oceanic commerce (or, in the later language of the 1760s, the "external" affairs) of the colony. The assembly was not challenging England's navigation acts, which regulated major aspects of colonial commerce. No such claim would have been accepted by the duke or the king's ministers. Because Parliament had not yet attempted to legislate for the "internal" concerns of the settlers, that question was not yet at issue.

[7] This clause implicitly distinguishes between adjourning, proroguing, and dissolving the assembly. The assembly could adjourn itself for short periods. When it resumed its session after an adjournment, all proceedings picked up where they had left off. The governor retained the power to prorogue or dissolve the assembly. A prorogation brought a session to an end without requiring new elections. It terminated all existing business. At the next session, all bills or resolutions would have to be introduced anew. A dissolution ended the life of the existing assembly. A new one could meet only after a general election.

[8] The charter here affirms a hard-fought privilege claimed by the House of Commons. In 1641, Charles I had led a band of soldiers into the House to arrest five members who opposed his policies. This confrontation became a major trigger of the civil war that led to Charles' execution in 1649. Like the House of Commons, the New York assembly insists that it alone, not the governor, can expel a member or decide the result of a disputed election.

[9] The assemblymen here claim the conventional privileges of members of Parlia-

II. THAT All bills agreed upon by the said Representatives or the Major part of them shall be presented unto the Governour and his Councell for their Approbacon and Consent[,] All and Every which Said Bills soe approved of [or?] Consented to by the Governour and his Councell shall be Esteemed and accounted the Lawes of the province, Which said Lawes shall continue and remaine of force untill they shall be repealed by the authority aforesaid[,] that is to say the Governour Councell and Representatives in General Assembly by and with the Approbacon of his Royal Highnesse[,] or Expire by their owne Limittacons.[10]

12. THAT In all Cases of death or removall of any of the said Representatives The Governour shall issue out Sumons by Writt to the Respective Townes Cittyes Shires Countryes [i.e., counties] or Divisions for which he or they soe removed or deceased were Chosen[,] willing and requireing the Freeholders of the Same to Elect others in their place and stead.[11]

13. THAT Noe freeman shall be taken and imprisoned or be disseized of his Freehold or Libertye or Free Customes or be outlawed or Exiled or any other wayes destroyed nor shall be passed upon adjudged or condemned But by the Lawfull Judgment of his peers and by the Law of this province. Justice nor Right shall be neither sold denyed or deferred to any man within this province.[12]

14. THAT Noe aid, Tax, Tallage, Assessment, Custome, Loane, Benevoloence or Imposicon whatsovever shall be layed assessed imposed or levyed on any of his Majestyes Subjects within this province

---

ment, which in turn were designed to guarantee an environment in which the legislators could debate and discuss issues openly and fully without fear of reprisal from the executive. If the assemblymen themselves considered someone's speech treasonable or insulting, they, but not the king or governor, could expel him.

10 This clause is poorly drafted. The first half seems to deny that the duke can disallow a statute once the governor, council, and assembly have approved it. Only the New York legislature could undo a New York law. But the second half seems to take the duke's participation for granted. This discrepancy would become a serious issue when James, as king, disallowed the Charter of Liberties. In 1689, some of its supporters still considered it the law of the land.

11 This clause was a standard privilege of the House of Commons. The assembly is trying to ensure that no governor could gain control of its proceedings by manipulating the rate of attrition of its members. With no guarantee of frequent elections, that possibility was quite real.

12 This clause closely paraphrases Articles 39 and 40 of Magna Carta. For an English translation, see Carl Stephenson and Frederick George Markham, eds., *Sources of English Constitutional History: A Selection of Documents from A.D. 600 to the Present* (New York, 1937), 115–26 at 121. The phrase "disseized of his freehold" means "deprived of his landed property." The "Lawfull Judgment of his peers [i.e., equals]" means trial by jury.

or their Estates upon any manner of Colour or pretence but by the act and Consent of the Governour Councell and Representatives of the people in Generall Assembly mett and Assembled.[13]

15. THAT Noe man of what Estate or Condicon soever shall be putt out of his Lands or Tenements, nor taken, nor imprisoned, nor disherited, nor banished nor any wayes distroyed without being brought to Answere by due Course of Law.[14]

16. THAT A Freeman Shall not be amerced [i.e., fined] for a small fault, but after the manner of his fault and for a great fault after the Greatnesse thereof Saveing to him his freehold, And a husbandman saveing to him his Wainage and a merchant likewise saveing to him his merchandize[.] And none of the said Amerciaments shall be assessed but by the oath of twelve honest and Lawfull men of the Vicinage[,] provided the faults and misdemeanours be not in Contempt of Courts of Judicature.[15]

17. ALL Tryalls shall be by the verdict of twelve men, and as neer as may be peers or Equalls And of the neighbourhood and in the County Shire or Division where the fact Shall arise or grow Whether the same be by Indictment infermacon Declaracon or otherwise against the person Offender or Defendant.[16]

---

[13] This clause closely follows Parliament's Petition of Right (1628) which denounced certain practices of Charles I. In simple terms, it means "no taxation without representation." It tries to include nearly every device used by the kings of England since the Norman Conquest to raise revenue, except for a few that were utterly obsolete. A feudal lord could demand an "aid" from his vassals and freemen on three occassions— to ransom himself, upon the knighting of his eldest son, and at the first wedding of his eldest daughter. Tallage was an arbitrary tax upon the king's own tenants or an imposition upon royal boroughs. Assessments were general property taxes. Customs were import and export duties. Impositions were port duties levied by the Crown without parliamentary consent, traditionally to regulate trade and promote English manufactures, although the early Stuarts increasingly used them to raise revenue. Benevolences were forced gifts from wealthy subjects. Charles I had used forced loans in the 1620s. Those who refused to lend money to the king found themselves in prison. Stephenson and Marcham, *Sources,* 450–51 and, for impositions, J. P. Kenyon, ed., *The Stuart Constitution: Documents and Commentary* (Cambridge, England, 1969), 55 and passim.

[14] In other words, the ruler must follow established judicial procedures in trying, convicting, and punishing any subject.

[15] This clause paraphrases Article 20 of Magna Carta and regulates procedures in non-capital trials. See Stephenson and Marcham, eds., *Sources,* 119. In lay terms, it says that the punishment should fit the crime, that fines should be imposed only after a jury trial (except for contempt of court), and that fines should not deprive the offender of his livelihood—a landowner's freehold estate, a farmer's (or husbandman's) agricultural implements (wainage), or a merchant's stock in trade. To do so would only make the community responsible for supporting another family.

[16] In most American colonies in the 1680s, misdemeanor trials rarely went to a jury.

18. THAT In all Cases Capitall or Criminall there shall be a grand Inquest who shall first present the offence and then twelve men of the neighbourhood to try the Offender who after his plea to the Indictment shall be allowed his reasonable Challenges.[17]

19. THAT In all cases whatsoever Bayle by sufficient Suretyes Shall be allowed and taken unlesse for treason or felony plainly and specially Expressed and menconed in the Warrant of Committment[,] provided Always that nothing herein contained shall Extend to discharge out of prison upon bayle any person taken in Execucon for debts or otherwise legally sentenced by the Judgment of any of the Courts of Record within the province.[18]

20. THAT no Freeman shall be compelled to receive any Marriners or Souldiers into his house and there suffer them to Sojourne, against their [i.e., the freemen's] willes[,] provided Always it be not in time of Actuall Warr within this province.[19]

This clause requires that all criminal trials, whether for capital offenses or misdemeanors, be decided by local juries, regardless of how the prosecution was initiated—through indictment by a grand jury, direct action (information) by a government prosecutor (usually the attorney general or, at the county level, the duke's or king's attorney), or direct prosecution by the victim (declaration). Proceedings by information were rare, unpopular, and often political. Almost by definition, they occurred only when the public prosecutor doubted that a grand jury would support an indictment. The charter guarantees that in such a case the accused would have the benefit of a petit jury.

[17] The word "Criminall" must mean "felonious" in this article, if only because the previous article sanctions other ways of bringing accused persons to trial than by grand jury. This clause requires an indictment or presentment by a grand jury (or grand inquest) before proceeding further in any trial for a capital offense (the technical meaning of "felony" in England and New York, but not all other colonies). This provision also gives the accused the right to challenge jurors after pleading guilty or not guilty. Technically, an indictment was a grand jury accusation put into Latin by a court official. It was almost never used in America. Its English-language equivalent, the presentment, was by far the most common device for beginning a prosecution. Note that the charter does not give an accused felon the right to an attorney. In seventeenth-century England, that privilege was available only for misdemeanors, not capital offenses.

[18] In the seventeenth century, with rare exceptions, jails existed, not to punish criminals, but to incarcerate debtors who refused to pay (on the assumption that they were really concealing assets somewhere) and to hold accused persons while awaiting trial. For this reason, a criminal tribunal was usually called a "court of assize and general gaol [jail] delivery." Whatever the results of the trials, the court delivered people from confinement, either to be acquitted or punished (executed, whipped, or fined). This clause of the charter grants bail to those accused of less than capital offenses, provided they can find "sureties"—persons who will post bond on their behalf promising to pay the amount of the bail if the accused fails to appear for trial. The clause also makes it clear that persons imprisoned for debt (a civil, not a criminal matter) have no claim to bail. A court of record was any common-law court, as against a court of equity, an ecclesiastical court, or a vice-admiralty court.

[19] This clause against the compulsory quartering of soldiers and sailors in private

21. THAT Noe Commissions for proceeding by Marshall Law against any of his Majestyes Subjects within this province shall issue forth to any person or persons whatsoever[,] Least [i.e., lest] by Colour of them any of his Majestyes Subjects bee destroyed or putt to death[,] Except all such officers persons and Soldiers in pay throughout the Government.[20]

22. THAT from hence forward Noe Lands Within this province shall be Esteemed or accounted a Chattle or personall Estate but an Estate of Inheritance according to the Custome and practice of his Majesties Realme of England.[21]

23. THAT Noe Court or Courts within this province have or at any time hereafter Shall have any Jurisdiccon power or authority to grant out any Execucon or other writt whereby any mans Land may be sold or any other way disposed off without the owners Consent[,] provided Always That the issues or meane proffitts of any mans Lands shall or may be Extended by Execucon or otherwise to satisfye just debts[,] Any thing to the Contrary hereof in any wise Notwithstanding.[22]

24. THAT Noe Estate of a feme Covert shall be sold or conveyed But by Deed acknowledged by her in Some Court of Record[,] the Woman being secretly Examined if She doth it freely without threats or Compulsion of her husband.[23]

---

homes is a greatly abbreviated version of a paragraph in Parliament's Petition of Right (1628). The last portion, making an exception in time of war within the province, is not in the English original. See Stephenson and Marcham, *Sources*, 451–52.

[20] This clause exempts civilians from trials by courts-martial, which can only be used against soldiers and officers receiving pay for active service. In 1683, that category included only the province's small redcoat garrison. In time of war, it presumably would also apply to provincial units in actual service, but not to the unpaid local militia.

[21] In suits for debt and similar obligations, English common law gave much stronger protection to landed than to personal property. The charter claims these benefits for New Yorkers.

[22] This clause clarifies the previous one. A person's landed property cannot be forfeited for debt without the debtor's consent, but the income derived from the property is liable to forfeiture.

[23] Under English common law, an unmarried woman was a *feme sole* (single female). When she married she became a *feme covert*, that is, her legal personality was submerged in or "covered" by her husband's. Only through him could she act in a legally binding way, such as to sue or be sued—except, of course, to answer for a crime she had personally committed. If she brought landed property to the marriage or inherited it while married, this clause gave her some protection should her husband try to sell that land. Before a common law court (court of record), with her husband not present (secretly), she would have to give her consent to the transaction. Up to the reforms of 1683, most Dutch women in New York had continued to function under Dutch law, which gave women far greater control over property. Even with the protection of this clause, the Charter of Liberties threatened to narrow those rights drastically.

25. THAT All Wills in writeing attested by two Credible Witnesses shall be of the same force to convey Lands as other Conveyances[,] being registered in the Secretaryes Office within forty dayes after the testators death.

26. THAT A Widdow after the death of her husband shall have her Dower And shall and may tarry in the Cheife house of her husband forty dayes after the death of her husband within which forty dayes her Dower shall be assigned her[.] And for her Dower shall be assigned unto her the third part of all the Lands of her husband dureing Coverture, Except shee were Endowed of Lesse before Marriage.[24]

27. THAT All Lands and Heritages within this province and Dependencyes shall be free from all fines and Lycences upon Alienacons, and from all Herriotts[,] Ward Shipps[,] Liveryes[,] primer Seizins[,] yeare day and Wast[,] Escheats and forfeitures upon the death of parents and Ancestors naturall[,] unaturall[,] casuall or Judiciall, and that forever; Cases of High treason only Excepted.[25]

28. THAT Noe person or persons which professe Faith in God by Jesus Christ Shall at any time be any wayes molested punished disquieted or called in Question for any Difference in opinion or Matter of Religious Concernment, who doe not actually disturb the Civill peace of the province, But that all and Every such person or persons may from time to time and at all times freely have and fully enjoy his or their

[24] This clause derives from Article 10 of Magna Carta. A *dower* was a woman's claim to a share of her husband's property after his death. It was distinct from the *dowry*, the property she brought into the marriage. In most cases, the dowry was personal property (her father's land nearly always went to her brothers), but her dower rights included a life-interest in her husband's landed property, usually a third of it.

[25] This clause abolishes feudal impediments to the inheritance and sale (alienation) of lands. Some of these feudal customs actually took hold on New York manors around the middle of the eighteenth century. This paragraph also abolishes the forfeiture of landed property upon conviction of a crime, except treason. Fines and licenses were amounts owed to a feudal superior upon the sale of land. A heriot was an obligation owed by an estate to a feudal superior upon the death of an occupant. A wardship was the superior's right to the income of an inferior's estate while the heir was a minor. Livery was the legal process by which the ward claimed possession from his superior and guardian. *Primer seisin* gave the superior a claim to a year's profit from an estate when it passed to an adult heir. Year, day, and waste gave the king the profits for a year and a day from the estates of people convicted of petty treason or felony. He also had the right to lay waste any tenements on the property, which then reverted to the convicted person's lord. Escheat today means the reversion of property to the state when no lawful heir can be found. In medieval England, it also meant the reversion of land to a feudal superior when the holder was convicted of a serious crime, which is presumably the form of escheat here abolished. In this context, forfeiture was interchangeable with that meaning of escheat. Deaths "natural, unnatural, casual or judicial" cover all possibilities—ordinary death, suicide, accidental death, and execution for crime.

Judgments or Consciencyes in matters of Religion throughout all the
province, they behaveing themselves peaceably and quietly and not
useing this Liberty to Lycentiousnesse nor to the civill Injury or outward
disturbance of others[;] provided Alwayes that this liberty or any thing
contained therein to the Contrary shall never be Construed or improved
to make void the Settlement of any publique Minister on Long Island
Whether Such Settlement be by two thirds of the voices in any Towne
thereon which shall alwayes include the Minor part[,] Or by Subscripcons of Perticuler Inhabitants in Said Townes provided they are the
two thirds thereon[,] Butt that all such agreements Covenants and
Subscripcons that are there already made and had Or that hereafter
shall bee in this Manner Consented to agreed and Subscribed shall at
all time and times hereafter be firme and Stable[.] And in Confirmacon
hereof It is Enacted by the Governour Councell and Representatives;
That all Such Sumes of money soe agreed on Consented to or Subscribed as aforesaid for maintenance of said publick Ministers by the
two thirds of any Towne on Long Island Shall always include the Minor
part who shall be regulated thereby[.] And also Such Subscripcons and
agreements as are before menconed are and Shall be always ratified
performed and paid, And if any Towne on said Island in their publick
Capacity of agreement with any Such minister or any perticuler persons
by their private Subscripcons as aforesaid Shall make default deny or
withdraw from Such payment Soe Covenanted to agreed upon and
Subscribed[,] That in Such Case upon Complaint of any Collector
appointed and Chosen by two thirds of Such Towne upon Long Island
unto any Justice of that County Upon his hearing the Same he is here
by authorized impowered and required to issue out his warrant unto
the Constable or his Deputy or any other person appointed for the
Collection of Said Rates or agreement to Levy upon the goods and
Chattles of the Said Delinquent or Defaulter all such Sumes of money
Soe covenanted and agreed to be paid by distresse with Costs and
Charges without any further Suite in Law Any Lawe Custome or usage
to the Contrary in any wise Notwithstanding.

PROVIDED Alwayes the said sume or sumes be under forty shillings
otherwise to be recovered as the Law directs.[26]

---

[26] This clause grants freedom of worship to all Christians willing to live peacefully
with one another. It makes no provision for New York's small Jewish community of the
1680s, but under James, Jews also enjoyed the benefits of toleration. The rest of the
paragraph protects all existing arrangements among New England settlers on Long Island
to pay ministers' salaries with public taxes, requires a two-thirds vote to establish such
a relationship (under the Duke's Laws of 1665, a majority vote had been sufficient),

AND WHEREAS All the Respective Christian Churches now in practice within the City of New Yorke and the other places of this province doe appeare to be priviledged Churches and have been Soe Established and Confirmed by the former authority of this Government[,] BEE it hereby Enacted by this Generall Assembly and by the authority thereof That all the Said Respective Christian Churches be hereby Confirmed therein And that they and Every of them Shall from henceforth forever be held and reputed as priviledged Churches and Enjoy all their former freedomes of their Religion in Divine Worshipp and Church Discipline And that all former Contracts made and agreed upon for the maintenances of the severall ministers of the Said Churches shall stand and continue in full force and virtue[.] And that all Contracts for the future to be made Shall bee of the same power[.] And all persons that are unwilling to performe their part of the said Contract Shall be Constrained thereunto by a warrant from any Justice of the peace provided it be under forty Shillings Or otherwise as this Law directs[.] [P]rovided allsoe that all Christian Churches that Shall hereafter come and settle within this province shall have the Same priviledges.[27]

---

binds any dissenting minority to pay the tax voted by such a majority, and empowers tax collectors to foreclose on the personal (not landed) property of tax delinquents for as much as 40 shillings without a need for trial. Of the various denominations in New York at the time, Quakers and Jews had the strongest reasons to find these arrangements potentially threatening. Quakers opposed all taxes for the support of religion.

[27] This clause offered public recognition and some kind of legal support to all Christian denominations, including the Roman Catholic Church. With the consent of two-thirds of the voters, any Long Island community, Dutch or English, could agree to provide tax support for a single church, and all taxpayers would have to contribute to that church. Religious minorities on Long Island could work out contractual arrangements between their members and their clergy, and these agreements would also be enforceable in law, but these people would have to pay support for two churches—the one locally established, and the one to which they belonged. In the rest of the province, contractual arrangements between minister and congregation, enforceable at law, would be the norm. The drafters clearly expected different denominations to become established churches in different parts of the province—the Dutch Reformed Church in Albany and King's County, the Congregational Church among most of the New England population of Long Island, and probably both the Dutch Reformed and Anglican churches in New York City. In many ways, this plan anticipated modern Canada's formula for religious liberty, rather than the separation of church and state that has taken hold in the United States since the American Revolution.

[The New York Charter of Liberties]

[1691]

First Session of The First Assembly To Meet
After the Restoration of Royal Government in 1691

An Act declareing what are the Rights and Priviledges of their Majesties Subjects inhabiting within their Province of new York.

[Passed, May 13, 1691]

Forsasmuch as the Representatives of this their Majesties Province of New York now Convened in Generall Assembly are deeply sensible of their Matys most gratious favour in restoring to them the undoubted Rights and Priviledges of Englishemen by declareing their Royall will and pleasure in their Letters Pattents to his Excellcy who they have appointed their Captaine generall and Governour in Chief over this their Province; that he should with the advice and consent of their Councill from time to time as need shall require to summon and call generall Assemblys of the Inhabitants being freeholders according to the usage of their Majesties other Plantations in America. And that this most excellent constitution soe necessary and soe much Esteemed by our Ancestors may ever continue unto their Majesties Subjects within this Province of New York; the Representatives of this their Majesties Province Convened in Generall Assembly doe with all duty and Submission humbly pray that the rights, Priviledges Libertyes and franch-eses according to the Lawes and statues of their Majesties Realm of England may be confirmed unto their Majesties most dutyfull and loyall Subjects Inhabiting within this their Province of New York by Authority of his generall assembly.[28]

Be it Therefore Enacted by the Governour and Councill and the Representatives mett in generall Assembly. And it is hereby enacted and declared by the Authority of the same,

---

[28] The letters patent were the royal commission to Henry Sloughter making him governor of New York and empowering him to summon an elective assembly. Under James II, New York had once again been governed without such a legislature from 1686 to 1689. For most purposes, these years marked a reversion to the pattern of government under the Duke of York from 1664 to 1683. Jacob Leisler's revolutionary regime (1689–91) seemed arbitrary to many settlers, particularly the English community in New York City. The assembly of 1691 was dominated by Anti-Leislerians. The preamble to the new Charter of Liberties thus claims that New Yorkers were deprived of "the undoubted Rights and Privileges of Englishmen" under both James II and Leisler.

1. That the supreame Legislative power and authorite under their Majesties William and Mary King and Queene of England &c shall forever be and reside in A Governour in Chief and Councill appointed by their Majesties their Heires and successours; And the people by their Representatives mett and Convened in generall Assembly;[29]

2. That the exercice and administration of the government over the said Province shall, persuant to their Majesties Letters Pattents[,] be in the said Governour in Chief, and Councill with whose advice and consent or with att least five of them, he is to rule and Govern the same, according to the lawes therof, and for any defect therein according to the Laws of England and not otherwise.[30]

3. That in Case the Governour in Chief shall Dye or be Absent out of the Province; and that there be noe person within the said Province Commissionated by their Majesties their heires or Successors to be governour or Commander in Chief[,] that then the Councill for the time being or soe many of them as are in the said Province doe take upon them the administration of the government and the Execution of the Lawes therof and powers and authorities belonging to the Governour in Chief and Councill, the first in nomination in which Councill is to preside untill the said Governour shall return and arrive in the said Province againe, or the pleasure of their Majestyes their heires or Successors be further known.[31]

4. That for the good government and rule of their Majestys Subjects a session of a generall Assembly be held in this Province once in every yeare.[32]

5. That every freeholder within this province and freeman in any Corporation shall have his free Choice and voat in the electing, of the Representatives without any manner of Constraint or Imposition; And that in all elections the Majority of votes shall carry itt, and by freeholders is to be understood every one who shall have fourty shillings P Annum in freehold.[33]

---

[29] This clause makes explicit what was implicit in 1683, that the council would be an appointive body.

[30] The most important new feature of this article is the provision that imposes the laws of England on the colony wherever New York law was silent or uncertain. This requirement threatened to challenge any Dutch customs that had managed to survive within the legal system.

[31] Unlike its 1683 counterpart, this clause explicitly recognizes the power of the Crown to name a lieutenant governor as well as a governor.

[32] The 1683 charter had required only one session every three years. The 1691 version demands annual sessions but still imposes no requirement about the frequency of elections. Except for one year, New York's assembly did meet annually for the rest of the colonial period.

[33] The 1683 charter left the traditional English freehold undefined. The 1691 revision

6. That the persons to be elected to Sitt as Representatives in the Generall Assembly from time to time for the severall Cittys, Towns, Countys, Shires, Divitions or Mannors of this province and all places within the same shall be according to the proportion and number hereafter expressed, that is to say for the Citty and County of New Yorke foure[,] for Suffolk County two[,] for Queens County two[,] for Kings County two, for the County of Richmond two, for the County of West-Chester two, for the County of Ulster two, for the Citty and County of Albany two, for the Colloney of Renslaerswick, one, Dukes County two; and as many more as their Majesties their heires and successors shall think fitt to establish.[34]

7. That all persons Chosen and Assembled in manner aforesaid or the Major part of them shall be deemed and accounted the representatives of this Province in generall assembly.

8. That the Representatives convened in generall Assembly may appoint their own times of meeting during their sessions and may adjourn their house from time to time as to them shall seem meet and convenient.

9. That the said representatives as aforesaid Conven'd are the sole Judges of the Qualifications of their own Members, and likewise of all undue Ellections, and may from time to time purg the house As they shall see occation[.]

10. That noe member of the generall assembly or their Servants dureing the Time of their Sessions and whilst they shall be going to and returning from the said Assembly shall be arrested, sued, Imprisoned or any wayes molested or troubled or be Compelled to make answer to any suite, bill, plaint Declaration or otherwise, Cases of high Treason and fellony onely Excepted.

11. That all Bills agreed upon by the Representatives or the Major part of them shall be presented unto the Governour and the Councill for their approbation and Consent[,] all and every which said Bills soe approved of and consented to by the Governour and the Councill shall be Esteemed and accounted the Laws of this province which said Lawes

---

makes the 40-shilling requirement for voters an explicit provision. "P Annum" is the Latin per annum, or yearly rental value.

[34] Rensselaerswyck was a patroonship (the Dutch equivalent of an English manor) in the upper Hudson Valley and the first of New York's manors to acquire the privilege of electing its own representative to the assembly. Because the Massachusetts charter of 1691 had not yet been issued when this assembly met, New York still claimed Martha's Vineyard (Dukes County) but not eastern Maine where the French and Indians had recently overwhelmed the English garrison at Pemaquid.

shall continue and remaine in force untill they be dissalowed by their Majesties their heirs and successors or expire by their own limitation.[35]

12. That in All Cases of death or Absence of any of the said Representatives the Governour for the time being, shall Issue out A writt of Summons to the Respective Cittys Towns Countys Division or Mannors; for which he or they so deceased or absent were Chosen, willing and requireing the freeholders of the same, to Elect others in their places and stead[.]

13. That noe freemen shall be taken and Imprisoned or be desiezed of his freehold, or liberty or free Custom's, or out Law'd or Exiled or any other wayes destroyed, nor shall be passed upon, adjudged or Condemned but by the Lawfull Judgement of his peers and by the Law of this Province[.] Justice nor right shall be neither sold denied or delayed to any person within this Province.

14. That noe Aid, tax, tollage [tallage], assessment, Custome[,] Loan, Benevolence gift, Excise[,] duty or Imposition whatsoever shall be laid assessed Imposed, Levyed or required of or on any of their Majtys Subjects within this Province &c or their estates upon any manor of Colour or pretence whatsoever but by the Act and Consent of the governor and Councill and Representatives of the people in generall Assembly mett and Convened;[36]

15. That noe man of what estate or Condition soever shall be put out of his Lands, tenements, nor taken nor Imprisoned nor disinherited nor banished nor any wayes destroyed or molested without first being brought to Answer by due Course of Law.

16. That A Freeman shall not be Amerced [fined] for A small fault but after the maner of his fault, And for A great fault after the greatness thereof, saveing to him his freehold[;] and A husbandman saveing to him his wainage; and A merchant saveing to him his Merchandize; and none of the said Amercements shall be Assessed but by the Oath of twelve honest and Lawfull men of the Vicinage[,] provided the faults and Misdemeaners be not in Contempt of Courts of Judicature.

17. All tryalls shall be by the verdict of Twelve men and as nere as may be peares [peers] or equalls of the neighbourhood of the place

[35] Unlike the 1683 charter, this version explicitly recognized the power of the Crown to disallow a law that had been approved by governor, council, and assembly in New York. No disallowance took effect until it was publicly proclaimed in the colony.

[36] Compared with the 1683 list, the new form of taxation included in 1691 is the excise, a tax on the consumption of a commodity, such as tobacco or alcohol taxes today. The word "duty" is also new. It was usually synonomous with "customs." The author of this clause probably intended to include all such obligations—customs on imports and exports, and tonnage duties, which were levied on ships rather than cargoes.

where the fact shall arise or grow; whether the same be by Indictment declaracon or Information or otherwise against the person or defendant.

18. That in all cases capitall or criminall there shall be a grand Inquest who shall first present the offence; and then twelve good men of the neighbourhood, to try the offendor, who after his plea to the Indictment shall be allowed his reasonable challenges.

19. That in all Cases whatsoever bayle by sufficient suretyes shall be allowed and taken unless for Treason or fellony plainely and specially expressed and mentioned in the Warrant of Committment; and that the Fellony be such as is restrained from Bayle by the Law of England.[37]

20. That noe freeman shall be Compelled to receive any souldiers or Marrinors; Except Inholders and other houses of Publique entertainment; who are to Quarter for Ready money into his house and their Suffer them to Sojourne against their Wills, Provided it be not in time of actuall warr within this Province.[38]

21. That noe Commission for proceeding by Martiall Law against any of his Majesties Subjects within this Province &c shall Issue forth to any person or persons whatsoever[,] least [i.e., lest] by Colour of them any of his Majesties Subjects be destroyed or put to death. Except all such officers and souldiers that are in Garrison and pay dureing the time of actuall Warr.

22. That all the lands within this Province shall be esteemed and accounted Land of Freehold and Inheritance in free and Common soccage according to the tenure of East Greenwich in their Ma[jes]tys Realm of England.[39]

23. [Omitted in the 1691 version.]

24. That noe Estate of A feme Covert shall be sold or Conveyed but by deed acknowledged by her in Some Court of Record[,] the

[37] The new provision in 1691 is the last part of this article. English law granted bail to some accused felons. That benefit now became available in New York.

[38] The poor syntax of this clause makes it a confusing provision. Unlike the 1683 version, it apparently intends to empower the government to compel innholders or tavernkeepers to quarter soldiers whether or not they were willing to receive them, but private homes were still exempt from quartering, except in time of "actuall" war. Whether "actuall" had any legal meaning is unclear.

[39] This provision, a routine clause in most colonial charters, replaced paragraphs 22 and 23 in the 1683 charter. "Free and Common soccage according to the tenure of East Greenwich" was the most generous form of land tenure that English law had yet devised. Medieval lawyers contrasted free socage with all forms of military tenure on the one hand, and with servile socage on the other. Socage meant the obligation a tenant owed to his lord in exchange for secure tenure. In the manor of East Greenwich these obligations had all but disappeared. To hold land under such a title thus placed no restrictions on the owners' right to sell and also implied strong protections against forfeiture for debt.

woman being secretly examined if She doth itt freely without threats or Compulsion of her husband.

25. That All wills in writeing; attested by three or more Credible Witnesses shall be of the same force to Convey Lands as other Conveyances[,] being proved and Registred in the proper offices in each County within dayes after the Testators death

26. [Omitted in the 1691 version.[40]]

27. That all Lands and heritages within this Province and dependencies shall be free from all fines, licences upon Alienations; and from all hariotts, ward shipps, leveries primer, Seizins[,][41] yeare and day waist[,] Escheat and forfeitures upon the death of parents and Ancestors, naturall, unnaturall[,] Cassuall or Judiciall and that for ever. Cases of high treason onely excepted.

28. That noe person of what degree or Condition soever throughout this Province Choosen appointed Commisionated to Officiate or Execute any office or place Civill or Military within this Province &c shall be capable in the Law to take upon him the Charge of such places before he hath first taken the oaths appointed by act of Parliament to be taken in Lieu of the Oaths of Supremacie and allegiance and Subscribes the test.[42]

29. That noe p[er]son or p[er]sons which profess faith in God by Jesus Christ his onely sonn shall at any time be any wayes molested punished disturbed disquieted or called in question for any difference in opinion, or matter of Conscience in Religious Concernment who doe not under that pretence disturb the Civill peace of the Province[,] and that all and every such Person or persons may from time to time and at all times hereafter freely and fully Enjoy his or their opinion persuasions Judgements in matters of conscience and Religion throughout

[40] The 1691 assembly probably did not consider a woman's dower rights to be in danger or even a political issue. The omission of this article did not change existing inheritance practices.

[41] The proper form of the last three words is probably "liveries, primer seisin." In short, the comma is misplaced.

[42] This article had no counterpart in the 1683 charter. It tried to ban Roman Catholics from public office in New York by requiring officials to take oaths disavowing the papacy and the Catholic doctrine of transubstantiation, the belief that during the Mass the priest changes bread and wine into the real body and blood of Christ. This article also imposed Parliament's Test Act of 1673 upon the colony. That law required officeholders to receive the Lord's Supper according to the rites of the Church of England at least once a year. A literal interpretation of the Test Act could have banned everyone but a handful of Anglicans from public life. In all probability the assembly meant to require any Protestant form of the Lord's Supper, not the specific Anglican ritual. However, even this reading of the provision would exclude Quakers and Jews as well as Catholics. The Quakers had abolished all of the sacraments.

all this Province and freely meet at Convenient places within this Province, and there worshipp according to their respective perswasions without being hindred or molested, they behaveing themselves peaceably Quietly, modestly and religiously, and not useing this Liberty to Licentiousness nor to the Civill Injury or outward disturbance of others. Always provided that noething herein, mentioned or Contained shall extend to give Liberty for any persons of the Romish Religion to exercise their manor of worshipp Contrary to the Laws and Statues of their Majesties Kingdon of England.[43]

---

[43] This article is the 1691 counterpart of Article 28 in the 1683 charter. By adding "his onely sonn" after "Jesus Christ" it excluded Socinians (early Unitarianians) from toleration. Nearly everyone but the victims probably agreed with the goal of Article 29 (1691) to ban Catholics from office. But the original assembly version of Article 29 had no provision denying toleration to Catholics. The council added that portion, and the assembly accepted the amendment. Unlike the 1683 version of the charter, this revision made no provision of any kind for the public support of Christian churches, a question that became a heated issue over the next twenty years.

V

The New York City Charter

1686

COMMENTARY BY LEO HERSHKOWITZ

ON APRIL 27, 1686, GOVERNOR THOMAS DONGAN signed and sealed his charter, under instructions of James II, King of England, which granted to citizens of the "ancient Citty" of New York all "Libertyes priviledges franchises Rights . . . and immunityes" held by custom, tradition, and law. While hardly an "ancient city," New York cheerfully received the document, surely recognizing, as did Chancellor James Kent, 150 years later, that the charter provided "the basis for a plan of government for a great city."[1] It certainly was in keeping with James's intent to grant to the city, named after him when he was ducal proprietor, "immunities and privileges beyond what other parts of my territory doe enjoy."[2]

This favored status was shared by few other English or colonial cities. Perhaps James II recognized the long history of struggle for self-government in New York and wished to avoid similar conflict, for as a Catholic he realized the seriousness of Protestant resistance to his authority in England. Or perhaps he saw in Dongan, also a Catholic, whom he had appointed governor on September 30, 1682, an ally whose term of service could be made politic and successful.

---

[1] James Kent, *The Charter of the City of New York With Notes Thereon* (New York, 1836), 118, cited in Hendrick Hartog, *Public Property and Private Power: The Corporation of the City of New York in American Law, 1730–1870* (Chapel Hill, 1983), 21.

[2] Quoted in James G. Wilson, ed., *Memorial History of the City of New York* 4 vols. (New York, 1892–93), I: 411.

The forty-eight-year-old, Irish-born Dongan was a good choice. He had served in the French army and was familiar with French and Dutch customs. He had been lieutenant governor in Tangier, Africa, during 1678–79. His patron, the Duke of York, later James II, invited him to court and was surely very pleased to sign his commission.[3]

The new governor arrived in New York on Saturday, August 25, 1683, after an overland journey from Massachusetts with a considerable retinue including Thomas Harvey, an English Jesuit. The first Catholic mass held in the city was celebrated in Fort James, the old Fort Amsterdam at the tip of Manhattan Island. New York was now a small city having fewer than 4,000 inhabitants, but as Dongan observed they "grow more numerous daily and are of a turbulent disposition."[4] That turbulence could be attested to by Peter Stuyvesant. It was as much a part of New York as the wall of Wall Street or the expanse of *Heere Weg*, "Gentleman's Way," soon to be Broadway. Dutch was still the colony's principal language, while its inhabitants' religions were drawn from around the world—French Huguenots, Dutch Reformed, Anglicans, Calvinists, Lutherans, a few Catholics, Jews, Anabaptists, Sabbatarians, Anti-Sabbatarians, and Quakers (including those of Singing or Ranting persuasions). Bears and wolves were plentiful north of the city proper; indeed, a bear hunt took place in an orchard between present Cedar Street and Maiden Lane,[5] in the center of today's canyons of finance. It was a small city but truly at odds, especially in the political arena.

One of the first matters of business facing Dongan was to establish, in accordance with his instructions from the Duke of York, "a General Assembly of all the Freeholders by the persons whom they shall choose to represent them." Such was scheduled to meet in New York City on October 17, 1683, and on October 30 passed a new law, "The Charter of Libertyes and priviledges." This charter for the entire province of New York, signed by Governor Dongan on October 31, 1683, established rights of assembly, representative elections, majority rule, and the principle of taxation by consent. Though signed by the duke in England, the original document was never returned to New York and by 1685 was, in fact, repealed. However, its basic provisions remained—including the creation of twelve counties, among them the City and County of New York.

New Yorkers took quick advantage of the generosity of James in granting their city special immunities and privileges. On November 9,

[3] Wilson, 1: 399–401.
[4] Wilson, 1: 402.
[5] Wilson, 1: 402–3.

1683, Dongan received a petition, signed by Mayor William Beekman and six aldermen, requesting the continuation of the "ancient customs, privileges and immunities" granted on June 12, 1665, by Governor Richard Nicolls in the first English charter for the city. That charter had incorporated New York and placed it under the administration of a mayor, aldermen, and sheriff. A second charter of the same date which had appointed Thomas Willet mayor along with five aldermen and a sheriff had been confirmed by the Duke of York. The 1683 petition requested the division of the city into six wards with annual elections ·ᵓy freemen in each ward. It also asked for annual appointments by the governor and his council not only of a mayor and a recorder, but also of a sheriff, town clerk, and coroner. The corporation would appoint its own treasurer and be given control of ferries, docks, and other municipal functions, including the sole right of bolting flour.

After some hesitation, the petition was granted and on December 10, 1684, Dongan ordered that the new corporation be put in effect "until such time as his Royal Highness' pleasure shall be further known therein." City officials in the meantime quickly created wards and the new city government immediately passed numerous ordinances, including those meant to keep the Sabbath; for example, "No youths, maydes [maides], or other persons may meete together on the Lord's Day for sport or play, under fine of one shilling."[6] Slaves or Indians could not bear arms; landlords of public houses were to report strangers; a bounty was posted on wolves. On October 13, 1684, members of the new bicameral common council were chosen for the six wards. Six aldermen were elected to the council's upper house; six assistant aldermen (or assistants) to the lower house. The next day, Gabriel Manvielle was selected mayor.[7]

When Charles II died early in February 1685, the Duke of York, his brother, succeeded to the throne as James II and the colony became a Crown dependency. A new charter for the city was now necessary—especially since the grant to an assembly had been withheld. New Yorkers were uneasy that their "ancient privileges" would be threatened—that years of struggle to gain corporate recognition, from the Dutch first and then from the English, would be jeopardized. There were citizens who could recall those "ancient" times.

In 1647, Director General Peter Stuyvesant, basically on orders from the Dutch West India Company, had allowed New Amsterdam to select eighteen persons from whom the director would choose nine to form a

---

6 Wilson, 1: 412–13. David T. Valentine, ed., *Manual of the Corporation of the City of New York for the years 1844–45* (New York, 1844), 312–13.

7 Wilson, 1: 413, 419.

council to advise him "as is customary in Fatherland."[8] This representative authority was enlarged in 1652 when the West India Company
granted to New Amsterdam a municipal government consisting of a
schout (sheriff), two burgomasters, and five *schepens* elected by the citizens "in the manner usual in the City of Amsterdam." The right to
pass laws was granted subsequently on February 2, 1653, when a charter
was granted the city.[9] It was a hard-won victory, one not easily to be
given away. The right of self-government was recognized at the time
of the surrender in 1664 by the Nicolls charter. In October 1675, after
the short-lived Dutch reoccupation of 1673–74, and operating under the
duke's instructions, Governor Edmund Andros vested the mayor, aldermen, and sheriff with full power "to rule and govern all the inhabitants
of this city and corporation, and with all strangers."[10] Surely by 1686
rights of self-government were well-established and the Dongan charter
restated traditional principles, or so New Yorkers hoped.

The 1686 charter is often seen as the "beginning of modern governmental history of New York City,"[11] largely because the city was
given specific property rights which confirmed New York's control of
its own affairs free from systematic external interference. However, that
authority was always derivative and dependent upon the Crown. Autonomy granted was always partial and incomplete. Further, the charter
never received the royal seal as did the later Montgomerie Charter of
1730. Thus, it was often argued that, like the 1664 Nicolls charter,
Dongan's grant failed to convey proper proof of title both to property
and to government.[12] Still, its provisions were indeed the foundations
for a great city.

The preamble to the 1686 charter again describes New York as an
"ancient" city. The next two sections confirm "privileges and immunities" to mayor, aldermen, sheriff, and citizens. The corporation was
given right and title to the city hall and its grounds, two market houses,
wharves, the "Great Dock," the bridge into the dock (later Moore
Street), the new burial place outside the city gate (Wall Street), and
Long Island ferry with its rents and profits. A grant was made to all
existing streets, watercourses, alleys, bridges, and highways, with power
to establish, make, lay out, and repair all thoroughfares "necessary
needfull and Convenient for the inhabitants." There followed a proviso
which upheld private property rights and provided further that a person's

[8] Murray Hoffman, *A Treatise upon the Estate and Rights of the Corporation of the City
of New York as Proprietors* (New York, 1853), 17.
[9] Hoffman, 18.
[10] Hoffman, 20.
[11] Hartog, 14.
[12] Hartog, 20, 31–32.

property could not be taken away without "his [or] her" consent. For Chancellor James Kent this protection of private property "did honor to the character of the charter."[13]

The second and third sections of the charter grant the corporation all waste or vacant land, unpatented and unappropriated lands in Manhattan extending to low water, as well as "Royaltyes" of "fishing fowling Hunting, Hawking [and] minerals," excepting gold and silver mines. These lands were granted on condition that an annual quit rent of one beaver skin or its monetary equivalent would be paid to the Crown on March 25th of each year (the first day of the New Year according to the old Roman or Julian calendar) as recognition of inherent royal ownership. This was also confirmed by the Montgomerie Charter of 1730.

The next section deals with the limits and jurisdictions of the city and the right of the corporation to all rights and franchises without interference on the part of the colonial government. Section five designates city offices by title and character. These included the mayor, recorder, town clerk, six aldermen, six assistants, a chamberlain or treasurer, marshall, coroner, clerk of the market, high constable (a city official), seven sub-constables, one sheriff (a county official), and two nonfunctioning positions (marshall and "Serjaint at Mace") to be "appointed Chosen and Sworne" as hereafter mentioned.

The sixth section incorporates the "Mayor Aldermen and Commonalty of the Citty of New Yorke" and provides for perpetual succession of the corporation. It also allows city officials to purchase, hold, sell, rent, or give any lands and chattel or real property of any kind and to be sued or sue as well as to alter and make a common seal (a technical term meaning that such officials could act on behalf of the city—a benefit of its corporate status). Next, city officers were appointed by name— Nicholas Bayard as mayor; James Graham as recorder; John West as town clerk; Andrew Bowne, John Robinson, William Beekman, John Delevall, Abraham De Peyster, and Johannes Kipp as aldermen; with Nicholas De Meyer, John De Bryn, Johannes Von Brugh, Tunisse DeKay, Abraham Corbett, and Wolfert Webber as assistant aldermen. The corporation was given power to make, enforce, and repeal necessary laws. This section was superseded by the 1730 charter which enlarged these necessary powers.[14]

The eighth and ninth sections provide, among other matters, that the aldermen, assistants, and constables be chosen by a "majority of voices" of each ward on election day—the first day of Saint Michael, September 29th. Voting in New York was done *viva voce* (by voice).

13 Kent, 109.
14 For a discussion, see Kent, 132–33.

More voices meant more votes, numerical count was a rare occurrence. It was also provided that all officials "Shall be persons of good capacity and understanding," though this was more often a wish than a reality. The mayor, recorder, and aldermen also served as justices of the peace and were empowered to try persons for treason and other felonies including high and petty treason or suspicion of treason and disturbance of the peace. The mayor was also given the power to grant annual licenses to tavern keepers, innkeepers (these provided bed and drink), ordinary (eating house) keepers, victuallers (another name for inn, tavern, or ordinary keepers), and all sellers of wine, strong waters, cider, or any sort of liquors by retail. The fee could not exceed thirty shillings for such license. The income from fees was to be applied for public use without any account to be rendered to the governor or any provincial official.

The eleventh section allowed the mayor, recorder, aldermen, or the mayor and any three aldermen to appoint free citizens. Freemanship permitted a person to vote and to carry on a retail trade or to exercise "any art trade mistery or manuall occupation" without being subject to a fine. Freemen had to be native born or duly naturalized by the general assembly or by letters of denization granted by the governor or the lieutenant governor.

Section twelve repeats the authority of the corporation to purchase and hold land in fee having title though theoretically still held by the Crown. Today, "in fee" usually means absolute title in theory and fact. This section restricts ownership of land to a sum not exceeding £1000 per annum. This was raised to £3000 in 1730. Section thirteen authorizes the corporation to hold market days Tuesday, Thursday, and Saturday. The next section grants power to the corporation to lay out lands on Manhattan up to the low water line. These water lots were extended by the charter of 1730. Section fifteen gives the mayor, recorder, and aldermen or any three of them, the right to hold a court of common pleas, for all action of debt, transfers, and other civil suits according to the "Rules of Common Law," on Tuesday of every week.

Section sixteen confirms all of the city's privileges, franchises, and powers not inconsistent with laws of the land enjoyed within the past twenty years. This included everything conferred by the Nicolls Charter and all other grants. It held for the Crown certain lands as the Governour's Garden "without the Gate called the Kings farme with the swamp next to the same land, by the fresh water." This farm and the late Trinity Church farm located on the Hudson were part of the earlier Dutch West India Company garden. The mentioned swamp was probably the adjacent Lispinard swamp. The "fresh water" emptied into the Beekman Swamp adjoining the East River, from Collect Pond, but this area seems never to have been part of the "farme." Fort James at the end of the island was also reserved by the Crown for use of the governor and garrison.

The last clause of the charter saves all prior grants of land to "persons and charitable uses" from any "contrivances." Specific grants do not appear. However, assuming these were mainly grants to churches, these were confirmed whether in the hands of the corporation or of any citizen.

The framework of the Dongan Charter was widened and improved over the years, especially by the Montgomerie Charter of 1730. However, the Dongan Charter did confirm basic principles of government, including those of majority vote and representative government. It also confirmed the city's "ancient" corporate rights to own property. At a time when the rights of English boroughs to "privilege and immunity" were questioned and guardedly given, if at all, New York was granted a "liberal" charter.

Some have suggested that New York City received such a favored charter because James II desired a strong government in New York City partly to reinforce his authority as king and "only a grant of property rights through a charter would suit his purposes. No other form of power for legal governance would have been plausible." The partiality given to the city at a time James sought to limit chartered rights and privileges throughout the dominions is considered to have resulted from the "personal character and influence of Dongan," as well as to that of leading citizens of New York.[15] By contrast, Chancellor James Kent held that the City's charter was granted in an "enlightened sense." Whatever the reasons, it provided a sure and stable government for the City of New York with the sanctity of corporate and private rights carefully considered. With it, New York was on its way to becoming a great city.[16]

A Note on the Printing of the Charter

The original Dongan Charter written on parchment is now in the New York Public Library, where it was deposited in 1899 on loan from the city by Comptroller Bird S. Coler along with many other city documents. It was received by librarian Wilberforce Eames. In 1693, this charter was entered in the manuscript minutes of the common council. It was first published in 1694 by William Bradford, New York's earliest printer.

---

[15] Hartog, 29. Martha J. Lamb, *History of the City of New York, Its Origin, Rise, and Progress* 2 vols. (New York, 1877–80), 1: 318.
[16] Kent, 118.

Rarely re-printed in the eighteenth century (John Peter Zenger's 1735
imprint of the charter is an exception), it did not appear in the edition
of the laws of New York published by James Parker (1752) or Thomas
Greenleaf (1788). It was reprinted, however, in Hugh Gaines, *Laws and
Ordinances . . . of the City of New York, New York 1793*, as it appeared in
the Montgomerie Charter of 1730. It was also published in New York
in 1801 by John Tiebout, "bookseller and stationer," and again in 1805
by James Cheetham in his volume on the *Charter of the City of New
York*. In 1836, it appeared once more as part of the Montgomerie Charter
in James Kent's *The Charter of the City of New York . . . and the Journal
of the City Convention*, prepared at the request of the Common Council.

One of the first mentions of reprinting the Dongan charter occurred
near the end of the nineteenth century when the New York State
Statutory Revision Commission was directed by Chapter 125 of the New
York State Laws of 1891 to republish verbatim, preserving the original
spelling and punctuation, the statutes of the Colony of New York from
foundation to 1788. The resulting five-volume edition contained the first
complete publication of New York's colonial laws and was printed in Albany in 1894. The Dongan Charter appears in Volume I at pages 181–95.

The most accurate of the transcriptions appears in Jerrold Seymann's *Colonial Charters Patents and Grants to the Communities Comprising
the City of New York* which was published by the New York City Board
of Statutory Consolidation in 1939. Seymann's effort was part of a national program joined by many legal scholars and the newly formed
Society of American Archivists which aimed at preserving and publishing
this country's legal history. This is the transcription used in the present
volume.

For Further Reading

Thomas J. Archdeacon. *New York City, 1664–1710: Conquest and Change.*
   Ithaca, N.Y., 1976.
Joyce Diane Goodfriend. " 'Too Great a Mixture of Nations': The De-
   velopment of New York City Society in the Seventeenth Century."
   Ph.D. Dissertation: UCLA, 1975.
Stephen L. Mershon. *English Crown Grants.* New York, 1918.
Arthur E. Peterson and George W. Edwards. *New York as an Eighteenth
   Century Municipality.* New York, 1917.
Jerrold Seymann. *Colonial Charters Patents and Grants to the Communities
   Comprising the City of New York.* New York, 1939.
James G. Wilson, ed. *Memorial History of the City of New York,* 4 vols.
   New York, 1892–93.

[The New York City Charter]

[1686]

Thomas Dongan Leiutenant Governour and Vice Admirall of New Yorke and its Dependencyes under his Majestye James the Second By the Grace of God of England Scotland France and Ireland King Defender of the faith Supreme Lord and proprietor of the collony and province of New Yorke and its Dependencyes in America &c, To ALL to whom this shall come, SENDETH GREETINGS: WHEREAS the Citty of New Yorke is an ancient Citty within the said province, And the Cittizens of the said Citty have antiently been a body politique and corporate And the Cittizens of the said Citty have held used and Enjoyed As well within the same as Elsewhere in the said province Diverse and sundry Rights Libertyes priviledges ffranchises ffree Customes, preheminences advantages Jurisdiccons Emoluments And Immunityes, as well by prescripcon As by Charter Letters pattents Grants and Confirmacons not only of Divers Governours and Comanders in Cheife in the said province But also of severall Governours Directors Generalls, and Comanders in Chiefe of the Nether Dutch Nation Whilst the same was or has beene under their power and subjeccon AND WHEREAS Diverse Lands Tenements and Heriditaments Jurisdiccons Libertyes immunityes and priviledges, have heretofore been given and Granted or mencioned to be given and granted to the Citizens and inhabitants of the Said Citty sometimes by name of Schout Burgomasters and Schepens of the Citty of New Amsterdam And sometimes by the name of the Mayor Alderman and Comonalty of the Citty of New Yorke sometimes by the name of the Mayor Aldermen and Sherriffe of the Citty of New Yorke sometimes by the name of the Mayor and Aldermen of the Citty of New Yorke and by Diverse other names As by their severall Letters pattents Charters Grants writeings Records and muniments amongst other things may more fully appear AND WHEREAS the Citizens and inhabitants of the said Citty have Erected built and appropriated at their Owne propper Costs and Charges severall publique buildings Accomodations and Conveniences for the said Citty, (that is to say) The

Reprinted from Jerrold Seymann, *Colonial Charters Patents and Grants to the Communities Comprising the City of New York* (New York, 1939), 216–36. The editor has supplied section numbers within brackets for reference purposes.

Citty Hall or Stathouse with the ground thereunto belonging, Two markett houses, the bridge into the Dock, The wharfes or Dock with their appurtenances And the new Buriall place without the Gate of the Citty and have Established and setled one fferry from the said Citty of New Yorke to Long Island for the Acomodačon and conveniency of passengers the said Citizens and Travellers.

AND WHEREAS severall the inhabitants of the said Citty and of Manhattans Island doe hold from and under his most sacred Majesty Respectively As well by severall and Respective Letters Pattents Grants Charters and Conveyances made and granted by the Late Leiutenants Governours or Comanders in Cheifs of the said province as otherwise severall and respective messuages Lands tenements and Heriditaments upon Manhattans Island and in the Citty of New Yorke aforesaid And that As well the said Mayor Aldermen and Comonalty of the said Citty and their successours As alsoe the inhabitants of the said Manhattans Island and Citty of New Yorke aforesaid and their heires and Assignes respectivly may hold Excercise and Enjoy not only such and the same Libertyes priviledges and ffranchises Rights Rolaytyes ffree Customes Jurisdiccons and immunityes as they have anciently had used held and Enjoyed but also such publique buildings Accomodations Convenienes Messuages tenements Lands and Heriditaments in the said Citty of New Yorke, and upon Manhattans Island aforesaid which as aforesaid have beene by the Citizens and inhabitants erected and built or which have as aforesaid been held Enjoyed granted and Conveyed unto them or any of them Respectively.

[1] KNOW YE THEREFORE That I the said Thomas Dongan by Virtue of the Comičon and Authority unto me given and power in me resideing at the humble Petičon of the now Mayor Aldermen and Comonalty of the said Citty of New Yorke and for diverse other good Causes and Considerations me thereunto moveing have given Granted, Ratifyed and Confirmed And by these presents for and on the behalfe of his most sacred majestye aforesaid his heires Successours and Assignes Do give grant ratifye and Confirme unto the said Mayor Aldermen and Comonalty of the said Citty All and Every such and the same Libertyes priviledges ffranchises Rights Royalties ffree Customes jurisdiccons and immunityes which they by the name of the Mayor Aldermen and Comonalty or otherwise have anciently had held used or Enjoyed PROVIDED Alwayes that none of the said Libertyes priviledges ffranchises Rights ffree Customes Jurisdiccons or immunityes be inconsistent with or Repugnant to the Laws of his Majestyes Kingdome of England or any other the Laws of the Generall Assembly of this province And the

aforesaid publique buildings accomodations and Conveniencyes in the said Citty. (that is to say) The aforesaid Citty Hall or statthouse with the ground thereunto belonging, Two markett houses, The Bridge into the Dock, The wharfes or Dock The said New Buriall place and the aforemenċoned fferry with their and Every of their rights members and appurtenances Together with all the profitts benefitts and advantages which shall or may accrue and arrise at all times hereafter for Dockage or wharfage within the said Dock with all and Singular the rents issues profitts gaines and advantages which shall or may arrise grow or accrue by the said Citty Hall or Statthouse and ground thereunto belonging markett houses bridge Dock Burying place fferry and other the above menconed premisess or any of them And alsoe all and Every the Streets Lanes Highways and Alleys within the said Citty of New Yorke and Manhattans Island aforesaid for the publick use and service of the said Mayor Aldermen and Comonalty of the said Citty and of the inhabitants of Manhattans Island aforesaid and travellers there Together with full power Lycence and authority to the said Mayor Aldermen and Comonalty and their successours forever to Establish appoint order and Direct the Establishing makeing layeing out ordering Amending and repairing of all streets Lanes-alleys highwayes water courses fferry and Bridges in and throughout the said Citty of New Yorke and Manhattans Island aforesaid necessary needfull and Convenient for the inhabitants of the said Citty and Manhattans Island aforesaid and for all travellers and passengers there PROVIDED Alwayes That this said Licence soe as above granted for the Establishing makeing laying out of streets Lanes Alleys Highwayes fferry and bridges be not Extended or be construed to Extend to the takeing away of any person or persons right or property without his her or their Consent or by some knowne Law of the said province And for the Consideraċons aforesaid I doe likewise give grant ratifye and confirme unto all and Every the respective inhabitants of the said Citty of New Yorke and of Manhattans Island aforesaid and their severall and Respective heires and Assignes all and Every the severall and respective messuages tenements lands and hereditaments scituate lyeing and being in the said Citty and Manhattans Island aforesaid to them severally and respectively granted conveyed and Confirmed by any the Late Governours Leiutenants or Comanders in Cheife of the said province or by any of the former Mayors or Deputy Mayors and Aldermen of the said Citty of New Yorke by Deed grant conveyance or otherwise howsoever To hold to their severall and Respective heires and Assigns forever.

[2] AND I doe by these presents give and graunt unto the said Mayor Aldermen and Comonalty of the said Citty of New Yorke All

the Wast Vacant unpattented and unappropriated Lands lyeing and being within the said Citty of New Yorke and on Manhattans Island aforesaid Extending and reaching to the Low water marke in by and through all parts of the said Citty of New Yorke And Manhattans Island aforesaid together with all Rivers Rivoletts Coves Creeks ponds waters and watercourses in the said Citty and Island or either of them not heretofore Given or granted by any of the former Governours Leiutenants or Comanders in cheife under their or some of their hands and seals or seal of the province or by any of the former Mayors or Deputy Mayors and Aldermen of the said Citty of New Yorke to some respective person or persons Late inhabitants of the said Citty of New Yorke or Manhattans Island or of other parts of the said province

[3] AND I doe by these pʳsents give grant and Confirme unto the said Mayor Aldermen and Comonalty of the said Citty of New Yorke and their successours forever the Royaltyes of fishing fowling Hunting Hawking mineralls and other Royaltyes and priviledges belonging or Appertaining to the Citty of New Yorke and Manhattans Island aforesaid (Gold and silver Mines only Excepted) To HAVE HOLD and Enjoy all and singular the premisses to the said Mayor Aldermen and Comonalty of the said Citty of New Yorke and their successours forever RENDRING AND PAYING therefor unto his most sacred Majestye his heires successours or Assignes or to such officer or OFFICERS As shall be appointed to receive the same yearly forever hereafter the annuall quittrent or acknowledgement of one Beaver Skin or the Value thereof in currant mony of this province in the said Citty of New Yorke on the five and twentith day of March yearly forever

[4] AND Moreover I will and by these presents doe grant appoint and declare That the said Citty of New Yorke and the compasse precincts and Limitts thereof and the jurisdiccon of the same shall from henceforth Extend and Reach itselfe and may and shall be able to reach forth and extend itself as well in Length and in breadth as in circuit to the furthest Extent of and in and throughout all the Said Island Manhattans and in and upon all the Rivers Rivoletts Coves Creeks and waters and watercourses belonging to the same Island as farre as lowe water Mark And I doe alsoe for and on behalfe of his Most Sacred Majesty aforesaid his heires and successors firmly Enjoyne and Comand That the aforesaid Mayor Aldermen and Comonalty of the Citty aforesaid and their Successours Shall and may freely and quietly have hold use and Enjoy the aforesaid Libertyes Authorities Jurisdiccons ffranchises Rights Royaltyes priviledges Exempçons Lands tenements Heriditaments and pʳmisses aforesaid in manner and forme aforesaid ac-

cording to the Tenour and Effect of the aforesaid Grants pattents
Customs and Letters pattentts of Grant and Confirmaĉon without the
Let hinderance or impediment of me or any of my Successours Gov-
ernours Leiutenants or other Officers whatsoever

[5] AND alsoe I Doe for and on the behalfe of his most sacred
Majestye aforesaid his heirs and Successours Grant To the Mayor Aldermen and Comonalty of the said Citty of New Yorke and their successours by these presents That for the better Government of the said
Citty Libertyes and pᵣcints thereof there Shall be forever hereafter
within the said Citty A Mayor and Recorder Town clerke and six Aldermen and six assistants to be appointed nominated Elected Chosen
and Sworne as hereinafter is perticulerly and respectively menĉoned
who shall be forever hereafter called the Mayor Aldermen and Com-
onaltye of the Citty of New Yorke And that there shall be forever One
chamberlaine or Treasurer one Sherriffe one Coroner one Clerke of the
Market one high Constable seven subconstables and one Marshall or
Serjaint at Mace to be appointed Chosen and Sworne in manner hereinafter menĉoned.

[6] AND I Doe by these presents for and on the behalfe of his most
Sacred Majesty aforesaid his heires Successours and Assignes declare
Constitute grant and appoint That the Mayor Recorder Aldermen and
Assistants of the said Citty of New Yorke for the time being And they
which hereafter shall be the Mayor Recorder and Aldermen and assistants of the said Citty of New Yorke for the time being and their
Successours forever hereafter be and shall be by force of these pᵣsents
one body Corporate and pollitique in Deed fact and name by the name
of the Mayor Aldermen and Comonalty of the Citty of New Yorke And
them by the name of, the Mayor Aldermen and Comonalty of the Citty
of New Yorke one body Corporate and pollitique in Deed fact and name
I Doe really and fully Create ordaine make Constitute and Confirme
by these presents And that by the name of the Mayor Aldermen and
Comonalty of the Citty of New Yorke they may have perpetuall succession And that they and their successors forever by the name of the
Mayor Aldermen and Comonalty of the Citty of New Yorke be and
shall be forever hereafter persons able and in Law Capable To have
gett receive and possesse lands tenements Rents Libertyes Jurisdicĉons
ffranchises and hereditaments to them and their Successours in ffee
Simple or for terme of life lives or yeares or otherwise and alsoe goods
and Chattells and alsoe other things of what nature kind or quality
soever And also to give grant Lett sett and Assigne the same Lands
tenements heriditaments goods and chattels and to doe and execute all

other things about the same by the name aforesaid And also that they be and forever shall be hereafter persons able in Law Capable to plead and be impleaded answer and be answered unto defend and be defended in all or any of the Courts of his said Majestye and other places whatsoever and before any Judges Jusstices and other person or persons whatsoever in all and all manner of acc̄ons suitss complaints demands pleas Causes and matters whatsoever of what nature kind or quality soever in the same and in the like manner and forme as other people of the said province being persons able and in Law Capable may plead and be impleaded answer and be answered unto defend and be defended by any Lawfull wayes and meanes whatsoever AND That the Said Mayor Aldermen and Comonalty of the said Citty of New Yorke and their successours Shall and may forever hereafter have one comon seale to serve for the sealing of all and singular their affaires and businesses touching or Concerning the said Corporac̄on AND it shall and may be Lawfull to and for the said Mayor Aldermen and Commonalty of the said Citty of New Yorke and their successours as they shall see Cause to Breake Change alter and new make their said Comon Seale when and as often as to them it shall seeme convenient

[7] AND FURTHER, KNOW YEE That I have assigned named ordained and Constituted and by these presents doe assigne name ordaine and Constitute Nicholas Bayard now Mayor of the said Citty of New Yorke to be p^rsent Mayor of the said Citty And that the said Nicholas Bayard shall remaine and Continue in the office of Mayor there untill another fitt person shall be appointed and Sworne in the said office according to the usage and Custome of the said Citty and as in and by these p^rsents is hereafter menconed and directed AND I have assigned named ordeined and Constituted, AND by the presents doe assigne name ordaine and Constitute create and Declare James Graham Esq to be the present Recorder of the said Citty to doe and Execute all things which unto the Office of Recorder of the Said Citty doth or may any ways appertaine or belong AND I have assigned named ordained and Constituted and by these p^rsents doe assigne name ordaine Constitute Create and declare John West Esq Towne Clerke of the said Citty to doe and Execute all things which unto the office of Towne Clerke may any wayes appertaine or belong AND I have named assigned Constituted and made and by these p^rsents doe assigne name Constitute and make Andrew Bowne John Robinson William Beakman John Delavall Abraham De Peister and Johannes Kipp Cittizens and inhabitants of the said Citty of New Yorke to be the present Aldermen of the said Citty AND also I have made assigned named and Constituted and by these p^rsents Doe assigne name Constitute and make Nicholas De Meyer Johannes

Van Brugh John De Bruijn Tunisse Decay Abraham Corbett and Wolfert
Webber Cittizens and inhabitants of the said Citty to be the present
assistants of the said Citty And alsoe I have assigned Chosen named
and Constituted and by these prsents Doe assigne Choose name and
Constitute Peter De LaNoy Cittizen and inhabitant of the said Citty
to be the present Chamberlaine or Treasurer of the Citty aforesaid AND
I have assigned named Constituted and appointed and by these prsents
Doe assigne name Constitute and appoint John Knight Esq one other
of the said Cittizens there to be prsent Sherriffe of the said Citty AND
I have assigned named Constituted and appointed and by these presents
doe assigne name Constitute and appoint Jarvis Marshall one other of
the said Cittizens there to be the present Marshall of the said Citty
AND I Doe by these prsents Grant to the said Mayor Aldermen and
Comonalty of the said Citty of New Yorke and their successours that
the Mayor Recorder Aldermen and Assistants of the said Citty for time
being or the Mayor Recorder and any three or more of the Aldermen
and any three or more of the assistants for the time being be and shall
be Called the Comon Councell of the said Citty And that they or the
Greater part of them shall or may have full power and authority by
Virtue of these presents from time to time to call and hold comon
councell within the Comon Councell house or Citty Hall of the said
Citty and there as occaċon shall be to make Laws Orders Ordinances
and Constituċons in writing and to add alter Diminish or reforme them
from time to time as to them shall seem necessary and Convenient (not
repugnant to the prerogative of his most sacred Majesty aforesaid his
heirs and successours or to any the laws of the Kingdome of England
or other the Laws of the Generall Assembly of the province of New
Yorke) for the good rule oversight correcċon and Government of the
said Citty and Libertyes of the same and of all the officers thereof And
for the Severall tradesmen Victuallers artificers and of all other the
people and inhabitants of the said Citty Libertys and precincts aforesaid
And for the better preservaċon of Government and Disposall of all the
Lands tenements and heriditaments goods and Chattells of the said
Corporaċon Which Laws Orders Ordinances and Constituċons shall be
binding to all the inhabitants of the said Citty, Libertyes and precincts
aforesaid And which Laws orders ordinances and Constituċons So by
them made as aforesaid shall be and remaine in force for the Space of
three months and noe longer unlesse they shall be allowed of and
Confirmed by the Governour and Councell for the time being AND I
Doe further on the behalfe of his sacred Majestye aforesaid his heires
and Successours appoint and Grant that the said Comon Councell of
the said Citty for the time being As often as they make ordaine and
Establish such Laws orders ordinances and Constituċons as aforesaid

shall or may make ordaine Limitt provide sett impose and tax reasonable fines and Amerciaments AGAINST and upon all persons offending against such Laws Orders Ordinances and Constituĉons as aforesaid or any of them to be made ordeined and Established as aforesaid and the said fines and amerciaments shall and may require demand levy take and receive by warrants under the Coɱon seale To and for the use and behoofe of the Mayor Aldermen and Coɱonalty of the said Citty and their successors either by distresse and sale of the goods and Chattells of the offendour therein if such goods and Chattells may be found within the said Citty Libertyes and precincts thereof Rendering to such of-fendor and offendors the Overplus or by any other Lawful wayes or means whatsoever

[8] AND I doe by these presents appoint and ordaine the assigning naming and appointment of the Mayor and Sherriffe of the said Citty that it shall be as followeth (vizt) upon the feast day of St Michael the Archangell yearly the Leiutenant Governour or Commander in Cheife for the time being by and with the Advice of his Councell Shall nominate and appoint such person as he shall think fitt to be Mayor of the said Citty for the year next ensueing And one other person of sufficient Ability in Estate and of good Capacity in understanding to be Sherriffe of the said Citty of New Yorke for the year next Ensueing AND That such person as shall be named assigned and appointed Mayor and such person as shall be named assigned and appointed Sherriffe of the said Citty as aforesaid shall on the fourteenth day of October then next following take their severall and respective Corporall oaths before the Governour and Councell for the time being for the due execuĉon of their Respective offices as aforesaid And that the said Mayor and Sher-riffe soe to be nominated assigned and appointed as aforesaid shall remaine and continue in their Said Respective offices until another fitt person shall be nominated appointed and sworne in the place of Mayor and one other person shall be nominated and appointed in the place of Sherriffe of the said Citty in manner aforesaid AND further That according to the now usage and custome of the said Citty the Recorder Towne Clerke and Clerke of the market of the said Citty Shall be persons of good capacity and understanding And such persons as his most sacred Majesty aforesaid his heires and successours Shall, in the Said respective offices of Recorder Town clerke and Clerke of the mar-kett appoint and Comissionate And for defect of such appointment and comissionateing, by his most sacred Majestye aforesaid his heires and successors to be such persons as the Leiutenent Governour or Comander in cheife of the said province for the time being shall appoint and Comissionate which persons soe Comissionated to the said offices of

Recorder Town clerke and clerke of the markett shall have hold and
Enjoy the said Offices according to the Tenour and Effect of their said
Comissions, and not otherwise AND further That the Recorder Town
clerke Clerke of the Markett Aldermen Assistants Chamberlain high
Constable petty constables and all other Officers of the said Citty before
they or any of them shall be admitted to enter upon and execute their
respective Offices shall be sworn faithfully to execute the same before
the Mayor or any three or more of the Aldermen for the time being
AND I doe by these presents for and on the behalfe of his most sacred
Majestye his heirs and successors grant and give power and authority
to the Mayor and Recorder of the said Citty, for the time being to
administer the same respective Oaths to them accordingly AND further
I doe by these p'sents grant, for and on the behalfe of his most sacred
Majesty aforesaid his heires and successors That the Mayor and Recorder of the said Citty for the time being and three or more of the
Aldermen of the said Citty not exceeding five shall be Justices and
keepers of the peace of his most sacred majesty his heires and successors, and Justices to hear and Determine matters and causes within the
said Citty and libertyes and precincts thereof AND that they or any three
or more of them whereof the Mayor and Recorder, or one of them, for
the time being to be there shall and may forever hereafter have power
and authority by virtue of these presents to hear and determine all and
all manner of Petty Larcenyes Riots routs oppressions extortions and
other tresspasses and offences whatsoever within the said Citty of New
Yorke and the Libertyes and precincts aforesaid from time to time
arriseing and happening and which arise or happen and any wayes
belong to the offices of justices of the peace and the Correcčon and
punishment of the offences aforesaid and every of them according to
the Laws of England and the Laws of the said Province and to doe and
execute all other things in the said Citty Libertyes and precincts aforesaid soe fully and in ample manner as to the Comisõners assigned and
to be assigned for the keeping of the peace in the said County of New
Yorke doth or may belong

[9] AND MOREOVER I doe by these presents for and on the behalfe
of his most sacred Majesty aforesaid his heirs and successors appoint
That the Aldermen assistants High Constable and Petty Constables
within the said Citty be yearly Chosen on the feast day of Saint Michael
the Archangell forever (viz`t`) one Alderman one assistant and one Constable, for each respective Ward and one Constable for each Division
in the Outward in such publique place in the said Respective wards as
the Aldermen for the time being for each Ward shall direct and appoint

And that the Aldermen assistants and Petty Constables be chosen by
Majority of voices of the inhabitants of each ward And that the High
Constable be appointed by the Mayor of the said Citty for the time
being AND That the Chamberlain shall be yearly Chosen on the said
feast day in the Citty Hall of the said Citty by the Mayor and Aldermen
and assistants, or by the Mayor or three or more of the Aldermen and
three or more of the Assistants of the said Citty for the time being AND
I doe by these presents Constitute and appoint the said John West to
be the present Town clerke Clerke of the peace and Clerke of the
Court of pleas to be holden before the Mayor Recorder and Aldermen
within the said Citty and the Libertyes and precincts thereof AND further I doe by these presents for and on the behalf of his most sacred
Majestye aforesaid his heires and successours require and strictly Charge
and Command That the Sherriffe Town clerke Clerke of the peace
High Constable petty Constables and all other subordinate Officers in
the said Citty for the time being and every of them respectively jointly
and severally as cause shall require shall attend upon the said Mayor
Recorder and Aldermen of the said Citty for the time being and every
or any of them according to the duty of their Respective places in and
about the executeing of such the Comands precepts warrants and pro-
cesse of them and every of them as belongeth and appertaineth to be
done or executed And that the aforesaid Mayor Recorder and Aldermen
and every of them as Justices of the peace for the time being by their
or any of their warrants all and every person and persons for High treason
or Petty treason or for suspicõn thereof or for other felonies whatsoever
and all malefactors and Disturbers of the peace and other offendors for
other misdemeanours who shall be apprehended within the said Citty
or Libertyes thereof shall and may send and Comitt or cause to be sent
and Comitted to the Comõn goale [jail] of the said Citty there to
remaine and be kept in safe Custody by the keeper of the said Goale
[jail] or his Deputy for the time being until such offender and offenders
shall be lawfully delivered thence AND I doe by these presents for and
on the behalfe of his most sacred Majestye aforesaid his heires and
successors Charge and require the keeper and keepers of the said Goale
for the time being and his and their Deputy and Deputyes to receive
take and in safe Custody to keep all and singular such person and
persons soe apprehended or to be apprehended sent and Comitted to
the said Goale by warrant of the said justices or any of them as aforesaid
until he and they soe sent and Comitted to the said Goale shall from
thence be delivered by due course of law

[10] AND further I doe grant and Confirme for and on the behalfe
of his most sacred Majestye aforesaid his heires and successours that

the said Mayor of the said Citty for the time being and no other (according to the usage and Custome practised in the said Citty of New Yorke in the times of my predecessours the several Leiutenants Governours and Comanders in Cheife of this Province) shall have power and authority to give and grant Lycences annually under the publique seale of the said Citty to all Taverne Keepers Innkeepers Ordinary Keepers Victuallers and all publique sellers of wine strong waters sider beer or any other sort of Liquors by retaile within the Citty aforesaid Manhattans Island or their Libertyes and Precincts thereof AND That it shall and may be Lawful to and for the said Mayor of the said Citty for the time being to ask demand and receive for such License by him to be given and granted as aforesaid such sume or sumes of money as he and the person to whom such Lycence shall be given or granted shall agree for not exceeding the sum of thirty Shillings for each Lycence All which mony as by the said Mayor shall be soe received shall be used and applyed to the publique use of the said Mayor Aldermen and Comonalty of the said Citty of New Yorke and their successours without any account thereof to be rendered made or done to any of the Leiutenants or Governours of this Province for the time being or any of their Deputyes

[II] AND KNOW YE That FOR the better Government of the said Citty and for the welfare of the said Cittizens tradesmen and inhabitants thereof Doe by these pᵣsents for and on the behalf of his most sacred Majesty his heires and successors Give and Grant to the said Mayor Aldermen and Comonalty of the said Citty and their successors that the Mayor Recorder and Aldermen or the Mayor and any three or more of the Aldermen for the time being shall from time to time and all times hereafter have full power and authority under the Comon seale to make ffree Cittizens of the said Citty, and Libertyes thereof and no person or persons whatsoever other than such free Citizens shall hereafter use any art trade mistery or manuall occupation within the said Citty Libertyes and precincts thereof saving in the times of fairs there to be kept and during the continuance of such fairs only AND in case any person or persons whatsoever not being free Cittizens of the said Citty as aforesaid shall at any time hereafter use or exercise any art trade mistery or manual occupaĉon or shall by himselfe themselves or others sell or expose to sale any manner of merchandize or wares whatsoever by retaile in any house shopp or place, or standing within the said Citty or the Libertyes or precincts thereof noe fair being then kept in the said Citty and shall persist therein after warning to him or them given or left by the appointment of the Mayor of the said Citty for the time being at the place or places where such person or persons shall

soe use or exercise any art trade mistery or manual occupacon or shall
sell or expose to sale any wares or merchandizes as aforesaid by retaile
then it shall be lawful for the Mayor of the said Citty for the time being
to cause such shopp windows to be shutt up and also to impose such
reasonable fine for such offence not exceeding five pounds for every
respective offence and the same fine and fines soe imposed to levy and
take by warrant under the comon seale of the said Citty for the time
being by distresse and sale of the goods and chattels of the person or
persons soe offending in the premises found within the libertyes or
precincts of the said Citty rendering to the party or partys the overplus
or by any other lawful ways or means whatsoever to the only use of the
said Mayor Alderman and Comonalty of the said Citty of New Yorke
and their successors without any account to be rendered made or done
to the Lieutenants Governors or Comanders in Cheife of this province
for the same PROVIDED That no person or persons shall be made free
as aforesaid but such as are his Majestyes naturall borne subjects or
such as shall first be Naturalized by act of General Assembly or shall
have obtained Letters of Denizacon under the hand of the Leiutenant
Governour or Comander in Cheife for the time being and seale of the
province AND that all persons to be made free as aforesaid shall and
Doe pay for the publique use of the said Mayor Aldermen and Comonalty of the said Citty such sume and sumes of mony as heretofore
hath beene used and accustomed to be paid and received on their being
admitted freemen as aforesaid provided it is not exceeding the sume
of five pounds

[12] AND FURTHER, I Doe by these presents for and on the behalfe
of his most sacred Majestye aforesaid his heires and successours grant
to the Mayor Aldermen, and Comonalty of the said Citty that they and
their successours be forever persons able and capable and shall have
power to purchase have take and possesse in ffee simple Lands tenements rents and other possessions within or without the same Citty to
them and their successors forever soe as the same exceed not the yearly
value of one thousand pounds/annum the statute of Mortmaine or any
other Law to the Contrary notwithstanding and the same lands tenements hereditaments and premises or any part thereof to demise grant
lease set over assigne and dispose at their owne will and pleasure and
to make seale and accomplish any Deed or Deeds Lease or Leases
evidences or writings for or Concerning the same or any part thereof
which shall happen to be made and granted by the said Mayor Aldermen
and Comonalty of the said Citty for the time being

[13] AND FURTHER I Doe by these presents for and on the behalf
of his most sacred Majestye aforesaid his heirs and successors Grant to

the said Mayor Aldermen and Comonalty^e That they and their successors shall and may forever hereafter hold and keep within the said Citty in every week of the year three markett days the one upon Tuesday the other upon Thursday and the other on Saturday weekly for ever

[14] AND ALSO I Doe by these presents, for and on the behalf of his most sacred Majestye aforesaid his heires and successors grant to the Mayor Aldermen and Comonalty of the said Citty that they and their successours and Assignes shall and may at any time or times hereafter when it to them shall seeme fitt and Convenient take in fill and make up and laye out all and singular the land and ground in and about the said Citty and Island Manhattans and the same to build upon or make use of in any other manner or way as to them shall seem fitt as farr into the Rivers thereof, and that encompasse the same at low water marke aforesaid

[15] AND I doe by these presents for and on the behalfe of his most sacred Majestye aforesaid his heires and successors Give and grant unto the aforesaid Mayor Aldermen and Comonalty of the said Citty of New Yorke and their successours That they and their successours shall and may have hold and keep within the said Citty and Libertys and precincts thereof in every week in every year forever upon Tuesday one Court of Comon Pleas for all accons of debt trespasse trespasse upon the Case detinue ejectment and other personal accons and the same to be held before the Mayor Recorder and Aldermen or any three of them whereof the Mayor or Recorder to be one who shall have power to hear and Determine the same pleas and Accons according to the Rules of the Comon Law and acts of Generall Assembly of the said province

[16] AND I doe by these presents for and on behalfe of his most sacred Majestye aforesaid his heires and successours Grant to the said Mayor Alderman and Comonalty of the said Citty of New Yorke and their successours That the said Mayor Aldermen and Comonalty of the said Citty and their successours shall have and enjoy all the priviledges franchises and powers that they have and use or that any of their predecessours at any time within the space of twenty years last past had took or enjoyed or ought to have had by reason or under pretence of any former Charter Grant prescripcon or any other Right Custome or usage although the same have been forfeited lost or have been ill used or not used or abused or discontinued albeit they be not particularly mencçoned And that no Officer shall disturbe them thyr'n under any pretence whatsoever not only for their future but their present enjoyment thereof PROVIDED Alwayes that the said priviledges franchises and

powers be not inconsistent with or repugnant to the laws of his Majestyes Kingdome of England or other the Laws of the General Assembly of this province as aforesaid And saving to his most sacred Majestye aforesaid his heirs successours and Assignes and the Lieutenants Governors and Comanders in Cheife and other officers under him and them in FORT JAMES in or by the Citty of New Yorke and in all the Libertyes boundaryes extents priviledges thereof for the maintenance of the said ffort and Garrison there all the right use title and Authority which they or any of them have had used or exercised there And alsoe one messuage or tenement next the Citty Hall and one Messuage by the ffort now in the possession of Thomas Coker Gentleman The peice of ground by the Gate called the Governours Garden and the land without the Gate called the Kings ffarme with the swamp next to the same land, by the ffresh water And saving the severall rents and Quitt rents reserved due and payable from severall persons inhabiting within the said Citty and Island Manhattans by virtue of former grants to them made and Given And saving to all other persons bodyes politique and Corporate their heires successours and Assignes all such Right title and claime possessions Rents services Comons emoluments interest in and to any thing which is theirs (save only the ffranchises aforesaid) in as ample manner as if this Charter had not beene made

[17] AND FURTHER I Doe appoint and declare that the incorporačon to be founded by this Charter SHALL not at any time hereafter doe or suffer to be done any thing by means whereof the lands tenements of hereditaments stock goods or Chattells thereof or in the hands Custody possession of any of the cittizens of the said Citty such as have been sett lett Given granted or collected to and for pious and charitable uses shall be wasted or misemployed Contrary to the Trust or intent of the founder or giver thereof And that such and no other construcčon shall be made thereof Than that which may tend most to advantage Religion Justice, and the publique good and to suppresse all Acts and Contrivances to be invented or putt in use Contrary thereunto IN WITNESS Whereof I have Caused these presents to be entered in the Secretaryes Office and the seale of the said Province to be hereunto affixed this seven and twentieth day of Aprill in the Second year of the Reigne of his most Sacred Majestye aforesaid And in the year of our Lord God One thousand Six hundred and Eightysix.

THOMAS DONGAN.

[On the reverse side of the Charter appears the following indorsements.]

May it Please Yo^r Honor

The Aturney Generall Hath perused This Pattent, And Finds Nothing Contained therein prejudiciall To his Majestyes Interest

Ja: Graham

Examined Aprile 27th

Secr.

1686

Recorded in the secretaryes office for the province of New Yorke in the N^o I: booke of pattents begun 1684 from page 278: to 309:

J. Spragge Secr.

New York Novr ye 5th 1713

Rece^d of Mr Saml^e Bayard the City Treasurer Twenty Seven beavers Skins in full for Twenty Seven Years Quit rent of ye within Charter to ye 27th of Aprile last as wittness my hand

T Byerky Co^H

I Archebald Kennedy Esqr his Majestyes Collector and Receivor General of the Province of New York Do hereby acknowledge to have Received of Cornelius Depeyster Esqr Treasurer of the City of New York by Order of the Mayor Aldermen and Commonality of the Corporation within Mentioned Sixteen Beaver Skins in full for Sixteen years quit Rent of the within Charter due and ending the twenty seventh day of April last past

Wittness my hand this eleventh day of December Anno Dom. 1729. I say sixteen Beaver Skins for sixteen years quit Rent

Arch^d Kennedy

Rec^r Gen^H

VI

The Albany Plan of Union

1754

COMMENTARY BY THOMAS E. BURKE

AT ALBANY, NEW YORK, DURING THE SUMMER of 1754, representatives from seven northern colonies turned their inventive political minds to the task of creating a plan of union which would serve to join the colonies of England's North American empire for the purpose of defense against France and its Indian allies without sacrificing the balance of local interests.

In the years after 1690, England fought three wars with its European opponents. In a fourth conflict, the Seven Years' War (1756–63), known in the colonies as the French and Indian War, America was the central theater of war. The immediate cause of the Seven Years' War sprang from a series of clashes between French troops trying to secure the Ohio River Valley and soldiers from Virginia which claimed the territory based on its original seventeenth-century charter. The French built Fort Duquesne at the junction of the Ohio, Allegheny, and Monongahela rivers. A small force under Major George Washington failed to dislodge them.

Anticipating a scale of conflict greater than that of any of the previous wars, delegates of seven colonies met at Albany in 1754, in an effort to coordinate defense plans among themselves and with their Indian allies.

Reprinted from Thomas E. Burke, "The Albany Congress and Constitution-making in Early America," *New York Notes* (Albany, 1988).

On the morning of June 19, 1754, twenty-three commissioners appeared at the Albany City Hall. In the presence of Lieutenant Governor John DeLancey, they presented the instructions which they had received from their individual colonies. The powers vested in the commissioners varied greatly. Those given to the Massachusetts Bay delegation were the most liberal, permitting it not only to make a treaty with the Indians but to enter "into articles of Union and Confederation."

New York's position, however, was peculiar. Although Lieutenant Governor DeLancey was present, as were four members of the Council, they did not appear as commissioners and had no special powers to act in behalf of their colony's government. Nevertheless, the New York members participated in the activities of the Congress as though fully qualified to do so. Their immediate concern was an intercolonial agreement for the installation of military posts in the Indian country, the expense of which would be shared among the colonies.

Lieutenant Governor DeLancey insisted on organizing the conference and controlling its proceedings as the presiding officer. This high-handed conduct, however, seems to have been resented by only the delegation from Massachusetts Bay.

All of the colonies represented at Albany had at least one common objective: the re-establishment of friendly relations between the Iroquois and the British. At the opening of the Congress, the delegates were made aware of the danger that the Six Nations (Mohawk, Oneida, Onondaga, Cayuga, Tuscarora, and Seneca) might be lost to the enemy. Only a small number of Indians appeared and their behavior indicated a calculated coldness and air of hostility.

Although DeLancey made it plain that he did not want the other commissioners to examine the details of New York's past relations with the Iroquois, the grievances of the Six Nations having to do with the fur trade and the disposal of their land could not be hidden.

There followed a series of meetings between the commissioners and the Iroquois. By July 9, these official negotiations had been concluded. The Iroquois now proclaimed the strength of their loyalty to the English cause. Most soon left, so loaded down with presents that thirty wagons were required to transport the gifts to the Indian country.

As early as June 24, however, the question had been raised as to "whether a Union of all the Colonies is not at present absolutely necessary for their security and defence." The idea was not a new one. During the seventeenth century the New England Confederation had maintained itself from 1643 until 1684. In 1686, at the order of King James II, the governments of Massachusetts, Connecticut, Rhode Island, and Plymouth Colony were consolidated; and, in 1688 New York and New Jersey were added to what became known as the Dominion of New England. The life of this union was brief, however. The Glorious Revolution in England, which overthrew James II, was followed by political disturbances within the colonies, such as Leisler's Rebellion in New York in 1689. By 1690, the dominion was dead.

During Queen Anne's War in 1709, the Crown worked out a plan for providing quotas of troops from neighboring colonies for an expedition against Canada which was to depart from Albany. Similarly, in King George's War during the 1740s, there was a "concert" of the New England colonies to provide troops and supplies to attack the French at Cape Breton. Given this past experience of intercolonial co-operation, it is not surprising that when the question of a union was raised at Albany, it was passed by the commissioners "in the affirmative unanimously."

Each delegation was called upon to choose one of its members to serve on a committee to prepare plans of union. The members included Thomas Hutchinson for Massachusetts Bay, Theodore Atkinson for New Hampshire, William Pitkin for Connecticut, Stephen Hopkins for Rhode Island, William Smith for New York, Benjamin Tasker for Maryland, and Benjamin Franklin for Pennsylvania.

As early as 1751, Franklin had produced a rough outline for a colonial union which embodied many of the ideas which would later be found in the 1754 plan. This plan of union was included in a pamphlet on Indian affairs printed by Archibald Kennedy the same year (1751). Kennedy, who had been receiver general and collector of customs for New York since the 1720s, was a faithful servant of the Crown whose interests corresponded with those of Franklin. Kennedy wrote six tracts concerning imperial defense, Indian policy, and the northern colonies between 1750 and 1755.

In his *Pennsylvania Gazette* on May 9, 1754, Franklin had written about the difficulties which the separate colonies faced in dealing with the French. The article was illustrated by the first American political cartoon—a woodcut of a snake separated into parts, representing the colonies, with the motto beneath it: "Join or Die." In going to Albany, Franklin was already committed to the general idea of establishing a union of the colonies.

Franklin arrived at New York City on June 5, and busied himself with meetings with prominent New Yorkers. He also took time to set down a scheme of union. He called his plan, "Short Hints toward a Scheme for Uniting the Northern Colonies." It included many features of his earlier plan of 1751. One important feature which it discarded was the idea of a voluntary union. Now he favored that the plan be sent to

England and established by an act of Parliament. In this manner, the colonies would have the union imposed on them.

The "Short Hints" called for the appointment by the king of a "Governor General" who would be paid by the Crown and who could veto all acts of the grand council. The members of the council were to be chosen by the colonial assemblies with each colony having at least one representative and the larger colonies, several.

Franklin's "Short Hints," however, was not the only plan submitted for consideration by the Congress. Richard Peters of the Pennsylvania delegation also prepared "A Plan for a General Union of the British Colonies of North America." This plan provided for the colonies to be grouped into four divisions: one for New England; another for New York and New Jersey; a third for Virginia, Maryland, and Pennsylvania; a fourth for Georgia, South Carolina, and North Carolina. Each colony would appoint a "Committee of Union" to correspond with the committees of the other twelve colonies. Also, each division would hold an annual meeting of the committees within it which would recommend necessary measures to each of the governments within that division. Each colony was to raise a company of one hundred men, "the Union regiment." There was to be a "Union Fund" raised by the issue of paper money and a "Fort Fund" to finance the building of forts to protect the frontiers.

Finally, at least one more plan was formulated, apparently by Thomas Hutchinson of Massachusetts. His plan, like Peters', adhered more closely to existing colonial arrangements than did Franklin's. Hutchinson suggested grouping the colonies into two unions, a northern and a southern, which would come into existence through an act of Parliament.

Initially, the Congress busied itself with Indian affairs and did not turn to the issue of union until June 28. By that time, the committee on plans of union had concluded to make Franklin's "Short Hints" the basis for the proposed union. The plan was debated for two days. On July 2, the question was put, "whether the Board should proceed to form a plan of Union of the Colonies by Act of Parliamt," and passed in the affirmative.

Although the commissioners had no power to bind their respective colonies, the vote represented the consensus of opinion of the most representative and politically capable and experienced body of colonials from the thirteen colonies to meet prior to the Stamp Act Congress of 1765.

On July 9, the committee on plans submitted its "Representation on the Present State of the Colonies." This was considered paragraph by paragraph. After referring to the need to regulate Indian affairs, certain broad recommendations were presented: that the encroachments of the French be removed; that the Indians be placed under some superintendency; that forts be built within each of the Indian nations; that the sale of Indian lands be regulated; and, finally, that there be a "Union of His Majtys several Governts on the Continent, that so their Councils, Treasure and strength may be employed in due proportion agst their common enemy."

The final draft of the "Plan of Union" seems to have been a fusion of ideas expressed in Franklin's "Short Hints," and the "Plan of a Proposed Union" formulated by Hutchinson. It called for a union of all the continental colonies except for the buffer colonies of Nova Scotia and Georgia. This union would be established by an act of Parliament. The conflict of interests among the colonies suggested to Franklin and some of the other commissioners that this was the only practical means of procuring a lasting plan of union. The "Representation" was forwarded by DeLancey to England to the Board of Trade, together with the other papers relating to the Congress.

Under the "Plan of Union," provision was made for a president general to be appointed and supported by the Crown. Also, there would be a grand council, the members of which were to be chosen by the respective assemblies with the following allotments: Massachusetts and Virginia, seven representatives each; Pennsylvania, six; Connecticut, five; New York, Maryland, North Carolina, and South Carolina, four each; New Jersey, three, and New Hampshire and Rhode Island, two each. The grand council was to meet at least once a year with the place of meeting, initially, at Philadelphia. To do business, a quorum of twenty-five was needed with one or more members from a majority of the colonies.

The "Plan" directed the president general, with the advice of the grand council, to direct all Indian treaties, to make peace or declare war with the Indians, to provide laws for regulating the Indian trade, and to settle outstanding land claims with the Indians.

To defend the colonies, the president general and the grand council were to raise and support soldiers and to build forts and equip war vessels. For these purposes they were to levy whatever duties, imports, or taxes appeared equal and just. However, it was provided that all acts of the grand council must receive the assent of the president general, and were to be sent to England for the approval of the privy council, which could disallow such acts within a period of three years.

Finally, a general treasurer and individual treasurers for each government would be appointed by joint action of the president general and the grand council who together could order sums of money in colonial treasuries to be placed in the general treasury. All accounts were to be reported yearly to the assemblies of the colonies.

Historians have seen in this plan certain features that underlay the subsequent establishment of Indian superintendents and the Proclamation Line of 1763, and also the idea of creation of trans-Appalachian colonies and commonwealths as embodied in the Northwest Ordinance of 1787. Historians also have noted that in many respects this plan goes beyond the provincialism of the Articles of Confederation of 1781.

Although Philadelphia, because of its convenient location, was to be the usual meeting place of the grand council, provision was made for its gathering in any colony which might be in need of assistance. Nothing, however, referred to the residence of the president general.

According to a report made by the Massachusetts Bay commissioners to Governor William Shirley of that colony, those attending the Congress were "very near unanimous" on three points: first, that a general union of the colonies was necessary to save them from the French; second, that a scheme for union could only be placed into execution by Parliament; third, that the proportion of the general expense that each colony should bear was to be estimated by the number of members allotted to each on the grand council. Finally, the commissioners agreed that taxation of the colonies should be through measures adopted by the grand council and not by Parliament.

Having completed their work, the commissioners returned home to give an accounting. Except for the Massachusetts delegation, those attending the Congress only had authority to deal with Indian affairs, and had not been specifically delegated by their governments to establish a colonial confederacy. This may explain why most took a passive attitude toward their achievement. Moreover, they did not have long to wait for opposition to their recommendations to develop.

Almost unanimously, the plan of union was ignored or rejected on both sides of the ocean. Colonial governors and assemblies either took no notice of the plan or, like Governor Dinwiddie of Virginia, waited to see how it was received in England. The assemblies in the various colonies refused to transfer their power to a new intercolonial agency.

At the time of the Albany Congress, the subject of Indian relations and of colonial defense was being discussed in England. In April 1754, the Board of Trade suggested that the English should build forts all along the disputed frontier, that the colonies should garrison them, and that these forts should serve both for defense against the French and as warehouses for Indian goods and trade.

On June 14, 1754, King George II ordered the Board of Trade to prepare a plan for the common defense of the colonies. However, in passing on the Albany plan of union to the king, the Board of Trade made no comment except to note, as a serious defect, that not enough provision had been made for the management of Indian affairs. The board recommended that Indian affairs be taken out of the hands of the separate colonies and placed under the domain of commissioners. It specifically suggested that William Johnson of New York, who already carried on extensive trade and diplomatic relations with the Iroquois and other tribes from his estate at today's Johnstown, be given command over the Six Nations. The Board of Trade also was fearful that the proposed intercolonial government would take power away from the Crown. Finally, the outbreak of war with France diverted attention to more immediate issues.

The Albany Plan survived as the basic idea of federalism during the years after 1754. At the first Continental Congress in 1774, Joseph Gallaway, a conservative Pennsylvanian, proposed a plan of union that was similar to that proposed at Albany except that both Parliament and the intercolonial legislature would be able to legislate for the colonies, each to have a veto on the other. This proposal was narrowly defeated by a vote of six states to five.

At the Second Continental Congress, in June 1775, Benjamin Franklin proposed a plan of confederation also based on the Albany Plan. Franklin argued for a scheme of representation proportional to population. Although his plan substituted for the provision granting powers of taxation to the grand council a proposal to allow Congress the right to make requisitions, Congress was to exercise wide power in other areas "necessary to the general welfare." However, this proposal was set aside and not given further consideration.

As finally adopted, the Articles of Confederation preserved that part of the Albany Plan which included control of the West by the general government. Franklin tried to introduce the idea of representation in proportion to population, but the Articles continued the voting equality of the states established by the First Continental Congress. In failing to go as far as the Albany Plan of Union in limiting the sovereignty of the states, the Articles fell short of what the commissioners at Albany had proposed more than twenty years earlier. However, a significant achievement representing a principal objective of the Albany Congress— federal control of the western territories—occurred in 1787 with the passage of the Northwest Ordinance in which Congress set up a government for the territories and provided for the admission of new states.

Finally, at Philadelphia in 1787 some of the basic concepts of the Albany Plan of Union were attained at the Constitutional Convention. In 1754, it was proposed that members of the council were to be elected by the colonial legislatures. In a similar manner, in 1787 the United States Constitution provided that two senators were to represent each state and that the senators were to be chosen by the state legislatures.

A system of checks and balances was embodied in the Albany Plan of Union as in the federal Constitution. The council was to have the authority to raise, equip, and pay an army and navy, with the consent of the president general. But the president general was to have the power to appoint the officers subject to the council's approval. Similarly, as regards the veto power, even if the president general approved a bill, it still could have been disallowed by the Crown. In this sense, Franklin's plan included the idea of a limit to legislative authority.

The Albany Congress produced a document which, although failing to receive acceptance at the time, foreshadowed the adjustment of power, authority, and interest represented in the constitutional compact achieved at Philadelphia over three decades later.

For Further Reading

Lawrence Henry Gipson. *The British Empire Before the American Revolution*. 15 vols. New York, rev. ed., 1958–1970, Vol 5.

Ralph L. Ketcham, ed. *The Political Thought of Benjamin Franklin*. Indianapolis, Ind., 1965.

R. C. Newbold. *The Albany Congress and the Plan of Union of 1754*. New York, 1955.

Carl Van Doren. *Benjamin Franklin*. New York, 1938.

[The Albany Plan of Union]

[1754]

Plan of a proposed Union of the Several Colonies of Massachusetts Bay, New Hampshire, Connecticut, Rhode Island, New York, New Jersey, Pensilvania, Maryland, North Carolina, and South Carolina, for their mutual defence & Security & for the Extending the British Settlements in North America.

That humble application be made for an act of the Parliament of Great Britain by virtue of which one General Government may be formed in America including all the said Colonies within & under which Government each Colony may retain it present constitution except in the Perticulars wherein a Change may be directed by the said act as Hereafter follows.—

That the said General Government be administered by a President General to be appointed & supported by the Crown, & a Grand Council to be chosen by the Representatives of the People of the several Colonies met in their respective Assemblies.

That within —— Months after the passing of such act, the House of Representatives in the several Assemblies that happens to be sitting within that time or that shall be exspecially for that purpose convened may & Shall chuse Members for the Grand Council in the following proportions that is to say.

Massachusetts Bay	7
New Hampshire	2
Connecticut	5
Rhode Island	2
New York	4
New Jersey	3
Pensilvania	6
Maryland	4

Reprinted from Robert C. Newbold, *The Albany Congress and Plan of Union of 1754* (New York, 1955), 184–87. The Albany Plan of Union as given here is a text facsimile from the manuscript copy of the Proceedings of the Albany Congress (pp. 43–46) preserved in the Archives of the Secretary of State of Rhode Island. Only paragraph indentations have been added for clarity.

Virginia	7
North Carolina	4
South Carolina	4
	48

Who shall meet for the first time at the City of Philadelphia in Pensilvania being called by the President General as soon as conveniently may be after his Appointment.

That there shall be a new Election of members for the Grand Council every three Years, & on the Death or resignation of any Member, his place shall be Supplyed by a new choice at the next sitting of the Assembly of the Colony he represented.

That after the first three years when the proportion of Money arising out of each Colony, to the General Treasury can be known, the Number of Members to be chosen for each Colony shall from time to time in all Ensuing Elections be regulated by that proportion yet so as that the Number to be chosen by any one Province be not more than Seven nor less than two.

That the Grand Council shall meet once in every year and oftener if occasion require at such time & place as they shall adjourn to at the last preceding meeting or as they shall be called to meet at by the President General on any Emergency he having first obtained in Writing the consent of Seven of the Members to such Call, & sent due & timely notice to the whole.

That the Grand Council have power to chuse their Speaker & shall neither be dissolved, prorogued, nor continue Sitting longer than Six Weeks at one time, without the[ir] own consent or the Special Command of the Crown.

That the Members of the Grand Council shall be allowed for their Service ten Shillings Sterling per diem during their Sessions and Journey to & from the place of meeting; twenty Miles to be reckoned a Days Journey.

That the assent of the President General be requisite to all Acts of the Grand Council, & that it be his Office & duty to cause them to be Carried into Execution.

That the President General with the advice of the Grand Council hold or direct all Indian Treaties in which the General Interest or Welfare of the Colonies may be concerned, & to make Peace or declare War with Indian Nations. That they make such Laws as they judge necessary for regulating all Indian Trade. That they make all purchases from Indians for the Crown, of Lands now not within the bounds of particular Colonies or that Shall not be within their Bounds when some of them are reduced to more Convenient Dimensions. That they make New Settlements on such Purchases by Granting Lands in the Kings name reserving a Quit Rent to the Crown for the use of the General Treasury. That they make Laws for Regulating & Governing such new Settlements till the Crown shall think fit to form them into particular Governments. That they may raise & pay Soldiers, and build Forts for the Defence of any of the Colonies, & equip Vessels of force to guard the Coast and protect the Trade on the Ocean Lakes or great Rivers, but they shall not impress men in any Colony without the consent of its Legislature—That for these Purposes they have power to make Laws, & lay, & levy such General Dutys Imposts or Taxes as to themselves appear most equal & just considering the ability & other Circumstances of the Inhabitants in the Several Colonies, & such as may be collected with the least Inconvenience to the People, rather discorageing Luxury, than loading Industry with unnecessary Burthens—that they may appoint a general Treasurer, and a perticular Treasurer in each Government when necessary and from time to time may order the Sums in the Treasuries of each Government into the General Treasury, or draw on them for special Payments as they find most convenient, Yet no money to Issue but by joint orders of the President General and Grand Council except where Sums have been appropriated to perticular purposes, and the President General is previously impowered by an Act to draw for Such Sums—That the General Accounts shall be yearly settled & reported to the Several Assemblies.—that a Quorum of the Grand Counsil, impowered to Act with the President General do consist of Twenty Five Members among who there shall be one or more from a Majority of the Colonies.—That the Laws made by them for the purposes aforesaid shall not be repugnant but as near as may be agreeable to the Laws of England and shall be transmitted to the King in Council for approbation as soon as may be after their passing and if not disapproved within three years after presentation to remain in force.—That in case of the Death of the President General the Speaker of the Grand Council for the time being shall Succeed and be vested with the same power and authorities & continue till the Kings pleasure be known.

That all Military Commission Officers whether for Land or Sea Service to act under this General Constitution Shall be nominated by the President General, but the approbation of the Grand Council is to be obtained before they receive their Commissions And all civil Officers are to be nominated by the Grand Council, and to receive the President Generals approbation before they officiate But in case of Vacancy by Death or removal of any Officer civil or Military under this Constitution, the Governor of the Provinces in which such Vacancy happens may appoint till the Pleasure of the President General and Grand Council be known.—That the perticular Military as well as civil Establishments in each Colony remain in their present State, this General Constitution notwithstanding; and that on Sudden Emergenceys any Colony may defend itself, and lay the Accounts of Expence Thence arisen before the President General and Grand Council, who may allow and order payment of the same as far as they judge such Accounts just and reasonable.

VII

John Adams's
Thoughts on Government

1776

COMMENTARY BY RICHARD B. BERNSTEIN

THE DOCUMENTS EXAMINED HERE are two of the catalysts of the American experiment with constitutional government in the states. Even before the Declaration of Independence from Great Britain, Americans set out to frame new forms of government for themselves, in order to protect their liberties and to preserve peace and domestic tranquility. These political experiments gave rise to many of the most important devices and practices of American constitutionalism.

The framing of new state constitutions grew out of the organization of American resistance to Great Britain in the 1760s and 1770s. In the decade following the Stamp Act Congress of 1765, Americans who opposed British colonial policy pieced together a network of committees of correspondence and public safety. Resistance began with these local committees, which then named provincial congresses, which in turn chose delegates to the First and Second Continental Congresses. By 1775, there existed alternative structures of government ready to fill the vacuum that would be created by the abrogation of British colonial rule. The process of building revolutionary "shadow governments" was well under way more than a year before the Continental Congress actually declared American independence.[1]

This commentary is adapted from Richard B. Bernstein with Kym S. Rice, *Are We to Be a Nation? The Making of the Constitution* (Cambridge, Mass., 1987), chapter 3.
[1] See, e.g., Pauline Maier, *From Resistance to Revolution: Colonial Radicals and the*

Months before the break with Britain became a legal reality as well as a practical necessity, Americans realized the need for new, legitimate sources of governmental authority to replace those soon to be toppled or swept aside by the Revolution. Because there was as yet no constitutional or legal sanction for an American union—the Continental Congresses being extralegal if not illegal organizations—and because most American political figures still considered their primary constituencies to be the individual colonies, this concern with establishing legitimate government focused on the individual colonies.

In late 1775 and early 1776, the provincial congresses of Massachusetts, New Hampshire, South Carolina, and Virginia asked the Second Continental Congress for advice on what to do about the unsettled condition of government caused by the outbreak of war with Britain. Congress agreed that there was a crisis of authority, but recommended only the convening of popularly elected assemblies to set up interim measures for exercising governmental authority to last until the establishment of a reconciliation with Great Britain.

In the congressional debates on these requests, John Adams of Massachusetts and like-minded colleagues urged Congress to act more decisively by recommending the establishment of alternative structures of authority as early as possible before any final break with Britain. Conservative delegates such as John Dickinson of Pennsylvania and James Duane and John Jay of New York argued in opposition that adopting new forms of government would be tantamount to declaring independence and would prevent reconciliation with the mother country.

It was not until May 10, 1776, that the Second Continental Congress finally adopted the following resolution drafted by John Adams. Five days later Congress accepted a preamble to the act also written by Adams and reprinted below.[2]

Development of American Opposition to Great Britain, 1763–1776 (New York, 1972); Jack N. Rakove, *The Beginnings of National Politics: An Interpretive History of the Continental Congress* (New York, 1979); Jerrilyn Green Marston, *King and Congress: The Transfer of Political Legitimacy, 1774–1776* (Princeton, 1988); and especially Willi Paul Adams, *The First American Constitutions* (Chapel Hill, 1980). Adams's book and Donald S. Lutz, *Popular Consent and Popular Control: Whig Political Theory and the State Constitutions* (Baton Rouge, La., 1980), are the best modern studies of the Revolutionary generation's state constitution-making.

[2] The text of this resolution is taken from The New York Public Library's copy of the official broadside publication, printed in Philadelphia in May 1776 by John Dunlap, the perennial printer to the Continental and Confederation Congresses. This copy is in the Library's Rare Books and Manuscripts Division. Spelling and punctuation are as in the original. Bracketed numbers before each part of the resolution have been inserted to facilitate reference. On this resolution, see generally Adams, *First American Constitutions*, 59–62.

IN CONGRESS,
MAY 15, 1776

[1] WHEREAS his Britannic Majesty, in conjunction with the Lords and
Commons of Great-Britain, has, by a late Act of Parliament, excluded
the inhabitants of these United Colonies from the protection of his
crown: [2] And whereas no answer whatever to the humble petition
of the Colonies for redress of grievances, and reconciliation with Great-
Britain has been or is likely to be given, but the whole force of that
kingdom, aided by foreign mercenaries, is to be exerted for the destruction of the good people of these Colonies: [3] And whereas it
appears absolutely irreconcileable to reason and good conscience, for
the people of these Colonies now to take the oaths and affirmations
necessary for the support of any government under the Crown of
Great-Britain; and it is necessary that the exercise of every kind of
authority under the said Crown should be totally suppressed, and all
the powers of government exerted under the authority of the people
of the Colonies for the preservation of internal peace, virtue, and good
order, as well as for the defence of their lives, liberties and properties,
against the hostile invasions and cruel depredations of their enemies:
Therefore

RESOLVED, [4] That it be recommended to the respective Assemblies and Conventions of the United Colonies, where no Government sufficient to the exigencies of their affairs has been hitherto
established, to adopt such Government as shall in the opinion of the
Representatives of the People best conduce to the happiness and
safety of their Constituents in particular, and America in general.

Extract from the Minutes,
CHARLES THOMSON, SECRETARY
Philadelphia: Printed by JOHN DUNLAP.

A close examination of this resolution enables us to reconstruct the
political and constitutional arguments of the Second Continental Congress. The first numbered clause of the preamble squarely placed the
blame for the rupture between the mother country and the colonies on
George III, acting in concert with the House of Lords and the House
of Commons of the British Parliament. The Act of Parliament mentioned there was the British response to the Olive Branch Petition
adopted by Congress on July 5, 1775—the "humble petition" cited in
the second clause. This petition, adopted at the insistence of delegates
such as Dickinson and Jay, sought (as modern lawyers would say) to
"exhaust the remedies" available to the colonists under the British
constitution by making one last appeal to the King. His refusal of the
petition, and his request that Parliament declare the American colonies
out of his allegiance and protection, made American independence all
but inevitable. The second numbered clause also contained language
(about the "destruction of the good people of these Colonies") recycled

by Thomas Jefferson into one of the specifications of charges against George III in both the Declaration of Independence and the preamble to the Virginia Constitution of 1776. The third numbered clause removed whatever ambiguity remained about the Americans' attitudes towards British authority. This part of Adams's preamble evaded the issue of whether establishing new constitutions would constitute a declaration of independence, placing the onus of the step on the British. In effect, the preamble contended, British measures excluding the colonies from the Crown's protection had compelled the colonists to throw off the Crown's authority. Adams and his contemporaries considered this resolution to be the effective instrument of American independence.[3]

Read carefully, the fourth numbered clause—the actual resolution adopted on May 10—did not direct the colonies to adopt republican governments, but the delegates assumed (and most Americans thought) that the Revolution was a struggle for republican government under the principles of the English constitution. Nonetheless, Congress chose not to recommend or impose a particular form of republican government or model constitution to be adopted by all the colonies. The delegates agreed that the people of each colony should adopt a form of government best suited to their needs, local conditions, and ideas of what a government should be. The Americans believed, as did most educated and politically active men of their time, that there was an intimate connection between a people's values and habits, on the one hand, and their institutions of government and systems of law, on the other.[4]

Congress's decision not to prescribe a model constitution for the colonies did not prevent individual delegates from writing constitutions or making recommendations. For example, in May and June of 1776, Thomas Jefferson drafted a constitution for Virginia and sent it home with his mentor George Wythe, only to discover that the Virginia convention of 1776 had anticipated him; however, as pointed out by Donald S. Lutz in his commentary in this volume, the convention grafted Jefferson's preamble, with its vigorous denunciation of George III (later incorporated into the Declaration of Independence), onto its own version as a statement of the justification for adopting a new constitution. Constitution-making engrossed delegates to Congress and their colleagues back home. Some delegates to Congress even began to complain about the lack of attention to the exigencies of the Revolution resulting from their fellow delegates' obsession with constitution-making.[5]

---

[3] Adams, *First American Constitutions*, 61.

[4] Adams, *First American Constitutions*, 49–62.

[5] On the fever of constitution-making, see George Dargo, *Law in the New Republic: Private Law and the Public Estate* (New York, 1983), 10; Adams, *First American Consti-*

The Americans' emphasis on written constitutions was rooted in American colonial history and the circumstances of the Revolution.[6] The term *constitution* in English usage denoted the whole complex of laws, common-law rules, customs, usages, and traditions that shape the political relations, rights, and responsibilities of the polity and its members. As part of the founding of colonies in North America, the Crown granted—or the colonists wrote—colonial charters setting forth the guidelines under which political power would be exercised; these new societies were at the same time extensions of England and distinct political communities with their own concerns and unique local conditions. Disputes between the colonists and representatives of the Crown over the extent of Crown authority and colonial self-government often focused on these written instruments of government; this mode of constitutional and political argument was still fresh in American memories at the outbreak of the constitutional crisis of the 1760s and 1770s. With the drift toward independence, the Americans again recognized the need to specify the basis for their new, independent political organizations in written instruments of government. This perceived necessity accorded with their sense that principles of government were immutable laws of nature, and thus had to be fixed in writing in a form distinct from and superior to mere statutes; by contrast, the unwritten English constitution, subject to the shifts and convulsions of ordinary politics, was not a sufficient bulwark against oppression.[7]

Of all the advice and suggestions produced for writing constitutions in the early years of the Revolution, perhaps the most important and influential was John Adams's *Thoughts on Government*.[8] Adams long had

---

tutions, 49–98; Allan Nevins, *The American States During and After the Revolution, 1776–1789* (New York, 1924), 117–70. See also, Jackson Turner Main, *The Sovereign States, 1775–1783* (New York, 1973), a useful supplement to Nevins. The manuscript of the third draft of Jefferson's constitution is in the Rare Books and Manuscripts Division, The New York Public Library; it is reprinted, with annotations and commentary, in Julian P. Boyd, Charles T. Cullen, and John Catanzariti, eds., *The Papers of Thomas Jefferson*, 21 vols. to date (Princeton, 1950–), I: 356–65; the first two drafts are reprinted in *ibid.*, 329–86. On the idea of a written constitution see Dargo, *Law in the New Republic*, 13–17; on the colonial heritage of written charters see also George Dargo, *Roots of the Republic: A New Perspective on Early American Constitutionalism* (New York, 1974), chap. 3. See also the works by Lutz cited below in note 6.

[6] On this, see Donald S. Lutz's fine monographs, *Popular Consent and Popular Control*, already cited, and *The Origins of American Constitutionalism* (Baton Rouge, La., 1988).

[7] See notes 6 and 7 above.

[8] On this pamphlet, the first of Adams's great writings on American constitutionalism (his newspaper and pamphlet writings on the constitutional controversy with Great Britain are contributions to British constitutional thought), see generally John R. Howe,

been fascinated by the intricacies of constitutional issues and had acquired a reputation for his extensive study of the subject. The story of the composition of *Thoughts on Government* illustrates the Americans' tendency to seize upon practical political crises as occasions to articulate their theoretical assumptions and arguments on constitutional questions.

In November of 1775, congressional delegate Richard Henry Lee of Virginia asked his fellow delegate John Adams for his thoughts on the structures of government that Americans should adopt if a break with Great Britain should occur, and Adams penned a brief sketch of what a new constitution should contain. In March 1776, two North Carolina delegates to Congress, John Penn and William Hooper, also approached Adams for advice when they received instruction to return home to help draft that state's constitution. Adams described his response in a letter to his friend and close political ally James Warren:[9]

> The Time was very Short. However the Gentleman thinking it an opportunity, providentially thrown in his Way, of communicating Some Hints upon a subject, which seems not to have been sufficiently considered in the southern Colonies, and so of turning the Thought of Gentlemen that way, concluded to borrow a little Time from his sleep and accordingly wrote with his own Hand, a Sketch, which he copied, giving the original to Mr. Hooper and the copy to Mr. Penn, which they carried with them to Carolina.

Adams's "Sketch" attracted more attention from his colleagues in Congress than he had expected. The respected lawyer and jurist George Wythe of Virginia caught sight of either Penn's or Hooper's copy, and Adams obligingly wrote out another version at Wythe's request. Then Jonathan Dickinson Sargeant of New Jersey asked for a copy. Adams prepared a revised and expanded version (now lost) for Sargeant. When Richard Henry Lee, who had received the earliest articulation of Adams's thinking, asked for a copy of his March 1776 letter, Adams borrowed back Wythe's copy and authorized Lee to arrange for its publication as an anonymous pamphlet, perhaps to stimulate his fellow

---

Jr., *The Changing Political Thought of John Adams* (Princeton, 1966), 59–101; Peter Shaw, *The Character of John Adams* (Chapel Hill, 1976), 92–97; Timothy H. Breen, "John Adams' Fight against Innovation in the New England Constitution: 1776," *New England Quarterly* 40 (1967): 501–20; Adams, *First American Constitutions*, 121–24. See also the account in L. H. Butterfield, ed., *The Diary and Autobiography of John Adams*, 4 vols. (Cambridge, Mass., 1961), 3: 331–32.

9 John Adams to James Warren, April 20, 1776, in Robert J. Taylor et al., eds., *Papers of John Adams*, 8 vols. to date (Cambridge, Mass., 1977–), 4: 130–32 (quote at 131).

delegates' consideration of the resolution they finally passed the next month.[10] *Thoughts on Government: Applicable to the Present State of the American Colonies. In a Letter from a Gentleman to his Friend* appeared in Philadelphia in late April of 1776 and was published several months later in Boston.[11]

Adams declared that his "Design [in *Thoughts on Government*] is to mark out a Path, and putt Men upon thinking."[12] In part he wrote his pamphlet in opposition to Thomas Paine's *Common Sense*, published in January 1776. Paine's first order of business was to invoke the republican sentiments of the American colonists to encourage resistance to British authority, but he also sketched his idea of the proper mode of government to replace the British colonial system. Paine suggested the creation of unicameral legislatures for each of the colonies, to be subordinate to a unicameral continental congress. Neither level of government would have an independent executive. Paine discarded separation of powers and checks and balances as important principles of republican government; he believed that the legislature, representing the whole people, should exercise all functions of government. Because there was no need to check the voice of the people by creating a second or upper house, Paine said, legislatures should be unicameral.

Adams and other moderate Revolutionary leaders valued *Common Sense* for its vigorous arguments against British rule, but they disliked Paine's radical plan for organizing governments. In contrast to Paine, Adams maintained that the new governments should preserve the best of the Anglo-American traditions of government—especially the idea of separation of powers. *Thoughts on Government* thus represents the moderate brand of Revolutionary constitutionalism.[13]

Like Paine, Adams scoffed at Alexander Pope's lines in *An Essay on Man*:[14]

---

[10] In a prefatory note written in 1811, Adams explained that he had decided to keep his name off the pamphlet because "if [my name] should appear, it would excite a continental clamor among the tories, that I was erecting a battering-ram to demolish the royal government and render independence indispensable." Charles Francis Adams, ed., *The Life and Works of John Adams*, 10 vols. (Boston, 1850–56), 4: 189.

[11] The history of the drafting and publication of *Thoughts on Government* receives its most detailed analysis in Taylor et al., *Papers of John Adams*, 4: 65–73.

[12] John Adams to James Warren, April 20, 1776, in Taylor et al., *Papers of John Adams*, 4: 132.

[13] This paragraph and the one preceding is indebted to Willi Paul Adams's suggestive juxtaposition of *Common Sense* with *Thoughts on Government* in Adams, *First American Constitutions*, 121–24. The phrase "revolutionary constitutionalism" comes from the short but valuable discussion in Alfred H. Kelly, Winfred Harbison, and Herman Belz, *The American Constitution: Its Origins and Development*, 6th ed. (New York, 1983), 68–85.

[14] Alexander Pope, *An Essay on Man*, Epistle III, lines 303–04.

> For forms of government let fools contest,
> That which is best administered is best.

He declared:

Nothing can be more fallacious than this: But poets read history to collect flowers not fruits—they attend to fanciful images, not the effects of social institutions. Nothing is more certain from the history of nations, and the nature of man, than that some forms of government are better fitted for being well administered than others.

Adams argued that only a republic could achieve the proper end of government—the promotion of human happiness, which he equated with virtue, the guiding principle of a republic. But determining the best *form* of a republic is just as important as choosing to create a republic in the first place. Adams thus rejected Paine's reliance on a one-house legislature as the sole institution of government in a republic. Noting the many faults of constructing a republican government consisting of a single assembly, Adams cited three as particular threats to republicanism: (1) A single assembly is susceptible to "all the vices, follies and frailties of an individual." (2) A single assembly cannot exercise the executive power "for want of two essential properties, secrecy and dispatch." (3) It cannot exercise the judicial power because it has too many members, works too slowly, and is "too little skilled in the laws." Developing these points he added that it was unsound to lodge only the power of legislation in a unicameral assembly, for the conflicts between a unitary executive and a unicameral assembly would destroy a republic. The judiciary could not act as a referee between the executive and legislature, because it was under the control of the legislature. Thus, a second house of the legislature was needed to act as mediator between the executive and the lower house in the process of legislation—incidentally, replicating the structure of King, Lords, and Commons familiar to generations of English lawyers, politicians, and voters. Adams suggested establishing a representative assembly, which would elect a council (his term for the upper house, derived from the colonial charters' structure of governor, council, and assembly); both houses would then elect a governor. The governor would be armed with an absolute veto over legislation and would have the power to appoint "Judges, Justices and all other officers, civil and military" with the consent of the council. To preserve their independence, judges would have tenure for life during good behavior, breaches of which would be punished by impeachment and removal from office. Adams recom-

mended that the governor and all members of both houses of the legislature be elected annually; this limitation "will teach them the great
political virtues of humility, patience, and moderation, without which
every man in power becomes a ravenous beast of prey." Finally, Adams
proposed areas in which the new government should legislate—including
public education, the militia, and sumptuary laws (such laws, first enacted in ancient Rome, were designed to tax what we would call conspicuous consumption to guard against the diseases of luxury and corruption, as well as to generate revenue for the government).

Adams reminded his readers that they should not hesitate to rework
their new constitutions should actual practice reveal defects in the design; he suggested such reforms as replacing annual elections with
longer terms of office, electing the governor and council by popular
vote, and giving both houses of the legislature a say in appointing judges
and other officers of government. Nonetheless, he predicted that the
government whose outlines he set forth in *Thoughts on Government*
would confirm the people in their attachment to republican government
and improve them in their daily lives as well.

It is difficult to estimate the influence that *Thoughts on Government*
had on the first state constitutions. Adams had intended his pamphlet
to spur constitution-making in the southern states in the direction of
republicanism in the hope that they would adopt governments as democratic as those of New England. But *Thoughts on Government* found
readers beyond Adams's intended southern audience as well. In his
home state, it was frequently quoted in newspaper essays throughout
Massachusetts and even reprinted once in the Newburyport *Essex Journal.* Adams's friend Benjamin Rush drew extensively on *Thoughts on
Government* in his attacks on the radical, Pennsylvania Constitution of
1776 with its unicameral assembly; and that document's defenders also
quoted Adams to refute Rush's invocation of his authority. Several of
the state constitutions framed after Adams wrote were consistent with
his prescription, and his friends and colleagues in Virginia, North Carolina, New Jersey, and New York assured him that they had made good
use of his advice—assurances which later scholars have confirmed.[15] The
constitutions of all these states established bicameral legislatures and
executives headed by a single governor, although most of these governors were weak and dependent on the legislature; Adams's belief in
an independent executive as an essential element of republican checks
and balances ran counter to the prevailing American distrust of executive power.

[15] See the valuable discussion in Taylor et al., *Papers of John Adams,* 4: 69–73.

Adams's pamphlet was widely and respectfully read and studied, even by his political and intellectual opponents. It helped to crystallize what many of Adams's fellow constitution-makers believed. Moreover, when Adams got the chance to prepare the draft of the Massachusetts Constitution of 1780, he followed many of the prescriptions set forth in his 1776 pamphlet; in turn, many of the provisions of that document shaped by the recommendations of *Thoughts on Government* helped to shape the framing of the United States Constitution in 1787.[16] Finally, Adams's statement in that pamphlet of the intellectual challenge and excitement of constitution-making stands as an eloquent summary of the spirit of the age:

> You and I, my dear Friend, have been sent into life, at a time when the greatest law-givers of antiquity would have wished to have lived. How few of the human race have ever enjoyed an opportunity of making an election of government more than of air, soil, or climate, for themselves or their children. When! Before the present epoch, had three millions of people full power and a fair opportunity to form and establish the wisest and happiest government that human wisdom can contrive?

In the 1990s, an era in which the nations of Eastern Europe are engaged in drafting or revising their constitutions and when the nations of Europe hope to create by 1992 a European confederation on a scale unprecedented in human history, the pages of *Thoughts on Government* have renewed relevance.

For Further Reading

Willi Paul Adams. *The First American Constitutions*. Chapel Hill, 1980.
Timothy H. Breen. "John Adams' Fight against Innovation in the New England Constitution: 1776." *New England Quarterly* 40. 1967.
L. H. Butterfield, ed. *The Diary and Autobiography of John Adams*, 4 vols. Cambridge, Mass., 1961.
John R. Howe, Jr. *The Changing Political Thought of John Adams*. Princeton, 1966.
Donald S. Lutz. *Popular Consent and Popular Control: Whig Political Theory and the State Constitutions*. Baton Rouge, La., 1980.

---

[16] On the pamphlet's influence on the framing of the Massachusetts constitution of 1780, see Taylor et al., *Papers of John Adams*, 4: 71–72.

Pauline Maier. *From Resistance to Revolution: Colonial Radicals and the Development of American Opposition to the Great Britain, 1763–1776.* New York, 1972.

Jerrilyn Green Marston. *King and Congress: The Transfer of Political Legitimacy, 1774–1776.* Princeton, 1988.

Jack N. Rakove. *The Beginnings of National Politics: An Interpretive History of the Continental Congress.* New York, 1979.

Peter Shaw. *The Character of John Adams.* Chapel Hill, 1976.

[John Adams's
Thoughts on Government]

[1776]

My dear Sir,

If I was equal to the task of forming a plan for the government of a colony, I should be flattered with your request, and very happy to comply with it; because as the divine science of politicks is the science of social happiness, and the blessings of society depend entirely on the constitutions of government, which are generally institutions that last for many generations, there can be no employment more agreeable to a benevolent mind, than a research after the best. POPE flattered tyrants too much when he said,

> "For forms of government let fools contest,
> That which is best administered is best."[1]

Nothing can be more fallacious than this: But poets read history to collect flowers not fruits—they attend to fanciful images, not the effects of social institutions. Nothing is more certain from the history of nations, and the nature of man, than that some forms of government are better fitted for being well administered than others.

WE ought to consider, what is the end of government, before we determine which is the best form.—Upon this point all speculative politicians will agree, that the happiness of society is the end of government, as all Divines and moral Philosophers will agree that the happiness of the individual is the end of man. From this principle it will follow, that the form of government, which communicates ease, comfort, security,

---

The full title of the text is *Thoughts on Government: Applicable to the Present State of the American Colonies. In a Letter from a Gentleman to his Friend* and is taken from Robert J. Taylor et al., eds., *Papers of John Adams*, 8 vols. to date (Cambridge, Mass., 1977–), 4: 86–93, which in turn is based on the Boston reprint of the first pamphlet edition published in Philadelphia in 1776 by John Dunlap.

[1] As noted in the commentary above, this verse comes from Alexander Pope, *An Essay on Man*, Epistle III, lines 303–04. Note that Alexander Hamilton also quoted these lines to criticize them in *The Federalist No. 68*, but then qualified his criticism by pointing out that the true test of a good government is its aptitude and tendency to produce a good administration, a point presaged by Adams at the close of this first paragraph.

or in one word happiness to the greatest number of persons, and in the greatest degree, is the best.[2]

ALL sober enquiries after truth, ancient and modern, Pagan and Christian, have declared that the happiness of man, as well as his dignity consists in virtue. Confucius, Zoroaster, Socrates, Mahomet, not to mention authorities really sacred, have agreed in this.

IF there is a form of government then, whose principle and foundation is virtue, will not every sober man acknowledge it better calculated to promote the general happiness than any other form?

FEAR is the foundation of most governments; but is so sordid and brutal a passion, and renders men, in whose breasts it predominates, so stupid, and miserable, that Americans will not be likely to approve of any political institution which is founded on it.

HONOUR is truly sacred, But holds a lower rank in the scale of moral excellence than virtue.—Indeed the former is but a part of the latter, and consequently has not equal pretensions to support a frame of government productive of human happiness.

THE foundation of every government is some principle or passion in the minds of the people.—The noblest principles and most generous affections in our nature then, have the fairest chance to support the noblest and most generous models of government.

A MAN must be indifferent to the sneers of modern Englishmen to mention in their company, the names of Sidney, Harrington, Locke, Milton, Nedham, Neville, Burnet, and Hoadley.[3]—No small fortitude

[2] Compare this paragraph's discussion of the greatest happiness to the greatest degree for the greatest number as the end of government with Jeremy Bentham's 1776 *Fragment on Government* and his *Introduction to the Principles of Morals and Legislation*.

[3] The historical figures cited here by Adams are all heroes of the seventeenth-century English struggles against the tyranny, real or feared, of the Stuart kings. They include the martyr Algernon Sidney (1622–1683), executed by the government of Charles II for the manuscript of his posthumously published *Discourses concerning Government*; John Harrington (1611–1677), whose utopian work *Oceana* was a landmark in the history of English republican thought; John Locke (1634–1704), the renowned author of the *Essay Concerning Human Understanding* and the *Two Treatises of Government*; Marchamont Nedham (1620–1678), whose *The Excellencie of a Free State* and other works on republican government John Adams reviewed and commented on in his three-volume *A Defence of the Constitutions of Government of the United States* (1787–1788); Henry Neville (1620–1694), a contemporary and intellectual ally of Harrington, and the author of *Plato Redivivus*; the prominent Whig historian and bishop of Salisbury Gilbert Burnet (1643–1715), who preached the coronation sermon at the coronation of William and Mary in 1689; and Benjamin Hoadly (1675–1761), bishop of Bangor, Hereford, Salisbury, and Winchester, and another noted Whig controversialist. The best study of these figures and their intellectual and political context is Caroline Robbins, *The Eighteenth-Century Commonwealthman: Studies in the Transmission, Development and Circumstance of English Liberal Thought from the Restoration of Charles II until the War with the Thirteen Colonies* (Cambridge, Mass., 1959; paperback, with new preface, New York, 1968).

is necessary to confess that one has read them. The wretched condition of this country, however, for ten or fifteen years past, has frequently reminded me of their principles and reasonings. They will convince any candid mind, that there is no good government but what is Republican. That the only valuable part of the British constitution is so; because the very definition of a Republic, is "an Empire of Laws, and not of men."[4] That, as a Republic is the best of governments, so that particular arrangement of the powers of society, or in other words that form of government, which is best contrived to secure an impartial and exact execution of the laws, is the best of Republics.

Of Republics, there is an inexhaustible variety, because the possible combinations of the powers of society, are capable of innumerable variations.[5]

As good government, is an empire of laws, how shall your laws be made? In a large society, inhabiting an extensive country, it is impossible that the whole should assemble, to make laws: The first necessary step then, is, to depute power from the many, to a few of the most wise and good.—But by what rules shall you choose your Representatives? Agree upon the number and qualifications of persons, who shall have the benefit of choosing, or annex this privilege to the inhabitants of a certain extent of ground.

The principal difficulty lies, and the greatest care should be employed in constituting this Representative Assembly. It should be in miniature, an exact portrait of the people at large.[6] It should think, feel, reason, and act like them. That it may be the interest of this Assembly to do strict justice at all times, it should be an equal representation, or in other words equal interest among the people should have equal interest in it.—Great care should be taken to effect this, and to prevent unfair, partial, and corrupt elections. Such regulations, however, may be better made in times of greater tranquility than the present, and they will spring up of themselves naturally, when all the powers

---

[4] Compare Article XXX of the Declaration of Rights of the Massachusetts Constitution of 1780, which enshrined the principle of separation of powers "to the end it may be a government of laws and not of men." See the commentary by Richard B. Bernstein on the Massachusetts Constitution of 1780 in this volume.

[5] For a modern discussion of the varying types of republicanism and the varying forms of government that can be deduced from this range of republican principles, see Forrest McDonald, *Novus Ordo Seclorum: The Intellectual Origins of the Constitution* (Lawrence, Kans., 1985), 66–87.

[6] Note Adams's insistence that the representative assembly "be in miniature, an exact portrait of the people at large." On theories of representation, see generally Hanna Fenichel Pitkin, *The Concept of Representation* (Berkeley, 1967), and John Phillip Reid, *The Concept of Representation in the Age of the American Revolution* (Chicago, 1988).

of government come to be in the hands of the peoples friends. At present it will be safest to proceed in all established modes to which the people have been familiarised by habit.

A REPRESENTATION of the people in one assembly being obtained, a question arises whether all the powers of government, legislative, executive, and judicial, shall be left in this body? I think a people cannot be long free, nor ever happy, whose government is in one Assembly.[7] My reasons for this opinion are as follow.

1. A SINGLE Assembly is liable to all the vices, follies and frailties of an individual.—Subject to fits of humour, starts of passion, flights of enthusiasm, partialities of prejudice, and consequently productive of hasty results and absurd judgments: And all these errors ought to be corrected and defects supplied by some controuling power.

2. A SINGLE Assembly is apt to be avaricious, and in time will not scruple to exempt itself from burthens which it will lay, without compunction, on its constituents.

3. A SINGLE Assembly is apt to grow ambitious, and after a time will not hesitate to vote itself perpetual. This was one fault of the long parliament, but more remarkably of Holland, whose Assembly first voted themselves from annual to septennial, then for life, and after a course of years, that all vacancies happening by death, or otherwise, should be filled by themselves, without any application to constituents at all.

4. A REPRESENTATIVE Assembly, altho' extremely well qualified, and absolutely necessary as a branch of the legislature, is unfit to exercise the executive power, for want of two essential properties, secrecy and dispatch.[8]

5. A REPRESENTATIVE Assembly is still less qualified for the judicial power; because it is too numerous, too slow, and too little skilled in the laws.[9]

---

[7] Compare the comment of Thomas Jefferson on the Virginia Constitution of 1776:

All the powers of government, legislative, executive, and judiciary, result to the legislative body. The concentrating these in the same hands is precisely the definition of despotic government. It will be no alleviation that these powers will be exercised by a plurality of hands, and not by a single one. 173 despots will surely be as oppressive as one.

Thomas Jefferson, *Notes on the State of Virginia*, edited by William Peden (Chapel Hill, 1955), Query XIII, 120. This passage from Jefferson was quoted by James Madison in *The Federalist No. 48*.

[8] On the qualities of secrecy and dispatch as characteristic of a good executive, see also Alexander Hamilton's discussion in *The Federalist No. 70* and the commentary by Richard B. Bernstein on *The Federalist Nos. 15, 70, and 78* in this volume.

[9] On the qualities needed for a good judiciary, see also Alexander Hamilton's

6. BECAUSE a single Assembly, possessed of all the powers of government, would make arbitrary laws for their own interest, execute all laws arbitrarily for their own interest, and adjudge all controversies in their own favour.

BUT shall the whole power of legislation rest in one Assembly? Most of the foregoing reasons apply equally to prove that the legislative power ought to be more complex—to which we may add, that if the legislative power is wholly in one Assembly, and the executive in another, or in a single person, these two powers will oppose and enervate upon each other, until the contest shall end in war, and the whole power, legislative and executive, be usurped by the strongest.

THE judicial power, in such case, could not mediate, or hold the balance between the two contending powers, because the legislative would undermine it.[10]—And this shews the necessity too, of giving the executive power a negative upon the legislative, otherwise this will be continually encroaching upon that.

To avoid these dangers let a distant[11] Assembly be constituted, as a mediator between the two extreme branches of the legislature, that which represents the people and that which is vested with the executive power.

LET the Representative Assembly then elect by ballot, from among themselves or their constituents, or both, a distinct Assembly, which for the sake of perspicuity we will call a Council. It may consist of any number you please, say twenty or thirty, and should have a free and independent exercise of its judgment, and consequently a negative voice in the legislature.

THESE two bodies thus constituted, and made integral parts of the legislature, let them unite, and by joint ballot choose a Governor, who, after being stripped of most of those badges of domination called prerogatives, should have a free and independent exercise of his judgment, and be made also an integral part of the legislature. This I know is liable to objections, and if you please you may make him only President

---

discussion in *The Federalist No. 78* and the commentary by Richard B. Bernstein on *The Federalist Nos. 15, 70,* and *78* in this volume.

[10] Compare Adams's ideas about the judiciary with Hamilton's in *The Federalist No. 78,* and see the commentary by Richard B. Bernstein on *The Federalist Nos. 15, 70,* and *78* in this volume. Ideas of separation of powers and checks and balances changed greatly between 1776 and 1787, according to Gordon S. Wood, *The Creation of the American Republic, 1776–1787* (Chapel Hill, 1969).

[11] The editors of the *Papers of John Adams* suggest that this word should be "direct" rather than "distant."

of the Council, as in Connecticut:[12] But as the Governor is to be invested with the executive power, with consent of Council, I think he ought to have a negative upon the legislative. If he is annually elective, as he ought to be, he will always have so much reverence and affection for the People, their Representatives and Councillors, that although you give him an independent exercise of his judgment, he will seldom use it in opposition to the two Houses, except in cases the public utility of which would be conspicuous, and some such cases would happen.

IN the present exigency of American affairs, when by an act of Parliament we are put out of the royal protection, and consequently discharged from our allegiance; and it has become necessary to assume government for our immediate security, the Governor, Lieutenant-Governor, Secretary, Treasurer, Commissary, Attorney-General, should be chosen by joint ballot, of both Houses. And these and all other elections, especially of Representatives and Councillors, should be annual, there not being in the whole circle of the sciences, a maxim more infallible than this, "Where annual elections end, there slavery begins."

THESE great men, in this respect, should be, once a year

> "Like bubbles on the sea of matter borne,
> They rise, they break, and to that sea return."[13]

This will teach them the great political virtues of humility, patience, and moderation, without which every man in power becomes a ravenous beast of prey.

THIS mode of constituting the great offices of state will answer very well for the present, but if, by experiment, it should be found inconvenient, the legislature may at its leisure devise other methods of creating them, by elections of the people at large, as in Connecticut, or it may enlarge the term for which they shall be chosen to seven years, or three years, or for life, or make any other alterations which the society shall find productive of its ease, its safety, its freedom, or in one word, its happiness.

A ROTATION of all offices, as well as of Representatives and Councillors, has many advocates, and is contended for with many plausible arguments. It would be attended no doubt with many advantages, and

[12] Adams referred here to the Fundamental Orders of Connecticut of 1639, which, revised slightly in 1776, served as the constitution of the state until 1818. See the commentary on the Fundamental Orders of Connecticut by Donald S. Lutz in this volume (Chapter 2 above).

[13] These lines come from Alexander Pope, An Essay on Man, Epistle III, lines 19–20. As made clear in the text, Adams cited Pope to illustrate and support the principle of rotation in office.

if the society has a sufficient number of suitable characters to supply the great number of vacancies which would be made by such a rotation, I can see no objection to it. These persons may be allowed to serve for three years, and then be excluded three years, or for any longer or shorter term.

ANY seven or nine of the legislative Council may be made a Quorum, for doing business as a Privy Council, to advise the Governor in the exercise of the executive branch of power, and in all acts of state.

THE GOVERNOR should have the command of the militia, and of all your armies. The power of pardons should be with the Governor and Council.

JUDGES, Justices and all other officers, civil and military, should be nominated and appointed by the Governor, with the advice and consent of Council, unless you choose to have a government more popular; if you do, all officers, civil and military, may be chosen by joint ballot of both Houses, or in order to preserve the independence and importance of each House, by ballot of one House, concurred by the other. Sheriffs should be chosen by the freeholders of counties—so should Registers of Deeds and Clerks of Counties.

ALL officers should have commissions, under the hand of the Governor and seal of the Colony.

THE dignity and stability of government in all its branches, the morals of the people and every blessing of society, depends so much upon an upright and skillful administration of justice, that the judicial power ought to be distinct from both the legislative and executive, and independent upon both, that so it may be a check upon both, as both should be checks upon that. The Judges therefore should always be men of learning and experience in the laws, of exemplary morals, great patience, calmness, coolness and attention. Their minds should not be distracted with jarring interests; they should not be dependent upon any man, or body of men. To these ends they should hold estates for life in their offices, or in other words their commissions should be during good behaviour, and their salaries ascertained and established by law.[14] For misbehaviour the grand inquest of the Colony, the House of Representatives, should impeach them before the Governor and Council, where they should have time and opportunity to make their defence, but if convicted should be removed from their offices, and subjected to such other punishment as shall be thought proper.

[14] Compare Adams's discussion of judicial power with Alexander Hamilton's fuller and more elaborate analysis in *The Federalist Nos. 78–83*, and see Richard B. Bernstein's commentary on *The Federalist Nos. 15, 70,* and *78* in this volume.

A MILITIA LAW requiring all men, or with very few exceptions, besides cases of conscience, to be provided with arms and ammunition, to be trained at certain seasons, and requiring counties, towns, or other small districts to be provided with public stocks of ammunition and entrenching utensils, and with some settled plans for transporting provisions after the militia, when marched to defend their country against sudden invasions, and requiring certain districts to be provided with field pieces, companies of matrosses, and perhaps some regiments of light horse, is always a wise institution, and in the present circumstances of our country indispensible.[15]

LAWS for the liberal education of youth, especially of the lower class of people, are so extremely wise and useful, that to a humane and generous mind, no expence for this purpose would be thought extravagant.[16]

THE very mention of sumptuary laws will excite a smile. Whether our countrymen have wisdom and virtue enough to submit to them I know not. But the happiness of the people might be greatly promoted by them, and a revenue saved sufficient to carry on this war forever. Frugality is a great revenue, besides curing us of vanities, levities and fopperies which are real antidotes to all great, manly and warlike virtues.

BUT must not all commissions run in the name of a King? No. Why may they not as well run thus, "The Colony of   to A. B. greeting," and be tested by the Governor?

WHY may not writs, instead of running in the name of a King, run thus, "The Colony of   to the Sheriff," &c. and be tested by the Chief Justice.

WHY may not indictments conclude, "against the peace of the Colony of   and the dignity of the same?"

A CONSTITUTION, founded on these principles, introduces knowledge among the People, and inspires them with a conscious dignity, becoming Freemen. A general emulation takes place, which causes good humour, sociability, good manners, and good morals to be general. That elevation of sentiment, inspired by such a government, makes the common people brave and enterprizing. That ambition which is inspired by it makes them sober, industrious and frugal. You will find among them some elegance, perhaps, but more solidity; a little pleasure, but

[15] This passage casts interesting light on the Second Amendment to the United States Constitution. See John P. Kaminski and Richard B. Bernstein's commentary on the Bill of Rights in this volume in Chapter 18 below.

[16] On governmental responsibility for education, compare Chapter V of the frame of government of the Massachusetts Constitution of 1780, and see Richard B. Bernstein's commentary on the Massachusetts Constitution of 1780 in Chapter 11 below.

a great deal of business—some politeness, but more civility. If you compare such a country with the regions of domination, whether Monarchial or Aristocratical, you will fancy yourself in Arcadia or Elisium.

IF the Colonies should assume governments separately, they should be left entirely to their own choice of the forms, and if a Continental Constitution should be formed, it should be a Congress, containing a fair and adequate Representation of the Colonies, and its authority should sacredly be confined to these cases, viz. war, trade, disputes between Colony and Colony, the Post-Office, and the unappropriated lands of the Crown, as they used to be called.[17]

THESE Colonies, under such forms of government, and in such a union, would be unconquerable by all the Monarchies of Europe.

YOU and I, my dear Friend, have been sent into life, at a time when the greatest lawgivers of antiquity would have wished to have lived.—How few of the human race have ever enjoyed an opportunity of making an election of government more than of air, soil, or climate, for themselves or their children.—When! Before the present epocha, had three millions of people full power and a fair opportunity to form and establish the wisest and happiest government that human wisdom can contrive? I hope you will avail yourself and your country of that extensive learning and indefatigable industry which you possess, to assist her in the formations of the happiest governments, and the best character of a great People.—For myself, I must beg you to keep my name out of sight, for this feeble attempt, if it should be known to be mine, would oblige me to apply to myself those lines of the immortal John Milton, in one of his sonnets,

> "I did but teach the age to quit their cloggs
> By the plain rules of ancient Liberty,
> When lo! a barbarous noise surrounded me,
> Of owls and cuckoos, asses, apes and dogs."[18]

---

[17] Note the limited purposes for which Adams suggested the necessity of a "Continental Constitution." A person holding such views eleven years later, in 1787, would be an Antifederalist. Note, however, Adams's willingness to assign authority over the "unappropriated lands of the Crown, as they used to be called," to the Congress. See, on this point, the commentary on the Northwest Ordinance of 1787 by Peter S. Onuf in Chapter 13 of volume.

[18] These lines are slightly misquoted from John Milton, "On the Detraction Which Followed upon My Writing Certain Treatises," second part, "On the Same," lines 1–4. They exhibit John Adams's concern, a constant throughout his life but especially in the difficult months before the declaration of American independence in July 1776, that his countrymen were ready to scorn him rather than listen to him.

VIII

The Declaration of Independence

1776

COMMENTARY BY DONALD S. LUTZ

COLONIAL AMERICANS WERE IN THE HABIT of using political compacts and constitutions as founding documents for establishing communities, churches, and colonies. After independence, Americans used the same forms to establish their state governments. It is not surprising that they used the same form at the national level. The Declaration of Independence and the Articles of Confederation together constituted our first national political compact; and when the Articles were replaced by the United States Constitution of 1787, we moved to the political compact under which we now live. The Declaration of Independence and the preamble to the Constitution together create a people, lay out its fundamental values and commitments, and establish a government. The body of the Constitution describes the institutions for collective decision-making.

The Declaration of Independence was not written in a vacuum. It did not suddenly spring from the mind of a few men. Thomas Jefferson himself said in a letter to Henry Lee written on May 8, 1825: "Neither aiming at originality of principles or sentiments, nor yet copied from any particular and previous writing, it was intended to be an expression of the American Mind." Apparently Jefferson attempted to summarize what he felt were the beliefs generally held by Americans on the basis of what was written in their political documents, newspaper articles, and political pamphlets. It could not have succeeded otherwise. Any political document intended to be the basis for common commitments must use language and ideas that are both familiar and widely shared. In such situations, there is very little receptivity to original ideas or new, unusual phrases. Those signing the Declaration of Independence saw themselves as proxies or representatives for the people of America. The language and meaning had to be that which the American people understood and approved. The immediate and total acceptance of the Declaration of Independence is evidence that Jefferson wrote the truth in 1825.

One does not need to take Jefferson's word for it. About three-fourths of the Declaration consists of a list of grievances against the king. At the beginning of the Virginia Constitution, passed the month before, there is a list of grievances that contains most of what is in the Declaration's list. Examining the lists of grievances at the beginning of the other state constitutions passed before Virginia's, we would find these and other grievances as well. If we examined the newspapers, beginning in 1774, we would find the Declaration's list of grievances in various combinations dozens of times. Jefferson needed to do no more than open a newspaper from that week to find his list.

The Virginia Declaration of Rights reveals that much of the famous first two paragraphs of the Declaration of Independence are in the Virginia document. An examination of the newspapers and pamphlets of the previous years would show these to be relatively standard sentiments. The last sentence of the Declaration is lifted from the Mecklenburgh Resolutions of North Carolina (May 20, 1775), as are other portions of the first and last paragraphs. North Carolinians referred to their Resolutions as a declaration of independence, so Jefferson had a good model from the previous year from which to work.

The first paragraph of Jefferson's Declaration explains the document's purpose—a justification for the colonies' break with Britain. The first paragraph also refers to the creation of a new people who are dissolving the political bands connecting them with another people. In early colonial covenant and compacts, it was the practice for a people to be defined by all those signing the document. At the end of the Declaration there is a list of signatures, and the last paragraph tells us that the signatures are those of the representatives of the "united States of America" acting "in the Name, and by Authority of the good People of the Colonies."

From the very beginning, the document begs the important question of whether this is an agreement among the states, and thus among thirteen different peoples, or whether it is an agreement creating one united people at the national level. One can point to evidence in the

Declaration to support both sides. Evidence that the document is creating one national people includes the opening statement where "one people" is separating from another, capitalizing and using the singular "People" when referring in the last paragraph to the "good People of these Colonies." Evidence for the other side includes the reference in the last paragraph to "Free and Independent States," and the use of the plural when referring to the states in the list of grievances. The delegates also signed the Declaration by state delegations, starting with New Hampshire in the far right column and then, in their north to south fashion, completing each column and beginning a new column to the left.

Of course, Americans today possess something like dual citizenship whereby they are simultaneously citizens of the United States and of their respective states. One could view the Declaration of Independence as containing implicitly the first statement of dual citizenship by more or less balancing references to a national people and to state peoples, thereby implying that both are created at the same time. It is interesting that the document tends to use group language for the creation of a single people toward the beginning and language for multiple state peoples toward the end. The list of grievances refers at times to things the king has done to hurt a colony or a colonial government, and at other times to things he has done to harm all Americans.

The textual ambiguity reflects not only a fundamental aspect of American politics—the simultaneous existence of state and national governments or federalism. It also reflects a fundamental aspect of the situation faced in 1776. If the document unambiguously reflected the creation of only one national people, it would have denied the existence of state governments, and would not have been acceptable to the majority who felt closer to a state than to the national government. If the Declaration had created only thirteen separate peoples, the document would have made no sense, for in it the states create a common cause. It is most useful to view the Declaration of Independence as effectively creating with the same act a national people and thirteen state peoples. The relationship between the national people and state peoples remains to be worked out institutionally, first in the Articles of Confederation and finally in the Constitution.

Such a simultaneous creation of peoples is reflected most interestingly in the title: "The unanimous Declaration of the thirteen united States of America." There are thirteen states, but they are united. Furthermore, the Declaration reflects a unity that is unanimous. There is a very important point to be made concerning the presence of the word "unanimous" in the title. The Declaration that was adopted on

July 4, 1776, was not unanimous, and the word did not appear in the title of the first version printed in July. Nor were the names at the end affixed in that version—so as to protect the signers from British retaliation for as long as possible. New York did not approve it, and not all of the eventual signers were present on July 4th.

On July 15, 1776, the delegates from New York approved the Declaration, and an official signing of an engrossed copy was held on August 2, 1776. Fifty men signed on that day. Five more added their names separately during the fall. Finally, on January 18, 1777, the Continental Congress authorized the printing of the Declaration of Independence, this time with the names of the signers included, although the fifty-sixth signature, that of Thomas McKean, had not yet been affixed by that date but would be added later. Also, the word "unanimous" was added to the title of this version, which became the official version.

The change in the title was an attempt to present a united front against Britain. One can also view the insistence upon unanimity as recognition that a compact does not bind those who do not sign it or agree to it. If we are to have a national people, a national social compact, both John Locke and the American colonial constitutional tradition required that the agreement be unanimous. Otherwise the people of a non-signing state would not be part of the national people. The insistence upon unanimity is one piece of evidence that the Declaration of Independence is a political compact.

The first paragraph states that upon dissolving the bands tying them with Britain, the American people take up a "separate and equal station to which the Laws of Nature and of Nature's God entitle them." American newspapers and political pamphlets were full of statements to the effect that the American people considered themselves equal to the British people. They were equal because, according to American political theory, every person has the inalienable right to give and withhold his or her consent because God dispensed the ability equally to all. Thus, any group of people can join together by political compact and be made equal to any other people regardless of the size of the community. Just as in the Christian tradition, a poor person and a rich one are equal in the sight of God, a small nation is equal to the largest nation once it forms itself by a compact based upon unanimous consent. Whereas today we are inclined to read "all men are created equal" as referring to individuals, those signing the document also read it to mean that "the American people are equal to the British people."

In 1776 few people saw a contradiction between what they read in John Locke and what they read in the Bible. When, in the second paragraph, the Declaration says "We hold these truths to be self-evident," it was self-evident on both biblical and rationalist grounds. The first paragraph referred to "Nature and Nature's God," a formulation acceptable at the time to those who believed in God as well as to those who did not but thought natural rights were just that—part of human nature and thus natural even without God. To the careful reader, the document contains abundant evidence of a religious as well as a more "enlightened" nature.

Locke had a natural connection with those of the Declaration. However, the language and ideas for the document are just as likely to have come from another Englishman, Algernon Sidney. Locke, in fact, borrowed many of Sidney's ideas. Sidney's essays, written prior to Locke's, had language that is closer to that used in the Declaration than does Locke's. The language in the Declaration resembles that found in half a dozen authors who wrote before or after Locke, but most importantly it resembles the language used in American publications between 1774 and 1776. There was no one writer from whom the ideas of the Declaration were taken.

The grievances against the king form an important part of the document and must be examined carefully. Viewed one way, the charges against the king express reasons for breaking with Britain. Viewed another way, they comprise a list of American political commitments.

The first six charges deal with the legislature and legislative process, which is appropriate given the long-standing American preference for legislative supremacy. The legislature was supposed to engage in a deliberative process for the common good. The king had disrupted the legislatures, interfered with their internal processes, dissolved them, called them together under circumstances not conducive to deliberation, placed conditions upon the laws they passed, refused to assent to laws, or failed to enforce ones properly passed. Every one of the first six charges either explicitly or implicitly rested upon the king threatening, thwarting, or neglecting the common good of the colonists. The third charge was notable also for expressing a strong desire for the continued westward expansion of the country.

The seventh charge against the king held that he had interfered with immigration to America. Freedom of movement, commitment to an easy naturalization process, viewing immigration as positive rather than negative, and a commitment to westward expansion were all part of this paragraph.

Charges eight and nine had to do with the king interfering with the judicial process. The Americans here asserted their preference for separating the judiciary from executive interference, and upholding the principle of judges serving under good behavior rather than at the pleasure of some other part of the government.

The tenth charge stated the American attachment to frugality as an essential principle of government. The swarms of officers were not objected to out of opposition to a bureaucracy, but because these men would "eat out their substance"—use up too much of the common wealth.

English common law contained a prohibition against a standing army in times of peace and also provided that the military was to be subordinate to the civil power. As part of this concept, soldiers were subject to both military tribunals and civil courts of law, and if there was a conflict as to which court had precedence the civil court was to prevail. Also, troops were not to be quartered among the people in peacetime. The eleventh, twelfth, fourteenth, and fifteenth charges held that these aspects of common law had been contravened. The American preference for a citizen militia and for civil control of the military were thus enunciated, prefiguring the Second and Third Amendments to the Constitution.

Halfway through the list it should be apparent that the list of charges, when read a certain way, amounts to a bill of rights. Like a bill of rights, the list of charges laid out a self-definition of the people created by the document and enunciated basic values and commitments. One basic commitment running through the entire list was a commitment to two sets of government. Most of the charges dealt with the king's actions against one or several of the colonies rather than against all of them. This implies rather strongly a commitment to protect state government, and prefigures the republican guarantee clause of the United States Constitution.

The thirteenth charge is in certain respects what the Declaration is all about. It held that the king had joined with Parliament to make laws for the colonies even though the colonies had their own legislatures. If a colonial legislature levied a tax, that was tolerable for the colonists since it would be an act of their own creation. If Parliament passed a tax affecting Americans, this was taxation without representation and a crime against all of America. It reflects the most fundamental political commitment of all: government must be based upon the consent of the governed and beholding to a majority of the people who constitute the government.

The sixteenth and seventeenth charges were precise glosses upon the thirteenth. American trade with the rest of the world was subject to a host of regulations passed by Parliament dating back to the Navigation Act of 1660. On the one hand, this was a further statement of the idea that government is and must be based upon the consent of the people; but it was also an anti-mercantilist statement that upheld the principle of free trade. The imposition of taxes without the consent of the colonial legislatures was another specification of the thirteenth charge.

English common law included many guarantees surrounding trial by jury. Charges eighteen and nineteen argued that the right to a trial by a jury of one's peers had been denied to Americans in a variety of ways. The commitment to jury trials was here expressed and later became part of the Constitution and Bill of Rights.

The twentieth charge referred to the institution of a Roman system of law in Quebec in place of the common law and to the geographical extension of Quebec into what later became the Northwest Territory of the United States. This last fact was most consternating as it was a threat to westward expansion. The twentieth charge thus reinforced the commitment found in the seventh charge to the westward growth of the United States.

The twenty-first and twenty-second charges expressed once again the fundamental commitment to government based upon the consent of the people and no other force. If charters of government were ignored, important laws altered, the form of government changed, and legislatures suspended, what would become of popular sovereignty, popular consent, and majority rule? This struck at the heart of 150 years of constitutional theory as practiced in America. The rejection of such behavior was an affirmation of some of the most fundamental of all American commitments.

The next five charges listed all the ways that the king had made war on the colonists. They together expressed what was felt to be one of the most important jobs of government—to protect the people from foreign and domestic violence. In effect, the king had withdrawn his protection and thereby ceased to provide legitimate government. The implication was that the king, not the American people, had broken the ties.

There was another paragraph at this point that was deleted by the Second Continental Congress before the Declaration was approved. Jefferson had a lengthy diatribe against the African slave trade and the king's refusal to allow colonies to prohibit it. South Carolina and Georgia, however, did not want to relinguish this trade, and some northeastern states were embarrassed about their long involvement in importing slaves; consequently, the clause was deleted.

The twenty-eighth charge, and the long paragraph that follows, revealed the American commitment to deliberative processes. Echoing the paragraph immediately preceding the list of charges—that important changes in government ought not to be undertaken lightly, and that all avenues should be pursued before having to make drastic change—the

Declaration here noted that all means, legal and informal, had been pursued for solving the problems short of drastic change, and that all such attempts had been rebuffed or ignored. A long train of abuses, just enumerated, had finally worn down American patience and exhausted the deliberative process.

The last paragraph contained another interesting phrase in the context of our earlier discussion. Any document calling on God as a witness would technically be a covenant. As previously suggested, American constitutionalism had its roots in the covenant form that was secularized into the compact. The last paragraph of the Declaration reads " . . . appealing to the Supreme Judge of the world for the rectitude of our intentions, do, in the Name, and by Authority of the good People of these Colonies. . . ." Because God has been called as a witness, the Declaration of Independence is in fact a covenant. The wording is peculiar, however, and while the form of an oath is present, the words stop short of the traditional form. Nonetheless, the close juxtaposition of an oath-like phrase with the reference to the popular sovereignty of a single people constitutes a very intricate textual dance around the covenant and compact form. The Declaration of Independence may be a covenant. It is definitely part of a compact in the old American political tradition.

For Further Reading

Carl L. Becker. *The Declaration of Independence*. New York, 1922.
Daniel J. Elazar and John Kincaid. *The Declaration of Independence: The Founding Covenant of the American People*. Philadelphia, 1980.
Dumas Malone. *Jefferson and His Time* 6 vols. Boston, 1948–1981.
Merrill D. Peterson. *Thomas Jefferson and the New Nation*. New York, 1970.
John Phillip Reid. *The Concept of Liberty in the Age of the American Revolution*. Chicago, 1989.
John Phillip Reid. *The Constitutional History of the American Revolution: The Authority of Rights*. Madison, 1986.
John Phillip Reid. *The Constitutional History of the American Revolution: The Authority to Tax*. Madison, 1987.
John Phillip Reid. "The Irrelevance of the Declaration." In *Law in the American Revolution and the Revolution in the Law*, edited by Hendrik Hartog. New York, 1981.
Garry Wills. *Inventing America: Jefferson's Declaration of Independence*. New York, 1978.

[The Declaration of Independence]

[1776]

In CONGRESS, July 4, 1776.

The unanimous Declaration of the thirteen united States of America,

When in the Course of human events, it becomes necessary for one people to dissolve the political bands which have connected them with another, and to assume among the powers of the earth, the separate and equal station to which the Laws of Nature and of Nature's God entitle them, a decent respect to the opinions of mankind requires that they should declare the causes which impel them to the separation.— We hold these truths to be self-evident, that all men are created equal, that they are endowed by their Creator with certain unalienable Rights, that among these are Life, Liberty and the pursuit of Happiness.—That to secure these rights, Governments are instituted among Men, deriving their just powers from the consent of the governed,—That whenever any Form of Government becomes destructive of these ends, it is the Right of the People to alter or to abolish it; and to institute new Government, laying its foundation on such principles and organizing its powers in such form, as to them shall seem most likely to effect their Safety and Happiness. Prudence, indeed, will dictate that Governments long established should not be changed for light and transient causes; and accordingly all experience hath shewn, that mankind are more disposed to suffer, while evils are sufferable, than to right themselves by abolishing the forms to which they are accustomed. But when a long train of abuses and usurpations, pursuing invariably the same Object evinces a design to reduce them under absolute Despotism, it is their right, it is their duty, to throw off such Government, and to provide new Guards for their future security.—Such has been the patient sufferance of these Colonies; and such is now the necessity which constrains them to alter their former Systems of Government. The history of the present King of Great Britain is a history of repeated injuries and usurpations, all having in direct object the establishment of an absolute Tyranny over these States. To prove this, let Facts be submitted to a

Engrossed manuscript, National Archives. Reprinted from Merrill Jensen et al., eds., *The Documentary History of the Ratification of the Constitution* (Madison, Wisc., 1976), I.

candid world.—He has refused his Assent to Laws, the most wholesome and necessary for the public good.—He has forbidden his Governors to pass Laws of immediate and pressing importance, unless suspended in their operation till his Assent should be obtained; and when so suspended, he has utterly neglected to attend to them.—He has refused to pass other Laws for the accommodation of large districts of people, unless those people would relinquish the right of Representation in the Legislature, a right inestimable to them and formidable to tyrants only.—He has called together legislative bodies at places unusual, uncomfortable, and distant from the depository of their public Records, for the sole purpose of fatiguing them into compliance with his measures.—He has dissolved Representative Houses repeatedly, for opposing with manly firmness his invasions on the rights of the people.—He has refused for a long time, after such dissolutions, to cause others to be elected; whereby the Legislative powers, incapable of Annihilation, have returned to the People at large for their exercise; the State remaining in the mean time exposed to all the dangers of invasion from without, and convulsions within.—He has endeavoured to prevent the population of these States; for that purpose obstructing the Laws for Naturalization of Foreigners; refusing to pass others to encourage their migration hither, and raising the conditions of new Appropriations of Lands.—He has obstructed the Administration of Justice, by refusing his Assent to Laws for establishing Judiciary powers—He has made Judges dependent on his Will alone, for the tenure of their offices, and the amount and payment of their salaries.—He has erected a multitude of New Offices, and sent hither swarms of Officers to harrass our people, and eat out their substance.—He has kept among us, in times of peace, Standing Armies without the Consent of our legislatures.—He has affected to render the Military independent of and superior to the Civil power.— He has combined with others to subject us to a jurisdiction foreign to our constitution, and unacknowledged by our laws; giving his Assent to their Acts of pretended Legislation:—For Quartering large bodies of armed troops among us:—For protecting them, by a mock Trial, from punishment for any Murders which they should commit on the Inhabitants of these States:—For calling off our Trade with all parts of the world:—For imposing Taxes on us without our Consent:—For depriving us in many cases, of the benefits of Trial by Jury:—For transporting us beyond Seas to be tried for pretended offences—For abolishing the free System of English Laws in a neighbouring Province, establishing therein an Arbitrary government, and enlarging its Boundaries so as to render it at once an example and fit instrument for introducing the same absolute rule into these Colonies:—For taking away our Charters, abolishing our most valuable Laws, and altering fundamentally the Forms of our Governments:—For suspending our own Legislatures, and declaring themselves invested with power to legislate for us in all cases whatsoever.—He has abdicated Government here, by declaring us out of his Protection and waging War against us.—He has plundered our seas, ravaged our Coasts, burnt our towns, and destroyed the Lives of our people.—He is at this time transporting large Armies of foreign Mercenaries to compleat the works of death, desolation and tyranny, already begun with circumstances of Cruelty & perfidy scarcely paralleled in the most barbarous ages, and totally unworthy the Head of a civilized nation.—He has constrained our fellow Citizens taken Captive on the high Seas to bear Arms against their Country, to become the executioners of their friends and Brethren, or to fall themselves by their Hands.—He has excited domestic insurrections amongst us, and has endeavoured to bring on the inhabitants of our frontiers, the merciless Indian Savages, whose known rule of warfare, is an undistinguished destruction of all ages, sexes and conditions. In every stage of these Oppressions We have Petitioned for Redress in the most humble terms: Our repeated Petitions have been answered only by repeated injury. A Prince, whose character is thus marked by every act which may define a Tyrant, is unfit to be the ruler of a free people. Nor have We been wanting in attentions to our Brittish brethren. We have warned them from time to time of attempts by their legislature to extend an unwarrantable jurisdiction over us. We have reminded them of the circumstances of our emigration and settlement here. We have appealed to their native justice and magnanimity, and we have conjured them by the ties of our common kindred to disavow these usurpations, which, would inevitably interrupt our connections and correspondence They too have been deaf to the voice of justice and of consanguinity. We must, therefore, acquiesce in the necessity, which denounces our Separation, and hold them, as we hold the rest of mankind, Enemies in War, in Peace Friends.—

We, therefore, the Representatives of the united States of America, in General Congress, Assembled, appealing to the Supreme Judge of the world for the rectitude of our intentions, do, in the Name, and by Authority of the good People of these Colonies, solemnly publish and declare, That these United Colonies are, and of Right ought to be Free and Independent States; that they are Absolved from all Allegiance to the British Crown, and that all political connection between them and the State of Great Britain, is and ought to be totally dissolved; and that as Free and Independent States, they have full Power to levy War, conclude Peace, contract Alliances, establish Commerce, and to do all

other Acts and Things which Independent States may of right do.—
And for the support of this Declaration, with a firm reliance on the
protection of divine Providence, we mutually pledge to each other our
Lives, our Fortunes and our sacred Honor.

NEW HAMPSHIRE
  Josiah Bartlett
  Wm. Whipple
  Matthew Thornton
MASSACHUSETT BAY
  John Hancock
  Saml. Adams
  John Adams
  Robt. Treat Paine
  Elbridge Gerry
RHODE ISLAND
  Step. Hopkins
  William Ellery
CONNECTICUT
  Roger Sherman
  Sam'el Huntington
  Wm. Williams
  Oliver Wolcott
NEW YORK
  Wm. Floyd
  Phil. Livingston
  Frans. Lewis
  Lewis Morris
NEW JERSEY
  Richd. Stockton
  Jno. Witherspoon
  Fras. Hopkinson
  John Hart
  Abra. Clark
PENNSYLVANIA
  Robt. Morris
  Benjamin Rush
  Benja. Franklin
  John Morton
  Geo. Clymer

  Jas. Smith
  Geo. Taylor
  James Wilson
  Geo. Ross
DELAWARE
  Caesar Rodney
  Geo. Read
  Tho. M'Kean
MARYLAND
  Samuel Chase
  Wm. Paca
  Thos. Stone
  Charles Carroll
    of Carrollton
VIRGINIA
  George Wythe
  Richard Henry Lee
  Th. Jefferson
  Benja. Harrison
  Ths. Nelson, Jr.
  Francis Lightfoot Lee
  Carter Braxton
NORTH CAROLINA
  Wm. Hooper
  Joseph Hewes
  John Penn
SOUTH CAROLINA
  Edward Rutledge, Jr.
  Thos. Heyward, Junr.
  Thomas Lynch, Junr.
  Arthur Middleton
GEORGIA
  Button Gwinnett
  Lyman Hall
  Geo. Walton

IX

The Virginia Declaration of Rights and Constitution

1776

COMMENTARY BY DONALD S. LUTZ

THE VIRGINIA CONSTITUTION IS PLACED HERE with the New York Constitution to facilitate comparison of these state documents, but such placement has the effect of moving the Virginia document slightly out of historical sequence since it was written and adopted before the Declaration of Independence. The matter of sequence is not a minor consideration since the Declaration was deeply influenced by the Virginia Constitution, and not the other way around. In June 1776, while a delegate to the Second Continental Congress, Thomas Jefferson framed at least three drafts of a constitution for Virginia. Jefferson's fellow delegate and former law teacher George Wythe carried a copy of Jefferson's third, most finished draft to the Virginia revolutionary convention. By the time Wythe arrived, the convention had already drafted a constitution, but the delegates liked Jefferson's preamble so much they added it to their own version. Jefferson later "recycled" his draft preamble as the body of charges against George III in the Declaration of Independence.

Virginia did not write the first state constitution. Massachusetts effectively made its 1691 charter a state constitution on June 19, 1775; New Hampshire adopted a newly written preliminary state constitution on January 5, 1776; South Carolina adopted its new constitution on March 26, 1776; on May 4, Rhode Island declared its colonial charter of 1663 to be the state constitution; and Connecticut continued to live under its 1662 charter as a functioning constitution without any formal readoption, although its title was changed to "constitution" in October of 1776. When Virginia adopted its Declaration of Rights on June 12, 1776, and its new constitution on June 29, it was not only the sixth state in line, it barely missed being seventh, when New Jersey adopted its constitution on July 2, 1776.

Still, the Virginia Constitution deeply influenced later constitutions, especially those written by states south of Pennsylvania, and its Declaration of Rights was a virtual dress rehearsal for the contents of the Declaration of Independence and the Pennsylvania Constitution. The Declaration of Rights placed at the beginning of the Virginia Constitution was written largely by George Mason. Mason also penned the constitution proper, but this part of the document also reflected the strong influence of James Madison, Edmund Pendleton, Richard Bland, Patrick Henry, and Edmund Randolph.

Although there were important differences in the way politics was practiced in Virginia as opposed to other colonies like Connecticut, Massachusetts, Pennsylvania, and New York, there were surprising similarities between the constitutions of most states. Each state codified the political system it had developed as a colony, and this tendency to codify what had come before not only was a shared trait but also indicated that the colonies had evolved some very similar institutions long before independence.

In most colonies, provincial politics had revolved around a struggle between an assembly elected by the colonists and a governor appointed by the king. The legislatures had gradually gained the upper hand and, for this and other reasons, the state constitutions often made the legislature the central and most powerful political institution. They created weak executives whose power was limited and circumscribed by controls from the legislature.

In the Virginia Constitution, compare legislative powers and limits with a list of the powers granted to the executive and the limits placed on him. For example, in Virginia the governor could call up the militia only with the consent of the privy council, and the privy council was selected by the legislature and composed primarily of legislators. Another example of a limit on executive power was the inability of the governor to "prorogue" the legislature (end or discontinue its session) or even to adjourn it for a few days. Such powers had traditionally been part of the executive power in British law for centuries; but, the early state constitutions created clear legislative supremacy instead of the more balanced powers we tend to take for granted in the United States Constitution and later state constitutions.

A list of powers normally associated with the executive branch would include the appointment of judges and other posts in the executive branch (under English practice the judiciary was under the executive branch), the pardoning of crimes, the calling up and leading of the militia and armed forces, the veto power, the approval of treaties, and the ability to temporarily suspend laws in times of emergency. These are some of the powers that had traditionally belonged to the executive but were withheld or limited by the Virginia Constitution.

Other common aspects of early state constitutions included a bicameral legislature with the upper house serving as the equivalent of the advisory council to the governor, annual elections by a broad electorate, clear limits on government in a bill of rights, and institutional reliance upon, as well as rhetorical celebration of, popular sovereignty. Early state constitutions not only provided that the people have ultimate control of government, but they also provided ways in which the actual institutions created the ability of the people to control their government.

Structurally, the Declaration of Rights is followed by a list of grievances against the king that form an extension of the bill of rights by listing those rights that have been attacked. Both are similar to the Declaration of Independence and the United States Bill of Rights. The preamble to the constitution follows the list of grievances, and begins "We therefore, the delegates. . . ." Compare this preamble with the opening words of the Mayflower Compact and the Fundamental Orders of Connecticut. The Virginia Constitution creates a people, lays out the basic values of the people, creates a government or civil body politic, and then describes the institutions of that government. What we find in the Virginia Constitution of 1776 recalls earlier American documents of political foundation as well as prefigures later ones.

Note that the Declaration of Rights is the first part of the document, followed by what is called the "constitution or form of government." The description of political institutions in state constitutions was invariably termed the constitution, whereas the preamble and bill of rights usually came first and were not covered by the term constitution (although in the Virginia document the preamble is so included.) What, then, is the entire document if only part of it was considered a constitution? The answer, not found in this particular document but in others such as the Massachusetts Constitution of 1780, is that the document is a compact. A compact was a secularized covenant—a covenant without an oath calling God as a witness. This means that what we call a constitution was really understood by its authors during the 1700s as a compact, of which the second part, or institutional description, was the constitution proper. The early state constitutions are an important part of the evidence pointing to the Declaration of Independence together with the Articles of Confederation as our first national compact, and the Declaration of Independence and United States Constitution of 1787 as the national compact under which we now operate.

State constitutions are important in their own right. Because every United States citizen has a double citizenship, state constitutions define one-half of every American's citizenship. The early state constitutions, like the ones examined in this volume, are important because they predated the United States Constitution, strongly influenced its form and content, and laid the foundation for the rest of our citizenship as represented in later state constitutions. State constitutions also both textually and contextually link the United States Constitution with colonial documents.

For Further Reading

John E. Selby. *The Revolution in Virginia, 1775–1783*. Williamsburg, Va., 1988.

John E. Selby. "Richard Henry Lee, John Adams, and the Virginia Constitution of 1776," *Virginia Magazine of History and Biography* LXXXIV (1976): 387–400.

George B. Oliver. "A Constitutional History of Virginia, 1776–1860." Ph.D. dissertation, Duke University, 1959.

Robert P. Sutton. *Revolution to Secession: Constitution Making in the Old Dominion*. Charlottsville, Va., 1989.

William J. Van Schreeven, Robert L. Scribner, and Brent Tarter, eds. *Revolutionary Virginia, The Road to Independence: A Documentary Record*. Charlottesville, Va., 1973–1983.

[The Virginia Declaration of Rights and Constitution]

[1776]

[THE VIRGINIA DECLARATION OF RIGHTS]

A DECLARATION *of* RIGHTS *made by the representatives of the good people of* Virginia, *assembled in full and free Convention; which rights do pertain to them, and their posterity, as the basis and foundation of government.*

1. That all men are by nature equally free and independent, and have certain inherent rights, of which, when they enter into a state of society, they cannot, by any compact, deprive or divest their posterity; namely, the enjoyment of life and liberty, with the means of acquiring and possessing property, and pursuing and obtaining happiness and safety.[1]

2. That all power is vested in, and consequently derived from, the people; that magistrates are their trustees and servants, and at all times amenable[2] to them.

3. That government is, or ought to be, instituted for the common benefit, protection, and security, of the people, nation, or community, of all the various modes and forms of government that is best, which is capable of producing the greatest degree of happiness and safety, and is most effectually secured against the danger of mal-administration;

Reprinted from John P. Kaminski and Gaspare J. Saladino, eds. *The Documentary History of the Ratification of the Constitution*, Vol. VIII, *Ratification of the Constitution by the States, Virginia (1)* (Madison, Wisc. 1988), 530–37.

[1] Parts of both the Declaration of Independence and the United States Bill of Rights were copied more or less directly from the Virginia Declaration of Rights. However, a comparison between the wording here and the similar wording in the Declaration of Independence indicates some potentially important alterations. In the Declaration of Independence, for example, Jefferson used "life, liberty, and happiness" instead of "life, liberty, and property" as it was commonly put by thinkers such as John Locke. Did Jefferson equate the ownership of property with happiness, or did he not see the ownership of property as an inherent right the way Geroge Mason does here in the Virginia Declaration of Rights?

[2] "Amenable" here means "answerable."

and that whenever any government shall be found inadequate or contrary to these purposes, a majority of the community hath an indubitable, unalienable, and indefeasible right, to reform, alter, or abolish it, in such manner as shall be judged most conducive to the public weal.[3]

4. That no man, or set of men, are entitled to exclusive or separate emoluments[4] or privileges from the community, but in consideration of publick services; which, not being descendible,[5] neither ought the offices of magistrate, legislator, or judge, to be hereditary.

5. That the legislative and executive powers of the state should be separate and distinct from the judiciary; and that the members of the two first may be restrained from oppression, by feeling and participating the burthens of the people, they should at fixed periods, be reduced to a private station, return into that body from which they were originally taken,[6] and the vacancies be supplied[7] by frequent, certain, and regular elections, in which all, or any part of the former members, to be again eligible, or ineligible, as the laws shall direct.

6. That elections of members to serve as representatives of the people, in assembly, ought to be free; and that all men, having sufficient evidence of permanent common interest with, and attachment to, the community, have the right of suffrage,[8] and cannot be taxed or deprived

---

[3] Whereas the first section listed inherent individual rights, this section lists two fundamental community rights: government is to protect and benefit the entire community and not only some portion of it. The majority speaks for the community and may replace the government when it so wishes. Section 3, by enunciating popular sovereignty, majority rule, and communitarianism as it does, raises the question of what is to be done if and when the individual rights in Section 1 come in conflict with the community rights.

[4] "Exclusive or separate emoluments" refers to payments, income, or rewards of the kind that were sometimes claimed by the aristocracy as their due as a result of title or social rank. For example, a lord might claim the privilege of being the county judge and be entitled to payment from the community for his services.

[5] "Descendible" means capable of being inherited. This is the other half of the prohibition. No one may claim either a position or money due a position as a result of heredity.

[6] The members of the legislative and executive branches should be returned to the great body of citizens, or people, after a fixed, limited period of time. Throughout the document there are provisions requiring that all government officials, except for judges, serve a limited term of office, after which they may not run again for a certain number of years. The framers felt that they should experience the effects of the laws they have passed. This provision also seeks to prevent government officials from becoming too entrenched in their role. These two principles fall under the general label of "rotation in office," which was an important political principle during the Revolutionary and early national periods.

[7] Read this as saying "and the vacancies be filled . . . ."

[8] It was common at the time to require the ownership of property in order to vote.

of their property for publick uses without their own consent, or that of their representatives so elected, nor bound by any law to which they have not, in like manner, assented, for the publick good.

7. That all power of suspending laws, or the execution of laws, by any authority without consent of the representatives of the people, is injurious to their rights, and ought not to be exercised.[9]

8. That in all capital or criminal prosecutions a man hath a right to demand the cause and nature of his accusation, to be confronted with the accusers and witnesses, to call for evidence in his favour, and to a speedy trial by an impartial jury of his vicinage,[10] without whose unanimous consent he cannot be found guilty, nor can he be compelled to give evidence against himself; that no man be deprived of his liberty except by the law of the land, or the judgment of his peers.

9. That excessive bail ought not to be required, nor excessive fines imposed, nor cruel and unusual punishments inflicted.

10. That general warrants, whereby any officer or messenger may be commanded to search suspected places without evidence of a fact committed, or to seize any person or persons not named, or whose offence is not particularly described and supported by evidence, are grievous and oppressive, and ought not to be granted.

11. That in controversies respecting property, and in suits between man and man, the ancient trial by jury is preferable to any other, and ought to be held sacred.

12. That the freedom of the press is one of the great bulwarks of liberty, and can never be restrained but by despotick governments.

This provision was not designed to exclude people, but rather, as it says here, to establish that the person was sufficiently attached to the community to cast an informed vote. It was also assumed that such a person was financially independent so that he was not susceptible to bribes. Since English common law had protected the right of no taxation without representation from Magna Carta, the right to vote and ownership of taxable property went together. Whereas in Britain only about 6 percent of white, adult males could vote under this common law provision, in America well over a majority of white, adult males were enfranchised—perhaps as many as 75 percent. Even free blacks who owned property could vote in some states. Finally, the property test was minimal, and if a person was known locally as a sober, productive member of the community, he was usually allowed to vote even if he did not own property. In some states, such as New York, exceptions to property ownership were granted for tenants paying a certain amount of rent or for laborers paying a minimal poll tax.

[9] This provision is directed at the executive branch.

[10] "Of his vicinage" means twelve men from his vicinity both in the sense of living nearby and in the sense of having a similar station in life—i.e., average-income farmers would not be tried by a jury full of rich people. Today, we speak of trial by a jury of one's peers.

13. That a well regulated militia, composed of the body of the people, trained to arms, is the proper, natural, and safe defence of a free state; that standing armies, in time of peace, should be avoided, as dangerous to liberty: and that, in all cases, the military should be under strict subordination to, and governed by, the civil power.[11]

14. That the people have a right to uniform government; and therefore, that no government separate from, or independent of, the government of *Virginia*, ought to be erected or established within the limits thereof.

15. That no free government, or the blessing of liberty, can be preserved to any people but by a firm adherence to justice, moderation, temperance, frugality, and virtue, and by frequent recurrence to fundamental principles.

16. That religion, or the duty which we owe to our CREATOR, and the manner of discharging it, can be directed only by reason and conviction, not by force or violence, and therefore all men are equally entitled to the free exercise of religion, according to the dictates of conscience; and that it is the mutual duty of all to practice Christian forbearance, love, and charity, towards each other.

[THE VIRGINIA CONSTITUTION]

The CONSTITUTION, *or* FORM *of* GOVERNMENT, *agreed to and resolved upon by the Delegates and Representatives of the several counties and corporations of* VIRGINIA.

Whereas *George* the third, king of *Great Britain* and *Ireland*, and elector of *Hanover*, heretofore intrusted with the exercise of the kingly office in this government, hath endeavoured to pervert the same into a detestable and insupportable tyranny, by putting his negative on laws[12] the most wholesome and necessary for the publick good:

By denying his governours permission to pass laws of immediate and pressing importance, unless suspended in their operation for his assent,[13] and, when so suspended, neglecting to attend to them for many years:

---

[11] Compare this section with the Second Amendment in the United States Constitution. Both deal with the right of the state to maintain a citizen militia to protect itself from a national standing army. Ownership of guns is therefore attached to membership in the militia, and the United States Supreme Court has consistently upheld this interpretation.

[12] "Putting his negative on laws" means vetoing laws passed by the colonial legislatures.

[13] "Assent" means approval.

By refusing to pass certain other laws, unless the persons to be benefited by them would relinquish the inestimable right of representation in the legislature:

By dissolving legislative Assemblies repeatedly and continually, for opposing with manly firmness his invasions of the rights of the people:[14]

When dissolved, by refusing to call others for a long space of time, thereby leaving the political system without any legislative head:

By endeavouring to prevent the population of our country, and, for that purpose, obstructing the laws for the naturalization of foreigners:

By keeping among us, in times of peace, standing armies and ships of war:

By affecting to render the military independent of, and superiour to, the civil power:

By combining with others to subject us to a foreign jurisdiction, giving his assent to their pretended acts of legislation:[15]

For quartering large bodies of armed troops among us:

For cutting off our trade with all parts of the world:

For imposing taxes on us without our consent:

For depriving us of the benefits of trial by jury:

For transporting us beyond seas, to be tried for pretended offences:

For suspending our own legislatures, and declaring themselves invested with power to legislate for us in all cases whatsoever:

By plundering our seas, ravaging our coasts, burning our towns, and destroying the lives of our people:

By inciting insurrections of our fellow subjects, with the allurements of forfeiture and confiscation:

By prompting our negroes to rise in arms among us, those very negroes whom, by an inhuman use of his negative, he hath refused us permission to exclude by law:

By endeavouring to bring on the inhabitants of our frontiers the merciless *Indian* savages, whose known rule of warfare is an undistinguished destruction of all ages, sexes, and conditions of existence:

By transporting, at this time, a large army of foreign mercenaries,[16] to complete the works of death, desolation, and tyranny, already begun

---

[14] The grammar of this sentence might seem garbled. It means, in effect, "By dissolving the assemblies because they opposed his violation of the people's rights."

[15] "Others" refer here to Parliament and its "pretended acts of legislation" which the colonists did not recognize.

[16] The king had obtained conscript soldiers (often incorrectly termed "mercenaries") from the Earl of Hesse in Germany to fight in America under British leadership. These troops were known as "Hessians," although many of them came from elsewhere in Germany.

with circumstances of cruelty and perfidy unworthy the head of a civilized nation:

By answering our repeated petitions for redress with a repetition of injuries:

And finally, by abandoning the helm of government, and declaring us out of his allegiance and protection.

By which several acts of misrule, the government of this country, as formerly exercised under the crown of *Great Britain*, is TOTALLY DISSOLVED.

We therefore, the delegates and representatives of the good people of *Virginia*, having maturely considered the premises, and viewing with great concern the deplorable condition to which this once happy country must be reduced, unless some regular adequate mode of civil polity is speedily adopted, and in compliance with a recommendation of the General Congress,[17] do ordain and declare the future form of government of *Virginia* to be as followeth:

The legislative, executive, and judiciary departments, shall be separate and distinct, so that neither exercise the powers properly belonging to the other; nor shall any person exercise the powers of more than one of them at the same time, except that the justices of the county courts shall be eligible to either House of Assembly.

The legislative shall be formed of two distinct branches, who, together, shall be a complete legislature. They shall meet once, or oftener, every year, and shall be called the GENERAL ASSEMBLY OF VIRGINIA.

One of these shall be called the HOUSE OF DELEGATES, and consist of two representatives to be chosen for each county, and for the district of *West Augusta*, annually, of such men as actually reside in and are freeholders[18] of the same, or duly qualified according to law, and

---

[17] The "General Congress" referred to here is the Second Continental Congress, which had recommended on May 10, 1776, that all colonies not yet having a permanent constitution based upon the authority of the people provide themselves with one. Some consider this recommendation by the Continental Congress to have in effect been a declaration of independence. See Bernstein's comments (Chapter 7).

[18] English common law defined a freehold as a piece of land sufficient in size to earn forty shillings a year in rent, if it were rented out. The definition of a freehold came from a common law doctrine dating back to the early 1400s, and since that time the amount of land needed to meet the requirement had generally varied between forty and sixty acres (fifty acres was the most commonly used figure). Unlike England, where long settlement and a wealthy aristocracy and gentry left little land to be distributed among most of the people, the freehold provision in America was an easy one to meet with millions of acres of land available and few prior claims. One could move further west, gain title to land by working it and then using the income to purchase it at a few pennies per acre. As noted earlier, some men did not have to own land in order to vote, but be "duly qualified" as it is noted in the Virginia Constitution.

also [of] one delegate or representative to be chosen annually for the city of *Williamsburg*, and one for the borough of *Norfolk*, and a representative for each of such other cities and boroughs as may hereafter be allowed particular representation by the legislature; but when any city or borough shall so decrease as that the number of persons having right of suffrage therein shall have been for the space of seven years successively less than half the number of voters in some one county in *Virginia*,[19] such city or borough thenceforward shall cease to send a delegate or representative to the Assembly.

The other shall be called the SENATE, and consist of twenty four members, of whom thirteen shall constitute a House[20] to proceed on business, for whose election the different counties shall be divided into twenty four districts, and each county of the respective district, at the time of the election of its delegates, shall vote for one Senator, who is actually a resident and freeholder within the district, or duly qualified according to law, and is upwards of twenty five years of age; and the sheriffs of each county, within five days at farthest[21] after the last county election in the district, shall meet at some convenient place, and from the poll[22] so taken in their respective counties return as a Senator the man who shall have the greatest number of votes in the whole district. To keep up this Assembly by rotation, the districts shall be equally divided into four classes, and numbered by lot. At the end of one year after the general election, the six members elected by the first division shall be displaced, and the vacancies thereby occasioned supplied from such class or division, by new election, in the manner aforesaid. This rotation shall be applied to each division, according to its number, and continued in due order annually.[23]

---

[19] This provision is a bit unclear. The intent was to prevent the situation that often occurred in Britain where some boroughs (a borough is a township or small town) declined in population to the point where five or six voters were electing a member of Parliament. This provision most likely means that each county gets two representatives, towns and boroughs larger in population than one-half the population of the smallest county can elect one representative, and towns or boroughs smaller than one-half the population of the smallest county shall have no representative.

[20] Read this to mean "shall constitute a quorum." A quorum is the minimum number of legislators that must be present for the proceedings to be legal and enforceable. In effect, then, a quorum is the minimum necessary for the body to be considered sitting legally as a house of the legislature.

[21] Read "farthest" to mean "at most."

[22] "Poll" here means "vote."

[23] Six of the twenty-four senate seats were subject to election every year so that every four years the entire senate would come up for election. This means the senators would each serve four years, except after the first election. After the first election, in

The right of suffrage in the election of members for both Houses shall remain as exercised at present, and each House shall choose its own speaker, appoint its own officers, settle its own rules of proceeding, and direct writs of election for supplying intermediate vacancies.

All laws shall originate in the House of Delegates, to be approved or rejected by the Senate, or to be amended with the consent of the House of Delegates; except money bills, which in no instance shall be altered by the Senate, but wholly approved or rejected.

A Governour, or chief magistrate, shall be chosen annually, by joint ballot of both Houses, to be taken in each House respectively, deposited in the conference room, the boxes examined jointly by a committee of each House, and the members severally reported to them, that the appointments may be entered (which shall be the mode of taking the joint ballot of both Houses in all cases) who shall not continue in that office longer than three years successively, nor be eligible until the expiration of four years after he shall have been out of that office. An adequate, but moderate salary, shall be settled on him during his continuance in office; and he shall, with the advice of a Council of State, exercise the executive powers of government according to the laws of this commonwealth; and shall not, under any pretence, exercise any power or prerogative by virtue of any law, statute, or custom, of *England:* But he shall, with the advice of the Council of State, have the power of granting reprieves or pardons, except where the prosecution shall have been carried on by the House of Delegates, or the law shall otherwise particularly direct; in which cases, no reprieve or pardon shall be granted, but by resolve of the House of Delegates.

Either House of the General Assembly may adjourn themselves respectively. The Governour shall not prorogue[24] or adjourn the Assembly during their sitting, nor dissolve them at any time; but he shall, if necessary, either by advice of the Council of State, or on application of a majority of the House of Delegates, call them before the time to which they shall stand prorogued or adjourned.

A Privy Council, or Council of State, consisting of eight members, shall be chosen by joint ballot of both Houses of Assembly, either from their own members or the people at large, to assist in the administration

---

which all twenty-four senators would be elected at once for the only time, six would be be randomly assigned a one-year term, six would be assigned a two-year term, six would be randomly assigned a three-year term, and the last six would have a four-year term. This established the rotation so that from then on every year would see the election of six senators for four-year terms. The institution of staggered elections for the United States Senate was taken from the several state constitutions where it was first developed.

[24] "Prorogue" means to end or discontinue a session.

of government. They shall annually choose out of their own members a president, who, in case of the death, inability, or necessary absence of the Governour from the government, shall act as Lieutenant-Governour. Four members shall be sufficient to act, and their advice and proceedings shall be entered of record, and signed by the members present (to any part whereof any member may enter his dissent) to be laid before the General Assembly, when called for by them. This Council may appoint their own clerk, who shall have a salary settled by law, and take an oath of secrecy in such matters as he shall be directed by the board to conceal. A sum of money appropriated to that purpose shall be divided annually among the members, in proportion to their attendance; and they shall be incapable, during their continuance in office, of sitting in either House of Assembly. Two members shall be removed by joint ballot of both Houses of Assembly at the end of every three years, and be ineligible for the three next years.[25] These vacancies, as well as those occasioned by death or incapacity, shall be supplied by new elections, in the same manner.

The delegates for *Virginia* to the Continental Congress shall be chosen annually, or superseded in the mean time by joint ballot of both Houses of Assembly.

The present militia officers shall be continued, and vacancies supplied by appointment of the Governour, with the advice of the Privy Council, on recommendations from the respective county courts; but the Governour and Council shall have a power of suspending any officer, and ordering a court-martial on complaint of misbehaviour or inability, or to supply vacancies of officers happening when in actual service. The Governour may embody[26] the militia, with the advice of the Privy Council; and, when embodied, shall alone have the direction of the militia under the laws of the country.

The two Houses of Assembly shall, by joint ballot, appoint Judges of the Supreme Court of Appeals, and General Court, Judges in Chan-

---

[25] Like the senate, the privy council had staggered terms of office for its members, only here the eight council members were replaced at the rate of two every three years giving them a twelve-year term of office. Even though a member of the privy council may not be reelected for three years after serving a term, and must resign his legislative seat when elected to the privy council, these men would be very powerful because of their ability to block almost all actions of the executive, and because their long terms of office enabled them to outlast the governor by many years. This unusual institution not only reflected the common distrust of all executives, but also reflected the blurring of executive and legislative roles common at the time. It also reflected, in the case of Virginia, the preference for vesting power in a group of the "better sort" to balance democratic tendencies.

[26] "Embody" in this instance means call out or assemble.

cery, Judges of Admiralty, Secretary, and the Attorney-General, to be commissioned by the Governour, and continue in office during good behaviour. In case of death, incapacity, or resignation, the Governour, with the advice of the Privy Council, shall appoint persons to succeed in office, to be approved or displaced by both Houses. These officers shall have fixed and adequate salaries, and, together with all others holding lucrative offices, and all ministers of the Gospel of every denomination, be incapable of being elected members of either House of Assembly, or the Privy Council.

The Governour, with the advice of the Privy Council, shall appoint Justices of the Peace for the counties; and in case of vacancies, or a necessity of increasing the number hereafter, such appointments to be made upon the recommendation of the respective county courts. The present acting Secretary in *Virginia*, and Clerks of all the County Courts, shall continue in office. In case of vacancies, either by death, incapacity, or resignation, a Secretary shall be appointed as before directed, and the Clerks by the respective courts. The present and future Clerks shall hold their offices during good behaviour, to be judged of and determined in the General Court. The Sheriffs and Coroners shall be nominated by the respective courts, approved by the Governour with the advice of the Privy Council, and commissioned by the Governour. The Justices shall appoint Constables, and all fees of the aforesaid officers be regulated by law.

The Governour, when he is out of office, and others offending against the state, either by mal-administration, corruption, or other means by which the safety of the state may be endangered, shall be impeachable by the House of Delegates. Such impeachment to be prosecuted by the Attorney-General, or such other person or persons as the House may appoint in the General Court, according to the laws of the land. If found guilty, he or they shall be either for ever disabled to hold any office under government, or removed from such office *pro tempore*, or subjected to such pains or penalties as the law shall direct.[27]

If all, or any of the Judges of the General Court, shall, on good grounds (to be judged of by the House of Delegates) be accused of any of the crimes or offences before-mentioned, such House of Delegates may, in like manner, impeach the Judge or Judges so accused, to

---

[27] Compare this with the impeachment provision of the United States Constitution. As in other state constitutions, one could be impeached not only for crimes and corruption, but also for poor judgment, bad luck, or anything else that the legislature thought "endangered" the safety of the state. In short, one could be impeached for political reasons. To be impeached and then convicted is not to be declared a criminal, but to be removed from office. One is still subject to criminal trial in the courts.

be prosecuted in the Court of Appeals; and he or they, if found guilty, shall be punished in the same manner as is prescribed in the preceding clause.

Commissions and grants shall run, *In the name of the* COMMONWEALTH *of* VIRGINIA, and bear test by the Governour with the seal of the commonwealth annexed. Writs shall run in the same manner, and bear test by the clerks of the several courts. Indictments shall conclude, *Against the peace and dignity of the commonwealth.*

A Treasurer shall be appointed annually, by joint ballot of both Houses.

All escheats,[28] penalties, and forfeitures, heretofore going to the king, shall go to the commonwealth, save only such as the legislature may abolish, or otherwise provide for.

The territories contained within the charters erecting the colonies *of Maryland, Pennsylvania, North* and *South Carolina,* are hereby ceded, released, and for ever confirmed to the people of those colonies respectively,[29] with all the rights of property, jurisdiction, and government, and all other rights whatsoever which might at any time heretofore have been claimed by *Virginia,* except the free navigation and use of the rivers *Potowmack* and *Pohomoke,*[30] with the property of the *Virginia* shores or strands bordering on either of the said rivers, and all improvements which have been or shall be made thereon. The western and northern extent of *Virginia* shall in all other respects stand as fixed by the charter of king *James* the first, in the year one thousand six hundred and nine, and by the publick treaty of peace between the courts of *Great Britain* and *France* in the year one thousand seven hundred and sixty three; unless, by act of legislature, one or more territories shall hereafter be laid off, and governments established westward of the *Allegheny* moun-

---

[28] When someone died in England with no legal heirs, that person's property belonged to the Crown. This was known as the law of escheat. However, this provision in the Virginia Constitution held that all money going to government as a result of criminal fines, forfeiture of property, escheats, etc. would go to the common treasury of the people rather than to one person or the disposal of any one officer.

[29] One very serious problem among the colonies, and later the states, was that of conflicting territorial claims wherein several states claimed the same land. A little-noted but extremely important achievement of the Articles of Confederation was to resolve these conflicts peacefully to the satisfaction of the contending state. The State of Virginia here cedes all such conflicting claims, as long as it has continued free navigation along two border rivers.

[30] The two rivers in question are the Potomac and the Pokomoke which form the northern Virginia boundary with Maryland. The Pokomoke is on the eastern shore of Virginia and actually goes into Maryland, but Virginia was most concerned with free use of the fishing beds in Pokomoke Sound at the mouth of the river and with free navigation in the Chesapeake Bay.

tains. And no purchase of lands shall be made of the *Indian* natives but on behalf of the publick, by authority of the General Assembly.

In order to introduce this government, the representatives of the people met in Convention shall choose a Governour and Privy Council, also such other officers directed to be chosen by both Houses as may be judged necessary to be immediately appointed. The Senate to be first chosen by the people, to continue until the last day of *March* next, and the other officers until the end of the succeeding session of Assembly. In case of vacancies, the speaker of either House shall issue writs for new elections.

X

The New York State Constitution

1777

COMMENTARY BY STEPHEN L. SCHECHTER

MASSACHUSETTS AND VIRGINIA WERE FOUNDED as commonwealths by Whigs, who, despite their theological differences, were committed to the idea of a constitution as a compact binding its members into a community of virtue. By contrast, New York was founded by Dutch merchants and acquired by the English Crown as a commercial republic committed to the idea of a constitution as a framework of rules protecting individual liberty and property in a secular society of diverse interests.

The New York tradition of constitutionalism is both the least romantic and the most undervalued of American state constitutional traditions.[1] It provided a laboratory for Federalist constitution-makers, a prototype for the United States Constitution of 1787, and proof that a republic could be based on a respect for diversity and the pursuit of commerce.

---

[1] For background on early state constitutions, see Willi Paul Adams, *The First American Constitutions: Republican Ideology and the Making of State Constitutions in the Revolutionary Era* (Chapel Hill, 1980); Donald S. Lutz, *Popular Consent and Popular Control: Whig Political Theory in the Early State Constitutions* (Baton Rouge, La., 1980); and Donald S. Lutz, *The Origins of American Constitutionalism* (Baton Rouge, La., 1988).

State Constitutions in the Revolution

"The blessings of society," wrote John Adams in 1776, "depend entirely on the constitutions of government."[2] Agreeing with this sentiment, the Second Continental Congress adopted a resolution on May 10, 1776: "That it be recommended to the respective Assemblies and Conventions of the United Colonies, where no government sufficient to the exigencies of their affairs has been hitherto established, to adopt such Government as shall in the opinion of the Representatives of the People, best conduce to the happiness and safety of their Constituents in particular, and America in general."[3]

Three weeks later, on May 31, George Washington warned of the vastness of the task: "To form a new Government requires infinite care and unbounded attention," Washington stated, "for if the foundation is badly laid, the superstructure must be bad. . . . A matter of such moment cannot be the Work of a day."

Washington's advice notwithstanding, each of the thirteen original states had adopted a constitution within one year of the congressional resolution urging them to do so. New Hampshire adopted a provisional constitution even before the call from Congress (on January 5, 1776). South Carolina acted on March 26, before receiving news of the congressional resolution. As a corporate colony, Rhode Island converted its colonial charter into a state constitution on May 4 by removing all references to royal authority. On June 29, Virginia adopted a constitution on which it had begun to work before the congressional resolution of May. Next came New Jersey on July 2, the same day that the Continental Congress declared independence. Most of the remaining states adopted constitutions before the end of 1776. Only two states delayed until 1777, largely owing to the exigencies of war: Georgia on February 5 and New York on April 20.

The foregoing account reminds us that the American Revolution required constitution-making as well as war-making. During the fifteen-year period, from 1776 to 1791, Americans adopted fourteen first state constitutions, seven revised state constitutions, one federal constitution (that is, the Articles of Confederation), one national constitution (that is, the United States Constitution of 1787), and its first ten amendments (collectively known as the Bill of Rights).

---

2 John Adams, *Thoughts on Government.* For the full text and discussion of this pamphlet, see Chapter 7.

3 This resolution, included in the prefatory material of New York's constitution, also appears in Chapter 7 .

The principles which these constitutions have in common are based on the republican theory of popular consent. What distinguishes these constitutions is the type of republican constitutional tradition on which they rest. Two traditions were employed: the older Whig tradition on which most state constitutions were based, and the federalist tradition widened most clearly in the United States Constitution of 1787. As Daniel J. Elazar explains:

> One was based on older *Whig* republican forms brought to American shores by the first British and northwest European colonists and further developed in the intervening four or five generations. The Whig tradition emphasized a communitarian polity and the importance of republican virtue. Individualism was tempered and legislatures as representatives of the community could intervene and regulate behavior in ways which would now be regarded as infringements of individual rights. At the same time, the Whig tradition placed great emphasis on direct, active, continuous, and well-nigh complete popular control over the legislature and government in general, through such devices as small electoral districts, short tenures of office, many elective offices, sharp separations of power, and procedures approaching constituent instruction of elected representatives.
>
> In facing the task of framing a national constitution, however, a new republican or *federalist* conception of constitutionalism emerged primarily through the work of James Madison. While the federalist idea agreed with the Whig tradition that all powers of government be derived from the people, Madison added the pregnant phrase, 'either directly or indirectly.' This reflected the federalist effort to cope with the problems of establishing an extended and diverse democratic republic compounded of constituent polities—particularly the problem of majority tyranny. The federalist conception of republican remedies for republican diseases placed greater emphasis on balancing individual and group interests and refining the interests and opinions of the people through such devices as large electoral districts, indirect senatorial elections, longer tenures of office, limited numbers of elective offices and a system of separated but shared powers. The federalist view also saw commerce as a partial way of solving the problem of republican virtue in a large republic.[4]

The New York State Constitutional Experience

New York's Constitution of 1777 is distinctive, in part, because it was the last of the first wave of Revolutionary state constitutions adopted

---

[4] Daniel J. Elazar, *State Constitutional Design in Federal Systems*, a special issue of *Publius* edited by Daniel J. Elazar and Stephen L. Schechter 12, no. 1 (1982): 13.

by the original states and the first to provide for a relatively strong chief executive directly elected by the people. However, the principal feature distinguishing the New York Constitution of 1777 is that it was the first state constitution to experiment with the newly emerging federalist tradition of constitutionalism. Several factors help explain how this came about. These factors are those of war, conservatism, pluralism, and New York's own tradition as a commercial republic.

The exigencies of war were particularly severe in New York.[5] Because of the threat of British attack, the Fourth Provincial Congress met at White Plains, on July 9, 1776, rather than in New York City, for the purpose of establishing "such a government that they shall deem calculated to secure the rights, liberties and happiness of the good people of this colony; and to continue in force until a future peace with Great Britain shall render the same unnecessary."[6] On August 1, the Fourth Provincial Congress, renamed "the Convention of the Representatives of the State of New-York," assigned the task of drafting a constitution to a committee of thirteen—John Jay, Gouverneur Morris, Robert R. Livingston, John Sloss Hobart, William Smith (of Suffolk County), William Duer, John Broome, John Morin Scott, Abraham Yates, Jr., Henry Wisner, Samuel Townsend, Charles DeWitt of Ulster County, and Robert Yates. James Duane was later added.

British advances forced the convention northward, first to Fishkill in Dutchess County, and finally to Kingston in Ulster County. Although the constitution-drafting committee was initially ordered to report a draft by August 26, 1776, it did not do so until March 12 of the following year. Beyond the problems caused by the need for constant flight, the committee found it difficult to assemble a quorum because many of the committee members had active military commands, local government responsibilities, or other convention committee assignments.

Wartime conditions were not the only cause for delay. The politics of delay was a tactic of conservatives on this issue in much the same way as Antifederalists and Federalists alike were to use it ten years later in the ratification of the United States Constitution. In a letter to William Duer of June 12, 1777, Robert R. Livingston confided that he and his allies made use of "well timed delays, indefatigable industry,

---

[5] The following historical review draws from the excellent history by William A. Polf, *1777: The Politial Revolution and New York's First Constitution* (Albany, 1977; reprinted in Stephen L. Schechter and Richard B. Bernstein, eds., *New York and the Union: Contributions to the American Constitutional Experience* (Albany, 1990).

[6] As quoted in Polf, *1777*, 2.

and a minute attention to every favorable circumstance"[7] in order to prevent the adoption of a radical constitution patterned after that of Pennsylvania's constitution in which the fear of executive power had eliminated the office of governor altogether. John Jay, the principal draftsman of the New York Constitution, virtually admitted as much when he remarked to his son William that "another turn of the winch would have cracked the cord."[8]

Conservatives and reluctant republicans (many of whom had been Loyalists and later would become Federalists) considered themselves "friends of order" and supporters of energetic government and a strong executive. By contrast, Whigs (many of whom would later become Antifederalists) considered themselves "friends of liberty" and saw little need for an independent executive in a system in which the legislature represented the people in a mirror-like fashion.

New York state politics was unpredictable because conservative leaders (including city merchants and rural manor lords) believed that they could attract the interest of commercially minded tradesmen in the city and rent-paying tenant farmers in the country. Toward this end, New York conservatives during the Revolutionary period found it to be in their interests to work for both a strong executive and an expanded electorate. This strategy was complicated by the British occupation of New York City, which attracted Loyalists to it and drove radicals out of it.

Another element of New York state politics is and always has been the great diversity of its population. The Revolution further divided New Yorkers in their sentiments, interests, and regions. So sharp were these divisions that the state might have degenerated into civil war had it not been for the British occupation of New York City and the consequent flight of Loyalists to it. Within this context, New York State took so long to adopt a constitution because it had little choice. Practically speaking, it took time for conservatives like John Jay and Gouverneur Morris and Whigs like John Morin Scott to learn how to work with one another as members of a drafting committee. Likewise, it took time to reconcile differences over ideology, religion, class, and region.

---

[7] Livingston Collection, New-York Historical Society, as quoted in Bernard Mason, *The Road to Independence: The Revolutionary Movement in New York, 1773–1777* (Lexington, Mass., 1966), 231.

[8] John Jay to Gouverneur Morris and Robert R. Livingston, April 29, 1777, as quoted in Mason, *The Road to Independence*, 230.

The Significance of the Constitution

The provision for a strong yet popularly elected governor was part of the greatest innovation of and compromise between the friends of liberty and order. By this compromise, the New York assembly became the Whiggish safeguard of liberty. Annual elections were expected to keep its members sensitive to as well as representative of their electors, and its electorate was broadened to include: farmers with freehold (real property) worth at least 20 pounds, land-renting tenants who paid annual rents of 2 pounds, and tradesmen recognized as "freemen" by the cities of Albany and New York. The governor became an acceptable component of energetic government. The state constitution also established a council of revision, in which the governor was forced to share the veto power with the chancellor and state supreme court justices, and a council of appointment, in which the governor was forced to share the appointment power with state senators.

The framers of New York's first constitution also helped to fashion seven building blocks of a federalist constitution, which would receive fuller expression in the United States Constitution drafted a decade later.

First, the 1777 Constitution provided for a legislature based on proportional representation, representative of often excluded segments of society—including tenant farmers, city workers, and free blacks.

Second, that document provided for a popularly elected executive with the power to govern energetically. The governor's term of office was three years, long by comparison with the other state constitutions, with no limit on reelection, and the office was vested with "the supreme executive power" (Article XVII); that is, "to take care that the laws are faithfully executed to the best of his ability; and to expedite all such measures as may be resolved upon by the legislature" (Article XIX).

Third, the constitution experimented with power-sharing arrangements, involving the judiciary in the review of legislation (subject to a two-thirds override by both houses) and the senate in the approval of appointments; both of these experiments found later expression in the U.S. Constitution.

Fourth, the judiciary was given more power than in any other state to date—a share in the review of legislation, a share in impeachments, and control of court officers.[9]

---

[9] Willi Paul Adams, *The First American Constitutions*, 268.

Fifth, although the 1777 Constitution contained no separate bill of rights, underscoring the state's reliance on a common-law basis of rights, it did provide a strong guarantee for the free exercise of religion, for trial by jury, for the right to vote, and for due process. (On January 26, 1787, the New York legislature passed a bill of rights as an ordinary statute rather than a constitutional amendment.)

Sixth, the constitution provided for the separation of church and state by barring clergyman from holding public office and rejecting a religious test for holding office and by prohibiting the 'adoption of any form of religious establishment.

Seventh, the constitution anticipated population growth in a commercial society by providing for legislative reapportionment based on a septennial census and the naturalization of immigrants.

In all these respects, the state Constitution of 1777 anticipated the national constitution written ten years later.[10] In this sense, it can properly be regarded as our first federalist constitution.

For Further Reading

Elisha P. Douglass. *Rebels and Democrats; the Struggle for Equal Political Rights and Majority Rule during the American Revolution.* Chapel Hill, 1955.

Charles Z. Lincoln. *The Constitutional History of New York from the beginning of the Colonial Period to the Year 1905.* Rochester, N.Y., 1906 (Volume 1: 471–595).

Bernard Mason. *The Road to Independence: The Revolutionary Movement in New York, 1773–1777.* Lexington, Mass., 1966.

William A. Polf. *1777: The Political Revolution and New York's First Constitution.* Albany, 1977; reprinted in Stephen L. Schechter and Richard B. Bernstein, eds. *New York and the Union: Contributions to the American Constitutional Experience.* Albany, 1990.

[10] For an analysis of borrowed state provisions, see Charles Warren, *Congress, The Constitution, and The Supreme Court* (Boston, 1935), 22–34.

[The New York State Constitution]

[1777]

WHEREAS the many tyrannical and oppressive usurpations of the King and Parliament of Great Britain, on the rights and liberties of the people of the American colonies, had reduced them to the necessity of introducing a government by Congresses and Committees, as temporary expedients, and to exist no longer than the grievances of the people should remain without redress.

AND WHEREAS the Congress of the colony of New-York, did on the thirty-first day of May now last past, resolve as follows, *viz.*

"WHEREAS the present government of this colony by Congress and Committees, was instituted while the former government under the crown of Great-Britain existed in full force; and was established for the sole purpose of opposing the usurpation of the British Parliament, and was intended to expire on a reconciliation with Great-Britain, which it was then apprehended would soon take place, but is now considered as remote and uncertain.

"AND WHEREAS many and great inconveniences attend the said mode of government by Congress and Committees, as of necessity, in many instances, legislative, judicial, and executive powers have been vested therein, especially since the dissolution of the former government by the abdication of the late Governor, and the exclusion of this colony from the protection of the King of Great-Britain.

"AND WHEREAS the Continental Congress did resolve as followeth, *to wit,*

[Text of the Continental Congress Resolution of May 1776 omitted.[1]]

"AND WHEREAS doubts have arisen whether this Congress are invested with sufficient power and authority to deliberate and determine

Reprinted from William A. Polf, *1777: The Political Revolution and New York's First Constitution* (Albany, 1977). According to Polf, "The constitution of 1777 is transcribed from the first edition printed in Fishkill by Samuel Loudon shortly after adoption. Only the text of the Declaration of Independence has been omitted.... The current rules of punctuation have been followed for hyphenating words at the end of the line. Otherwise, spelling, capitalization, and punctuation are reproduced exactly as they appear in the Loudon edition."

[1] For the text and a discussion of this resolution see Richard B. Bernstein's commentary, Chapter 7 above.

on so important a subject as the necessity of erecting and constituting a new form of government and internal police, to the exclusion of all foreign jurisdiction, dominion and controul whatever.—And whereas it appertains of right solely to the people of this colony to determine the said doubts, Therefore

"RESOLVED, That it be recommended to the electors in the several counties in this colony, by election in the manner and form prescribed for the election of the present Congress, either to authorize (in addition to the powers vested in this Congress) their present deputies, or others in the stead of their present deputies, or either of them, to take into consideration the necessity and propriety of instituting such new government as in and by the said resolution of the Continental Congress is described and recommended: And if the majority of the counties, by their deputies in Provincial Congress, shall be of opinion that such new government ought to be instituted and established; then to institute and establish such a government as they shall deem best calculated to secure the rights, liberties and happiness of the good people of this colony; and to continue in force until a future peace with Great-Britain shall render the same unnecessary. And

"RESOLVED, that the said elections in the several counties, ought to be had on such day and at such place or places, as by the Committee of each county respectively shall be determined.—And it is recommended to the said Committees, to fix such early days for the said elections, as that all the deputies to be elected have sufficient time to repair to the city of New-York by the second Monday in July next; on which day all the said deputies ought punctually to give their attendance.

"AND WHEREAS the object of the aforegoing resolutions is of the utmost importance to the good people of this colony,—

"RESOLVED, That it be, and it is hereby earnestly recommended to the Committees, freeholders, and other electors in the different counties in this colony, diligently to carry the same into execution."

AND WHEREAS the good people of the said colony, in pursuance of the said resolution, and reposing special trust and confidence in the members of this Convention, have appointed, authorized and empowered them for the purposes, and in the manner, and with the powers in and by the said resolve specified, declared and mentioned.

AND WHEREAS the delegates of the United American States, in general Congress convened, did on the fourth day of July now last past, solemnly publish and declare, in the words following, *viz.*

[Text of the Declaration of Independence omitted.[2]]

AND WHEREAS this Convention having taken this declaration into their most serious consideration, did on the ninth day of July last past, unanimously resolve, that the reasons assigned by the Continental Congress, for declaring the United Colonies, free and independent States, are cogent and conclusive: And that while we lament the cruel necessity which has rendered that measure unavoidable we approve the same, and will at the risque of our lives and fortunes join the other Colonies in supporting it.

By virtue of which several acts, declarations and proceedings, mentioned and contained in the afore recited resolves or resolutions of the General Congress of the United American States, and of the Congresses or Conventions of this State, all power whatever therein hath reverted to the people thereof, and this Convention hath by their suffrages and free choice been appointed, and among other things authorized to institute and establish such a government, as they shall deem best calculated to secure the rights and liberties of the good people of this State, most conducive of the happiness and safety of their constituents in particular, and of America in general.

I. This Convention therefore, in the name and by the authority of the good people of this State, doth ORDAIN, DETERMINE and DECLARE, that no authority shall on any pretence whatever be exercised over the people or members of this State, but such as shall be derived from and granted by them.

II. This Convention doth further in the name and by the authority of the good people of this State, ORDAIN, DETERMINE and DECLARE, that the supreme legislative power, within this State, shall be vested in two separate and distinct bodies of men; the one to be called the Assembly of the State of New-York; the other to be called the Senate of the State of New-York; who together shall form the legislature, and meet once at least in every year for the dispatch of business.

III. AND WHEREAS, Laws inconsistent with the spirit of this constitution, or with the public good, may be hastily and unadvisedly passed; BE IT ORDAINED, that the Governor for the time being, the Chancellor and the Judges of the Supreme Court, or any two of them, together with the Governor, shall be, and hereby are, constituted a Council to revise all bills about to be passed into laws by the legislature. And for that purpose shall assemble themselves, from time to time, when the

[2] For the text and discussion of the Declaration of Independence see Chapter 8 above.

legislature shall be convened; for which nevertheless, they shall not receive any salary or consideration under any pretence whatever. And that all bills which have passed the Senate and Assembly, shall, before they become laws, be presented to the said Council for their revisal and consideration; and if upon such revision and consideration, it should appear improper to the said Council, or a majority of them, that the said bill should become a law of this State, that they return the same, together with their objections thereto, in writing, to the Senate, or House of Assembly, in whichsoever the same shall have originated, who shall enter the objections sent down by the Council, at large, in their minutes, and proceed to reconsider the said bill. But if after such reconsideration, two thirds of the said Senate or House of Assembly, shall, notwithstanding the said objections, agree to pass the same, it shall, together with the objections, be sent to the other branch of the legislature, where it shall also be reconsidered, and if approved by two thirds of the members present, shall be a law.

And in order to prevent any unnecessary delays, BE IT FURTHER ORDAINED, that if any bill shall not be returned by the Council, within ten days after it shall have been presented, the same shall be a law, unless the legislature shall, by their adjournment render a return of the said bill within ten days impracticable; in which case the bill shall be returned on the first day of the meeting of the legislature, after the expiration of the said ten days.[3]

IV. That the Assembly shall consist of at least seventy members, to be annually chosen in the several counties, in the proportions following, viz.[4]

---

[3] The Council of Revision was unique to New York. It served as an executive-judicial check on the legislature, but it could also be viewed as a third branch of the legislature that did not possess the authority to initiate legislation. The Council of Revision intrigued James Madison, who supported such a body in the Constitutional Convention in 1787. Madison wanted every bill enacted by Congress to be considered immediately by a national council of revision with power to strike down acts of Congress before they operated. He preferred this to judicial review, which could only strike down laws once they had begun to operate and only because they were unconstitutional. During its lifetime, the New York Council of Revision considered 6,590 bills and rejected 128. The legislature overrode the veto only seventeen times. See Alfred B. Street, *The Council of Revision of the State of New York* ... (Albany, 1859).

[4] New York County included present-day Manhattan. The boundaries of Kings and Richmond counties remain about the same. Queens County included present-day Nassau and Queens counties, while Suffolk County boundaries remain about the same two centuries later. Westchester County included present-day Westchester and The Bronx; Orange County included present-day Rockland and much of Orange counties; and Dutchess County included present-day Dutchess and Putnam counties. Ulster County extended to the Delaware River and included all of present-day Ulster and Sullivan counties

For the city and county of New York,	nine;
The city and county of Albany,	ten;
The county of Dutchess	seven;
The county of West-chester,	six;
The county of Ulster,	six;
The county of Suffolk,	five;
The county of Queens,	four;
The county of Orange,	four;
The county of Kings,	two;
The county of Richmond,	two;
The county of Tryon,	six;
The county of Charlotte,	four;
The county of Cumberland,	three;
The county of Gloucester,	two.

V. That as soon after the expiration of seven years, subsequent to the termination of the present war as may be, a Census of the electors and inhabitants in this State be taken, under the direction of the legislature. And if on such Census it shall appear, that the number of representatives in Assembly from the said counties, is not justly proportioned to the number of electors in the said counties respectively, that the legislature do adjust and apportion the same by that rule. And further, that once in every seven years, after the taking of the said first Census, a just account of the electors resident in each county shall be taken; and if it shall thereupon appear, that the number of electors in any county, shall have encreased or diminished one or more seventieth parts of the whole number of electors, which on the said first Census shall be found in this State, the number of representatives for such county shall be increased or diminished accordingly, that is to say, one representative for every seventieth part as aforesaid.

VI. AND WHEREAS, an opinion hath long prevailed among divers of the good people of this State, that voting at elections by Ballot, would tend more to preserve the liberty and equal freedom of the people, than voting *viva voce*. To the end therefore that a fair experiment be made, which of those two methods of voting is to be preferred:

---

and parts of Orange, Delaware and Greene counties. Tryon County included the lands between the treaty line of 1768 on the west and the 1777 counties of Ulster, Albany, and Charlotte on the east up to the Canadian border. Albany County included all of present-day Albany, Columbia, Rensselaer, Schenectady, and Saratoga counties, and parts of Greene, Schoharie, and Washington counties. Charlotte included the lands north of Albany County and east of Tryon into present-day Vermont. Cumberland and Gloucester included, respectively, the southern and northern parts of the remainder of present-day Vermont each to the Connecticut River.

BE IT ORDAINED, that as soon as may be, after the termination of the present war, between the United States of America and Great-Britain, an act, or acts be passed by the legislature of this State, for causing all elections thereafter to be held in this State for Senators and Representatives in assembly, to be by Ballot, and directing the manner in which the same shall be conducted. AND WHEREAS, it is possible, that after all the care of the legislature, in framing the said act or acts, certain inconveniences and mischiefs, unforeseen at this day, may be found to attend the said mode of electing by Ballot:

IT IS FURTHER ORDAINED, that if after a full and fair experiment shall be made of voting by Ballot aforesaid, the same shall be found less conducive to the safety or interest of the State, than the method of voting *viva voce,* it shall be lawful and constitutional for the legislature to abolish the same; provided two thirds of the members present in each House, respectively shall concur therein: And further, that during the continuance of the present war, and until the legislature of this State shall provide for the election of Senators and Representatives in assembly by Ballot, the said elections shall be made *viva voce.*

VII. That every male inhabitant of full age, who shall have personally resided within one of the counties of this State, for six months immediately preceding the day of election, shall at such election, be entitled to vote for representatives of the said county in assembly; if during the time aforesaid, he shall have been a Freeholder, possessing a Freehold of the value of twenty pounds, within the said county, or have rented a tenement therein of the yearly value of forty shillings, and been rated and actually paid taxes to this State: Provided always, that every person who now is a freeman of the city of Albany, or who was made a freeman of the city of New-York, on or before the fourteenth day of October, in the year of our Lord one thousand seven hundred and seventy-five, and shall be actually and usually resident in the said cities respectively, shall be entitled to vote for Representatives in assembly within his said place of residence.

VIII. That every elector before he is admitted to vote, shall, if required by the returning officer or either of the inspectors, take an oath, or if of the people called Quakers, an affirmation, of allegiance to the State.

IX. That the assembly thus constituted, shall chuse their own Speaker, be judges of their own members, and enjoy the same privileges and proceed in doing business, in like manner as the assemblies of the colony of New-York of *right* formerly did; and that a majority of the said members, shall, from time to time constitute a House to proceed upon business.

X. And this Convention doth further, in the name and by the authority of the good people of this State, ORDAIN, DETERMINE and DECLARE, that the Senate of the State of New-York, shall consist of twenty-four freeholders, to be chosen out of the body of the freeholders, and that they be chosen by the freeholders of this State, possessed of freeholds of the value of one hundred pounds, over and above all debts charged thereon.

XI. That the members of the Senate be elected for four years, and immediately after the first election, they be divided by lot into four classes, six in each class, and numbered one, two, three and four; that the seats of the members of the first class shall be vacated at the expiration of the first year, the second class the second year, and so on continually, to the end that the fourth part of the Senate, as nearly as possible, may be annually chosen.

XII. That the election of Senators shall be after this manner; that so much of this State as is now parcelled into counties, be divided into four great districts; the southern district to comprehend the city and county of New-York, Suffolk, Westchester, Kings, Queens and Richmond counties; the middle district to comprehend the counties of Dutchess, Ulster and Orange; the western district the city and county of Albany, and Tryon county; and the eastern district, the counties of Charlotte, Cumberland and Gloucester. That the Senators shall be elected by the freeholders of the said districts, qualified as aforesaid, in the proportions following, *to wit,* in the southern district nine, in the middle district six, in the western district six, and in the eastern district three. And BE IT ORDAINED, that a Census shall be taken as soon as may be, after the expiration of seven years from the termination of the present war, under the direction of the legislature: And if on such Census it shall appear, that the number of Senators is not justly proportioned to the several districts, that the legislature adjust the proportion as near as may be, to the number of freeholders qualified as aforesaid, in each district. That when the number of electors within any of the said districts, shall have increased one twenty-fourth part of the whole number of electors, which by the said Census, shall be found to be in this State, an additional Senator shall be chosen by the electors of such district. That a majority of the number of Senators to be chosen as aforesaid, shall be necessary to constitute a Senate, sufficient to proceed upon business, and that the Senate shall in like manner with the assembly, be the judges of its own members. And BE IT ORDAINED, that it shall be in the power of the future legislatures of this State for the convenience and advantage of the good people thereof, to divide the same into such further and other counties and districts, as shall to them appear necessary.

XIII. And this Convention doth further, in the name and by the authority of the good people of this State, ORDAIN, DETERMINE and DECLARE, that no member of this State, shall be disfranchised, or deprived of any of the rights or privileges secured to the subjects of this State, by this constitution, unless by the law of the land, or the judgment of his peers.

XIV. That neither the assembly or the senate shall have power to adjourn themselves for any longer time than two days, without the mutual consent of both.

XV. That whenever the Assembly and Senate disagree, a conference shall be held in the presence of both, and be managed by Committees to be by them respectively chosen by ballot. That the doors both of the Senate and Assembly shall at all times be kept open to all persons, except when the welfare of the State shall require their debates to be kept secret. And the Journals of all their proceedings shall be kept in the manner heretofore accustomed by the General Assembly of the colony of New-York, and except such parts as they shall as aforesaid, respectively determine not to make public, be from day to day (if the business of the legislature will permit) published.

XVI. It is nevertheless provided, that the number of Senators shall never exceed one hundred, nor the number of Assembly three hundred; but that whenever the number of Senators shall amount to one hundred, or of the Assembly to three hundred, then and in such case, the legislature shall from time to time, thereafter, by laws for that purpose, apportion and distribute the said one hundred Senators and three hundred Representatives, among the great districts and counties of this State in proportion to the number of their respective electors; so that the representation of the good people of this State, both in the Senate and Assembly, shall for ever remain proportionate and adequate.

XVII. And this Convention doth further, in the name and by the authority of the good people of this State, ORDAIN, DETERMINE and DECLARE, that the supreme executive power, and authority of this State, shall be vested in a Governor; and that statedly once in every three years, and as often as the seat of government shall become vacant, a wise and discreet freeholder of this State, shall be by ballot elected Governor, by the freeholders of this State, qualified as before described to elect Senators; which elections shall be always held at the times and places of choosing representatives in assembly for each respective county; and that the person who hath the greatest number of votes within the said State, shall be Governor thereof.[5]

---

[5] New York's governor had the longest term of office of any of the state chief executives and was one of six governors who was eligible to be reelected without limit.

XVIII. That the Governor shall continue in office three years, and shall, by virtue of his office, be General and Commander in Chief of all the militia, and Admiral of the Navy of this State; that he shall have power to convene the Assembly and Senate on extraordinary occasions, to prorogue them from time to time, provided such prorogations shall not exceed sixty days in the space of any one year; and at his discretion to grant reprieves and pardons to persons convicted of crimes, other than treason or murder, in which he may suspend the execution of the sentence, until it shall be reported to the legislature at their subsequent meeting; and they shall either pardon or direct the execution of the criminal, or grant a further reprieve.

XIX. That it shall be the duty of the Governor to inform the legislature, at every sessions, of the condition of the State, so far as may respect his department; to recommend such matters to their consideration as shall appear to him to concern its good government, welfare and prosperity; to correspond with the Continental Congress, and other States; to transact all necessary business with the officers of government, civil and military; to take care that the laws are faithfully executed to the best of his ability; and to expedite all such measures as may be resolved upon by the legislature.

XX. That a Lieutenant-Governor shall, at every election of a Governor, and as often as the Lieutenant-Governor shall die, resign, or be removed from office, be elected in the same manner with the Governor, to continue in office, until the next election of a Governor; and such Lieutenant-Governor shall, by virtue of his office, be President of the Senate, and, upon an equal division, have a casting voice in their decisions, but not vote on any other occasion.

And in case of the impeachment of the Governor, or his removal from office, death, resignation, or absence from the State, the Lieutenant-Governor shall exercise all the power and authority appertaining to the office of Governor, until another be chosen, or the Governor absent or impeached shall return, or be acquitted. Provided that where the Governor shall, with the consent of the legislature, be out of the State, in time of war, at the head of a military force thereof, he shall still continue in his command of all the military force of this State, both by sea and land.

XXI. That whenever the Government shall be administered by the Lieutenant-Governor, or he shall be unable to attend as President of the Senate, the senators shall have power to elect one of their own members to the office of President of the Senate, which he shall exercise *pro hac vice*. And if, during such vacancy of the office of Governor, the Lieutenant-Governor shall be impeached, displaced, resign, die, or be absent from the State, the President of the Senate, shall in like manner as the Lieutenant-Governor administer the government, until others shall be elected by the suffrage of the people at the succeeding election.

XXII. And this Convention doth further, in the name and by the authority of the good people of this State, ORDAIN, DETERMINE and DE-CLARE, that the Treasurer of this State shall be appointed by act of the legislature, to originate with the assembly: Provided that he shall not be elected out of either branch of the legislature.

XXIII. That all officers, other than those, who by this constitution are directed to be otherwise appointed, shall be appointed in the manner following, *to wit,* The assembly shall, once in every year, openly nom-inate and appoint one of the Senators from each great district, which Senators shall form a council for the appointment of the said officers, of which the Governor for the time being, or the Lieutenant-Governor, or the President of the Senate, when they shall respectively administer the government, shall be President, and have a casting voice, *but no other vote*; and with the advice and consent of the said council, shall appoint all the said officers; and that a majority of the said council be a quorum. And further, the said Senators shall not be eligible to the said council for two years successively.[6]

XXIV. That all military officers be appointed during pleasure; that all commissioned officers civil and military, be commissioned by the Governor, and that the Chancellor, the Judges of the supreme court, and first Judge of the county court in every county, hold their offices during good behaviour, or until they shall have respectively attained the age of sixty years.

XXV. That the Chancellor and Judges of the supreme court, shall not at the same time hold any other office, excepting that of Delegate to the General Congress, upon special occasions; and that the first Judges of the county courts in the several counties, shall not at the same time hold any other office, excepting that of Senator, or Delegate to the General Congress: But if the Chancellor or either of the said

[6] The Council of Appointment was also unique to New York. In the 1789 guber-natorial election, Alexander Hamilton charged Governor George Clinton with an arrogant misinterpretation of the state constitution by claiming over the past twelve years the exclusive power to nominate officers in the council. In 1794 when Federalists captured both houses of the legislature for the first time, the four anti-Clinton senators elected to the council assumed the power to nominate, therefore making the governor almost a non-functioning member of the council. When John Jay was elected governor in 1795, he tried unsuccessfully to restore the executive's exclusive power of nomination. See Hugh M. Flick, "The Council of Appointment in New York State, The First Attempt to Regulate Political Patronage, 1777–1822," *Proceedings of the New York State Historical Association* XXXII (1934): 253–80.

Judges be elected or appointed to any other office, excepting as is before excepted, it shall be at his option in which to serve.

XXVI. That Sheriffs and Coroners be annually appointed; and that no person shall be capable of holding either of the said offices more than four years successively, nor the Sheriff of holding any other office at the same time.

XXVII. AND BE IT FURTHER ORDAINED, that the register and clerks in chancery be appointed by the Chancellor; the clerks of the supreme court by the Judges of the said court; the clerk of the court of probates, by the Judge of the said court; and the register and marshall of the court of admiralty, by the Judge of the admiralty.—The said marshall, registers and clerks, to continue in office during the pleasure of those, by whom they are to be appointed, as aforesaid.

And that all Attorneys, Solicitors and Counsellors at Law, hereafter to be appointed, be appointed by the court, and licensed by the first judge of the court in which they shall respectively plead or practice; and be regulated by the rules and orders of the said courts.

XXVIII. AND BE IT FURTHER ORDAINED, that where by this Convention the duration of any office shall not be ascertained, such office shall be construed to be held during the pleasure of the Council of Appointment: Provided that new commissions shall be issued to judges of the county courts (other than to the first judge) and to justices of the peace, once at the least in every three years.

XXIX. That town clerks, supervisors, assessors, constables and collectors, and all other officers heretofore eligible by the people, shall always continue to be so eligible, in the manner directed by the present or future acts of legislature.

That loan officers, county treasurers, and clerks of the supervisors, continue to be appointed in the manner directed by the present or future acts of the legislature.

XXX. That Delegates to represent this State, in the General Congress of the United States of America, be annually appointed as follows, *to wit,* The Senate and Assembly shall each openly nominate as many persons as shall be equal to the whole number of Delegates to be appointed; after which nomination, they shall meet together, and those persons named in both lists shall be Delegates; and out of those persons whose names are not in both lists, one half shall be chosen by the joint ballot of the Senators and Members of Assembly, so met together as aforesaid.

XXXI. That the stile of all laws shall be as follows, *to wit,* BE IT ENACTED *by the people of the State of New-York, represented in Senate and Assembly.* And that all writs and other proceedings shall run in the name of *the people of the State of New-York,* and be tested in the name of the Chancellor or Chief Judge of the court from whence they shall issue.

XXXII. And this Convention doth further, in the name and by the authority of the good people of this State, ORDAIN, DETERMINE and DE-CLARE, that a court shall be instituted for the trial of Impeachments, and the Correction of Errors, under the regulations which shall be established by the legislature; and to consist of the President of the Senate, for the time being, and the Senators, Chancellor, and Judges of the Supreme Court, or the major part of them; except that when an impeachment shall be prosecuted against the Chancellor, or either of the Judges of the Supreme Court, the person so impeached shall be suspended from exercising his office, until his acquittal: And in like manner, when an appeal from a decree in equity shall be heard, the Chancellor shall inform the court of the reasons of his decree, but shall not have a voice in the final sentence. And if the cause to be determined shall be brought up by writ of error on a question of law, on a judgment in the Supreme Court, the Judges of that Court shall assign the reasons of such their judgment, but shall not have a voice for its affirmance or reversal.

XXXIII. That the power of impeaching all officers of the State, for mal and corrupt conduct in their respective offices, be vested in the representatives of the people in assembly; but that it shall always be necessary that two third parts of the members present shall consent to and agree in such impeachment. That previous to the trial of every impeachment, the members of the said court shall respectively be sworn, truly and impartially to try and determine the charge in question, according to evidence; and that no judgement of the said court shall be valid, unless it shall be assented to by two third parts of the members then present; nor shall it extend farther than to removal from office, and disqualification to hold or enjoy any place of honour, trust or profit, under this State. But the party so convicted, shall be, nevertheless, liable and subject to indictment, trial, judgment and punishment, according to the laws of the land.

XXXIV. AND IT IS FURTHER ORDAINED, that in every trial on impeachment or indictment for crimes or misdemeanors, the party impeached or indicted, shall be allowed counsel, as in civil actions.

XXXV. And this Convention doth further, in the name and by the authority of the good people of this State, ORDAIN, DETERMINE and DE-CLARE, that such parts of the common law of England, and of the statute law of England and Great-Britain, and of the acts of the legislature of the colony of New-York, as together did form the law of the said colony on the nineteenth day of April,[7] in the year of our Lord one thousand seven hundred and seventy-five, shall be and continue the law of this State; subject to such alterations and provisions, as the legislature of this State shall, from time to time, make concerning the same. That such of the said acts as are temporary, shall expire at the times limited for their duration respectively. That all such parts of the said common law, and all such of the said statutes, and acts aforesaid, or parts thereof, as may be construed to establish or maintain any particular denomination of Christians, or their Ministers, or concern the allegiance heretofore yielded to, and the supremacy sovereignty, government or prerogatives, claimed or exercised by the King of Great-Britain and his predecessors, over the colony of New-York and its inhabitants, or are repugnant to this constitution, be, and they hereby are, abrogated and rejected. And this Convention doth farther ordain, that the resolves or resolutions of the Congresses of the colony of New-York, and of the Convention of the State of New-York, now in force, and not repugnant to the government established by this Constitution, shall be considered as making part of the laws of this State; subject, nevertheless to such alterations and provisions, as the legislature of this State may from time to time make concerning the same.

XXXVI. AND BE IT FURTHER ORDAINED, that all grants of land within this State, made by the King of Great-Britain, or persons acting under his authority, after the fourteenth day of October, one thousand seven hundred and seventy-five, shall be null and void: But that nothing in this constitution contained, shall be construed to affect any grants of land, within this State, made by the authority of the said King or his predecessors, or to annul any charters to bodies politic, by him or them or any of them, made prior to that day. And that none of the said charters, shall be adjudged to be void by reason of any non-user or misuser of any of their respective rights or privileges, between the ninetee[n]eth day of April, in the year of our Lord one thousand seven hundred and seventy-five, and the publication of this constitution. And further, that all such of the officers described in the said charters respectively, as by the terms of the said charters, were to be appointed by the Governor of the colony of New-York, with or without the advice and consent of the Council of the said King, in the said colony, shall henceforth be appointed by the Council established by this constitution, for the appointment of officers in this State, until otherwise directed by the legislature.

---

[7] The battles of Lexington and Concord occurred on April 19, 1775; therefore this date includes the beginning of war between Great Britain and the colonies.

XXXVII. AND WHEREAS it is of great importance to the safety of this State, that peace and amity with the Indians within the same, be at all times supported and maintained. AND WHEREAS, the frauds too often practised towards the said Indians, in contracts made for their lands, have in divers instances been productive of dangerous discontents and animosities; BE IT ORDAINED, that no purchases or contracts for the sale of lands made since the fourteenth day of October, in the year of our Lord, one thousand seven hundred and seventy-five, or which may hereafter be made with or of the said Indians, within the limits of this State, shall be binding on the said Indians, or deemed valid, unless made under the authority, and with the consent of the legislature of this State.

XXXVIII. AND WHEREAS we are required by the benevolent principles of rational liberty, not only to expel civil tyranny, but also to guard against that spiritual oppression and intolerance, wherewith the bigotry and ambition of weak and wicked priests and princes, have scourged mankind: This Convention doth further, in the name and by the authority of the good people of this State, ORDAIN, DETERMINE and DECLARE, that the free exercise and enjoyment of religious profession and worship, without discrimination or preference, shall for ever hereafter be allowed within this State to all mankind. Provided that the liberty of conscience hereby granted, shall not be so construed, as to excuse acts of licentiousness, or justify practices inconsistent with the peace or safety of this State.

XXXIX. AND WHEREAS the ministers of the gospel, are by their profession dedicated to the service of God and the cure of souls, and ought not to be diverted from the great duties of their function; therefore no minister of the gospel, or priest of any denomination whatsoever, shall at any time hereafter, under any pretence or description whatever, be eligible to, or capable of holding any civil or military office or place, within this State.

XL. AND WHEREAS it is of the utmost importance to the safety of every State, that it should always be in a condition of defence; and it is the duty of every man, who enjoys the protection of society, to be prepared and willing to defend it; this Convention therefore, in the name and by the authority of the good people of this State, doth ORDAIN, DETERMINE and DECLARE, that the militia of this State, at all times hereafter, as well in peace as in war, shall be armed and disciplined, and in readiness for service. That all such of the inhabitants of this State, being of the people called Quakers, as from scruples of conscience, may be averse to the bearing of arms, be therefrom excused by the legislature; and do pay to the State such sums of money in lieu of their personal service, as the same may, in the judgment of the legislature, be worth: And that a proper magazine of warlike stores, proportionate to the number of inhabitants, be, for ever hereafter, at the expence of this State, and by acts of the legislature, established, maintained, and continued in every county in this State.

XLI. And this Convention doth further ORDAIN, DETERMINE and DECLARE, in the name and by the authority of the good people of this State, that trial by jury, in all cases in which it hath heretofore been used in the colony of New-York, shall be established, and remain inviolate forever. And that no acts of attainder shall be passed by the legislature of this State for crimes, other than those committed before the termination of the present war; and that such acts shall not work a corruption of blood. And further, that the legislature of this State shall, at no time hereafter, institute any new court or courts, but such as shall proceed according to the course of the common law.

XLII. And this Convention doth further, in the name and by the authority of the good people of this State, ORDAIN, DETERMINE and DE-CLARE, that it shall be in the discretion of the legislature to naturalize all such persons, and in such manner as they shall think proper; provided all such of the persons, so to be by them naturalized, as being born in parts beyond sea, and out of the United States of America, shall come to settle in, and become subjects of this State, shall take an oath of allegiance to this State, and abjure and renounce all allegiance and subjection to all and every foreign King, Prince, Potentate and State, in all matters ecclesiastical as well as civil.

By order.
LEONARD GANSEVOORT, Pres. pro tem.

XI

The Massachusetts Constitution

1780

COMMENTARY BY RICHARD B. BERNSTEIN

IN THE REVOLUTIONARY PERIOD, constitution making on the state level reached its most mature stage of development in Massachusetts, where the people wrangled over the proper mechanism and procedures for framing a new form of government for nearly five years. The result, the Massachusetts Constitution of 1780, was generally considered the best of the state constitutions and the fullest working out of the theoretical issues of Revolutionary constitutionalism.

Prelude: The Rejected Constitution of 1778

In Massachusetts, the vacuum of authority created by the suspension of the colonial government in 1775 was filled at first by the provincial legislature or General Court, reconstituted as a provisional government under the Charter of 1691 as modified for the emergency. However, town meetings and county conventions petitioned the General Court for a permanent instead of a provisional constitution. In the fall of 1776, the towns rejected the General Court's proposal that the towns authorize

This commentary is a revised and greatly expanded version of pages 56–64 of Richard B. Bernstein with Kym S. Rice, *Are We to Be a Nation? The Making of the Constitution* (Cambridge, Mass., 1987).

it to write a new constitution; the resolutions of Concord, Lexington, and Pittsfield added important new ideas to the controversy. Concord demanded the election of a constitutional convention to write a new constitution, pointing out that "a Constitution [made and] alterable by the Supreme Legislature is no Security at all to the Subject against any Encroachment of the Governing part on any or on all of their Rights & privileges."[1] Lexington and Pittsfield suggested (in the words of the Lexington resolution) that the constitution, once drafted, be submitted to "the Inhabitants, as Towns, or Societies, to express their Approbation, or the Contrary."[2]

Instead of following Concord's suggestion, the General Court resolved on April 4, 1777, that, at the next election for the legislature, the voters would choose their representatives with the knowledge that these men would be authorized to write a constitution. The resolution also adopted the suggestion of the Lexington and Pittsfield resolutions; it provided that the constitution written by the General Court armed with this constituent power (that is, the power to frame or constitute a government) would be submitted to the town meetings, and that every free adult male inhabitant could vote to accept or reject the constitution.

In early 1778, the General Court announced a constitution providing for a two-house legislature and a popularly elected governor who would be a member of the upper house but would have no veto power over legislation. The constitution lacked a bill of rights and a preamble setting forth the theoretical justification for a constitution, and it contained a provision barring "negroes, Indians, and mulattoes" from the franchise. For the first time in American history, a constitution was put to the test of the votes of all adult male citizens of the political community. The proposed constitution was defeated by a vote of more than three to one—9,972 to 2,083, with 129 town meetings failing to provide any returns at all. The returns from the town meetings cited among the reasons for rejection the absence of a bill of rights, the restrictions on the franchise, and the complex and unfair apportionment of seats in the General Court. Another equally powerful argument invoked in many of the returns was the impropriety of assigning the drafting of a constitution to the legislature rather than to a specially chosen convention. Foremost among the statements of the town meetings in detail,

---

[1] Quoted in Robert J. Taylor, ed., *Massachusetts, Colony to Commonwealth: Documents on the Foundation of the Constitution 1775–1780* (Chapel Hill, 1961), 45.

[2] Quoted in Oscar Handlin and Mary Handlin, eds., *The Popular Sources of Political Authority: Documents on The Massachusetts Constitution of 1780* (Cambridge, Mass., 1966), 150.

organization, and intellectual sophistication was the "Essex Result," a pamphlet expressing the views of the Essex County convention and written by Theophilus Parsons, a young lawyer from Newburyport. John Adams, then serving abroad with Benjamin Franklin in Paris, noted that the reasoning of the "Essex Result" was close to that of his influential 1776 pamphlet on constitution-making, *Thoughts on Government*, and was put out that the pamphlet did not acknowledge its debt to the earlier work.[3]

The Constitutional Convention of 1780

The demand for a convention continued after the failure of the Constitution of 1778. Focused in Berkshire County and other parts of western Massachusetts, the Constitutionalist movement insisted that the courts could not open until they had legitimate, constitutional authority. Despite their opponents' claims that they merely wanted to keep the courts closed to avoid suits for debt, the Constitutionalists acted for principled as well as economic reasons. A convention of towns in Hampshire County demanded the calling of a new convention on March 30, 1779:[4]

> We are of Opinion that by Delaying and Putting off the Forming of a Bill of Rights and a free Constitution for this State, we are Deprived of a Great Blessing viz Civil Government and Good wholsom Laws— Founded thereon, whereby the Virtuous may be Protected in their Liberty and Property, and Transgressors Brought to proper Punishment.

The month before, the General Court had given in to the demands for action and resolved that the town meetings should be polled for their views on the calling of a constitutional convention. Presented with a vote of better than two to one in favor, the legislature issued a call in June 1779 for elections to a convention; all adult freemen could participate in this election and in the vote on the constitution itself. The returns from the towns, voting on the constitution article by article, would be submitted to a final session of the convention, which would determine whether the constitution had been adopted by the necessary two-thirds vote.

---

[3] Documents on the 1779 constitution may be found in Handlin and Handlin, *Popular Sources*, and in Taylor, *Massachusetts*. For *Thoughts on Government*, see Bernstein, Chapter 7 above.

[4] Resolutions of Hampshire Convention, March 30, 1779, Hawley Papers, box 1, Rare Books and Manuscripts Division, New York Public Library.

During the first week of September 1779, the first session of the convention met in Cambridge. The convention appointed a drafting committee of thirty members, which in turn named a subcommittee of three members—John Adams, Samuel Adams, and James Bowdoin. The subcommittee assigned John Adams the task of drafting the constitution, and Adams rose to the challenge, producing what one historian has described as "the most eloquent of all American constitutions."[5] The convention reassembled on October 28 and met until November 17, when it adjourned yet again, scheduling its next session for January 5, 1780, in Boston. The convention did not resume full sessions until February 27, and continued its work for only a few days, adjourning again on March 2 after submitting the constitution to the towns. On June 7, the convention held its last session to count the returns of the votes taken at the town meetings. For nearly two weeks the delegates wrestled with the confusing job of tallying the votes on each article; Samuel Eliot Morison suggested that the convention juggled the vote returns in order to arrive at the conclusion that the constitution in fact had been adopted by the needed two-thirds vote.[6] On June 16, the convention declared the new constitution adopted and announced that it would go into effect on October 25, 1780.

The Constitution of 1780

Unlike the failed Constitution of 1778 and most of the earlier state constitutions, the Massachusetts Constitution of 1780 embodied a full, coherent system of ideas about government, the people, and the individual citizen. Its preamble set forth the view that the constitution represented a "social compact" entered into for the benefit and protection of the people and requiring the solemnity and certainty of a written constitution.

The constitution itself had two parts, a Declaration of Rights in thirty articles and a Frame of Government. Most of the provisions of the Declaration of Rights, even those that on their face invoked individual rights, actually stated principles of government that were essen-

[5] Ronald M. Peters, Jr., *The Massachusetts Constitution of 1780: A Social Compact* (Amherst, Mass., 1980), 14.
[6] Samuel Eliot Morison, "The Struggle over the Adoption of The Constitution of Massachusetts, 1780," *Massachusetts Historical Society Proceedings* 30 (1916–1917): 353–412. presents this argument. The returns from the town meetings are conveniently assembled in Handlin and Handlin, *Popular Sources*; a selection appears in Taylor, *Massachusetts*.

tial building blocks of Revolutionary constitutionalism. The most famous provision of the Declaration of Rights was Article XXX:

> In the government of this Commonwealth, the legislative department
> shall never exercise the executive and judicial powers, or either of
> them: The executive shall never exercise the legislative and judicial
> powers, or either of them: The judicial shall never exercise the leg-
> islative and executive powers, or either of them: to the end it may be
> a government of laws and not of men.

Article XXX's classic statement of the doctrine of separation of
powers captures the essence of the Frame of Government. It created
a popularly elected, bicameral General Court containing a senate and
a house of representatives, an independent and popularly elected governor and lieutenant governor, and a council drawn from the senate and
elected by the General Court to advise the governor and assume executive responsibilities should both the governor and lieutenant governor be outside the state. The governor had the power to veto legislation, but two-thirds of both houses of the General Court could override
his veto. A divergence from Adams's preference for an absolute executive veto, this provision was influenced by the New York Constitution
of 1777. The structure of the judiciary was not specified; by implication,
the constitution preserved the judicial system that had evolved since
colonial times, though leaving the legislature free to alter that system
if necessary.

Chapter V of the Frame of Government was the only state constitutional provision to address the subject of governmental responsibility
for education. Section I transformed Harvard College into a university
and reorganized and systematized the state's supervisory authority, leaving the legislature free to change Harvard's structure for its future
benefit "and the interest of the republic of letters." Section II commanded all state and local officeholders "to cherish the interests of
literature and the sciences, and all seminaries of them" because of the
importance of diffusing "[w]isdom, and knowledge, as well as virtue
. . . generally among the body of the people . . . and . . . spreading the
opportunities and advantages of education in the various parts of the
country, and among the different orders of the people. . . ."

John Adams could attend only the convention's first session; just
after he finished his draft constitution, he had to leave for Paris to take
up his duties as the first American envoy to negotiate a treaty of peace
with Great Britain. Nonetheless, his handiwork was much on his mind,
especially as his frustration at having nothing to do and his feelings of

humiliation at the hands of the French increased. On February 23, 1780, he penned a wistful letter to Samuel Adams:[7]

> I hope you will be so good as to inform me of what passes, particularly what progress the Convention makes in the Constitution. I assure you it is more comfortable making Constitutions in the dead of Winter at Cambridge or Boston, than Sailing in a leaky Ship, or climbing on foot or upon Mules over the Mountains of Gallicia or the Pyrenees.

Adams had good reason to look back with fondness upon the convention, for it gave him the chance to present his idea of a perfect commonwealth, suited to the special needs, customs, and habits of his native state and its people. He drew equally upon his constitutional theory and his practical political experience. Relishing the role of framer, in the constitution's preamble Adams even described God as "the Great Legislator of the Universe."

In September, when Samuel Adams informed him of the adoption of the constitution, he could barely contain his pride despite his Puritan upbringing.[8] His pride and anxiety for the constitution were still lively even two years later, when he was immersed in the negotiation of treaties of friendship and commerce with The Netherlands. As he wrote to Samuel Adams in June of 1782:[9]

> Pray, how does your Constitution work? How does the privy Council play its Part? Are there no Inconveniences found in it?—it is the Part which I have been most anxious about least it should become un-popular and Gentlemen should be averse to Serve in it.—This Form of Government has a very high reputation in Europe, and I wish it may be as well approved in Practice as it is in Theory.

Most Americans shared John Adams's pride in their new consti-tutions. Soon collected and published in omnibus volumes, the docu-ments were widely read and extensively discussed on both sides of the Atlantic. Two in particular, the New York Constitution of 1777 and the Massachusetts Constitution of 1780, influenced the framing of the Fed-eral Constitution in 1787.[10] These constitutions were authoritative proof

---

[7] John Adams to Samuel Adams, February 23, 1780, Bancroft Collection, Rare Book and Manuscripts Division, New York Public Library.

[8] John Adams to Samuel Adams, September 20, 1780, Bancroft Collection, Rare Book and Manuscripts Division, New York Public Library.

[9] John Adams to Samuel Adams, June 15, 1782, Bancroft Collection, Rare Book and Manuscripts Division, New York Public Library.

[10] See the discussion in Charles Warren, *Congress, the Constitution, and the Supreme Court*, rev. ed. (Boston, 1935), 1–40, esp. 30–34; Willi Paul Adams, *The First American Constitutions* (Chapel Hill, 1980), 4; George Dargo, *Law in the New Republic: Private Law and the Public Estate* (New York, 1983), 13.

that the Americans were making the most sweeping and creative contributions of their time to what John Adams called "the divine science of politics."[11]

For Further Reading

Willi Paul Adams, *The First American Constitutions: Republicn Ideologies and the Making of State Constitutions in the Revolutionary Era.* Chapel Hill, 1980.
Edward S. Corwin. "The Progress of Constitutional Theory between the Declaration of Independence and the Meeting of the Philadelphia Convention." *American Historical Review*, 1925.
George Dargo. *Law in the New Republic: Private Law and the Public Estate.* New York, 1983.
Oscar Handlin and Mary Handlin, eds., *The Popular Sources of Political Authority: Documents on the Massachusetts Constitution of 1780* (Cambridge, Mass., 1966).
Samuel Eliot Morison, "The Struggle Over the Adoption of the Constitution of Massachusetts, 1780." *Massachusetts Historical Society Proceedings* 30 (1916–1917).
Samuel Eliot Morison. "Symposium: The Massachusetts Constitution of 1780." *Suffolk University Law Review* 14, 1980.
Ronald M. Peters, Jr. *The Massachusetts Constitution of 1780: A Social Compact.* Amherst, Mass., 1980.
Robert J. Taylor, ed. *Massachusetts, Colony to Commonwealth: Documents on the Foundation of Its Constitution, 1775–1780.* Chapel Hill, 1961.
Correa M. Walsh. *The Political Science of John Adams.* New York, 1915.
Charles Warren. *Congress, the Constitution, and the Supreme Court*, rev. ed. Boston, 1935.

[11] Quoted in Correa M. Walsh, *The Political Science of John Adams* (New York, 1915), 1. See also the classic study by Edward S. Corwin, "The Progress of Constitutional Theory between the Declaration of Independence and the Meeting of the Philadelphia Convention," *American Historical Review* 30 (1925): 511–36.

[The Massachusetts Constitution of 1780]

A *CONSTITUTION OR FRAME OF GOVERNMENT, Agreed upon by the Delegates of the People of the STATE OF MASSACHUSETTS-BAY,—*In Convention,*—Begun and held at Cambridge, on the First of September, 1779, and continued by Adjournments to the Second of March, 1780.*

Preamble

The end of the institution, maintenance and administration of government, is to secure the existence of the body-politic; to protect it; and to furnish the individuals who compose it, with the power of enjoying, in safety and tranquillity, their natural rights, and the blessings of life: And whenever these great objects are not obtained, the people have a right to alter the government, and to take measures necessary for their safety, prosperity and happiness.[1]

The body-politic is formed by a voluntary association of individuals: It is a social compact, by which the whole people covenants with each citizen, and each citizen with the whole people, that all shall be governed by certain laws for the common good. It is the duty of the people, therefore, in framing a Constitution of Government, to provide for an equitable mode of making laws, as well as for an impartial interpretation, and a faithful execution of them; that every man may, at all times, find his security in them.

We, therefore, the people of Massachusetts, acknowledging, with grateful hearts, the goodness of the Great Legislator of the Universe, in affording us, in the course of His providence, an opportunity, delib-

---

The text of the Massachusetts Constitution of 1780 is reprinted by permission of the publisher from the Appendix to Ronald M. Peters, *The Massachusetts Constitution of 1780: A Social Compact* (Amherst, Mass: University of Massachusetts Press, 1980), 195–224. Peters in turn reprinted it from *The Journal of the Convention, for Framing a Constitution of Government for the State of Massachusetts-Bay* (Boston, 1832), 222–249.

[1] Compare the language of the preamble's first paragraph with that of the opening sentences of the Declaration of Independence. See Donald S. Lutz's commentary on the Declaration (Chapter 8 above).

erately and peaceably, without fraud, violence or surprise, of entering into an original, explicit, and solemn compact with each other; and of forming a new Constitution of Civil Government, for ourselves and posterity; and devoutly imploring His direction in so interesting a design, DO agree upon, ordain and establish, the following *Declaration of Rights, and Frame of Government,* as the CONSTITUTION of the COMMONWEALTH of MASSACHUSETTS.

Part the First

A Declaration of the Rights of the Inhabitants of the Commonwealth of Massachusetts.[2]

Art. I. All men are born free and equal, and have certain natural, essential, and unalienable rights; among which may be reckoned the right of enjoying and defending their lives and liberties; that of acquiring, possessing, and protecting property; in fine, that of seeking and obtaining their safety and happiness.

II. It is the right as well as the duty of all men in society, publicly, and at stated seasons, to worship the SUPREME BEING, the great creator and preserver of the universe. And no subject shall be hurt, molested, or restrained, in his person, liberty, or estate, for worshipping GOD in the manner and season most agreeable to the dictates of his own conscience; or for his religious profession or sentiments; provided he doth not disturb the public peace, or obstruct others in their religious worship.[2]

---

[2] In reviewing the Declaration of Rights, note that virtually all its provisions used "ought" or "ought not" rather than "shall" or "shall not." As Lutz points out in his commentaries, this language indicated that the Declaration of Rights codified political principles for the easy reference of the citizenry, who could then make decisions about electing or refusing to elect officials based on their compliance with these principles.

[3] Articles II and III of the Declaration of Rights comprised the constitutional authorization for the establishment of religion in Massachusetts. This may strike modern readers as a contradiction of the purpose of a declaration of rights, but the Declaration of Rights listed responsibilities as well as rights, and included provisions designed to enable (and, indeed, require) the citizens to conduct their lives in conformity with the need to preserve the liberties and virtue of the Commonwealth. See generally William G. McLoughlin, *New England Dissent: The Baptists and the Separation of Church and State,* 2 vols. (Cambridge, Mass., 1970); Thomas J. Curry, *The First Freedoms* (New York, 1986).

Note throughout these provisions, and the constitution generally, the emphasis on local government. These provisions and phrases in the Massachusetts Constitution of 1780 reflected the reality of life in the New England states—specifically, the centrality of participation in the life of one's town or other community. See, e.g., Michael Zuckerman, *Peaceable Kingdoms: New England Towns in the Eighteenth Century* (New York, 1970); William E. Nelson, *Americanization of the Common Law: The Impact of Legal Change on Massachusetts Society, 1760–1830* (Cambridge, Mass., 1975).

III. As the happiness of a people, and the good order and preservation of civil government, essentially depend upon piety, religion and morality; and as these cannot be generally diffused through a community, but by the institution of the public worship of GOD, and of public instructions in piety, religion and morality: Therefore, to promote their happiness and to secure the good order and preservation of their government, the people of this Commonwealth have a right to invest their legislature with power to authorize and require, and the legislature shall, from time to time, authorize and require, the several towns, parishes, precincts, and other bodies-politic, or religious societies, to make suitable provision, at their own expense, for the institution of the public worship of GOD, and for the support and maintenance of public protestant teachers of piety, religion and morality, in all cases where such provision shall not be made voluntarily.

And the people of this Commonwealth have also a right to, and do, invest their legislature with authority to enjoin upon all the subjects and attendance upon the instructions of the public teachers aforesaid, at stated times and seasons, if there be any on whose instructions they can conscientiously and conveniently attend.

Provided notwithstanding, that the several towns, parishes, precincts, and other bodies-politic, or religious societies, shall, at all times, have the exclusive right of electing their public teachers, and of contracting with them for their support and maintenance.

And all monies paid by the subject to the support of public worship, and of the public teachers aforesaid, shall, if he require it, be uniformly applied to the support of the public teacher or teachers of his own religious sect or denomination, provided there be any on whose instructions he attends: otherwise it may be paid towards the support of the teacher or teachers of the parish or precinct in which the said monies are raised.

And every denomination of christians, demeaning themselves peaceably, and as good subjects of the Commonwealth, shall be equally under the protection of the law: And no subordination of any one sect or denomination to another shall ever be established by law.

IV. The people of this Commonwealth have the sole and exclusive right of governing themselves as a free, sovereign, and independent state; and do, and forever hereafter shall, exercise and enjoy every power, jurisdiction, and right, which is not, or may not hereafter, be by them expressly delegated to the United States of America, in Congress assembled.

V. All power residing originally in the people, and being derived from them, the several magistrates and officers of government, vested with authority, whether legislative, executive, or judicial, are their substitutes and agents, and are at all times accountable to them.[4]

VI. No man, nor corporation, or association of men, have any other title to obtain advantages, or particular and exclusive privileges, distinct from those of the community, than what arises from the consideration of services rendered to the public; and this title being in nature neither hereditary, nor transmissible to children, or descendants, or relations by blood, the idea of a man born a magistrate, lawgiver, or judge, is absurd and unnatural.

VII. Government is instituted for the common good; for the protection, safety, prosperity and happiness of the people; and not for the profit, honor, or private interest of any one man, family, or class of men: Therefore the people alone have an incontestible, unalienable, and indefeasible right to institute government; and to reform, alter, or totally change the same, when their protection, safety, prosperity and happiness require it.

VIII. In order to prevent those, who are vested with authority, from becoming oppressors, the people have a right, at such periods and in such manner as they shall establish by their frame of government, to cause their public officers to return to private life; and to fill up vacant places by certain and regular elections and appointments.[5]

IX. All elections ought to be free; and all the inhabitants of this Commonwealth, having such qualifications as they shall establish by their frame of government, have an equal right to elect officers, and to be elected, for public employments.

X. Each individual of the society has a right to be protected by it in the enjoyment of his life, liberty and property, according to standing laws. He is obliged, consequently, to contribute his share to the expense of this protection; to give his personal service, or an equivalent, when necessary: But no part of the property of any individual, can, with justice, be taken from him, or applied to public uses without his own consent, or that of the representative body of the people: In fine, the people of this Commonwealth are not controlable by any other laws, than those to which their constitutional representative body have given their consent. And whenever the public exigencies require, that the

---

[4] Article V of the Declaration of Rights stated the principle of political accountability or responsibility. See also the discussion of this point in Richard B. Bernstein's commentary on *The Federalist Nos. 15, 70*, and *78* (Chapter 16 below).

[5] Article VIII of the Declaration of Rights stood for the principle of rotation in office. See also the discussion of this point in Lutz's commentary on the Articles of Confederation (Chapter 12 below).

property of any individual should be appropriated to public uses, he shall receive a reasonable compensation therefor.

XI. Every subject of the Commonwealth ought to find a certain remedy, by having recourse to the laws, for all injuries or wrongs which he may receive in his person, property, or character. He ought to obtain right and justice freely, and without being obliged to purchase it; completely, and without any denial; promptly, and without delay; conformably to the laws.

XII. No subject shall be held to answer for any crime or offence, until the same is fully and plainly, substantially and formally, described to him; or be compelled to accuse, or furnish evidence against himself. And every subject shall have a right to produce all proofs, that may be favorable to him; to meet the witnesses against him face to face, and to be fully heard in his defence by himself, or his council, at his election. And no subject shall be arrested, imprisoned, despoiled, or deprived of his property, immunities, or privileges, put out of the protection of the law, exiled, or deprived of his life, liberty, or estate; but by the judgment of his peers, or the law of the land.[6]

And the legislature shall not make any law, that shall subject any person to a capital or infamous punishment, excepting for the government of the army and navy, without trial by jury.

XIII. In criminal prosecutions, the verification of facts in the vicinity where they happen, is one of the greatest securities of the life, liberty, and property of the citizen.

XIV. Every subject has a right to be secure from all unreasonable searches, and seizures of his person, his houses, his papers, and all his possessions. All warrants, therefore, are contrary to this right, if the cause or foundation of them be not previously supported by oath or affirmation; and if the order in the warrant to a civil officer, to make search in suspected places, or to arrest one or more suspected persons, or to seize their property, be not accompanied with a special designation of the persons or objects of search, arrest, or seizure: and no warrant ought to be issued but in cases, and with the formalities, prescribed by the laws.[7]

---

[6] Article XII of the Declaration of Rights used "shall" language rather than "ought" language, probably because it dealt with that sphere where the state might have greatest power over the individual citizen—power in desperate need of limitation in a free society. Note the similar definite language in Articles XIV, XV, and XXVI—for similar reasons.

Compare Article XII with the Fifth and Sixth Amendments to the United States Constitution. See also Leonard W. Levy, *The Origins of the Fifth Amendment* (New York, 1968).

[7] Compare Article XIV with the Fourth Amendment to the United States Consti-

XV. In all controversies concerning property, and in all suits between two or more persons, except in cases in which it has heretofore been otherways used and practised, the parties have a right to a trial by jury; and this method of procedure shall be held sacred, unless, in causes arising on the high-seas, and such as relate to mariners wages, the legislature shall hereafter find it necessary to alter it.

XVI. The liberty of the press is essential to the security of freedom in a state: it ought not, therefore, to be restrained in this Commonwealth.[8]

XVII. The people have a right to keep and to bear arms for the common defence. And as in time of peace armies are dangerous to liberty, they ought not to be maintained without the consent of the legislature; and the military power shall always be held in an exact subordination to the civil authority, and be governed by it.[9]

XVIII. A frequent recurrence to the fundamental principles of the constitution, and a constant adherence to those of piety, justice, moderation, temperance, industry, and frugality, are absolutely necessary to preserve the advantages of liberty, and to maintain a free government: The people ought, consequently, to have a particular attention to all those principles, in the choice of their officers and representatives: And they have a right to require of their law-givers and magistrates, an exact and constant observance of them, in the formation and execution of the laws necessary for the good administration of the Commonwealth.

XIX. The people have a right, in an orderly and peaceable manner, to assemble to consult upon the common good; give instructions to their representatives; and to request of the legislative body, by the way of addresses, petitions, or remonstrances, redress of the wrongs done them, and of the grievances they suffer.[10]

XX. The power of suspending the laws, or the execution of the laws, ought never to be exercised but by the legislature, or by authority derived from it, to be exercised in such particular cases only as the legislature shall expressly provide for.

---

tution. The people of Massachusetts had particular familiarity with the abuses against which this provision was intended to guard. See, for further discussion, M. H. Smith, *The Writs of Assistance Case* (Berkeley, 1978).

[8] Compare Article XVI with the First Amendment to the United States Constitution. See generally Leonard W. Levy, *Emergence of a Free Press* (New York, 1985).

[9] Compare Article XVII with the Second Amendment to the United States Constitution. Note in particular the limitation of the purpose of the right to keep and bear arms—"for the common defence." Note also the statement of the principle of civil supremacy over the military.

[10] Compare Article XIX with the First Amendment to the United States Constitution.

XXI. The freedom of deliberation, speech and debate, in either house of the legislature, is so essential to the rights of the people, that it cannot be the foundation of any accusation or prosecution, action or complaint, in any other court or place whatsoever.[11]

XXII. The legislature ought frequently to assemble for the redress of grievances, for correcting, strengthening, and confirming the laws, and for making new laws, as the common good may require.

XXIII. No subsidy, charge, tax, impost, or duties, ought to be established, fixed, laid, or levied, under any pretext whatsoever, without the consent of the people, or their representatives in the legislature.

XXIV. Laws made to punish for actions done before the existence of such laws, and which have not been declared crimes by preceding laws, are unjust, oppressive, and inconsistent with the fundamental principles of a free government.[12]

XXV. No subject ought, in any case, or in any time, to be declared guilty of treason or felony by the legislature.

XXVI. No magistrate or court of law shall demand excessive bail or sureties, impose excessive fines, or inflict cruel or unusual punishments.[13]

XXVII. In time of peace no soldier ought to be quartered in any house without the consent of the owner; and in time of war such quarters ought not to be made but by the civil magistrate, in a manner ordained by the legislature.[14]

XXVIII. No person can in any case be subjected to law-martial, or to any penalties or pains, by virtue of that law, except those employed in the army or navy, and except the militia in actual service, but by authority of the legislature.[15]

XXIX. It is essential to the preservation of the rights of every individual, his life, liberty, property and character, that there be an impartial interpretation of the laws, and administration of justice. It is

[11] Compare Article XXI with Article I, section 6, clause 1 of the United States Constitution. These provisions gave constitutional status to the unwritten British constitution's principle of "parliamentary privilege."

[12] Compare Article XXIV with Article I, sections 9 and 10 of the United States Constitution. These constitutional provisions barred *ex post facto* laws. On this point, see also Lutz's commentary on the United States Constitution (Chapter 14 below).

[13] Compare Article XXVI with the Eighth Amendment to the United States Constitution.

[14] Compare Article XXVII with the Third Amendment to the United States Constitution. The people of Massachusetts also had extensive experience in the years between 1765 and 1775 with the abuses which this provision was intended to guard against.

[15] Article XXVIII reinforced the statement of civil supremacy over the military in Article XVII. Again, note the definite language of the provision.

the right of every citizen to be tried by judges as free, impartial and independent as the lot of humanity will admit. It is therefore not only the best policy, but for the security of the rights of the people, and of every citizen, that the judges of the supreme judicial court should hold their offices as long as they behave themselves well; and that they should have honorable salaries ascertained and established by standing laws.[16]

XXX. In the government of this Commonwealth, the legislative department shall never exercise the executive and judicial powers, or either of them: The executive shall never exercise the legislative and judicial powers, or either of them: The judicial shall never exercise the legislative and executive powers, or either of them: to the end it may be a government of laws and not of men.[17]

Part the Second

The Frame of Government.

The people, inhabiting the territory formerly called the Province of Massachusetts-Bay, do hereby solemnly and mutually agree with each other, to form themselves into a free, sovereign, and independent body-politic or state, by the name of THE COMMONWEALTH OF MASSACHUSETTS.

Chapter I. The Legislative Power.[18]
Section I. The General Court.

Art. I. The department of legislation shall be formed by two branches, a *Senate* and *House of Representatives:* each of which shall have a negative on the other.

---

[16] Article XXIX provided that judges shall hold their offices during good behavior, a provision echoed in Article III, section 1 of the United States Constitution. Article XXIX's requirement of fixed judicial salaries was also echoed in Article III, section 1.

The issue of salaries for government officials was a powerful one in colonial politics. At times, the lower houses of the colonial legislatures used their power over salaries to coerce executive and judicial officials; often, colonial royal governors and judges sought to have their salaries paid by the Crown in order to deprive the lower houses of such power. See, e.g., Jack P. Greene, *The Quest for Power* (Chapel Hill, 1963).

[17] Compare the United States Constitution's creation of a system of separated institutions sharing certain powers. On the intellectual history of the doctrine of separation of powers, see generally M. J. C. Vile, *Constitutionalism and the Separation of Powers* (Oxford, 1967); W. B. Gwyn, *The Meaning of the Separation of Powers*, Tulane Studies in Political Science, IX (New Orleans, La., 1965); and Benjamin F. Wright, "The Origins of the Separation of Powers in America," *Economica* 13 (1933): 169–85.

[18] Chapter I of the Frame of Government is called the "Legislative Power;" Chapter

The legislative body shall assemble every year, on the last Wednesday in May, and at such other times as they shall judge necessary; and shall dissolve and be dissolved on the day next preceding the said last Wednesday in May; and shall be styled, THE GENERAL COURT OF MASSACHUSETTS.

II. No bill or resolve of the Senate or House of Representatives shall become a law, and have force as such, until it shall have been laid before the Governor for his revisal: And if he, upon such revision, approve thereof, he shall signify his approbation by signing the same. But if he have any objection to the passing of such bill or resolve, he shall return the same, together with his objections thereto, in writing, to the Senate or House of Representatives, in which soever the same shall have originated; who shall enter the objections sent down by the Governor, at large, on their records, and proceed to reconsider the said bill or resolve: But if, after such reconsideration, two thirds of the said Senate or House of Representatives, shall, notwithstanding the said objections, agree to pass the same, it shall, together with the objections, be sent to the other branch of the legislature, where it shall also be reconsidered, and if approved by two thirds of the members present, shall have the force of a law: But in all such cases the votes of both houses shall be determined by yeas and nays; and the names of the persons voting for, or against, the said bill or resolve, shall be entered upon the public records of the Commonwealth.

And in order to prevent unnecessary delays, if any bill or resolve shall not be returned by the Governor within five days after it shall have been presented, the same shall have the force of a law.[19]

III. The General Court shall forever have full power and authority to erect and constitute judicatories and courts of record, or other courts, to be held in the name of the Commonwealth, for the hearing, trying, and determining of all manner of crimes, offences, pleas, processes, plaints, actions, matters, causes and things, whatsoever, arising or happening within the Commonwealth, or between or concerning persons inhabiting, or residing, or brought within the same; whether the same be criminal or civil, or whether the said crimes be capital or not capital, and whether the said pleas be real, personal, or mixt; and for the awarding and making out of execution thereupon: To which courts and ju-

---

II is called the "Executive Power;" and Chapter III is called the "Judiciary Power." This set of titles underscored the principle set forth in Article XXX of the Declaration of Rights.

[19] Chapter I, section I, article II of the Frame of Government influenced the provision on the qualified veto power of the president in Article I, section 7, clause 2 of the United States Constitution.

dicatories are hereby given and granted full power and authority, from time to time, to administer oaths or affirmations, for the better discovery of truth in any matter in controversy or depending before them.[20]

IV. And further, full power and authority are hereby given and granted to the said General Court, from time to time, to make, ordain, and establish, all manner of wholesome and reasonable orders, laws, statutes, and ordinances, directions and instructions, either with penalties or without; so as the same be not repugnant or contrary to this Constitution, as they shall judge to be for the good and welfare of this Commonwealth, and for the government and ordering thereof, and of the subjects of the same, and for the necessary support and defence of the government thereof; and to name and settle annually, or provide by fixed laws, for the naming and settling all civil officers within the said Commonwealth, the election and constitution of whom are not hereafter in this Form of Government otherwise provided for; and to set forth the several duties, powers and limits; of the several civil and military officers of this Commonwealth, and the forms of such oaths or affirmations as shall be respectively administered unto them for the execution of their several offices and places, so as the same be not repugnant or contrary to this Constitution; and to impose and levy proportional and reasonable assessments, rates, and taxes, upon all the inhabitants of, and persons resident, and estates lying, within the said Commonwealth; and also to impose, and levy reasonable duties and excises, upon any produce, goods, wares, merchandize, and commodities whatsoever, brought into, produced, manufactured, or being within the same; to be issued and disposed of by warrant, under the hand of the Governor of this Commonwealth for the time being, with the advice and consent of the Council, for the public service, in the necessary defence and support of the government of the said Commonwealth, and the protection and preservation of the subjects thereof, according to such acts as are or shall be in force within the same.

And while the public charges of government, or any part thereof, shall be assessed on polls and estates, in the manner that has hitherto been practised, in order that such assessments may be made with equality, there shall be a valuation of estates within the Commonwealth taken anew once in every ten years at least, and as much oftener as the General Court shall order.[21]

---

[20] Compare Chapter I, section I, article III of the Frame of Government with Article III, sections 1 and 2, of the United States Constitution.

[21] Chapter I, section I, article IV of the Frame of Government was a grant of general legislative authority, as opposed to Article I, section 8 of the United States Constitution, which is a limited though extensive grant of legislative authority.

Chapter I
Section II. Senate.[22]

Art. I. There shall be annually[23] elected by the freeholders and other inhabitants of this Commonwealth, qualified as in this Constitution is provided, forty persons to be Counsellors and Senators for the year ensuing their election; to be chosen by the inhabitants of the districts, into which the Commonwealth may from time to time be divided by the General Court for that purpose: And the General Court, in assigning the numbers to be elected by the respective districts, shall govern themselves by the proportion of the public taxes paid by the said districts; and timely make known to the inhabitants of the Commonwealth, the limits of each district, and the number of Counsellors and Senators to be chosen therein; provided, that the number of such districts shall never be less than thirteen; and that no district be so large as to entitle the same to choose more than six Senators.

And the several counties in this Commonwealth shall, until the General Court shall determine it necessary to alter the said districts, be districts for the choice of Counsellors and Senators, (except that the counties of Dukes County and Nantucket shall form one district for that purpose) and shall elect the following number for Counsellors and Senators, viz:

Suffolk	Six	York	Two
Essex	Six	Dukes County	
Middlesex	Five	and Nantucket	One
Hampshire	Four	Worcester	Five
Plymouth	Three	Cumberland	One
Barnstable	One	Lincoln	One
Bristol	Three	Berkshire	Two.

II. The Senate shall be the first branch of the legislature; and the Senators shall be chosen in the following manner, viz: There shall be a meeting on the first Monday in April annually, forever, of the inhabitants of each town in the several counties of this Commonwealth; to

[22] On upper houses in state constitutions, see generally Jackson Turner Main, *The Upper House in Revolutionary America* (Madison, Wisc. 1967).
[23] Chapter I, section II, article I of the Frame of Government (one-year term for senators) built into the Massachusetts Constitution of 1780 the principle, "Where annual elections end, tyranny begins." See also Chapter I, section III, article V of the Frame of Government (representatives); Chapter II, section I, article II (the governor); Chapter II, section II, article II (lieutenant governor); Chapter II, section III, article II (council); Chapter II, section IV, article I (other state officials in the executive branch).

be called by the Selectmen, and warned in due course of law, at least seven days before the first Monday in April, for the purpose of electing persons to be Senators and Counsellors: And at such meetings every male inhabitant of twenty-one years of age and upwards, having a free- hold estate within the Commonwealth, of the annual income of three pounds, or any estate of the value of sixty pounds, shall have a right to give in his vote for the Senators for the district of which he is an inhabitant.[24] And to remove all doubts concerning the meaning of the word "inhabitant" in this constitution, every person shall be considered as an inhabitant, for the purpose of electing and being elected into any office, or place within this State, in that town, district, or plantation, where he dwelleth, or hath his home.

The Selectmen of the several towns shall preside at such meetings impartially; and shall receive the votes of all the inhabitants of such towns present and qualified to vote for Senators, and shall sort and count them in open town meeting, and in presence of the Town Clerk, who shall make a fair record in presence of the Selectmen, and in open town meeting, of the name of every person voted for, and of the number of votes against his name; and a fair copy of this record shall be attested by the Selectmen and the Town-Clerk, and shall be sealed up, directed to the Secretary of the Commonwealth for the time being, with a su- perscription, expressing the purport of the contents thereof, and deliv- ered by the Town-Clerk of such towns, to the Sheriff of the county in which such town lies, thirty days at least before the last Wednesday in May annually; or it shall be delivered into the Secretary's office sev- enteen days at least before the said last Wednesday in May; and the Sheriff of each county shall deliver all such certificates by him received, into the Secretary's office seventeen days before the said last Wednesday in May.

And the inhabitants of plantations unincorporated, qualified as this Constitution provides, who are or shall be empowered and required to assess taxes upon themselves toward the support of government, shall have the same privilege of voting for Counsellors and Senators, in the plantations where they reside, as town inhabitants have in their re- spective towns; and the plantation-meetings for that purpose shall be held annually on the same first Monday in April, at such place in the plantations respectively, as the Assessors thereof shall direct; which Assessors shall have like authority for notifying the electors, collecting and returning the votes, as the Selectmen and Town-Clerks have in

---

[24] Note the property qualification established for voting for senators and counsellors in Chapter I, section II, article II of the Frame of Government.

their several towns, by this Constitution. And all other persons living in places unincorporated (qualified as aforesaid) who shall be assessed to the support of government by the Assessors of an adjacent town, shall have the privilege of giving in their votes for Counsellors and Senators, in the town where they shall be assessed, and be notified of the place of meeting by the Selectmen of the town where they shall be assessed, for that purpose, accordingly.

III. And that there may be a due convention of Senators on the last Wednesday in May annually, the Governor, with five of the Council, for the time being, shall, as soon as may be, examine the returned copies of such records; and fourteen days before the said day he shall issue his summons to such persons as shall appear to be chosen by a majority of voters, to attend on that day, and take their seats accordingly: Provided nevertheless, that for the first year the said returned copies shall be examined by the President and five of the Council of the former Constitution of Government; and the said President shall, in like manner, issue his summons to the persons so elected, that they may take their seats as aforesaid.

IV. The Senate shall be the final judge of the elections, returns and qualifications of their own members, as pointed out in the Constitution; and shall, on the said last Wednesday in May annually, determine and declare who are elected by each district, to be Senators, by a majority of votes: And in case there shall not appear to be the full number of Senators returned elected by a majority of votes for any district, the deficiency shall be supplied in the following manner, viz. The members of the House of Representatives, and such Senators as shall be declared elected, shall take the names of such persons as shall be found to have the highest number of votes in such district, and not elected, amounting to twice the number of Senators wanting, if there be so many voted for; and, out of these, shall elect by ballot a number of Senators sufficient to fill up the vacancies in such district: And in this manner all such vacancies shall be filled up in every district of the Commonwealth; and in like manner all vacancies in the Senate, arising by death, removal out of the State, or otherwise, shall be supplied, as soon as may be after such vacancies shall happen.[25]

V. Provided nevertheless, that no person shall be capable of being elected as a Senator, who is not seized in his own right of a freehold within this Commonwealth, of the value of three hundred pounds at

[25] Compare Chapter I, section II, articles IV, VI, and VII (and Chapter I, section III, article X) of the Frame of Government with Article I, section 5 of the United States Constitution.

least, or possessed of personal estate to the value of six hundred pounds at least, or of both to the amount of the same sum, and who has not been an inhabitant of this Commonwealth for the space of five years immediately preceding his election, and, at the time of his election, he shall be an inhabitant in the district, for which he shall be chosen.[26]

VI. The Senate shall have power to adjourn themselves, provided such adjournments do not exceed two days at a time.

VII. The Senate shall choose its own President, appoint its own officers, and determine its own rules of proceeding.

VIII. The Senate shall be a court with full authority to hear and determine all impeachments made by the House of Representatives, against any officer or officers of the Commonwealth, for misconduct and mal-administration in their offices. But, previous to the trial of every impeachment, the members of the Senate shall respectively be sworn, truly and impartially to try and determine the charge in question, according to evidence. Their judgment, however, shall not extend further than to removal from office and disqualification to hold or enjoy any place of honor, trust, or profit, under this Commonwealth: But the party, so convicted, shall be, nevertheless, liable to indictment, trial, judgment, and punishment, according to the laws of the land.[27]

IX. Not less than sixteen members of the Senate shall constitute a quorum for doing business.

Chapter I.
Section III. House of Representatives.

Art. I. There shall be in the Legislature of this Commonwealth, a representation of the people, annually elected, and founded upon the principle of equality.

II. And in order to provide for a representation of the citizens of this Commonwealth, founded upon the principle of equality, every corporate town, containing one hundred and fifty rateable polls, may elect one Representative: Every corporate town, containing three hundred

[26] Compare the property qualification established by Chapter I, section II, article V of the Frame of Government for office-holding in the senate with the decision not to include an analogous provision in the United States Constitution.

[27] Compare the power to try impeachments granted to the senate in Chapter I, section II, article VIII of the Frame of Government with the analogous provision in Article I, section 3, clause 6 of the United States Constitution. As in Article I, section 2, clause 5 of the United States Constitution, the Massachusetts house of representatives had the power to initiate impeachments. See Chapter I, section III, article VI of the Frame of Government.

and seventy-five rateable polls, may elect two Representatives: Every corporate town, containing six hundred rateable polls, may elect three Representatives; and proceeding in that manner, making two hundred and twenty-five rateable polls the mean increasing number for every additional Representative.

Provided nevertheless, that each town now incorporated, not having one hundred and fifty rateable polls, may elect one Representative: but no place shall hereafter be incorporated with the privilege of electing a Representative, unless there are within the same one hundred and fifty rateable polls.

And the House of Representatives shall have power, from time to time, to impose fines upon such towns as shall neglect to choose and return members to the same, agreeably to this Constitution.

The expenses of travelling to the General Assembly, and returning home, once in every session, and no more, shall be paid by the government, out of the public treasury, to every member who shall attend as seasonably as he can, in the judgment of the House, and does not depart without leave.

III. Every member of the House of Representatives shall be chosen by written votes; and for one year at least next preceding his election shall have been an inhabitant of, and have been seized in his own right of a freehold of the value of one hundred pounds within the town he shall be chosen to represent, or any rateable estate to the value of two hundred pounds; and he shall cease to represent the said town immediately on his ceasing to be qualified as aforesaid.

IV. Every male person, being twenty-one years of age, and resident in any particular town in this Commonwealth for the space of one year next preceding, having a freehold estate within the same town, of the annual income of three pounds, or any estate of the value of sixty pounds, shall have a right to vote in the choice of a Representative or Representatives for the said town.[28]

V. The members of the House of Representatives shall be chosen annually in the month of May, ten days at least before the last Wednesday of that month.

VI. The House of Representatives shall be the Grand Inquest of this Commonwealth; and all impeachments made by them shall be heard and tried by the Senate.

[28] Chapter I, section III, article IV of the Frame of Government established not only the property and other qualifications for voting to elect members of the house of representatives; by Article I, section 2, clause 1 of the United States Constitution, it established the qualifications for voters in elections for the Massachusetts members of the U.S. House of Representatives.

VII. All money-bills shall originate in the House of Representatives; but the Senate may propose or concur with amendments, as on other bills.[29]

VIII. The House of Representatives shall have power to adjourn themselves; provided such adjournment shall not exceed two days at a time.

IX. Not less than sixty members of the House of Representatives shall constitute a quorum for doing business.

X. The House of Representatives shall be the judge of the returns, elections, and qualifications of its own members, as pointed out in the constitution; shall choose their own Speaker; appoint their own officers, and settle the rules and orders of proceeding in their own house: They shall have authority to punish by imprisonment, every person, not a member, who shall be guilty of disrespect to the House, by any disorderly, or contemptuous behaviour, in its presence; or who, in the town where the General Court is sitting, and during the time of its sitting, shall threaten harm to the body or estate of any of its members, for any thing said or done in the House; or who shall assault any of them therefor; or who shall assault, or arrest, any witness, or other person, ordered to attend the House, in his way in going, or returning; or who shall rescue any person arrested by the order of the House.

And no member of the House of Representatives shall be arrested, or held to bail on mean process, during his going unto, returning from, or his attending, the General Assembly.

XI. The Senate shall have the same powers in the like cases; and the Governor and Council shall have the same authority to punish in like cases. Provided, that no imprisonment on the warrant or order of the Govenor, Council, Senate, or House of Representatives, for either of the above described offences, be for a term exceeding thirty days.

And the Senate and House of Representatives may try, and determine, all cases where their rights and privileges are concerned, and which, by the Constitution, they have authority to try and determine, by committees of their own members, or in such other way as they may respectively think best.[30]

---

[29] Article I, section 7, clause 1 of the United States Constitution is virtually identical to Chapter I, section III, article VII of the Frame of Government.

[30] Note the sweeping power to punish offenses against the general court and the governor and council set forth in Chapter I, section III, articles X and XI of the Frame of Government.

Chapter II. Executive Power.
Section I. Governor.[31]

Art. I. There shall be a Supreme Executive Magistrate, who shall be styled, THE GOVERNOR OF THE COMMONWEALTH OF MASSACHUSETTS; and whose title shall be—HIS EXCELLENCY.[32]

II. The Governor shall be chosen annually: And no person shall be eligible to this office, unless at the time of his election, he shall have been an inhabitant of this Commonwealth for seven years next preceding; and unless he shall, at the same time, be seized in his own right, of a freehold within the Commonwealth, of the value of one thousand pounds; and unless he shall declare himself to be of the christian religion.

III. Those persons who shall be qualified to vote for Senators and Representatives within the several towns of this Commonwealth, shall, at a meeting, to be called for that purpose, on the first Monday of April annually, give in their votes for a Governor, to the Selectmen, who shall preside at such meetings; and the Town Clerk, in the presence and with the assistance of the Selectmen, shall, in open town meeting, sort and count the votes, and form a list of the persons voted for, with the number of votes for each person against his name; and shall make a fair record of the same in the town books, and a public declaration thereof in the said meeting; and shall, in the presence of the inhabitants, seal up copies of the said list, attested by him and the Selectmen, and transmit the same to the Sheriff of the county, thirty days at least before the last Wednesday in May; and the thirty days at least before the last Wednesday in May, and the Sheriff shall transmit the same to the Secretary's office seventeen days at least before the said last Wednesday in May; or the Selectmen may cause returns of the same to be made to the office of the Secretary of the Commonwealth seventeen days at least before the said day; and the Secretary shall lay the same before the Senate and the House of Representatives, on the last Wednesday in May, to be by them examined: And in case of an election by a majority of all the votes returned, the choice shall be by them declared and published: But if no person shall have a majority of votes, the House of Representatives shall, by ballot, elect two out of four persons who had the highest number of votes, if so many shall have been voted for;

---

[31] Compare Chapter II, section I of the Frame of Government with Article II of the United States Constitution.

[32] This title was the title given to colonial royal governors as well.

but, if otherwise, out of the number voted for; and make return to the Senate of the two persons so elected; on which, the Senate shall proceed, by ballot, to elect one, who shall be declared Governor.[33]

IV. The Governor shall have authority, from time to time, at his discretion, to assemble and call together the Counsellors of this Commonwealth for the time being; and the Governor, with the said Counsellors, or five of them at least, shall, and may, from time to time, hold and keep a Council, for the ordering and directing the affairs of the Commonwealth, agreeably to the Constitution and the laws of the land.

V. The Governor, with advice of Council, shall have full power and authority, during the session of the General Court, to adjourn or prorogue the same to any time the two Houses shall desire; and to dissolve the same on the day next preceding the last Wednesday in May; and, in the recess of the said Court, to prorogue the same from time to time, not exceeding ninety days in any one recess; and to call it together sooner than the time to which it may be adjourned or prorogued, if the welfare of the Commonwealth shall require the same: And in case of any infectious distemper prevailing in the place where the said Court is next at any time to convene, or any other cause happening whereby danger may arise to the health or lives of the members from their attendance, he may direct the session to be held at some other time the most convenient place within the State.

And the Governor shall dissolve the said General Court on the day next preceding the last Wednesday in May.

VI. In cases of disagreement between the two Houses, with regard to the necessity, expediency or time of adjournment, or prorogation, the Governor, with advice of the Council, shall have a right to adjourn or prorogue the General Court, not exceeding ninety days, as he shall determine the public good shall require.

VII. The Governor of this Commonwealth, for the time being, shall be the commander-in-chief of the army and navy, and of all the military forces of the State, by sea and land; and shall have full power, by himself, or by any commander, or other officer or officers, from time to time, to train, instruct, exercise and govern the militia and navy; and, for the special defence and safety of the Commonwealth, to assemble in martial

---

[33] Chapter II, section I, article III of the Frame of Government provided for direct popular election of the governor, as did the New York Constitution of 1777. These two constitutions cut against the prevailing current of the earlier state constitutions of 1776 and 1777, but the converted colonial charters of Connecticut and Rhode Island as well as those constitutions adopted after the Massachusetts Constitution of 1780, such as the New Hampshire Constitution of 1784, the Pennsylvania Constitution of 1790, and the Georgia Constitution of 1790, called for an elected chief executive officer.

array, and put in warlike posture, the inhabitants thereof, and to lead and conduct them, and with them, to encounter, repel, resist, expel and pursue, by force of arms, as well as by sea as by land, within or without the limits of this Commonwealth, and also to kill, slay and destroy, if necessary, and conquer, by all fitting ways, enterprizes and means whatsoever, all and every such person and persons as shall, at any time hereafter, in a hostile manner, attempt or enterprize the destruction, invasion, detriment, or annoyance of this Commonwealth; and to use and exercise, over the army and navy, and over the militia in actual service, the law martial, in time of war or invasion, and also in time of rebellion, declared by the legislature to exist, as occasion shall necessarily require; and to take and surprise by all ways and means whatsoever, all and every such person or persons, with their ships, arms, ammunition and other goods, as shall, in a hostile manner, invade, or attempt the invading, conquering, or annoying this Commonwealth; and that the Governor be intrusted with all these and other powers, incident to the offices of Captain-General and Commander-in-Chief, and Admiral, to be exercised agreeably to the rules and regulations of the Constitution, and the laws of the land, and not otherwise.

Provided, that the said Governor shall not, at any time hereafter, by virtue of any power by this Constitution granted, or hereafter to be granted to him by the legislature, transport any of the inhabitants of this Commonwealth, or oblige them to march out of the limits of the same, without their free and voluntary consent, or the consent of the General Court; except so far as may be necessary to march or transport them by land or water, for the defence of such part of the State, to which they cannot otherwise conveniently have access.

VIII. The power of pardoning offences, except such as persons may be convicted of before the Senate by an impeachment of the House, shall be in the Governor, by and with the advice of Council: But no charter of pardon, granted by the Governor, with advice of the Council, before conviction, shall avail the party pleading the same, notwithstanding any general or particular expressions contained therein, descriptive of the offence, or offences intended to be pardoned.[34]

IX. All judicial officers, the Attorney-General, the Solicitor-General, all Sheriffs, Coroners, and Registers of Probate, shall be nominated and appointed by the Governor, by and with the advice and consent of

---

[34] Compare the pardoning power conferred on the governor by Chapter II, section I, article VIII of the Frame of Government with that conferred by Article II, section 2, clause 1 of the United States Constitution.

the Council; and every such nomination shall be made by the Governor, and made at least seven days prior to such appointment.[35]

X. The Captains and subalterns of the militia shall be elected by the written votes of the train-band and alarm list of their respective companies, of twenty-one years of age and upwards: The field-officers of Regiments shall be elected by the written votes of the captains and subalterns of their respective regiments: The Brigadiers shall be elected in like manner, by the field officers of their respective brigades: And such officers, so elected, shall be commissioned by the Governor, who shall determine their rank.

The Legislature shall, by standing laws, direct the time and manner of convening the electors, and of collecting votes, and of certifying to the Governor the officers elected.

The Major-Generals shall be appointed by the Senate and House of Representatives, each having a negative upon the other; and be commissioned by the Governor.

And if the electors of Brigadiers, field-officers, captains or subalterns, shall neglect or refuse to make such elections, after being duly notified, according to the laws for the time being, then the Governor, with advice of Council, shall appoint suitable persons to fill such offices.

And no officer, duly commissioned to command in the militia, shall be removed from his office, but by the address of both houses to the Governor, or by fair trial in court martial, pursuant to the laws of the Commonwealth for the time being.

The commanding officers of regiments shall appoint their Adjutants and Quarter-masters; the Brigadiers their Brigade-Majors; and the Major-Generals their Aids: and the Governor shall appoint the Adjutant General.

The Governor, with advice of Council, shall appoint all officers of the continental army, whom by the confederation of the United States it is provided that this Commonwealth shall appoint,—as also all officers of forts and garrisons.

The divisions of the militia into brigades, regiments and companies, made in pursuance of the militia laws now in force, shall be considered as the proper divisions of the militia of this Commonwealth, until the same shall be altered in pursuance of some future law.

XI. No monies shall be issued out of the treasury of this Commonwealth, and disposed of (except such sums as may be appropriated

[35] Compare the nominating power of the governor and council in Chapter II, section I, article IX of the Frame of Government with that of the president and the Senate in Article II, section 2, clause 2 of the United States Constitution.

for the redemption of bills of credit or Treasurer's notes, or for the payment of interest arising thereon) but by warrant under the hand of the Governor for the time being, with the advice and consent of the Council, for the necessary defence and support of the Commonwealth; and for the protection and preservation of the inhabitants thereof, agreeably to the acts and resolves of the General Court.

XII. All public boards, the Commissary-General, all superintending officers of public magazines and stores, belonging to this Commonwealth, and all commanding officers of forts and garrisons within the same, shall, once in every three months, officially and without requisition, and at other times, when required by the Governor, deliver to him an account of all goods, stores, provisions, ammunition, cannon with their appendages, and small arms with their accoutrements, and of all other public property whatever under their care respectively; distinguishing the quantity, number, quality and kind of each, as particularly as may be; together with the condition of such forts and garrisons: And the said commanding officer shall exhibit to the Governor, when required by him, true and exact plans of such forts, and of the land and sea, or harbour or harbours adjacent.

And the said boards, and all public officers, shall communicate to the Governor, as soon as may be after receiving the same, all letters, dispatches, and intelligences of a public nature, which shall be directed to them respectively.

XIII. As the public good requires that the Governor should not be under the undue influence of any of the members of the General Court, by a dependence on them for his support—that he should, in all cases, act with freedom for the benefit of the public—that he should not have his attention necessarily diverted from that object to his private concerns—and that he should maintain the dignity of the Commonwealth in the character of its chief magistrate—it is necessary that he should have an honorable stated salary, of a fixed and permanent value, amply sufficient for those purposes, and established by standing laws: And it shall be among the first acts of the General Court, after the Commencement of this Constitution, to establish such salary by law accordingly.[36]

Permanent and honorable salaries shall also be established by law for the Justices of the Supreme Judicial Court.

And if it shall be found, that any of the salaries aforesaid, so established, are insufficient, they shall, from time to time, be enlarged, as the General Court shall judge proper.

[36] Compare Chapter II, section I, article XIII of the Frame of Government with Article II, section 1, clause 7 of the United States Constitution.

Chapter II.
Section II. Lieutenant-Governor.[37]

Art. I. There shall be annually elected a Lieutenant-Governor of the Commonwealth of Massachusetts, whose title shall be HIS HONOR—and who shall be qualified, in point of religion, property, and residence in the Commonwealth, in the same manner with the Governor: And the day and manner of his election, and the qualifications of the electors, shall be the same as are required in the election of a Governor. The return of the votes for this officer, and the declaration of his election, shall be in the same manner: And if no one person shall be found to have a majority of all the votes returned, the vacancy shall be filled by the Senate and House of Representatives, in the same manner as the Governor is to be elected, in case no one person shall have a majority of the votes of the people to be Governor.

II. The Governor, and in his absence the Lieutenant-Governor, shall be President of the Council, but shall have no vote in Council: And the Lieutenant-Governor shall always be a member of the Council, except when the chair of the Governor shall be vacant.

III. Whenever the chair of the Governor shall be vacant, by reason of his death, or absence from the Commonwealth, or otherwise, the Lieutenant-Governor, for the time being, shall, during such vacancy, perform all the duties incumbent upon the Governor, and shall have and exercise all the powers and authorities, which by this Constitution the Governor is vested with, when personally present.

Chapter II.
Section III. Council, and the Manner of Settling Elections by the Legislature.[38]

Art. I There shall be a Council for advising the Governor in the executive part of government, to consist of nine persons besides the Lieu-

---

[37] Chapter II, section II provided a far more detailed description of the powers and duties of the lieutenant governor than the comparable provisions of the United States Constitution did for the powers and duties of the vice president. Note in particular that, under Chapter II, section II, article III, the lieutenant governor could only exercise the powers and perform the duties of the governor when the office of governor was vacant; it is likely that the short term of office for all offices made it unnecessary for the lieutenant governor in such cases to become governor.

[38] Chapter II, section III continued the longstanding practice in colonial charters and the early state constitutions of associating the governor with a council. The governor of Massachusetts was, by comparison with governors in the other states, comparatively independent of his council.

tenant-Governor, whom the Governor, for the time being, shall have full power and authority, from time to time, at his discretion, to assemble and call together. And the Governor, with the said Counsellors, or five of them at least, shall and may, from time to time, hold and keep a council, for the ordering and directing the affairs of the Commonwealth, according to the laws of the land.

II. Nine Counsellors shall be annually chosen from among the persons returned for Counsellors and Senators, on the last Wednesday in May, by the joint ballot of the Senators and Representatives assembled in one room: And in case there shall not be found, upon the first choice, the whole number of nine persons who will accept a seat in the Council, the deficiency shall be made up by the electors aforesaid from among the people at large; and the number of Senators left shall constitute the Senate for the year. The seats of the persons thus elected from the Senate, and accepting the trust, shall be vacated in the Senate.

III. The Counsellors, in the civil arrangements of the Commonwealth, shall have rank next after the Lieutenant-Governor.

IV. Not more than two Counsellors shall be chosen out of any one district of this Commonwealth.

V. The resolutions and advice of the Council shall be recorded in a register, and signed by the members present; and this record may be called for at any time by either House of the Legislature; and any member of the Council may insert his opinion contrary to the resolution of the majority.

VI. Whenever the office of the Governor and Lieutenant-Governor shall be vacant, by reason of death, absence, or otherwise, then the Council or the major part of them, shall, during such vacancy, have full power and authority, to do, and execute, all and every such acts, matters and things, as the Governor or the Lieutenant-Governor might or could, by virtue of this Constitution, do or execute, if they, or either of them, were personally present.

VII. And whereas the elections appointed to be made by this Constitution, on the last Wednesday in May annually, by the two Houses of the Legislature, may not be completed on that day, the said elections may be adjourned from day to day until the same shall be completed. And the order of elections shall be as follows; the vacancies in the Senate, if any, shall first be filled up; the Governor and Lieutenant-Governor shall then be elected, provided there should be no choice of them by the people: And afterwards the two Houses shall proceed to the election of the Council.

Chapter II.
Section IV. Secretary, Treasurer, Commissary, etc.

Art. I. The Secretary, Treasurer and Receiver-General, and the Commissary-General, Notaries-Public, and Naval-Officers, shall be chosen annually, by joint ballot of the Senators and Representatives in one room. And that the citizens of this Commonwealth may be assured, from time to time, that the monies remaining in the public Treasury, upon the settlement and liquidation of the public accounts, are their property, no man shall be eligible as Treasurer and Receiver-General more than five years successively.

II. The records of the Commonwealth shall be kept in the office of the Secretary, who may appoint his Deputies, for whose conduct he shall be accountable, and he shall attend the Governor and Council, the Senate and House of Representatives, in person, or by his deputies, as they shall respectively require.

Chapter III. Judiciary Power.

Art. I. The tenure that all commission officers shall by law have in their offices, shall be expressed in their respective commissions. All judicial officers, duly appointed, commissioned and sworn, shall hold their offices during good behaviour, excepting such concerning whom there is different provision made in this Constitution: Provided, nevertheless, the Governor, with consent of the Council, may remove them upon the address of both Houses of the Legislature.[39]

II. Each branch of the Legislature, as well as the Governor and Council, shall have authority to require the opinions of the Justices of the Supreme Judicial Court, upon important questions of law, and upon solemn occasions.[40]

III. In order that the people may not suffer from the long continuance in place of any Justice of the Peace, who shall fail of discharging

[39] Chapter III, article I of the Frame of Government authorized the removal of judges by the governor after an address requesting such removal by both houses of the legislature. By contrast, read together, Article III, section 1 and Article II, section 4 of the United States Constitution make clear that the only way to remove a federal judge from office is the impeachment process.

[40] Chapter III, article II of the Frame of Government authorized the issuing of advisory opinions by the justices of the Massachusetts supreme judicial court—that the "judiciary power" was not bound by a requirement that there be an actual case or controversy. Compare the limited grant of judicial power in Article III, section 2 of the United States Constitution; see Lutz's commentary on the federal judicial powers (Chapter 14 below).

the important duties of his office with ability or fidelity, all commissions of Justices of the Peace shall expire and become void, in the term of seven years from their respective dates; and, upon the expiration of any commission, the same may, if necessary, be renewed, or another person appointed, as shall most conduce to the well being of the Commonwealth.

IV. The Judges of Probate of Wills, and for granting letters of administration, shall hold their courts at such place or places, on fixed days, as the convenience of the people shall require. And the Legislature shall, from time to time, hereafter appoint such times and places; until which appointments, the said Courts shall be holden at the times and places which the respective Judges shall direct.

V. All causes of marriage, divorce and alimony, and all appeals from the Judges of Probate, shall be heard and determined by the Governor and Council until the Legislature shall, by law, make other provision.

Chapter IV. Delegates to Congress.[41]

The delegates of this Commonwealth to the Congress of the United States, shall, sometime in the month of June annually, be elected by the joint ballot of the Senate and House of Representatives, assembled together in one room; to serve in Congress for one year, to commence on the first Monday in November then next ensuing. They shall have commissions under the hand of the Governor, and the great seal of the Commonwealth; but may be recalled at any time within the year, and others chosen and commissioned, in the same manner, in their stead.

Chapter V. The University at Cambridge, and Encouragement of Literature, etc. Section I. The University.

Art. I Whereas our wise and pious ancestors, so early as the year one thousand six hundred and thirty six, laid the foundation of Harvard-College, in which University many persons of great eminence have, by the blessing of GOD, been initiated in those arts and sciences, which qualified them for public employments, both in Church and State: And whereas the encouragement of Arts and Sciences, and all good literature, tends to the honor of GOD, the advantage of the christian religion, and

[41] Chapter IV of the Frame of Government was superseded by the adoption of the United States Constitution.

the great benefit of this, and the other United States of America—It is declared, That the PRESIDENT AND FELLOWS OF HARVARD-COLLEGE, in their corporate capacity, and their successors in that capacity, their officers and servants, shall have, hold, use, exercise and enjoy, all the powers, authorities, rights, liberties, privileges, immunities and franchises, which they now have, or are entitled to have, hold, use, exercise and enjoy: And the same are hereby ratified and confirmed unto them, the said President and Fellows of Harvard-College, and to their successors, and to their officers and servants, respectively, forever.

II. And whereas there have been at sundry times, by divers persons, gifts, grants, devises of houses, lands, tenements, goods, chattels, legacies and conveyances, heretofore made, either to Harvard-College in Cambridge, in New-England, or to the President and Fellows of Harvard-College, or to the said College, by some other description, under several charters successively: IT IS DECLARED, That all the said gifts, grants, devises, legacies and conveyances, are hereby forever confirmed unto the President and Fellows of Harvard-College, and to their successors, in the capacity aforesaid, according to the true intent and meaning of the donor or donors, grantor or grantors, devisor or devisors.

III. And whereas by an act of the General Court of the Colony of Massachusetts-Bay, passed in the year one thousand six hundred and forty-two, the Governor and Deputy-Governor, for the time being, and all the magistrates of that jurisdiction, were, with the President, and a number of the clergy in the said act described, constituted the Overseers of Harvard-College: And it being necessary, in this new Constitution of Government, to ascertain who shall be deemed successors to the said Governor, Deputy-Governor and Magistrates: IT IS DECLARED, That the Governor, Lieutenant-Governor, Council and Senate of this Commonwealth, are, and shall be deemed, their successors; who, with the President of Harvard-College, for the time being, together with the ministers of the congregational churches in the towns of Cambridge, Watertown, Charlestown, Boston, Roxbury, and Dorchester, mentioned in the said act, shall be, and hereby are, vested with all the powers and authority belonging, or in any way appertaining to the overseers of Harvard-College; PROVIDED, that nothing herein shall be construed to prevent the Legislature of this Commonwealth from making such alterations in the government of the said university, as shall be conducive to its advantage, and the interest of the republic of letters, in as full a manner as might have been done by the Legislature of the late Province of the Massachusetts-Bay.

Chapter V.
Section II. The Encouragement of Literature, etc.[42]

Wisdom, and knowledge, as well as virtue, diffused generally among the body of the people, being necessary for the preservation of their rights and liberties; and as these depend on spreading the opportunities and advantages of education in the various parts of the country, and among the different orders of the people, it shall be the duty of legislators and magistrates, in all future periods of this Commonwealth, to cherish the interests of literature and the sciences, and all seminaries of them; especially the university at Cambridge, public schools, and grammar schools in the towns; to encourage private societies and public institutions, rewards and immunities, for the promotion of agriculture, arts, sciences, commerce, trades, manufactures, and a natural history of the country; to countenance and inculcate the principles of humanity and general benevolence, public and private charity, industry and frugality, honesty and punctuality in their dealings; sincerity, good humour, and all social affections, and generous sentiments among the people.

Chapter VI. Oaths and Subscriptions; Incompatibility of and Exclusion from Offices; Pecuniary Qualifications; Commissions; Writs; Confirmation of Laws; Habeas Corpus; The Enacting Style; Continuance of Officers; Provision for a future Revisal of the Constitution, etc.

Art. I. Any person chosen Governor, Lieutenant-Governor, Counsellor, Senator, or Representative, and accepting the trust, shall, before he proceed to execute the duties of his place or office, make and subscribe the following declaration, viz.—

"I, A. B. do declare, that I believe the christian religion, and have a firm persuasion of its truth; and that I am seized and possessed, in my own right, of the property required by the Constitution as one qualification for the office or place to which I am elected."[43]

[42] Chapter V, section II of the Frame of Government stated a basic principle of the political thought of the Revolutionary generation—that an informed and enlightened citizenry was a precondition of free society and republican government.
[43] In setting forth the oath of office, Chapter VI, article I of the Frame of Government also supplemented Articles II and III of the Declaration of Rights in establishing a religious test for officeholding—that only Christians could hold political office in Massachusetts. Compare Article VI, section 3 of the United States Constitution, forbidding religious test oaths for officeholding.

And the Governor, Lieutenant-Governor, and Counsellors, shall make and subscribe the said declaration, in the presence of the two Houses of Assembly; and the Senators and Representatives first elected under this Constitution, before the President and five of the Council of the former Constitution, and, forever afterwards, before the Governor and Council for the time being.

And every person chosen to either of the places or offices aforesaid, as also any person appointed or commissioned to any judicial, executive, military, or other office under the government, shall, before he enters on the discharge of the business of his place or office, take and subscribe the following declaration, and oaths or affirmations, viz.—

"I, A. B. do truly and sincerely acknowledge, profess, testify and declare, that the Commonwealth of Massachusetts is, and of right ought to be, a free, sovereign and independent State; and I do swear, that I will bear true faith and allegiance to the said Commonwealth, and that I will defend the same against traitorous conspiracies and all hostile attempts whatsoever: And that I do renounce and adjure all allegiance, subjection and obedience to the King, Queen or Government of Great Britain, (as the case may be) and every other foreign power whatsoever: And that no foreign Prince, Person, Prelate, State or Potentate, hath, or ought to have, any jurisdiction, superiority, pre-eminence, authority, dispensing or other power, in any matter, civil, ecclesiastical or spiritual, within this Commonwealth; except the authority and power which is or may be vested by their Constituents in the Congress of the United States: And I do further testify and declare, that no man or body of men hath or can have any right to absolve or discharge me from the obligation of this oath, declaration or affirmation; and that I do make this acknowledgment, profession, testimony, declaration, denial, re-nunciation and abjuration, heartily and truly, according to the common meaning and acceptation of the foregoing words, without any equivo-cation, mental evasion, or secret reservation whatsoever. So help me GOD."[44]

"I, A. B. do solemnly swear and affirm, that I will faithfully and impartially discharge and perform all the duties incumbent on me

[44] Chapter VI, article I's second oath of office served several functions. First, it was a loyalty oath, designed to weed out Loyalist sympathizers from the class of potential officeholders in Massachusetts. Second, its requirement that the oath-taker renounce all allegiances to and deny all authority of any "foreign Prince, Person, Prelate, State or Potentate" in "any matter, civil, ecclesiastical or spiritual" disqualified all members of the Roman Catholic Church from holding office under the constitution. This point was emphasized by the statement that no individual or group could release the oath-taker from this obligation—a reference to the presumed power of the pope to relieve Catholics from oaths contrary to the doctrines of the church.

as   ; according to the best of my abilities and understanding, agreeably to the rules and regulations of the Constitution, and the laws of this Commonwealth." "So help me GOD."

PROVIDED always, that when any person, chosen or appointed as aforesaid, shall be of the denomination of the people called Quakers, and shall decline taking the said oaths, he shall make his affirmation in the foregoing form, and subscribe the same, omitting the words "*I do swear,*" "*and adjure,*" "*oath or,*" "*and abjuration,*" in the first oath; and in the second oath, the words "*swear and;*" and in each of them the words "*So help me* GOD;" subjoining instead thereof, "*This I do under the pains and penalties of perjury.*"[45]

And the said oaths or affirmations shall be taken and subscribed by the Governor, Lieutenant Governor, and Counsellors, before the President of the Senate, and the presence of the two Houses of Assembly; and by the Senators and Representatives first elected under this Constitution, before the President and five of the Council of the former Constitution; and forever afterwards before the Governor and Council for the time being: And by the residue of the officers aforesaid, before such persons and in such manner as from time to time shall be prescribed by the Legislature.

II. No Governor, Lieutenant Governor, or Judge of the Supreme Judicial Court, shall hold any other office or place, under the authority of this Commonwealth, except such as by this Constitution they are admitted to hold, saving that the Judges of the said Court may hold the offices of Justices of the Peace through the State; nor shall they hold any other place or office, or receive any pension or salary from any other State or Government or Power whatever.

No person shall be capable of holding or exercising at the same time, within this State, more than one of the following offices, viz:— Judge of Probate—Sheriff—Register of Probate—or Register of Deeds— and never more than any two offices which are to be held by appointment of the Governor, or the Governor and Council, or the Senate, or the House of Representatives, or by the election of the people of the State at large, or of the people of any county, military offices and the offices of Justices of the Peace excepted, shall be held by one person.

No person holding the office of Judge of the Supreme Judicial Court—Secretary—Attorney General—Solicitor General—Treasurer or Receiver General—Judge of Probate—Commissary General—President,

[45] Chapter VI, article I also represented something of a gain in religious liberty in its permission to Quakers, who do not believe in taking oaths, to make affirmations instead.

Professor, or Instructor of Harvard College—Sheriff—Clerk of the House of Representatives—Register of Probate—Register of Deeds—Clerk of the Supreme Judicial Court—Clerk of the Inferior Court of Common Pleas—or Officer of the Customs, including in this description Naval Officers—shall at the same time have a seat in the Senate or House of Representatives; but their being chosen or appointed to, and accepting the same, shall operate as a resignation of their seat in the Senate or House of Representatives; and the place so vacated shall be filled up.

And the same rule shall take place in case any judge of the said Supreme Judicial Court, or Judge of Probate, shall accept a seat in Council; or any Counsellor shall accept of either of those offices or places.

And no person shall ever be admitted to hold a seat in the Legislature, or any office of trust or importance under the Government of this Commonwealth, who shall, in the due course of law, have been convicted of bribery or corruption in obtaining an election or appointment.[46]

III. In all cases where sums of money are mentioned in this Constitution, the value thereof shall be computed in silver at six shillings and eight pence per ounce: And it shall be in the power of the Legislature from time to time to increase such qualifications, as to property, of the persons to be elected to offices, as the circumstances of the Commonwealth shall require.

IV. All commissions shall be in the name of the Commonwealth of Massachusetts, signed by the Governor, and attested by the Secretary or his Deputy, and have the great seal of the Commonwealth affixed thereto.

V. All writs, issuing out of the clerk's office in any of the Courts of law, shall be in the name of the Commonwealth of Massachusetts: They shall be under the seal of the Court from whence they issue: They shall bear test of the first Justice of the Court to which they shall be returnable, who is not a party, and be signed by the clerk of such court.[47]

VI. All the laws which have heretofore been adopted, used and approved in the Province, Colony or State of Massachusetts Bay, and

[46] On the problem of plural officeholding in colonial Massachusetts, an abuse against which Chapter VI, article II of the Frame of Government was directed, see Eileen Brennan, *Plural Office-Holding in Massachusetts* (Chapel Hill, 1943). Compare also Article I, section 6, clause 2 of the United States Constitution, which bars plural officeholding crossing the lines between legislative, executive, and judicial branches.

[47] Chapter VI, articles IV and V of the Frame of Government replaced the colonial practice of having all writs and commissions run in the name of the king or queen of Great Britain. At the federal level, this matter was dealt with by statute.

usually practiced on in the Courts of law, shall still remain and be in full force, until altered or repealed by the Legislature; such parts only excepted as are repugnant to the rights and liberties contained in this Constitution.[48]

VII. The privilege and benefit of the writ of *habeas corpus* shall be enjoyed in the Commonwealth in the most free, easy, cheap, expeditious and ample manner; and shall not be suspended by the Legislature, except upon the most urgent and pressing occasions, and for a limited time not exceeding twelve months.[49]

VIII. The enacting style, in making and passing all acts, statutes and laws, shall be—"Be it enacted by the Senate and House of Representatives, in General Court assembled, and by the authority of the same."

IX. To the end there may be no failure of justice or danger arise to the Commonwealth from a change of the Form of Government—all officers, civil and military, holding commissions under the government and people of Massachusetts Bay in New-England, and all other officers of the said government and people, at the time this Constitution shall take effect, shall have, hold, use, exercise and enjoy all the powers and authority to them granted or committed, until other persons shall be appointed in their stead: And all courts of law shall proceed in the execution of the business of their respective departments; and all the executive and legislative officers, bodies and powers shall continue in full force, in the enjoyment and exercise of all their trusts, employments and authority; until the General Court and the supreme and executive officers under this Constitution are designated and invested with their respective trusts, powers and authority.

X. In order the more effectually to adhere to the principles of the Constitution, and to correct those violations which by any means may be made therein, as well as to form such alterations as from experience shall be found necessary—the General Court, which shall be in the year of our Lord one thousand seven hundred and ninety-five, shall issue

[48] Chapter VI, articles VI and VIII of the Frame of Government govern the transition from the revamped colonial charter to the new constitution.

[49] Compare the precise language of Chapter VI, article VII—conferring only on the legislature a limited power to suspend the writ of habeas corpus (a writ by which a court can inquire into the legality of the reason for which a person is being detained by government)—with Article I, section 9, clause 2 of the United States Constitution, which is silent on which officer or institution of the federal government may suspend the writ. In the first year of the Civil War, President Abraham Lincoln argued that the lack of a specific limit on this power meant that he could exercise it; however, he later secured legislation from Congress that approved the suspension retroactively. See generally William Duker, *A Constitutional History of Habeas Corpus* (Westport, Conn., 1980).

precepts to the Selectmen of the several towns, and to the Assessors of the unincorporated plantations, directing them to convene the qualified voters of their respective towns and plantations for the purpose of collecting their sentiments on the necessity or expediency of revising the Constitution, in order to amendments.

And if it shall appear by the returns made, that two thirds of the qualified voters throughout the State, who shall assemble and vote in consequence of the said precepts, are in favor of such revision or amendment, the General Court shall issue precepts, or direct them to be issued from the Secretary's office to the several towns, to elect Delegates to meet in Convention for the purpose aforesaid.

The said Delegates to be chosen in the same manner and proportion as their Representatives in the second branch of the Legislature are by this Constitution to be chosen.[50]

XI. This form of government shall be enrolled on parchment, and deposited in the Secretary's office, and be a part of the laws of the land—and printed copies thereof shall be prefixed to the book containing the laws of this Commonwealth, in all future editions of the said laws.

JAMES BOWDOIN, *President.*
Attest. SAMUEL BARRETT, *Secretary.*

---

[50] Chapter VI, article X of the Frame of Government was the sole part of the Massachusetts Constitution of 1780 to deal with the question of amending or revising the constitution. Compare Article V of the United States Constitution.

XII

The Articles of Confederation

1781

COMMENTARY BY DONALD S. LUTZ

THE SECOND CONTINENTAL CONGRESS RESOLVED on June 11, 1776, to create a committee to draft articles of confederation. The debate on the proposal continued intermittently in Congress as the committee from time to time presented pieces of its work. The overall proposal was approved by Congress on November 15, 1777; and on June 26, 1778, a form for ratification by the states was finally presented. Eight states signed it almost immediately, but other ratifications dribbled in until March 1, 1781, when Maryland became the last to ratify. The next day, Congress assembled for the first time under the Articles of Confederation, America's first national constitution.

The text of the Articles of Confederation looked both forward and backward. The very first line said "we the undersigned," the traditional style for opening foundation documents since the Mayflower Compact (1620). At the end, there was a list of signatures in the form commonly used during the colonial era. These signatures were grouped by state, and at the beginning of the Articles the fact that the agreement was made by delegates of states rather than individuals was underscored by listing the states in geographical order from north to south, not once but twice. Article I contains the phrase "The United States of America," which had been used in the Declaration of Independence for the first time in American history. This phrase also resonates with the opening line in the preamble to the United States Constitution, but in the

Articles of Confederation the phrase was not designed to echo other documents as much as it was to indicate that the agreement was one among states. This point was reinforced by Article II which provided that "Each state retains its sovereignty, freedom and independence," as well as any powers not expressly granted to the United States.

The Articles of Confederation emphasized so heavily its status as a compact among the states that the framers felt a need to provide language reminding readers that they were indeed engaged in a common cause as well. Articles III and IV referred to the states entering into "a firm league of friendship" to "perpetuate mutual friendship and intercourse." The preamble called the document "Articles of Confederation and perpetual Union," and perpetual union was mentioned again in Article XIII.

There were curious echoes of colonial documents. For example, Article V provided in part that "No state shall be represented in Congress by less than two, nor by more than seven Members," which was the range suggested by Benjamin Franklin in the Albany Plan of Union in 1754, and more or less followed in the Continental Congress before the adoption of the Articles. Franklin's idea for three-year terms was also echoed in Article V insofar as no delegate could serve more than three one-year terms over any six-year period. In practice, this meant that delegates usually served for three years and then went out of office for at least three years. This provision for rotation in office and the prohibition on multiple office-holding were common provisions in state constitutions.

The Articles of Confederation had several significant flaws. The single-house Congress had absolutely no coercive power over states or individuals. Congress could apportion federal expenses among the states according to its system of land values, but it could not force states to pay their quotas. Throughout the revolutionary era, a few states paid as much as 70 percent of their allocations, but most paid far less. Georgia, in fact, never contributed a penny toward its federal tax bill. Therefore, although the Articles of Confederation authorized Congress to borrow money, Congress had no means to repay its debt. Congress could also ask the states to raise soldiers to fight the war; but, depending upon their military and financial situations, the states either complied or ignored Congress's requests.

Congress had the power to enter into treaties but it could not enforce them. The states flagrantly violated the Treaty of Paris of 1783 that ended the war with Great Britain, thus affording an excuse for the British retention of forts on American territory. Since Congress had no mechanism to regulate commerce, states were free to establish their own trade patterns, both foreign and interstate. A labyrinth of customs duties developed as states enacted tariffs against each others goods. The failure to establish a unified trade policy meant that Congress could not effectively counteract discriminatory British and Spanish practices, especially those acts that barred American goods and ships from their traditional trading partners in the West Indies.

To correct these shortcomings, Congress repeatedly tried to amend the Articles of Confederation. Article XIII provided that Congress propose amendments and that all state legislatures be required to adopt any alteration. Every attempt to amend the Articles failed—some amendments never got out of Congress, while those that were submitted to the states never received the necessary unanimous ratification. Several amendments were adopted by eleven or twelve states, but a small minority always thwarted efforts to correct glaring problems.

Despite its weaknesses, the Articles contained beneficial provisions, many of which were incorporated into the Constitution of 1787. That the Articles were wholly replaced by the Constitution of 1787 is not exactly the case. It would be more accurate to say that the 1787 document, although providing for a fundamentally different kind of government, was generally constructed around an amended Articles of Confederation. Depending upon how one counts words and provisions, from one-half to two-thirds of what appears in the Articles was retained in the Federalist Constitution of 1787.

For example, sections 1 and 2 of Article IV in the Constitution were taken almost entirely from Article IV of the Articles of Confederation, including the wording for "full faith and credit," "privileges and immunities," and the return of interstate fugitives. The admission of new states found in section 3 of Article IV has its counterpart in Article XI of the Articles. The republican guarantee of section 4 of Article IV has its counterpart in Article III of the Articles. Article IX of the Articles is a specific grant of power to Congress, and while it was not nearly as broad a grant as found in the Constitution, it was structurally similar. Toward the end of Article IX there was a list of prohibitions on national powers similar to that found in Article I, Section 9 of the Constitution. Article VI was a list of prohibitions on state governments that paralleled Article I, Section 10 of the Constitution.

Buried in Article IV of the Articles was an innovation of considerable importance for the later United States Constitution, but whose implications were not fully utilized in the Articles. Article IV in the Articles of Confederation states: ". . . the free inhabitants of each of these states . . . shall be entitled to all the privileges and immunities of free citizens in the several states." These privileges and immunities were then enumerated as applying to the ability to move between states whether this movement was to change residence or simply to visit, to engage in trade and commerce on an equal footing with the other citizens in the state to which one may have travelled, to be subject to the same taxes and restrictions as other citizens of the state entered, and to move one's property from one state to another.

The implication of a *United* States of America was that one had privileges and immunities that one might not have without a federal government. The extent of such privileges and immunities constituted the basis for a federal citizenship as opposed to citizenship in a given state, because one carried these privileges and immunities across state borders. These ideas took ultimate shape in Section 2 of Article IV of the Constitution: "The Citizens of each State shall be entitled to all privileges and immunities of Citizens in the several States." This is a fundamental expression of federalism because it means that every American is simultaneously a citizen of the United States and of the state wherein he or she resides. One of the many implications of Section 2 is that Americans are directly subject to laws made by either Congress or their state legislature, and face trial in either a state or federal court system.

The Articles set up what amounts to a national court system in Article IX. This court system functioned only to adjudicate disputes between states, not individuals, because the Confederation Congress could pass no laws directly affecting individuals. Therefore, its courts could not hold individuals to account for anything. When Congress was given the power by the Constitution of 1787 to affect individuals directly, the notion of dual citizenship was revolutionized. National citizenship was expanded to the extent that the national government could directly affect individuals. By the same token, the invention of dual citizenship in the Articles of Confederation structured the way in which national citizenship operated later in the United States Constitution. The invention of dual citizenship in the Articles, and then the transfer of this concept to the national Constitution in 1787, was the legal basis for the operation of federalism in all of its many manifestations, including a dual court system.

Without the Articles of Confederation, and thus without dual citizenship, there was no certainty that the United States Constitution would have taken its present form. Indeed, it is possible that something other than the extremes—a unitary government without states or a loose league of independent, sovereign states—would have been very difficult to visualize in either theory or practice. Put another way, the Articles of Confederation was like a vessel waiting to be loaded. Not only did its contents, when experienced in practice, suggest what needed to be added; but when the new substance of the United States Constitution was added, the older vessel determined the basic shape.

The structure of government under the Articles differed from that of the national government of 1789 in four basic respects: the Confederation Congress had a narrower grant of power; it was a unicameral legislature where each state had one vote. Congress was presided over by a single president chosen annually by the delegates. The president served as a sort of speaker of the house. When Congress was not in session its executive was a Committee of the States, not a single executive, comprised of one delegate from each state; and the court was directly a creature of Congress. By comparison, the state constitutions were characterized by a weak executive, often under the sway of a committee appointed or elected by the legislature, and a court system directly under the legislature. In these important respects, the Articles of Confederation was more reflective of existing institutions in state constitutions than of any independent theorizing about the best institutions for a national government. Both with respect to the limited grant of power and the style of institutions described, the Articles of Confederation represented a straightforward extension of colonial American political thought to national government.

The looseness of the Confederation and its inherent weakness resembled the Iroquois Confederation, except in one important respect. The Iroquois Confederation required tribal unanimity for all concerted action; the Articles of Confederation required unanimity only when amending the document. Otherwise, approval by seven states for most matters and nine states for important legislation was required. Approval by nine of the states in the Committee of the States was also required to execute any of the powers given it by the United States in Congress assembled. Admission of new states also required the approval of nine states.

This brings us to an interesting aspect of the Articles in comparison with the Constitution. James Madison made much in *The Federalist No. 10* of something known as the extended republic. Modern analysts credit the notion of the extended republic as being at the heart of the Madisonian model and thus an integral part of the theory underlying the United States Constitution. The extended republic was two constitutional provisions—the requirement that nine states approve the Constitution before it is ratified, and the provision for admitting new states. With either of these two provisions missing, there would have been no extended republic. They were the document's necessary and sufficient conditions.

First, why did the framers of the Constitution pick the number nine instead of, say, a majority of seven? Why not conclude that any two or more states ratifying would constitute the United States? The answer to the last question is rather obvious. A nation of two, three, or four states would have left at least nine or ten independent nations, only a marginal improvement over thirteen. A majority of seven would have been better still, but what if these seven were composed of only small states or states from only two regions? The delegates to the Constitutional Convention knew that the new nation had to have all three of the states with the largest populations—Massachusetts, Pennsylvania, and Virginia, as well as the strategically located state of New York. With anything less, the nation would be too small and too fragmented for the system to work as designed. The number nine seemed to offer a good chance that three of the most populous states would be included, especially when they did not expect Rhode Island to go along with any plan. A random list of nine out of twelve seemed to provide for a combination of states that would be extensive in size and population because most of the large states were probably included.

Familiarity with state politics led the Federalists to expect ratification by Pennsylvania, but the situation in Massachusetts, Virginia, and especially New York was far from reassuring. It was also hoped that as more states ratified, the remaining holdouts would be caught in a bandwagon effect. Thus, simple political calculations told them that at least nine states would be needed for the new nation to survive, and such a nation would inevitably be extensive.

At the same time, there was considerable experience with a nine-state requirement in the Confederation Congress. As flawed as the Articles of Confederation had been, it had structured an experience that led Americans to expect a nine-state approval as the standard for agreement. Nine states constituted almost a two-thirds majority. This was a litmus test the framers understood; it was a majority that helped lead the framers in 1787 to adopt a similar requirement for ratifying the Constitution. If it worked, they would have an extended republic.

Yet another reason justified the nine states requirement of Article V. The requirement of unanimous consent by all thirteen states for amendment of the Articles effectively doomed all attempts to amend the Articles between 1781 and its replacement by the Constitution in 1789. And yet the framers of the Constitution recognized that so important a decision as the replacement of one national constitution by another required a margin of acceptance greater than a simple majority. Nine states seemed to strike the balance between these competing beliefs—exceeding a simple majority by enough to recognize the importance of the step being taken, yet not so great as to present an insurmountable obstacle to success. (Similar considerations governed the amendment procedure set forth in Article V of the Constitution.)

Without the Articles of Confederation, the extended republic would have had to be borrowed from the writings of Europeans as an untested experiment with little chance of acceptance by a skeptical public, and the decision rule for ratification would have been based on something other than reasonable expectations derived from past political experience. On the other hand, Americans had learned from a decade of experience that government on a continental basis was possible, in certain respects desireable; and that a stable, effective national government required more than an extended republic—it also needed some power that could be applied directly to individual citizens. Experience also convinced them that the national government should have limited powers, and that state governments could not be destroyed. There was a logic to experience that no amount of reading in political theory could shake.

Providing for an amendment process was one of the most innovative aspects of both federal constitutions. Even more daring was the provision for admitting new states. History showed few instances when a nation added new territory without treating it as a conquered land. Even when new units were added on an equal footing, these were already existing states. Contrary to such standard historical practice, the founders proposed the addition in future years of new states from territories which were then only sparsely, if at all, settled. (In the Articles, provision was also made for adding Canada.) Today, we take the possibility of adding new states for granted, but the Articles of Confederation was of major historical importance for first containing this extraordinarily liberal provision, and for passing it on to the United States Constitution of 1787. It guaranteed the building of an extensive republic.

Both provisions in the Federalist Constitution that served to create Madison's extended republic were also found in the Articles of Confederation. If the Articles of Confederation already defined an extended republic, then what was the major advantage of the Constitution? Why did Madison make so much of something already found in a document he did not respect? He did so, not because the proposed Constitution created an extensive republic, but because the national government would affect the citizens of this extended republic *directly*. It was the combination of an extensive republic and direct power over individual citizens that produced the effect Madison wanted. Madison may have borrowed the language of David Hume to describe the advantages of an extended republic, but the fact of an extended republic was handed to him through the Articles of Confederation, and his own experience as a citizen in an extended republic had to be decisive. Furthermore, the experience of living under the Articles provided him with the best possible school for understanding the crucial element that needed to be added if we were to have a stable, effective government for an extended republic—a direct connection between the national government and its citizens. This, in turn, required dual citizenship, the basis for which already existed in the Articles of Confederation, because experience showed the state governments would have to remain.

As noted above the Declaration of Independence and Articles of Confederation together formed America's first national compact. The Declaration of Independence and the United States Constitution of 1787 together formed the second national compact under which Americans still live today. The second compact, did not so much replace the first as evolve it. The second compact built upon the first one as a revision in an earlier experiment that had been found to be flawed. The United States of America was not simply founded in 1787, but refounded upon a base that had been laid earlier in the Articles of Confederation.

For Further Reading

Merrill Jensen. *The Articles of Confederation: An Interpretation of the Socio-Constitutional History of the American Revolution, 1774–1781.* Madison, Wisc., 1940.

Merrill Jensen. *The New Nation: A History of the United States During the Confederation, 1781–1789.* New York, 1950.

Forrest McDonald. *E Pluribus Unum: The Formation of the American Republic, 1776–1790.* Boston, 1965.

Andrew C. McLaughlin. *Confederation and Constitution, 1781–1789.* New York, 1906.

Richard B. Morris. *The American Revolution Reconsidered.* New York, 1967.

Richard B. Morris. *The Forging of the Union, 1781–1789.* New York, 1987.

Jack N. Rakove. *The Beginnings of National Politics: An Interpretative History of the Continental Congress.* New York, 1979.

Gordon S. Wood. *The Creation of the American Republic, 1776–1787.* Chapel Hill, 1969.

[Articles of Confederation]

[NOVEMBER 15, 1787]

To all to whom these Presents shall come, we the under signed Delegates of the States affixed to our Names send greeting. Whereas the Delegates of the United States of America in Congress assembled did on the fifteenth day of November, in the Year of Our Lord One Thousand Seven Hundred and Seventy seven, and in the Second Year of the Independence of America agree to certain articles of Confederation and perpetual Union between the States of Newhampshire, Massachusetts-bay, Rhodeisland and Providence Plantations, Connecticut, New York, New Jersey, Pennsylvania, Delaware, Maryland, Virginia, North-Carolina, South-Carolina and Georgia in the Words following, viz, "Articles of Confederation and perpetual Union between the States of Newhampshire, Massachusetts-bay, Rhodeisland and Providence Plantations, Connecticut, New-York, New-Jersey, Pennsylvania, Delaware, Maryland, Virginia, North-Carolina, South-Carolina and Georgia.

Article I. The Stile of this confederacy shall be "The United States of America."

Article II. Each state retains its sovereignty, freedom and independence, and every Power, Jurisdiction and right, which is not by this confederation expressly delegated to the United States, in Congress assembled.[1]

Engrossed manuscript, Papers of Continental Congress, National Archives. Reprinted from Merrill Jensen et al., eds. *The Documentary History of the Ratification of the Constitution* (Madison, Wisc., 1976), I: 86–94. According to Jensen, "The engrossed document does not have a title. This heading is endorsed on the outside of the document. The title page of the printed pamphlet sent to the states reads 'Articles of Confederation and Perpetual Union Between the States of,' followed by the names of the states from New Hampshire to Georgia. For a careful analysis of the test of the engrossed Articles, see Julian P. Boyd, *The Articles of Confederation and Perpetual Union* (*Old South Leaflets*, Nos. 228–29 [Boston, Mass., 1960])."

[1] This "reserved powers" clause was left out of the United States Constitution as originally written, but added later as the Tenth Amendment. Compare the wording here with that amendment and note the important omission of the word "expressly" which severely narrowed the delegation of the Confederation Congress's powers.

Article III. The said states hereby severally[2] enter into a firm league of friendship with each other, for their common defence, the security of their Liberties, and their mutual and general welfare, binding themselves to assist each other, against all force offered to, or attacks made upon them, or any of them, on account of religion, sovereignty, trade, or any other pretence whatever.

Article IV. The better to secure and perpetuate mutual friendship and intercourse among the people of the different states in this union, the free inhabitants of each of these states, paupers, vagabonds and fugitives from Justice excepted, shall be entitled to all privileges and immunities of free citizens in the several states; and the people of each state shall have free ingress and regress[3] to and from any other state, and shall enjoy therein all the privileges of trade and commerce, subject to the same duties, impositions[4] and restrictions as the inhabitants thereof respectively,[5] provided that such restriction shall not extend so far as to prevent the removal of property imported into any state, to any other state of which the Owner is an inhabitant; provided also that no imposition, duties or restriction shall be laid by any state, on the property of the united states, or either of them.

If any Person guilty of, or charged with treason, felony, or other high misdemeanor in any state, shall flee from Justice, and be found in any of the united states, he shall upon demand of the Governor or executive power, of the state from which he fled, be delivered up and removed to the state having jurisdiction of his offence.

Full faith and credit shall be given in each of these states to the records, acts and judicial proceedings of the courts and magistrates of every other state.[6]

Article V. For the more convenient management of the general interests of the united states,[7] delegates shall be annually appointed in

---

[2] "Severally" means "separately" and here implies both that the states were separate entities and that they entered into the agreement through their own consent and without being forced.

[3] Free to enter and leave.

[4] An "imposition" is a tax or a fine.

[5] A citizen of each state shall have the same privileges and immunities as a citizen of the United States—the latter here described as a citizen of the "several states." The privileges and immunities described in this section are thus protected in state courts as well as in federal court, and neither state nor national legislatures may take them away.

[6] Compare all of Article IV here with Article IV of the United States Constitution of 1787. They are essentially the same, with a change in the order and wording of the provisions.

[7] For the most part, delegates to the Confederation Congress were elected by their

such manner as the legislature of each state shall direct, to meet in Congress on the first Monday in November, in every year, with a power reserved to each state, to recal its delegates, or any of them, at any time within the year, and to send others in their stead, for the remainder of the Year.

No state shall be represented in Congress by less than two, nor by more than seven Members;[8] and no person shall be capable of being a delegate for more than three years in any term of six years; nor shall any person, being a delegate, be capable of holding any office under the united states,[9] for which he, or another for his benefit receives any salary, fees or emolument[10] of any kind.

Each state shall maintain its own delegates in a meeting of the states, and while they act as members of the committee of the states.[11]

In determining questions in the united states, in Congress assembled, each state shall have one vote.[12]

---

state legislatures. In Connecticut and Rhode Island, however, congressional delegates were elected directly by the people. Under the Constitution of 1787, legislative election of United States senators was retained until changed to popular election by the Seventeenth Amendment.

[8] This refers to the size of each state's delegation in Congress. Each state had only one vote in the proceedings, so the state would cast its vote according to the wishes of the majority of the delegation from that state. This was done, presumably, to allow for a more representative body while at the same time providing for the equality of states. The larger a state, the more diverse it was presumed to be, and thus the more delegates were needed to represent the different interests within the state. For example, when Connecticut had a legislature evenly divided into two factions, it would send a delegate from each faction and a third one who either belonged to neither faction or was trusted by both. Still, this gave the larger states more influence since they had more people who could speak in Congress, more people to go around convincing others to support their position, and more chance to send outstanding leaders to argue its position. Most states elected four or five delegates. Since serving in Congress was sometimes onerous, states were usually represented at one time by only three or four delegates at any one time. Some states went for long periods without a delegation.

[9] This prohibition on holding more than one office was known at that time as the separation of powers. The term is not used here, but the prohibition against multiple officeholding that was common in state constitutions is borrowed here and later became the basis for the separation of powers in the United States Constitution of 1787.

[10] An "emolument" is any kind of payment received for work whether in the form of salary, wages, fees, or prizes.

[11] "Maintain" here indicates that each state shall pay the living expenses of its delegates to Congress if they belong to the Committee of States, which meets almost continuously, as well as if they are attending Congress, which meets annually.

[12] How many votes each state should have was a critical issue. As mentioned before, although the size of a state's delegation could vary between two and seven, each state would be equal when it came time for casting a vote. In the United States Constitution a compromise was reached by having two houses in Congress with the upper house, or Senate, giving each state an equal vote, and the House of Representatives giving a number of votes proportional to a state's population.

Freedom of speech and debate in Congress shall not be impeached or questioned in any Court, or place out of Congress, and the members of congress shall be protected in their persons from arrests and imprisonments, during the time of their going to and from, and attendance on congress, except for treason, felony, or breach of the peace.[13]

Article VI.[14] No state without the Consent of the united states in congress assembled, shall send any embassy to, or receive any embassy from, or enter into any conferrence, agreement, alliance or treaty with any King prince or state; nor shall any person holding any office of profit or trust under the united states, or any of them, accept of any present, emolument, office or title of any kind whatever from any king, prince or foreign state; nor shall the united states in congress assembled, or any of them, grant any title of nobility.

No two or more states shall enter into any treaty, confederation or alliance whatever between them, without the consent of the united states in congress assembled, specifying accurately the purposes for which the same is to be entered into, and how long it shall continue.

No state shall lay any imposts[15] or duties, which may interfere with any stipulations in treaties, entered into by the united states in congress assembled, with any king, prince or state, in pursuance of any treaties already proposed by congress, to the courts of France and Spain.

No vessels of war shall be kept up in time of peace by any state, except such number only, as shall be deemed necessary by the united states in congress assembled, for the defence of such state, or its trade; nor shall any body of forces be kept up by any state, in time of peace, except such number only, as in the judgment of the united states, in congress assembled, shall be deemed requisite to garrison the forts necessary for the defence of such state; but every state shall always keep up a well regulated and disciplined militia, sufficiently armed and accoutred,[16] and shall provide and constantly have ready for use, in public stores, a due number of field pieces and tents, and a proper quantity of arms, ammunition and camp equipage.[17]

---

[13] See Article I, Section 6 of the United States Constitution.

[14] Article VI here basically becomes Article I, Section 10 of the United States Constitution.

[15] An "impost" is a tax levied on imported goods, now often called a "customs duty."

[16] The preferred spelling now is "accoutered" and means to be equipped, especially for military duty.

[17] This is the French word for equipment, although it implies especially things like tents, furnishings, wagons, and horses.

No state shall engage in any war without the consent of the united states in congress assembled, unless such state be actually invaded by enemies, or shall have received certain advice of a resolution being formed by some nation of Indians to invade such state, and the danger is so imminent as not to admit of a delay, till the united states in congress assembled can be consulted: nor shall any state grant commissions to any ships or vessels of war, nor letters of marque[18] or reprisal, except it be after a declaration of war by the united states in congress assembled, and then only against the kingdom or state and the subjects thereof, against which war has been so declared, and under such regulations as shall be established by the united states in congress assembled, unless such state be infested by pirates, in which case vessels of war may be fitted out for that occasion, and kept so long as the danger shall continue, or until the united states in congress assembled shall determine otherwise.

Article VII. When land-forces are raised by any state for the common defence, all officers of or under the rank of colonel, shall be appointed by the legislature of each state respectively by whom such forces shall be raised, or in such manner as such state shall direct, and all vacancies shall be filled up by the state which first made the appointment.[19]

Article VIII. All charges of war, and all other expences that shall be incurred for the common defence or general welfare, and allowed by the united states in congress assembled, shall be defrayed out of a common treasury, which shall be supplied by the several states, in proportion to the value of all land within each state, granted to or surveyed for any Person, as such land and the buildings and improvements thereon shall be estimated according to such mode as the united states in congress assembled, shall from time to time direct and appoint.[20] The taxes for paying that proportion shall be laid and levied

[18] "Marque" is a French word pronounced like the name Mark. "Letters of marque" refers to a government document authorizing a ship to pursue and raid enemy vessels on the high seas. It, in essence, transformed a private merchant vessel into a military one sanctioned by one country to attack ships of another for profit. The letter of marque made piracy in the service of the state legal. Many of the ships that fought the British navy during the American Revolution were privateers operating under letters of marque.

[19] By implication, all higher officers (generals) were to be commissioned by the federal government. At that time, a colonel commanded a regiment, so regiments of volunteers, usually coming from the same locale, could elect their officers, or have them appointed by their own representatives.

[20] This is an important provision because it was the most serious weakness of the Articles. The national government could not tax American citizens directly, but had to

by the authority and direction of the legislatures of the several states within the time agreed upon by the united states in congress assembled.

Article IX.[21] The united states in congress assembled, shall have the sole and exclusive right and power of determining on peace and war, except in the cases mentioned in the sixth article—of sending and receiving ambassadors—entering into treaties and alliances, provided that no treaty of commerce shall be made whereby the legislative power of the respective states shall be restrained from imposing such imposts and duties on foreigners, as their own people are subjected to, or from prohibiting the exportation or importation of any species of goods or commodities whatsoever—of establishing rules for deciding in all cases, what captures on land or water shall be legal, and in what manner prizes taken by land or naval forces in the service of the united states shall be divided or appropriated—of granting letters of marque and reprisal in times of peace[22]—appointing courts for the trial of piracies and felonies committed on the high seas and establishing courts for receiving and determining finally appeals in all cases of captures, provided that no member of congress shall be appointed a judge of any of the said courts.

The united states in congress assembled shall also be the last resort on appeal in all disputes and differences now subsisting or that hereafter may arise between two or more states concerning boundary, jurisdiction or any other cause whatever; which authority shall always be exercised in the manner following.[23] Whenever the legislative or executive authority or lawful agent of any state in controversy with another shall present a petition to congress stating the matter in question and praying[24] for a hearing, notice thereof shall be given by order of congress to the legislative or executive authority of the other state in controversy,

---

obtain funds from each state government. This section contains the agreement that each state will normally expect to pay a portion of expenses proportional to the assessed valuation of property in the state compared to the total value of property in all states combined. Needless to say, most states were slow to pay their share, if they did at all.

[21] Article IX here became the basis for Article I, Section 8 in the United States Constitution. Here, as there, it is a list of powers, (known as *enumerated* powers) that are expressly given only to the national government. This is an important aspect of limited government since those powers not given were considered denied to the government. The concept of limited powers contained in an explicit list was first developed in the Articles of Confederation.

[22] In Article VI, this power was explicitly denied to the states. Here it is expressly granted to the national government.

[23] In the United States Constitution of 1787 the power to settle disputes between states was given to the Supreme Court in Article III of that document.

[24] "Praying" here means asking or petitioning.

and a day assigned for the appearance of the parties by their lawful
agents, who shall then be directed to appoint by joint consent, commissioners or judges to constitute a court for hearing and determining
the matter in question:[25] but if they cannot agree, congress shall name
three persons out of each of the united states, and from the list of such
persons each party shall alternately strike out one,[26] the petitioners
beginning, until the number shall be reduced to thirteen; and from that
number not less than seven, nor more than nine names as congress
shall direct, shall in the presence of congress be drawn out by lot,[27] and
the persons whose names shall be so drawn or any five of them,[28] shall
be commissioners or judges, to hear and finally determine the controversy, so always as a major part of the judges who shall hear the cause
shall agree in the determination:[29] and if either party shall neglect to
attend at the day appointed, without shewing reasons, which congress
shall judge sufficient, or being present shall refuse to strike,[30] the congress shall proceed to nominate three persons out of each state, and
the secretary of congress shall strike in behalf of such party absent or
refusing; and the judgment and sentence of the court to be appointed,
in the manner before prescribed, shall be final and conclusive; and if
any of the parties shall refuse to submit to the authority of such court,
or to appear or defend their claim or cause, the court shall nevertheless

[25] These commissioners or judges are the functional equivalent of the Supreme
Court. There were no national trial courts under the Articles of Confederation for the
simple reason that since the Congress could not pass laws that directly affected citizens,
citizens could not break national laws, and thus there was no need for a national trial
court. (The only court that might be considered a national one having an existence
separate from Congress was the Court of Appeals in Cases of Capture, the jurisdiction
of which was limited to admirality cases.)

[26] To "strike out" here means to cross out one of the names on the list of nominees.

[27] To select someone by lot is to use some means of picking people at random.

[28] This rather complicated system for picking a "court" to settle disputes between
states is designed to make the process so honest and unbiased that the "court's" decision
would be followed. Presumably, the provision for "any five of them" is a response to
the possibility that some of those selected might not want to serve, cannot make it to
the proceedings in time, or are ill. After seven to nine have been selected by lot, at
least five of these must be present in order for the proceedings to be considered legitimate.

[29] "Determination" here means "decision." After the complicated selection process
to ensure a sense of fairness, the use of majority rule means that a minimum of three
commissioners would be sufficient to reach a decision if only five attended. The Supreme
Court created by the United States Constitution also uses majority rule.

[30] This part of the provision takes into account the possibility that one of the
parties might attempt to thwart the process by refusing to take part—either by not
showing up or refusing to engage in the process of striking names from the list of thirteen
nominees. If one party did not perform its role in the process, someone else did it for
them.

proceed to pronounce sentence, or judgment, which shall in like manner be final and decisive, the judgment or sentence and other proceedings being in either case transmitted to congress, and lodged among the acts of congress for the security of the parties concerned:[31] provided that every commissioner, before he sits in judgment, shall take an oath to be administered by one of the judges of the supreme or superior court of the state, where the cause shall be tried, "well and truly to hear and determine the matter in question, according to the best of his judgment, without favour, affection or hope of reward:" provided also that no state shall be deprived of territory for the benefit of the united states.

All controversies concerning the private right of soil claimed under different grants of two or more states, whose jurisdictions as they may respect such lands, and the states which passed such grants are adjusted, the said grants or either of them being at the same time claimed to have originated antecedent to such settlement of jurisdiction, shall on the petition of either party to the congress of the united states, be finally determined as near as may be in the same manner as is before prescribed for deciding disputes respecting territorial jurisdiction between different states.[32]

The united states in congress assembled shall also have the sole and exclusive right and power of regulating the alloy[33] and value of coin struck by their own authority, or by that of the respective states—fixing the standard of weights and measures throughout the united states—regulating the trade and managing all affairs with the Indians, not members of any of the states,[34] provided that the legislative right of any state

[31] Although every effort was made to create an unbiased process so that everyone would be inclined to accept its decisions, there was this final provision which allowed Congress to pass a law enforcing the court's decision if either side failed to abide by it. Of course, there was no way the court could force Congress to pass such a law, but the implicit threat was still there. Furthermore, Congress had no means with which to enforce its laws.

[32] The United States Constitution also gives the Supreme Court jurisdiction over cases and controversies between citizens of different states. (See Article III, Section 2.) However, since under the Articles of Confederation the federal government could not act directly upon individual citizens, disputes between citizens were changed into disputes between states by determining which state had the right to make the grant of land. Presumably, whichever state had the right, the citizen acquiring the land under the authority of that state won.

[33] This means that the Confederation Congress can determine the metallic composition of money, setting the standard for how much silver, for example, must be in a coin in order for it to have a specific value.

[34] The status of Indians was even more ambiguous then than it is now. Some were considered citizens and others were not, depending upon where they lived, what their treaty provided, and what the particular state's law said. This provision allowed the federal government to affect only those Indians who were not by some definition citizens of a state.

within its own limits be not infringed or violated—establishing or regulating post-offices from one state to another, throughout all the united
states, and exacting such postage on the papers passing thro' the same
as may be requisite to defray the expences of the said office—appointing
all officers of the land forces, in the service of the united states, excepting regimental officers—appointing all the officers of the naval
forces, and commissioning all officers whatever in the service of the
united states—making rules for the government and regulation of the
said land and naval forces, and directing their operations.

The united states in congress assembled shall have authority to
appoint a committee, to sit in the recess of congress,[35] to be denominated
"A Committee of the States,"[36] and to consist of one delegate from
each state; and to appoint such other committees and civil officers as
may be necessary for managing the general affairs of the united states
under their direction—to appoint one of their number to preside,[37] provided that no person be allowed to serve in the office of president more
than one year in any term of three years; to ascertain the necessary
sums of Money to be raised for the service of the united states, and to
appropriate and apply the same for defraying the public expences—to
borrow money, or emit[38] bills on the credit of the united states, transmitting every half year to the respective states an account of the sums
of money so borrowed or emitted,—to build and equip a navy—to agree
upon the number of land forces, and to make requisitions from each
state for its quota, in proportion to the number of white inhabitants in
such state;[39] which requisition shall be binding, and thereupon the leg-

[35] This clause means "while Congress is not in session."

[36] The sole institution of the executive branch clearly authorized by the Articles
was a committee composed of thirteen members of Congress, one from each state. This
collective leadership, with one of their members acting as president, could be compared
to the parliamentary system where the executive is part of the legislature. However, in
this instance the executive branch was very weak, even more than the weak executives
in the state constitutions.

[37] The Committee of States elected one of their members to be president, but
his primary duty was simply to preside over meetings of the Committee of States—
hardly a powerful position. The American dislike for strong executives during the founding era is still reflected in the name we call our chief executive, president, which comes
from the root word "preside." By implication the chief executive presides rather than
leads.

[38] To "emit bills" is to print and circulate money.

[39] This article seems in direct conflict with Article VIII which says that the treasury
collections will be apportioned according to the value of land and property in a state,
whereas here it is to be done on the basis of the number of white inhabitants. However,
Article IX was concerned only with the expenses of the Revolutionary War, whereas
Article VIII included general military expenses as well as all expenses for the "general

islature of each state shall appoint the regimental officers, raise the men and cloath,[40] arm and equip them in a soldier like manner, at the expence of the united states, and the officers and men so cloathed, armed and equipped shall march to the place appointed, and within the time agreed on by the united states in congress assembled: But if the united states in congress assembled shall, on consideration of circumstances judge proper that any state should not raise men, or should raise a smaller number than its quota, and that any other state should raise a greater number of men than the quota thereof, such extra number shall be raised, officered, cloathed, armed and equipped in the same manner as the quota of such state, unless the legislature of such state shall judge that such extra number cannot be safely spared out of the same, in which case they shall raise officer, cloath, arm and equip as many of such extra number as they judge can be safely spared. And the officers and men so cloathed, armed and equipped, shall march to the place appointed, and within the time agreed on by the united states in congress assembled.

The united states in congress assembled shall never engage in a war, nor grant letters of marque and reprisal in time of peace, nor enter into any treaties or alliances, nor coin money, nor regulate the value thereof, nor ascertain the sums and expences necessary for the defence and welfare of the united states, or any of them, nor emit bills, nor borrow money on the credit of the united states, nor appropriate money, nor agree upon the number of vessels of war, to be built or purchased, or the number of land or sea forces to be raised, nor appoint a commander in chief of the army or navy, unless nine states assent to the same: nor shall a question on any other point, except for adjourning from day to day be determined, unless by the votes of a majority of the united states in congress assembled.[41]

---

welfare." Article VIII was a provision for peacetime since only after the war's end would there be time and opportunity to engage in the lengthy and complicated process of property valuation. By contrast, the population of each state was easier to estimate, although a complete and accurate census was not taken until 1790. Article I, Section 8, paragraph 1 of the United States Constitution brings together the welfare clause of the Articles and the common defense clause as it was in Article VIII.

    [40] Clothe.

    [41] This paragraph establishes two categories of issues, each with a different decision rule. The issues listed require nine out of thirteen states for approval, whereas all issues not so listed require only a simple majority of the states represented in Congress. This constitutional principle—of extraordinary majorities for important matters—was also used in the United States Constitution. See, for example, the majority required to amend the United States Constitution as described in Article V of that document and the majority required to override presidential vetoes.

The congress of the united states shall have power to adjourn to any time within the year, and to any place within the united states, so that no period of adjournment be for a longer duration than the space of six Months, and shall publish the Journal of their proceedings monthly, except such parts thereof relating to treaties, alliances or military operations, as in their judgment require secresy; and the yeas and nays of the delegates of each state on any question shall be entered on the Journal, when it is desired by any delegate; and the delegates of a state, or any of them, at his or their request shall be furnished with a transcript of the said Journal, except such parts as are above excepted, to lay before the legislatures of the several states.

Article X. The committee of the states, or any nine of them, shall be authorized to execute, in the recess of congress, such of the powers of congress as the united states in congress assembled, by the consent of nine states, shall from time to time think expedient to vest them with; provided that no power be delegated to the said committee, for the exercise of which, by the articles of confederation, the voice of nine states in the congress of the united states assembled is requisite.[42]

Article XI. Canada acceding to this confederation, and joining in the measures of the united states, shall be admitted into, and entitled to all the advantages of this union: but no other colony shall be admitted into the same, unless such admission be agreed to by nine states.[43]

Article XII. All bills of credit emitted, monies borrowed and debts contracted by, or under the authority of congress, before the assembling of the united states, in pursuance of the present confederation, shall be deemed and considered as a charge against the united states, for payment and satisfaction whereof the said united states, and the public faith are hereby solemnly pledged.

Article XIII. Every state shall abide by the determinations of the united states in congress assembled, on all questions which by this confederation are submitted to them. And the Articles of this confed-

---

[42] The Committee of States was a continuous body, and in its role as executive could sometimes, with a two-thirds majority of its members, act as if it were the entire Congress while the Congress was not in session. The Committee of States could do this, however, only in those matters on which the entire Congress could act with a simple majority of the states. When it came to those issues listed in Article IX, requiring a vote of nine states, the Committee of States could not act at all on its own.

[43] Canada could join the Union and be on an equal footing with the other states. Any other colonies seeking admission required approval by nine states and were not guaranteed equal status with the original thirteen states.

eration shall be inviolably observed by every state, and the union shall be perpetual; nor shall any alteration at any time hereafter be made in any of them; unless such alteration be agreed to in a congress of the united states, and be afterwards confirmed by the legislatures of every state.[44]

And Whereas it hath pleased the Great Governor of the World[45] to incline the hearts of the legislatures we respectively represent in congress, to approve of, and to authorize us to ratify the said articles of confederation and perpetual union. Know Ye that we the undersigned delegates, by virtue of the power and authority to us given for that purpose, do by these presents, in the name and in behalf of our respective constituents, fully and entirely ratify and confirm each and every of the said articles of confederation and perpetual union, and all and singular the matters and things therein contained: And we do further solemnly plight and engage[46] the faith of our respective constituents, that they shall abide by the determinations[47] of the united states in congress assembled, on all questions, which by the said confederation are submitted to them. And that the articles thereof shall be inviolably observed by the states we respectively represent, and that the union shall be perpetual. In Witness whereof we have hereunto set our hands in Congress. Done at Philadelphia in the state of Pennsylvania the ninth Day of July, in the Year of our Lord one Thousand seven Hundred and Seventy-eight, and in the third year of the independence of America.

[44] The amendment process is also an historical innovation, although this institution was invented first in state constitutions. Note that unanimity of the states is required to amend the Articles, referred to here and elsewhere in the document as a "perpetual union." It appears, therefore, that amending the Articles is the most serious issue of all.

[45] In the Declaration of Independence, God is referred to as "Nature's God," "Divine Providence," "the Creator," and "the Supreme Judge." He is referred to in state constitutions as "the Author of existence," the "Supreme Being," "almighty God," and a variety of other titles including the "Great Legislator." He is the "Great Governor of the World" here in Article XIII of the Articles. God is mentioned, but not called upon as a witness.

[46] "Plight and engage" here means "pledge and promise."

[47] "Determinations" here means "decisions."

On the Part & behalf
of the State of
New Hampshire[48]

{ Josiah Bartlett
John Wentworth Junr
August 8th 1778

On the part and behalf
of the State of
Massachusetts Bay

{ John Hancock
Samuel Adams
Elbridge Gerry
Francis Dana
James Lovell
Samuel Holten

On the part and behalf of
the State of Rhode-Island
and Providence Plantations

{ William Ellery
Henry Marchant
John Collins

on the Part and behalf
of the State of
Connecticut

{ Roger Sherman
Samuel Huntington
Oliver Wolcott
Titus Hosmer
Andrew Adams

On the Part and Behalf
of the State of New York

{ Jas. Duane
Fras. Lewis
Wm: Duer
Gouvr. Morris

On the Part and in Behalf
of the State of New
Jersey Novr. 26, 1778.—

{ Jno Witherspoon
Nathl. Scudder

On the part and behalf
of the State of
Pennsylvania

{ Robt Morris,
Daniel Roberdeau
Jona: Bayard Smith.
William Clingan
Joseph Reed,
[22d.?] July 1778

On the part & behalf
of the State of
Delaware

{ Thos McKean, Feby 22, 1779
John Dickinson, May 5th-1779
Nicholas Van Dyke,

on the part and behalf
of the State of Maryland

{ John Hanson, March 1st, 1781
Daniel Carroll, do

[48] As was usual for documents written by the Continental Congresses, the states are listed from north to south with the delegates linked to their respective states.

On the Part and Behalf
of the State of
Virginia

{ Richard Henry Lee
John Banister
Thomas Adams
Jno Harvie
Francis Lightfoot Lee

On the part and Behalf
of the State of No.
Carolina

{ John Penn, July 21st 1778
Corns. Harnett
Jno. Williams

On the part & behalf
of the State of
South-Carolina

{ Henry Laurens.
William Henry Drayton
Jno. Mathews
Richd. Hutson
Thos: Heyward, junr:

On the part & behalf
of the State of Georgia

{ Jno Walton 24th. July 1778
Edwd. Telfair
Edwd Langworthy.

XIII

The Northwest Ordinance

1787

COMMENTARY BY PETER S. ONUF

THE NORTHWEST ORDINANCE, passed by the Confederation Congress on July 13, 1787, established the basic framework of the American territorial system. Congress had devoted much of its rapidly diminishing energy to the West over the previous few years. In 1784 it adopted an ordinance for territorial government, largely the work of Thomas Jefferson, that provided for the orderly admission of new states on a basis of full equality with the original members of the union. But with the subsequent adoption in 1785 of an ordinance for the sale of federal lands, congressmen became convinced that Jefferson's scheme was inadequate. Potential purchasers of federal lands demanded a more elaborate system of "temporary" territorial government that would guarantee law and order and secure land titles during the pre-statehood period. There was also growing sentiment that Jefferson's plans for ten new states north of the Ohio River were based on overly optimistic assessments of the region's potential population. The Northwest Ordinance thus marked the culmination of a protracted reassessment of western policy. The timing of its enactment undoubtedly was a direct result of simultaneous negotiations with land companies—most notably with the Ohio Associates, whose lobbyist Manasseh Cutler was busily cultivating support in Congress.

The enlightened colonial policy set forth in the ordinance promised purchasers of federal lands that, after a temporary period of congressional rule, the new settlements ultimately would be formed into self-governing states with all the rights and privileges of the original members of the union. In this way, the Ordinance filled a crucial gap in the national Constitution then being drafted at Philadelphia.

Article IV, section III of the Constitution provides that Congress may admit new states and that it has the power to establish appropriate "rules and regulations" for the government of federal territory. However, Congress is not constitutionally required to make the territories into states. By providing this missing connection, the Ordinance guaranteed that the new American union would expand far beyond its original borders.

Commentary on the Northwest Ordinance usually begins with the question of its relationship to the Constitution. From a functional perspective, the two documents are *complementary*; the Ordinance defines and limits Congress's constitutional powers over the national domain. However, the chronology is backward. The Confederation Congress passed the Ordinance *before* the Constitution was drafted or ratified. How could an ordinary act of legislation by that Congress control future congresses acting under the authority of the new Constitution? In 1850, Chief Justice Roger B. Taney wrote the U.S. Supreme Court's answer in *Strader* v. *Graham*: the Ordinance, reenacted by the First Federal Congress in 1789, simply represented the exercise of Congress's plenary authority over national territory and therefore could be revised, rescinded, or simply ignored by subsequent congresses.

Taney's verdict was historically accurate. It also reflected the conventional wisdom of his day; in the American system, the national Constitution clearly was paramount. The test of the Constitution also provided the authoritative standard of constitutionality. The Northwest Ordinance simply did not measure up; its authors did not act under any specific constitutional mandate, nor was their work in turn sanctioned by the sovereign people. Hastily written and poorly organized, the Ordinance did not compare favorably with the skillfully constructed national Constitution.

The case against the Ordinance as a "constitutional" text seems compelling—almost too compelling. How could the Ordinance's authors have been such poor draftsmen, so oblivious to the document's obvious defects? A fresh reading of the Ordinance in its historical context—and with due regard to its authors' original intentions—suggests that Taney's perspective is fundamentally anachronistic. The Ordinance was never intended to be a "constitution," properly speaking; yet neither was it supposed to be merely statutory legislation. What did Congressman Nathan Dane of Massachusetts, who drafted the final version of the ordinance, and his congressional colleagues think they were doing when they drafted the Ordinance?

Western Policy

In formulating its western policy, Congress acted under authority derived from the cession of state title claims to the region north and west of the Ohio River and to the Mississippi River, the limit of the United States under the Treaty of Paris. In these cessions, landed states such as Virginia (in 1784) required Congress to develop western lands for the common benefit of the entire Union and to provide for the formation of new equal states. Although congressmen were well aware of the limits of their legislative competence in other area, they had no misgivings about their authority to lay down conditions under which federal property could be sold and held. As the recognized holder of property rights in the region, Congress's power was absolute. The question then was how the subsequent creation of private rights would modify Congress's power. In the land ordinance of May 20, 1785, the Confederation Congress promised to make its lands available on specified terms. Responding to pressures from potential purchasers—namely, the Ohio Associates of New England—Congress set forth a plan for the temporary government of the region in the Northwest Ordinance. Clearly imperative was the timely introduction of institutions that could effectively guarantee law and order, secure land titles, and protect settlers from the Indians.

Self-government during the first phase of territorial development was antithetical to the interests of prospective land purchasers. The establishment of territorial government in fact represented an alternative to the lawless, anarchic frontier conditions in which unauthorized settlers acknowledged no superior authority and "governed" themselves. Security of private rights depended at the outset on what proponents of territorial self-government would later characterize as the arbitrary and tyrannical power of officials appointed by Congress to govern the Northwest Territory. While the Ordinance promised that settlers would eventually govern themselves, the fundamental premise of congressional western policy was that pioneer settlers were incapable of managing their own affairs.

The primacy of property rights in western policy and Congress's role as the sovereign source of good titles suggest that the modern idea of "constitution" is inappropriate to the Northwest Ordinance. The more appropriate model for the Ordinance is the colonial charter, through which the British Crown announced terms under which lands

could be taken up and authorized the establishment of local governments within specified boundaries. There was no question that Congress
had the authority to govern the Northwest as it saw fit and that, through
the creation of private property rights and the gradual extension of
political rights to settlers, it could set limits on its own power.

The only constitutional problem raised by the Northwest Ordinance
concerned the statehood promise. The Articles of Confederation strictly
defined the conditions under which new members could be added to
the union: Canada and other (presumably British) colonies were wel-
come, but the admission of any other new state depended on the unanimous consent of the states—or, in other words, on the amendment of
the Articles themselves. From this perspective, Article IV, section III
of the national Constitution could be seen as remedying this defect in
the Articles, thus giving full effect to the Ordinance according to its
authors' original intentions. The reenactment of the Ordinance in 1789
by the First Federal Congress resolved a few formal discrepancies resulting from the institution of the new federal regime. It did not
supersede or invalidate the basic framework for territorial government
established by the Ordinance of 1785 on land and that of 1787 on government.

As noted above, Congress derived its title to the Northwest Territory from the cession of state claims in the region. Congress first called
for cessions in September 1780; in October, it pledged to dedicate revenues from the sale of its new domain to the common benefit of all the
states and promised that new states would be formed in the region.
These resolutions set the basic framework for western policy subsequently elaborated in the land and government ordinances. They also
implicitly disavowed any intention by Congress to assert its jurisdiction
over the western lands in the face of conflicting state claims. Congress's
title in the area was established only when *all* state claims were extinguished—most notably Virginia's, ceded in 1784. Congressional authority
over the national domain was uncontested precisely because it was built
on state claims: by acknowledging the priority and primacy of the sovereign states, Congress was able to exercise absolute power in the
Northwest.

Yet the western land cessions also guaranteed that congressional
power over the national domain would serve the interests of the em-
bryonic new states. Congress's agreement to receive the cessions created
contractual obligations. Congressmen were not troubled by the supposedly defective form of the Northwest Ordinance as mere legislation
because they understood that they were authorized to act by the cession
agreements. In other words, the Ordinance by itself was not intended

to be a complete and self-sufficient constitutional text. It presupposed the prior "compact" agreements with the ceding states on which the national title to the western lands was built. Therefore, any *further* state action authorizing Congress to create a system of territorial government would have been redundant, except perhaps at the point when one of the new states presented itself for admission to the union. The states understood that Congress was bound to exercise its power toward specific ends and thus was, in some broad sense, constitutionally limited. But these limitations did not depend on the specific form of the Ordinance, or on the powers explicitly delegated to its authors.

The text of the Northwest Ordinance should be seen as part of a larger complex of texts, including the original congressional call for cessions, the subsequent state cession acts, and Congress's agreements to accept them. This larger context helps explain why the specific provisions of the land and government ordinances were thought to be within the discretionary authority of Congress and therefore were not controversial. Congress's mandate was permissive: it had the unquestioned authority to revise its policies so long as they conformed to the broad purposes laid down in the cession compacts. No one expected the territorial ordinances to remain unchanged, and there was no perceived need to provide procedures for their amendment. The development of western policy between 1784, when the report of a congressional committee on territorial government headed by Thomas Jefferson was adopted, and the passage of the Northwest Ordinance in 1787 demonstrates that Congress had no misgivings about revising its western policy. The process of revision would continue after 1787 as well.

Yet, the actual settlement and political development of the Northwest Territory revealed the ambiguous status of the Ordinance *in relation to the citizens of the "new states."* Congress may have had broad discretion in fulfilling its obligations to the ceding states and to the existing members of the union generally. But, as a kind of charter for the development of American colonies, the Ordinance also held forth specific promises to settlers. Significantly, these promises were elaborated in the self-proclaimed "compact articles." (See Articles One to Six of Section 14 of the Northwest Ordinance below.) Presumably, if individual settlers, or groups of settlers in the new states, accepted Congress's terms, those terms would then be binding on Congress. In other words, the complex of texts in which the Ordinance was situated included future acts of territorial citizens, acting individually, as purchasers of federal lands, and collectively, as founders of new states. The compact articles would then become "constitutional" in a more specific and conventional sense.

The Ordinance and its Provisions

The Northwest Ordinance incorporated basic principles set forth in the 1784 government ordinance as well as a series of amendments proposed by subsequent congressional committees. The first part of the Ordinance, including provisions for the inheritance of property (Section 2) and for the temporary government of territorial citizens prior to statehood (Sections 3–12), was added by the final congressional committee. The articles of compact that follow recapitulated the main provisions of earlier proposals, with some significant revisions. The most important of these, the prohibition of slavery in Article Six, was a last-minute addition to the text. Southern congressmen were willing to prohibit slavery from the Northwest Territory to forestall economic competition from a potential plantation economy. In addition, the ban on slavery may have been a concession to the antislavery sentiments of the New Englanders in the Ohio Company who planned the first legal American settlement in the region. However, Article Six also provided that fugitive slaves in the Northwest Territory could be lawfully reclaimed.

A brief review of the main features of the Ordinance shows how difficult it is to establish its authorship, a crucial issue for most later commentators. The final draft of the Ordinance is in the hand of Massachusetts Congressman Nathan Dane, a leading member of the final congressional committee. Dane later claimed credit for the guarantees of individual rights, most notably in Article Two. As a prominent lawyer sensitive to the interests of prospective landholders, Dane was also undoubtedly responsible for the elaborate provisions for inheritance. Even in these sections, it is unclear whether Dane was anticipating or responding to demands from his friends in the Ohio Company. In the case of the slavery prohibition, Dane probably incorporated a proposal by Manasseh Cutler, the Ohio Company's lobbyist at Congress.

The authorship of Article Six of the compact continues to generate controversy among commentators on the Ordinance. Debate has centered on the supposed connection between Jefferson's earlier proposal to ban slavery throughout the West, beginning in 1800, and Article Six. By a narrow vote, Jefferson's proposal was excluded from the 1784 government ordinance. But the limited geographical scope of Article Six (confined as it was to the Northwest), its supposedly immediate operation, and its belated insertion in the text of the Ordinance (during the third and final reading) suggest that the links to Jefferson are tenuous at best. Jefferson's legacy is much more apparent in the principle of new state equality carried over from the 1784 Ordinance (Section 13 and Article Five) and 18). Jefferson was also concerned with establishing the boundaries of projected new states, thereby giving the statehood promise concreteness and specificity. In this case, however, the Jefferson committee's proposal for ten new states in the region north of the Ohio was modified by a successor committee, headed by Jefferson's protégé James Monroe, which first recommended the creation of three to five new states (in 1786) that was repeated in Article Five.

The importance of the 1784 ordinance lay in articulating a broad conception of the American Union based on the equality of the member states, thus precluding the establishment of second-class states or colonies in the process of westward expansion. This conception of the union—and therefore the credibility of claims that Jefferson was the true "author" of the Ordinance—survived through successive reformulations of congressional western policy. But later committees had to accommodate to new circumstances that Jefferson and his colleagues had not confronted. Most significant was the growing recognition that a successful land sales policy depended on establishing an effective system of territorial government. It was not enough to provide for the eventuality of statehood alone; the growth of population and the recruitment of an orderly and industrious class of settlers depended on keeping squatters out of the region and on guaranteeing secure titles and safe conditions to purchasers of federal lands.

By requiring the prior survey of federal lands, the 1785 land ordinance mandated an extensive federal presence—including surveying parties, defense forces, and, as the system was subsequently developed, officials to administer the land office. Here, in short, were the rudiments of territorial "government." The Northwest Ordinance extended these government provisions in logical fashion. Not coincidentally, the first substantive section of the Ordinance—after designating the region a "territory, for the purpose of temporary government"—is dedicated to the transmission of land titles (Section 2). Implicit in this paragraph is that Congress had the responsibility to define and enforce private property rights *beyond* the point of passing title to purchasers of its lands. And in fact the entire scheme of territorial government outlined in the following paragraphs—including governor (Sections 3–8), judges (Sections 4–5), and legislature (Sections 9–11)—is previewed in this section on inheritance.

Considered as a single "constitutional" text, the Ordinance is exceedingly awkward and ungainly: why did Dane and his coauthors specify the powers and responsibilities of the respective branches *before* laying down the basic structure of territorial government? Seen historically, however, the section on inheritance is a natural continuation of the 1785 land ordinance. Furthermore, the precedence of property rights

over the elaboration of provisions for government reflects the fundamental premises of liberal social contract theory as well as the actual
process of policy formulation.

The sections of the Ordinance providing for the temporary government of the region—and particularly those describing the extensive
powers of the territorial governor—inspired the most controversy during
the early years of the territorial system. This is hardly surprising, given
the supposedly "temporary" duration of the system (Section 1) and the
Ordinance's provision for successive stages of development. Once the
governor was satisfied that there were "five thousand free male inhabitants of full age in the district," he was authorized to call elections for
a territorial house of representatives (Section 19). Until that time, however, officials appointed by Congress wielded unlimited political power,
checked only by the bill of rights written into Article Two of the Ordinance. (This first stage lasted until 1799 in the original Northwest
Territory.)

In the next stage, power was to some, always controversial, degree
shared between territorial officials and locally elected representatives
(see esp. Section 11). Given Congress's basic commitment to the political
development of the territory, it can be argued that the entire first section
of the Ordinance (Section 3-12) was designed to self-destruct. The very
arbitrariness of the governor's powers—the apparent discretion he enjoyed at each stage of development—spurred into action a political opposition that prepared the Northwest Territory for self-government and
membership in the union.

The subsequent history of the government provisions is best understood in terms of the political development they authorized and of the
continuing process of revision of those provisions resulting from political
activity in the territories. Historians agree that the Wisconsin Organic
Act of 1836 marks the complete supersession of the original scheme of
territorial government by a more "democratic" regime that gave territorial citizens wide control over local politics and a measure of political
autonomy or quasi-statehood from the very outset.

In contrast to the first part of the Ordinance, the "articles of compact, between the original States and the people and States in the said
territory" were supposed to "forever remain unalterable" (Section 14).
That this promise would not, in fact, be fulfilled, at least in detail, is
clearly demonstrated by a review of the process of state creation and
subsequent political and constitutional controversy, most significantly
over the slavery ban in Article Six. In theory, the notion of a "compact"
between old and new states would limit the actions of future congresses,
thus limiting the plenary grant of authority in Article IV, section 3 of

the U.S. Constitution. But the Ordinance failed to provide effective recourse against Congress when that body apparently violated its obligations; the U.S. Supreme Court subsequently ruled that such questions were "political," and therefore beyond its jurisdiction. Furthermore, Congress never would acknowledge any limitations on its control over its own membership, notwithstanding any pledges made to settlers in the national domain.

The defects of the Northwest Ordinance as a constitutional instrument were obvious to later generations of politicians and lawyers operating within the framework of the national Constitution. The specific provisions of the Ordinance were *not* authoritative: the scheme for temporary government was soon revised beyond recognition, and the compact articles were generally either modified or ignored. But it is a mistake to read the Ordinance too closely. The authors of the Ordinance did not intend their work as the final or definitive formulation of American western policy.

According to the state land cessions, Congress was bound to develop the national domain in the common interest and to create new states; fulfillment of these responsibilities might well require the reformulation of its specific policies. Thus, in the Northwest Ordinance, Congress reserved the right to admit a smaller or greater number of new states (Section 19), depending on the subsequent and unforeseeable rate of population growth and economic development. To insist on the larger number, congressmen feared, might mean that the scattered settlers in these new "states" would never be sufficiently numerous to qualify for admission to the union, thereby defeating the statehood promise. Nor was there anything fixed or "constitutional" about the 60,000 population requirement. In 1787, a state with this population and with prospects for continuing growth could make a credible claim to equality with the old states. But this might not be the case at a later time. Congressional discretion therefore was a logical necessity in providing for the continuing expansion of a union of equal states.

From a later perspective, there was no clear distinction between Congress's discretionary trusteeship over the national domain and the absolute, sovereign authority implied in the U.S. Constitution. As a result, commentators such as Chief Justice Taney concluded that there was nothing "constitutional" about the Ordinance at all; it was inferior to the Constitution and depended for whatever force it possessed on the continuing will of Congress, the constitutional authority. But the authors of the Ordinance intended both more and less for the document: the text may not have been constitutional, but the principles it implemented *were* fundamental, and Congress's commitment to those principles constituted the United States as an expanding union of equal states.

The people of the territories understood the Ordinance in these general terms, even when they sought relief from its specific provisions. So, too, congressmen never imagined that their discretion could ever be exercised in ways that would undercut the eventual achievement of statehood or diminish the rights of American citizens in the territories. Indeed, the most significant revisions of the Ordinance's text showed congressional responsiveness to demands for more extensive political participation during the territorial period. When the larger crisis of the Union over the slavery issue did come to block the regular and orderly admission of new states, congressmen recognized that the breakdown of the territorial system violated fundamental principles. The Northwest Ordinance may not have bound Congress in a strictly constitutional sense, but Congress's failure to implement the principles it embodied foretold the ultimate rupture of the Union during the Civil War.

For Further Reading

Robert F. Berkhofer, Jr. "Jefferson, the Ordinance of 1784, and the Origins of the American Territorial System," *William and Mary Quarterly*, 3rd ser., 29 (1972), 231–62

Andrew R. L. Cayton. *The Frontier Republic: Ideology and Politics in the Ohio Country, 1780–1825*. Kent, Ohio, 1986.

Jack Ericson Eblen. *The First and Second United States Empires: Governors and Territorial Government, 1784–1912*. Pittsburgh, 1968.

Merrill Jensen. "The Creation of the National Domain, 1781–1784," *The Mississippi Valley Historical Review* 26 (1939), 323–42.

Peter S. Onuf. *The Origins of the Federal Republic: Jurisdictional Controversies in the United States, 1775–1787*. Philadelphia, 1983.

Peter S. Onuf. *Statehood and Union: A History of the Northwest Ordinance*. Bloomington, Ind., 1987.

Francis Philbrick. "Introduction," *Laws of the Illinois Territory, 1809–1818*. Springfield, Ill., 1950.

David Curtis Skaggs, ed. *The Old Northwest in the American Revolution: An Anthology*. Madison, Wisc., 1977.

[Northwest Ordinance]

[1787]

An ORDINANCE for the GOVERNMENT of the TERRITORY of the UNITED STATES Northwest of the RIVER OHIO

[1] Be it ordained by the United States in Congress assembled, That the said territory, for the purposes of temporary government, be one district; subject, however, to be divided into two districts, as future circumstances may, in the opinion of Congress, make it expedient.

[2] Be it ordained by the authority aforesaid, That the estates both of resident and non-resident proprietors in the said territory, dying intestate, shall descend to, and be distributed among, their children, and the descendants of a deceased child in equal parts; the descendants of a deceased child or grand-child, to take the share of their deceased parent in equal parts among them: And where there shall be no children or descendants, then in equal parts to the next of kin, in equal degree; and among collaterals, the children of a deceased brother or sister of the intestate shall have in equal parts among them their deceased parents share; and there shall in no case be a distinction between kindred of the whole and half blood; saving in all cases to the widow of the intestate, her third part of the real estate for life, and one third part of the personal estate; and this law relative to descents and dower, shall remain in full force until altered by the legislature of the district.—And until the governor and judges shall adopt laws as herein after mentioned, estates in the said territory may be devised or bequeathed by wills in writing, signed and sealed by him or her, in whom the estate may be, (being of full age) and attested by three witnesses;—and real estates may be conveyed by lease and release, or bargain and sale, signed, sealed, and delivered by the person being of full age, in whom the estate may be, and attested by two witnesses, provided such wills be duly proved, and such conveyances be acknowledged, or the execution thereof duly proved, and be recorded within one year after proper magistrates, courts, and registers shall be appointed for that purpose; and personal property may be transferred by delivery, saving, however, to

Broadsheet, RG 360, Papers of the Continental Congress, No. 59, I: 229–30, National Archives. (Two pages.)

the French and Canadian inhabitants, and other settlers of the Kaskaskies, Saint Vincent's, and the neighbouring villages, who have heretofore professed themselves citizens of Virginia, their laws and customs now in force among them, relative to the descent and conveyance of property.

[3] Be it ordained by the authority aforesaid, That there shall be appointed from time to time, by Congress, a governor, whose commission shall continue in force for the term of three years, unless sooner revoked by Congress; he shall reside in the district, and have a freehold estate therein, in one thousand acres of land, while in the exercise of his office.

[4] There shall be appointed from time to time, by Congress, a secretary, whose commission shall continue in force for four years, unless sooner revoked, he shall reside in the district, and have a freehold estate therein, in five hundred acres of land, while in the exercise of his office; it shall be his duty to keep and preserve the acts and laws passed by the legislature, and the public records of the district, and the proceedings of the governor in his executive department; and transmit authentic copies of such acts and proceedings, every six months, to the secretary of Congress: There shall also be appointed a court to consist of three judges, any two of whom to form a court, who shall have a commonlaw jurisdiction, and reside in the district, and have each therein a freehold estate in five hundred acres of land, while in the exercise of their offices; and their commissions shall continue in force during good behaviour.

[5] The governor and judges, or a majority of them, shall adopt and publish in the district, such laws of the original states, criminal and civil, as may be necessary, and best suited to the circumstances of the district, and report them to Congress, from time to time, which laws shall be in force in the district until the organization of the general assembly therein, unless disapproved of by Congress; but afterwards the legislature shall have authority to alter them as they shall think fit.

[6] The governor for the time being, shall be commander in chief of the militia, appoint and commission all officers in the same, below the rank of general officers; all general officers shall be appointed and commissioned by Congress.

[7] Previous to the organization of the general assembly, the governor shall appoint such magistrates, and other civil officers, in each county or township, as he shall find necessary for the preservation of the peace and good order in the same: After the general assembly shall

be organized, the powers and duties of magistrates and other civil officers shall be regulated and defined by the said assembly; but all magistrates and other civil officers, not herein otherwise directed, shall, during the continuance of this temporary government, be appointed by the governor.

[8] For the prevention of crimes and injuries, the laws to be adopted or made shall have force in all parts of the district, and for the execution of process, criminal and civil, the governor shall make proper divisions thereof—and he shall proceed from time to time, as circumstances may require, to lay out the parts of the district in which the Indian titles shall have been extinguished, into counties and townships, subject, however, to such alterations as may thereafter be made by the legislature.

[9] So soon as there shall be five thousand free male inhabitants, of full age, in the district, upon giving proof thereof to the governor, they shall receive authority, with time and place, to elect representatives from their counties or townships, to represent them in the general assembly; provided that for every five hundred free male inhabitants there shall be one representative, and so on progressively with the number of free male inhabitants, shall the right of representation increase, until the number of representatives shall amount to twenty-five, after which the number and proportion of representatives shall be regulated by the legislature; provided that no person be eligible or qualified to act as a representative, unless he shall have been a citizen of one of the United States three years and be a resident in the district, or unless he shall have resided in the district three years, and in either case shall likewise hold in his own right, in fee simple, two hundred acres of land within the same:—Provided also, that a freehold in fifty acres of land in the district, having been a citizen of one of the states, and being resident in the district; or the like freehold and two years residence in the district shall be necessary to qualify a man as an elector of a representative.

[10] The representatives thus elected, shall serve for the term of two years, and in case of the death of a representative, or removal from office, the governor shall issue a writ to the county or township for which he was a member, to elect another in his stead, to serve for the residue of the term.

[11] The general assembly, or legislature, shall consist of the governor, legislative council, and a house of representatives. The legislative council shall consist of five members, to continue in office five years,

unless sooner removed by Congress, any three of whom to be a quorum, and the members of the council shall be nominated and appointed in the following manner, to wit: As soon as representatives shall be elected, the governor shall appoint a time and place for them to meet together, and when met, they shall nominate ten persons, resident in the district, and each possessed of a freehold in five hundred acres of land, and return their names to Congress; five of whom Congress shall appoint and commission to serve as aforesaid; and whenever a vacancy shall happen in the council, by death or removal from office, the house of representatives shall nominate two persons, qualified as aforesaid, for each vacancy, and return their names to Congress; one of whom Congress shall appoint and commission for the residue of the term; and every five years, four months at least before the expiration of the time of service of the members of the council, the said house shall nominate ten persons, qualified as aforesaid, and return their names to Congress, five of whom Congress shall appoint and commission to serve as members of the council five years, unless sooner removed. And the governor, legislative council, and house of representatives, shall have authority to make laws in all cases for the good government of the district, not repugnant to the principles and articles in this ordinance established and declared. And all bills having passed by a majority in the house, and by a majority in the council, shall be referred to the governor for his assent; but no bill or legislative act whatever, shall be of any force without his assent. The governor shall have power to convene, prorogue and dissolve the general assembly, when in his opinion it shall be expedient.

[12] The governor, judges, legislative council, secretary, and such other officers as Congress shall appoint in the district, shall take an oath or affirmation of fidelity, and of office, the governor before the president of Congress, and all other officers before the governor. As soon as a legislature shall be formed in the district, the council and house, assembled in one room, shall have authority by joint ballot to elect a delegate to Congress, who shall have a seat in Congress, with a right of debating, but not of voting, during this temporary government.

[13] And for extending the fundamental principles of civil and religious liberty, which form the basis whereon these republics, their laws and constitutions are erected; to fix and establish those principles as the basis of all laws, constitutions and governments, which for-ever hereafter shall be formed in the said territory;—to provide also for the establishment of states, and permanent government therein, and for their admission to a share in the federal councils on an equal footing

with the original states, at as early periods as may be consistent with the general interest:

[14] It is hereby ordained and declared by the authority aforesaid, That the following articles shall be considered as articles of compact between the original states and the people and states in the said territory, and forever remain unalterable, unless by common consent, to wit:

[15] *Article the First.* No person, demeaning himself in a peaceable and orderly manner, shall ever be molested on account of his mode of worship or religious sentiments, in the said territory.

[16] *Article the Second.* The inhabitants of the said territory shall always be entitled to the benefits of the writ of habeas corpus, and of the trial by jury; of a proportionate representation of the people in the legislature, and of judicial proceedings according to the course of the common law; all persons shall be bailable unless for capital offences, where the proof shall be evident, or the presumption great; all fines shall be moderate, and no cruel or unusual punishments shall be inflicted; no man shall be deprived of his liberty or property but by the judgment of his peers, or the law of the land; and should the public exigencies make it necessary for the common preservation to take any person's property, or to demand his particular services, full compensation shall be made for the same;—and in the just preservation of rights and property it is understood and declared, that no law ought ever to be made, or have force in the said territory, that shall in any manner whatever interfere with, or affect private contracts or engagements, bona fide, and without fraud previously formed.

[17] *Article the Third.* Religion, morality, and knowledge, being necessary to good government and the happiness of mankind, schools and the means of education shall forever be encouraged. The utmost good faith shall always be observed towards the Indians; their lands and property shall never be taken from them without their consent; and in their property, rights and liberty, they never shall be invaded or disturbed, unless in just and lawful wars authorized by Congress; but laws founded in justice and humanity shall from time to time be made, for preventing wrongs being done to them, and for preserving peace and friendship with them.

[18] *Article the Fourth.* The said territory, and the states which may be formed therein, shall forever remain a part of this confederacy of the United States of America, subject to the articles of confederation,

and to such alterations therein as shall be constitutionally made; and to all the acts and ordinances of the United states in Congress assembled, conformable thereto. The inhabitants and settlers in the said territory, shall be subject to pay a part of the federal debts contracted or to be contracted, and a proportional part of the expences of government, to be apportioned on them by Congress, according to the same common rule and measure by which apportionments thereof shall be made on the other states; and the taxes for paying their proportion, shall be laid and levied by the authority and direction of the legislatures of the district or districts or new states, as in the original states, within the time agreed upon by the United States in Congress assembled. The legislatures of those districts, or new states, shall never interfere with the primary disposal of the soil by the United States in Congress assembled, nor with any regulations Congress may find necessary for securing the title in such soil to the bona fide purchasers. No tax shall be imposed on lands the property of the United States; and in no case shall non-resident proprietors be taxed higher than residents. The navigable waters leading into the Missisippi and St. Lawrence, and the carrying places between the same shall be common highways, and forever free, as well to the inhabitants of the said territory, as to the citizens of the United States, and those of any other states that may be admitted into the confederacy, without any tax, impost or duty therefor.

[19] *Article the Fifth.* There shall be formed in the said territory, not less than three nor more than five states; and the boundaries of the states, as soon as Virginia shall alter her act of cession and consent to the same, shall become fixed and established as follows, to wit: The western state, in the said territory, shall be bounded by the Missisippi, the Ohio and Wabash rivers; a direct line drawn from the Wabash and Post Vincent's due north, to the territorial line between the United States and Canada, and by the said territorial line to the lake of the Woods and Missisippi. The middle state shall be bounded by the said direct line, the Wabash from Post Vincent's to the Ohio; by the Ohio, by a direct line drawn due north from the mouth of the Great Miami to the said territorial line, and by the said territorial line. The eastern state shall be bounded by the last mentioned direct line, the Ohio, Pennsylvania, and the said territorial line: Provided however, And it is further understood and declared, that the boundaries of these three states, shall be subject so far to be altered, that if Congress shall hereafter find it expedient, they shall have authority to form one or two states in that part of the said territory which lies north of an east and west line drawn through the southerly bend or extreme of lake Michigan: and whenever any of the said states shall have sixty thousand free

inhabitants therein, such state shall be admitted by its delegates into the Congress of the United states, on an equal footing with the original states in all respects whatever; and shall be at liberty to form a permanent constitution and state government: Provided the constitution and government so to be formed, shall be republican, and in conformity to the principles contained in these articles; and so far as it can be consistent with the general interest of the confederacy, such admission shall be allowed at an earlier period, and when there may be a less number of free inhabitants in the state than sixty thousand.

[20] *Article the Sixth.* There shall be neither slavery nor involuntary servitude in the said territory, otherwise than in punishment of crimes whereof the party shall have been duly convicted: Provided always, that any person escaping into the same, from whom labor or service is lawfully claimed in any one of the original states, such fugitive may be lawfully reclaimed and conveyed to the person claiming his or her labor or service as aforesaid.

Be it ordained by the authority aforesaid, That the resolutions of the 23d of April, 1784, relative to the subject of this ordinance, be, and the same are hereby repealed and declared null and void.

DONE by the UNITED STATES in CONGRESS assembled, the 13th day of July, in the year of our Lord 1787, and of their sovereignty and independence the 12th.

XIV

The United States Constitution

1787

COMMENTARY BY DONALD S. LUTZ

EXCEPT FOR THE MASSACHUSETTS CONSTITUTION of 1780, the United States Constitution of 1787 is the oldest founding document still in use. The national document is also one of the shortest ever written. Perhaps because of its age and the veneration that has grown up around it, the sometimes unfamiliar terminology from another era, its succinctness, and the technical treatment it has received from the Supreme Court, many people approach the document as if it is some mysterious puzzle understandable only to lawyers.

This view is inappropriate for two reasons. First, the whole point of a written constitution is to make available to the average citizen a description of the institutions and rules whereby a people govern themselves. Any constitution that cannot be understood by its citizens is, in effect, *not* a constitution. Second, this attitude is inappropriate because it tends to produce what is known as a "self-fulfilling prophecy"— something which, when believed, makes what is believed come true. Anyone who approaches the Constitution as if it is not understandable is unlikely to take the time or exert the effort that is needed to understand the document.

In a sense the Constitution is both a simple, straightforward document and a vague, complicated set of principles that can be and has been interpreted differently at various times. The Constitution is really composed of two parts: an outline for a plan of government and a theoretical blueprint setting forth basic principles for that government. The intricate plan of government delineated in the Constitution is understood relatively easily; the theoretical basis for this government, however, is more complex. Four organizing principles of the Constitution, taken together, form a coherent theory of politics. These four constitutional principles are federalism, the extended republic, separation of powers, and checks and balances.

Federalism

Federalism, the division and sharing of power between state and national governments, rests in turn upon three concepts—popular sovereignty, limited government, and dual citizenship. Limited government and dual citizenship are specific applications of the general concept of popular sovereignty.

Popular sovereignty is the idea that the people have the final say in political matters, that they are ultimately in control and government exists to serve them, not *vice versa*. We know that popular sovereignty is an assumption underlying the Constitution because the Declaration of Independence tells us so; because, the preamble to the Constitution says that "We the People of the United States" created the government; and because all offices rest ultimately upon elections or upon those who are elected. We also know that popular sovereignty is a fact of American political life because the fate of most political decisions ultimately turns on some vote of *popular consent*, the corollary of popular sovereignty. There are no hereditary offices, offices reserved for special groups of people, or offices that can be bought with wealth. Implicit in the opening sentence of the preamble is the notion that the sovereign people acting here are the citizens of the United States, not the citizens of the states. The existence of state constitutions can be made compatible with the simultaneous existence of a national government precisely because there is popular sovereignty. That is, because the people have ultimate power, they can divide up political power and parcel it out to whatever government they wish, or keep some of it in their hands and give it to no government. The parceling out of power by constitutional means two different governments, each serving a different geographical configuration of the American body politic, is known as federalism. Keeping some power away from government altogether is known as limited government.

Limited government flows from popular sovereignty in the sense that if the people have ultimate power, and the citizens create government, government is limited to only those powers given to it by the people in the Constitution. Article I, Section 8 is a list of those powers given to the national government. Article I, Section 9 is a list of those powers which might go with the powers in Section 8, but which are denied to the national government. Article I, Section 10 is a list of those powers denied to the state governments. These three sections, plus the Bill of Rights, limit the powers available to the national and state governments. State governments, in turn, are empowered and further limited by their respective constitutions and bills of rights.

Dual citizenship means that the people in our country are citizens twice. They are simultaneously citizens of the United States and of the state wherein they reside. That is, the people use their popular sovereignty twice—as a whole people to create the national government and then divided into smaller publics to create a state government for each state public. Dual citizenship is found in Article IV, Section 2 of the Constitution where a distinction is made between "The Citizens of each State" and "Citizens in several States." The latter phrase means the citizens of all the states or of the United States. Dual citizenship is also implicit in Article I, sections 8, 9, and 10 which distribute power between national and state governments. The only way that section 10 can deny powers to states at the same time that sections 8 and 9 can grant and limit power to the national government is if it is the same people who have power over both sets of government. The same people have a true citizenship in relation to both the national and state governments not only because they create both governments, but also because they can be parties in state courts for laws passed by the state governments just as they can in national courts for laws passed by the national government. That every American has sovereignty over two governments, lives under two constitutions, elects people to two legislatures, is bound by two sets of laws, and can go to either of two court systems is the institutional basis for dual citizenship.

Federalism and the dual citizenship underlying it inform many other parts of the Constitution. For example, Article I, Section 2 of the Constitution declares the electorate for the House of Representatives to be the same as that for the lower house in the respective state legislatures. The electorate for the House would thus be defined by the states. Also, the same state-defined electorate would be electing the state legislatures, which would in turn be electing the United States Senate. The Senate is apportioned to give each state equal representation. The Senate thus represents the states and brings federalism into the national legislature.

Federalism underlies the amendment process, set forth in Article V, which involves action by both national and state institutions. The president is elected by an electoral college apportioned according to state population, elected by the citizens of the different states, with electors assembling in their states to decide how to cast their votes. If the electoral college fails to produce a winner in the presidential election, the election is thrown into the United States House of Representatives where the representatives are grouped into their state delegations with each state having one vote. Federalism is also stated explicitly in the Tenth Amendment, which provides that powers not delegated to the national government in Article I, Section 8, nor denied to the states in Article I, Section 10, are reserved to the states, or to the people (another link joining the ideas of federalism, limited government, and popular sovereignty).

These are just a few examples of how federalism runs through and ties together virtually every part of the Constitution. In fact, the states are relevant, either by being mentioned or by direct implication, at least fifty times in forty-two separate sections of the document, not counting the amendments. Federalism not only underlies and ties the document together; without federalism there never would have been a United States Constitution to begin with, for the idea of the extended republic required federalism, a fact that is unaltered by any changes inthe operation of the federal system since 1789.

The Extended Republic

The Constitution had twin goals—to preserve liberty and to create a stable, effective government. Liberty already existed in America in 1787 and did not have to be created, only preserved. Ineffectiveness of government at the national level had two sources: the powers granted the Congress under the Articles of Confederation were insufficient, and Congress could not use its powers to control improper state actions or to affect individual citizens directly. However, directness was a two-way street in American constitutionalism. In order for government to act directly upon the citizens, the founders had to open up the government to be acted upon directly by the citizens. Any constitution that solved the problem of ineffective national government would have to be approved by the citizens and involve citizens in national elections—otherwise the first principle of popular sovereignty would not be met. However, what was to prevent the same dangers of majority tyranny that some saw at the state level from arising at the national level? Expanding national powers would remove certain important matters from state majorities but expose those matters to national majorities and thus the threat of national tyranny. The solution offered by the United States Constitution was to expand national power, to have those powers act directly upon the citizens, *and* to so structure national government that it would check majority tyranny and its danger to liberty.

The founders decided that majority tyranny could be controlled through two means: representation and the extended republic. Representation filters upward men of greater virtue. Virtuous men are those who seek the common good rather than the partial good of any one faction. However, the framers of the Constitution and their allies did not believe that virtuous men always would be elected. Even if they were, this solution would be inadequate to prevent a tyrannical majority from getting its way for the majority elects these men and can unelect them.

Ultimately the solution to the problem of majority tyranny lay in a republic so extended, so large, with such a diverse population, that the existence of a natural majority was rendered highly unlikely, if not impossible. With no natural majority on a given issue, but only a large number of minority factions, *and with the requirement for majority rule to pass policy*, any majority must be a coalition constructed from different minorities. The creation of a majority coalition will take time, the majority will be temporary for that issue only, and there will be no basis for a common passion sufficient for the majority to seek to harm the vital interests of any minority. The process of constructing a majority would create enough delay to result in policy based upon calm calculations of interest rather than passion. Hence, a stable and effective government would be produced and preserved.

The extended republic was created by two constitutional provisions—the ratification requirement of at least nine states in Article VII and the provision in Article IV, Section 3 for the admission of new states. There is nothing else in the Constitution relevant for creating an *extended* republic, and the two provisions that are relevant are taken directly from the Articles of Confederation which the Constitution was supposed to correct. Why is it that the solution to the ineffectiveness of the Articles, the extended republic, was already to be found in the Articles?

The answer lies in the second word in the phrase "extended republic." The nation created by the Articles of Confederation was extensive, but it was not a republic because the Congress did not embody the republican principle—direct election by the people. What made the Constitution a solution for ineffective government was that the House of Representatives in Congress was to be elected directly by the people, *and thus Congress could pass laws directly affecting those who elected them.*

The Articles of Confederation created an extended confederacy, but
the Constitution created an *extended republic*. The key to the solution,
then, is not only the size of the country, but the fact that a national
citizenry has a direct role in the government of a large country. Article
I, Section 2 which provides for direct election of the House of Representatives was thus of great importance since it established the relationship necessary for the extended republic to be, in fact, a republic.

The extended republic would not have come into existence without
federalism, which made possible both its extended and republican qualities. First of all, it was politically unrealistic to adopt a unitary government. No proposal that destroyed state governments would have
been ratified. The state governments could not be made simply to
disappear. Federalism allowed many states to be linked, creating a large
or extended republic, without destroying state government. Furthermore, the national government could not be republican in form unless
its legislature was elected by the people. This, in turn, was not possible
unless the government and people had a direct relationship. The creation of dual citizenship permitted a direct relationship between citizens
and without federalism there would have been no extended republic.

Separation of Powers

Having controlled the problem of majority tyranny, the founders also
needed a solution for *governmental* tyranny—defined as the use of arbitrary power by those in government over the people. The solution
for governmental tyranny was structurally similar to that for majority
tyranny. The powers given to the national government were divided
among the two houses of the legislature and the three branches of the
government such that power was fragmented. No one part of the government had a "majority" of the power, but the various branches had
to cooperate to govern. Consensus on the common good, among the
branches of government as among the various groups comprising the
American people, was thus a precondition for action by the national
government.

Separation of powers had its roots at least partly in the colonial
attempt to prevent the crown-appointed governors from buying off members of the legislature. Those governors, in imitation of the king in
England, would offer well paying positions in the executive branch to
key members of the legislature. The colonists successfully resisted the
attempts by the governors to divide them through patronage and instituted prohibitions on multiple officeholding. Most of the explicit ref-

erences to separation of powers in the early state constitutions reflect
more the colonial experience than the adoption of a coherent theory of
separation of powers.

Montesquieu was full of praise for the separation of powers in
England, and although his analysis of the English constitution in theory
had little resemblance to its actual operation, he still deeply impressed
Americans. The United States Constitution bears the imprint of his
ideas, most notably in the separate judiciary. English practice was to
make the judiciary part of the executive, which made the crown the
final court of appeal. The American colonial system followed the English
model, but after independence the state constitutions usually made the
judiciary the creature of the legislature, which made the legislature the
final court of appeal. The idea of a separate judiciary probably came
from Montesquieu. However, most state constitutions had already provided for a separate judiciary by barring judges from holding other state
office. And, contrary to Montesquieu's recommendation, the Supreme
Court was made a permanent body with its members serving on good
behavior instead of being frequently replaced.

Although the founders heeded Montesquieu and made separation
of powers an important feature of the Constitution, the document in
the end did not describe simply a separation-of-powers system. The
Americans were responding to different circumstances, and they developed a different, more complex system than the one Montequieu
described. For one thing, in the American context, the phrase "separation of powers" was a misnomer. A more accurate phrase would have
been "separation of functions with shared powers." If the powers had
really been separated, the three branches would have nothing to do
with each other, whereas in the Constitution they were all interlocked
like an intricate machine. The separated functions were linked through
a system of checks and balances that resulted in shared powers.

Checks and Balances

There are a considerable number of checks in the United States Constitution. For example, the president can veto legislation, and the legislature can override the veto with a two-thirds majority. The Senate
must approve treaties made by the president, and it also approves appointments made by the president. Judicial review is not provided for
explicitly in the Constitution, and thus is not a formal constitutional
check, but Congress can make or unmake lower courts, decide the size
of the Supreme Court, determine its appellate jurisdiction, and set the

salaries for the executive and judiciary. It also has the power to impeach members of the executive and judicial branches.

If one counts up all of the checks, and considers their implications, it becomes clear that the primary result of the system of checks was to permit the legislature to keep a leash on the other two branches. The executive had real power, unlike the executives in most of the state constitutions, and the Supreme Court had an historically unprecedented level of independence. But, not completely trusting a separate and independently powerful executive or judiciary, the architects of the Constitution built in a series of leashes, most of which led back to Congress. The executive, legislative, and judicial powers were separated to a certain degree, but then linked firmly in a partial remixing, and Congress was dominant in the mix.

In a sense, the Senate does check the House of Representatives, but by the same token the House checks the Senate. Furthermore, most of the Senate's explicit checks are aimed not at the House but at the executive such as in its power to approve or reject treaties and appointments. Having the vice president preside over the Senate, and giving him a vote in evenly balanced and therefore probably politically sensitive matters, provides a check by the executive upon the Senate. Although most checks have the effect of enhancing control by the legislature, they also have the effect of linking the three branches and thus undercutting the strict separation of powers.

In addition to having the vice president serve as the president of the Senate, the Constitution furthers the mixing of powers by involving the Supreme Court—specifically, the chief justice of the United States—in the impeachment of the president and by the impeachment process itself. By implication, this involved the legislature in the execution and adjudication of laws. Congress historically backed off from using the instrument of impeachment for this purpose, and we now have an institution of impeachment whose meaning has evolved through historical practice rather than formal constitutional amendment. Even if impeachment was intended to be used only in instances of criminal behavior, Congress would be involved in a judicial proceeding, although limited to removal from office and disqualification from future officeholding as a penalty.

The standard practice is to put "checks" together with "balances" almost as if they are one word; but they are not the same, or even similar. Nor does the term "balance" refer to balances within the national government such as a balance between the two houses or the balance between the president and Congress. The term has little to do with balance in the sense of scales and equilibrium. Rather it refers to a mechanism or mechanisms for regulating the speed at which something occurs—a mechanistic definition similar to that used during the eighteenth century by clockmakers or physicists like Isaac Newton. The first major balance comprises the different terms of office for the major institutions. Let us suppose that a faction is attempting to gain control of the national government for its own ends and manages to inflame a good portion of the electorate into joining them. First, they must gain a majority in the House of Representatives. Say they manage to win a majority of the House in the next election. Only one-third of the Senate was up for reelection that year, so they must wait two more years to gain control of the Senate. They also must wait until then in order to win the presidency. Otherwise the president might veto the legislation, and without a majority in the Senate, let alone two-thirds, the veto could not be overridden. Then there is the Supreme Court. The justices must be replaced or reformed if they are not to fight a rearguard action against the desired changes in public policy. Here is one example of how checks come into play to support balances. The different terms of office mean that a faction must put together a majority faction, and keep it together for at least four years, probably longer. Like a clock balance, this constitutional balance keeps the system moving at a more or less regular speed that cannot be hurried.

The second major balance results from the different constituencies to which each part of the government is beholden. Each member of the House has a relatively small, compact constituency that is concerned mostly with local issues. Any faction attempting to gain control of the House must find either an issue that cuts across a majority of congressional districts, an unlikely event in an extended republic, or some way of linking their cause to different local issues in a majority of congressional districts. Then, the faction must win over a majority in each of a majority of state legislatures to gain control of the Senate, as was envisioned in the original Constitution. The framers believed that state legislators were likely to be more virtuous, in the sense of having political, intellectual, and moral abilities to a higher degree than that found in the general population. These legislators would be harder to fool or convince than the average voter in congressional districts, and winning them over would take a different kind of campaigning. Also, these legislators have state interests that must be addressed. Then, a faction would have to convince a majority in the electoral college to vote for its presidential candidate. The constituency for the Supreme Court is the president plus the Senate. Each constituency has different characteristics, requires a different kind of approach, and (as one moves up the ladder) requires more careful argumentation to persuade. If a faction, after four or more years, manages to gain control of the two houses of Congress and the presidency, then it deserves to get its legislation. Once again a balance has the effect of producing a process that moves forward only in a steady, deliberative fashion.

The two balances interact with each other, the many constitutional checks, the extended republic, and federalism to produce an interlocking effect. This effect resembles the workings of a clock or some other machine with gears, levers, and springs. At no point does the model assume that virtuous men will prevent majority tyranny, only that every one following their own interest will result in a highly deliberative (and thus slow) process.

We see, in discussing the balances, how the various parts of the Constitution work together to produce a coherent effect. The effect is not anti-majoritarian. In fact, we can see now why the checks generally run in favor of Congress. The president and Supreme Court are the easiest branches to capture through covert politics. Majority will is expressed most directly at the national level through Congress, and the majority in control of Congress at the time can rein in either or both of the other branches if they get too far out of line. In the long run, majorities composed of those whose permanent, aggregate interests are threatened will remain intense long enough to gain control of the government. These majorities ought to win.

The net effect of the complicated structure of institutions to prevent governmental tyranny was to induce delay in the political process. Americans had a deep love for deliberative processes, and here they made the process very deliberative. Some today see the institutions of delay as a means of thwarting majority will, even of preventing majority rule. However, the entire system assumes ultimate majority rule or else the process will not work. In fact, the value of deliberation for adequate "reflection and choice" by the public forms the starting point for *The Federalist*, examined in the next two chapters. If the founders did not intend for the majority to rule, why did they even worry about preventing majority tyranny? Directly electing the House of Representatives, compared with the Articles of Confederation where Congress was elected by the state legislatures, does not look like a step away from majority rule but rather a step toward it. This and other aspects of the United States Constitution argue against an elitist interpretation of it.

The political system established by the Constitution is rather strange by European standards. Initially, it looks like a separation of powers document, but then it turns out that the functions, not the powers, are separated. Another quick glance appears to show a government with the branches in balance. Further analysis shows the branches not to be balanced. Instead, a preponderance of checks are given to the legislature to keep a rein on the other branches. The checks that are supposed to balance are here used to unbalance the powers and mix them. The resulting political system resembles a hopeless confusion by European standards. What the United States Constitution seems most like is an evolved version of state constitutions, particularly the Massachusetts Constitution of 1780, although one can recognize a similar, less evolved pattern in the 1776 Virginia and 1777 New York constitutions. We also see how much the Constitution owes to the Articles of Confederation for both form and content. Finally, we can see a more long-term debt to colonial documents, especially with respect to popular sovereignty, federalism, the creation and self-definition of a people, and even the idea of a constitution—that there should be a single document containing a description of governmental institutions and processes that is binding on all citizens, rulers and ruled alike.

For Further Reading

Charles A. Beard. *An Economic Interpretation of the Constitution of the United States.* New York, 1913.

Christopher Collier and James Lincoln Collier. *Decision in Philadelphia: The Constitutional Convention of 1787.* New York, 1986.

Patrick T. Conley and John P. Kaminski, eds. *The Constitution and the States: The Role of the Original Thirteen in the Framing and Adoption of the Federal Constitution.* Madison, Wisc., 1988.

Leonard W. Levy, Kenneth L. Karst, and Dennis J. Mahoney, eds. *Encyclopedia of the American Constitution* 4 vols. New York, 1986.

John P. Kaminski and Richard Leffler, eds. *Federalists and Antifederalists: The Debate Over the Ratification of the Constitution.* Madison, Wisc., 1989.

Michael Kammen, ed. *The Origins of the American Constitution: A Documentary History.* New York, 1986.

Forrest McDonald. *Novus Ordo Seclorum: The Intellectual Origins of the Constitution.* Lawrence, Kan., 1985.

Jackson Turner Main. *The Antifederalists: Critics of the Constitution, 1781–1788.* Chapel Hill, 1961.

Clinton Rossiter. *1787: The Grand Convention.* New York, 1966.

Jeffery St. John. *Constitutional Journal: A Correspondent's Report from the Convention of 1787.* Ottawa, Ill., 1987.

Carl Van Doren. *The Great Rehearsal: The Story of the Making and Ratifying of the Constitution of the United States.* New York, 1948.

The United States Constitution

We the People of the United States, in Order to form a more perfect[1] Union, establish Justice, insure domestic Tranquility, provide for the common defence, promote the general Welfare,[2] and secure the Blessings of Liberty to ourselves and our Posterity, do ordain and establish this Constitution for the United States of America.

Article. I.

Section. 1. All legislative Powers herein granted shall be vested in a Congress of the United States, which shall consist of a Senate and House of Representatives.

Section. 2. The House of Representatives shall be composed of Members chosen every second Year by the People of the several States, and the Electors[3] in each State shall have the Qualifications requisite for Electors of the most numerous Branch of the State Legislature.

No Person shall be a Representative who shall not have attained to the Age of twenty five Years, and been seven Years a Citizen of the United States, and who shall not, when elected, be an Inhabitant of that State in which he shall be chosen.

Representatives and direct Taxes[4] shall be apportioned among the several States which may be included within this Union, according to their respective Numbers, which shall be determined by adding to the whole Number of free Persons, including those bound to Service for a Term of Years, and excluding Indians not taxed, three fifths of all other Persons.[5] The actual Enumeration[6] shall be made within three Years

Engrossed manuscript, Record Group II, National Archives. Reprinted from Merrill Jensen, ed., *The Documentary History of the Ratification of the Constitution* (Madison, Wisc., 1976), I: 306–17.

[1] "More perfect" suggests the idea of perfectability in government.

[2] The word "Welfare" did not refer then to what we now call "welfare programs." Rather, "general Welfare" meant "common good."

[3] "Electors" here means "voters" as in those who elect.

[4] "Direct Taxes" refers to taxing individuals directly through such means as a property tax or an income tax.

[5] "Those bound to service" refers to indentured servants. Some Indians paid taxes and were considered citizens of the states wherein they resided. Most did not pay taxes and so, even though they were free persons could not be counted for purposes of apportioning either taxes or representatives to Congress. See footnote 35 to the Articles

after the first Meeting of the Congress of the United States, and within every subsequent Term of ten Years, in such Manner as they shall by Law direct. The Number of Representatives shall not exceed one for every thirty Thousand, but each State shall have at Least one Representative; and until such enumeration shall be made, the State of New Hampshire shall be entitled to chuse three, Massachusetts eight, Rhode-Island and Providence Plantations one, Connecticut five, New-York six, New Jersey four, Pennsylvania eight, Delaware one, Maryland six, Virginia ten, North Carolina five, South Carolina five, and Georgia three.

When vacancies happen in the Representation from any State, the Executive Authority thereof shall issue Writs of Election to fill such Vacancies.

The House of Representatives shall chuse their Speaker and other Officers; and shall have the sole Power of Impeachment.

Section. 3. The Senate of the United States shall be composed of two Senators from each State, chosen by the Legislature thereof, for six Years; and each Senator shall have one Vote.

Immediately after they shall be assembled in Consequence of the first Election, they shall be divided as equally as may be into three Classes. The Seats of the Senators of the first Class shall be vacated at the Expiration of the second Year, of the second Class at the Expiration of the fourth Year, and of the third Class at the Expiration of the sixth Year, so that one third may be chosen every second Year; and if Vacancies happen by Resignation, or otherwise, during the Recess of the Legislature of any State, the Executive thereof may make temporary Appointments until the next Meeting of the Legislature, which shall then fill such Vacancies.

---

of Confederation. Just as every state (with the exception of Massachusetts) in 1789 had at least a few slaves, every state also had at least a few free blacks, and those paying taxes could vote. The number of blacks who were slaves was reduced by two-fifths for purposes of assessing taxes and representation to the states. This clause seemed to have the effect of making a slave three-fifths of a free person, and has often been so read, both by those denouncing the Constitution as a pro-slavery document and by those claiming that the Constitution accorded slaves at least partial status as human beings. Both readings are incorrect; the framers of the document recognized that slaves were both human beings and property. The three-fifths ratio was taken from an amendment proposed to the Articles of Confederation in April 1783 that would have apportioned federal expenses by population (with three-fifths of the slaves counted) instead of by the value of property. Eleven of the thirteen states had ratified this amendment; and, although not officially adopted, the Confederation Congress used population as the basis for apportioning expenses among the states in 1786.

6 "Enumeration" here refers to taking a census of the population for purposes of allotting taxes and representation to the states.

No Person shall be a Senator who shall not have attained to the Age of thirty Years, and been nine Years a Citizen of the United States, and who shall not, when elected, be an Inhabitant of that State for which he shall be chosen.

The Vice President of the United States shall be President of the Senate, but shall have no Vote, unless they be equally divided.

The Senate shall chuse their other Officers, and also a President pro tempore,[7] in the Absence of the Vice President, or when he shall exercise the Office of President of the United States.

The Senate shall have the sole Power to try all Impeachments. When sitting for that Purpose, they shall be on Oath or Affirmation.[8] When the President of the United States is tried, the Chief Justice shall preside: And no Person shall be convicted without the Concurrence of two thirds of the Members present.

Judgment in Cases of Impeachment shall not extend further than to removal from Office, and disqualification to hold and enjoy any Office of honor, Trust or Profit under the United States: but the Party convicted shall nevertheless be liable and subject to Indictment, Trial, Judgment and Punishment, according to Law.

Section. 4. The Times, Places and Manner of holding Elections for Senators and Representatives, shall be prescribed in each State by the Legislature thereof; but the Congress may at any time by Law make or alter such Regulations, except as to the Places of chusing Senators.

The Congress shall assemble at least once in every Year, and such Meeting shall be on the first Monday in December, unless they shall by Law appoint a different Day.

Section. 5. Each House shall be the Judge of the Elections, Returns and Qualifications of its own Members, and a Majority of each shall constitute a Quorum to do Business; but a smaller Number may adjourn from day to day, and may be authorized to compel the Attendance of absent Members, in such Manner, and under such Penalties as each House may provide.

Each House may determine the Rules of its Proceedings, punish its members for disorderly Behaviour, and, with the Concurrence of two thirds, expel a Member.

---

[7] *"Pro tempore"* is a Latin phrase meaning "temporary." The president *pro tempore* of the Senate presides temporarily in the absence of the vice president of the United States who is the actual president of the Senate.

[8] Many people then and now, such as Quakers, have personal and religious grounds for refusing to take an oath. These people are allowed to provide "affirmation" that they are telling the truth without calling upon God or using God's name. Note that the presidential oath in the last paragraph of Article I, Section 1 of the Constitution is consistent with the practice of allowing an affirmation.

Each House shall keep a Journal of its Proceedings, and from time to time publish the same, excepting such Parts as may in their Judgment require Secrecy; and the Yeas and Nays of the Members of either House on any question shall, at the Desire of one fifth of those Present, be entered on the Journal.

Neither House, during the Session of Congress, shall, without the Consent of the other, adjourn for more than three days, nor to any other Place than that in which the two Houses shall be sitting.

Section. 6. The Senators and Representatives shall receive a Compensation for their Services, to be ascertained by Law, and paid out of the Treasury of the United States. They shall in all Cases, except Treason, Felony and Breach of the Peace, be privileged from Arrest during their Attendance at the Session of their respective Houses, and in going to and returning from the same; and for any Speech or Debate in either House, they shall not be questioned in any other Place.

No Senator or Representative shall, during the Time for which he was elected, be appointed to any civil Office under the Authority of the United States which shall have been created, or the Emoluments[9] whereof shall have been encreased during such time; and no Person holding any Office under the United States, shall be a Member of either House during his Continuance in Office.

Section. 7. All Bills for raising Revenue shall originate in the House of Representatives; but the Senate may propose or concur with Amendments as on other Bills.

Every Bill which shall have passed the House of Representatives and the Senate shall, before it become a Law, be presented to the President of the United States; If he approve he shall sign it, but if not he shall return it, with his Objections to that House in which it shall have originated, who shall enter the Objections at large on their Journal, and proceed to reconsider it. If after such Reconsideration two thirds of that House shall agree to pass the Bill, it shall be sent, together with the Objections, to the other House, by which it shall likewise be reconsidered, and if approved by two thirds of that House, it shall become a Law. But in all such Cases the Votes of both Houses shall be determined by yeas and Nays, and the Names of the Persons voting for and against the Bill shall be entered on the Journal of each House respectively. If any Bill shall not be returned by the President within ten Days (Sundays excepted) after it shall have been presented to him, the Same shall be a Law, in like Manner as if he had signed it, unless the Congress

---

[9] An "emolument" is any kind of payment received for work whether in the form of salary, wages, fees, or prizes.

by their Adjournment prevent its Return, in which Case it shall not be a Law.

Every Order, Resolution, or Vote to which the Concurrence of the Senate and House of Representatives may be necessary (except on a question of Adjournment) shall be presented to the President of the United States; and before the Same shall take Effect, shall be approved by him, or being disapproved by him, shall be repassed by two thirds of the Senate and House of Representatives, according to the Rules and Limitations prescribed in the Case of a Bill.

Section. 8. The Congress shall have Power To lay and collect Taxes, Duties, Imposts and Excises,[10] to pay the Debts and provide for the common Defence and general Welfare of the United States; but all Duties, Imposts and Excises shall be uniform throughout the United States;

To borrow Money on the credit of the United States;

To regulate Commerce with foreign Nations, and among the several States, and with the Indian Tribes;

To establish an uniform Rule of Naturalization, and uniform Laws on the subject of Bankruptcies throughout the United States;

To coin Money, regulate the Value thereof, and of foreign Coin, and fix the Standard of Weights and Measures;

To provide for the Punishment of counterfeiting the Securities and current Coin of the United States;

To establish Post Offices and post Roads;

To promote the Progress of Science and useful Arts, by securing for limited Times to Authors and Inventors the exclusive Right to their respective Writings and Discoveries;

To constitute Tribunals inferior to the supreme Court;

To define and punish Piracies and Felonies committed on the high Seas, and Offences against the Law of Nations;

To declare War, grant Letters of Marque[11] and Reprisal, and make Rules concerning Captures on Land and Water;

---

[10] Strictly speaking, an "impost" is a tax levied on imported goods; a "duty" is a tax levied on imports or exports (usually manufactured goods); and an "excise" is a tax levied on commodities like tobacco and liquor as they are made, sold, or consumed in the country. Today, there is often an excise on services as well, such as phone calls or electricity usage. This is to be distinguished from a sales tax, because an excise tax is applied to an activity while a sales tax is applied to an economic transaction. An excise can also refer to a fee paid for a license to carry on a certain occupation.

[11] "Letters of marque" refers to a government document authorizing an individual to make reprisals on the subjects or citizens of an enemy nation. (See footnote 19 to The Articles of Confederation.)

To raise and support Armies, but no Appropriation of Money to that Use shall be for a longer Term than two Years;

To provide and maintain a Navy;

To make Rules for the Government and Regulation of the land and naval Forces;

To provide for calling forth the Militia to execute the Laws of the Union, suppress Insurrections and repel Invasions;

To provide for organizing, arming, and disciplining, the Militia, and for governing such Part of them as may be employed in the Service of the United States, reserving to the States respectively, the Appointment of the Officers, and the Authority of training the Militia according to the discipline prescribed by Congress;

To exercise exclusive Legislation in all Cases whatsoever, over such District (not exceeding ten Miles square)[12] as may, by Cession of particular States,[13] and the Acceptance of Congress, become the Seat of the Government of the United States, and to exercise like Authority over all Places purchased by the Consent of the Legislature of the State in which the same shall be, for the Erection of Forts, Magazines, Arsenals, dock-Yards, and other needful Buildings;—And

To make all Laws which shall be necessary and proper for carrying into Execution the foregoing Powers, and all other Powers vested by this Constitution in the Government of the United States, or in any Department or Officer thereof.

Section. 9. The Migration or Importation of such Persons as any of the States now existing shall think proper to admit, shall not be prohibited by the Congress prior to the Year one thousand eight hundred and eight, but a Tax or duty may be imposed on such Importation, not exceeding ten dollars for each Person.

The Privilege of the Writ of Habeas Corpus[14] shall not be suspended, unless when in Cases of Rebellion or Invasion the public Safety may require it.

---

[12] This does not say ten square miles, but a square district no larger than ten miles on a side, which is 100 square miles.

[13] The seat of national government will be in a district, now called the District of Columbia, which must be territory ceded by one or more states.

[14] *Habeas corpus* is a latin term meaning "here is the body." In law it is a writ or order requiring that a prisoner be brought before a court at a stated time, in public, to determine whether detention or imprisonment is legal. This is to protect one against false arrest or illegal detention, and resulted in reaction to the practice of certain English kings who arrested enemies and other people, for unstated reasons, who were never seen again.

No Bill of Attainder[15] or ex post facto Law[16] shall be passed.

No Capitation,[17] or other direct, Tax shall be laid, unless in Proportion to the Census or Enumeration herein before directed to be taken.

No Tax or Duty shall be laid on Articles exported from any State.

No Preference shall be given by any Regulation of Commerce or Revenue to the Ports of one State over those of another: nor shall Vessels bound to, or from, one State, be obliged to enter, clear, or pay Duties in another.

No Money shall be drawn from the Treasury, but in Consequence of Appropriations made by Law; and a regular Statement and Account of the Receipts and Expenditures of all public Money shall be published from time to time.

No Title of Nobility shall be granted by the United States: And no Person holding any Office of Profit or Trust under them, shall, without the Consent of the Congress, accept of any present, Emolument, Office, or Title, of any kind whatever, from any King, Prince, or foreign State.

Section. 10. No State shall enter into any Treaty, Alliance, or Confederation; grant Letters of Marque and Reprisal; coin Money; emit Bills of Credit; make any Thing but gold and silver Coin a Tender in Payment of Debts; pass any Bill of Attainder, ex post facto Law, or Law impairing the Obligation of Contracts, or grant any Title of Nobility.

No State shall, without the Consent of the Congress, lay any Imposts or Duties on Imports or Exports, except what may be absolutely necessary for executing it's inspection Laws: and the net Produce of all Duties and Imposts, laid by any State on Imports or Exports, shall be for the Use of the Treasury of the United States; and all such Laws shall be subject to the Revision and Controul of the Congress.

---

[15] A "bill of attainder" is a law by which a legislature imposes a penalty directly on an individual—and thus contradicts the fundamental principle of Anglo-American law that punishments can only be imposed after due process of law. The term also indicates that such bills "attainted the blood" (that is, the family) of the subject of the bill; descendants of a person targeted by a bill of attainder suffered side effects of the penalties imposed by that bill, such as the loss of rights to inherit the attainted person's property. Note that, although in theory bills of attainder contradict fundamental notions of due process in Anglo-American law, in practice the British Parliament in the seventeenth century could and did enact bills of attainder.

[16] An *ex post facto* law is one that makes a crime out of an action performed before the law was passed.

[17] A tax or fee of so much per head, ie., a poll tax.

No State shall, without the Consent of Congress, lay any Duty of Tonnage, keep Troops, or Ships of War in time of Peace, enter into any Agreement or Compact with another State, or with a foreign Power, or engage in War, unless actually invaded, or in such imminent Danger as will not admit of delay.

Article. II.

Section. 1. The executive Power shall be vested in a President of the United States of America. He shall hold his Office during the Term of four Years, and, together with the Vice President, chosen for the same Term, be elected, as follows

Each State shall appoint, in such Manner as the Legislature thereof may direct, a Number of Electors,[18] equal to the whole Number of Senators and Representatives to which the State may be entitled in the Congress: but no Senator or Representative, or Person holding an Office of Trust or Profit under the United States, shall be appointed an Elector.

The Electors shall meet in their respective States and vote by Ballot for two Persons, of whom one at least shall not be an Inhabitant of the same State with themselves. And they shall make a List of all the Persons voted for, and of the Number of Votes for each; which List they shall sign and certify, and transmit sealed to the Seat of the Government of the United States, directed to the President of the Senate. The President of the Senate shall, in the Presence of the Senate and House of Representatives, open all the Certificates, and the Votes shall then be counted. The Person having the greatest Number of Votes shall be the President, if such Number be a Majority of the whole Number of Electors appointed; and if there be more than one who have such Majority, and have an equal Number of Votes, then the House of Representatives shall immediately chuse by Ballot one of them for President; and if no Person have a Majority, then from the five highest on the List the said House shall in like Manner chuse the President. But in chusing the President, the Votes shall be taken by States, the Representation from each State having one Vote; A quorum for this Purpose shall consist of a Member or Members from two thirds of the States, and a Majority of all the States shall be necessary to a Choice. In every Case, after the Choice of the President, the Person having the greatest Number of Votes of the Electors shall be the Vice President. But if

[18] "Electors" here does not refer to all voters, but rather to those elected to the Electoral College who would in turn elect the president.

there should remain two or more who have equal Votes, the Senate shall chuse from them by Ballot the Vice President.

The Congress may determine the Time of chusing the Electors, and the Day on which they shall give their Votes; which Day shall be the same throughout the United States.

No Persons except a natural born Citizen, or a Citizen of the United States, at the time of the Adoption of this Constitution, shall be eligible to the Office of President; neither shall any Person be eligible to that Office who shall not have attained to the Age of thirty five Years, and been fourteen Years a Resident within the United States.

In Case of the Removal of the President from Office, or of his Death, Resignation, or Inability to discharge the Powers and Duties of the said Office, the Same shall devolve[19] on the Vice President, and the Congress may by Law provide for the Case of Removal, Death, Resignation or Inability, both of the President and Vice President, declaring what Officer shall then act as President, and such Officer shall act accordingly, until the Disability be removed, or a President shall be elected.

The President shall, at stated Times, receive for his Services, a Compensation, which shall neither be encreased nor diminished during the Period for which he shall have been elected, and he shall not receive within that Period any other Emolument from the United States, or any of them.

Before he enter on the Execution of his Office, he shall take the following Oath or Affirmation:—"I do solemnly swear (or affirm) that I will faithfully execute the Office of President of the United States, and will to the best of my Ability, preserve, protect and defend the Constitution of the United States."

Section. 2. The President shall be Commander in Chief of the Army and Navy of the United States, and of the Militia of the several States, when called into the actual Service of the United States; he may require the Opinion, in writing, of the principal Officer in each of the executive Departments, upon any Subject relating to the Duties of their respective Offices, and he shall have Power to grant Reprieves and Pardons for Offences against the United States, except in Cases of Impeachment.

He shall have Power, by and with the Advice and Consent of the Senate, to make Treaties, provided two thirds of the Senators present concur; and he shall nominate, and by and with the Advice and Consent of the Senate, shall appoint Ambassadors, other public Ministers and Consuls, Judges of the supreme Court, and all other Officers of the

[19] "Devolve on the Vice President" means "be passed on to the Vice President."

United States, whose Appointments are not herein otherwise provided for, and which shall be established by Law: but the Congress may by Law vest the Appointment of such inferior Officers, as they think proper, in the President alone, in the Courts of Law, or in the Heads of Departments.

The President shall have Power to fill up all Vacancies that may happen during the Recess of the Senate, by granting Commissions which shall expire at the End of their next Session.

Section. 3. He shall from time to time give to the Congress Information of the State of the Union, and recommend to their Consideration such Measures as he shall judge necessary and expedient; he may, on extraordinary Occasions, convene both Houses, or either of them, and in Case of Disagreement between them, with Respect to the Time of Adjournment, he may adjourn them to such Time as he shall think proper; he shall receive Ambassadors and other public Ministers; he shall take Care that the Laws be faithfully executed, and shall Commission all the Officers of the United States.

Section. 4. The President, Vice President and all civil Officers of the United States, shall be removed from Office on Impeachment for, and Conviction of Treason, Bribery, or other high Crimes and Misdemeanors.[20]

Article. III.

Section. 1. The judicial Power of the United States, shall be vested in one supreme Court, and in such inferior Courts as the Congress may from time to time ordain and establish. The Judges, both of the supreme and inferior Courts, shall hold their Offices during good Behaviour, and shall, at stated Times, receive for their Services, a Compensation, which shall not be diminished during their Continuance in Office.

Section. 2. The judicial Power shall extend to all Cases, in Law and Equity,[21] arising under this Constitution, the Laws of the United

[20] The phrase "high Crimes and Misdemeanors" has been the subject of political and scholarly controversy for two centuries. Some argue that impeachable offenses can only be violations of criminal law. Others argue that impeachable offenses can also be offenses against the spirit of the Constitution.

[21] This section of the Constitution recognizes the traditional Anglo-American distinction between law and equity. In cases at law the remedy sought by the party bringing suit is money damages, whereas in cases at equity the remedy sought by the party bringing suit is *equitable relief* —that is, a court order either requiring that the defendant do something (usually called a *mandatory injunction*) or barring the defendant from doing

States, and Treaties made, or which shall be made, under their Authority;—to all Cases affecting Ambassadors, other public Ministers and Consuls;[22]—to all Cases of admiralty and maritime Jurisdiction;[23]—to Controversies to which the United States shall be a Party;—to Controversies between two or more States;—between a State and Citizens of another State;—between Citizens of different States,—between Citizens of the same State claiming Lands under Grants of different States, and between a State, or the Citizens thereof, and foreign States, Citizens or Subjects.

In all Cases affecting Ambassadors, other public Ministers and Consuls, and those in which a State shall be Party, the supreme Court shall have original Jurisdiction. In all the other Cases before mentioned, the supreme Court shall have appellate Jurisdiction, both as to Law and Fact, with such Exceptions, and under such Regulations as the Congress shall make.

The Trial of all Crimes, except in Cases of Impeachment, shall be by Jury; and such Trial shall be held in the State where the said Crimes shall have been committed; but when not committed within any State, the Trial shall be at such Place or Places as the Congress may by Law have directed.

Section. 3. Treason against the United States, shall consist only in levying War against them, or in adhering to their Enemies, giving them Aid and Comfort. No Person shall be convicted of Treason unless on the Testimony of two Witnesses to the same overt Act, or on Confession in open Court.

---

something (usually called a *prohibitory injunction*). Until the late nineteenth and twentieth centuries, Anglo-American law made sharp distinctions between law and equity, and there were two different court systems, law courts and chancery courts, to handle these different kinds of disputes. The federal courts have always had both law and equity jurisdiction, as authorized by this section of the Constitution.

22 A "consul" is someone hired by a government to look after its citizens in another country. A consulate, therefore, is the institution concerned with the business, safety, and other needs of citizens from the consulate's country.

23 Cases falling within the Supreme Court's "original Jurisdiction" can and must begin in the Supreme Court itself; cases falling within its "appellate Jurisdiction" come to the Supreme Court from lower federal or state courts. The constitutional limitation "with such Exceptions, and under such Regulations as the Congress shall make" gives Congress the power to control the jurisdiction of the Supreme Court and other federal courts. In the late 1860s, for example, Congress took away the Supreme Court's jurisdiction to hear appeals challenging the validity of the statutes giving effect to "Congressional Reconstruction" policies; in the decades since the Court's 1962 and 1963 school prayer and Bible-reading cases, Congress has often discussed but never enacted legislation to exclude such types of cases from the jurisdiction of the federal courts.

The Congress shall have Power to declare the Punishment of Treason, but no Attainder of Treason shall work Corruption of Blood, or Forfeiture except during the Life of the Person attainted.[24]

Article. IV.

Section. 1. Full Faith and Credit shall be given in each State to the public Acts, Records, and judicial Proceedings of every other State. And the Congress may by general Laws prescribe the Manner in which such Acts, Records and Proceedings shall be proved, and the Effect thereof.

Section. 2. The Citizens of each State shall be entitled to all privileges and Immunities of Citizens in the several States.

A Person charged in any State with Treason, Felony, or other Crime, who shall flee from Justice, and be found in another State, shall on Demand of the executive Authority of the State from which he fled, be delivered up, to be removed to the State having Jurisdiction of the Crime.

No Person held to Service or Labour in one State, under the Laws thereof, escaping into another, shall, in Consequence of any Law or Regulation therein, be discharged from such Service or Labour, but shall be delivered up on Claim of the Party to whom such Service or Labour may be due.

Section. 3. New States may be admitted by the Congress into this Union; but no new State shall be formed or erected within the Jurisdiction of any other State; nor any State be formed by the Junction[25] of two or more States, or Parts of States, without the Consent of the Legislatures of the States concerned as well as of the Congress.

The Congress shall have Power to dispose of and make all needful Rules and Regulations respecting the Territory or other Property belonging to the United States; and nothing in this Constitution shall be so construed as to Prejudice any Claims of the United States, or of any particular State.

Section. 4. The United States shall guarantee to every State in this Union a Republican Form of Government, and shall protect each of them against Invasion; and on Application of the Legislature, or of the

---

[24] "Corruption of blood" was a practice used in England whereby those related "by blood" to someone accused or convicted of treason or other serious crimes paid the same or similar penalties, usually in the form of confiscated property or fines. Children, grandchildren, and other descendents were often included.

[25] "Junction" here means "joining" or "uniting."

Executive (when the Legislature cannot be convened) against domestic Violence.

Article. V.

Congress, whenever two thirds of both Houses shall deem it necessary, shall propose Amendments to this Constitution, or, on the Application of the Legislatures of two thirds of the several States, shall call a Convention for proposing Amendments, which, in either Case, shall be valid to all Intents and Purposes, as Part of this Constitution, when ratified by the Legislatures of three fourths of the several States, or by Conventions in three fourths thereof, as the one or the other Mode of Ratification may be proposed by the Congress; Provided that no Amendment which may be made prior to the Year One thousand eight hundred and eight shall in any Manner affect the first and fourth Clauses in the Ninth Section of the first Article; and that no State, without its Consent, shall be deprived of it's equal Suffrage in the Senate.[26]

Article. VI.

All Debts contracted and Engagements entered into, before the Adoption of this Constitution, shall be as valid against the United States under this Constitution, as under the Confederation.

This Constitution, and the Laws of the United States which shall be made in Pursuance thereof; and all Treaties made, or which shall be made, under the Authority of the United States, shall be the supreme Law of the Land; and the Judges in every State shall be bound thereby, any Thing in the Constitution or Laws of any State to the Contrary notwithstanding.

The Senators and Representatives before mentioned, and the Members of the several State Legislatures, and all executive and judicial Officers; both of the United States and of the several States, shall be bound by Oath or Affirmation, to support this Constitution; but no religious Test shall ever be required as a Qualification to any Office or public Trust under the United States.

---

[26] Only two parts of the Constitution may not be amended. One is that provision prohibiting Congress from stopping the importation of slaves until 1808. Most states had, however, already prohibited their citizens from participating in the foreign slave trade. Because it is not to be expected that any state will consent to losing its equal vote in the Senate, this clause of Article V effectively immunizes that provision of the Constitution giving each state two Senators from constitutional amendment.

Article. VII.

Ratification of the Conventions of nine States, shall be sufficient for the Establishment of this Constitution between the States so ratifying the Same.

Done in Convention by the Unanimous Consent of the States present the Seventeenth Day of September in the Year of our Lord one thousand seven hundred and Eighty seven and of the Independance of the United States of America the Twelfth In Witness whereof We have hereunto subscribed our Names,

Attest William Jackson Secretary   Go: Washington—Presidt.
                                                                    and deputy from Virginia

Delaware	Geo: Read Gunning Bedford junr John Dickinson Richard Bassett Jaco: Broom	New Hampshire	John Langdon Nicholas Gilman
		Massa- chusetts	Nathaniel Gorham Rufus King
Maryland	James McHenry Dan of St Thos. Jenifer Danl Carroll	Connecticut	Wm: Saml. Johnson Roger Sherman
Virginia	John Blair— James Madison Jr.	New York	Alexander Hamilton
North Carolina	Wm. Blount Richd. Dobbs Spaight. Hu Williamson	New Jersey	Wil: Livingston David Brearley Wm. Paterson. Jona: Dayton
South Carolina	J. Rutledge Charles Cotesworth Pinckney Charles Pinckney Pierce Butler	Pennsylvania	B Franklin Thomas Mifflin Robt Morris Geo. Clymer Thos. FitzSimons Jared Ingersoll James Wilson Gouv. Morris
Georgia	William Few Abr Baldwin		

XV

The Federalist
on Federalism

1787–1788

Commentary by Stephen L. Schechter

ESSENTIAL TO UNDERSTANDING THE PURPOSE of a masterpiece like *The Federalist* is that it is actually three documents in one. It is a campaign document, designed to win popular approval among the voters of New York State for the proposed Constitution; a serious work of political thought, analyzing the nature of free societies; and the authoritative commentary on the Constitution, reflecting the intent of the Framers of the Constitution.

The multifaceted character of *The Federalist* is what makes it such a challenge to read with comprehension. To understand *The Federalist*, one must understand its historical context, the rhetoric (i.e., political language of that time), the political theory of *The Federalist*, the place of that theory in the history of political thought, and how these elements can reinforce one another on the printed page. Based on these criteria, it is difficult to fully understand *The Federalist*; but one can apply these criteria to improve one's understanding of it.

Revised version of a paper prepared for the Center for the Study of Federalism, Temple University, with the support of a grant from the National Endowment for the Humanities.

Historical Background

On February 21, 1787, the Confederation Congress called for a convention to revise the Articles of Confederation. That convention, known as the Constitutional Convention, met in Philadelphia from May 25 to September 17. The product of its summer efforts was a new Constitution, debated in the Congress, September 26–28, and sent without approval to the states.[1]

By the end of 1787, four states beginning with Delaware had ratified the Constitution. By June of 1788, four more states ratified. Then, on June 21, New Hampshire became the ninth state to ratify, bringing the Constitution into effect.

New York was not among those first nine states. In fact, New York did not ratify the Constitution until July 26, 1788, becoming the eleventh to do so. The state legislature delayed the process, first, by waiting until February 1, 1788, to call the convention, and then by scheduling the election for the end of April and the convention for mid-June. But why did the state legislature choose to delay the process? To understand *The Federalist* as a campaign document, one must first understand why New York waited so long to ratify.

New York was a reluctant state because neither Federalist nor Antifederalist leaders were willing to risk an early decision. As the state's minority party, Federalists wanted late elections in the hope of swaying new voters to their side; they wanted a late convention because they believed that, given time, they could win over moderate Antifederalist delegates. And if these two efforts failed, there would be no early defeat in New York to hurt Federalist efforts in other states.

Antifederalists had their own reasons for delay. They were led by George Clinton, the state's first governor, undefeated in every election bid since 1777. Clinton was a smart politician who left nothing to chance. He realized his forces might have won an early contest, but they also might have lost. He wanted time to assess his statewide strength on this particular issue and to organize the diversity of interests needed to win in a state like New York. He also hoped that, with time, Antifederalists could build an interstate movement for a second constitutional convention. Finally, Clinton did not want New York to be the first big state to reject the Constitution.[2]

---

[1] Article 7 of the proposed Constitution requires the "Ratification [consent] of the conventions [not legislatures] of nine States [i.e., over two-thirds of the thirteen states]" to establish the Constitution.

[2] For a full account, see John P. Kaminski, "New York: the Reluctant Pillar," in *The Reluctant Pillar: New York and the Adoption of the Federal Constitution*, ed. Stephen L. Schechter (1985; Albany, 1987).

How and Why *The Federalist* Was Written

The proposed Constitution was first printed in New York on September 21, 1787, and within a week the debate over its adoption began. A commentary by a Federalist appeared in a New York City newspaper, *The Daily Advertiser*, on September 24. It was answered three days later in the city's only blatantly Antifederalist newspaper, *The New-York Journal* in "Cato" I, the first of seven of his essays attributed by some to Governor Clinton. Several days later, "Cato" was attacked in a newspaper essay by "Caesar" (once thought to be Alexander Hamilton), and the debate was well underway, nurturing two basic tools of American campaign politics—the print media and the political party.

The Federalist was an important part of the New York debate, with the first essay appearing on October 27, 1787, two days after the unanswered charges of "Cato" III were published.[3] The decision to write the essays was made by Alexander Hamilton and fellow New Yorker John Jay. Though little is known about that decision, it is likely that Hamilton recognized the need for an authoritative series of essays in defense of the proposed Constitution to counter the early onslaught of Antifederalists like "Cato," and that *The Federalist* was intended to serve that purpose.

The essays were written by Alexander Hamilton, John Jay, and James Madison of Virginia under the pseudonym "Publius."[4] Eighty-four essays were printed in New York City between October 27, 1787 and May 28, 1788. The essays were first published in New York City newspapers. They were then widely circulated in other newspapers until January 1788 when it was announced that the M'Lean brothers would print the essays in book form. (The first of the two-volume set was published on March 22, 1788; the second, on May 28.)

The essays were addressed to the "People of the State of New York" and intended to convince New Yorkers of the necessity of ratifying the new Constitution. In particular, the essays were intended to

---

[3] Then, on November 8, 1788, Thomas Greenleaf, the Antifederalist printer, advertised the first pamphlet of . . . *Letters From the Federal Farmer to the Republican*, considered then and today to be one of the best Antifederalist commentaries.

[4] Many commentaries on the Constitution were written under pseudonyms, both to protect the author and to make full use of available symbols. Heroes of the Roman Republic were popular choices, because many were well-known symbols of republicanism. (Plutarch's *Lives of the Noble Romans* was widely read at that time.) Publius Valerius established stable republican government after the overthrow of Tarquia, the last Roman king. The choice of this hero was undoubtedly Hamilton's since he had used that pseudonym nearly ten years earlier.

show, in Hamilton's words:

> "The utility of the *UNION* to your political prosperity—The insuffi-
> ciency of the present Confederation to preserve that Union—The ne-
> cessity of a government at least equally energetic with the one pro-
> posed to the attainment of this object—The conformity of the proposed
> constitution to the true principles of republican government—Its anal-
> ogy to your own state constitution—*and lastly,* The additional security,
> which its adoption will afford to the preservation of that species of
> government, to liberty and to property."[5]

The essays were written on a tight schedule: at first, two were
printed each week; later, the schedule was increased to four per week.
This did not leave much time for careful study or coordination. As James
Madison explained near the end of his life in a private memorandum,
the essays "were written most of them in great haste, and without any
special allotment [assignment] of the different parts of the subject to
the several writers, J. M. [James Madison] being at the time a member
of the then Congress [of the Confederation in New York City], and A.
H. [Alexander Hamilton] being also a member, and occupied moreover
in his profession at the bar [as a lawyer], which occasionally took him
up to Albany."[6]

At the time of their publication, *The Federalist* papers were widely
recognized by Federalist and Antifederalist alike as one of the most
serious and sophisticated defenses of the Constitution. Federalists generally regarded the essays as the best analysis of the Constitution,
though some admitted that they were too "elaborate" and not "well
calculated for the common people." (In other words, even friendly
readers of the day found them heavy and, at times, difficult reading.)

Today, *The Federalist* is widely regarded as the authoritative statement of the intent of the framers of the Constitution. It is used by
lawyers, legal scholars, and judges to interpret the meaning of particular
clauses of the Constitution, and by theorists to understand the meaning
of the Constitution as a whole. However, its impact on its intended
audience—the people of New York—was negligible. A majority of New
York voters cast their ballots for Antifederalist convention delegates,
and there is no evidence that any of those Antifederalist delegates who

[5] *The Federalist No. 1,* pp. 6–7. All quotes from *The Federalist* are from the Jacob E.
Cooke edition (Middletown, Conn., 1961), now distributed by Harper & Row.

[6] As quoted in John P. Kaminski and Gaspare J. Saladino, eds., *The Documentary
History of the Ratification of the Constitution, Commentaries,* Volume I (Madison, Wisc.,
1981), 487. This excellent series presents the commentaries on the Constitution in chronological order and with useful annotations and footnotes.

later decided to switch their final vote for ratification were influenced by *The Federalist*.

How *The Federalist* Begins

With this background in mind, consider how *The Federalist* begins. The first paragraph of the very first essay begins:

> It has been frequently remarked, that it seems to have been reserved to the people of this country, by their conduct and example, to decide the important question, whether societies of men are really capable or not, of establishing good government from reflection and choice, or whether they are forever destined to depend, for their political constitutions, on accident and force.

Written by Hamilton, this sentence can be read in two ways; namely, as the opening statement of a campaign document and as a work of political thought.

As the opening statement of a campaign document, this sentence is a classic "gambit"—an opening move designed to occupy a favorable position (in this case, the "high ground") with a minimal amount of sacrifices. Consider how the same sentence might read in terms of today's political rhetoric:

> Once again, my fellow Americans, we have an historic opportunity to show the world that we are a thoughtful people capable of creating good government by careful planning and popular consent, not by being forced to do it or by accidentally blundering into it.

The opening sentence gains added dimension as a campaign statement when its political context is recalled. The overall context was shaped by the desire to buy time, and what better way to do that than to appeal to the "reflective" nature of the voters? The particular context is the newspapers of New York City and what was being printed that week by the opposition.[7]

As an opening statement of political thought, the first sentence of *The Federalist No. 1* suggests that politicians (and Hamilton was one of

---

[7] Piecing together this context is not as difficult as it might seem. *The Documentary History* noted above is arranged in chronological order, so one can simply look up *The Federalist No. 1* and begin reading the previous documents looking for cross-references. For a fine analysis of the media's role in the convention itself see John K. Alexander, *The Selling of the Constitutional Convention, A History of News Coverage* (Madison, Wisc., 1990).

the best) do not campaign simply to win the votes of the people, they also campaign to govern; in this instance, to inform the public (and by that I mean giving shape and form to the public mind as well as providing it with bits of information) about the better world that will be possible under the new Constitution. This involves the selection and use of words not merely as tactics in an overall strategy but also as concepts (ideas) in an overall theory.

In this sense, the opening sentence contains two basic ideas that shape America's theory of constitutionalism.[8] Hamilton elegantly phrased those ideas but he did not invent them. In fact, they were so much a part of the eighteenth-century American mind that they were widely used by Federalists and Antifederalists alike.

The two ideas used to introduce *The Federalist* address the political question: If society is governed by laws, how can laws (and in this instance, the Constitution) be made in a way that the members of society will obey willingly? The answer to this question is, in Hamilton's words, "reflection and choice."

Reflection is the Enlightenment idea that humankind is a thinking species, capable of improving its lot by thinking before it acts. This idea was shared by both sides in the debate, and it is one of the reasons why the campaign remained a peaceful debate. It was used in *The Federalist No. 1*, but it was also used in Antifederalist "Cato" I: "Deliberate, therefore, on this new national government with coolness; analize it with criticism; and reflect on it with candour. . . . Beware of those who wish to influence your passions, and to make you dupes to their resentments and little interests . . . ." And "Cato" II wrote of the Federalist author "Caesar": "he shuts the door of true deliberation and discussion."

This is not to say that all matters of politics were objects of reason. Reprinted from a Philadelphia statement of August 29, 1787, in the *New Jersey Journal* on September 5, 1787, while the Constitutional Convention was still in session, is an interesting distinction: "The principles of liberty and the principles of government . . . are distinct things: Many understand the former which are matters of feeling, who know nothing of the latter, which are objects of reflection and reason."

Choice is the republican idea of popular consent. It occurs time and time again throughout *The Federalist* and all other commentaries on the Constitution by Federalists and Antifederalists; and it stands for the complex yet simple notion that people will obey laws of their own

---

[8] Constitutionalism is the belief that society should be governed by laws, of which the Constitution is the most fundamental.

making (or by representatives of their own choosing), so long as they have confidence in themselves and their representatives. In the heat of debate, some Federalists accused Antifederalists of pandering to the people, while some Antifederalists accused the other side of forgetting the people. However, virtually all were advocates of popular government; and, rhetoric aside, most were advocates of popular government by some form of elected representation.[9]

In sum, then, Federalists and Antifederalists agreed on the need for delay, the worth of cool and reasoned debate, and the goal of government by popular consent. On what did they disagree and how did federalism figure into that debate?

The Antifederalist Platform: A Confederacy of Small Republics[10]

Federalists and Antifederalists were both advocates of popular government in its republican form. Where they differed was in the type of republican society they wanted and the type of federal system they thought best suited to secure that society.

Antifederalists were opposed to the proposed Constitution in its original form; like any group bound by opposition, it would have been difficult for them to agree on what they stood *for*. It is for this reason that they are remembered as "men of little faith." However, as one reads their writings, one builds a sense that Antifederalists were against the Constitution as proposed because they were for a type of society that they felt would be threatened by the new Constitution; and, as they read what "Publius" had to say, especially in essays such as *The Federalist No. 10*, their fears were undoubtedly confirmed, because "Publius" was quite clear about the different type of society he envisioned.

Much of Antifederalist opinion was united behind the idea that republics had to be small (like ancient Greek city-states, medieval Swiss cantons, or modern American states) to survive. Undoubtedly, part of this opinion was shaped by a desire to preserve the existing status quo.

[9] In the language of the day, popular government had two species: a republic in which governmental decisions were made by the people's representatives; and a democracy in which governmental decisions were made by the people directly (as in a town meeting).

[10] For more information see Herbert J. Storing, *What the Anti-Federalists Were For* (Chicago, 1981). This slim volume reviews Antifederalist political thought and introduces the multi-volume collection of Antifederalist writing, *The Complete Anti-Federalist*, edited by Storing.

However, another part was an idea which they drew from the French philosopher Montesquieu: the basis of republican government (i.e., popular consent) required a small and intimate setting where citizens (1) knew one another, (2) shared similar habits and values, and (3) did not have the opportunity to become too unequal in their fortunes. Without these three bonds, people would not trust one another enough to agree on anything (including how to protect themselves against tyranny). Note how "Cato" III relies on these same three bonds in his explanation:

> The strongest principle of union resides within our domestic walls. The ties of the parent exceed that of any other; as we depart from home, the next general principle of union is amongst citizens of the same state, where acquaintance, habits, and fortunes, nourish affection, and attachment; enlarge the circle still further, &, as citizens of different states, though we acknowledge the same national denomination, we lose the ties of acquaintance, habits, and fortunes, and thus, by degrees, we lessen in our attachments, till, at length, we no more than acknowledge a sameness of species.

"Cato" assumed the existence of a union (see line 1 of the quote) and of national ties (see line 7). What "Cato" could not accept was the idea of a national government. Like other Antifederalists, "Cato" advocated a federal or confederal union of the states. In the eighteenth century, "federal" and "confederal" were used as synonyms. Both terms referred to relations among equals (in this instance, states) entered into voluntarily by compact or covenant. They could be loose relations (as in an alliance or league) or they could be stronger, as in the perpetual union formed by the Articles of Confederation. However, Antifederalists rejected the Federalist argument that federal relations could exist with a national government in the same system.

The Federalist Platform:
An Extended and Compound Republic

Federalists, including "Publius," believed "Cato" was wrong. In fact, much of what made the Federalist argument so new to the eighteenth-century mind was (1) the idea that republics should be large and complex, not small and simple; and (2) the constitutional means for accomplishing that task.

In *The Federalist No. 10*, James Madison, as "Publius," sets out the step-by-step reasons for a large, compound republic, focusing more on the large-republic element. He resumes this theoretical discussion in

The Federalist No. 51, focusing on the compound-republic element. In *Nos. 37* and *39*, he considers the constitutional means for securing a large, compound republic. There are other writings where the Federalist experiment is explained,[11] but it is Madison's Tenth, like Beethoven's Fifth, which is most frequently studied and, hence, most widely known. For this reason, let us review Madison's Tenth to discover the reasons for wanting a large, compound republic, and then proceed to *Nos. 51*, *37*, and *39* to complete the Madisonian model of republican government.

The Madisonian Model Outlined

The Federalist No. 10 and the Large Republic

1. The greatest danger facing popular government is factionalism, which occurs when a majority or minority unites around a passion or interest adverse to individual rights or the public good.[12]
2. Madison rejects the idea of controlling factionalism by removing its causes.
   a. Controlling the people by denying their liberties would be unwise, much like throwing the baby out with the bathwater.
   b. Telling people how to think would not work because no one would listen unless they were forced to do so, and that option was rejected.
3. Madison accepts the idea of controlling factionalism by controlling its effects.
4. The effects of *minority* factions can be controlled relatively simply by the republican principle of popular consent, by which the majority would defeat the minority faction at the polls. Perhaps, however, Madison worried too little about minority factions and some of their effects.

---

[11] Hamilton sets out the theoretical argument for a large, compound republic in *The Federalist No. 9*. John Jay, often forgotten in his role as "Publius," wrote the more politically persuasive version in a pamphlet entitled *An Address to the People of the State of New York*, signed by "A Citizen of New-York," and published on April 15, 1788.

[12] *Number 10* was the first essay that Madison wrote, but, in the reader's mind, it was still the tenth essay written by "Publius." Since Hamilton had spoken of factions in *Number 9*, and since factionalism was generally accepted as a major danger facing republics, Madison might well have decided to focus on factions as a way of beginning his own case while appearing to continue the argument set out in the previous essay.

5. The real problem facing popular governments and the "great object" of his essay is how to control the *majority* when it becomes factious.
6. There are two basic ways to control majority factions: control the motives that inspire them and the opportunities for them to organize. These are taken up in (8) and (9) below, respectively, after Madison introduces the distinction between democracies and republics.
7. Of the two forms of popular government, a republic is more likely than a democracy to control majority factions, partly because democracies are by their very nature inclined toward instability. Also, republics allow for representation and increased size of population and territory. These last two factors are considered below.
8. Republics make it possible to have elected representatives, and good ones can refine the factious spirit that might spread among the majority. Large republics are more likely than small republics to elect good representatives for two reasons:
   a. Regardless of their size, all republics need the same number of legislators in order to avoid the clubiness of too few and the confusion of too many. But in a large republic, there will be more options to fill those seats with qualified people.
   b. Since the size of the constituency is greater in the large republic, it will be less susceptible to deception by unworthy candidates. (Is it harder to fool 100,000 people than 10,000?)
   c. However, on this as on other points, one must strive for the mean. If the constituency is too large, the representative will not be sufficiently aware of local conditions. If the constituency is too small, the representative will be tied to local conditions and unable to see the larger picture or pursue the national interest. The Constitution forms a "happy combination" that refers "great and aggregate interests" to the federal Congress and "local and particular" interests to the state legislatures. (Is there one optimum ratio of representative to be represented for a national legislature, and another optimum for state legislatures? And is this a guarantor that the states are "closer" to the people?)[13]
9. Republics make it possible to increase the size of the citizenry and territory, and larger republics make it less likely that majority factions will form.

---

[13] The Constitution specifies in Article I, Section 2 that the number of representatives in the House of Representatives cannot be more than one for every 30,000 people. This means there cannot be two per 30,000, but there could be one per 100,000, reflecting the Framers' fear of localism. In 1929, Congress fixed the number of representatives at 435, and the ratio has steadily increased to one to over 500,000.

a. The larger the society, the greater the variety of parties and interests.
b. The greater the diversity of interests in society, the less likely a majority will have a single passion or interest. Put differently, majorities in large societies are more likely to be coalitions of various interests than a monolithic force of one interest.
c. The larger the number of citizens and territory, the more difficult it will be for those who could form a factious majority to discover one another and come together.

10. The Union is more likely to control the effects of faction than are the states composing it.

a. Members of Congress are more likely to possess the enlightened views and virtuous sentiments needed to override local prejudice. (If "Cato" had a localistic "small town" bias, does Madison suffer from a cosmopolitan bias?)
b. The greater variety of parties in the Union as a whole will prevent any one party from outnumbering the others. For example, a factious leader may be able to take over one state but not the Union; a religious sect may become a factious majority in one region, but other sects will prevent its spread; a particular fad or disruptive element or wicked group is less likely to take over the whole system than a part of it.

11. "In the extent and proper structure of the Union, therefore, we behold a Republican remedy for the diseases most incident to Republican Government." Madison fully considered the extent of the Union, but he did not go as far in addressing its "proper structure" (i.e., its compound nature); a matter which is introduced in point ten and continued in *The Federalist No. 51*.

The Federalist No. 51 and the Principle of the Compound Republic

1. Madison continues the theoretical discussion of *No. 10* shifting attention from controlling minority and majority factions to controlling all factions and government itself. At the end of the fourth paragraph, he notes: "A dependence on the people is no doubt the primary controul on the government; but experience has taught mankind the necessity of auxiliary precautions."
2. Madison identifies three "auxiliary precautions": limited government, framed by laws; divided government, with one "department" checked by another; and a compound republic, providing the double security of two sets of limited and divided governments.

3. All three precautions are governed by the same policy of "checks and balances." As Madison notes in paragraph five: "This policy, of supplying by opposite and rival interests, the defect of better motives, might be traced through the whole system of human affairs, private as well as public." (Historians of science find this view of the political world similar to Newton's view of the universe.)

4. In a classic statement of human nature, Madison explains the need for auxiliary precautions (see the middle of paragraph four):

   a. Ambition must be made to counteract ambition.[14]

   b. If men were angels, no government would be necessary. If angels governed men, no controls on government would be necessary. (Consider how this compares with Hamilton's view in *The Federalist No. 6*, paragraph three.)

   c. In framing a government of men over men, one must first empower the government to control the people, and then oblige it to control itself. A dependence on the people is the best control over the government, but other safeguards are necessary.

The Federalist No. 37 and the Task of Forming a Compound Republic

1. Madison addresses the difficulties of forming a compound republic.

2. The first challenge is to insure a proper balance among three seemingly contradictory principles:

   a. Energetic government, which seems to require concentrating power in a single hand;

   b. Stability, which seems to require a long duration in office; and

   c. Republican liberty, which seems to require widely distributing power among many hands holding office for short periods of time.

3. The second set of challenges is the task of deciding the proper distribution of authority between general and state governments,[15] and among legislative, executive, and judicial branches.

4. The final set of challenges has to do with mediating the differences between large and small states, and among other combinations of states (e.g., North vs. South, and East vs. West).

---

[14] Since the time of the ancient Greeks, political philosophers have focused on ambition (the desire to achieve something important and win lasting recognition for it) as the single most important motivation for entering the world of politics.

[15] It was a common practice up to the Civil War to refer to the federal government as the "general" government, and the term has much to recommend it. It suggests a government of general scope, avoids the status element in the term "central" government, and nicely sidesteps the choice between "federal" and "national" government.

The Federalist No. 39 and the New Federalism

1. In this essay, Madison finally gets down to the specific ways in which the Constitution establishes a government that is both republican and federal.

2. In the first six paragraphs, Madison offers a specific definition of republican government and, in textbook fashion, shows how the new government is fully republican in form.

3. Madison then responds to the charge that the Framers should have "preserved the *federal* form, which regards the union as a *confederacy* of sovereign States; instead of which, they have framed a *national* government, which regards the union as a *consolidation* of the States." (Recall the way these terms were used in 1787: "federal" and "confederal" were synonyms referring to the lateral relations among states.)

4. Madison's answer is a perfect combination of campaign rhetoric and political theory. The new Constitution, explains Madison, keeps the federal element of interstate relations and simply adds to it a national element. The result, Madison cleverly concludes, "is in strictness neither a national nor a federal constitution; but a composition of both."

5. Madison's answer nicely elaborates the Constitution as a compound of federal and national elements:

   a. The ratification of the Constitution is a federal act, with the people electing delegates and the delegates voting on the Constitution, both as members of their respective states.

   b. The source of powers for the new government is partly federal and partly national, with the House of Representatives elected nationally, the Senate elected by the states (i.e., federally), and the president elected by an electoral college which accumulates national majorities on a state-by-state basis.

   c. The operation of the new government is national, because it acts directly on the individual citizen.

   d. The extent or scope of the new government is federal, because it is supreme not over all things but only with regard to the enumerated powers granted to it, while the states remain supreme within their respective sphere.

   e. Finally, the amendment process is neither wholly federal, nor wholly national, requiring special majorities of both the Congress and the states.[16]

[16] Readers interested in identifying other occurrences of terms like "federal" and

Conclusion

Federalism occupies a critical position in *The Federalist*, both as a campaign document and a serious work of political thought. In one master stroke, Madison preempts the federal principle, taking it away from the sole preserve of Antifederalist opposition, while at the same time redirecting it toward the goals of building a new nation and expanding the republic. In this effort, Madison provides a bridge from the way federalism had been defined to the way federalism is understood today.

For Further Reading

George Carey. *The Federalist: Design for a Constitutional Republic.* Urbana, Ill., 1989.
Trevor Colburn, ed. *Fame and the Founding Fathers: Essays of Douglass Adair* New York, 1974.
David F. Epstein. *The Political Theory of The Federalist.* Chicago, 1984.
Morton White. *Philosophy, The Federalist, and the Constitution.* New York, 1987.

"national" in *The Federalist* can consult Thomas S. Engeman, Edward J. Erler, and Thomas B. Hofeller, eds., *The Federalist Concordance* (Middletown, Conn., 1980; paperback ed., Chicago, 1988), which lists all key words in their contextual occurrences.

The Federalist No. I

ALEXANDER HAMILTON[1]

October 27, 1787

To the People of the State of New York.

AFTER an unequivocal experience of the inefficacy of the subsisting Foederal Government, you are called upon to deliberate on a new Constitution for the United States of America. The subject speaks its own importance; comprehending in its consequences, nothing less than the existence of the UNION, the safety and welfare of the parts of which it is composed, the fate of an empire, in many respects, the most interesting in the world. It has been frequently remarked, that it seems to have been reserved to the people of this country, by their conduct and example, to decide the important question, whether societies of men are really capable or not, of establishing good government from reflection and choice, or whether they are forever destined to depend, for their political constitutions, on accident and force. If there be any truth in the remark, the crisis, at which we are arrived, may with propriety be regarded as the æra in which that decision is to be made; and

Reprinted with permission from Jacob E. Cooke, ed., *The Federalist* (Hanover, N.H.: University Press of New England, 1982), copyright © 1961 by Wesleyan University Press. The Cooke edition is generally regarded as the most reliable edition of the text. Cooke collated the first book edition published in New York by John and Archibald M'Lean in 1788 with the texts printed in the New York newspapers in 1787–88 and with later editions prepared under Alexander Hamilton's (New York: George Hopkins, 1802) and James Madison's (Washington, D.C.: Jacob Gideon, 1818) supervision. The first note to each essay, specifying its source and publication history, is taken from Cooke as well.

    All numbered notes to the essay following the first are the commentator's notes, and were prepared with the assistance of Richard B. Bernstein; all notes indicated by symbols are the original notes by "Publius."

    There were eighty-four essays in *The Federalist* published in New York City newspapers, but the numbering of essays in the M'Lean edition does not correspond with that of the newspaper versions for two reasons: *No. 31* was divided into two essays because of its length (thus making a total of eighty-five essays), and *No. 35* was originally published as the twenty-eighth essay in the newspapers. Virtually all editions, including Cooke's, follow the numbering of the M'Lean edition, and that numbering is also followed here.

[1] From *The Independent Journal*, October 27, 1787. This essay appeared on October 30 in both *The New-York Packet* and *The Daily Advertiser.*

a wrong election of the part we shall act, may, in this view, deserve to be considered as the general misfortune of mankind.[2]

This idea will add the inducements of philanthropy to those of patriotism to heighten the solicitude, which all considerate and good men must feel for the event. Happy will it be if our choice should be directed by a judicious estimate of our true interests, unperplexed and unbiassed by considerations not connected with the public good. But this is a thing more ardently to be wished, than seriously to be expected. The plan offered to our deliberations, affects too many particular interests, innovates upon too many local institutions, not to involve in its discussion a variety of objects foreign to its merits, and of views, passions and prejudices little favourable to the discovery of truth.

Among the most formidable of the obstacles which the new Constitution will have to encounter, may readily be distinguished the obvious interest of a certain class of men in every State to resist all changes which may hazard a diminution of the power, emolument and consequence of the offices they hold under the State-establishments—and the perverted ambition of another class of men, who will either hope to aggrandise themselves by the confusions of their country, or will flatter themselves with fairer prospects of elevation from the subdivision of the empire into several partial confederacies, than from its union under one government.[3]

It is not, however, my design to dwell upon observations of this nature. I am well aware that it would be disingenuous to resolve indiscriminately the opposition of any set of men (merely because their situations might subject them to suspicion) into interested or ambitious views: Candour will oblige us to admit, that even such men may be actuated by upright intentions; and it cannot be doubted that much of the opposition which has made its appearance, or may hereafter make its appearance, will spring from sources, blameless at least, if not respectable, the honest errors of minds led astray by preconceived jealousies and fears. So numerous indeed and so powerful are the causes, which serve to give a false bias to the judgment, that we upon many

[2] Compare the opening passage of "Brutus" I, which similarly evokes the importance of the decision on the Constitution in terms going beyond the particular importance of the question to the American republic and which similarly takes "the high road" of political discourse.

[3] This passage summarizes the Federalist explanation why such notable politicians as Patrick Henry, George Clinton, and John Hancock (who were primarily active in state politics) opposed the proposed Constitution. As Ralph Ketcham makes clear in his commentary on Antifederalist writings, the foes of the Constitution believed that they were upholding human liberty and the principles of the Revolution (see Chapter 17).

occasions, see wise and good men on the wrong as well as on the right side of questions, of the first magnitude to society. This circumstance, if fully attended to, would furnish a lesson of moderation to those, who are ever so much persuaded of their being in the right, in any controversy. And a further reason for caution, in this respect, might be drawn from the reflection, that we are not always sure, that those who advocate the truth are influenced by purer principles than their antagonists. Ambition, avarice, personal animosity, party opposition, and many other motives, not more laudable than these, are apt to operate as well upon those who support as upon those who oppose the right side of a question. Were there not even these inducements to moderation, nothing could be more illjudged than that intolerant spirit, which has, at all times, characterized political parties. For, in politics as in religion, it is equally absurd to aim at making proselytes by fire and sword. Heresies in either can rarely be cured by persecution.

And yet however just these sentiments will be allowed to be, we have already sufficient indications, that it will happen in this as in all former cases of great national discussion. A torrent of angry and malignant passions will be let loose. To judge from the conduct of the opposite parties, we shall be led to conclude, that they will mutually hope to evince the justness of their opinions, and to increase the number of their converts by the loudness of their declamations, and by the bitterness of their invectives. An enlightened zeal for the energy and efficiency of government will be stigmatized, as the off-spring of a temper fond of despotic power and hostile to the principles of liberty. An overscrupulous jealousy of danger to the rights of the people, which is more commonly the fault of the head than of the heart, will be represented as mere pretence and artifice; the bait for popularity at the expence of public good. It will be forgotten, on the one hand, that jealousy is the usual concomitant of violent love, and that the noble enthusiasm of liberty is too apt to be infected with a spirit of narrow and illiberal distrust. On the other hand, it will be equally forgotten, that the vigour of government is essential to the security of liberty; that, in the contemplation of a sound and well informed judgment, their interest can never be separated; and that a dangerous ambition more often lurks behind the specious mask of zeal for the rights of the people, than under the forbidding appearance of zeal for the firmness and efficiency of government. History will teach us, that the former has been found a much more certain road to the introduction of despotism, than the latter, and that of those men who have overturned the liberties of republics the greatest number have begun their carreer, by paying an obsequious court to the people, commencing Demagogues and ending Tyrants.

In the course of the preceeding observations I have had an eye, my Fellow Citizens, to putting you upon your guard against all attempts, from whatever quarter, to influence your decision in a matter of the utmost moment to your welfare by any impressions other than those which may result from the evidence of truth. You will, no doubt, at the same time, have collected from the general scope of them that they proceed from a source not unfriendly to the new Constitution. Yes, my Countrymen, I own to you, that, after having given it an attentive consideration, I am clearly of opinion, it is your interest to adopt it. I am convinced, that this is the safest course for your liberty, your dignity, and your happiness. I effect not reserves, which I do not feel. I will not amuse you with an appearance of deliberation, when I have decided. I frankly acknowledge to you my convictions, and I will freely lay before you the reasons on which they are founded. The consciousness of good intentions disdains ambiguity. I shall not however multiply professions on this head. My motives must remain in the depository of my own breast: My arguments will be open to all, and may be judged of by all. They shall at least be offered in a spirit, which will not disgrace the cause of truth.

I propose in a series of papers to discuss the following interesting particulars—*The utility of the* UNION *to your political prosperity—The insufficiency of the present Confederation to preserve that Union—The necessity of a government at least equally energetic with the one proposed to the attainment of this object—The conformity of the proposed constitution to the true principles of republican government—Its analogy to your own state constitution*—and lastly, *The additional security, which its adoption will afford to the preservation of that species of government, to liberty and to property.*[4]

In the progress of this discussion I shall endeavour to give a satisfactory answer to all the objections which shall have made their appearance that may seem to have any claim to your attention.

It may perhaps be thought superfluous to offer arguments to prove the utility of the UNION, a point, no doubt, deeply engraved on the hearts of the great body of the people in every state, and one, which it may be imagined has no adversaries. But the fact is, that we already hear it whispered in the private circles of those who oppose the new constitution, that the Thirteen States are of too great extent for any

---

[4] Hamilton, Madison, and Jay generally followed Hamilton's outline of *The Federalist* given here. In *The Federalist No. 85*, Hamilton made clear that "that species of government" referred to republican government rather than the New York constitution of 1777. He also pointed out that although there is no single essay in *The Federalist* addressing the similarities between the state constitution and the United States Constitution, the authors addressed this theme throughout the essays.

general system, and that we must of necessity resort to separate confederacies of distinct portions of the whole.* This doctrine will, in all
probability, be gradually propagated, till it has votaries enough to countenance an open avowal of it. For nothing can be more evident, to those
who are able to take an enlarged view of the subject, than the alternative
of an adoption of the new Constitution, or a dismemberment of the
Union. It will therefore be of use to begin by examining the advantages
of that Union, the certain evils and the probable dangers, to which every
State will be exposed from its dissolution.[5] This shall accordingly constitute the subject of my next address.

PUBLIUS.

The Federalist No. 10[6]

JAMES MADISON

November 22, 1787

To the People of the State of New York.

AMONG the numerous advantages promised by a well constructed Union,
none deserves to be more accurately developed than its tendency to
break and control the violence of faction.[7] The friend of popular governments, never finds himself so much alarmed for their character and
fate, as when he contemplates their propensity to this dangerous vice.

[5] For a discussion of this point, see Richard B. Bernstein's commentary on *The
Federalist Nos. 15, 70,* and *78* (Chapter 16 below).
[6] From *The Daily Advertiser,* November 22, 1787. This essay appeared in *The New-
York Packet* on November 23 and in *The Independent Journal* on November 24.
[7] Madison's essay, the most famous in *The Federalist* as a contribution to political
theory, has an important place in the first division of *The Federalist*—that devoted to
extolling the American Union and showing that no form of government less powerful
than the proposed Constitution will suffice to preserve the Union.

* *The same idea, tracing the arguments to their consequences, is held out in several of the
late publications against the New Constitution* (Publius).

He will not fail therefore to set a due value on any plan which, without violating the principles to which he is attached, provides a proper cure for it. The instability, injustice and confusion introduced into the public councils, have in truth been the mortal diseases under which popular governments have every where perished; as they continue to be the favorite and fruitful topics from which the adversaries to liberty derive their most specious declamations. The valuable improvements made by the American Constitutions on the popular models, both ancient and modern, cannot certainly be too much admired; but it would be an unwarrantable partiality, to contend that they have as effectually obviated the danger on this side as was wished and expected. Complaints are every where heard from our most considerate and virtuous citizens, equally the friends of public and private faith, and of public and personal liberty; that our governments are too unstable; that the public good is disregarded in the conflicts of rival parties; and that measures are too often decided, not according to the rules of justice, and the rights of the minor party; but by the superior force of an interested and overbearing majority. However anxiously we may wish that these complaints had no foundation, the evidence of known facts will not permit us to deny that they are in some degree true. It will be found indeed, on a candid review of our situation, that some of the distresses under which we labor, have been erroneously charged on the operation of our governments; but it will be found, at the same time, that other causes will not alone account for many of our heaviest misfortunes; and particularly, for that prevailing and increasing distrust of public engagements, and alarm for private rights, which are echoed from one end of the continent to the other. These must be chiefly, if not wholly, effects of the unsteadiness and injustice, with which a factious spirit has tainted our public administrations.

By a faction I understand a number of citizens, whether amounting to a majority or minority of the whole, who are united and actuated by some common impulse of passion, or of interest, adverse to the rights of other citizens, or to the permanent and aggregate interests of the community.

There are two methods of curing the mischiefs of faction: the one, by removing its cause; the other, by controling its effects.

There are again two methods of removing the causes of faction: the one by destroying the liberty which is essential to its existence; the other, by giving to every citizen the same opinions, the same passions, and the same interests.

It could never be more truly said than of the first remedy, that it is worse than the disease. Liberty is to faction, what air is to fire, an aliment without which it instantly expires. But it could not be a less folly to abolish liberty, which is essential to political life, because it nourishes faction, than it would be to wish the annihilation of air, which is essential to animal life, because it imparts to fire its destructive agency.

The second expedient is as impracticable, as the first would be unwise. As long as the reason of man continues fallible, and he is at liberty to exercise it, different opinions will be formed. As long as the connection subsists between his reason and his self-love, his opinions and his passions will have a reciprocal influence on each other; and the former will be objects to which the latter will attach themselves. The diversity in the faculties of men from which the rights of property originate, is not less an insuperable obstacle to a uniformity of interests. The protection of these faculties is the first object of Government. From the protection of different and unequal faculties of acquiring property, the possession of different degrees and kinds of property immediately results: and from the influence of these on the sentiments and views of the respective proprietors, ensues a division of the society into different interests and parties.

The latent causes of faction are thus sown in the nature of man; and we see them every where brought into different degrees of activity, according to the different circumstances of civil society. A zeal for different opinions concerning religion, concerning Government and many other points, as well of speculation as of practice; an attachment to different leaders ambitiously contending for pre-eminence and power; or to persons of other descriptions whose fortunes have been interesting to the human passions, have in turn divided mankind into parties, inflamed them with mutual animosity, and rendered them much more disposed to vex and oppress each other, than to co-operate for their common good. So strong is this propensity of mankind to fall into mutual animosities, that where no substantial occasion presents itself, the most frivolous and fanciful distinctions have been sufficient to kindle their unfriendly passions, and excite their most violent conflicts. But the most common and durable source of factions, has been the various and unequal distribution of property.[8] Those who hold, and those who are

---

[8] Charles A. Beard and his followers focused on this passage in arguing that Madison was an early exponent of economic determinism. See generally Charles A. Beard, *An Economic Interpretation of the Constitution of the United States* (New York, 1913). Douglass Adair's pathbreaking essay "The Tenth Federalist Revisited" chronicles the intellectual history of the essay from its first publication to the 1940s, focusing on the rise, popularity, and deficiencies of the "economic determinist" reading of *The Federalist No. 10*. Adair's

without property, have ever formed distinct interests in society. Those
who are creditors, and those who are debtors, fall under a like discrimination. A landed interest, a manufacturing interest,[9] a mercantile interest, a monied interest, with many lesser interests, grow up of necessity in civilized nations and divide them into different classes,
actuated by different sentiments and views. The regulation of these
various and interfering interests forms the principal task of modern
Legislation, and involves the spirit of party and faction in the necessary
and ordinary operations of Government.

No man is allowed to be a judge in his own cause; because his
interest would certainly bias his judgment, and, not improbably, corrupt
his integrity. With equal, nay with greater reason, a body of men, are
unfit to be both judges and parties, at the same time; yet, what are
many of the most important acts of legislation, but so many judicial
determinations, not indeed concerning the rights of single persons, but
concerning the rights of large bodies of citizens; and what are the different classes of legislators, but advocates and parties to the causes
which they determine? Is a law proposed concerning private debts? It
is a question to which the creditors are parties on one side, and the
debtors on the other. Justice ought to hold the balance between them.
Yet the parties are and must be themselves the judges; and the most
numerous party, or, in other words, the most powerful faction must be
expected to prevail. Shall domestic manufactures be encouraged, and
in what degree, by restrictions on foreign manufactures? are questions
which would be differently decided by the landed and the manufacturing

---

sequel, " 'That Politics May Be Reduced to a Science': David Hume, James Madison,
and the Tenth Federalist," also broke new ground in tracing the intellectual origins of
ideas advanced in *The Federalist*. Trevor Colbourn has edited a valuable collection of
Adair's essays: *Fame and the Founding Fathers: Essays of Douglass Adair* (New York, 1974).
Adair's unpublished doctoral dissertation, "The Intellectual Origins of Jeffersonian Democracy: Republicanism, Class Struggle, and the Virtuous Farmer" (New Haven, 1943)
is of enduring importance.

Although Madison said that economics was the principal cause of factions, he did
not say that economics was the sole cause of factions. He drew his examples of causes
of factionalism from his political experience in Virginia or his close and troubled observations of politics in the other colonies and states. For example, his experience during
the Virginia disestablishment struggle of the 1780s informed his observations on religious
sources of factionalism; his opposition to the faction organized and led by Patrick Henry
underlay his identification of allegiance to one or another political leader as another
source of factional strife.

[9] Madison's mention of manufacturers is ironic in light of his and his Jeffersonian
Republican allies' opposition to the plan for promoting American manufacturers ad-
vanced by Alexander Hamilton as secretary of the treasury. See Drew McCoy, *The Elusive
Republic: Political Economy in Jeffersonian America* (Chapel Hill, 1980).

classes; and probably by neither, with a sole regard to justice and the public good. The apportionment of taxes on the various descriptions of property, is an act which seems to require the most exact impartiality; yet, there is perhaps no legislative act in which greater opportunity and temptation are given to a predominant party, to trample on the rules of justice. Every shilling with which they over-burden the inferior number, is a shilling saved to their own pockets.

It is in vain to say, that enlightened statesmen will be able to adjust these clashing interests, and render them all subservient to the public good. Enlightened statesmen will not always be at the helm: Nor, in many cases, can such an adjustment be made at all, without taking into view indirect and remote considerations, which will rarely prevail over the immediate interest which one party may find in disregardng the rights of another, or the good of the whole.

The inference to which we are brought, is, that the *causes* of faction cannot be removed; and that relief is only to be sought in the means of controling its *effects.*

If a faction consists of less than a majority, relief is supplied by the republican principle, which enables the majority to defeat its sinister views by regular vote: It may clog the administration, it may convulse the society; but it will be unable to execute and mask its violence under the forms of the Constitution. When a majority is included in a faction, the form of popular government on the other hand enables it to sacrifice to its ruling passion or interest, both the public good and the rights of other citizens. To secure the public good, and private rights, against the danger of such a faction, and at the same time to preserve the spirit and the form of popular government, is then the great object to which our enquiries are directed: Let me add that it is the great desideratum, by which alone this form of government can be rescued from the opprobrium under which it has so long labored, and be recommended to the esteem and adoption of mankind.

By what means is this object attainable? Evidently by one of two only. Either the existence of the same passion or interest in a majority at the same time, must be prevented; or the majority, having such coexistent passion or interest, must be rendered, by their number and local situation, unable to concert and carry into effect schemes of oppression. If the impulse and the opportunity be suffered to coincide, we well know that neither moral nor religious motives can be relied on as an adequate control. They are not found to be such on the injustice and violence of individuals, and lose their efficacy in proportion to the number combined together; that is, in proportion as their efficacy becomes needful.

From this view of the subject, it may be concluded, that a pure Democracy, by which I mean, a Society, consisting of a small number of citizens, who assemble and administer the Government in person, can admit of no cure for the mischiefs of faction. A common passion or interest will, in almost every case, be felt by a majority of the whole; a communication and concert results from the form of Government itself; and there is nothing to check the inducements to sacrifice the weaker party, or an obnoxious individual. Hence it is, that such Democracies have ever been spectacles of turbulence and contention; have ever been found incompatible with personal security, or the rights of property; and have in general been as short in their lives, as they have been violent in their deaths. Theoretic politicians, who have patronized this species of Government, have erroneously supposed, that by reducing mankind to a perfect equality in their political rights, they would, at the same time, be perfectly equalized and assimilated in their possessions, their opinions, and their passions.

A Republic, by which I mean a Government in which the scheme of representation takes place, opens a different prospect, and promises the cure for which we are seeking. Let us examine the points in which it varies from pure Democracy, and we shall comprehend both the nature of the cure, and the efficacy which it must derive from the Union.

The two great points of difference between a Democracy and a Republic are, first, the delegation of the Government, in the latter, to a small number of citizens elected by the rest: secondly, the greater number of citizens, and greater sphere of country, over which the latter may be extended.[10]

The effect of the first difference is, on the one hand to refine and enlarge the public views, by passing them through the medium of a chosen body of citizens, whose wisdom may best discern the true interest of their country, and whose patriotism and love of justice, will be least likely to sacrifice it to temporary or partial considerations. Under such a regulation, it may well happen that the public voice pronounced by the representatives of the people, will be more consonant to the public good, than if pronounced by the people themselves convened for the purpose. On the other hand, the effect may be inverted. Men of factious tempers, of local prejudices, or of sinister designs, may by intrigue, by corruption or by other means, first obtain the suffrages, and then betray the interests of the people. The question resulting is, whether small or extensive Republics are most favorable to the election of proper guard-

---

[10] In *The Federalist No. 14*, Madison took the measure of the United States to prove that it could be governed as an extended republic.

ians of the public weal: and it is clearly decided in favor of the latter by two obvious considerations.

In the first place it is to be remarked that however small the Republic may be, the Representatives must be raised to a certain number, in order to guard against the cabals of a few; and that however large it may be, they must be limited to a certain number, in order to guard against the confusion of a multitude. Hence the number of Representatives in the two cases, not being in proportion to that of the Constituents, and being proportionally greatest in the small Republic, it follows, that if the proportion of fit characters, be not less, in the large than in the small Republic, the former will present a greater option, and consequently a greater probability of a fit choice.

In the next place, as each Representative will be chosen by a greater number of citizens in the large than in the small Republic, it will be more difficult for unworthy candidates to practice with success the vicious arts, by which elections are too often carried; and the suffrages of the people being more free, will be more likely to center on men who possess the most attractive merit, and the most diffusive and established characters.

It must be confessed, that in this, as in most other cases, there is a mean, on both sides of which inconveniences will be found to lie. By enlarging too much the number of electors, you render the representative too little acquainted with all their local circumstances and lesser interests; as by reducing it too much, you render him unduly attached to these, and too little fit to comprehend and pursue great and national objects. The Federal Constitution forms a happy combination in this respect; the great and aggregate interests being referred to the national, the local and particular, to the state legislatures.

The other point of difference is, the greater number of citizens and extent of territory which may be brought within the compass of Republican, than of Democratic Government; and it is this circumstance principally which renders factious combinations less to be dreaded in the former, than in the latter. The smaller the society, the fewer probably will be the distinct parties and interests composing it; the fewer the distinct parties and interests, the more frequently will a majority be found of the same party; and the smaller the number of individuals composing a majority, and the smaller the compass within which they are placed, the more easily will they concert and execute their plans of oppression. Extend the sphere, and you take in a greater variety of parties and interests; you make it less probable that a majority of the whole will have a common motive to invade the rights of other citizens; or if such a common motive exists, it will be more difficult for all who feel it to discover their own strength, and to act in unison with each other. Besides other impediments, it may be remarked, that where there is a consciousness of unjust or dishonorable purposes, communication is always checked by distrust, in proportion to the number whose concurrence is necessary.

Hence it clearly appears, that the same advantage, which a Republic has over a Democracy, in controling the effects of faction, is enjoyed by a large over a small Republic—is enjoyed by the Union over the States composing it. Does this advantage consist in the substitution of Representatives, whose enlightened views and virtuous sentiments render them superior to local prejudices, and to schemes of injustice? It will not be denied, that the Representation of the Union will be most likely to possess these requisite endowments. Does it consist in the greater security afforded by a greater variety of parties, against the event of any one party being able to outnumber and oppress the rest? In an equal degree does the encreased variety of parties, comprised within the Union, encrease this security. Does it, in fine, consist in the greater obstacles opposed to the concert and accomplishment of the secret wishes of an unjust and interested majority? Here, again, the extent of the Union gives it the most palpable advantage.

The influence of factious leaders may kindle a flame within their particular States, but will be unable to spread a general conflagration through the other States: a religious sect, may degenerate into a political faction in a part of the Confederacy; but the variety of sects dispersed over the entire face of it, must secure the national Councils against any danger from that source: a rage for paper money, for an abolition of debts, for an equal division of property, or for any other improper or wicked project, will be less apt to pervade the whole body of the Union, than a particular member of it; in the same proportion as such a malady is more likely to taint a particular county or district, than an entire State.

In the extent and proper structure of the Union, therefore, we behold a Republican remedy for the diseases most incident to Republican Government. And according to the degree of pleasure and pride, we feel in being Republicans, ought to be our zeal in cherishing the spirit, and supporting the character of Federalists.

PUBLIUS

The Federalist No. 37[11]

James Madison

January 11, 1788

To the People of the State of New York.

IN reviewing the defects of the existing Confederation, and shewing that they cannot be supplied by a Government of less energy than that before the public, several of the most important principles of the latter fell of course under consideration. But as the ultimate object of these papers is to determine clearly and fully the merits of this Constitution, and the expediency of adopting it, our plan cannot be compleated without taking a more critical and thorough survey of the work of the Convention; without examining it on all its sides; comparing it in all its parts, and calculating its probable effects. That this remaining task may be executed under impressions conducive to a just and fair result, some reflections must in this place be indulged, which candor previously suggests. It is a misfortune, inseparable from human affairs, that public measures are rarely investigated with that spirit of moderation which is essential to a just estimate of their real tendency to advance or obstruct the public good; and that this spirit is more apt to be diminished than prompted, by those occasions which require an unusual exercise of it. To those who have been led by experience to attend to this consideration, it could not appear surprising, that the act of the Convention which recommends so many important changes and innovations, which may be viewed in so many lights and relations, and which touches the springs of so many passions and interests, should find or excite dispositions unfriendly both on one side, and on the other, to a fair discussion and accurate judgment of its merits. In some, it has been too evident from their own publications, that they have scanned the proposed Constitution, not only with a predisposition to censure; but with a predetermination to condemn: as the language held by others betrays an opposite predetermination or bias, which must render their opinions also of little moment in the question. In placing however, these different

---

[11] From *The Daily Advertiser*, January 11, 1788. This essay appeared on January 12 in *The Independent Journal*, on January 15 in *The New-York Packet*, and on January 19 in *The New-York Journal*. It was numbered 37 in the M'Lean edition and 36 in the newspapers.

characters on a level, with respect to the weight of their opinions, I wish not to insinuate that there may not be a material difference in the purity of their intentions. It is but just to remark in favor of the latter description, that as our situation is universally admitted to be peculiarly critical, and to require indispensibly, that something should be done for our relief, the predetermined patron of what has been actually done, may have taken his bias from the weight of these considerations, as well as from considerations of a sinister nature. The predetermined adversary on the other hand, can have been governed by no venial motive whatever. The intentions of the first may be upright, as they may on the contrary be culpable. The views of the last cannot be upright, and must be culpable. But the truth is, that these papers are not addressed to persons falling under either of these characters. They solicit the attention of those only, who add to sincere zeal for the happiness of their country, a temper favorable to a just estimate of the means of promoting it.

Persons of this character will proceed to an examination of the plan submitted by the Convention, not only without a disposition to find or to magnify faults; but will see the propriety of reflecting that a faultless plan was not to be expected. Nor will they barely make allowances for the errors which may be chargeable on the fallibility to which the Convention, as a body of men, were liable; but will keep in mind that they themselves also are but men, and ought not to assume an infallibility in rejudging the fallible opinions of others.[12]

With equal readiness will it be perceived, that besides these inducements to candor, many allowances ought to be made for the difficulties inherent in the very nature of the undertaking referred to the Convention.

The novelty of the undertaking immediately strikes us. It has been shewn in the course of these papers, that the existing Confederation is founded on principles which are fallacious;[13] that we must consequently change this first foundation, and with it, the superstructure resting upon it. It has been shewn, that the other confederacies which could be consulted as precedents, have been viciated by the same erroneous principles, and can therefore furnish no other light than that of beacons,

---

[12] Madison pursued in this essay a curious and, to our eyes, somewhat disingenuous strategy. Unable to reveal his identity as Publius, he could not disclose that he had been a delegate to the Federal Convention. His use of "must have," "must have been," and "should have been" cloaked his actual involvement in the debates and disagreements that he catalogued.

[13] See *The Federalist Nos. 15–22.*

which give warning of the course to be shunned, without pointing out that which ought to be pursued.[14] The most that the Convention could do in such a situation, was to avoid the errors suggested by the past experience of other countries, as well as of our own; and to provide a convenient mode of rectifying their own errors, as future experience may unfold them.

Among the difficulties encountered by the Convention, a very important one must have lain, in combining the requisite stability and energy in Government, with the inviolable attention due to liberty, and to the Republican form. Without substantially accomplishing this part of their undertaking, they would have very imperfectly fulfilled the object of their appointment, or the expectation of the public: Yet, that it could not be easily accomplished, will be denied by no one, who is unwilling to betray his ignorance of the subject. Energy in Government is essential to that security against external and internal danger, and to that prompt and salutary execution of the laws, which enter into the very definition of good Government.[15] Stability in Government, is essential to national character, and to the advantages annexed to it, as well as to that repose and confidence in the minds of the people, which are among the chief blessings of civil society. An irregular and mutable legislation, is not more an evil in itself, than it is odious to the people; and it may be pronounced with assurance, that the people of this country, enlightened as they are, with regard to the nature, and interested, as the great body of them are, in the effects of good Government, will never be satisfied, till some remedy be applied to the vicissitudes and uncertainties, which characterize the State administrations. On comparing, however, these valuable ingredients with the vital principles of liberty, we must perceive at once, the difficulty of mingling them together in their due proportions. The genius of Republican liberty, seems to demand on one side, not only that all power should be derived from the people; but, that those entrusted with it should be kept in dependence on the people, by a short duration of their appointments; and, that even during this short period, the trust should be placed not in a few, but in a number of hands. Stability, on the contrary, requires, that the hands, in which power is lodged, should continue for a length of time, the same. A frequent change of men will result from a frequent return of electors, and a frequent change of measures, from a frequent change of men: whilst energy in Government requires not only a certain duration of power, but the execution of it by a single hand. How far

[14] See *The Federalist Nos. 18–20.*
[15] See *The Federalist No. 70* on this same point.

the Convention may have succeeded in this part of their work, will better appear on a more accurate view of it. From the cursory view, here taken, it must clearly appear to have been an arduous part.

Not less arduous must have been the task of marking the proper line of partition, between the authority of the general, and that of the State Governments. Every man will be sensible of this difficulty, in proportion, as he has been accustomed to contemplate and discriminate objects, extensive and complicated in their nature. The faculties of the mind itself have never yet been distinguished and defined, with satisfactory precision, by all the efforts of the most acute and metaphysical Philosophers. Sense, perception, judgment, desire, volition, memory, imagination, are found to be separated by such delicate shades, and minute gradations, that their boundaries have eluded the most subtle investigations, and remain a pregnant source of ingenious disquisition and controversy. The boundaries between the great kingdoms of nature, and still more, between the various provinces, and lesser portions, into which they are subdivided, afford another illustration of the same important truth. The most sagacious and laborious naturalists have never yet succeeded, in tracing with certainty, the line which separates the district of vegetable life from the neighboring region of unorganized matter, or which marks the termination of the former and the commencement of the animal empire. A still greater obscurity lies in the distinctive characters, by which the objects in each of these great departments of nature, have been arranged and assorted. When we pass from the works of nature, in which all the delineations are perfectly accurate, and appear to be otherwise only from the imperfection of the eye which surveys them, to the institutions of man, in which the obscurity arises as well from the object itself, as from the organ by which it is contemplated; we must perceive the necessity of moderating still farther our expectations and hopes from the efforts of human sagacity. Experience has instructed us that no skill in the science of Government has yet been able to discriminate and define, with sufficient certainty, its three great provinces, the Legislative, Executive and Judiciary; or even the privileges and powers of the different Legislative branches. Questions daily occur in the course of practice, which prove the obscurity which reigns in these subjects, and which puzzle the greatest adepts in political science. The experience of ages, with the continued and combined labors of the most enlightened Legislators and jurists, have been equally unsuccessful in delineating the several objects and limits of different codes of laws and different tribunals of justice. The precise extent of the common law, the statute law, the maritime law, the ecclesiastical law, the law of corporations and other local laws and customs, remain still to be clearly and finally established in Great-Britain, where accuracy in such subjects has been more industriously pursued than in any other part of the world. The jurisdiction of her several courts, general and local, of law, of equity, of admiralty, &c. is not less a source of frequent and intricate discussions, sufficiently denoting the indeterminate limits by which they are respectively circumscribed. All new laws, though penned with the greatest technical skill, and passed on the fullest and most mature deliberation, are considered as more or less obscure and equivocal, until their meaning be liquidated and ascertained by a series of particular discussions and adjudications. Besides the obscurity arising from the complexity of objects, and the imperfection of the human faculties, the medium through which the conceptions of men are conveyed to each other, adds a fresh embarrassment. The use of words is to express ideas. Perspicuity therefore requires not only that the ideas should be distinctly formed, but that they should be expressed by words distinctly and exclusively appropriated to them. But no language is so copious as to supply words and phrases for every complex idea, or so correct as not to include many equivocally denoting different ideas. Hence, it must happen, that however accurately objects may be discriminated in themselves, and however accurately the discrimination may be considered, the definition of them may be rendered inaccurate by the inaccuracy of the terms in which it is delivered. And this unavoidable inaccuracy must be greater or less, according to the complexity and novelty of the objects defined. When the Almighty himself condescends to address mankind in their own language, his meaning, luminous as it must be, is rendered dim and doubtful, by the cloudy medium through which it is communicated. Here then are three sources of vague and incorrect definitions; indistinctness of the object, imperfection of the organ of conception, inadequateness of the vehicle of ideas. Any one of these must produce a certain degree of obscurity. The Convention, in delineating the boundary between the Federal and State jurisdictions, must have experienced the full effect of them all.

To the difficulties already mentioned, may be added the interfering pretensions of the larger and smaller States. We cannot err in supposing that the former would contend for a participation in the Government, fully proportioned to their superior wealth and importance; and that the latter would not be less tenacious of the equality at present enjoyed by them. We may well suppose that neither side would entirely yield to the other, and consequently that the struggle could be terminated only by compromise. It is extremely probable also, that after the ratio of representation had been adjusted, this very compromise must have produced a fresh struggle between the same parties, to give such a turn to the organization of the Government, and to the distribution of its powers, as would encrease the importance of the branches, in forming which they had respectively obtained the greatest share of influence. There are features in the Constitution which warrant each of these suppositions; and as far as either of them is well founded, it shews that the Convention must have been compelled to sacrifice theoretical propriety to the force of extraneous considerations.

Nor could it have been the large and small States only which would marshal themselves in opposition to each other on various points. Other combinations, resulting from a difference of local position and policy, must have created additional difficulties. As every State may be divided into different districts, and its citizens into different classes, which give birth to contending interests and local jealousies; so the different parts of the United States are distinguished from each other, by a variety of circumstances, which produce a like effect on a larger scale. And although this variety of interests, for reasons sufficiently explained in a former paper,[16] may have a salutary influence on the administration of the Government when formed; yet every one must be sensible of the contrary influence which must have been experienced in the task of forming it.

Would it be wonderful if under the pressure of all these difficulties, the Convention should have been forced into some deviations from that artificial structure and regular symmetry, which an abstract view of the subject might lead an ingenious theorist to bestow on a Constitution planned in his closet or in his imagination? The real wonder is, that so many difficulties should have been surmounted; and surmounted with a unanimity almost as unprecedented as it must have been unexpected. It is impossible for any man of candor to reflect on this circumstance, without partaking of the astonishment. It is impossible for the man of pious reflection not to perceive in it, a finger of that Almighty hand which has been so frequently and signally extended to our relief in the critical stages of the revolution. We had occasion in a former paper, to take notice of the repeated trials which have been unsuccessfully made in the United Netherlands,[17] for reforming the baneful and notorious vices of their Constitution. The history of almost all the great councils and consultations, held among mankind for reconciling their discordant opinions, assuaging their mutual jealousies, and adjusting their respective interests, is a history of factions, contentions, and disappointments; and may be classed among the most dark and degrading pictures which

[16] See *The Federalist No. 10.*
[17] See *The Federalist No. 20.*

display the infirmities and depravities of the human character. If, in a few scattered instances, a brighter aspect is presented, they serve only as exceptions to admonish us of the general truth; and by their lustre to darken the gloom of the adverse prospect to which they are contrasted. In revolving the causes from which these exceptions result, and applying them to the particular instance before us, we are necessarily led to two important conclusions. The first is, that the Convention must have enjoyed in a very singular degree, an exemption from the pestilential influence of party animosities; the diseases most incident to deliberative bodies, and most apt to contaminate their proceedings. The second conclusion is, that all the deputations composing the Convention, were either satisfactorily accommodated by the final act; or were induced to accede to it, by a deep conviction of the necessity of sacrificing private opinions and partial interests to the public good, and by a despair of seeing this necessity diminished by delays or by new experiments.[18]

PUBLIUS.

[18] Madison's peroration in *The Federalist No. 37* parallels Benjamin Franklin's closing speech to the Federal Convention:

I doubt too whether any other Convention we can obtain may be able to make a better Constitution. For when you assemble a number of men to have the advantage of their joint wisdom, you inevitably assemble with those men, all their prejudices, their passions, their errors of opinion, their local interests, and their selfish views. From such an assembly can a perfect production be expected? It therefore astonishes me, Sir, to find this system approaching as near to perfection as it does; and I think it will astonish our enemies. . . . Thus I consent, Sir, to the Constitution because I expect no better, and because I am not sure, that it is not the best.

Max Farrand, ed., *Records of the Federal Convention of 1787*, rev. ed., 4 vols. (New Haven, Conn., 1987), II, 641–43 (speech of Benjamin Franklin on September 17, 1787).

The Federalist No. 39[19]

James Madison

January 16, 1788

To the People of the State of New York.

THE last paper having concluded the observations which were meant to introduce a candid survey of the plan of government reported by the Convention, we now proceed to the execution of that part of our undertaking. The first question that offers itself is, whether the general form and aspect of the government be strictly republican? It is evident that no other form would be reconcileable with the genius of the people of America; with the fundamental principles of the revolution; or with that honorable determination, which animates every votary of freedom, to rest all our political experiments on the capacity of mankind for self-government. If the plan of the Convention therefore be found to depart from the republican character, its advocates must abandon it as no longer defensible.

What then are the distinctive characters of the republican form? Were an answer to this question to be sought, not by recurring to principles, but in the application of the term by political writers, to the constitutions of different States, no satisfactory one would ever be found. Holland, in which no particle of the supreme authority is derived from the people, has passed almost universally under the denomination of a republic. The same title has been bestowed on Venice, where absolute power over the great body of the people, is exercised in the most absolute manner, by a small body of hereditary nobles. Poland, which is a mixture of aristocracy and of monarchy in their worst forms, has been dignified with the same appellation. The government of England, which has one republican branch only, combined with a hereditary aristocracy and monarchy, has with equal impropriety been frequently placed on the list of republics. These examples, which are nearly as

[19] From *The Independent Journal*, January 16, 1788. This essay appeared on the same day in *The Daily Advertiser* on January 18 in *The New-York Packet*, and on January 30 in *The New-York Journal*. It was numbered 39 in the M'Lean edition and 38 in the newspapers, with the exception of *The New-York Journal*, where it was numbered 37 and was the last essay to appear in that newspaper.

dissimilar to each other as to a genuine republic, shew the extreme inaccuracy with which the term has been used in political disquisitions. If we resort for a criterion, to the different principles on which different forms of government are established, we may define a republic to be, or at least may bestow that name on, a government which derives all its powers directly or indirectly from the great body of the people; and is administered by persons holding their offices during pleasure, for a limited period, or during good behaviour. It is *essential* to such a government that it be derived from the great body of the society, not from an inconsiderable proportion, or a favored class of it; otherwise a handful of tyrannical nobles, exercising their oppressions by a delegation of their powers, might aspire to the rank of republicans, and claim for their government the honorable title of republic. It is *sufficient* for such a government, that the persons administering it be appointed, either directly or indirectly, by the people; and that they hold their appointments by either of the tenures just specified; otherwise every government in the United States, as well as every other popular government that has been or can be well organized or well executed, would be degraded from the republican character. According to the Constitution of every State in the Union, some or other of the officers of government are appointed indirectly only by the people. According to most of them the chief magistrate himself is so appointed. And according to one, this mode of appointment is extended to one of the coordinate branches of the legislature. According to all the Constitutions also, the tenure of the highest offices is extended to a definite period, and in many instances, both within the legislative and executive department, to a period of years. According to the provisions of most of the constitutions, again, as well as according to the most respectable and received opinions on the subject, the members of the judiciary department are to retain their offices by the firm tenure of good behaviour.

On comparing the Constitution planned by the Convention, with the standard here fixed, we perceive at once that it is in the most rigid sense conformable to it. The House of Representatives, like that of one branch at least of all the State Legislatures, is elected immediately by the great body of the people. The Senate, like the present Congress, and the Senate of Maryland, derives its appointment indirectly from the people. The President is indirectly derived from the choice of the people, according to the example in most of the States. Even the judges, with all other officers of the Union, will, as in the several States, be the choice, though a remote choice, of the people themselves. The duration of the appointments is equally conformable to the republican standard, and to the model of the State Constitutions. The House of

Representatives is periodically elective as in all the States: and for the period of two years as in the State of South-Carolina. The Senate is elective for the period of six years; which is but one year more than the period of the Senate of Maryland; and but two more than that of the Senates of New-York and Virginia. The President is to continue in office for the period of four years; as in New-York and Delaware, the chief magistrate is elected for three years, and in South-Carolina for two years. In the other States the election is annual. In several of the States however, no constitutional provision is made for the impeachment of the Chief Magistrate. And in Delaware and Virginia, he is not impeachable till out of office. The President of the United States is impeachable at any time during his continuance in office. The tenure by which the Judges are to hold their places, is, as it unquestionably ought to be, that of good behaviour. The tenure of the ministerial offices generally will be a subject of legal regulation, conformably to the reason of the case, and the example of the State Constitutions.

Could any further proof be required of the republican complextion of this system, the most decisive one might be found in its absolute prohibition of titles of nobility, both under the Federal and the State Governments; and in its express guarantee of the republican form to each of the latter.

But it was not sufficient, say the adversaries of the proposed Constitution, for the Convention to adhere to the republican form. They ought, with equal care, to have preserved the *federal* form, which regards the union as a *confederacy* of sovereign States; instead of which, they have framed a *national* government, which regards the union as a *consolidation* of the States. And it is asked by what authority this bold and radical innovation was undertaken. The handle which has been made of this objection requires, that it should be examined with some precision.

Without enquiring into the accuracy of the distinction on which the objection is founded, it will be necessary to a just estimate of its force, first to ascertain the real character of the government in question; secondly, to enquire how far the Convention were authorised to propose such a government; and thirdly, how far the duty they owed to their country, could supply any defect of regular authority.

First. In order to ascertain the real character of the government it may be considered in relation to the foundation on which it is to be established; to the sources from which its ordinary powers are to be drawn; to the operation of those powers; to the extent of them; and to the authority by which future changes in the government are to be introduced.

On examining the first relation, it appears on one hand that the Constitution is to be founded on the assent and ratification of the people of America, given by deputies elected for the special purpose; but on the other, that this assent and ratification is to be given by the people, not as individuals composing one entire nation; but as composing the distinct and independent States to which they respectively belong. It is to be the assent and ratification of the several States, derived from the supreme authority in each State, the authority of the people themselves. The act therefore establishing the Constitution, will not be a *national* but a *federal* act.

That it will be a federal and not a national act, as these terms are understood by the objectors, the act of the people as forming so many independent States, not as forming one aggregate nation, is obvious from this single consideration that it is to result neither from the decision of a *majority* of the people of the Union, nor from that of a *majority* of the States. It must result from the *unanimous* assent of the several States that are parties to it, differing no other wise from their ordinary assent than in its being expressed, not by the legislative authority, but by that of the people themselves. Were the people regarded in this transaction as forming one nation, the will of the majority of the whole people of the United States, would bind the minority; in the same manner as the majority in each State must bind the minority; and the will of the majority must be determined either by a comparison of the individual votes; or by considering the will of a majority of the States, as evidence of the will of a majority of the people of the United States. Neither of these rules has been adopted. Each State in ratifying the Constitution, is considered as a sovereign body independent of all others, and only to be bound by its own voluntary act. In this relation then the new Constitution will, if established, be a *federal* and not a *national* Constitution.

The next relation is to the sources from which the ordinary powers of government are to be derived. The house of representatives will derive its powers for the people of America, and the people will be represented in the same proportion, and on the same principle, as they are in the Legislature of a particular State. So far the Government is *national* not *federal*. The Senate on the other hand will derive its powers from the States, as political and co-equal societies; and these will be represented on the principle of equality in the Senate, as they now are in the existing Congress. So far the government is *federal*, not *national*. The executive power will be derived from a very compound source. The immediate election of the President is to be made by the States in their political characters. The votes allotted to them, are in a com-

ROOTS OF THE REPUBLIC

pound ratio, which considers them partly as distinct and co-equal societies; partly as unequal members of the same society. The eventual election, again is to be made by that branch of the Legislature which consists of the national representatives; but in this particular act, they are to be thrown into the form of individual delegations from so many distinct and co-equal bodies politic. From this aspect of the Government, it appears to be of a mixed character presenting at least as many *federal* as *national* features.

The difference between a federal and national Government as it relates to the *operation of the Government* is supposed to consist in this, that in the former, the powers operate on the political bodies composing the confederacy, in their political capacities: In the latter, on the individual citizens, composing the nation, in their individual capacities.[20] On trying the Constitution by this criterion, it falls under the *national*, not the *federal* character; though perhaps not so compleatly, as has been understood. In several cases and particularly in the trial of controversies to which States may be parties, they must be viewed and proceeded against in their collective and political capacities only. So far the national countenance of the Government on this side seems to be disfigured by a few federal features. But this blemish is perhaps unavoidable in any plan; and the operation of the Government on the people in their individual capacities, in its ordinary and most essential proceedings, may on the whole designate it in this relation a *national* Government.

But if the Government be national with regard to the *operation* of its powers, it changes its aspect again when we contemplate it in relation to the *extent* of its powers. The idea of a national Government involves in it, not only an authority over the individual citizens; but an indefinite supremacy over all persons and things, so far as they are objects of lawful Government. Among a people consolidated into one nation, this supremacy is compleatly vested in the national Legislature. Among communities united for particular purposes, it is vested partly in the general, and partly in the municipal Legislatures. In the former case, all local authorities are subordinate to the supreme; and may be controuled, directed or abolished by it at pleasure. In the latter the local or municipal authorities form distinct and independent portions of the supremacy, no more subject within their respective spheres to the general authority, than the general authority is subject to them, within its

---

[20] Compare *The Federalist No. 15*, which emphasizes as the principal defect of the Articles of Confederation its failure to confer power on the general government to operate directly on individuals.

own sphere. In this relation then the proposed Government cannot be deemed a *national* one; since its jurisdiction extends to certain enumerated objects only, and leaves to the several States a residuary and inviolable sovereignty over all other objects. It is true that in controversies relating to the boundary between the two jurisdictions, the tribunal which is ultimately to decide, is to be established under the general Government. But this does not change the principle of the case. The decision is to be impartially made, according to the rules of the Constitution; and all the usual and most effectual precautions are taken to secure this impartiality. Some such tribunal is clearly essential to prevent an appeal to the sword, and a dissolution of the compact; and that it ought to be established under the general, rather than under the local Governments; or to speak more properly, that it could be safely established under the first alone, is a position not likely to be combated.

If we try the Constitution by its last relation, to the authority by which amendments are to be made, we find it neither wholly *national*, nor wholly *federal*. Were it wholly national, the supreme and ultimate authority would reside in the *majority* of the people of the Union; and this authority would be competent at all times, like that of a majority of every national society, to alter or abolish its established Government. Were it wholly federal on the other hand, the concurrence of each State in the Union would be essential to every alteration that would be binding on all. The mode provided by the plan of the Convention is not founded on either of these principles. In requiring more than a majority, and particularly, in computing the proportion by *States*, not by *citizens*, it departs from the *national*, and advances towards the *federal* character: In rendering the concurrence of less than the whole number of States sufficient, it loses again the *federal*, and partakes of the *national* character.

The proposed Constitution therefore is in strictness neither a national nor a federal constitution; but a composition of both. In its foundation, it is federal, not national; in the sources from which the ordinary powers of the Government are drawn, it is partly federal, and partly national: in the operation of these powers, it is national, not federal: In the extent of them again, it is federal, not national: And finally, in the authoritative mode of introducing amendments, it is neither wholly federal, nor wholly national.

PUBLIUS.

The Federalist No. 51[21]

James Madison

February 6, 1788

To the People of the State of New York.

To what expedient then shall we finally resort for maintaining in practice the necessary partition of power among the several departments, as laid down in the constitution? The only answer that can be given is, that as all these exterior provisions are found to be inadequate, the defect must be supplied, by so contriving the interior structure of the government, as that its several constituent parts may, by their mutual relations, be the means of keeping each other in their proper places. Without presuming to undertake a full development of this important idea, I will hazard a few general observations, which may perhaps place it in a clearer light, and enable us to form a more correct judgment of the principles and structure of the government planned by the convention.

In order to lay a due foundation for that separate and distinct exercise of the different powers of government, which to a certain extent, is admitted on all hands to be essential to the preservation of liberty, it is evident that each department should have a will of its own; and consequently should be so constituted, that the members of each should have as little agency as possible in the appointment of the members of the others. Were this principle rigorously adhered to, it would require that all the appointments for the supreme executive, legislative, and judiciary magistracies, should be drawn from the same fountain of authority, the people, through channels, having no communication whatever with one another. Perhaps such a plan of constructing the several departments would be less difficult in practice than it may in contemplation appear. Some difficulties however, and some additional expence, would attend the execution of it. Some deviations therefore from the principle must be admitted. In the constitution of the judiciary department in particular, it might be inexpedient to insist rigorously on

---

[21] From *The Independent Journal*, February 6, 1788. This essay appeared on February 8 in *The New-York Packet* and on February 11 in *The Daily Advertiser*. It was numbered 51 in the M'Lean edition and 50 in the newspapers.

the principle; first, because peculiar qualifications being essential in the members, the primary consideration ought to be to select that mode of choice, which best secures these qualifications; secondly, because the permanent tenure by which the appointments are held in that department, must soon destroy all sense of dependence on the authority conferring them.[22]

It is equally evident that the members of each department should be as little dependent as possible on those of the others, for the emoluments annexed to their offices. Were the executive magistrate, or the judges, not independent of the legislature in this particular, their independence in every other would be merely nominal.

But the great security against a gradual concentration of the several powers in the same department, consists in giving to those who administer each department, the necessary constitutional means, and personal motives, to resist encroachments of the others. The provision for defence must in this, as in all other cases, be made commensurate to the danger of attack. Ambition must be made to counteract ambition. The interest of the man must be connected with the constitutional rights of the place. It may be a reflection on human nature, that such devices should be necessary to controul the abuses of government. But what is government itself but the greatest of all reflections on human nature? If men were angels, no government would be necessary. If angels were to govern men, neither external nor internal controuls on government would be necessary. In framing a government which is to be administered by men over men, the great difficulty lies in this: You must first enable the government to controul the governed; and in the next place, oblige it to controul itself. A dependence on the people is no doubt the primary controul on the government; but experience has taught mankind the necessity of auxiliary precautions.

This policy of supplying by opposite and rival interests, the defect of better motives, might be traced through the whole system of human affairs, private as well as public. We see it particularly displayed in all the subordinate distributions of power; where the constant aim is to divide and arrange the several offices in such a manner as that each may be a check on the other; that the private interest of every individual, may be a centinel over the public rights. These inventions of prudence cannot be less requisite in the distribution of the supreme powers of the state.

But it is not possible to give to each department an equal power of self defence. In republican government the legislative authority, nec-

---

[22] Compare Hamilton's discussion of the judiciary in *The Federalist No. 78.*

essarily, predominates. The remedy for this inconveniency is, to divide the legislature into different branches; and to render them by different modes of election, and different principles of action, as little connected with each other, as the nature of their common functions, and their common dependence on the society, will admit. It may even be necessary to guard against dangerous encroachments by still further precautions. As the weight of the legislative authority requires that it should be thus divided, the weakness of the executive may require, on the other hand, that it should be fortified. An absolute negative, on the legislature, appears at first view to be the natural defence with which the executive magistrate should be armed. But perhaps it would be neither altogether safe, nor alone sufficient. On ordinary occasions, it might not be exerted with the requisite firmness; and on extraordinary occasions, it might be perfidiously abused. May not this defect of an absolute negative be supplied, by some qualified connection between this weaker department, and the weaker branch of the stronger department, by which the latter may be led to support the constitutional rights of the former, without being too much detached from the rights of its own department?

If the principles on which these observations are founded be just, as I persuade myself they are, and they be applied as a criterion, to the several state constitutions, and to the federal constitution, it will be found, that if the latter does not perfectly correspond with them, the former are infinitely less able to bear such a test.

There are moreover two considerations particularly applicable to the federal system of America, which place that system in a very interesting point of view.

First. In a single republic, all the power surrendered by the people, is submitted to the administration of a single government; and usurpations are guarded against by a division of the government into distinct and separate departments. In the compound republic of America, the power surrendered by the people, is first divided between two distinct governments, and then the portion allotted to each, subdivided among distinct and separate departments. Hence a double security arises to the rights of the people. The different governments will controul each other; at the same time that each will be controuled by itself.

Second.[23] It is of great importance in a republic, not only to guard the society against the oppression of its rulers; but to guard one part of the society against the injustice of the other part. Different interests

---

[23] The balance of *The Federalist No. 51* echoes the analysis presented in *The Federalist No. 10.*

necessarily exist in different classes of citizens. If a majority be united by a common interest, the rights of the minority will be insecure. There are but two methods of providing against this evil: The one by creating a will in the community independent of the majority, that is, of the society itself; the other by comprehending in the society so many separate descriptions of citizens, as will render an unjust combination of a majority of the whole, very improbable, if not impracticable. The first method prevails in all governments possessing an hereditary or self appointed authority. This at best is but a precarious security; because a power independent of the society may as well espouse the unjust views of the major, as the rightful interests, of the minor party, and may possibly be turned against both parties. The second method will be exemplified in the federal republic of the United States. Whilst all authority in it will be derived from and dependent on the society, the society itself will be broken into so many parts, interests and classes of citizens, that the rights of individuals or of the minority, will be in little danger from interested combinations of the majority. In a free government, the security for civil rights must be the same as for religious rights. It consists in the one case in the multiplicity of interests, and in the other, in the multiplicity of sects. The degree of security in both cases will depend on the number of interests and sects; and this may be presumed to depend on the extent of country and number of people comprehended under the same government. This view of the subject must particularly recommend a proper federal system to all the sincere and considerate friends of republican government: Since it shews that in exact proportion as the territory of the union may be formed into more circumscribed confederacies or states, oppressive combinations of a majority will be facilitated, the best security under the republican form, for the rights of every class of citizens, will be diminished; and consequently, the stability and independence of some member of the government, the only other security, must be proportionally increased. Justice is the end of government. It is the end of civil society. It ever has been, and ever will be pursued, until it be obtained, or until liberty be lost in the pursuit. In a society under the forms of which the stronger faction can readily unite and oppress the weaker, anarchy may as truly be said to reign, as in a state of nature where the weaker individual is not secured against the violence of the stronger: And as in the latter state even the stronger individuals are prompted by the uncertainty of their condition, to submit to a government which may protect the weak as well as themselves: So in the former state, will the more powerful factions or parties be gradually induced by a like motive, to wish for a government which will protect all parties, the weaker as well as the more powerful. It can be little doubted, that if the state of Rhode Island was separated from the confederacy, and left to itself, the insecurity of rights under the popular form of government within such narrow limits, would be displayed by such reiterated oppressions of factious majorities, that some power altogether independent of the people would soon be called for by the voice of the very factions whose misrule had proved the necessity of it.[24] In the extended republic of the United States, and among the great variety of interests, parties and sects which it embraces, a coalition of a majority of the whole society could seldom take place on any other principles than those of justice and the general good; and there being thus less danger to a minor from the will of the major party, there must be less pretext also, to provide for the security of the former, by introducing into the government a will not dependent on the latter; or in other words, a will independent of the society itself. It is no less certain than it is important, notwithstanding the contrary opinions which have been entertained, that the larger the society, provided it lie within a practicable sphere, the more duly capable it will be of self government. And happily for the *republican cause*, the practicable sphere may be carried to a very great extent, by a judicious modification and mixture of the *federal principle*.

PUBLIUS.

[24] It was a popular Federalist polemical tactic to invoke the instability and turbulence of Rhode Island politics, and to suggest that without the Constitution the entire nation would subside into similar anarchy. See generally Irwin Polishook, *Rhode Island and the Union, 1774–1795* (Evanston, Ill., 1969).

XVI

The Federalist
on Energetic Government

1787–1788

COMMENTARY BY RICHARD B. BERNSTEIN

By 'constitutionalism,' I mean a complex of ideas, attitudes, and patterns of behavior elaborating the principle that the authority of government derives from and is limited by a body of fundamental law. For Americans, distinctively, the word 'constitution' had come to mean a single document embodying the sovereign will of the people—a document that established or reorganized a government, prescribing its structure and endowing it with power, while at the same time restricting that power in the interest of personal liberty.[1]

THIS PASSAGE BY DON E. FEHRENBACHER sets forth valuable definitions of "constitutionalism" and "constitution." The relevance of Fehrenbacher's definitions underscores a serious limit of many other historians' and political scientists' interpretations of constitutionalism in general, of American constitutionalism in particular, and especially of the version of American constitutionalism presented in *The Federalist*.

Most modern scholars view constitutionalism solely as a source of limitations on the power of government, overlooking its equally significant function as a theory of the origins and exercise of legitimate governmental power.[2] This deficiency is rooted in the inclination of con-

[1] Don E. Fehrenbacher, *Constitutions and Constitutionalism in the Slaveholding South* (Athens, Ga., 1989), 1.
[2] See, e.g., Walter H. Mead, *The United States Constitution: Personalities, Principles, Issues* (Columbia, S.C., 1987), and Jon Elster, "Introduction," in Jon Elster and Rune Slagstad, eds., *Constitutionalism and Democracy* (Cambridge, England, 1988).

temporary constitutional theorists to focus their attention on the limitation of governmental power and the protection of individual rights, the central problems of constitutional government in the modern era. If we are to understand American constitutionalism in its historical context, however, we should not neglect its importance as a theory of sovereignty—a component of constitutionalism which the Revolutionary generation of Americans never forgot.

We can condense and restate the basic principles of the American variant of constitutionalism thus: the Constitution, a document established by and incarnating the principle of popular sovereignty, creates a form of government that is energetic enough to protect national interests and achieve national goals. At the same time, the Constitution so limits that form of government, by reason of (i) its limited grants of power to the general government, (ii) its preservation of a sphere for the state governments, and (iii) the system of checks and balances built into the general government, that that government will not endanger individual liberty or popular sovereignty. The terms of what might be called the equation of American constitutionalism given above recur, in varying forms, throughout the founding documents of the American constitutional tradition, among them *The Federalist*.[3] The originality of *The Federalist's* examination of the recurring problems of limiting the power of government justifies the traditional emphasis on this subject in *Federalist* scholarship. However, partly as a consequence of the incomplete understanding of constitutionalism mentioned above, students of *The Federalist* tend either to overlook the essays' equally significant arguments for the necessity of energetic government or to minimize those arguments' theoretical importance. This is an ironic omission, for the authors of *The Federalist* sought to defend, on theoretical as well as practical grounds, the scope and types of power that the framers of the Constitution sought to vest in the government of the United States.

Another source of the tendency to slight *The Federalist's* arguments for energetic government is the perception that "Publius," the ostensible voice of *The Federalist*, is a split personality, speaking as an advocate of energetic government through the writings of Alexander Hamilton and John Jay and as an advocate of limited government through the writings of James Madison.[4] Although this distinction is valuable and

---

[3] My discussion is indebted to Donald S. Lutz, *The Origins of American Constitutionalism* (Baton Rouge, La., 1988), which stands in contrast to the conventional, more limited view.

[4] The principal source for this view is Alpheus Thomas Mason, "*The Federalist*—A Split Personality," *American Historical Review* 57 (1952): 625–43. Mason (following Douglass Adair) states these views more precisely and circumspectly, and therefore more persuasively, than do those following him.

suggestive, later scholars have expanded it beyond its plausible limits. The late Clinton Rossiter made the soundest response to the over-drawing of this distinction:

> Publius was, on any large view, at least as whole a personality as any reasonable man can be when he has to deal with the everlasting ten-sions of free government. His own tensions, it might be argued, are only an honest reflection of those built into the Constitution.[5]

The task this commentary performs is twofold. First, it sketches the emphasis in *The Federalist* on the need for energy in government—a requirement addressed by all three authors of *The Federalist*. Second, it recovers the historical, political, and intellectual contexts for *The Federalist's* general justification of energetic government and for its ex-planations and defenses of executive power and judicial review—two types of governmental energy often challenged by Antifederalist critics of the Constitution and their intellectual heirs.

This commentary examines three of the finest and most influential of Hamilton's essays as "Publius": *No. 15* lists the ways in which the principal defect of the Articles of Confederation—a want of energy in the general government—imperiled the American Union. *No. 70* ex-plains and defends the Constitution's provision for a single chief ex-ecutive, the president of the United States. *No. 78* sets forth the case for a federal judiciary vested with the power of judicial review.

Although scholars have agreed that all three of these essays are both pivotal in the general argument of *The Federalist* and influential in American constitutional history, many have read them solely as au-thoritative expositions of the meaning of the Constitution, and have assumed that they were written for that purpose.[6] Of course, *The Fed-eralist* is the first great work in the line of American constitutional commentaries; Hamilton, Madison, and Jay have pride of place on sub-stantive as well as chronological grounds in that long, distinguished, and contentious tradition.

Understanding "Publius" as a constitutional commentator is only one possible way to read *The Federalist*, however. We can also regard

---

[5] Clinton Rossiter, "Introduction," in *The Federalist Papers* (New York, 1961), xv.

[6] But see Bruce Ackerman, "Discovering the Constitution—The Storrs Lectures," *Yale Law Journal* 93 (1984): 1013–72, a preview of his work-in-progress on American constitutional theory featuring an acute and historically sensitive reading of *The Federalist*. This article advances what Ackerman calls a "Neo-*Federalist*" theory of the Constitution legitimizing judicial review. See also Bruce Ackerman, "Constitutional Politics/Consti-tutional Law," *Yale Law Journal* 99 (1989): 453–548.

ROOTS OF THE REPUBLIC

the essays as masterful polemics intended to win approval for the proposed Constitution—a "debater's handbook," in a phrase favored by
Douglass Adair, Alpheus Thomas Mason, and Clinton Rossiter.[7] Or we
can consider them a means of entry into the world of late eighteenth-
century political thought, one that at the same time presents enduring
philosophical reflections on the problems of politics.[8] As Adair, Rossiter,
and Morton White have suggested, combining these three techniques
may well bring us closest to the essence of "Publius." This essay,
therefore, comments on the types of argument employed by Hamilton
and the methods of reading that best convey the flavor of The Federalist.

The selections from The Federalist and the Antifederalist writings
included here are not formal constitutional documents like the Mayflower Compact, the Albany Plan of Union, or the Articles of Confederation. Nor are they official expressions of political philosophy and
national identity like the Declaration of Independence. Nonetheless,
these works of political argument belong in a compilation of founding
documents because the Constitution was founded in debate and in
argument.

Founding a form of government—or a constitutional document delineating a form of government—is a political act. The method by which
we establish a government shapes the character of that government and
of political behavior and decision-making under it. By submitting the
Constitution to the vote of the people in the state ratifying conventions,
the Revolutionary generation of American politicians helped to invent
a national political community. They also incorporated reasoned political and constitutional argument as a key component of this national
political community and its constitutional governance. Thus, the writings of advocates and opponents of the Constitution designed to influence the people's decision to adopt or to reject it are as much founding
documents as the Constitution itself.

---

[7] For this point, see, e.g., Mason, "The Federalist"; Trevor Colbourn, ed., Fame
and the Founding Fathers: Essays of Douglass Adair (New York, 1974); and Clinton J.
Rossiter, "Introduction," The Federalist Papers. Albert Furtwangler stresses the essays'
rhetorical strategies rather than the substance of their arguments in The Authority of
Publius (Ithaca, N.Y., 1984), emphasizing the character of The Federalist as a typical
eighteenth-century periodical series of letters comparable to The Spectator.

[8] See, e.g., Fame and the Founding Fathers in which Adair traces intellectual influences of such writers as Plutarch and David Hume; Garry Wills, Explaining America: The
Federalist (New York, 1981) (stressing influence of Hume); Morton White, Philosophy,
The Federalist, and the Constitution (New York, 1987), examining The Federalist's treatment
of philosophical issues while recognizing the essays' limits as works in philosophy.

Establishing the Context

The Federalist No. 15

[F]acts too stubborn to be resisted have produced a species of general assent to the abstract proposition that there exist material defects in our national system; but the usefulness of the concession, on the part of the old adversaries of fœderal measures, is destroyed by a strenuous opposition to a remedy, upon the only principles, that can give it a chance of success. While they admit that the Government of the United States is destitute of energy; they contend against conferring upon it those powers which are requisite to supply that energy. . . .

Alexander Hamilton
The Federalist No. 15

Before we examine the arguments of *No. 15*, we must set it in its context as part of *The Federalist*. This essay began the second phase of "Publius's" argument for the Constitution. The first fourteen essays extolled the virtues and blessings of the American Union. "Publius" lauded the Union as a safeguard of liberty, republican government, and national identity against foreign threats, internal subversion, and "diseases," such as factionalism and civil war, that had always proved fatal to republican governments in the past.

Hamilton, Madison, and Jay celebrated the glories and benefits of the Union for a definite polemical purpose. They used the Union as the basis for two linked arguments:

First, the preservation of the American Union required a government with energy adequate to that goal. The Constitution conformed to this prescription for American happiness far more closely than did the Articles of Confederation could, for no informed American could deny the faults of the Articles of Confederation or the government it established.

Second, "Publius" contended, some Americans conceded that the Articles had to be replaced but were not willing to adopt a form of government fitting the needs of the United States. Instead, because they feared that republican government and liberty could not be preserved on the scale of the American Union, they contended that the United States should be broken up into three or four regional confederacies. Although some politicians may have made such arguments in private during the mid-1780s, nobody did so during the ratification controversy. This opening stratagem of "Publius's" argument for the Constitution was thus an exercise in deception. Nonetheless, the argument against breaking up the Union served valuable rhetorical purposes, as it gave

Hamilton, Madison, and Jay an obvious means to link the preservation of the Union with the ratification of the Constitution.

Having established the value of the Union and the need for its preservation, *The Federalist* argued that the Articles of Confederation were insufficient to preserve the Union. *The Federalist Nos. 15–22* presented the case against the Articles with devastating force. Those advocates of the Constitution who used *The Federalist* as a "debater's handbook" in state ratifying conventions probably resorted most frequently to these essays. The Publian indictment of the Articles had an even greater influence on historians of the making of the Constitution in the nineteenth and early twentieth centuries. Only in the past fifty years have historians abandoned the reflexive condemnation of the Articles associated with John Fiske and Andrew C. McLaughlin.[9]

Hamilton's angry, eloquent assault on the Articles in *The Federalist No. 15* was the culmination of a train of thought that he had begun to pursue in 1780, while he was still a staff officer in the Continental Army under General George Washington. As Washington's confidential aide, Hamilton had experienced first-hand the deficiencies of administration under the Continental Congress. Nothing he saw of the workings of the Confederation—including his year as a New York delegate to the Confederation Congress (1782–83)—or of the conduct of American politics under the Articles changed his mind. Indeed, Hamilton's experience during the 1780s as the Confederation's receiver of taxes in New York only confirmed his contempt for the Articles.

Hamilton's opening paragraphs catalogued the failings of American public policy, at the level of the Confederation and at the level of the states, using these examples as support for his main argument: The chief defect of the Articles of Confederation was the lack of power of the United States to operate directly on individuals. In Hamilton's view, this flaw was no accident; rather, it was one of the basic principles of the form of government established by the Articles of Confederation. Hamilton's analysis assumed—and later scholars have agreed—that the Articles were a product of the American revolution against British centralized government. The Americans' experience in resisting parlia-

[9] John Fiske, *The Critical Period in American History* (Boston, 1889); Andrew C. McLaughlin, *Confederation and Constitution, 1783–1789* (New York, 1906). Merrill Jensen, *The Articles of Confederation* (Madison, 1940) and Merrill Jensen, *The New Nation: A History of the United States under the Confederation, 1781–1789* (New York, 1950), began the reconsideration of the Articles. Richard B. Morris, *The Forging of the Union, 1781–1789* (New York, 1987) and Jack N. Rakove, *The Beginnings of National Politics* (New York, 1979) present the latest, most balanced evaluations of the Confederation. See generally the commentary on the Articles by Donald S. Lutz in this volume.

mentary and ministerial usurpations left them with a profound fear and distrust of energetic, centralized government that, in turn, shaped the framing of the Articles.

The Confederation's supposed ability to operate on states was no remedy for its want of power to operate on individuals, Hamilton contended. Only coercion of individuals was effective in upholding national interests; moreover, as confirmed by experience, the Confederation lacked any real power to command the obedience of the state governments. Thus, Hamilton concluded, this central flaw of the Articles had generated a host of difficulties for the American republic—difficulties whose solution could be made possible only by replacing the Articles with the Constitution. Because the Constitution would confer on the United States the power to operated directly on individuals, Hamilton noted, it would enable the general government to raise its own revenue, to regulate commerce, to make and enforce its own laws, to develop solutions for the ever-present problem of the national debt, and to vindicate national honor against challenges by both friendly and hostile foreign nations.

The Federalist Nos. 16–22 developed the indictment of the Articles begun in *No. 15.* "Publius" maintained, among other things, that the tendency of the states to encroach on the general authority would be a greater threat to the success of the Constitution than would be any tendency of the general government to encroach on the authority of the states. Later scholars have derided this claim as a false prophecy. When considered against the background of American politics in the 1770s and 1780s, however, "Publius's" prediction seems a natural deduction based on what the authors of *The Federalist* already knew.

Hamilton brought this second stage of the argument to a close in *The Federalist No. 22.* Reviewing the flaws of the Articles, Hamilton cited the Confederation's lack of an executive power and a judiciary power. That the Articles did not provide for either an executive branch or a judicial branch was no accident. Once again, the reason for these omissions was the Americans' distrust of centralized power—in particular, centralized executive and judicial power. We explore below Hamilton's defense of the creation of executive and judicial branches by Articles II and III of the proposed Constitution.

Executive Power

The Federalist No. 70

A feeble executive implies a feeble execution of the government. A feeble execution is but another phrase for a bad execution: And a gov-

ernment ill executed, whatever it may be in theory, must be in practice a bad government.

Alexander Hamilton
The Federalist No. 70

The Federalist No. 70 is the centerpiece of the eleven essays—*Nos.
67–77*—examining and justifying the office of president of the United
States as described in Article II of the Constitution.
Hamilton observed of the presidency in *No. 67*:

> There is hardly any part of the system which could have been at-
> tended with greater difficulty in the arrangement than this; and there
> is perhaps none, which has been inveighed against with less candor, or
> criticized with less judgment.

James Madison's Virginia Plan, the basis of the Federal Convention's debates in 1787, had provided for a national executive but had left
a blank for the number of members it would have. When James Wilson
of Pennsylvania moved for a one-person chief executive, the delegates
greeted the motion with silence, broken only after Benjamin Franklin
urged his colleagues to express their views. Although Governor Edmund Randolph of Virginia had introduced the Virginia Plan, he led
those delegates opposing a unitary chief executive, calling it a "foetus
of monarchy." Nonetheless, the Convention was persuaded of the need
for a single executive, and having adopted Wilson's motion, they never
looked back.[10]

Executive power was a problematical matter in American politics
and constitution-making throughout the era of the Revolution.[11] The
colonists' frequent battles with royal governors combined with the prevailing American hostility to George III after 1775; the resulting distrust
of strong executives shaped the assumptions and goals that the Americans brought to the task of creating new state constitutions.

Virtually all the state constitutions adopted between 1776 and 1784
either discarded a unitary chief executive or created one dependent on

[10] Max Farrand, *The Records of the Federal Convention of 1787*, rev. ed. in 4 vols.
(New Haven, 1987), I: 64–69, 96–97; Charles Thach, *The Creation of the Presidency, 1775–
1789* (Baltimore, 1922); Thomas E. Cronin, ed., *Inventing the American Presidency* (Lawrence, Kans., 1989). Richard B. Bernstein with Kym S. Rice, *Are We to Be a Nation? The
Making of the Constitution* (Cambridge, Mass., 1987), 171–74, is a useful summary.

[11] See Ralph Ketcham, *Presidents Above Party: The First American Presidency, 1789–
1829* (Chapel Hill, 1984) for a valuable analysis of ideas of executive power in the Anglo-
American world in the seventeenth and eighteenth centuries.

the legislature for election and lacking independent authority.[12] Only the constitutions of New York (1777), Massachusetts (1780), and New Hampshire (1784) departed from this model. At the other end of the political spectrum was the Pennsylvania Constitution of 1776, which created a supreme executive council whose president had little more authority than the chairman of the board of directors of a large modern corporation. Most other state constitutions landed somewhere in the middle. Thus, it is not surprising that the presidency was a favorite target of the Constitution's opponents.

Hamilton himself was a popular focus of Antifederalists' scorn and loathing during the ratification controversy for reasons having direct relevance to the presidency. His fellow New York delegates, Robert Yates and John Lansing, Jr., had walked out of the Federal Convention in disgust—but not before hearing (and making notes of) Hamilton's marathon speech of June 18, 1787. In that speech, which may have caused Hamilton as much trouble with later historians as with his contemporaries, he dismissed both the Virginia Plan and the New Jersey Plan as inadequate to the emergency confronting the United States. Instead, he declared, the Convention should adopt a radically centralizing and high-toned national government in which the states would be reduced to administrative districts. Declaring his admiration for the British constitution, Hamilton conceded that the republican spirit of Americans would not tolerate its reintroduction. He sketched a version of that model adapted to American conditions: it included a bicameral legislature with a popularly elected lower house serving three-year terms and an indirectly elected upper house serving during good behavior, and a governor chosen by a two-step method of indirect election, also to serve during good behavior. Hamilton maintained that he had never advocated monarchy, and that his "governor" was distinguishable from a monarch because he could be removed for bad behavior and because he and his successors would be elected, albeit indirectly. Drawing on Yates's and Lansing's reports, however, Hamilton's opponents never let him off the hook, raising the charge of monarchy at every turn to impugn him and, by indirect association, the Constitution.[13]

[12] See generally Willi Paul Adams, *The First American Constitutions: Republican Ideology and the Making of the State Constitutions in the Revolutionary Era* (Chapel Hill, 1980).

[13] All available versions of Hamilton's speech appear in Farrand's *Records of the Federal Convention* I: 281–311; see also Harold C. Syrett, ed., *The Papers of Alexander Hamilton*, 27 vols. (New York, 1961–87), 4: 178–211. See also Bower Aly, *The Rhetoric of Alexander Hamilton* (1941; New York, 1958), 87–89; Forrest McDonald, *Alexander Hamilton: A Biography* (New York, 1979), 99–105.

Most of the essays on the presidency in *The Federalist* explained
and justified the process of electing the president and his term and
powers. *Nos. 67* and *76* deal with the president's power to appoint officers of the government. *No. 68* defends the electoral college system.
Nos. 71 and *72* support the four-year term of office and the Constitution's lack of a limit on the number of terms that a given president may
serve. *No. 73* examines both the provision for the president's salary
(which assures his independence of the Congress) and his qualified
veto power over legislation (noting the parallel between this provision
of the U.S. Constitution and that of the New York Constitution of
1777). *Nos. 74* and *75* treat the President's pardoning and treaty-making
powers, respectively. *No. 77* recapitulates the arguments of this group
of essays.

No. 69 presents a powerful comparative analysis of four executive
officers: the governor of New York, the governor of Massachusetts, the
king of Great Britain, and the president of the United States. This essay gave Hamilton an opportunity (even though it was anonymous) to
refute the imputation of monarchy against the proposed Constitution.
Hamilton concluded that the office of president bore almost no likeness
to the British Crown (thereby refuting that favorite Antifederalist
charge); rather, it closely resembled the governorship of New York,
then occupied by George Clinton, the single most popular figure in
New York politics and a decided Antifederalist, and the governorship of
Massachusetts, held by the well-regarded Antifederalist John Hancock.
If, Hamilton asked, the presidency so strongly paralleled these gover-
norships, surely the people of the United States had nothing to fear
from it. A tactic as shrewd as Hamilton's comparison of the presidency
to offices held by influential Antifederalists was his use of Sir William
Blackstone's classic *Commentaries on the Laws of England* (the book at
the heart of his own legal education) in his analysis of the Crown.[14]
Blackstone had made sweeping claims for the king's prerogative and
the powers derived from it. Hamilton's use of Blackstone in comparing
the powers of the Crown with the powers of the presidency thus made
the difference between the British monarch and the president even
greater than it already was.

As noted above, however, the pivotal essay in "Publius's" treatment of the presidency is *The Federalist No. 70*, which deals with the
single most troubling aspect of the presidency in the eyes of Antifederalists and undecided voters: its unity.

---

[14] On Blackstone's influence on Hamilton, see Gerald Stourzh, *Alexander Hamilton
and the Idea of Republican Government* (Stanford, 1970).

Hamilton began with the declaration that a vigorous executive is at least as necessary to a republican government as to any other. To substantiate this claim, he catalogued the areas in which a strong executive is of aid in preserving good government: war and foreign policy, impartial administration of the laws, defense of private property against faction, and protection of private liberties against factional convulsions.

Having proved the necessity and desirability of executive power, Hamilton then contended that the goal of a republican constitution incorporating a vigorous executive was to provide executive energy while at the same time securing "safety in the republican sense." The aim of *The Federalist No. 70* was to show that the American presidency satisfied both requirements. In essence, *No. 70* paralleled the general argument of *The Federalist* that the Constitution created a government of adequate energy hemmed in by requisite republican safeguards.

Hamilton identified two ways of destroying the necessary unity of the executive—creating a plural executive ("two or more magistrates of equal dignity and authority") or establishing a one-man executive but subjecting him "in part to the controul and co-operation, in the capacity of counsellors to him." The rest of the essay discredited the arguments for both measures.

In the course of his analysis, Hamilton took pains to distinguish between an executive and a legislature. Madison had noted in *The Federalist No. 51,* "In republican government the legislative authority, necessarily, predominates." Hamilton adopted and extended this point to demonstrate that the requisite energy needed for good government could not be vested in a legislature because a legislature could not by its nature possess the qualities to wield that executive power effectively. This reasoning against vesting executive power in a legislature, he continued, worked equally well against the proposal of vesting executive power in a plural executive or even in a single executive with a council.

Disposing of the idea of a plural executive by recounting the many conflicts between the two consuls of the Roman Republic, Hamilton shifted his attention to the more powerful and more threatening alternative: the executive plus a council.

Maintaining that the presidency was dangerous because the president was not associated with (and thus not limited by) a council, the Antifederalists compared the presidency to the chief executives and councils of most of the states. If most state constitutions incorporated such a safeguard, they insisted, it must be necessary; if the Constitution lacked this necessary check on executive power, it must be dangerous. Recognizing the facile persuasiveness of this argument, Hamilton concentrated his polemical and analytical skills on disproving it.

In one of the most original arguments to be found in *The Federalist,*
Hamilton showed that the institution of a council, far from being a safeguard of the people against executive usurpation, could become a mask
for tyranny or incompetence. In the former case, the people would have
no way to sort out who of several executive officials should be held accountable for oppressive acts. In the latter case, a president could take
shelter behind his council as an excuse for failing to act with sufficient
vigor to meet a national crisis. In either situation, Hamilton established, unity in the executive was the surest means to executive responsibility or accountability, which in turn was the surest means to control
a chief executive. Not only was a unitary executive necessary to reap
the full benefits of executive power—it was also necessary to ensure
that that power could be effectually controlled. These great desiderata,
he concluded, were amply provided by the proposed Constitution.

Like the argument for the extended republic as a bar to factionalism in *No. 10,* the case for a unitary executive in *No. 70* displays a distinctive method of argument in *The Federalist.* Rather than accepting
the "conventional wisdom" about government, "Publius" inverts it, de-
ducing consequences diametrically opposed to what that "conventional
wisdom" would teach. The ingenuity of reasoning in *No. 78,* and in *The
Federalist* as a whole, demonstrates its continuing value to students of
constitutional argument.

Judicial Review

The Federalist No. 78

In unfolding the defects of the existing confederation, the utility and
necessity of a federal judicature have been clearly pointed out.

Alexander Hamilton
The Federalist No. 78

This is perhaps the single most often cited essay in *The Federalist.* It
exerts a special fascination for those legal and constitutional scholars
preoccupied with defending or attacking the doctrine of judicial review,[15] in large part because in his landmark opinion for the U.S. Su-

---

[15] To provide a full list of even the most important contributions to the voluminous
literature on judicial review would fill a volume. The following is only a sampling: James
Bradley Thayer, "The Original Scope of the American Doctrine of Constitutional Law,"
Harvard Law Review 7 (1893): 127–56; Charles A. Beard, *The Supreme Court and the
Constitution* (New York, 1912); Charles Warren, *Congress, the Constitution, and the Supreme*

preme Court in *Marbury* v. *Madison*,[16] Chief Justice John Marshall followed the reasoning of this essay in declaring the authority of the
Supreme Court to pass on the constitutionality of acts of Congress.

The Federalist Nos. 78–83 deal with issues having to do with the federal judiciary as outlined in Article III. These essays are the vaguest to
be found in *The Federalist*—principally because the Federal Convention
spent little time on the structure and powers of the judiciary. Some
Framers, among them John Rutledge of South Carolina, maintained
that the new government did not need an independent court system;
they argued that the state courts could perform whatever judicial functions the new federal government might require. The majority disagreed, but could not reach an accord on the structure of the federal
court system or on the exact nature of its jurisdiction. Therefore, except for the specification that the federal court system shall have "one
supreme Court," Article III, Section 1 left to the first Congress to meet
under the Constitution the task of establishing a federal judiciary. Article III, Section 2 set forth a maximum grant of federal jurisdiction (or
judicial power), again leaving to the first Congress the delicate question
whether this provision conferred all specified types of federal jurisdiction on the new courts or was merely a limit which Congress need not
reach but beyond which Congress could not go. The Judiciary Act of
1789 embodied the latter view.

Court, rev. ed. (Boston, 1937); Charles Warren, *The Supreme Court in U.S. History*, rev.
ed. in 2 vols. (Boston, 1926); Louis B. Boudin, *Government by Judiciary*, 2 vols. (New
York, 1932); Alexander M. Bickel, *The Least Dangerous Branch: The Supreme Court at the
Bar of Politics* (Indianapolis, 1962); Raoul Berger, *Congress versus the Supreme Court* (Cam-
bridge, Mass., 1969); Charles L. Black, Jr., *Structure and Relationship in Constitutional
Law* (Baton Rouge, La., 1970); Laurence H. Tribe, *American Constitutional Law* (1978;
2d ed., Mineola, N.Y., 1988); John Hart Ely, *Democracy and Distrust: A Theory of Judicial
Review* (Cambridge, Mass., 1980); Jesse H. Choper, *Judicial Review and the National
Political Process* (Chicago, 1980); Laurence H. Tribe, *Constitutional Choices* (Cambridge,
Mass., 1985); and Christopher Wolfe, *The Rise of Modern Judicial Review* (New York,
1986). Richard Loss, ed., *Corwin on the Constitution*, 3 vols. (Ithaca, N.Y., 1981–1988),
presents the most important essays of Edward S. Corwin, one of the greatest constitutional scholars of the twentieth century. In addition, readers with access to law reviews
should consult the essays of Bruce A. Ackerman of Columbia Law School and Cass
Sunstein of the University of Chicago Law School, both of whom are preparing major
books on judicial review and American constitutional theory. A useful compilation with
extensive added bibliographies is John H. Garvey and T. Alexander Aleinikoff, eds.,
Modern Constitutional Theory: A Reader (St. Paul, Minn., 1989). John Phillip Reid, "Another Origin of Judicial Review: The Constitutional Crisis of 1776 and the Need for a
Dernier Judge," *New York University Law Review 64* (1989): 963–89, demonstrates the
influence of the experience of the American Revolution on the development of the
theory and practice of judicial review.

[16] 1 *Cranch* (5 U.S.) 137 (1803).

Of the other essays discussing the judiciary, *The Federalist No. 79* justifies the constitutional requirement that the federal judges receive a specified salary which could not be diminished. (This essay was prompted by the actions of several state legislatures in the 1780s which had used their powers over judicial appointments and salaries to bludgeon judges into compliance with the will of the legislature.) It also points out that federal judges are rendered responsible or accountable because they are subject to impeachment and adds some thoughts on judicial tenure and age. *Nos. 80–82* analyze technical questions of federal jurisdiction and the relations between the federal and state courts systems. Among other points, it refutes the suggestion that the state courts could perform the functions that the Constitution vests in whatever federal courts would be established by Congress. *No. 83* defends the Constitution against the Antifederalists' charge that it would take away the benefit of trial by jury—although the Sixth Amendment greatly strengthened the defects of Article III, Section 2 cited by the Antifederalists.

Clinton Rossiter declared: "Publius the constitutional lawyer, in the bold person of Hamilton, reached the peak of intellectual power and of historical influence" in *The Federalist No. 78*'s argument for judicial review.[17] This essay therefore deserves detailed exploration.

After a brief reference to the discussion already given in *Nos. 76* and *77* of the power to appoint officials (including judges), Hamilton began *No. 78* by defending the judges' holding of their office *"during good behaviour."* Citing the British and American experiences with the power of impeachment, Hamilton pointed out that service during good behavior will make it easier for the federal judges to do their job: "steady, upright and impartial administration of the laws." This point gave Hamilton the opening to expand his focus from the specified duties of the federal judiciary to its place in the constitutional system.

In part, Hamilton's aim was to allay the fears that many Antifederalists and other voters had of an all-powerful federal judiciary. The Antifederalists had evoked with great skill the difficulties the Americans had faced during the early days of the struggle against Great Britain at the hands of royal judges responsible only to royal governors or to the Crown; they contended that a new federal court system would revive these dangers to liberty. Hamilton declared, first, that federal judges were placed under adequate restraint because they were subject to the power of impeachment, and, second, that the power of federal

---

[17] Rossiter, "Introduction," in *The Federalist Papers*, xiii.

judges was nowhere so threatening to liberty as the Antifederalists feared.

At this stage of his argument Hamilton made his now-famous distinctions among the three branches of the federal government:

> The executive not only dispenses the honors, but holds the sword of the community. The legislature not only commands the purse, but prescribes the rules by which the duties and rights of every citizen are to be regulated. The judiciary on the contrary has no influence over either the sword or the purse, no direction either of the strength or of the wealth of the society, and can take no active resolution whatever. It may truly be said to have neither Force nor Will, but merely judgment; and must ultimately depend upon the aid of the executive arm even for the efficacy of its judgments.

Hamilton pointed out that, as the judiciary is so weak, it has no real power to injure the general liberty of the people. Indeed, its existence as an independent body is necessary, under a limited constitution, to protect the people from the other two branches of government. To indicate what he meant by a limited constitution, Hamilton cited provisions from the Constitution limiting the power of government to injure individual liberty (such as the bars on bills of attainder and *ex post facto* laws). Hamilton declared that the only way to give such provisions effect is the power of the federal courts to declare void an act of Congress. Thus, the courts protect both the Constitution and the people's liberty.

Hamilton's argument for judicial review is at the core of *The Federalist No. 78*. Hamilton rejected the idea that such a power would render the judiciary superior to the legislature. He explained that judicial review is simply the courts' power to give effect to the will of the people, as expressed in the Constitution, over the will of their elected representatives, as expressed in a statute. The people are the ultimate authority in the United States. The Constitution embodies the people's commissions to the institutions of the new government specifying those institutions' powers and the limits on those powers. How, then, can the Congress legitimately pass a law not only exceeding but violating the Constitution, Hamilton asked? To do so would be to exceed their authority, and the law would be void.

Hamilton acknowledged the objection that each institution of the new government, including Congress, could interpret the Constitution for itself and did not need the federal courts to impose their interpretations. In response, he asked the rhetorical question: How could the will of the people as codified in the Constitution be trumped by the will of the people's representatives as set forth in an ordinary law passed under the supposed authority of that Constitution? Hamilton urged that the Constitution properly should be regarded as a "fundamental law" which the courts are to interpret and apply in the course of their ordinary business, as they are to interpret and apply ordinary laws enacted by Congress. For this reason, he concluded, if the Constitution and an ordinary law come into conflict, "the constitution ought to be preferred to the statute, the intention of the people to the intention of their agents."

Seeking to render this power of judicial review a natural and easy consequence of a written constitution, Hamilton equated it with an ordinary principle of statutory construction, pointing out that courts regularly reconcile conflicting laws; judicial review is only a special category of that general task.

Hamilton returned to the charge that judicial review would lead to judicial supremacy. The power of a court to declare a law void because it violates the Constitution does not raise the judiciary above the legislature, he insisted; it only confirms that the people are superior to both the judiciary and the legislature. The people's solemn lawmaking act, the Constitution, is superior to any statute adopted by their representatives. Just as the Federalists maintained in expounding the federal nature of the Constitution that the people are sovereign and delegate parts of that sovereignty to one or more instrumentalities (federal and state governments), so, here, the people are sovereign and assign parts of the national share of sovereignty to the legislative and judicial branches (and, by implication, to the executive branch as well).

Hamilton also sought to refute the argument that the courts could use the power of judicial review indiscriminately, to establish themselves as an ultimate law-making body. In one of the weaker links in his chain of reasoning, he reminded his readers that the courts possessed the power of judgment rather than the legislative will; he suggested that if courts exercise will, they would be indistinguishable from legislators, and therefore we should have no courts independent from the legislature. (He might have argued that the power of impeachment in the hands of the House and the Senate might serve as a useful restraint on judicial law-making; in so arguing, he also might have pointed out that the courts, unlike practically any other government institution, are obliged not only to decide but to explain their decisions, and that such explanations must conform to the idea of judgment to retain legitimacy.)

Hamilton noted that the people themselves might desire or support ill-considered statutes that turn out to be unconstitutional. He stressed that only "some solemn and authoritative act" by the people, such as a constitutional amendment, could change the Constitution; in the absence of such a thorough consideration of the question by the people and their representatives, the courts should stand firm against momentary spasms of the popular will. Hamilton acknowledged wryly, "[I]t would require an uncommon portion of fortitude in the judges to do their duty as faithful guardians of the constitution, where legislative invasions of it had been instigated by the major voice of the community."

Returning to the question of judicial independence, Hamilton emphasized the need for an independent judiciary in ordinary lawsuits over private rights and in defending such rights against legislative infringement through hasty or partial laws. In the process, he again insisted that service during good behavior was a vital guard of the "firmness of the judicial magistracy."

Hamilton's final argument for tenure during good behavior was that the nation needed a learned and expert body of judges, who could only acquire the requisite abilities and familiarity with the laws they are to interpret and apply through long service on the bench. Those possessing the innate talents and inherent integrity required for a good judge would not turn from "lucrative" private practice to accept appointment unless they were assured of tenure during good behavior. Even here, however, Hamilton was careful to raise as the only possible alternative the specter of "an arbitrary discretion in the courts" and to remind his readers that most state constitutions, including those of Massachusetts and New York, provided for judicial service during good behavior. (*No. 79* mentions the provision of the New York Constitution of 1777 requiring judicial retirement at age sixty, but does so in order to criticize it.)

The Federalist No. 78 focuses on review by federal courts of acts of the national legislature or the national executive—what might be called *co-equal* judicial review. Hamilton distinguished co-equal judicial review, which several generations of constitutional scholars have deemed problematic, from what might be called *supervisory* judicial review— that is, review by a federal court of state laws or other actions. Hamilton discussed and defended supervisory judicial review in *The Federalist Nos. 80, 81*, and *82*.

Hamilton's role in the controversial 1784 case of *Rutgers* v. *Waddington* is relevant both to the general question of judicial review in the early national period and as a possible precursor of both supervisory and co-equal judicial review. Hamilton was counsel for a British defendant, Josiah Waddington, in an action brought by Elizabeth Rutgers in the New York City Mayor's Court under New York's Trespass Act of 1783; Mrs. Rutgers sought back rent and damages for Waddington's occupation of her brewery under British authority during the British occupation of New York City. Hamilton argued that the Trespass Act was void under the law of nations and as a violation of that part of the Treaty of Paris of 1783 barring state laws injuring the rights of Loyalists and British subjects; both the treaty and the law of nations, he maintained, were part and parcel of the law of New York. Waddington, Hamilton pointed out, occupied the brewery under license from British occupying authorities, which was standard practice under the laws of war. Mayor James Duane and his fellow judges interpreted the Trespass Act to make it consistent with the treaty and the law of nations, thus limiting the damages that Mrs. Rutgers could recover under the statute.

Whether *Rutgers* v. *Waddington* was a true judicial review case or just a deftly defused political time bomb, we can see Hamilton's position in that case as incorporating arguments for both supervisory judicial review—using a "national" or "American" enactment such as the 1783 treaty to strike down a state law—and co-equal judicial review—in that a state court could invalidate a state statute. Either way, Hamilton believed that supervisory judicial review (even by a state or local court) was vital to the preservation of the Union.[18] He used *The Federalist Nos. 80–82* to demonstrate that the supremacy clause of the Constitution justifies both the legitimacy and the necessity of supervisory judicial review.

Conclusion

Only in the decades since the Second World War have students of *The Federalist* come to appreciate it as a work of political theory.[19] To be sure, Hamilton, Madison, and Jay did not conceive of the essays of "Publius" as exercises in political philosophy. They had a concrete

---

[18] On *Rutgers* v. *Waddington*, see Richard B. Morris, ed., *Select Cases of the Mayor's Court of New York City, 1674–1784* (1935; reprint, Millwood, N.Y., 1975). A technical discussion with extensive documentation is in Julius Goebel, Jr., and Joseph H. Smith, eds., *The Law Practice of Alexander Hamilton*, 5 vols. (New York, 1964–80), I: 282–419. A more accessible discussion is in Richard B. Morris, *Seven Who Shaped Our Destiny: The Founding Fathers as Revolutionaries* (New York, 1973), 235–37.

[19] Douglass Adair made this point in perhaps his most famous essay, "The Tenth Federalist Revisited," reprinted in Colbourn, ed., *Fame and the Founding Fathers*. For a reassuring measure of how far *Federalist* scholarship has come since Adair's 1951 lament, see Charles R. Kesler, ed., *Saving the Revolution: The Federalist Papers and the American Founding* (New York, 1987).

objective in mind—the ratification of the Constitution—and used *The Federalist* as one of several means to that end. Nonetheless, as Morton White has shown, there is a great deal of sophisticated political philosophy as well as political argument in *The Federalist*.[20] For one thing, its authors devoted much time and care to thinking through the larger or "philosophical" consequences of their political goals; for another, they lived at a time when the realms of political philosophy and practical politics were closer to one another than ever before (or than they have been since). The essays rest on a framework of assumptions about human nature, society, government, and politics—sometimes explicit, sometimes hidden beneath the surface. Recent studies of *The Federalist* have sought to recover the matrix of ideas and assumptions undergirding the formal arguments of the essays, both to reconstruct the eighteenth-century intellectual world of Publius and to cast new light on the meaning of the essays.[21]

The essays considered in this commentary illustrate the value of keeping several levels of meaning and purpose in mind when we consider the words of "Publius." We may close most appropriately with a comment by George Washington, who acknowledged Hamilton's gift of a copy of *The Federalist* in words predicting the enduring significance of the essays:

> When the transient circumstances and fugitive performances which attended this Crisis shall have disappeared, That Work will merit the notice of posterity: because in it are candidly and ably discussed the principles of freedom and the topics of government, which will be always interesting to mankind so long as they shall be connected in Civil Society.[22]

For Further Reading

Ralph Ketcham, ed. *The Antifederalist Papers and Constitutional Debates.* New York, 1986.

[20] See generally White, *Philosophy, The Federalist, and the Constitution.*

[21] In addition to White, *Philosophy, The Federalist, and the Constitution,* see David F. Epstein, *The Political Theory of The Federalist* (Chicago, 1984); Wills, *Explaining America*; and George Carey, *The Federalist: Design for a Constitutional Republic* (Urbana, Ill., 1989).

[22] George Washington to Alexander Hamilton, August 28, 1788, in John C. Fitzpatrick, ed., *The Writings of George Washington...*, 39 vols. (Washington, D.C., 1931–44), 30: 66.

Jackson Turner Main. *The Antifederalists: Critics of the Constitution, 1781–1789.* Chapel Hill 1961.

Robert A. Rutland. *The Ordeal of the Constitution.* Boston, 1966, rev. ed. 1983.

Herbert J. Storing. *What the Anti-Federalists Were For* Chicago, 1981.

Herbert J. Storing with Murray Dry, eds. *The Complete Anti-Federalist.* 7 vols. Chicago, 1981.

Gordon S. Wood. *The Creation of the American Republic, 1776–1787.* Chapel Hill, 1969.

The Federalist No. 15

ALEXANDER HAMILTON

December 1, 1787

To the People of the State of New York.

IN the course of the preceding papers, I have endeavored, my Fellow Citizens, to place before you in a clear and convincing light, the importance of Union to your political safety and happiness. I have unfolded to you a complication of dangers to which you would be exposed should you permit that sacred knot which binds the people of America together to be severed or dissolved by ambition or by avarice, by jealousy or by misrepresentation. In the sequel of the inquiry, through which I propose to accompany you, the truths intended to be inculcated will receive further confirmation from facts and arguments hitherto unnoticed. If the road, over which you will still have to pass, should in some places appear to you tedious or irksome, you will recollect, that you are in quest of information on a subject the most momentous which can engage the attention of a free people: that the field through which you have to travel is in itself spacious, and that the difficulties of the journey have been unnecessarily increased by the mazes with which sophistry has beset the way. It will be my aim to remove the obstacles to your progress in as compendious a manner, as it can be done, without sacrificing utility to dispatch.[2]

  [1] From *The Independent Journal*, December 1, 1787. This essay appeared on December 4 in both *The Daily Advertiser* and *The New-York Packet.*

  [2] In this essay Hamilton pressed the Federalists' polemical advantage in the ratification controversy. If the impartial American voter conceded that the Articles of Confederation were radically defective, and that these defects imperiled the existence of the Union, the integrity and honor of the United States, and the success of the Revolution, then the Federalists succeeded in establishing the agenda of American politics. They also gained a "leg up" for the proposed Constitution because it was the only option on the agenda that offered a hope of solving this problem.

  The Federalists' strategy presented the Antifederalists with an uncomfortable

In pursuance of the plan, which I have laid down, for the discussion of the subject, the point next in order to be examined is the "insufficiency of the present confederation to the preservation of the Union." It may perhaps be asked, what need is there of reasoning or proof to illustrate a position, which is not either controverted or doubted; to which the understandings and feelings of all classes of men assent; and which in substance is admitted by the opponents as well as by the friends of the New Constitution? It must in truth be acknowledged that however these may differ in other respects, they in general appear to harmonise in this sentiment at least, that there are material imperfections in our national system, and that something is necessary to be done to rescue us from impending anarchy. The facts that support this opinion are no longer objects of speculation. They have forced themselves upon the sensibility of the people at large, and have at length extorted from those, whose mistaken policy has had the principal share in precipitating the extremity, at which we are arrived, a reluctant confession of the reality of those defects in the scheme of our Fœderal Government, which have been long pointed out and regretted by the intelligent friends of the Union.

We may indeed with propriety be said to have reached almost the last stage of national humiliation.[3] There is scarcely any thing that can

---

choice of untenable positions: (i) denying the problem's existence, (ii) conceding the problem's existence but denying its seriousness, and (iii) conceding the problem's existence and seriousness but attacking the only proposed solution on the agenda. Most Antifederalists opted for the second or third position.

[3] This paragraph refers to a wide range of issues at the heart of American politics and public policy during the Confederation period:

The "engagements" mentioned in the third sentence were pledges made in the Treaty of Paris of 1783 that the United States would not continue to punish Loyalists and British subjects nor enact new laws burdening them—but several states enacted and enforced statutes preventing Loyalist and British creditors from recovering debts owed by American debtors from before the Revolution or limiting what they could recover by barring recovery for interest for the period of the Revolution.

The "valuable territories and important posts" were in the Northwest Territory, ceded by Great Britain to the United States under the Treaty of Paris of 1783. The British refused to withdraw their forces from these forts and territories until the United States honored its commitment under the treaty to remove obstacles to lawsuits by British and Loyalist creditors. These points were not settled until Chief Justice John Jay's negotiation of the Jay Treaty with Great Britain in 1794.

Hamilton's reference to "the navigation of the Mississippi" was to the Jay-Gardoqui negotiations of 1786; Jay, the Confederation's secretary for foreign affairs, was unable to persuade the Spanish minister, Don Diego de Gardoqui, that Spain should permit American citizens in the western territories to make free use of the Mississippi River and the port city of New Orleans. Spain had required any Americans seeking this permission to swear allegiance to Spain, renouncing their American citizenship. Gardoqui offered wound the pride, or degrade the character of an independent nation, which we do not experience. Are there engagements to the performance of which we are held by every tie respectable among men? These are the subjects of constant and unblushing violation. Do we owe debts to foreigners and to our own citizens contracted in a time of imminent peril, for the preservation of our political existence? These remain without any proper or satisfactory provision for their discharge. Have we valuable territories and important posts in the possession of a foreign power, which by express stipulations ought long since to have been surrendered? These are still retained, to the prejudice of our interests not less than of our rights. Are we in a condition to resent, or to repel the aggression? We have neither troops nor treasury nor government.* Are we even in a condition to remonstrate with dignity? The just imputations on our own faith, in respect to the same treaty, ought first to be removed. Are we entitled by nature and compact to a free participation in the navigation of the Mississippi? Spain excludes us from it. Is public credit an indispensable resource in time of public danger? We seem to have abandoned its cause as desperate and irretrievable. Is commerce of importance to national wealth? Ours is at the lowest point of declension. Is respectability in the eyes of foreign powers a safeguard against foreign encroachments? The imbecility of our Government even forbids them to treat with us:[4] Our ambassadors abroad are the mere pageants of mimic sovereignty. Is a violent and unnatural decrease in the value of land a symptom of national distress? The price of improved land in most parts of the country is much lower than can be accounted for by the quantity of waste land at market, and can only be fully explained by that want of private and public confidence, which are so alarmingly prevalent among all ranks and which have a direct tendency to depreciate property of every kind. Is private credit the friend and

---

Jay trade concessions if the United States would relinquish its claimed right to navigate the Mississippi. When Jay asked the Confederation Congress for permission to accept Gardoqui's offer, the five Southern states voted *en masse* against the proposal, signaling their ability and readiness to block any trade treaty with Spain giving up navigation rights. (Under the Articles, the votes of nine of the thirteen states were needed to ratify treaties.) Jay, Hamilton, and their allies maintained that the weakness of the Articles was at the bottom of the failed Jay-Gardoqui negotiations. These problems persisted until the Pinckney Treaty of 1795 (which established both friendly trading conditions between the United States and Spain and American navigation rights along the Mississippi) and the Louisiana Purchase of 1803 (by which the United States acquired the entire Louisiana Territory from France, which had acquired it from Spain).

4 "Imbecility" means "want of power," the common eighteenth-century meaning, rather than its modern connotation of gross stupidity.

*I mean for the Union. (Publius)

patron of industry? That most useful kind which relates to borrowing and lending is reduced within the narrowest limits, and this still more from an opinion of insecurity than from the scarcity of money. To shorten an enumeration of particulars which can afford neither pleasure nor instruction it may in general be demanded, what indication is there of national disorder, poverty and insignificance that could befal a community so peculiarly blessed with natural advantages as we are, which does not form a part of the dark catalogue of our public misfortunes?

This is the melancholy situation, to which we have been brought by those very maxims and councils, which would now deter us from adopting the proposed constitution; and which not content with having conducted us to the brink of a precipice, seem resolved to plunge us into the abyss, that awaits us below. Here, my Countrymen, impelled by every motive that ought to influence an enlightened people, let us make a firm stand for our safety, our tranquility, our dignity, our reputation.[5] Let us at last break the fatal charm which has too long seduced us from the paths of felicity and prosperity.

It is true, as has been before observed, that facts too stubborn to be resisted have produced a species of general assent to the abstract proposition that there exist material defects in our national system; but the usefulness of the concession, on the part of the old adversaries of fœderal measures, is destroyed by a strenuous opposition to a remedy, upon the only principles, that can give it a chance of success. While they admit that the Government of the United States is destitute of energy; they contend against conferring upon it those powers which are requisite to supply that energy: They seem still to aim at things repugnant and irreconcilable—at an augmentation of Fœderal authority without a diminution of State authority—at sovereignty in the Union and complete independence in the members. They still in fine seem to cherish with blind devotion the political monster of an *imperium in imperio*.[6] This renders a full display of the principal defects of the con-

---

[5] Hamilton's linking of these concepts is a principal theme of his public and private political writings.

[6] *Imperium in imperio*—literally, an empire within an empire— was shorthand for what the conventional political wisdom of the eighteenth century regarded as a basic fallacy in political argument. There could not be an empire within an empire; put another way, two political entities in the same territory could not share sovereignty, or ultimate political authority, for one or the other necessarily would come to dominate. It is the point of *The Federalist*, as shown in Stephen L. Schechter's commentary, that the people of the United States are sovereign; they may delegate their sovereignty to one or more instrumentalities, whether the general government or the states. Thus, the Federalists concluded, the Constitution did not divide sovereignty, and the charge that the Constitution was an *imperium in imperio* was irrelevant and groundless.

federation necessary, in order to shew, that the evils we experience do
not proceed from minute or partial imperfections, but from fundamental
errors in the structure of the building which cannot be amended otherwise than by an alteration in the first principles and main pillars of the
fabric.

The great and radical vice in the construction of the existing Confederation is in the principle of LEGISLATION FOR STATES or GOVERN-
MENTS, in their CORPORATE OR COLLECTIVE CAPACITIES and as contrad-
istinguished from the INDIVIDUALS of whom they consist. Though this
principle does not run through all the powers delegated to the Union;
yet it pervades and governs those, on which the efficacy of the rest
depends. Except as to the rule of apportionment, the United States
have an indefinite discretion to make requisitions for men and money;
but they have no authority to raise either by regulations extending to
the individual citizens of America. The consequence of this is, that
though in theory their resolutions concerning those objects are laws,
constitutionally binding on the members of the Union, yet in practice
they are mere recommendations, which the States observe or disregard
at their option.

It is a singular instance of the capriciousness of the human mind,
that after all the admonitions we have had from experience on this head,
there should still be found men, who object to the New Constitution
for deviating from a principle which has been found the bane of the
old; and which is in itself evidently incompatible with the idea of GOV-
ERNMENT; a principle in short which if it is to be executed at all must
substitute the violent and sanguinary agency of the sword to the mild
influence of the Magistracy.

There is nothing absurd or impracticable in the idea of a league or
alliance between independent nations, for certain defined purposes precisely stated in a treaty; regulating all the details of time, place, circumstance and quantity; leaving nothing to future discretion; and depending for its execution on the good faith of the parties. Compacts of
this kind exist among all civilized nations subject to the usual vicissitudes of peace and war, of observance and non observance, as the interests or passions of the contracting powers dictate. In the early part
of the present century, there was an epidemical rage in Europe for this
species of compacts; from which the politicians of the times fondly hoped
for benefits which were never realised. With a view to establishing the
equilibrium of power and the peace of that part of the world, all the
resources of negotiation were exhausted, and triple and quadruple alliances were formed; but they were scarcely formed before they were
broken, giving an instructive but inflicting lesson to mankind how little

dependence is to be placed on treaties which have no other sanction than the obligations of good faith; and which oppose general considerations of peace and justice to the impulse of any immediate interest and passion.

If the particular States in this country are disposed to stand in a similar relation to each other, and to drop the project of a general DISCRETIONARY SUPERINTENDENCE, the scheme would indeed be pernicious, and would entail upon us all the mischiefs that have been enumerated under the first head; but it would have the merit of being at least consistent and practicable. Abandoning all views towards a confederate Government, this would bring us to a simple alliance offensive and defensive; and would place us in a situation to be alternately friends and enemies of each other as our mutual jealousies and rivalships nourished by the intrigues of foreign nations should prescribe to us.

But if we are unwilling to be placed in this perilous situation; if we will still adhere to the design of a national government, or which is the same thing of a superintending power under the direction of a common Council, we must resolve to incorporate into our plan those ingredients which may be considered as forming the characteristic difference between a league and a government; we must extend the authority of the union to the persons of the citizens,—the only proper objects of government.

Government implies the power of making laws. It is essential to the idea of a law, that it be attended with a sanction; or, in other words, a penalty or punishment for disobedience. If there be no penalty annexed to disobedience, the resolutions or commands which pretend to be laws will in fact amount to nothing more than advice or recommendation. This penalty, whatever it may be, can only be inflicted in two ways; by the agency of the Courts and Ministers of Justice, or by military force; by the COERTION of the magistracy, or by the COERTION of arms. The first kind can evidently apply only to men—the last kind must of necessity be employed against bodies politic, or communities or States. It is evident, that there is no process of a court by which their observance of the laws can in the last resort be enforced. Sentences may be denounced against them for violations of their duty; but these sentences can only be carried into execution by the sword. In an association where the general authority is confined to the collective bodies of the communities that compose it, every breach of the laws must involve a state of war, and military execution must become the only instrument of civil obedience. Such a state of things can certainly not deserve the name of government, nor would any prudent man choose to commit his happiness to it.

There was a time when we were told that breaches, by the States, of the regulations of the fœderal authority were not to be expected— that a sense of common interest would preside over the conduct of the respective members, and would beget a full compliance with all the constitutional requisitions of the Union. This language at the present day would appear as wild as a great part of what we now hear from the same quarter will be thought, when we shall have received further lessons from that best oracle of wisdom, experience. It at all times betrayed an ignorance of the true springs by which human conduct is actuated, and belied the original inducements to the establishment of civil power. Why has government been instituted at all? Because the passions of men will not conform to the dictates of reason and justice, without constraint. Has it been found that bodies of men act with more rectitude or greater disinterestedness than individuals? The contrary of this has been inferred by all accurate observers of the conduct of man- kind; and the inference is founded upon obvious reasons. Regard to reputation has a less active influence, when the infamy of a bad action is to be divided among a number, than when it is to fall singly upon one.[7] A spirit of faction which is apt to mingle its poison in the delib- erations of all bodies of men, will often hurry the persons of whom they are composed into improprieties and excesses, for which they would blush in a private capacity.

In addition to all this, there is in the nature of sovereign power an impatience of controul, that disposes those who are invested with the exercise of it, to look with an evil eye upon all external attempts to restrain or direct its operations. From this spirit it happens that in every political association which is formed upon the principle of uniting in a common interest a number of lesser sovereignties, there will be found a kind of excentric tendency in the subordinate or inferior orbs, by the operation of which there will be a perpetual effort in each to fly off from the common center. This tendency is not difficult to be accounted for. It has its origin in the love of power. Power controuled or abridged is almost always the rival and enemy of that power by which it is controuled or abridged. This simple proposition will teach us how little reason there is to expect, that the persons, entrusted with the admin- istration of the affairs of the particular members of a confederacy, will at all times be ready, with perfect good humour, and an unbiassed regard to the public weal, to execute the resolutions or decrees of the general

---

[7] Hamilton expanded upon this point in his discussion of the advantages of a unitary chief executive in *The Federalist No. 70.*

authority. The reverse of this results from the constitution of human nature.

If therefore the measures of the confederacy cannot be executed, without the intervention of the particular administrations, there will be little prospect of their being executed at all. The rulers of the respective members, whether they have a constitutional right to do it or not, will undertake to judge of the propriety of the measures themselves. They will consider the conformity of the thing proposed or required to their immediate interests or aims, the momentary conveniences or inconveniences that would attend its adoption. All this will be done, and in a spirit of interested and suspicious scrutiny, without that knowledge of national circumstances and reasons of state, which is essential to a right judgment, and with that strong predilection in favour of local objects, which can hardly fail to mislead the decision. The same process must be repeated in every member of which the body is constituted; and the execution of the plans, framed by the councils of the whole, will always fluctuate on the discretion of the ill-informed and prejudiced opinion of every part. Those who have been conversant in the proceedings of popular assemblies; who have seen how difficult it often is, when there is no exterior pressure of circumstances, to bring them to harmonious resolutions on important points, will readily conceive how impossible it must be to induce a number of such assemblies, deliberating at a distance from each other, at different times, and under different impressions, long to cooperate in the same views and pursuits.

In our case, the concurrence of thirteen distinct sovereign wills is requisite under the confederation to the complete execution of every important measure, that proceeds from the Union. It has happened as was to have been foreseen. The measures of the Union have not been executed; and the delinquencies of the States have step by step matured themselves to an extreme; which has at length arrested all the wheels of the national government, and brought them to an awful stand. Congress at this time scarcely possess the means of keeping up the forms of administration; 'till the States can have time to agree upon a more substantial substitute for the present shadow of a fœderal government. Things did not come to this desperate extremity at once. The causes which have been specified produced at first only unequal and disproportionate degrees of compliance with the requisitions of the Union. The greater deficiencies of some States furnished the pretext of example and the temptation of interest to the complying, or to the least delinquent States. Why should we do more in proportion than those who are embarked with us in the same political voyage? Why should we consent to bear more than our proper share of the common burthen?

These were suggestions which human selfishness could not withstand, and which even speculative men, who looked forward to remote consequences, could not, without hesitation, combat. Each State yielding to the persuasive voice of immediate interest and convenience has successively withdrawn its support, 'till the frail and tottering edifice seems ready to fall upon our heads and to crush us beneath its ruins.

PUBLIUS

The Federalist No. 70[8]

ALEXANDER HAMILTON

March 15, 1788

To the People of the State of New York

THERE is an idea, which is not without its advocates, that a vigorous executive is inconsistent with the genius of republican government. The enlightened well wishers to this species of government must at least hope that the supposition is destitute of foundation; since they can never admit its truth, without at the same time admitting the condemnation of their own principles. Energy in the executive is a leading character in the definition of good government. It is essential to the protection of the community against foreign attacks: It is not less essential to the steady administration of the laws, to the protection of property against those irregular and high handed combinations, which sometimes interrupt the ordinary course of justice, to the security of liberty against the enterprises and assaults of ambition, of faction and of anarchy. Every man the least conversant in Roman story knows how often that republic was obliged to take refuge in the absolute power of a single man, under the formidable title of dictator, as well against the intrigues of ambitious

[8] From *The Independent Journal*, March 15, 1788. This essay appeared on March 18 in *The New-York Packet*. It was numbered 70 in the McLean edition and 69 in the newspapers.

individuals, who aspired to the tyranny, and the seditions of whole classes of the community, whose conduct threatened the existence of all government, as against the invasions of external enemies, who menaced the conquest and destruction of Rome.[9]

There can be no need however to multiply arguments or examples on this head. A feeble executive implies a feeble execution of the government. A feeble execution is but another phrase for a bad execution: And a government ill executed, whatever it may be in theory, must be in practice a bad government.

Taking it for granted, therefore, that all men of sense will agree in the necessity of an energetic executive; it will only remain to inquire, what are the ingredients which constitute this energy—how far can they be combined with those other ingredients which constitute safety in the republican sense? And how far does this combination characterise the plan, which has been reported by the convention?

The ingredients, which constitute energy in the executive, are first unity, secondly duration, thirdly an adequate provision for its support, fourthly competent powers.

The circumstances which constitute safety in the republican sense are, Ist. a due dependence on the people, secondly a due responsibility.

Those politicians and statesmen, who have been the most celebrated for the soundness of their principles, and for the justness of their views,

---

[9] Hamilton's allusion to Roman history (like the other citations of ancient history throughout *The Federalist*) is nothing unusual in the political writing of the late eighteenth century. It was a commonplace of Enlightenment political thought that one could derive from the record of history general laws of human nature, society, government, and politics; thus, political writers felt free to cite examples from the full range of available historical knowledge. American political commentators of all points of view made extensive use of the histories of the ancient and modern republics because they believed that the histories of these republics contained lessons of special value for the American republic. History is a common resource for *The Federalist*; in particular, historical precedents are virtually the whole basis of the argument of Hamilton's *The Federalist No. 6* and Madison's and Hamilton's *The Federalist Nos. 18–20*. John Phillip Reid of New York University Law School has described this mode of argument as "forensic history." See John Phillip Reid, "Originalism and Subjectivism in the Bicentennial Year," *Social Science Quarterly* 68 (1987): 687–702 (especially 687–88).

As to Hamilton's mention of the "dictator," the constitution of the Roman Republic (which was like the unwritten British constitution rather than the written United States Constitution) provided that, in times of crisis, the Senate could appoint a one-man executive, known as a *dictator*, whose decrees and directives would have the force of law and who could command unquestioning obedience from the magistrates and the citizens of Rome. The dictator would give up his power at the close of the emergency. Of course, this practice posed a thorny problem: it is difficult to give up such absolute power and tempting to retain it, as the Romans learned to their cost. Hence, the term "dictator" has come to mean an official who wields unchecked political power and who cannot be removed from office short of violence.

have declared in favor of a single executive and a numerous legislature. They have with great propriety considered energy as the most necessary qualification of the former, and have regarded this as most applicable to power in a single hand; while they have with equal propriety considered the latter as best adapted to deliberation and wisdom, and best calculated to conciliate the confidence of the people and to secure their privileges and interests.

That unity is conducive to energy will not be disputed. Decision, activity, secrecy, and dispatch will generally characterize the proceedings of one man, in a much more eminent degree, than the proceedings of any greater number; and in proportion as the number is increased, these qualities will be diminished.

This unity may be destroyed in two ways; either by vesting the power in two or more magistrates of equal dignity and authority; or by vesting it ostensibly in one man, subject in whole or in part to the controul and co-operation of others, in the capacity of counsellors to him. Of the first the two consuls of Rome may serve as an example; of the last we shall find examples in the constitutions of several of the states. New-York and New-Jersey, if I recollect right, are the only states, which have entrusted the executive authority wholly to single men.*[10] Both these methods of destroying the unity of the executive have their partisans; but the votaries of an executive council are the most numerous. They are both liable, if not to equal, to similar objections; and may in most lights be examined in conjunction.

The experience of other nations will afford little instruction on this head. As far however as it teaches any thing, it teaches us not to be inamoured of plurality in the executive. We have seen that the Achæan

---

[10] As shown in Stephen L. Schechter's commentary on the New York Constitution of 1777 in this volume, the governor of New York had to share power and responsibility with two councils, one for appointments and one for revision (that is, a qualified veto power over legislation), but Hamilton only mentioned the council of appointment. He did discuss the council of revision, which consisted of the governor, the chancellor, and the judges of the supreme court, in *The Federalist Nos. 69 and 73.* In his discussion of chief executive offices in the American states, Hamilton also overlooked the Massachusetts Constitution of 1780, which created a one-man chief executive or governor. The governorship of Massachusetts under the state's 1780 constitution was the most powerful executive office in the United States before the establishment of the American presidency.

James Madison found the New York council of revision far more admirable than Hamilton did. Indeed, he urged the adoption of a similar institution at the Federal Convention of 1787.

New-York has no council except for the single purpose of appointing to offices; New-Jersey has a council, whom the governor may consult. But I think from the terms of the constitution their resolutions do not bind him. (Publius)

on an experiment of two Prætors, were induced to abolish one.[11] The Roman history records many instances of mischiefs to the republic from the dissentions between the consuls, and between the military tribunes, who were at times substituted to the consuls. But it gives us no specimens of any peculiar advantages derived to the state, from the circumstance of the plurality of those magistrates. That the dissentions between them were not more frequent, or more fatal, is matter of astonishment; until we advert to the singular position in which the republic was almost continually placed and to the prudent policy pointed out by the circumstances of the state, and pursued by the consuls, of making a division of the government between them. The Patricians engaged in a perpetual struggle with the Plebians for the preservation of their antient authorities and dignities; the consuls, who were generally chosen out of the former body, were commonly united by the personal interest they had in the defence of the privileges of their order. In addition to this motive of union, after the arms of the republic had considerably expanded the bounds of its empire, it became an established custom with the consuls to divide the administration between themselves by lot; one of them remaining at Rome to govern the city and its environs; the other taking the command in the more distant provinces. This expedient must no doubt have had great influence in preventing those collisions and rivalships, which might otherwise have embroiled the peace of the republic.

But quitting the dim light of historical research, and attaching ourselves purely to the dictates of reason and good sense, we shall discover much greater cause to reject than to approve the idea of plurality in the executive, under any modification whatever.

Wherever two or more persons are engaged in any common enterprize or pursuit, there is always danger of difference of opinion. If it be a public trust or office in which they are cloathed with equal dignity and authority, there is peculiar danger of personal emulation and even animosity. From either and especially from all these causes, the most bitter dissentions are apt to spring. Whenever these happen, they lessen the respectability, weaken the authority, and distract the plans and operations of those whom they divide. If they should unfortunately assail the supreme executive magistracy of a country, consisting of a plurality of persons, they might impede or frustrate the most important measures of the government, in the most critical emergencies of the state. And what is still worse, they might split the community into the most violent

---

[11] Hamilton referred to the discussion in *The Federalist No. 18.*

and irreconcilable factions, adhering differently to the different individuals who composed the magistracy.

Men often oppose a thing merely because they have had no agency in planning it, or because it may have been planned by those whom they dislike. But if they have been consulted and have happened to disapprove, opposition then becomes in their estimation an indispensable duty of self love. They seem to think themselves bound in honor, and by all the motives of personal infallibility to defeat the success of what has been resolved upon, contrary to their sentiments. Men of upright, benevolent tempers have too many opportunities of remarking with horror, to what desperate lengths this disposition is sometimes carried, and how often the great interests of society are sacrificed to the vanity, to the conceit and to the obstinacy of individuals, who have credit enough to make their passions and their caprices interesting to mankind. Perhaps the question now before the public may in its consequences afford melancholy proofs of the effects of this despicable frailty, or rather detestable vice in the human character.

Upon the principles of a free government, inconveniences from the source just mentioned must necessarily be submitted to in the formation of the legislature; but it is unnecessary and therefore unwise to introduce them into the constitution of the executive. It is here too that they may be most pernicious. In the legislature, promptitude of decision is oftener an evil than a benefit. The differences of opinion, and the jarrings of parties in that department of the government, though they may sometimes obstruct salutary plans, yet often promote deliberation and circumspection; and serve to check excesses in the majority. When a resolution too is once taken, the opposition must be at an end. That resolution is a law, and resistance to it punishable. But no favourable circumstances palliate or atone for the disadvantages of dissention in the executive department. Here they are pure and unmixed. There is no point at which they cease to operate. They serve to embarrass and weaken the execution of the plan or measure, to which they relate, from the first step to the final conclusion of it. They constantly counteract those qualities in the executive, which are the most necessary ingredients in its composition, vigour and expedition, and this without any counterballancing good. In the conduct of war, in which the energy of the executive is the bulwark of the national security, every thing would be to be apprehended from its plurality.

It must be confessed that these observations apply with principal weight to the first case supposed, that is to a plurality of magistrates of equal dignity and authority; a scheme the advocates for which are not likely to form a numerous sect: But they apply, though not with equal, yet with considerable weight, to the project of a council, whose concurrence is made constitutionally necessary to the operations of the ostensible executive. An artful cabal in that council would be able to distract and to enervate the whole system of administration. If no such cabal should exist, the mere diversity of views and opinions would alone be sufficient to tincture the exercise of the executive authority with a spirit of habitual feebleness and dilatoriness.

But one of the weightiest objections to a plurality in the executive, and which lies as much against the last as the first plan, is that it tends to conceal faults, and destroy responsibility.[12] Responsibility is of two kinds, to censure and to punishment. The first is the most important of the two; especially in an elective office. Man, in public trust, will much oftener act in such a manner as to render him unworthy of being any longer trusted, than in such a manner as to make him obnoxious to legal punishment. But the multiplication of the executive adds to the difficulty of detection in either case. It often becomes impossible, amidst mutual accusations, to determine on whom the blame or the punishment of a pernicious measure, or series of pernicious measures ought really to fall. It is shifted from one to another with so much dexterity, and under such plausible appearances, that the public opinion is left in suspense about the real author. The circumstances which may have led to any national miscarriage or misfortune are sometimes so complicated, that where there are a number of actors who may have had different degrees and kinds of agency, though we may clearly see upon the whole that there has been mismanagement, yet it may be impracticable to pronounce to whose account the evil which may have been incurred is truly chargeable.

"I was overruled by my council. The council were so divided in their opinions, that it was impossible to obtain any better resolution on the point." These and similar pretexts are constantly at hand, whether true or false. And who is there that will either take the trouble or incur the odium of a strict scrutiny into the secret springs of the transaction? Should there be found a citizen zealous enough to undertake the un-promising task, if there happen to be a collision between the parties concerned, how easy is it to cloath the circumstances with so much ambiguity, as to render it uncertain what was the precise conduct of any of those parties?

---

[12] Clinton Rossiter and Douglass Adair maintained that one of the most original and valuable contributions of *The Federalist* to political theory is its development of ideas of legislative and executive responsibility (or accountability). Madison's discussion of legislative responsibility appears in *The Federalist No. 63*; as noted in the commentary, this passage presents Hamilton's analysis of executive responsibility.

In the single instance in which the governor of this state is coupled with a council, that is in the appointment to offices, we have seen the mischiefs of it in the view now under consideration. Scandalous appointments to important offices have been made. Some cases indeed have been so flagrant, that ALL PARTIES have agreed in the impropriety of the thing. When enquiry has been made, the blame has been laid by the governor on the members of the council; who on their part have charged it upon his nomination: While the people remain altogether at a loss to determine by whose influence their interests have been committed to hands so unqualified, and so manifestly improper. In tenderness to individuals, I forbear to descend to particulars.[13]

It is evident from these considerations, that the plurality of the executive tends to deprive the people of the two greatest securities they can have for the faithful exercise of any delegated power; first, the restraints of public opinion, which lose their efficacy as well on account of the division of the censure attendant on bad measures among a number, as on account of the uncertainty on whom it ought to fall; and secondly, the opportunity of discovering with facility and clearness the misconduct of the persons they trust, in order either to their removal from office, or to their actual punishment, in cases which admit of it.

In England the king is a perpetual magistrate; and it is a maxim, which has obtained for the sake of the public peace, that he is unaccountable for his administration, and his person sacred. Nothing therefore can be wiser in that kingdom than to annex to the king a constitutional council, who may be responsible to the nation for the advice they give. Without this there would be no responsibility whatever in the executive department; an idea inadmissible in a free government. But even there the king is not bound by the resolutions of his council, though they are answerable for the advice they give. He is the absolute master of his own conduct, in the exercise of his office; and may observe or disregard the council given to him at his sole discretion.

But in a republic, where every magistrate ought to be personally responsible for his behaviour in office, the reason which in the British constitution dictates the propriety of a council not only ceases to apply, but turns against the institution. In the monarchy of Great-Britain, it furnishes a substitute for the prohibited responsibility of the chief magistrate; which serves in some degree as a hostage to the national justice

[13] In this passage, Hamilton could not resist a dig at George Clinton in describing the tendency of a council (in this case, the council of appointment) to dissipate responsibility; although, "[i]n tenderness to individuals," he did not name names, his readers in 1787–88 could name them for him.

for his good behaviour. In the American republic it would serve to destroy, or would greatly diminish the intended and necessary responsibility of the chief magistrate himself.

The idea of a council to the executive, which has so generally obtained in the state constitutions, has been derived from that maxim of republican jealousy, which considers power as safer in the hands of a number of men than of a single man. If the maxim should be admitted to be applicable to the case, I should contend that the advantage on that side would not counterballance the numerous disadvantages on the opposite side. But I do not think the rule at all applicable to the executive power. I clearly concur in opinion in this particular with a writer whom the celebrated "Junius"[14] pronounces to be "deep, solid and ingenious," that, "the executive power is more easily confined when it is one":[15] That it is far more safe there should be a single object for

[14] "Junius" was the pen-name used by the author of a series of sixty-nine newspaper essays attacking the Whig administration of the Earl of Grafton, Lord Mansfield and his colleagues on the English high judiciary (with the conspicuous exception of Charles Pratt, first Lord Camden), and most Tory politicians. The *Letters of Junius* appeared between 1769 and 1772, and were later collected into book form with a new preface and an "Address to the English Nation." "Junius," whose identity is still a matter of vigorous scholarly dispute, assailed the Grafton ministry as dangerously subservient to King George III. His essays display a deep distrust for the executive and judiciary and a profound reverence for the British constitution, which, he insisted, could be protected only through the extreme watchfulness of the British people and the liberty of the press. The *Letters of Junius* sparked major court cases in 1771 establishing some legal protection for the liberty of the press; they also contributed indirectly to the concession by Parliament of permission to report the debates of the House of Commons. The best modern edition is John Cannon, ed., *The Letters of Junius* (Oxford, 1978).

The *Letters of Junius* were extremely popular in the American colonies and became a model for the periodical essay series, a principal medium of American political argument in the 1770s, 1780s, and 1790s—of which *The Federalist* is perhaps the greatest example. In a tactic copied by many American polemical pamphleteers (such as the authorial team behind the mask of "Publius"), "Junius" took his pseudonym from Plutarch's *Lives of the Most Noble Grecians and Romans*—in particular, from the life of Junius Brutus, the leader of the Romans' revolt against the corrupt Etruscan kings which led to the establishment of the Roman Republic. On this point, see generally Douglass Adair, "A Note on Certain of Hamilton's Pseudonyms," in Trevor Colbourn, ed., *Fame and the Founding Fathers: Essays of Douglass Adair* (New York, 1974); and Gaspare J. Saladino, "Pseudonyms Used in the Newspaper Debate Over the Ratification of the United States Constitution in the State of New York, September 1787–July 1788," in Stephen L. Schechter and Richard B. Bernstein, eds., *New York and the Union: Contributions to the American Constitutional Experience* (Albany, N.Y., 1990). See also the discussion of this point in Stephen L. Schechter's commentary in this volume on *The Federalist Nos 1, 10, 37, 39* and *51.*

[15] The writer praised by "Junius" in his preface to the compilation of *The Letters of Junius* was Jean Louis De Lolme (misspelled De Lome in the newspaper publication), a Swiss lawyer and author of the widely reprinted 1775 work *The Constitution of England,*

the jealousy and watchfulness of the people; and in a word that all multiplication of the executive is rather dangerous than friendly to liberty.

A little consideration will satisfy us, that the species of security sought for in the multiplication of the executive is unattainable. Numbers must be so great as to render combination difficult; or they are rather a source of danger than of security. The united credit and influence of several individuals must be more formidable to liberty than the credit and influence of either of them separately. When power therefore is placed in the hands of so small a number of men, as to admit of their interests and views being easily combined in a common enterprise, by an artful leader, it becomes more liable to abuse and more dangerous when abused, than if it be lodged in the hands of one man; who from the very circumstance of his being alone will be more narrowly watched and more readily suspected, and who cannot unite so great a mass of influence as when he is associated with others. The Decemvirs of Rome, whose name denotes their number,* were more to be dreaded in their usurpation than any ONE of them would have been. No person would think of proposing an executive much more numerous than that body, from six to a dozen have been suggested for the number of the council. The extreme of these numbers is not too great for an easy combination; and from such a combination America would have more to fear, than from the ambition of any single individual. A council to a magistrate, who is himself responsible for what he does, are generally nothing better than a clog upon his good intentions; are often the instruments and accomplices of his bad, and are almost always a cloak to his faults.

I forbear to dwell upon the subject of expence; though it be evident that if the council should be numerous enough to answer the principal end, aimed at by the institution, the salaries of the members, who must be drawn from their homes to reside at the seat of government, would form an item in the catalogue of public expenditures, too serious to be incurred for an object of equivocal utility.

---

or an Account of the English Government; in which it is compared with the Republican Form of Government, and occasionally with the other Monarchies in Europe. The fourth edition of De Lolme (4th ed., Dublin, 1776) quotes "Junius's" praise on the verso page. The quotation from De Lolme used here by Hamilton is the title of Book II, Chapter 2 of *The Constitution of England.*

Here again, we see Hamilton's adroit use of examples and authority. If "Junius," who distrusted executive power and was valued by American readers for that reason, could praise De Lolme and recommend him as an authority on the English constitution, then De Lolme's comment that unity in the executive promotes control of the executive gains force and persuasiveness.

* *Ten.*

I will only add, that prior to the appearance of the constitution, I rarely met with an intelligent man from any of the states, who did not admit as the result of experience, that the UNITY of the Executive of this state was one of the best of the distinguishing features of our constitution.

PUBLIUS

The Federalist No. 78[16]

ALEXANDER HAMILTON

May 28, 1788

We proceed now to an examination of the judiciary department of the proposed government.

In unfolding the defects of the existing confederation, the utility and necessity of a federal judicature have been clearly pointed out.[17] It is the less necessary to recapitulate the considerations there urged; as the propriety of the institution in the abstract is not disputed: The only questions which have been raised being relative to the manner of constituting it, and to its extent. To these points therefore our observations shall be confined.

The manner of constituting it seems to embrace these several objects—1st. The mode of appointing the judges. 2d. The tenure by which they are to hold their places. 3d. The partition of the judiciary authority between different courts, and their relations to each other.

First. As to the mode of appointing the judges: This is the same with that of appointing the officers of the union in general, and has been so fully discussed in the two last numbers, that nothing can be said here which would not be useless repetition.

---

[16] From J. and A. M'Lean, *The Federalist,* II, 290–99, where this essay was first published on May 28, 1788, and numbered 78. It appeared on June 14 in *The Independent Journal* where it was numbered 77, and was begun on June 17 and concluded on June 20 in *The New-York Packet* (where it was numbered 78).

[17] See *The Federalist No. 22,* as mentioned in the commentary to *The Federalist No. 15.*

Second. As to the tenure by which the judges are to hold their places: This chiefly concerns their duration in office; the provisions for their support; and the precautions for their responsibility.

According to the plan of the convention, all the judges who may be appointed by the United States are to hold their offices *during good behaviour,* which is conformable to the most approved of the state constitutions; and among the rest, to that of this state. Its propriety having been drawn into question by the adversaries of that plan, is no light symptom of the rage for objection which disorders their imaginations and judgments. The standard of good behaviour for the continuance in office of the judicial magistracy is certainly one of the most valuable of the modern improvements in the practice of government. In a monarchy it is an excellent barrier to the despotism of the prince: In a republic it is a no less excellent barrier to the encroachments and oppressions of the representative body. And it is the best expedient which can be devised in any government, to secure a steady, upright and impartial administration of the laws.[18]

Whoever attentively considers the different departments of power must perceive, that in a government in which they are separated from each other, the judiciary, from the nature of its functions, will always be the least dangerous to the political rights of the constitution; because it will be least in a capacity to annoy or injure them. The executive not only dispenses the honors, but holds the sword of the community. The legislature not only commands the purse, but prescribes the rules by which the duties and rights of every citizen are to be regulated. The judiciary on the contrary has no influence over either the sword or the purse, no direction either of the strength or of the wealth of the society, and can take no active resolution whatever. It may truly be said to have neither Force nor Will, but merely judgment; and must ultimately depend upon the aid of the executive arm even for the efficacy of its judgments.

This simple view of the matter suggests several important consequences. It proves incontestably that the judiciary is beyond comparison

---

[18] Both in England and in the American colonies, the lower houses of legislatures used the power of impeachment as a rein on the power of executive and judicial officers; indeed, it was generally regarded as a powerful political weapon. The impeachment of Warren Hastings, governor-general of India, was taking place in London at the time of the Federal Convention of 1787 and influenced the debates of the framers of the Constitution on the impeachment power. For a history of impeachment in the colonial, Revolutionary, and early national periods, see Peter C. Hoffer and N. E. H. Hull, *Impeachment in America, 1638–1805* (New Haven, 1984). See also Raoul Berger, *Impeachment: The Constitutional Problems* (Cambridge, Mass., 1973).

the weakest of the three departments of power;*[19] that it can never attack with success either of the other two; and that all possible care is requisite to enable it to defend itself against their attacks. It equally proves, that though individual oppression may now and then proceed from the courts of justice, the general liberty of the people can never be endangered from that quarter: I mean, so long as the judiciary remains truly distinct from both the legislative and executive. For I agree that "there is no liberty, if the power of judging be not separated from the legislative and executive powers."** And it proves, in the last place, that as liberty can have nothing to fear from the judiciary alone, but would have every thing to fear from its union with either of the other departments; that as all the effects of such an union must ensue from a dependence of the former on the latter, notwithstanding a nominal and apparent separation; that as from the natural feebleness of the judiciary, it is in continual jeopardy of being overpowered, awed or influenced by its coordinate branches; and that as nothing can contribute so much to its firmness and independence, as permanency in office, this quality may therefore be justly regarded as an indispensable ingredient in its constitution; and in a great measure as the citadel of the public justice and the public security.

The complete independence of the courts of justice is peculiarly essential in a limited constitution. By a limited constitution I understand one which contains certain specified exceptions to the legislative authority; such for instance as that it shall pass no bills of attainder, no

---

[19] The French jurist and philosopher Charles Louis Secondat, Baron de Montesquieu (1690–1754) was the leading philosopher of government of the Age of Enlightenment; his stature was comparable to that of Isaac Newton. *The Spirit of the Laws* was Montesquieu's *magnum opus*. This huge, disorderly treatise, familiar to most Americans (including Hamilton and Madison) in the 1752 English translation by Thomas Nugent, was a grab-bag of information and ideas about politics and government; its aim was to determine the relationships among human nature, climate, economy, religion, society, and government.

Both quotations from Montesquieu in *The Federalist No. 78* are from Book XI, Chapter 6, "On the Constitution of England." The first of Hamilton's quotations is incorrect, as Roy Fairfield has pointed out in his edition of *The Federalist* (1961; 2d ed., Baltimore, 1981); Hamilton left out the qualifying words "in some measure." Whether this omission was deliberate on Hamilton's part, or a result of the haste with which the essays were written and published, or an indication of a common practice of eighteenth-century authors (who aimed for the sense of the quotation rather than its exact words), is hard to determine. A combination of the second and third reasons is most likely.

*The celebrated Montesquieu speaking of them says, "of the three powers above mentioned, the JUDICIARY is next to nothing." Spirit of Laws, vol. 1, page 186.

**Idem. page 181.

ex post facto laws, and the like.[20] Limitations of this kind can be preserved in practice no other way than through the medium of the courts of justice; whose duty it must be to declare all acts contrary to the manifest tenor of the constitution void. Without this, all the reservations of particular rights or privileges would amount to nothing.

Some perplexity respecting the right of the courts to pronounce legislative acts void, because contrary to the constitution, has arisen from an imagination that the doctrine would imply a superiority of the judiciary to the legislative power. It is urged that the authority which can declare the acts of another void, must necessarily be superior to the one whose acts may be declared void. As this doctrine is of great importance in all the American constitutions, a brief discussion of the grounds on which it rests cannot be unacceptable.

There is no provision which depends on clearer principles, than that every act of a delegated authority, contrary to the tenor of the commission under which it is exercised, is void. No legislative act therefore contrary to the constitution can be valid. To deny this would be to affirm that the deputy is greater than his principal; that the servant is above his master; that the representatives of the people are superior to the people themselves; that men acting by virtue of powers may do not only what their powers do not authorise, but what they forbid.

If it be said that the legislative body are themselves the constitutional judges of their own powers, and that the construction they put upon them is conclusive upon the other departments, it may be answered, that this cannot be the natural presumption, where it is not to be collected from any particular provisions in the constitution. It is not otherwise to be supposed that the constitution could intend to enable the representatives of the people to substitute their *will* to that of their constituents. It is far more rational to suppose that the courts were designed to be an intermediate body between the people and the legislature, in order, among other things, to keep the latter within the limits assigned to their authority. The interpretation of the laws is the proper and peculiar province of the courts. A constitution is in fact, and must be, regarded by the judges as a fundamental law. It therefore belongs to them to ascertain its meaning as well as the meaning of any particular act proceeding from the legislative body. If there should happen to be an irreconcileable variance between the two, that which has the superior obligation and validity ought of course to be preferred; or

[20] For definitions of bills of attainder and *ex post facto* laws, see the commentary on the U.S. Constitution by Donald S. Lutz in this volume.

in other words, the constitution ought to be preferred to the statute, the intention of the people to the intention of their agents.

Nor does this conclusion by any means suppose a superiority of the judicial to the legislative power. It only supposes that the power of the people is superior to both; and that where the will of the legislature declared in its statutes, stands in opposition to that of the people declared in the constitution, the judges ought to be governed by the latter, rather than the former. They ought to regulate their decisions by the fundamental laws, rather than by those which are not fundamental.

This exercise of judicial discretion in determining between two contradictory laws, is exemplified in a familiar instance. It not uncommonly happens, that there are two statutes existing at one time, clashing in whole or in part with each other, and neither of them containing any repealing clause or expression. In such a case, it is the province of the courts to liquidate and fix their meaning and operation: So far as they can by any fair construction be reconciled to each other; reason and law conspire to dictate that this should be done. Where this is impracticable, it becomes a matter of necessity to give effect to one, in exclusion of the other. The rule which has obtained in the courts for determining their relative validity is that the last in order of time shall be preferred to the first. But this is mere rule of construction, not derived from any positive law, but from the nature and reason of the thing. It is a rule not enjoined upon the courts by legislative provision, but adopted by themselves, as consonant to truth and propriety, for the direction of their conduct as interpreters of the law. They thought it reasonable, that between the interfering acts of an *equal* authority, that which was the last indication of its will, should have the preference.

But in regard to the interfering acts of a superior and subordinate authority, of an original and derivative power, the nature and reason of the thing indicate the converse of that rule as proper to be followed. They teach us that the prior act of a superior ought to be preferred to the subsequent act of an inferior and subordinate authority; and that, accordingly, whenever a particular statute contravenes the constitution, it will be the duty of the judicial tribunals to adhere to the latter, and disregard the former.

It can be of no weight to say, that the courts on the pretence of a repugnancy, may substitute their own pleasure to the constitutional intentions of the legislature. This might as well happen in the case of two contradictory statutes; or it might as well happen in every adjudication upon any single statute. The courts must declare the sense of the law; and if they should be disposed to exercise WILL instead of JUDGMENT, the consequence would equally be the substitution of their pleasure to that of the legislative body. The observation, if it proved any thing, would prove that there ought to be no judges distinct from that body.

If then the courts of justice are to be considered as the bulwarks of a limited constitution against legislative encroachments, this consideration will afford a strong argument for the permanent tenure of judicial offices, since nothing will contribute so much as this to that independent spirit in the judges, which must be essential to the faithful performance of so arduous a duty.

This independence of the judges is equally requisite to guard the constitution and the rights of individuals from the effects of those ill humours which the arts of designing men, or the influence of particular conjunctures, sometimes disseminate among the people themselves, and which, though they speedily give place to better information and more deliberate reflection, have a tendency in the mean time to occasion dangerous innovations in the government, and serious oppressions of the minor party in the community. Though I trust the friends of the proposed constitution will never concur with its enemies*[21] in questioning that fundamental principle of republican government, which admits the right of the people to alter or abolish the established constitution whenever they find it inconsistent with their happiness; yet it is not to be inferred from this principle, that the representatives of the

[21] The Antifederalist writings cited by Hamilton are, first, the protest adopted by the twenty-three delegates to the Pennsylvania ratifying convention who voted against adoption of the Constitution, and, second, the *Genuine Information* of Luther Martin of Maryland, a detailed and often verbose attack on the Constitution by a non-signing delegate to the Federal Convention. Both these publications challenged the legitimacy of the Federal Convention's action in proposing the Constitution; because, they maintained, the Confederation Congress had authorized the Federal Convention only to propose revisions to the Articles of Confederation, the Convention had exceeded its authority by proposing an entirely new Constitution. Moreover, they contended, the method of ratifying the Constitution violated the Articles by requiring less than unanimous ratification of the Constitution. At first, these were preferred Antifederalist tactics; indeed, as late as June of 1788 Patrick Henry still argued—albeit to no avail—that the Constitution was not legitimately before the Virginia ratifying convention.

The favorite Federalist response to this tactic (exemplified in James Wilson's speeches to the Pennsylvania ratifying convention and in James Madison's *The Federalist No. 40*) was to invoke the fundamental right of the people to alter or abolish their government as articulated in the Declaration of Independence. In 1776, they declared, the Americans acted to throw off an oppressive government whose exertions threatened liberty; in 1787, they continued, the framers of the Constitution acted, and the people of America should act, to abolish a government whose weaknesses were equally as threatening to liberty as British tyranny had been.

*Vide Protest of the minority of the convention of Pennsylvania, Martin's speech, &c.

people, whenever a momentary inclination happens to lay hold of a majority of their constituents incompatible with the provisions in the existing constitution, would on that account be justifiable in a violation of those provisions; or that the courts would be under a greater obligation to connive at infractions in this shape, than when they had proceeded wholly from the cabals of the representative body. Until the people have by some solemn and authoritative act annulled or changed the established form, it is binding upon themselves collectively, as well as individually; and no presumption, or even knowledge of their sentiments, can warrant their representatives in a departure from it, prior to such an act. But it is easy to see that it would require an uncommon portion of fortitude in the judges to do their duty as faithful guardians of the constitution, where legislative invasions of it had been instigated by the major voice of the community.

But it is not with a view to infractions of the constitution only that the independence of the judges may be an essential safeguard against the effects of occasional ill humours in the society. These sometimes extend no farther than to the injury of the private rights of particular classes of citizens, by unjust and partial laws.[22] Here also the firmness of the judicial magistracy is of vast importance in mitigating the severity, and confining the operation of such laws. It not only serves to moderate the immediate mischiefs of those which may have been passed, but it operates as a check upon the legislative body in passing them; who, perceiving that obstacles to the success of an iniquitous intention are to be expected from the scruples of the courts, are in a manner compelled by the very motives of the injustice they meditate, to qualify their attempts. This is a circumstance calculated to have more influence upon the character of our governments, than but few may be aware of. The benefits of the integrity and moderation of the judiciary have already been felt in more states than one; and though they may have

[22] Hamilton relied on his readers' knowledge of state legislatures' tendencies to enact laws injuring private rights, such as the Rhode Island paper money and tender laws that were at issue in the 1786 Rhode Island Supreme Court's decision in *Trevett* v. *Weeden*. For the decision itself, see James M. Varnum, *The Case, Trevett v. Weeden . . .* (Providence, 1786), 1–36; the case is discussed in Irwin Polishook, *Rhode Island and the Union, 1774–1795* (Evanston, Ill., 1969), 133–42. Hamilton also may have been thinking of the 1784 New York Mayor's Court case of *Rutgers* v. *Waddington,* described in the commentary to *No. 78.*

Madison recognized the importance of *Trevett* v. *Weeden*; indeed, he cited the case approvingly during the debates in the Federal Convention, see Max Farrand, ed., *The Records of the Federal Convention of 1787,* rev. ed. in 4 vols. (New Haven, 1987), II: 27–28 (remarks of James Madison on July 17, 1787), and the discussion in Warren, *Congress, the Constitution, and the Supreme Court,* 44 and 44 n.2.

displeased those whose sinister expectations they may have disappointed, they must have commanded the esteem and applause of all the virtuous and disinterested. Considerate men of every description ought to prize whatever will tend to beget or fortify that temper in the courts; as no man can be sure that he may not be tomorrow the victim of a spirit of injustice, by which he may be a gainer to-day. And every man must now feel that the inevitable tendency of such a spirit is to sap the foundations of public and private confidence, and to introduce in its stead, universal distrust and distress.[23]

That inflexible and uniform adherence to the rights of the constitution and of individuals, which we perceive to be indispensable in the courts of justice, can certainly not be expected from judges who hold their offices by a temporary commission. Periodical appointments, however regulated, or by whomsoever made, would in some way or other be fatal to their necessary independence. If the power of making them was committed either to the executive or legislature, there would be danger of an improper complaisance to the branch which possessed it; if to both, there would be an unwillingness to hazard the displeasure of either; if to the people, or to persons chosen by them for the special purpose, there would be too great a disposition to consult popularity, to justify a reliance that nothing would be consulted but the constitution and the laws.

There is yet a further and a weighty reason for the permanency of the judicial offices; which is deducible from the nature of the qualifications they require. It has been frequently remarked with great propriety, that a voluminous code of laws is one of the inconveniences necessarily connected with the advantages of a free government. To avoid an arbitrary discretion in the courts, it is indispensable that they should be bound down by strict rules and precedents, which serve to define and point out their duty in every particular case that comes before

---

[23] In the aftermath of *Trevett* v. *Weeden*, the Rhode Island legislature challenged the justices of the state supreme court to defend their decision on the tender law. Two of the five justices chose not to do so; the legislature refused to renew the appointment of the other three, including the chief justice, prompting a lawsuit. The lawsuit was delayed until the terms of the suing justices ran out, thereby rendering the case moot. See generally the discussion in Polishook, *Rhode Island and the Union*.

The Clintonian New York legislature censured the New York City Mayor's Court for its decision in *Rutgers* v. *Waddington*, even though the judges had not struck down the Trespass Act of 1783 but merely offered what lawyers call a "saving construction" that narrowed the statute's reach. In response to the public outcry, Hamilton wrote two of his most eloquent pamphlets, the *First* and *Second Letters of Phocion*, defending the decision and the principles embodied in it and denouncing the state's anti-Loyalist policies as unjust and as harmful to the interests of New York and the Union.

them; and it will readily be conceived from the variety of controversies which grow out of the folly and wickedness of mankind, that the records of those precedents must unavoidably swell to a very considerable bulk, and must demand long and laborious study to acquire a competent knowledge of them. Hence it is that there can be but few men in the society, who will have sufficient skill in the laws to qualify them for the stations of judges. And making the proper deductions for the ordinary depravity of human nature, the number must be still smaller of those who unite the requisite integrity with the requisite knowledge. These considerations apprise us, that the government can have no great option between fit characters; and that a temporary duration in office, which would naturally discourage such characters from quitting a lucrative line of practice to accept a seat on the bench, would have a tendency to throw the administration of justice into hands less able, and less well qualified to conduct it with utility and dignity. In the present circumstances of this country, and in those in which it is likely to be for a long time to come, the disadvantages on this score would be greater than they may at first sight appear; but it must be confessed that they are far inferior to those which present themselves under the other aspects of the subject.

Upon the whole there can be no room to doubt that the convention acted wisely in copying from the models of those constitutions which have established *good behaviour* as the tenure of their judicial offices in point of duration; and that so far from being blameable on this account, their plan would have been inexcuseably defective if it had wanted this important feature of good government. The experience of Great Britain affords an illustrious comment on the excellence of the institution.

PUBLIUS

XVII

Antifederalist Essays
and Speeches

1787-1788

COMMENTARY BY RALPH KETCHAM

THE PRESENTATION OF THE PROPOSED new Constitution of the United
States to the public on September 17, 1787, and its submission to the
states for their approval or disapproval eleven days later by the Confederation Congress, began the "ratification debate." For all practical
purposes, this debate ended on July 26, 1788, when New York became
the eleventh state to ratify the Constitution, assuring that it would soon
become the new form of government of the American Union. This
evolving political struggle linked the usual give-and-take of politics in
free societies with an intense war of words between friends and foes of
the new document. Each side had able and eloquent leaders, mustered
elaborate arguments, and organized within each state and across state
lines to further its cause.

The ratification struggle began with a clever move by the proponents of the new Constitution. Because sentiment in the United States,
hostile to the idea of a national government, preferred a confederation
or federation (the words were synonymous in the eighteenth century),
the proponents of the Constitution called themselves "Federalists."
They appropriated this term even though the new document, strictly
speaking, did not create a league of governments, as had the old Articles
of Confederation. As James Madison explained in *The Federalist No. 39*,
the government created by the Constitution would be a "composite,"
partly national in that it had power in some cases to operate directly

on the people and in those cases was directly responsible to the people (most notably the taxing power and the election of the House of Representatives), partly federal in that the states acted as constituent units of the general government (most notably in the election of the Senate). By appropriating the popular word "federal" to denote the new Constitution, its backers gained an important symbolic advantage for themselves and left the Constitution's opponents with the negative designation, "Antifederalists."

Newspapers throughout the nation began to publish "federal" and "antifederal" essays, sometimes as isolated letters and sometimes as part of more systematic treatments. Furthermore, as the people of each state elected ratification conventions and as these bodies began to meet, the conventions generated speeches, majority and minority reports, and proposed amendments which in turn fed the torrent of words in the public debate. The most famous pro-Constitution series of essays was *The Federalist*. Although no single antifederal publication matched "Publius" in comprehensiveness and intellectual power, there were several notable antifederal pamphlets and series of essays—among them the "Letters of Centinel" (October 1787 to April 1788), the "Letters of Cato" (September 1787 to January 1788), the "Letters from the Federal Farmer" (October 1787 to January 1788), and the "Essays of Brutus" (October 1787 to April 1788). "Centinel" was published in Philadelphia; all the rest listed above, as well as *The Federalist,* appeared first in New York.

The newspaper war took place at the same time as the series of political battles in each state comprising the struggle for ratification. Reflecting satisfaction over the Constitution's protection of state equality in the Senate, and anxiety for protection within a stronger union, conventions in three small states, Delaware, New Jersey, and Georgia, ratified early and unanimously. Connecticut, a Federalist stronghold, also ratified early and by a large margin (128–40). The vagaries of Pennsylvania politics, combined with the heavy-handedness of Federalist leaders and the zeal of James Wilson, produced an early Federalist victory there, too (46–23). When the closely divided Massachusetts convention met in January 1788, five states had already ratified and none had rejected the Constitution. After a long, spirited debate, and some clever maneuvering by the Federalists, the Massachusetts convention ratified the Constitution on February 16, 1788 (187–168).

This close vote, and the Antifederalists' strength in the critical states of Virginia and New York, created an air of uncertainty during the first six months of 1788. The easy ratifications by Maryland (63–11) and South

Carolina (149–73) cheered the Federalists; only one more state ratification was needed to put the new form of government into effect. However, Antifederalists were dominant in New Hampshire; Rhode Island and North Carolina were hostile; and there was real danger that Virginia and New York would not ratify. Thus, the issue was hanging in the balance in June 1788, when three state ratifying conventions—Virginia, New Hampshire, and New York—convened.

In the most important of the ratification contests, the Virginia convention, James Madison, Governor Edmund Randolph, and other Federalists narrowly triumphed in debate and in the voting over Patrick Henry and George Mason, and their Antifederalist supporters. Virginia voted to ratify (89–79) on June 25; in the meantime, on June 21, New Hampshire had voted (57–47) to adopt the Constitution as well. With ten states having ratified, the Constitution's victory was assured. Faced with this state of affairs, the New York ratifying convention (in which Antifederalists outnumbered Federalists 46 to 19) voted to ratify after a lengthy debate (30–27). The North Carolina ratifying convention even voted against deciding whether or not to ratify (193–75); the Rhode Island legislature refused even to call a convention, and the state's voters held a referendum on the Constitution in town meetings and rejected it by a margin of ten to one, although the Federalists in the major towns of Providence and Newport boycotted the proceedings. North Carolina eventually ratified the Constitution and joined the Union in November 1789; Rhode Island followed suit in May 1790.

Though the war of words that accompanied the political battles often focused on regional rivalries and petty details, each side also set forth a larger vision of what purposes of government were embodied in the proposed Constitution and what kind of nation might develop under it. The Federalist argument is well-known, due mostly to the enduring greatness of *The Federalist* as a work of constitutional interpretation and political theory. The Antifederalist argument also deserves analysis.

Antifederalists feared what Patrick Henry termed the "consolidated government" proposed by the new Constitution. They saw in Federalist hopes for commercial growth and international prestige only the lust of ambitious men for a "splendid empire" that, in the time-honored way of empires, would oppress the people with taxes, conscription, and military campaigns. Uncertain that any government over so vast a domain as the United States could be controlled by the people, Antifederalists saw in the enlarged powers of the general government only the familiar threats to the rights and liberties of the people. The federal judiciary, for example, seemed like just another magistracy removed from the people that would enforce harsh and arbitrary laws (see *Brutus No. 15* following this commentary). The broad power to lay and collect taxes, the president's role as commander in chief, Congress's authority to pass any laws "necessary and proper" to carry out its enumerated powers, and the "supreme law of the land" and treaty-making powers all seemed unbounded and at least potentially tyrannical (see *Brutus No. 1*). The Antifederalists' twin goals, therefore, were to withdraw some of the powers explicitly given to the general government and to restrain with further checks and balances the exercise of its remaining powers (see Patrick Henry's speeches in the Virginia convention). Antifederalists were, in a sense, "men of little faith" as both contemporary critics and later historians (principally Cecelia Kenyon) have charged, but this was true only in the context of their abiding fear that centralized power tended to become arbitrary and impersonal.

Antifederalists also had a positive vision of what the government of the United States should be—a republican vision which they thought was far closer to the principles and goals of the American Revolution than the political and commercial ambitions of the Federalists. The Antifederalists looked to the classical ideal of the small, pastoral republic where virtuous, self-reliant citizens managed their own affairs and shunned the power and glory of empire. To them, the victory in the American Revolution meant not so much the big chance to become a wealthy world power, but rather the opportunity to achieve a genuinely republican polity, far from the greed, lust for power, and tyranny that had generally characterized human society (see Patrick Henry's speeches in the Virginia convention).

To Antifederalists, the prescription for government that would preserve the virtue and happiness of the people—the preconditions for a republican polity that in turn would preserve liberty—was to retain as much as possible the vitality of local government, in which rulers and ruled could see, know, and understand one another. Thus, they prized the American Revolution's emphasis on state and local councils and committees; thus, they cherished the Articles of Confederation, whose structure rested entirely on the states, although they unitedly believed that the Articles needed to be amended to give Congress more power. In their view, the idea of self-government was tied inextricably to a quality of directness reminiscent of a town meeting or a state legislature composed of many representatives who were subject to annual elections and who would really know the people of their districts. Each such district, furthermore, would be a town or ward or region conscious of its own particular identity rather than some amorphous, arbitrary geographic entity. Only with such intimacy could the trust, good will, and deliberation essential to wise and virtuous public life be a reality. Anything else, even though resting in some fashion on the consent of the people, would not really be self-government (see Melancton Smith's speeches in the New York convention).

The Antifederalists' intense suspicions of corruption, greed, and lust for power were directed generally at those who ruled from on high and without restraint. Corruption and tyranny would be rampant as they always had been when those who exercised power felt little connection with the people. This would be true, moreover, for elected representatives, as well as for kings and nobles and bishops, who lived in a distant capital where power, wealth, and intrigue would exert their baneful influences. The more remote and distantly powerful a government was, the more it would be reminiscent of imperial Rome or Versailles or London with all their venality, cynicism, corruption, and neglect of the people. Would some future capital of the United States be filled with courtiers, courtesans, military heroes, and superfluous officeholders as was London or Paris or St. Petersburg? Antifederalists thought so under a constitution that consolidated power in a central government remote from the people.

On the other hand, the histories and legends of the Greek and Roman republics, the maturing ideology of natural rights, and the substantial experience of local self-government in the New World seemed to offer a far more alluring prospect. If the basic decency in human nature, most evident among ordinary people at the local level amid family, church, school, and other nourishing institutions, could impinge directly and continuously on government, then perhaps it too might be kept virtuous and worthy of confidence. Then, instead of endless suspicion and guarding against the evil and corruption of government, it might be possible to trust government and use it for the public benefit (see *Centinel No. 1*). The result might even be a society where honest, hardworking people could enjoy the fruits of their labor, where institutions encouraged and rested on virtue rather than greed, where officials were servants of the people rather than oppressors, and where peace and prosperity came from vigilant self-confidence rather than from conquest and dominion. Antifederalists saw mild, grass-roots, small-scale governments in sharp contrast to the splendid edifice and overweening ambition implicit in the new Constitution and heralded by "Publius" and its other advocates. The Antifederalist ideal of government left its citizens free to live their own lives and to cultivate the virtue (public and private) vital to republicanism; the second soon entailed taxes and drafts and offices and wars damaging to human dignity and thus fatal to self-government (see *Brutus No. 1*).

The Antifederalist ideal emerged most clearly and practically in its understanding of what representation and government by consent could really mean. Instead of seeking to insulate officials from popular influence (as, for example, "Publius" had argued in *The Federalist No. 78* regarding federal judges), Antifederalists sought to ensure the public good by requiring close association. If, for example, legislators rather than federal judges appointed for life had the power to interpret the Constitution, they would do so "at their peril"; if the people disapproved the interpretation, they "could remove them" (see *Brutus No. 15*). The ideal went beyond a close control of officials by the people. In a truly self-governing society, there would be such dialogue, empathy, and even intimacy that the very distinction between ruler and ruled would tend to disappear. Such a close link between the people and their officials could embody the idea of liberty as both a security of rights and a guard of the people's effective voice in public affairs. Antifederalists groped for mechanisms that would give reality to this idea: how could it be achieved, in substance as well as in form, in a large nation? (See *Centinel No. 1*.)

For Antifederalists, the bonds between the people and their representatives had to be trustworthy as well as close. Not only, as Melancton Smith put it, should "representatives resemble those they represent; they should be a true picture of the people"; they should possess especially the virtues most characteristic of ordinary people: temperance, morality, and restrained ambition. Smith acknowledged that "the same passions and prejudices govern all men," but it was also true that "circumstances . . . give a cast to human character." The wealthy and the powerful, sad to say, were inclined to cheat customers, disdain honest labor, raise armies, put on social airs, and oppress the people. Could they be expected to rule wisely and justly in the interests of all? Rather, it was necessary that people of the "middling sort"—average people, perhaps yeoman farmers—themselves take part in government, and perhaps even be elected to office in large enough numbers to "set the tone" in the capital. Smith observed that such people, in the daily round of their occupations, had "less temptations, [and] are inclined by habit, and by the company with whom they associate, to set bounds to their passions and appetites." He envisioned, then, a government of popular confidence and respect, vital at the local levels where the virtues of ordinary people could prevail. Though Smith articulated this more forthrightly than most Antifederalists (see Smith's June 21 speech in the New York convention), many others implied their agreement with this idea (see also Patrick Henry's speeches in the Virginia convention), and it was consistent with a moral and civic tradition long familiar in the Western world.

This was idealistic, of course, but Antifederalists thought the goal of the American Revolution was to end the ancient equation of power where arrogant, oppressive, and depraved rulers on one side produced subservience and a gradual erosion of the self-respect, capacities, and virtue of the people on the other side. The result was an increasing corruption and degeneracy in both rulers and ruled. Unless this cycle could be broken, independence would mean little more than the exchange of one tyranny for another. The aspirations of the Federalists for commercial growth, westward expansion, increased national power, and effective world diplomacy were in some ways attractive and worthy, but they also fitted an ominous, all-too-familiar pattern of "great, splendid, . . . consolidated government" and "Universal Empire" that the American Revolution had been fought to eradicate. Many Antifederalists were unwilling to abandon their ideal and the hope that the New World might be a different and better place to live.

The ratification contest, then, was at bottom a debate over the future of the nation. Beneath the disputes about detailed clauses were deep differences over what fulfillment of the American Revolution meant. To Federalists, it meant independence, growth of national power, and prosperity, all within a federal system of government retaining the states and deriving its authority from the people, but also competent to all the needs and exigencies of respectable, energetic nationhood. This was an attractive purpose for large numbers of Americans of all classes and walks of life; in their view, it was a legitimate outgrowth of the Revolution. The Antifederalists, on the other hand, sought a society where virtuous, hardworking, honest men and women lived simply in their own communities, enjoyed their families and their neighbors, were devoted to the common welfare, and had such churches, schools, trade associations, and local governments as they needed to sustain their values and achieve their goals. Though this intention was seldom fully or clearly articulated, it permeates Antifederalist writings enough to reveal what their positive ideal was.

Although there was no comprehensive work of Antifederal political thought comparable to Hamilton, Madison, and Jay's *The Federalist*, the speeches and essays presented here to exemplify Antifederalist thought do counter the arguments presented in the selections from *The Federalist*. Patrick Henry's speeches at the Virginia ratifying convention, for example, meet head-on those of "Publius" in *The Federalist No. 1* for a stronger union. Whereas "Publius" notes that "the vigor of government is essential to the security of liberty," and that "a dangerous ambition . . . often lurks behind the specious mask of zeal for the rights of the people," Henry's speeches denounce the consolidating and empowering clauses of the Constitution and uphold instead the more decentralized Articles of Confederation as the protector of liberty. Thus the reader can reflect on the relative contributions of strength in government and of human rights to effective freedom. Is Henry's criticism of a national government and its tendency toward "empire" a fair warning against "Publius's" desire for greater and more efficient national power?

"Centinel" No. 1 raises another profound issue: Is good government more likely to result from a variety of conflicting interests and checks and balances, as "Publius" argues in *The Federalist Nos. 10* and *51*, or from a simple form of government where public officials are held directly responsible, through frequent elections, to the people? Is democracy frustrated when, under complicated checks and balances, the people are "perplexed and divided in their sentiments about the sources of abuse and misconduct?" Do private motivations and "ambition [made to] counteract ambition" result in freedom and the good of the nation, as "Publius" maintains in *The Federalist No. 51*, or is "Centinel" correct in suggesting that the welfare and happiness of the community" can never come from a system of "jarring adverse interests"?

To the patient explanation offered by "Publius" in *The Federalist Nos. 37* and *39* of the need to combine "stability and energy" in government with republican freedom, and hence to have a "composition" of federal and national features in the new Constitution, "Brutus" asks "the Citizens of the State of New-York" to consider, in fact, the "absolute and uncontroulable power," legislative, executive, and judicial, implicit in two clauses of the Constitution—the "necessary and proper" clause (Article I, Section 8) and the "supreme law of the land" clause (Article VI). In questioning whether "the thirteen United States should be reduced to one great republic," "Brutus" challenges the whole idea that the proposed Constitution is a wise balance between state and national power. He questions whether a country as large as the United States can preserve the reality of free and responsible government if powers are consolidated at the center. "The opinion of the greatest men, and the experience of mankind," he asserted, rejected that idea.

To the eloquent argument of *The Federalist No. 70* that "Energy in the executive is a leading character in the definition of good government," and that an able, fully empowered, and responsible executive was the vital capstone of the new Constitution, Melancton Smith offered a more populist alternative. Speaking to the New York ratifying convention, Smith took direct aim at fellow convention delegate Alexander Hamilton, rejecting the high-toned idea that the people needed sophisticated and exceptional people to conduct their affairs. Rather, the reality of self-government required that public officials be close to the people, intimately aware of their needs and problems, and in constant touch with the ordinary people, who exemplified the desirable traits of industry and virtue more than did "conspicuous military, popular, civil or legal talents."

Finally, "Brutus" No. 15 contested the claims in *The Federalist No. 78* that an independent judiciary, insulated from popular passions and the "ill humors" of "designing" politicians, was necessary to uphold the "fundamental law" of the Constitution and "guard . . . the rights of individuals." Such elevation above popular control, "Brutus" argued, was incompatible with the very idea of responsible self-government. Thus "independent of the people, of the legislature, and of every power under heaven," judges so elevated would "soon feel themselves independent of heaven itself." Rather, the Constitution should receive its final interpretation from a legislative body elected by the people. Then, if the people disagreed with the interpretation of their Constitution, they could defeat the erring legislators at the next election. Only then could the proper chain of responsibility be maintained. Again, a basic issue had surfaced: was it dangerous, in a democratic government, to have important officers insulated from control by the people, or was it necessary to accept that risk in order to protect fundamental rights from infringement by popular passions or political intrigue? This argument also echoes the fundamental tension in the Declaration of Independence—and in American politics and law generally—between the existence of "certain unalienable rights" not to be violated by government and the need to make all decisions accord with "the consent of the governed."

In offering a searching and profound critique of many of the political axioms and devices of government proposed by the framers of the Constitution and defended by the Federalists, the Antifederalists made an important contribution to the evolution of the Constitution. The quick adoption of the Bill of Rights, the ready acceptance of the new Constitution by former Antifederalists, and the Jeffersonian Republicans' triumph in 1801 with its manifest Antifederalist overtones, all attest to the vigor and influence of Antifederalism and its ability to find fulfillment even under the document the Antifederalists opposed so vehemently in 1787–88. Antifederal ideas have also surfaced again and again in various guises among later generations of Americans. Their ideas are elements of the American political tradition as vital as the enticing prospects held out by "Publius" in *The Federalist*; both bodies of political thought are important components of the philosophy of the Constitution.

For Further Reading

John K. Alexander. *The Selling of the Constitutional Convention: A History of News Coverage.* Madison, Wisc., 1990.

Merrill Jensen, John P. Kaminski, and Gaspare J. Saladino, eds. *The Documentary History of the Ratification of the Constitution.* Madison, Wisc., 1976–.

Ralph Ketcham, ed. *The Antifederist Papers and the Constitutional Debates.* New York, 1986.

Jackson Turner Main. *The Antifederalists: Critics of the Constitution, 1781–1789.* Chapel Hill, 1961.

Robert A. Rutland. *The Ordeal of the Constitution.* Boston, 1966, rev. ed., 1983.

Herbert J. Storing. *What the Anti-Federalists Were For.* Chicago, 1981.

Herbert J. Storing with Murray Dry, eds. *The Complete Anti-Federalist.* 7 vols. Chicago, 1981.

Gordon S. Wood. *The Creation of the American Republic, 1776–1787.* Chapel Hill, 1969.

Patrick Henry
Speech in Virginia
Ratifying Convention

JUNE 5, 1788

I rose yesterday to ask a question, which arose in my own mind. When I asked the question, I thought the meaning of my interrogation was obvious: The fate of this question and America may depend on this: Have they said, we the States? Have they made a proposal of a compact between States? If they had, this would be a confederation: It is otherwise most clearly a consolidated government. The question turns, Sir, on that poor little thing—the expression, *We, the People,* instead of the States of America. I need not take much pains to show, that the principles of this system, are extremely pernicious, impolitic, and dangerous. Is this a Monarchy, like England—a compact between Prince and people; with checks on the former, to secure the liberty of the latter? Is this a Confederacy, like Holland—an association of a number of independent States, each of which retain its individual sovereignty? It is not a democracy, wherein the people retain all their rights securely. Had these principles been adhered to, we should not have been brought to this alarming transition, from a Confederacy to a consolidated Government. We have no detail of those great considerations which, in my opinion, ought to have abounded before we should recur to a government of this kind. Here is a revolution as radical as that which separated us from Great Britain. It is as radical, if in this transition our rights and privileges are endangered, and the sovereignty of the States be relinquished: And cannot we plainly see, that this is actually the case? The rights of conscience, trial by jury, liberty of the press, all your immunities and franchises, all pretensions to human rights and privileges, are rendered insecure, if not lost, by this change so loudly talked of by some, and inconsiderately by others. Is this same relinquishment of rights worthy of freemen? Is it worthy of that manly fortitude that ought to characterize republicans: It is said eight States have adopted this plan.

All of the documents in this chapter have been reprinted with permission from Herbert J. Storing, ed., *The Complete Anti-Federalist,* 7 vols. (Chicago: The University of Chicago Press, 1981), Vols. 2, 5 and 6.

I declare that if twelve States and an half had adopted it, I would with manly firmness, and in spite of an erring world, reject it. You are not to inquire how your trade may be increased, nor how you are to become a great and powerful people, but how your liberties can be secured; for liberty ought to be the direct end of your Government. Having premised these things, I shall, with the aid of my judgment and information, which I confess are not extensive, go into the discussion of this system more minutely. Is it necessary for your liberty, that you should abandon those great rights by the adoption of this system? Is the relinquishment of the trial by jury, and the liberty of the press, necessary for your liberty? Will the abandonment of your most sacred rights tend to the security of your liberty? Liberty the greatest of all earthly blessings—give us that precious jewel, and you may take everything else: But I am fearful I have lived long enough to become an old fashioned fellow: Perhaps an invincible attachment to the dearest rights of man, may, in these refined enlightened days, be deemed *old fashioned*: If so, I am contended to be so: I say, the time has been, when every pore of my heart beat for American liberty, and which, I believe, had a counterpart in the breast of every true American: But suspicions have gone forth—suspicions of my integrity—publicly reported that my professions are not real—23 years ago was I supposed a traitor to my country; I was then said to be a bane of sedition, because I supported the rights of my country: I may be thought suspicious when I say our privileges and rights are in danger: But, Sir, a number of the people of this country are weak enough to think these things are too true: I am happy to find that the Honorable Gentleman on the other side, declares they are groundless: But, Sir, suspicion is a virtue, as long as its object is the preservation of the public good, and as long as it stays within proper bounds: Should it fall on me, I am contented: Conscious rectitude is a powerful consolation: I trust, there are many who think my professions for the public good to be real. Let your suspicion look to both sides: There are many on the other side, who, possibly may have been per-suaded of the necessity of these measures, which I conceive to be dangerous to your liberty. Guard with jealous attention the public liberty. Suspect every one who approaches that jewel. Unfortunately, nothing will preserve it, but downright force: Whenever you give up that force, you are inevitably ruined. I am answered by Gentlemen, that though I might speak of terrors, yet the fact was, that we were sur-rounded by none of the dangers I apprehended. I conceive this new Government to be one of those dangers: It has produced those horrors, which distress many of our best citizens. We are come hither to preserve the poor Commonwealth of Virginia, if it can be possibly done: Something must be done to preserve your liberty and mine: The Confederation; this same despised Government, merits, in my opinion, the highest encomium: It carried us through a long and dangerous war: It rendered us victorious in that bloody conflict with a powerful nation: It has secured us a territory greater than any European Monarch possesses: And shall a Government which has been thus strong and vigorous, be accused of imbecility and abandoned for want of energy? . . . There is one thing in it which I never would acquiesce in. I mean the changing it into a Consolidated Government; which is so abhorrent to my mind. The Honorable Gentleman then went on to the figure we make with foreign nations; the contemptible one we make in France and Holland; which, according to the system of my notes, he attributes to the present feeble Government. An opinion has gone forth, we find, that we are a contemptible people: The time has been when we were thought otherwise: Under this same despised Government, we commanded the respect of all Europe: Wherefore are we now reckoned otherwise? The American spirit has fled from hence: It has gone to regions, where it has never been expected: It has gone to the people of France in search of a splendid Government—a strong energetic Government. Shall we imitate the example of those nations who have gone from a simple to a splendid Government? Are those nations more worthy of our imitation? What can make an adequate satisfaction to them for the loss they suffered in attaining such a Government for the loss of their liberty? If we admit this Consolidated Government it will be because we like a great splendid one. Some way or other we must be a great and mighty empire; we must have an army, and a navy, and a number of things: When the American spirit was in its youth, the language of America was different: Liberty, Sir, was then the primary object. We are descended from a people whose Government was founded on liberty: Our glorious forefathers of Great-Britain, made liberty the foundation of every thing. That country is become a great, mighty, and splendid nation; not because their Government is strong and energetic; but, Sir, because liberty is its direct end and foundation: We drew the spirit of liberty from our British ancestors; by that spirit we have triumphed over every difficulty: But now, Sir, the American spirit, assisted by the ropes and chains of consolidation, is about to convert this country to a powerful and mighty empire: If you make the citizens of this country agree to become the subjects of one great consolidated empire of America, your Government will not have sufficient energy to keep them together: Such a government is incompatible with the genius of republicanism: There will be no checks, no real balances, in this Government: What can avail your specious imaginary balances, your rope-dancing, chain-rattling, ridiculous ideal checks and contrivances? But, Sir, we are not feared by foreigners; we do not make nations tremble: Would this, Sir, constitute happiness, or secure liberty? I trust, Sir, our political hemisphere will ever direct their operations to the security of those objects. Consider our situation, Sir: Go to the poor man, ask him what he does; he will inform you, that he enjoys the fruits of his labour, under his own fig-tree, with his wife and children around him, in peace and security. Go to every other member of the society, you will find the same tranquil ease and content; you will find no alarms or disturbances: Why then tell us of dangers to terrify us into an adoption of this new Government? and yet who knows the dangers that this new system may produce; they are out of sight of the common people: They cannot foresee latent consequences: I dread the operation of it on the middling and lower class of people: It is for them I fear the adoption of this system.

Patrick Henry
Speech in Virginia
Ratifying Convention

JUNE 5, 1788

. . . In this scheme of energetic Government, the people will find two sets of tax-gatherers—the State and the Federal Sheriffs. This it seems to me will produce such dreadful oppression, as the people cannot possibly bear: The Federal Sheriff may commit what oppression, make what distresses he pleases, and ruin you with impunity: For how are you to tie his hands? Have you any sufficient decided means of preventing him from sucking your blood by speculations, commissions and fees? Thus thousands of your people will be most shamefully robbed: Our State Sheriffs, those unfeeling blood-suckers, have, under the watchful eye of our Legislature, committed the most horrid and barbarous ravages on our people: It has required the most constant vigilance of the Legislature to keep them from totally ruining the people: A repeated succession of laws has been made to suppress their inequitous speculations and cruel extortions; and as often have their nefarious ingenuity devised methods of evading the force of those laws: In the struggle they have generally triumphed over the Legislature. It is fact that lands have sold for five shillings, which were worth one hundred pounds: If Sheriffs thus immediately under the eye of our State Legislature and Judiciary, have dared to commit these outrages, what would they not have done if their masters had been at Philadelphia or New-York? If they perpetrate the most unwarrantable outrage on your persons or property, you cannot get redress on this side of Philadelphia or New-York: And how can you get it there? If your domestic avocations could permit you to go thither, there you must appeal to Judges sworn to support this Constitution, in opposition to that of any State, and who may also be inclined to favor their own officers: When these harpies are aided by excise men, who may search at any time your houses and most secret recesses, will the people bear it? If you think so you differ from me: Where I thought there was a possibility of such mischiefs, I would grant power with a niggardly hand; and here there is strong probability that these oppressions shall actually happen. I may be told, that it is safe to err on that side; because such regulations *may* be made by Congress, as shall restrain these officers, and because laws are made by our Representatives, and judged by righteous Judges: But, Sir, as these regulations may be made, so they may not; and many reasons there are to induce a belief that they will not: I shall therefore be an infidel on that point till the day of my death.

    This Constitution is said to have beautiful features; but when I come to examine these features, Sir, they appear to me horridly frightful: Among other deformities, it has an awful squinting; it squints toward monarchy: And does not this raise indignation in the breast of every American? Your President may easily become King: Your Senate is so imperfectly constructed that your dearest rights may be sacrificed by what may be a small minority; and a very small minority may continue forever unchangeably this Government, although horridly defective: Where are your checks in this Government? Your strong holds will be in the hands of your enemies: It is on a supposition that our American Governors shall be honest, that all the good qualities of this Government are founded: But its defective, and imperfect construction, puts it in their power to perpetrate the worst of mischiefs, should they be bad men: And, Sir, would not all the world, from the Eastern to the Western hemisphere, blame our distracted folly in resting our rights upon the contingency of our rulers being good or bad. Shew me that age and country where the rights and liberties of the people were placed on the sole chance of their rulers being good men, without a consequent loss of liberty? I say that the loss of that dearest privilege has ever followed with absolute certainty, every such mad attempt. If your American chief, be a man of ambition, and abilities, how easy is it for him to render himself absolute: The army is in his hands, and, if he be a man of address, it will be attached to him; and it will be the subject of long meditation with him to seize the first auspicious moment to accomplish his design; and, Sir, will the American spirit solely relieve you when this happens? I would rather infinitely, and I am sure most of this Convention are of the same opinion, have a King, Lords, and Commons, than a Government so replete with such insupportable evils. If we make a King, we may prescribe the rules by which he shall rule his people, and interpose such checks as shall prevent him from infringing them: But the President, in the field, at the head of his army, can prescribe the terms on which he shall reign master, so far that it will puzzle any American ever to get his neck from under the galling yoke. I cannot with patience, think of this idea. If ever he violates the laws, one of two things will happen: He shall come to the head of his army to carry every thing before him; or, he will give bail, or do what Mr. Chief Justice will order him. If he be guilty, will not the recollection of his crimes teach him to make one bold push for the American throne? Will not the immense difference between being master of every thing, and being ignominiously tried and punished, powerfully excite him to make this bold push? But, Sir, where is the existing force to punish him? Can he not at the head of his army beat down every opposition? Away with your President, we shall have a King: The army will salute him Monarch; your militia will leave you and assist in making him King, and fight against you: And what have you to oppose this force? What will then become of you and your rights? Will not absolute despotism ensue?

Centinel No. 1
[Samuel Bryan]

Philadelphia *Independent Gazetteer*
October 5, 1787

Mr. Oswald,
   As *the Independent Gazetteer seems free for the discussion of all public matters, I expect you will give the following a place in your next.*

To the Freemen of Pennsylvania.

Friends, Countrymen, and Fellow Citizens,
   Permit one of yourselves to put you in mind of certain *liberties* and *privileges* secured to you by the constitution of this commonwealth, and to beg your serious attention to his uninterested opinion upon the plan of federal government submitted to your consideration, before you surrender these great and valuable privileges up forever. Your present frame of government, secures to you a right to hold yourselves, houses, papers and possessions free from search and seizure, and therefore warrants granted without oaths or affirmations first made, affording sufficient foundation for them, whereby any officer or messenger may be commanded or required to search your houses or seize your persons or property, not particularly described in such warrant, shall not be granted. Your constitution further provides "that in controversies respecting property, and in suits between man and man, the parties have a right *to trial by jury, which ought to be held sacred.*" It also provides and declares, *"that the people have a right of* FREEDOM OF SPEECH, *and of* WRITING *and* PUBLISHING *their sentiments, therefore* THE FREEDOM OF THE PRESS OUGHT NOT TO BE RESTRAINED. The constitution of Pennsylvania is *yet* in existence, *as yet* you have the right to *freedom of speech*, and of *publishing your sentiments.* How long those rights will appertain to you, you yourselves are called upon to say, whether your *houses* shall continue to be your *castles;* whether your *papers*, your *persons* and your *property*, are to be held sacred and free from *general warrants*, you are now to determine. Whether the *trial by jury* is to continue as your birth-right, the freemen of Pennsylvania, nay, of all America, are now called upon to declare.
   Without presuming upon my own judgement, I cannot think it an unwarrantable presumption to offer my private opinion, and call upon

others for their's; and if I use my pen with the boldness of a freeman, it is because I know that *the liberty of the press yet remains unviolated,* and *juries yet are judges.*

The late Convention have submitted to your consideration a plan of a new federal government—The subject is highly interesting to your future welfare—Whether it be calculated to promote the great ends of civil society, *viz.* the happiness and prosperity of the community; it behoves you well to consider, uninfluenced by the authority of names. Instead of that frenzy of enthusiasm, that has actuated the citizens of Philadelphia, in their approbation of the proposed plan, before it was possible that it could be the result of a rational investigation into its principles; it ought to be dispassionately and deliberately examined, and its own intrinsic merit the only criterion of your patronage. If ever free and unbiassed discussion was proper or necessary, it is on such an occasion.—All the blessings of liberty and the dearest privileges of free-men, are now at stake and dependent on your present conduct. Those who are competent to the task of developing the principles of govern-ment, ought to be encouraged to come forward, and thereby the better enable the people to make a proper judgment; for the science of gov-ernment is so abstruse, that few are able to judge for themselves; without such assistance the people are too apt to yield an implicit assent to the opinions of those characters, whose abilities are held in the highest esteem, and to those in whose integrity and patriotism they can confide; not considering that the love of domination is generally in proportion to talents, abilities, and superior acquirements; and that the men of the greatest purity of intention may be made instruments of despotism in the hands of the *artful and designing.* If it were not for the stability and attachment which time and habit gives to forms of government, it would be in the power of the enlightened and aspiring few, if they should combine, at any time to destroy the best establishments, and even make the people the instruments of their own subjugation.

The late revolution having effaced in a great measure all former habits, and the present institutions are so recent, that there exists not that great reluctance to innovation, so remarkable in old communities, and which accords with reason, for the most comprehensive mind cannot foresee the full operation of material changes on civil polity; it is the genius of the common law to resist innovation.

The wealthy and ambitious, who in every community think they have a right to lord it over their fellow creatures, have availed them-selves, very successfully, of this favorable disposition; for the people thus unsettled in their sentiments, have been prepared to accede to any extreme of government; all the distresses and difficulties they experience, proceeding from various causes, have been ascribed to the impotency of the present confederation, and thence they have been led to expect full relief from the adoption of the proposed system of government; and in the other event, immediately ruin and annihilation as a nation. These characters flatter themselves that they have lulled all distrust and jealousy of their new plan, by gaining the concurrence of the two men in whom America has the highest confidence, and now triumphantly exult in the completion of their long meditated schemes of power and aggrandisement. I would be very far from insinuating that the two illustrious personages alluded to, have not the welfare of their country at heart; but that the unsuspecting goodness and zeal of the one, has been imposed on, in a subject of which he must be necessarily inexperienced, from his other arduous engagements; and that the weakness and indecision attendant on old age, has been practised on in the other.

I am fearful that the principles of government inculcated in Mr. Adam's treatise, and enforced in the numerous essays and paragraphs in the newspapers, have misled some well designing members of the late Convention.—But it will appear in the sequel, that the construction of the proposed plan of government is infinitely more extravagant.

I have been anxiously expecting that some enlightened patriot would, ere this, have taken up the pen to expose the futility, and counteract the baneful tendency of such principles. Mr. Adams's *sine qua non* of a good government is three balancing powers, whose repelling qualities are to produce an equilibrium of interests, and thereby promote the happiness of the whole community. He asserts that the administrators of every government, will ever be actuated by views of private interest and ambition, to the prejudice of the public good; that therefore the only effectual method to secure the rights of the people and promote their welfare, is to create an opposition of interests betweeen the members of two distinct bodies, in the exercise of the powers of government, and balanced by those of a third. This hypothesis supposes human wisdom competent to the task of instituting three co-equal orders in government, and a corresponding weight in the community to enable them respectively to exercise their several parts, and whose views and interests should be so distinct as to prevent a coalition of any two of them for the destruction of the third. Mr. Adams, although he has traced the constitution of every form of government that ever existed, as far as history affords materials, has not been able to adduce a single instance of such a government; he indeed says that the British constitution is such in theory, but this is rather a confirmation that his principles are chimerical and not to be reduced to practice. If such an organization of power were practicable, how long would it continue? not a day—for there is so great a disparity in the talents, wisdom and industry of mankind, that the scale would presently preponderate to one or the other body, and with every accession of power the means of further increase would be greatly extended. The state of society in England is much more favorable to such a scheme of government than that of America. There they have a powerful hereditary nobility, and real distinctions of rank and interests; but even there, for want of that perfect equallity of power and distinction of interests, in the three orders of government, they exist but in name; the only operative and efficient check, upon the conduct of administration, is the sense of the people at large.

Suppose a government could be formed and supported on such principles, would it answer the great purposes of civil society; if the administrators of every government are actuated by views of private interest and ambition, how is the welfare and happiness of the community to be the result of such jarring adverse interests?

Therefore, as different orders in government will not produce the good of the whole, we must recur to other principles. I believe it will be found that the form of government, which holds those entrusted with power, in the greatest responsibility to their constituents, the best calculated for freemen. A republican, or free government, can only exist where the body of the people are virtuous, and where property is pretty equally divided[;] in such a government the people are the sovereign and their sense or opinion is the criterion of every public measure; for when this ceases to be the case, the nature of the government is changed, and an aristocracy, monarchy or despotism will rise on its ruin. The highest responsibility is to be attained, in a simple structure of government, for the great body of the people never steadily attend to the operations of government, and for want of due information are liable to be imposed on.—If you complicate the plan by various orders, the people will be perplexed and divided in their sentiments about the source of abuses or misconduct, some will impute it to the senate, others to the house of representatives, and so on, that the interposition of the people may be rendered imperfect or perhaps wholly abortive. But if, imitating the constitution of Pennsylvania, you vest all the legislative power in one body of men (separating the executive and judicial) elected for a short period, and necessarily excluded by rotation from permanency, and guarded from precipitancy and surprise by delays imposed on its proceedings, you will create the most perfect responsibility for then, whenever the people feel a grievance they cannot mistake the authors, and will apply the remedy with certainty and effect, discarding them at the next election. This tie of responsibility will obviate all the dangers apprehended from a single legislature, and will the best secure the rights of the people. . . .

Brutus No. 1

New York Journal
October 18, 1787

To the Citizens of the State of New-York

When the public is called to investigate and decide upon a question in which not only the present members of the community are deeply interested, but upon which the happiness and misery of generations yet unborn is in great measure suspended, the benevolent mind cannot help feeling itself peculiarly interested in the result.

In this situation, I trust the feeble efforts of an individual, to lead the minds of a people to a wise and prudent determination, cannot fail of being acceptable to the candid and dispassionate part of the community. Encouraged by this consideration, I have been induced to offer my thoughts upon the present important crisis of our public affairs.

Perhaps this country never saw so critical a period in their political concerns. We have felt the feebleness of the ties by which these United-States are held together, and the want of sufficient energy in our present confederation, to manage, in some instances, our general concerns. Various expedients have been proposed to remedy these evils, but none have succeeded. At length a Convention of the states has been assembled, they have formed a constitution which will now, probably, be submitted to the people to ratify or reject, who are the fountain of all power, to whom alone it of right belongs to make or unmake constitutions, or forms of government, at their pleasure. The most important question that was ever proposed to your decision, or to the decision of any people under heaven, is before you, and you are to decide upon it by mean of your own election, chosen specially for this purpose. If the constitution, offered to your acceptance, be a wise one, calculated to preserve the invaluable blessings of liberty, to secure the inestimable rights of mankind, and promote human happiness, then, if you accept it, you will lay a lasting foundation of happiness for millions yet unborn; generations to come will rise up and call you blessed. You may rejoice in the prospects of this vast extended continent becoming filled with freemen, who will assert the dignity of human nature. You may solace yourselves with the idea, that society, in this favoured land, will fast advance to the highest point of perfection; the human mind will expand in knowledge and virtue, and the golden age be, in some measure, realised. But if, on the other hand, this form of government contains principles that will lead to the subversion of liberty—if it tends to establish a despotism, or, what is worse, a tyrannic aristocracy; then, if you adopt it, this only remaining assylum for liberty will be shut up, and posterity will execrate your memory.

Momentous then is the question you have to determine, and you are called upon by every motive which should influence a noble and virtuous mind, to examine it well, and to make up a wise judgment. It is insisted, indeed, that this constitution must be received, be it ever so imperfect. If it has its defects, it is said, they can be best amended when they are experienced. But remember, when the people once part with power, they can seldom or never resume it again but by force. Many instances can be produced in which the people have voluntarily increased the powers of their rulers; but few, if any, in which rulers have willingly abridged their authority. This is sufficient reason to induce you to be careful, in the first instance, how you deposit the powers of government.

With these few introductory remarks, I shall proceed to a consideration of this constitution:

The first question that presents itself on the subject is, whether a confederated government be the best for the United States or not? Or in other words, whether the thirteen United States should be reduced to one great republic, governed by one legislature, and under the direction of one executive and judicial; or whether they should continue thirteen confederated republics, under the direction and controul of a supreme federal head for certain defined national purposes only?

This enquiry is important, because, although the government reported by the convention does not go to a perfect and entire consolidation, yet it approaches so near to it, that it must, if executed, certainly and infallibly terminate in it.

This government is to possess absolute and uncontroulable power, legislative, executive and judicial, with respect to every object to which it extends, for by the last clause of section 8th, article 1st, it is declared "that the Congress shall have power to make all laws which shall be necessary and proper for carrying into execution the foregoing powers, and all other powers vested by this constitution, in the government of the United States; or in any department or office thereof." And by the 6th article, it is declared "that this constitution, and the laws of the United States, which shall be made in pursuance thereof, and the treaties made, or which shall be made, under the authority of the United States, shall be the supreme law of the land; and the judges in every state shall be bound thereby, any thing in the constitution, or law of any state to the contrary notwithstanding." It appears from these articles that there is no need of any intervention of the state governments, between the Congress and the people, to execute any one power vested in the general government, and that the constitution and laws of every state are nullified and declared void, so far as they are or shall be inconsistent with this constitution, or the laws made in pursuance of it, or with treaties made under the authority of the United States.—The government then, so far as it extends, is a complete one, and not a confederation. It is as much one complete government as that of New-York or Massachusetts, has as absolute and perfect powers to make and execute all laws, to appoint officers, institute courts, declare offences, and annex penalties, with respect to every object to which it extends, as any other in the world. So far therefore as its powers reach, all ideas of confederation are given up and lost. It is true this government is limited to certain objects, or to speak more properly, some small degree of power is still left to the states, but a little attention to the powers vested in the general government, will convince every candid man, that if it is capable of being executed, all that is reserved for the individual states must very soon be annihilated, except so far as they are barely necessary to the organization of the general government. The powers of the general legislature extend to every case that is of the least importance—there is nothing valuable to human nature, nothing dear to freemen, but what is within its power. It has authority to make laws which will affect the lives, the liberty, and property of every man in the United States; nor can the constitution or laws of any state, in any way prevent or impede the full and complete execution of every power given. The legislative power is competent to lay taxes, duties, imposts, and excises;—there is no limitation to this power, unless it be said that the clause which directs the use to which those taxes, and duties shall be applied, may be said to be a limitation; but this is no restriction of the power at all, for by this clause they are to be applied to pay the debts and provide for the common defence and general welfare of the United States; but the legislature have authority to contract debts at their discretion; they are the sole judges of what is necessary to provide for the common defence, and they only are to determine what is for the general welfare; this power therefore is neither more nor less, than a power to lay and collect taxes, imposts, and excises, at their pleasure; not only [is] the power to lay taxes unlimited, as to the amount they may require, but it is perfect and absolute to raise them in any mode they please. No state legislature, or any power in the state governments, have any more to do in carrying this into effect, than the authority of one state has to do with that of another. In the business therefore of laying and collecting taxes, the idea of confederation is totally lost, and that of one entire republic is embraced. It is proper here to remark, that the authority to lay and collect taxes is the most important of any power that can be granted; it connects with it almost all other powers, or at least will in process of time draw all other after it; it is the great mean of protection, security, and defence, in a good government, and the great engine of oppression and tyranny in a bad one. This cannot fail of being the case, if we consider the contracted limits which are set by this constitution, to the late governments, on this article of raising money. No state can emit paper money—lay any duties, or imposts, on imports, or exports, but by consent of the Congress; and then the net produce shall be for the benefit of the United States: the only mean therefore left, for any state to support its government and discharge its debts, is by direct taxation; and the United States have also power to lay and collect taxes, in any way they please. Every one who has thought on the subject, must be convinced that but small sums of money can be collected in any country, but direct taxe[s], when the fœderal government begins to exercise the right of taxation in all its parts, the legislatures of the several states will find it impossible to raise monies to support their governments. Without money they cannot be supported, and they must dwindle away, and, as before observed, their powers absorbed in that of the general government.

It might be here shewn, that the power in the federal legislative, to raise and support armies at pleasure, as well in peace as in war, and their controul over the militia, tend, not only to a consolidation of the government, but the destruction of liberty.—I shall not, however, dwell upon these, as a few observations upon the judicial power of this government, in addition to the preceding, will fully evince the truth of the position.

The judicial power of the United States is to be vested in a supreme court, and in such inferior courts as Congress may from time to time ordain and establish. The powers of these courts are very extensive; their jurisdiction comprehends all civil causes, except such as arise between citizens of the same state; and it extends to all cases in law and equity arising under the constitution. One inferior court must be established, I presume, in each state, at least, with the necessary executive officers appendant thereto. It is easy to see, that in the common course of things, these courts will eclipse the dignity, and take away from the respectability, of the state courts. These courts will be, in themselves, totally independent of the states, deriving their authority from the United States, and receiving from them fixed salaries; and in the course of human events it is to be expected, that they will swallow up all the powers of the courts in the respective states.

How far the clause in the 8th section of the 1st article may operate to do away all idea of confederated states, and to effect an entire consolidation of the whole into one general government, it is impossible to say. The powers given by this article are very general and comprehensive, and it may receive a construction to justify the passing almost any law. A power to make all laws, which shall be *necessary and proper,* for carrying into execution, all powers vested by the constitution in the government of the United States, or any department or officer thereof, is a power very comprehensive and definite [indefinite?], and may, for ought I know, be exercised in a such manner as entirely to abolish the state legislatures. Suppose the legislature of a state should pass a law to raise money to support their government and pay the state debt, may the Congress repeal this law, because it may prevent the collection of a tax which they may think proper and necessary to lay, to provide for the general welfare of the United States? For all laws made, in pursuance of this constitution, are the supreme law of the land, and the judges in every state shall be bound thereby, any thing in the constitution or laws of the different states to the contrary notwithstanding.— By such a law, the government of a particular state might be overturned at one stroke, and thereby be deprived of every means of its support.

It is not meant, by stating this case, to insinuate that the constitution would warrant a law of this kind; or unnecessarily to alarm the fears of the people, by suggesting, that the federal legislature would be more likely to pass the limits assigned them by the constitution, than that of an individual state, further than they are less responsible to the people. But what is meant is, that the legislature of the United States are vested with the great and uncontroulable powers, of laying and collecting taxes, duties, imposts, and excises; of regulating trade, raising and supporting armies, organizing, arming, and disciplining the militia, instituting courts, and other general powers. And are by this clause invested with the power of making all laws, *proper and necessary,* for carrying all these into execution; and they may so exercise this power as entirely to annihilate all the state governments, and reduce this country to one single government. And if they may do it, it is pretty certain they will; for it will be found that the power retained by individual states, small as it is, will be a clog upon the wheels of the government of the United States; the latter therefore will be naturally inclined to remove it out of the way. Besides, it is a truth confirmed by the unerring experience of ages, that every man, and every body of men, invested with power, are ever disposed to increase it, and to acquire a superiority over every thing that stands in their way. This disposition, which is implanted in human nature, will operate in the federal legislature to lessen and ultimately to subvert the state authority, and having such advantages, will most certainly succeed, if the federal government succeeds at all. It must be very evident then, that what this constitution wants of being a complete consolidation of the several parts of the union into one complete government, possessed of perfect legislative, judicial, and executive powers, to all intents and purposes, it will necessarily acquire in its exercise and operation.

Let us now proceed to enquire, as I at first proposed, whether it be best the thirteen United States should be reduced to one great republic, or not? It is here taken for granted, that all agree in this, that whatever government we adopt, it ought to be a free one; that it should be so framed as to secure the liberty of the citizens of America, and such an one as to admit of a full, fair, and equal representation of the people. The question then will be, whether a government thus constituted, and founded on such principles, is practicable, and can be exercised over the whole United States, reduced into one state?

If respect is to be paid to the opinion of the greatest and wisest men who have ever thought or wrote on the science of government, we shall be constrained to conclude, that a free republic cannot succeed over a country of such immense extent, containing such a number of inhabitants, and these encreasing in such rapid progression as that of the whole United States. Among the many illustrious authorities which might be produced to this point, I shall content myself with quoting only two. The one is the baron de Montesquieu, spirit of laws, chap. xvi. vol. I [book VIII]. "It is natural to a republic to have only a small territory, otherwise it cannot long subsist. In a large republic there are men of large fortunes, and consequently of less moderation; there are trusts too great to be placed in any single subject; he has interest of his own; he soon begins to think that he may be happy, great and glorious, by oppressing his fellow citizens; and that he may raise himself to grandeur on the ruins of his country. In a large republic, the public good is sacrificed to a thousand views; it is subordinate to exceptions, and depends on accidents. In a small one, the interest of the public is easier perceived, better understood, and more within the reach of every citizen; abuses are of less extent, and of course are less protected." Of the same opinion is the marquis Beccarari.

History furnishes no example of a free republic, any thing like the extent of the United States. The Grecian republics were of small extent; so also was that of the Romans. Both of these, it is true, in process of time, extended their conquests over large territories of country; and the consequence was, that their governments were changed from that of free governments to those of the most tyrannical that ever existed in the world.

Not only the opinion of the greatest men, and the experience of mankind, are against the idea of an extensive republic, but a variety of reasons may be drawn from the reason and nature of things, against it. In every government, the will of the sovereign is the law. In despotic governments, the supreme authority being lodged in one, his will is law, and can be as easily expressed to a large extensive territory as to a small one. In a pure democracy the people are the sovereign, and their will is declared by themselves; for this purpose they must all come together to deliberate, and decide. This kind of government cannot be exercised, therefore, over a country of any considerable extent; it must be confined to a single city, or at least limited to such bounds as that the people can conveniently assemble, be able to debate, understand the subject submitted to them, and declare their opinion concerning it.

In a free republic, although all laws are derived from the consent of the people, yet the people do not declare their consent by themselves in person, but by representatives, chosen by them, who are supposed to know the minds of their constituents, and to be possessed of integrity to declare this mind.

In every free government, the people must give their assent to the laws by which they are governed. This is the true criterion between a free government and an arbitrary one. The former are ruled by the will of the whole, expressed in any manner they may agree upon; the latter by the will of one, or a few. If the people are to give their assent to the laws, by persons chosen and appointed by them, the manner of the choice and the number chosen, must be such, as to possess, be disposed, and consequently qualified to declare the sentiments of the people; for if they do not know, or are not disposed to speak the sentiments of the people, the people do not govern, but the sovereignty is in a few. Now, in a large extended country, it is impossible to have a representation, possessing the sentiments, and of integrity, to declare the minds of the people, without having it so numerous and unwieldly, as to be subject in great measure to the inconveniency of a democratic government.

The territory of the United States is of vast extent; it now contains near three millions of souls, and is capable of containing much more than ten times that number. Is it practicable for a country, so large and so numerous as they will soon become, to elect a representation, that will speak their sentiments, without their becoming so numerous as to be incapable of transacting public interests? It certainly is not.

In a republic, sentiments, and interests of the people should be similar. If this be not the case, there will be a constant clashing of opinions; and the representatives of one part will be continually striving against those of the other. This will retard the operations of government, and prevent such conclusions as will promote the public good. If we apply this remark to the condition of the United States, we shall be convinced that it forbids that we should be one government. The United States includes a variety of climates. The productions of the different parts of the union are very variant, and their interests, of consequence, diverse. Their manners and habits differ as much as their climates and productions; and their sentiments are by no means coincident. The laws and customs of the several states are, in many respects, very diverse, and in some opposite; each would be in favor of its own interests and customs and, of consequence, a legislature, formed of representatives from the respective parts, would not only be too numerous to act with any care or decision, but would be composed of such heterogenous and discordant principles, as would constantly be contending with each other.

The laws cannot be executed in a republic, of an extent equal to that of the United States, with promptitude.

The magistrates in every government must be supported in the execution of the laws, either by an armed force, maintained at the public expence for that purpose; or by the people turning out to aid the magistrate upon his command, in case of resistance.

In despotic governments, as well as in all the monarchies of Europe, standing armies are kept up to execute the commands of the prince or the magistrate, and are employed for this purpose when occasion requires: But they have always proved the destruction of liberty, and [are] abhorrent to the spirit of a free republic. In England, where they depend upon the parliament for their annual support, they have always been complained of as oppressive and unconstitutional, and are seldom employed in executing of the laws; never except on extraordinary occasions, and then under the direction of a civil magistrate.

A free republic will never keep a standing army to execute its laws. It must depend upon the support of its citizens. But when a government is to receive its support from the aid of the citizens, it must be so constructed as to have the confidence, respect, and affection of the people. Men who, upon the call of the magistrate, offer themselves to execute the laws, are influenced to do it either by affection to the government, or from fear; where a standing army is at hand to punish offenders, every man is actuated by the latter principle, and therefore, when the magistrate calls, will obey; but, where this is not the case, the government must rest for its support upon the confidence and respect which the people have for their government and laws. The body of the people being attached, the government will always be sufficient to support and execute its laws, and to operate upon the fears of any faction which may be opposed to it, not only to prevent an opposition to the execution of the laws themselves, but also to compel the most of them to aid the magistrate; but the people will not be likely to have such confidence in their rulers, in a republic so extensive as the United States, as necessary for these purposes. The confidence which the people have in their rulers, in a free republic, arises from their knowing them, from their being responsible to them for their conduct, and from the power they have of displacing them when they misbehave; but in a republic of the extent of this continent, the people in general would be acquainted with very few of their rulers: the people at large would know little of their proceedings, and it would be extremely difficult to change them. The people of Georgia and New-Hampshire would not know one another's mind, and therefore could not act in concert to enable them to effect a general change of representatives. The different parts of so extensive a country could not possibly be made acquainted with the conduct of their representatives, nor be informed of the reasons upon which measures were founded. The consequence will be, they will have no confidence in their legislature, suspect them of ambitious views, be jealous of every measure they adopt, and will not support the laws they pass. Hence the government will be nerveless and inefficient, and no way will be left to render it otherwise, but by establishing an armed force to execute the laws at the point of the bayonet—a government of all others the most to be dreaded.

In a republic of such vast extent as the United-States, the legislature cannot attend to the various concerns and wants of its different parts. It cannot be sufficiently numerous to be acquainted with the local condition and wants of the different districts, and if it could, it is impossible it should have sufficient time to attend to and provide for all the variety of cases of this nature, that would be continually arising.

In so extensive a republic, the great officers of government would soon become above the controul of the people, and abuse their power to the purpose of aggrandizing themselves, and oppressing them. The

trust committed to the executive offices, in a country of the extent of
the United-States, must be various and of magnitude. The command
of all troops and navy of the republic, the appointment of officers, the
power of pardoning offences, the collecting of all the public revenues,
and the power of expending them, with a number of other powers, must
be lodged and exercised in every state, in the hands of a few. When
these are attended with great honor and emolument, as they always
will be in large states, so as greatly to interest men to pursue them,
and to be proper objects for ambitious and designing men, such men
will be ever restless in their pursuit after them. They will use the power,
when they have acquired it, to the purposes of gratifying their own
interest and ambition, and it is scarcely possible, in a very large republic,
to call them to account for their misconduct, or to prevent their abuse
of power.

These are some of the reasons by which it appears, that a free
republic cannot long subsist over a country of the great extent of these
states. If then this new constitution is calculated to consolidate the
thirteen states into one, as it evidently is, it ought not to be adopted.

Though I am of opinion, that it is a sufficient objection to this
government, to reject it, that it creates the whole union into one government, under the form of a republic, yet if this objection was obviated,
there are exceptions to it, which are so material and fundamental, that
they ought to determine every man, who is a friend to the liberty and
happiness of mankind, not to adopt it. I beg the candid and dispassionate
attention of my countrymen while I state these objections—they are
such as have obtruded themselves upon my mind upon a careful attention to the matter, and such as I sincerely believe are well founded.
There are many objections, of small moment, of which I shall take no
notice—perfection is not to be expected in any thing that is the production of man—and if I did not in my conscience believe that this
scheme was defective in the fundamental principles—in the foundation
upon which a free and equal government must rest—I would hold my
peace.

Brutus.

Brutus No. 15

New York Journal,
March 20, 1788

I said in my last number, that the supreme court under this constitution would be exalted above all power in the government, and subject to no controul. The business of this paper will be to illustrate this, and to shew the danger that will result from it. I question whether the world ever saw, in any period of it, a court of justice invested with such immense powers, and yet placed in a situation so little responsible. Certain it is, that in England, and in the several states, where we have been taught to believe, the courts of law are put upon the most prudent establishment, they are on a very different footing.

The judges in England, it is true, hold their offices during their good behaviour, but then their determinations are subject to correction by the house of lords; and their power is by no means so extensive as that of the proposed supreme court of the union.—I believe they in no instance assume the authority to set aside an act of parliament under the idea that it is inconsistent with their constitution. They consider themselves bound to decide according to the existing laws of the land, and never undertake to controul them by adjudging that they are inconsistent with the constitution—much less are they vested with the power of giving an *equitable* construction to the constitution.

The judges in England are under the controul of the legislature, for they are bound to determine according to the laws passed by them. But the judges under this constitution will controul the legislature, for the supreme court are authorised in the last resort, to determine what is the extent of the powers of the Congress; they are to give the constitution an explanation, and there is no power above them to set aside their judgment. The framers of this constitution appear to have followed that of the British, in rendering the judges independent, by granting them their offices during good behaviour, without following the constitution of England, in instituting a tribunal in which their errors may be corrected; and without adverting to this, that the judicial under this system have a power which is above the legislative, and which indeed transcends any power given to a judicial by any free government under heaven.

I do not object to the judges holding their commissions during good behaviour. I suppose it a proper provision provided they were made properly responsible. But I say, this system has followed the English government in this, while it has departed from almost every other principle of their jurisprudence, under the idea, of rendering the judges independent; which, in the British constitution, means no more than that they hold their places during good behaviour, and have fixed salaries, they have made the judges *independent*, in the fullest sense of the word. There is no power above them, to controul any of their decisions. There is no authority that can remove them, and they cannot be controuled by the laws of the legislature. In short, they are independent of the people, of the legislature, and of every power under heaven. Men placed in this situation will generally soon feel themselves independent of heaven itself. Before I proceed to illustrate the truth of these assertions, I beg liberty to make one remark—Though in my opinion the judges ought to hold their offices during good behaviour, yet I think it is clear, that the reasons in favour of this establishment of the judges in England, do by no means apply to this country.

The great reason assigned, why the judges in Britain ought to be commissioned during good behaviour, is this, that they may be placed in a situation, not to be influenced by the crown, to give such decisions, as would tend to increase its powers and prerogatives. While the judges held their places at the will and pleasure of the king, on whom they depended not only for their offices, but also for their salaries, they were subject to every undue influence. If the crown wished to carry a favorite point, to accomplish which the aid of the courts of law was necessary, the pleasure of the king would be signified to the judges. And it required the spirit of a martyr, for the judges to determine contrary to the king's will.—They were absolutely dependent upon him both for their offices and livings. The king, holding his office during life, and transmitting it to his posterity as an inheritance, has much stronger inducements to increase the prerogatives of his office than those who hold their offices for stated periods, or even for life. Hence the English nation gained a great point, in favour of liberty. When they obtained the appointment of the judges, during good behaviour, they got from the crown a concession, which deprived it of one of the most powerful engines with which it might enlarge the boundaries of the royal prerogative and encroach on the liberties of the people. But these reasons do not apply to this country, we have no hereditary monarch; those who appoint the judges do not hold their offices for life, nor do they descend to their children. The same arguments, therefore, which will conclude in favor of the tenor of the judge's offices for good behaviour, lose a considerable part of their weight when applied to the state and condition of America. But much less can it be shewn, that the nature of our government requires that the courts should be placed beyond all account more independent, so much so as to be above controul.

I have said that the judges under this system will be *independent* in the strict sense of the word: To prove this I will shew—That there is no power above them that can controul their decisions, or correct their errors. There is no authority that can remove them from office for any errors or want of capacity, or lower their salaries, and in many cases their power is superior to that of the legislature.

1st. There is no power above them that can correct their errors or controul their decisions.—The adjudications of this court are final and irreversible, for there is no court above them to which appeals can lie, either in error or on the merits.—In this respect it differs from the courts in England, for there the house of lords is the highest court, to whom appeals, in error, are carried from the highest of the courts of law.

2d. They cannot be removed from office or suffer a dimunition of their salaries, for any error in judgement or want of capacity.

It is expressly declared by the constitution,—"That they shall at stated times receive a compensation for their services which shall not be diminished during their continuance in office."

The only clause in the constitution which provides for the removal of the judges from office, is that which declares, that "the president, vice-president, and all civil officers of the United States, shall be re-moved from office, on impeachment for, and conviction of treason, brib-ery, or other high crimes and misdemeanors." By this paragraph, civil officers, in which the judges are included, are removable only for crimes. Treason and bribery are named, and the rest are included under the general terms of high crimes and misdemeanors.—Errors in judgement, or want of capacity to discharge the duties of the office, can never be supposed to be included in these words, *high crimes and misdemeanors.* A man may mistake a case in giving judgment, or manifest that he is incompetent to the discharge of the duties of a judge, and yet give no evidence of corruption or want of integrity. To support the charge, it will be necessary to give in evidence some facts that will shew, that the judges committed the error from wicked and corrupt motives.

3d. The power of this court is in many cases superior to that of the legislature. I have shewed, in a former paper, that this court will be authorised to decide upon the meaning of the constitution, and that, not only according to the natural and ob[vious] meaning of the words, but also according to the spirit and intention of it. In the exercise of this power they will not be subordinate to, but above the legislature.

For all the departments of this government will receive their powers, so far as they are expressed in the constitution, from the people immediately, who are the source of power. The legislature can only exercise such powers as are given them by the constitution, they cannot assume any of the rights annexed to the judicial, for this plain reason, that the same authority which vested the legislature with their powers, vested the judicial with theirs—both are derived from the same source, both therefore are equally valid, and the judicial hold their powers independently of the legislature, as the legislature do of the judicial.— The supreme court then have a right, independent of the legislature, to give a construction to the constitution and every part of it, and there is no power provided in this system to correct their construction or do it away. If, therefore, the legislature pass any laws, inconsistent with the sense the judges put upon the constitution, they will declare it void; and therefore in this respect their power is superior to that of the legislature. In England the judges are not only subject to have their decisions set aside by the house of lords, for error, but in cases where they give an explanation to the laws or constitution of the country, contrary to the sense of the parliament, though the parliament will not set aside the judgment of the court, yet, they have authority, by a new law, to explain a former one, and by this means to prevent a reception of such decisions. But no such power is in the legislature. The judges are supreme—and no law, explanatory of the constitution, will be binding on them.

From the preceding remarks, which have been made on the judicial powers proposed in this system, the policy of it may be fully developed.

I have, in the course of my observation on this constitution, affirmed and endeavored to shew, that it was calculated to abolish entirely the state governments, and to melt down the states into one entire government, for every purpose as well internal and local, as external and national. In this opinion the opposers of the system have generally agreed—and this has been uniformly denied by its advocates in public. Some individuals, indeed, among them, will confess, that it has this tendency, and scruple not to say, it is what they wish; and I will venture to predict, without the spirit of prophecy, that if it is adopted without amendments, or some such precautions as will ensure amendments immediately after its adoption, that the same gentlemen who have employed their talents and abilities with such success to influence the public mind to adopt this plan, will employ the same to persuade the people, that it will be for their good to abolish the state governments as useless and burdensome.

Perhaps nothing could have been better conceived to facilitate the abolition of the state governments than the constitution of the judicial.

They will be able to extend the limits of the general government gradually, and by insensible degrees, and to accommodate themselves to the temper of the people. Their decisions on the meaning of the constitution will commonly take place in cases which arise between individuals, with which the public will not be generally acquainted; one adjudication will form a precedent to the next, and this to a following one. These cases will immediately affect individuals only; so that a series of determinations will probably take place before even the people will be informed of them. In the mean time all the art and address of those who wish for the change will be employed to make converts to their opinion. The people will be told, that their state officers, and state legislatures are a burden and expence without affording any solid advantage, for that all the laws passed by them, might be equally well made by the general legislature. If to those who will be interested in the change, be added, those who will be under their influence, and such who will submit to almost any change of government, which they can be persuaded to believe will ease them of taxes, it is easy to see, the party who will favor the abolition of the state governments would be far from being inconsiderable.—In this situation, the general legislature, might pass one law after another, extending the general and abridging the state jurisdictions, and to sanction their proceedings would have a course of decisions of the judicial to whom the constitution has committed the power of explaining the constitution.—If the states remonstrated, the constitutional mode of deciding upon the validity of the law, is with the supreme court, and neither people, nor state legislatures, nor the general legislature can remove them or reverse their decrees.

Had the construction of the constitution been left with the legislature, they would have explained it at their peril; if they exceed their powers, or sought to find, in the spirit of the constitution, more than was expressed in the letter, the people from whom they derived their power could remove them, and do themselves right; and indeed I can see no other remedy that the people can have against their rulers for encroachments of this nature. A constitution is a compact of people with their rulers; if the rulers break the compact, the people have a right and ought to remove them and do themselves justice; but in order to enable them to do this with the greater facility, those whom the people chuse at stated periods, should have the power in the last resort to determine the sense of the compact; if they determine contrary to the understanding of the people, an appeal will lie to the people at the period when the rulers are to be elected, and they will have it in their power to remedy the evil; but when this power is lodged in the hands

of men independent of the people, and of their representatives, and
who are not, constitutionally, accountable for their opinions, no way is
left to controul them but *with a high hand and an outstretched arm.*

Brutus.

Melancton Smith
Speech in New York
Ratifying Convention

JUNE 21, 1788

. . . The idea that naturally suggests itself to our minds, when we speak
of representatives is, that they resemble those they represent; they
should be a true picture of the people; possess the knowledge of their
circumstances and their wants; sympathize in all their distresses, and
be disposed to seek their true interests. The knowledge necessary for
the representatives of a free people, not only comprehends extensive
political and commercial information, such as is acquired by men of
refined eduction, who have leisure to attain to high degrees of improvement, but it should also comprehend that kind of acquaintance with
the common concerns and occupations of the people, which men of the
middling class of life are in general much better competent to, than
those of a superior class. To understand the true commercial interests
of a country, not only requires just ideas of the general commerce of
the world, but also, and principally, a knowledge of the productions of
your own country and their value, what your soil is capable of producing[,] the nature of your manufactures, and the capacity of the
country to increase both. To exercise the power of laying taxes, duties
and excises with discretion, requires something more than an acquaintance with the abstruse parts of the system of finance. It calls for a
knowledge of the circumstances and ability of the people in general, a
discernment how the burdens imposed will bear upon the different
classes.

From these observations results this conclusion that the number of representatives should be so large, as that while it embraces men of the first class, it should admit those of the middling class of life. I am convinced that this Government is so constituted, that the representatives will generally be composed of the first class in the community, which I shall distinguish by the name of the natural aristocracy of the country. I do not mean to give offence by using this term. I am sensible this idea is treated by many gentlemen as chimerical. I shall be asked what is meant by the natural aristocracy—and told that no such distinction of classes of men exists among us. It is true it is our singular felicity that we have no legal or hereditary distinctions of this kind; but still there are real differences: Every society naturally divides itself into classes. The author of nature has bestowed on some greater capacities than on others—birth, education, talents and wealth, create distinctions among men as visible and of as much influence as titles, stars and garters. In every society, men of this class will command a superior degree of respect—and if the government is so constituted as to admit but few to exercise the powers of it, it will, according to the natural course of things, be in their hands. Men in the middling class, who are qualified as representatives, will not be so anxious to be chosen as those of the first. When the number is so small the office will be highly elevated and distinguished—the stile in which the members live will probably be high—circumstances of this kind, will render the place of a representative not a desirable one to sensible, substantial men, who have been used to walk in the plain and frugal paths of life.

Besides, the influence of the great will generally enable them to succeed in elections—it will be difficult to combine a district of country containing 30 or 40,000 inhabitants, frame your election laws as you please, in any one character; unless it be in one of conspicuous, military, popular, civil or legal talents. The great easily form associations; the poor and middling class form them with difficulty. If the elections be by plurality, as probably will be the case in this state, it is almost certain, none but the great will be chosen—for they easily unite their interest— The common people will divide, and their divisions will be promoted by the others. There will be scarcely a chance of their uniting, in any other but some great man, unless in some popular demagogue, who will probably be destitute of principle. A substantial yeoman of sense and discernment, will hardly ever be chosen. From these remarks it appears that the government will fall into the hands of the few and the great. This will be a government of oppression. I do not mean to declaim against the great, and charge them indiscriminately with want of principle and honesty.—The same passions and prejudices govern all men.

The circumstances in which men are placed in a great measure give a cast to the human character. Those in middling circumstances, have less temptation—they are inclined by habit and the company with whom they associate, to set bounds to their passions and appetites—if this is not sufficient, the want of means to gratify them will be a restraint—they are obliged to employ their time in their respective callings—hence the substantial yeomanry of the country are more temperate, of better morals and less ambition than the great. The latter do not feel for the poor and middling class; the reasons are obvious—they are not obliged to use the pains and labour to procure property as the other.—They feel not the inconveniences arising from the payment of small sums. The great consider themselves above the common people—entitled to more respect—do not associate with them—they fancy themselves to have a right of pre-eminence in every thing. In short, they possess the same feelings, and are under the influence of the same motives, as an hereditary nobility. I know the idea that such a distinction exists in this country is ridiculed by some—But I am not the less apprehensive of danger from their influence on this account—Such distinctions exist all the world over—have been taken notice of by all writers on free government—and are founded in the nature of things. It has been the principal care of free governments to guard against the encroachments of the great. Common observation and experience prove the existence of such distinctions. Will any one say, that there does exist in this country the pride of family, of wealth, of talents; and that they do not command influence and respect among the common people? Congress, in their address to the inhabitants of the province of Quebec, in 1775, state this distinction in the following forcible words quoted from the Marquis Beccaria. "In every human society, there is an essay continually tending to confer on one part the height of power and happiness, and to reduce the other to the extreme of weakness and misery. The intent of good laws is to oppose this effort, and to diffuse their influence universally and equally." We ought to guard against the government being placed in the hands of this class—They cannot have that sympathy with their constituents which is necessary to connect them closely to their interest: Being in the habit of profuse living, they will be profuse in the public expenses. They find no difficulty in paying their taxes, and therefore do not feel public burthens: Besides if they govern, they will enjoy the emoluments of the government. The middling class, from their frugal habits, and feeling themselves the public burdens, will be careful how they increase them.

But I may be asked, would you exclude the first class in the community, from any share in legislation? I answer by no means—they would be more dangerous out of power than in it—they would be factious—discontented and constantly disturbing the government—it would also be unjust—they have their liberties to protect as well as others—and the largest share of property. But my idea is, that the Constitution should be so framed as to admit this class, together with a sufficient number of the middling class to controul them. You will then combine the abilities and honesty of the community—a proper degree of information, and a disposition to pursue the public good. A representative body, composed principally of respectable yeomanry is the best possible security to liberty.—When the interest of this part of the community is pursued, the public good is pursued; because the body of every nation consists of this class. And because the interest of both the rich and the poor are involved in that of the middling class. No burden can be laid on the poor, but what will sensibly affect the middling class. Any law rendering property insecure, would be injurious to them.—When therefore this class in society pursue their own interest, they promote that of the public, for it is involved in it.

In so small a number of representatives, there is great danger from corruption and combination. A great politician has said that every man has his price: I hope this is not true in all its extent—But I ask the gentlemen to inform, what government there is, in which it has not been practised? Notwithstanding all that has been said of the defects in the Constitution of the antient Confederacies of the Grecian Republics, their destruction is to be imputed more to this cause than to any imperfection in their forms of government. This was the deadly poison that effected their dissolution. This is an extensive country, increasing in population and growing in consequence. Very many lucrative offices will be in the grant of the government, which will be the object of avarice and ambition. How easy will it be to gain over a sufficient number, in the bestowment of these offices, to promote the views and purposes of those who grant them! Foreign corruption is also to be guarded against. A system of corruption is known to be the system of government in Europe. It is practised without blushing. And we may lay it to our account it will be attempted amongst us. The most effectual as well as natural security against this, is a strong democratic branch in the legislature frequently chosen, including in it a number of the substantial, sensible yeomanry of the country. Does the house of representatives answer this description? I confess, to me they hardly wear the complexion of a democratic branch—they appear the mere shadow of representation. The whole number in both houses amounts to 91—Of these 46 make a quorum; and 24 of those being secured, may carry any point. Can the liberties of three millions of people be securely trusted in the hands of 24 men? Is it prudent to commit to so small a number the decision of the great questions which will come before them? Reason revolts at the idea.

The honorable gentleman from New York has said that 65 members in the house of representatives are sufficient for the present situation of the country, and taking it for granted that they will increase as one for 30,000, in 25 years they will amount to 200. It is admitted by this observation that the number fixed in the Constitution, is not sufficient without it is augmented. It is not declared that an increase shall be made, but is left at the discretion of the legislature, by the gentleman's own concession; therefore the Constitution is imperfect. We certainly ought to fix in the Constitution those things which are essential to liberty. If any thing falls under this description, it is the number of the legislature. To say, as this gentleman does, that our security is to depend upon the spirit of the people, who will be watchful of their liberties, and not suffer them to be infringed, is absurd. It would equally prove that we might adopt any form of government. I believe were we to create a despot, he would not immediately dare to act the tyrant; but it would not be long before he would destroy the spirit of the people, or the people would destroy him. If our people have a high sense of liberty, the government should be congenial to this spirit—calculated to cherish the love of liberty, while yet it had sufficient force to restrain licentiousness. Government operates upon the spirit of the people, as well as the spirit of the people operates on it—and if they are not conformable to each other, the one or the other will prevail. In a less time than 25 years, the government will receive its tone. What the spirit of the country may be at the end of that period, it is impossible to foretell: Our duty is to frame a government friendly to liberty and the rights of mankind, which will tend to cherish and cultivate a love of liberty among our citizens. If this government becomes oppressive it will be by degrees: It will aim at its end by disseminating sentiments of government opposite to republicanism; and proceed from step to step in depriving the people of a share in the government. A recollection of the change that has taken place in the minds of many in this country in the course of a few years, ought to put us upon our guard. Many who are ardent advocates for the new system, reprobate republican principles as chimerical and such as ought to be expelled from society. Who would have thought ten years ago, that the very men who risqued their lives and fortunes in support of republican principles, would now treat them as the fictions of fancy?—A few years ago we fought for liberty—We framed a general government on free principles—We placed the state legislatures, in whom the people have a full and fair representation, between Congress and the people. We were then, it is true, too cautious; and too much restricted the powers of the general government. But now it is proposed to go into the contrary, and a more dangerous extreme; to remove all barriers; to give the New Government free access to our pockets, and ample command of our persons; and that without providing for a genuine and fair representation of the people. No one can say what the progress of the change of sentiment may be in 25 years. The same men who now cry up the necessity of an energetic government, to induce a compliance with this system, may in much less time reprobate this in as severe terms as they now do the confederation, and may as strongly urge the necessity of going as far beyond this, as this is beyond the Confederation.—Men of this class are increasing—they have influence, talents and industry.—It is time to form a barrier against them. And while we are willing to establish a government adequate to the purposes of the union, let us be careful to establish it on the broad basis of equal liberty.

Melancton Smith Speech in New York Ratifying Convention

JUNE 27, 1778

. . . Another idea is in my mind, which I think conclusive against a simple government for the United States. It is not possible to collect a set of representatives, who are acquainted with all parts of the continent. Can you find men in Georgia who are acquainted with the situation in New-Hampshire? who know what taxes will best suit the inhabitants; and how much they are able to bear? Can the best men make laws for a people of whom they are entirely ignorant? Sir, we have no reason to hold our state governments in contempt, or to suppose them incapable of acting wisely. I believe they have operated more beneficially than most people expected, who considered that those governments were erected in a time of war and confusion, when they were very liable to errors in their structure. It will be a matter of astonishment to all unprejudiced men hereafter, who shall reflect upon our situation, to observe to what a great degree good government has prevailed. It is true some bad laws have been passed in most of the states; but they arose more from the difficulty of the times, than from any want of honesty or wisdom. Perhaps there never was a government, which in the course of ten years did not do something to be repented of. As for Rhode-Island, I do not mean to justify her—She deserves to be condemned—If there were in the world but one example of political depravity, it would be her's: And no nation ever merited or suffered a more genuine infamy, than a wicked administration has attached to her character. Massachusetts also has been guilty of errors; and has lately been distracted by an internal convulsion. Great-Britain, notwithstanding her boasted constitution, has been a perpetual scene of revolutions and civil war—Her parliaments have been abolished; her kings have been banished and murdered. I assert that the majority of the governments in the union have operated better than any body had reason to expect: and that nothing but experience and habit is wanting, to give the state laws all the stability and wisdom necessary to make them respectable. If these things be true, I think we ought not to exchange our condition, with a hazard of losing our state constitutions. We all agree that a general government is necessary: But it ought not to go so far, as to destroy the authority of the members. We shall be unwise, to make a new experiment in so important a manner, without some known and sure grounds to go upon. The state constitutions should be the guardians of our domestic rights and interests; and should be both the support and the check of the federal government.

. . . Sir, has any country which has suffered distresses like ours, exhibited within a few years, more striking marks of improvement and prosperity? How its population has grown; How its agriculture, commerce and manufactures have been extended and improved! How many forests have been cut down; How many wastes have been cleared and cultivated; How many additions have been made to the extent and beauty of our towns and cities! I think our advancement has been rapid. In a few years, it is to be hoped, that we shall be relieved from our embarrassments; and unless new, calamities come upon us, shall be flourishing and happy. . . .

XVIII

The Bill of Rights

1791

COMMENTARY BY JOHN P. KAMINSKI
AND RICHARD B. BERNSTEIN

FROM 1763 TO 1788, AMERICANS DEBATED the nature of government and how best to preserve liberty. Never before or since has such a prolonged public debate on freedom occurred. Midway in this debate, most Americans agreed that their liberties could not be secure while they remained part of the British Empire. In declaring their independence, Americans solemnly expressed the importance of retaining rights when forming new governments. In June 1776, Virginia adopted a new state constitution prefaced by a declaration of rights that proclaimed "That all men are by nature equally free and independent, and have certain inherent rights, of which, when they enter into a state of society, they cannot by any compact, deprive or divest their posterity; namely, the enjoyment of life and liberty, with the means of acquiring and possessing property, and pursuing and obtaining happiness and safety." A month later, the Second Continental Congress, meeting in Philadelphia, adopted the Declaration of Independence, which pronounced "these truths to be self-evident, that all men are created equal, that they are endowed by their Creator with certain unalienable Rights, that among these are Life, Liberty and the pursuit of Happiness."

The mere declaration of independence and the sacredness of rights, however, did not guarantee liberty. Americans had to fight an eight-year war to obtain their independence from Great Britain. During that time, Americans adopted state constitutions which they believed would

secure their liberties. Most of these new constitutions gave an inordi-
nately large share of political power to state assemblies, while governors
and state senates retained little of their colonial authority. On the federal
level, Congress proposed and the states adopted the Articles of Confederation, which created a federal government with no independent
executive or judiciary and a single-house Congress with no power over
individuals. States—not people—were represented in Congress, and
Congress had only limited power over the states. Article II provided
that "Each state retains its sovereignty, freedom, and independence,
and every Power, Jurisdiction and right, which is not by this confederation expressly delegated to the United States, in Congress assembled."

Within ten years after declaring their independence, most Americans believed that the Articles of Confederation had failed. Without the
power to tax or enforce its own laws and treaties, Congress had become
incapable of governing. The states, on the other hand, passed too many
laws, including laws that violated the rights of minorities and laws that
were repealed on an annual basis as new factions won control of the
legislatures. Disputes also arose between states over boundaries and
commercial matters. Violence threatened throughout the country and
conflicts actually flared between state militias on several occasions.

Adding to the country's problems, a serious economic depression
started in 1785 and, by 1787, social unrest filled the land. In September
1786 a mob of angry farmers surrounded the state legislature in Exeter,
New Hampshire, demanding the abolition of all debts and the enactment of government programs that would restore prosperity. The governor called out the state militia, and the mob was easily dispersed.
But similar incidents erupted all over the country. The largest uprising
occurred in Massachusetts, where angry farmers led by Daniel Shays
attempted to stop county courts from foreclosing on their mortgages.
The rebellion lasted more than half a year and created an atmosphere
of crisis. Alarmed at the news, George Washington sensed that there
were "cumbustibles in every state" ready to be ignited by a single
spark. Americans worried that a demagogue might come forth who
would promise to restore stability and prosperity. Tired of unrest, Americans might accept this benevolent dictator; and, in time, prosperity
would return and unrest disappear. But, within a short time, the new
ruler's benevolence would also disappear. Most people believed that
the desperate situation required that the Articles of Confederation
should be strengthened; others felt that the country needed an entirely
new form of government.

In May 1787, a Constitutional Convention met in Philadelphia to
address the country's problems. The delegates believed that their pri-

mary tasks were to strengthen the general government and to limit the powers of the state governments. Because the delegates focused on these goals, it is not surprising that the Constitutional Convention failed to propose a federal bill of rights. In their minds, the delegates believed that the problem facing America was an excess of democracy—not too little freedom. But the decision to omit a federal bill of rights almost proved fatal to the new Constitution. Opponents of the Constitution, called Antifederalists, used the omission of a bill of rights as proof that a conspiracy was afoot to subvert the principles of the Revolution and deprive Americans of their dear-bought rights. Defenders of the Constitution, called Federalists, devised various arguments—all rather unconvincing—to explain the lack of a bill of rights. The omission of a bill of rights became the single most important issue during the yearlong debate over the ratification of the Constitution.

Federalists primarily justified the lack of a bill of rights by arguing that the Constitution created a federal government with strictly delegated powers. Since the new federal government could only do those things which the Constitution specified, and since none of the specified powers threatened liberty, rights would not be endangered. Federalists also argued that Americans had become accustomed to certain liberties. The people would not sit idly by if government violated these rights. Bills of rights were necessary against kings, but not in republics where the people could elect new representatives, senators, and even a new president if these government officials threatened liberties. Parchment barriers, Federalists asserted, provided no protections. Only the people, ever watchful over their government, could guarantee their liberties. Furthermore, if certain rights were in fact protected in the Constitution, that would indicate that the government had implied powers over those rights, and that any right not listed might be considered as unprotected. Additionally, violations of parchment bills of rights, Federalists argued, would disparage not only the rights in question, but would degrade the Constitution itself.

Antifederalists drew on history and human nature to justify the need for a bill of rights. The corrupting nature of power required written protections for liberties specifying the boundaries which government could not cross. The new Constitution, Antifederalists asserted, did not create a government of delegated powers. Referring to the general welfare clause, the necessary and proper clause, and the supremacy clause, Antifederalists argued that the Constitution would create a government with dangerous, indefinite powers. When Congress possessed unlimited powers, and when the federal judiciary served as the final arbiter in disputed cases, state bills of rights would be useless in con-

426 ROOTS OF THE REPUBLIC

frontations with the federal government. Responding to Federalist arguments against a partial list of rights, Antifederalists pointed to several rights embodied in the proposed Constitution—prohibitions of bills of attainder, ex post facto laws, the suspension of the writ of habeas corpus, the granting of titles of nobility, etc. Why, Antifederalists asked, were these rights and no others protected in the Constitution? Federalists had no convincing explanation.

Article VII of the Constitution provided that the new plan of government should be considered by state ratifying conventions, whose duty it was to accept or reject the Constitution; once nine states adopted the new Constitution, it would go into effect among the ratifying states. Federalists asserted that the state conventions must adopt the Constitution in its entirety or reject it. The conventions, they argued, had no authority to propose amendments or to ratify with conditions. Having commanding majorities in the first conventions that met, Federalists easily obtained ratification by five states. The Federalist bandwagon, however, halted abruptly in Massachusetts, the second largest state in the Union. Unable to obtain an unconditional ratification, Federalists were forced to agree to a recommendation that Massachusetts' future representatives in the first federal Congress should seek nine amendments to the Constitution. Several of these amendments protected rights. Six of the remaining seven states ratified the Constitution with recommendations that similar (though many more) amendments be added to the Constitution after the establisment of the new government. The conventions in Virginia, New York, North Carolina, and later Rhode Island proposed two separate lists of amendments to the Constitution—one list of structural amendments and another list in the form of a bill of rights. Without the moderate Federalists' acknowledgment that amendments were needed, it is unlikely that the Constitution would have been adopted by the required nine states.

The first federal Congress under the Constitution convened in New York City in March 1789. In his inaugural address on April 30, President George Washington recommended that Congress consider amendments to the Constitution—amendments that would not alter the structure of the federal government but would protect "the characteristic rights of freemen" and restore public harmony. Within a week of the president's speech, Congressman James Madison of Virginia notified the House that he would soon introduce amendments to the Constitution. Most members of Congress opposed an early consideration of amendments because other pressing issues—the creation of the federal judiciary and the executive departments, the adoption of revenue bills, and so forth—demanded their immediate attention. But Madison would not be diverted. Virginia's convention had recommended amendments and Madison had promised his constituents that, if elected to Congress, he would advocate amendments. Consequently on June 8, 1789, Madison proposed a series of amendments which, taken together, made up a bill of rights.

Both Federalists and Antifederalists opposed Madison's amendments. The former repeated their previous arguments against bills of rights, calling them trifling things that offered no real security for liberty. The latter claimed that Madison's amendments were "Milk & Water Propositions" that would serve as "a Tub to the Whale," that is, a diversion from more significant structural amendments to the Constitution needed to change the very nature of the federal government. Antifederalists did not merely want to protect personal rights, they also wanted to reestablish a fairly weak general government based on the Articles of Confederation with a few significant additional powers for Congress.

Despite this opposition, Madison, himself a former opponent of a federal bill of rights, eloquently and adamantly argued his case. A bill of rights, he predicted, would empower the federal judiciary to become "an impenetrable bulwark against every assumption of power in the legislative or executive." The debate persisted, becoming so heated at times that some congressmen considered settling their disagreements with dueling pistols, but fortunately cooler heads prevailed. On July 21, Madison's amendments, as well as the almost 200 different amendments proposed by the state conventions, were sent to a committee which, a week later, reported seventeen amendments—basically Madison's amendments. More than three weeks elapsed before, on August 13, the full House of Representatives reconsidered the amendments. At times during the debate, Madison's amendments appeared to be doomed because they did not have the support of the necessary two-thirds majority of the representatives required by Article V of the Constitution. But, with support from President Washington, Madison was able to gain House acceptance of the amendments on August 24.

One important decision that some representatives at the time thought trifling was the matter of form. How should the amendments be added to the Constitution? Would they be placed at the end of the original document or would they be interspersed throughout, deleting passages of the original Constitution that were no longer applicable and altering others? Madison urged the latter, arguing that "there is a neatness and propriety in incorporating the amendments into the constitution itself." The Constitution, he argued, would "certainly be more simple, when the amendments are interwoven into those parts to which they naturally belong, than it will if they consist of separate and distinct parts." Congressman Roger Sherman of Connecticut, long a staunch opponent of a bill of rights, opposed this interweaving, arguing, "We might as well endeavor to mix brass, iron, and clay, as to incorporate such heterogeneous articles." Congressman James Jackson of Georgia, another opponent of a bill of rights, advocated "that the original constitution ought to remain inviolate, and not be patched up, from time to time, with various stuffs resembling Joseph's coat of many colors." On August 13 Madison's arrangement was approved only to be overturned by a two-thirds vote six days later.

On August 24, 1789, the House of Representatives approved the amendments and sent them to the Senate. The Senate began its consideration on September 2; within a week, the upper house had tightened the language and consolidated the House's seventeen amendments into a list of twelve. Significantly, the Senate eliminated the amendment which Madison considered "the most valuable one on the whole list" when it struck out the provision prohibiting the states from infringing on the freedoms of religion, speech, and the press, and the guarantee of jury trials. A conference committee worked out the differences between the two sets of amendments, and on September 24 the House of Representatives accepted the list of twelve amendments. The following day the Senate agreed to the revised amendments.

On October 2, 1789, President Washington sent the amendments to the states for their approval. Several state legislatures rejected the first two amendments which provided (1) a formula for the apportionment of the House of Representatives and (2) a restriction on the power of Congress to enact salary increases for its members. It took over two years for the other ten amendments to be adopted by the necessary three-quarters of the state legislatures. On December 15, 1791, Virginia became the eleventh state to ratify the amendments, and the Bill of Rights became part of the Constitution.

The Fourteenth Amendment and the Incorporation Controversy

In *Barron* v. *Mayor and City Council of Baltimore*, 7 Peters 248 (1833), Barron sued the City of Baltimore for ruining the use of his wharf in Baltimore harbor as a result of city construction work; Barron claimed that the city had violated his Fifth Amendment rights by taking his property for public use without just compensation. Chief Justice John

Marshall ruled in his last major constitutional opinion that the provisions of the federal Bill of Rights did not apply to state or local governments.

In 1868, the adoption of the Fourteenth Amendment added language to the Constitution that later jurists and scholars have invoked as incorporating key provisions of the federal Bill of Rights to restrict the powers of state and local governments. In *Adamson* v. *California*, 221 U.S., 67 (1947), Justice Hugo L. Black began his campaign for incorporation of the full Bill of Rights; his dissenting opinion in that case amassed historical evidence for the position that the Fourteenth Amendment did incorporate the Bill of Rights. Justice Felix Frankfurter issued an opinion in *Adamson* disputing Black's historical arguments, and thus began a long and bitter argument between his intellectual allies and heirs and Black's supporters.

The Court never followed Black's strategy of total incorporation, continuing the methodology of piecemeal incorporation that had begun with *Gitlow* v. *New York*, 268 U.S. 652 (1925), under which most of the key provisions of the Bill of Rights are now binding on the states; the few exceptions include the right to jury trial in civil cases, the right to be held answerable for a crime only through a grand jury indictment, and perhaps the right to bear arms. The incorporation controversy has dominated the legal scholarship on the origins of the Fourteenth Amendment.

The Bill of Rights

Congress shall make no law respecting an establishment of religion, or prohibiting the free exercise thereof; or abridging the freedom of speech, or of the press, or the right of the people peaceably to assemble, and to petition the Government for a redress of grievances.

The history of the First Amendment is one of continually expanding civil liberties and a heightened wall between church and state. Before the independence of the United States, most countries had an established religion supported by taxes; non-members of the established church were often disqualified from voting or holding public office. Individuals who disagreed with the teachings of the established church frequently were discriminated against and sometimes suffered severe persecution. Wars were often fought for religious reasons.

Although several of the American states had established religions, because America was composed of so many different religions, it was agreed not to establish one official religion for the country. The First Amendment originally had no effect on established churches in the states. Some state constitutions, however, such as New York's, prohibited established churches; other states, starting with Virginia in the mid-1780s, passed laws that espoused religious liberty, refused to create an established church (or churches), or disestablished their churches. Not until 1833 did Massachusetts eliminate its established church.

The First Amendment is now understood to mean that government (state or federal) may not create an official religion, favor any or all religions, or prevent people from worshipping (or not worshipping) in their own way.

Before the adoption of the First Amendment, freedom of the press meant only that the government could not require licences for printed matter or prevent anyone from printing anything (no prior restraint). However, once statements were made that criticized the government or public officials, whether true or false, the author could be charged with seditious libel. The First Amendment seems to have adopted this

Engrossed broadside, RG11, General Records of the United States Government, National Archives.

narrow defintion of freedom of the press. The Sedition Act of 1798 made truth a defense in seditious libel cases. Opponents of the act argued for a broader interpretation of the First Amendment, which they said prohibited any punishment for written or spoken expression.

Today the courts have given great latitude to freedom of the press and speech, but it is still not an absolute right. For instance, though the expression of ideas is protected, and seditious libel may be a thing of the past, one may still be held to account for libel, even libels against public figures, and pornography is still punishable.

Before the Declaration of Independence, the king refused to accept the right of Americans to petition directly for the correction of grievances. American petitions were viewed as impertinences if not treason. The right to assemble was also limited under the British mutiny laws. The First Amendment was originally meant to protect the right to gather together in peaceful meetings and to request government to correct abuses. The right to assemble also has been expanded to include the right to associate together in organizations.

AMENDMENT II

A well regulated Militia, being necessary to the security of a free State, the right of the people to keep and bear Arms, shall not be infringed.

The meaning of this amendment has become quite controversial. Today, some people and most judicial decisions interpreting the amendment read it to apply only to the right of the states to maintain militias (the national guard), which would allow government to regulate or even to prohibit individual ownership of weapons. The most recent scholarship indicates that it was meant not only to provide for a well-equipped militia, but also to protect the people's right to keep arms for hunting and for their own protection against criminals, tyrants, and foreign invaders. Most people agree that government can prohibit certain kinds of large and dangerous weapons from individual ownership and license and require the registration of smaller weapons.

AMENDMENT III

No Soldier shall, in time of peace be quartered in any house, without the consent of the Owner, nor in time of war, but in a manner to be prescribed by law.

Housing of soldiers in the homes of private citizens had been condemned in England in the Petition of Right (1628) and in the Bill of Rights (1689). Parliament's forced housing of soldiers in America contributed to the coming of the Revolution and was one of the grievances against King George III specified in the Declaration of Independence. The Third Amendment, which rarely has been used in courts, guarantees that government cannot force people to keep soldiers in their homes during peacetime, or in wartime unless required to do so by law.

Amendment IV

The right of the people to be secure in their persons, houses, papers, and effects, against unreasonable searches and seizures, shall not be violated, and no Warrants shall issue, but upon probable cause, supported by Oath or affirmation, and particularly describing the place to be searched, and the persons or things to be seized.

This amendment prohibited general warrants and writs of assistance which were commonly used in England and America before the Revolution. In the famous *North Briton, No. 45* case in 1763, one general warrant was used to search at least five houses, arrest forty-nine people (most of whom were innocent), and seize thousands of books and papers. The Fourth Amendment provides that people may not be arrested, have their houses searched, or their papers and property taken by the government unless a valid warrant is issued by a judge, or in other carefully limited situations in which warrantless searches may be "reasonable." The government must give the judge good reason (probable cause) to believe that a crime has been committed, and the warrant must specifically describe the place to be searched and what is expected to be found. Evidence obtained without a valid search warrant or by an unreasonable search is inadmissible in court (the exclusionary rule). These governmental restrictions have also been applied in cases of electronic surveillance, such as wiretapping. Search and arrest warrants are not required when a crime is in the process of being committed, when a moving vehicle is stopped and is suspected of containing illegal substances, and so forth. In these cases, authorities are required to show that a warrant could not reasonably have been obtained before the search or arrest.

Amendment V

No person shall be held to answer for a capital, or otherwise infamous crime, unless on a presentment or indictment of a Grand Jury, except in cases arising in the land or naval forces, or in the Militia, when in actual service in time of War or public danger; nor shall any person be subject for the same offence to be twice put in jeopardy of life or limb, nor shall be compelled in any criminal case to be a witness against himself, nor be deprived of life, liberty, or property, without due process of law; nor shall private property be taken for public use, without just compensation.

Many of these rights had evolved over years as part of the British common law and were incorporated into the legal system in colonial America. Their meanings have been expanded considerably. No person can be tried for a serious federal crime unless a grand jury charges that there is reason to believe that the accused is guilty. No person found innocent of a crime can be tried a second time for the same offense (double jeopardy). No person charged with a crime can be forced to testify in court against himself (self-incrimination). No person can be executed or deprived of his freedom or property without a fair hearing with all legal safeguards (procedural due process), and an expansion of the concept of liberty has been developed that is known as "substantive due process." Professor Laurence H. Tribe of Harvard Law School has aptly defined substantive due process:

> To say that governmental action violates "substantive due process" is to say that the action, while adhering to the forms of law, unjustifiably abridges the Constitution's fundamental constraints upon the content of what government may do to people in the name of "law." . . . It thus restricts government power, requiring coercive acts of the state to have public as opposed to merely private ends, defining certain means that government may not employ absent the most compelling necessity, and identifying certain aspects of behavior which it may not regulate without a clear showing that no less intrusive means could achieve government's legitimate public aims.[1]

Private property cannot be taken by the government for public use (using its power of eminent domain) unless the owner is paid a fair price. One expanded protection the courts have derived from the Fifth Amendment is that accused individuals must be informed of their rights not to answer questions while being interrogated and that any answers given could be used as evidence against them.

Amendment VI

In all criminal prosecutions, the accused shall enjoy the right to a speedy and public trial, by an impartial jury of the State and district wherein the crime

---

[1] Laurence H. Tribe, "Substantive Due Process of Law," in Leonard W. Levy, Kenneth Karst, and Dennis Mahoney, eds., *Encyclopedia of the American Constitution*, 4 vols. (New York, 1986), 3: 1796–1803 (quoted at 1796).

shall have been committed; which district shall have been previously ascer-
tained by law, and to be informed of the nature and cause of the accusation;
to be confronted with the witnesses against him; to have compulsory process
for obtaining Witnesses in his favor, and to have the Assistance of Counsel
for his defence.

The right to a speedy, public jury trial was first enunciated in 1215 in Magna Carta and was reasserted in the common law and in most of the Revolutionary War state constitutions and bills of rights. This right protected defendants from long periods of incarceration before trial, during which time witnesses might die or have their memories impaired. A person accused of a crime must be given a speedy public jury trial in the state and district where the crime occurred. Accused individuals must be informed of the charges against them and witnesses must testify in open court. The accused has the right to require witnesses in his favor to appear in court. The right to be represented by a lawyer has changed over time. At first, this right was interpreted to mean that legal assistance could not be denied an accused who wanted and could afford to hire a lawyer. Not until the 1930s, however, did the courts start to expand this right by requiring that government provide legal assistance for defendants who could not afford to hire their own lawyers. The right has also been expanded to mean that accused individuals should have attorneys at early stages in criminal investigations and that, in some cases, individuals may represent themselves in criminal trials.

Amendment VII

In Suits at common law, where the value in controversy shall exceed twenty
dollars, the right of trial by jury shall be preserved, and no fact tried by a
jury shall be otherwise re-examined in any Court of the United States, than
according to the rules of the common law.

This amendment satisfied two of the most serious objections that Antifederalists raised against the federal judiciary proposed in the new Constitution. The Constitutional Convention had guaranteed jury trials in all criminal cases, but, because many of the states had different provisions for handling civil cases, Convention delegates omitted a provision guaranteeing jury trials in these cases. This amendment provides that in civil cases involving more than $20, jury trial is guaranteed. Antifederalists also feared that the decisions of juries in the lower courts might be overturned by appellate courts without juries if the facts in the case could be re-examined. If a defendant is convicted and new evidence arises, the case should be tried again by a new jury. This guarantee provides that although courts (i.e., judges) may interpret the law, juries alone should determine the facts.

Amendment VIII

Excessive bail shall not be required, nor excessive fines imposed, nor cruel and unusual punishments inflicted.
The right to bail was first codified in England in the Statute of Westminster of 1275 and supplemented by the Habeas Corpus Act of 1679 and the Bill of Rights in 1689. The protection was incorporated in the Virginia Declaration of Rights in 1776 and in other state constitutions and bills of rights. When a person is arrested for a crime, the amount of bail (the posting of a sum of money or property to guarantee that the accused will appear for trial) must be reasonable in relation to the seriousness of the crime.

Throughout many years in England, government levied excessive fines and cruel and unusual punishments as a means of punishing criminals or political opponents. The Eighth Amendment prohibits both excessive fines and cruel and unusual punishments. The general meaning of these protections has remained unchanged since the amendment was proposed, but the appropriate use of bail and the constitutionality of capital punishment have become controversial when weighed against the protection society feels it needs from criminals.

Amendment IX

The enumeration in the Constitution, of certain rights, shall not be construed to deny or disparage others retained by the people.
One reason that Federalists gave for their opposition to a bill of rights was that the failure to list every right would leave all unlisted rights unprotected. To answer Federalists' criticism, the Ninth Amendment provides that the rights listed in the Constitution are not the only rights retained by the people. The courts have been reluctant to use the Ninth Amendment to protect rights because of its open-endedness. Many people, however, would like to base the right of privacy upon this amendment. In fact, the appellants in *Roe v. Wade*, 410 U.S. 113 (1973), invoked the Ninth Amendment in the U.S. Court of Appeals. The Ninth Amendment, however, was abandoned when *Roe v. Wade* came before the Supreme Court.

Amendment X

The powers not delegated to the United States by the Constitution, nor pro-
hibited by it to the States, are reserved to the States respectively, or to the
people.

The second article of the Articles of Confederation provided that
the Confederation Congress possessed only those powers that were
expressly granted to it by the Articles. All other powers were retained
by the states. Federalists maintained that the new federal government
under the Constitution would similarly be a government of powers
delegated by the Constitution. Antifederalists were skeptical, citing the
general welfare clause, the necessary and proper clause, and the supremacy clause. They wanted a specific provision in the new Constitution that would limit the federal government to delegated powers,
while reserving all other powers (that were not prohibited by the Constitution to the states) to the states or to the people. Chief Justice John
Marshall ruled in *McCulloch* v. *Maryland*, 4 Wheaton 316 (1819), that the
exclusion of the word "expressly" from the Tenth Amendment allowed
Congress to interpret its powers broadly. The expansion of the federal
government since the 1930s has diluted, if not totally evaporated, the
authority of the Tenth Amendment.

For Further Reading

General

Irving Brant. *The Bill of Rights*. Indianapolis, Ind. 1965.
Edward S. Corwin. *The Constitution and What It Means Today*. 14th ed.
   Princeton, 1978.
Edward Dumbauld. *The Bill of Rights and What It Means Today*. Norman,
   Okla., 1957.
John P. Kaminski. "The Making of the Bill of Rights," in *Contexts of*
   the Bill of Rights, ed. Stephen L. Schechter and Richard B. Bernstein.
   Albany, 1990.
Jon Kukla, ed. *The Bill of Rights: A Lively Heritage*. Richmond, 1987.
Leonard W. Levy, Kenneth L. Karst, and Dennis J. Mahoney, eds.
   Encyclopedia of the American Constitution. 4 volumes. New York, 1986.
Robert Allen Rutland. *The Birth of the Bill of Rights 1776–1791*. Chapel
   Hill, 1955.
Gaspare J. Saladino. "The Bill of Rights: A Bibliographic Essay," in
   Contexts of the Bill of Rights, ed. Stephen L. Schechter and Richard
   B. Bernstein. Albany, 1990.

Bernard Schwartz. *The Great Rights of Mankind: A History of the American Bill of Rights.* New York, 1977.

First Amendment

Glenn Abernathy. *The Right of Assembly and Association.* Columbia, 1961.

Walter Berns. *The First Amendment and the Future of American Democracy.* New York, 1976.

Zechariah Chafee, Jr. *Free Speech in the United States.* Cambridge, Mass., 1948.

Archibald Cox. *Freedom of Expression.* Cambridge, Mass., 1981.

Thomas J. Curry. *The First Freedoms: Church and State in America to the Passage of the First Amendment.* New York, 1986.

Milton Konvitz. *Fundamental Liberties of a Free People: Religion, Speech, Press, Assembly.* Ithaca, N.Y., 1957.

Leonard W. Levy. *Emergence of a Free Press.* New York, 1985.

Leonard W. Levy. *Freedom of Speech and Press in Early American History: Legacy of Suppression.* New York, 1963.

Leonard W. Levy. *The Establishment Clause: Religion and the First Amendment.* New York, 1986.

Alexander Meiklejohn. *Political Freedom: The Constitutional Powers of the People.* New York, 1960.

William Lee Miller. *The First Liberty: Religion and the American Republic.* New York, 1986.

Leo Pfeffer. *Church, State, and Freedom*; rev. ed. Boston, 1967.

Martin H. Redish. *Freedom of Expression: A Critical Analysis.* Charlottesville, Va., 1984.

Frederick Seaton Siebert. *Freedom of the Press in England, 1476–1776.* Urbana, Ill., 1952.

Anson Phelps Stokes. *Church and State in the United States.* 3 volumes. New York: Harper & Bros., 1950. rev. ed. with Leo Pfeffer. New York, 1964.

Second Amendment

Laurence Delbert Cress. "An Armed Community: The Origins and Meaning of the Right to Bear Arms," *Journal of American History* 71 (1984): 22–41.

Stephen P. Halbrook. *That Every Man Be Armed: The Evolution of a Constitutional Right.* Albuquerque, 1984.

Don B. Kates, Jr. "Handgun Prohibition and the Original Meaning of the Second Amendment," *Michigan Law Review* 82 (1983): 204–73.

Don B. Kates, Jr., ed. "Symposium on Gun Control," *Law and Contemporary Problems* 49 (1986): 1–267.

Joyce Malcolm. "The Right of the People to Keep and Bear Arms: The Common Law Tradition," *Hastings Constitutional Law Quarterly* 10 (1983): 285–314.

John Kenneth Rowland. "Origins of the Second Amendment: The Creation of the Constitutional Rights of Militia and of Keeping and Bearing Arms." Ph.D. dissertation: Ohio State University, 1978.

Robert E. Shalhope. "The Ideological Origins of the Second Amendment," *Journal of American History* 69 (1982): 599–614.

U.S. Senate, Subcommittee on the Constitution of the Committee on the Judiciary. *The Right to Keep and Bear Arms*, 97th Cong., 2d Sess. (1982).

Third Amendment

B. Carmon Hardy. "A Free People's Intolerable Grievance: The Quartering of Troops and the Third Amendment," in *The Bill of Rights: A Lively Heritage*, ed. Jon Kukla. Richmond, 1987: 66–82.

John Phillip Reid. *In Defiance of the Law: The Standing-Army Controversy, the Two Constitutions, and the Coming of the American Revolution.* Chapel Hill, 1981.

Fourth Amendment

William Cuddihy and B. Carmon Hardy. "A Man's House Was Not His Castle: Origins of the Fourth Amendment to the United States Constitution," *William and Mary Quarterly*, 3rd ser., 37 (1980): 371–400.

Oliver M. Dickerson. *Navigation Acts and the American Revolution.* Philadelphia, 1951.

Nelson Lasson. *The History . . . of the Fourth Amendment.* Baltimore, 1937.

M. H. Smith. *The Writs of Assistance Case.* Berkeley, Calif., 1978.

Fifth Amendment

Erwin N. Griswold. *The Fifth Amendment Today.* Cambridge, Mass., 1955.

Leonard W. Levy. *Origins of the Fifth Amendment: The Right Against Self-Incrimination.* New York 1968.

Sixth Amendment

Anthony G. Amsterdam. "Speedy Criminal Trial: Rights and Remedies," *Stanford Law Review* 27 (1975): 525–43.

John C. Godbold. "Speedy Trial—Major Surgery for a National Ill," *Alabama Law Review* 24 (1972): 265–94.

Wayne R. LaFave and Jedd H. Israel. *Criminal Procedure.* St. Paul, Minn., 1985.

Anthony Lewis. *Gideon's Trumpet.* New York, 1964.

Charles H. Whitebread. *Criminal Procedure.* Mineola, N.Y., 1980.

Seventh Amendment

Richard H. Helmholz and Thomas A. Green. *Juries, Libel, & Justice: The Role of English Juries in Seventeenth- and Eighteenth-Century Trials for Libel and Slander*. Los Angeles, 1984.

John H. Langbein. "Origins of Public Prosecution at Common Law," *American Journal of Legal History* 17 (1973): 313–33.

John M. Murrin and A. G. Roeber. "Trial by Jury," in *The Bill of Rights: A Lively Heritage*, ed. Jon Kukla. Richmond, 1987: 108–29.

Eighth Amendment

Larry Charles Berkson. *The Concept of Cruel and Unusual Punishments*. Lexington, Mass., 1975.

Anthony F. Granucci. " 'Nor Cruel and Unusual Punishments Inflicted': The Original Meaning," *California Law Review* 57 (1969): 839–85.

Richard A. Williamson. "Bail, Fines, and Punishment: The Eighth Amendment's Safeguards," in *The Bill of Rights: A Lively Heritage*, ed. Jon Kukla. Richmond, 1987: 130–39.

Ninth Amendment

Floyd Abrams. "The Ninth Amendment and the Protection of Unenumerated Rights," *Harvard Journal of Law & Public Policy* 11 (1988): 93–96.

Morris S. Arnold. "Doing More Than Remembering the Ninth Amendment," *Chicago-Kent Law Review* 64.1 (1988): 265–71.

Sotirios A. Barber. "The Ninth Amendment: Inkblot or Another Hard Nut to Crack?," *Chicago-Kent Law Review* 64.1 (1988): 67–89.

Randy E. Barnett. "Foreword: The Ninth Amendment and Constitutional Legitimacy," *Chicago-Kent Law Review* 64.1 (1988): 37–67.

Charles L. Black, Jr. *Decision According to Law*. New York, 1981.

Russell Caplan. "The History and Meaning of the Ninth Amendment," *Virginia Law Review* 69 (1983): 223–68.

Leslie W. Dunbar. "James Madison and the Ninth Amendment," *Virginia Law Review* 42 (1956): 627–43.

John P. Kaminski. "Restoring the Declaration of Independence: Natural Rights and the Ninth Amendment," in *The Bill of Rights: A Lively Heritage*, ed. Jon Kukla. Richmond, 1987: 140–50.

Calvin R. Massey. "Federalism and Fundamental Rights: The Ninth Amendment," *Hastings Law Journal* 38.2 (1987): 305–44.

Lawrence E. Mitchell. "The Ninth Amendment and the Jurisprudence of Original Intention," *Georgetown Law Journal* 74 (1986): 1719–42.

Bennett B. Patterson. *The Forgotten Ninth Amendment*. Indianapolis, Ind., 1955.

Gerald G. Watson. "The Ninth Amendment: Source of a Substantive Right to Privacy," *John Marshall Law Review* 19.4 (1986): 959–81.

Tenth Amendment

Walter Berns. "The Meaning of the Tenth Amendment," in *A Nation of States: Essays on the American Federal System*, ed. Robert A. Goldwin. Chicago, 1963: 133–37.

Edward S. Corwin. "The Passing of Dual Federalism," *Virginia Law Review* 36 (1950): 1–24.

Charles F. Hobson. "The Tenth Amendment and the New Federalism of 1789," in *The Bill of Rights: A Lively Heritage*, ed. Jon Kukla. Richmond, 1987: 152–63.

Herbert Wechsler. "The Political Safeguards of Federalism: The Role of the States in the Composition and Selection of the National Government," *Columbia Law Review* 54 (1954): 543–60.

The Fourteenth Amendment

Raoul Berger. *The Fourteenth Amendment and the Bill of Rights*. Norman, Okla., 1988.

Michael Kent Curtis. *No State Shall Abridge*. Durham, N. C., 1988.

William E. Nelson, *The Fourteenth Amendment: From Political Principle to Judicial Doctrine*. Cambridge, Mass., 1988.

——— Afterword ———

Thomas Jefferson's
Letter to Roger D. Weightman

——— June 24, 1826 ———

Commentary by Richard B. Bernstein

In June of 1826, Thomas Jefferson was eighty-three years old, nearly bankrupt, in failing health, and alarmed for the future of the American republic.[1] He had focused his attention during his retirement on the founding of the University of Virginia, an institution central to his dreams of an enlightened public educational system for an agrarian commonwealth. Jefferson not only planned the curriculum and designed the buildings, but served as that university's first rector.

Jefferson's private situation had been a source of abiding worry ever since his retirement from the presidency in 1809. He had continued his expensive hobby of redesigning and rebuilding Monticello and his other pursuits of experiments in agriculture and plantation management. He had hoped by some of these experiments to recover a measure of financial stability for his household, but these plans were shattered by a friend's defalcation: Wilson Cary Nicholas had persuaded Jefferson to cosign a note and had defaulted, leaving Jefferson to satisfy Nicholas's creditors. The former president found himself in the humiliating situation of having to petition the Virginia government for permission to sell Monticello to amass funds to satisfy the Nicholas obligation; Virginia instead authorized a lottery to raise the needed money.

This essay is for Henry Steele Commager.

[1] The finest study of Jefferson's last years is the sixth volume of Dumas Malone's magisterial biography, *Jefferson and His Times: The Sage of Monticello* (Boston, 1981).

Unable to free his slaves at his death as he had planned due to the harsh laws of his native state, Jefferson at the same time was plunged into gloom by his dread of an impending clash between the free states and the slave states and his abiding conviction that whites and blacks could not live side-by-side in equality and peace. Jefferson's fears led him to express such extreme state sovereignty views that some later historians identified him as an intellectual father of secession and the Civil War.

None of these worries is reflected in this confident letter, which Jefferson wrote in response to an invitation from Mayor Roger D. Weightman of Washington, D.C., to take part in the festivities honoring the fiftieth anniversary of the Declaration of Independence. By 1826, most of the leaders of the Revolution were dead or dying. Both Jefferson and John Adams had to decline Mayor Weightman's invitation to attend the jubilee celebration of the Declaration of Independence in the nation's capital. Each man took comfort in the thought that the other was attending the ceremony.

By the 1820s, the Declaration had assumed an importance as a national talisman that it had not possessed during the Revolution, Confederation, and early national periods. The Revolution itself was becoming the stuff of patriotic myth, the germ of what Henry Steele Commager has called the American "usable past."[2] A new generation, whose members either had been young children during the Revolutionary War or had not been born until after the winning of independence, had reached political maturity. They had assumed the responsibility of conserving and protecting the achievement of the Founders.

The surviving members of the Revolutionary generation were revered sages, deluged with inquiring visitors and letters of every description. Often called "the Fathers" by their admiring countrymen, they corresponded with one another to compare and preserve memories of the history they had made and witnessed, to correct errors and refute myths, and to seek and offer reassurance that their sacrifices had not been in vain.[3] Indeed, the reconciliation in 1812 between John Adams

[2] See generally Henry Steele Commager, *The Search for a Usable Past and Other Essays in Historiography* (New York, 1966).

[3] For two especially rich collections of letters of this sort, see Lester J. Cappon, ed., *The Adams-Jefferson Letters*, 2 vols. (Chapel Hill, 1959), and John A. Schutz and Douglass G. Adair, eds., *The Spur of Fame: Dialogues of John Adams and Benjamin Rush, 1805–1812* (San Marino, Calif., 1966). James Morton Smith is completing an edition of the correspondence of Thomas Jefferson and James Madison. See also the superb study by Drew R. McCoy, *The Last of the Fathers: James Madison and the Republican Legacy* (Cambridge, England, 1989).

and Thomas Jefferson was in large part an effort to form common cause
between witnesses of and fellow laborers in the creation of the American
republic.

Most citizens were determined to memorialize the achievements
of the Revolution, and enlisted the advice and support of the patriarchs
of the American experiment. The noted artist John Trumbull, for example, painted huge historical paintings of such events as the surrender
of General Cornwallis, Washington's delivery of his commission as commander-in-chief to the Confederation Congress on his resignation from
the army, and above all the declaration of American independence; in
addition, he published inexpensive line engravings of these paintings
for sale to the general public. Jefferson advised, applauded, and encouraged Trumbull's enterprise.[4]

Although preoccupied by national politics (despite his protests to
the contrary), by the affairs of the University of Virginia, and by his
own troubles, Jefferson had not neglected his place in history. He took
great care to preserve and arrange his papers for posterity, seeking at
the same time to establish his own reading of the history he had witnessed and helped to make. (This may help to explain the historio-
graphical advantage that Jefferson has had in the past fifty years over
Alexander Hamilton—both that Jefferson lived so much longer and thus
wrote so much more and that Hamilton's early death deprived him of
a comparable chance to present his life and career to posterity.[5]) Jefferson also copied out extracts from his papers and collections of documents for inquiring biographers and historians and answered hundreds
of their questions. Some of these letters, which are among Jefferson's
best, are incisive biographical essays replete with insight into such men
as George Washington, Benjamin Franklin, and George Wythe.[6]

More than any other political figure of his time, Jefferson used
letters as a means to propagate his ideas and to develop and refine his
thinking on important political, intellectual, and social questions. He
once estimated that he had written more than ten thousand letters—
only a fraction of which have been published. These letters constitute
one of the richest bodies of material from which historians can approach

[4] See the innovative monograph by Albert Furtwangler, *American Silhouettes: Rhetorical Identities of the Founders* (New Haven, 1987).

[5] I am indebted to Joanne B. Freeman for this point.

[6] See, e.g., Jefferson to Dr. Walter Jones, January 2, 1814 (on Washington); Jefferson
to Robert Walsh, December 4, 1816 (on Franklin); and Jefferson to John Saunderson,
August 31, 1820 (on Wythe). All these letters are conveniently reprinted in Adrienne
Koch and William Peden, eds., *The Life and Selected Writings of Thomas Jefferson* (New
York, 1943), 173–83.

the era of the American Revolution; they also comprise one of the greatest treasures of political wisdom available to us.

When asked to make a statement to be read at local Independence Day ceremonies, the ninety-year-old Adams declared, "I give you, 'IN-DEPENDENCE FOREVER!' " When asked whether he wanted to elaborate or expand on this sentiment, he said, "Not a word." Adams emphasized by this terse greeting that he thought that American independence was the most important legacy of the Revolution. Skeptical of progress, aware of the good and evil aspects of human nature, wary of sweeping generalizations about the applicability of the American experience to other nations, Adams held to the beliefs that he had preserved for half a century.

Unlike Adams, Jefferson was willing to maintain that the American Revolution had some larger significance for human history, and that the dream of human liberty was available to all human beings who reached out to grasp it. He therefore took the occasion of his apologetic letter to Mayor Weightman to convey his beliefs as to the promise of the Revolution. What turned out to be the last letter that Thomas Jefferson ever wrote was his valedictory statement to the American people.[7]

Monticello, June 24, 1826.

Respected Sir, —

[1] The kind invitation I receive from you on the part of the citizens of the city of Washington, to be present with them at their celebration on the 50th. anniversary of American Independence, as one of the surviving signers of an instrument, pregnant with our own, and the fate of the world, is most flattering to myself, and heightened by the honorable accompaniment proposed for the comfort of such a journey. [2] It adds sensibly to the sufferings of sickness, to be deprived by it of a personal participation in the rejoicings of that day. [3] But acquiescence is a duty, under circumstances not placed among those we are permitted to controul. [4] I should indeed, with peculiar delight, have met and exchanged there, congratulations personally, with the small band, the remnant of that host of worthies, who joined with us, on that day, in the bold and doubtful election we were to make, for our country, between submission, or the sword; and to have enjoyed with them the consolatory fact that our fellow citizens, after

---

[7] The text of this letter is taken from the Jefferson Papers in the Library of Congress. For a modern printing, see Merrill D. Peterson, ed., *Thomas Jefferson: Writings* (New York, 1984), 1516–17. Bracketed numbers have been added before each of the discussed sentences for easy reference. The first letter in every sentence has been capitalized, which Jefferson usually did not do.

half a century of experience and prosperity, continue to approve the choice we made. [5] May it be to the world what I believe it will be, (to some parts sooner, to others later, but finally to all,) the Signal of arousing men to burst the chains, under which Monkish ignorance and superstition had persuaded them to bind themselves, and to assume the blessings & security of self government. [6] That form which we have substituted restores the free right to the unbounded exercise of reason and freedom of opinion. [7] All eyes are opened, or opening to the rights of man. [8] The general spread of the light of science has already laid open to every view the palpable truth that the mass of mankind has not been born, with saddles on their backs, nor a favored few booted and spurred, ready to ride them legitimately, by the grace of god. [9] These are grounds of hope for others. [10] For ourselves let the annual return of this day, forever refresh our recollections of these rights, and an undiminished devotion to them.

I will ask permission here to express the pleasure with which I should have met my ancient neighbors of the City of Washington and it's vicinities, with whom I passed so many years of a pleasing social intercourse; an intercourse which so much relieved the anxieties of the public cares, and left impressions so deeply engraved in my affections, as never to be forgotten. With my regret that ill health forbids me the gratification of an acceptance, be pleased to receive for yourself and those for whom you write the assurance of my highest respect and friendly attachments.

Jefferson's last letter demonstrates once again that he was perhaps the most gifted writer of the Revolutionary generation; as John Adams had observed, Jefferson had "a happy talent for composition and a peculiar felicity of expression." A detailed analysis confirms that Jefferson's letter to Roger Weightman ranks with his own First Inaugural Address and with Abraham Lincoln's Gettysburg Address and Second Inaugural Address as statements of the significance of the American experience and the central truths of the American experiment in government.

Jefferson's first sentence signalled his belief that the American Revolution was an event that shaped not only the history of the United States but human history as well. His reference in the fourth sentence to "the small band, the remnant of that host of worthies" echoes the famous "Crispin's Day" oration of William Shakespeare's *Henry V*. The fourth sentence also voices Jefferson's idea (one central to his political thought) that each generation makes its own choices about politics and government, and his satisfaction that subsequent generations of Americans "continue to approve the choice we made." The fifth sentence evidences Jefferson's faith that the Revolution has enduring meaning for all peoples and nations, as well as his instinct for the haunting metaphor. Jefferson insisted here that human beings choose their form of government, even a tyrannical government, implying that the people always have the power to overthrow a tyranny. He also sought to refute the conventional wisdom that self-government is a turbulent and un-stable enterprise, stressing instead its "blessings & security." There is an irony about the Jeffersonian references to liberty and shackles when we recall that Jefferson died, as he had lived, an owner of slaves.[8] In this case, Jefferson's own life was a bitter case study of a larger tragedy disfiguring the American experiment.

Jefferson's emphasis in the sixth sentence on "the unbounded ex-ercise of reason and freedom of opinion" recalls the struggles between the Federalists and Republicans in 1798–1800 over the Alien and Se-dition Acts;[9] again, however, it is ironic in light of the powerful argument by Leonard Levy that Jefferson's devotion to civil liberties was erratic and inconsistent.[10] The last sentences of this paragraph are among the most famous from Jefferson's pen. They feature two metaphors: one of light and vision characteristic of the Age of Enlightenment (sentences seven and eight); the other (in sentence eight) drawn from the last speech of Colonel Richard Rumbold, a Whig martyr in the history of the English struggles against Stuart tyranny in the seventeenth century. Rumbold declared: "I am sure there was no Man born marked of God above another; for none comes into the World with a Saddle on his Back, nor any booted and spurr'd to Ride him."[11]

The ninth sentence restates Jefferson's hope that the American Revolution will have larger significance in the history of human liberty.

[8] For the spectrum of scholarly views on Jefferson and slavery, ranging from most charitable to most severe, see John C. Miller, *The Wolf by the Ears: Thomas Jefferson and Slavery* (New York, 1977); Robert McColley, *Slavery and Jeffersonian Virginia* (Urbana, Ill., 1964); and Winthrop D. Jordan, *White over Black: American Attitudes Towards Slavery and the Negro, 1550–1812* (Chapel Hill, 1968), 429–81. See also the posthumously published essay by Douglass Adair, "The Jefferson Scandals," in Trevor Colbourn, ed., *Fame and the Founding Fathers: Essays of Douglass Adair* (New York, 1974), 160–91.

[9] The most thorough study is James Morton Smith, *Freedom's Fetters: The Alien and Sedition Acts and American Civil Liberties* (1956; rev. ed., Ithaca, N.Y., 1963). See also John C. Miller, *Crisis in Freedom: The Alien and Sedition Acts* (Boston, 1955).

[10] See generally Leonard W. Levy, *Jefferson and Civil Liberties: The Darker Side* (Cambridge, Mass., 1963). The 1972 edition, with a new introduction replying to critics, has been reprinted in paperback (Chicago, 1989).

[11] See the brilliant essay by Douglass Adair, "Rumbold's Dying Speech, 1685, and Jefferson's Last Words on Democracy, 1826," *William and Mary Quarterly* 3d ser. 9 (1952): 521–31, and Douglass Adair, "Letter to the Editor," *William and Mary Quarterly* 3d ser. 23 (1966): 672. Both pieces are reprinted in Colbourn, ed., *Fame and the Founding Fathers*, 192–202.

The tenth sentence is Jefferson's contribution to the development of the Fourth of July as a holiday of ritual rededication to the ideals of the Revolution.

Thomas Jefferson died ten days later, on July Fourth. Both he and John Adams fought to live to the Fourth against what proved to be their last illnesses. Both men succeeded. Jefferson passed in and out of un-consciousness several times during his final days; his last words were the question, "Is it the Fourth?" Upon being assured that it was, he smiled and lapsed into his final coma, dying later that morning. Several hundred miles north, in Quincy, Massachusetts, John Adams murmured his last and best-remembered words a few hours after Jefferson's death: "Thomas Jefferson still survives."

* * * *

Although John Adams never had the chance to read Jefferson's letter to Mayor Weightman, posterity has linked Adams's last words about his old friend and adversary with Jefferson's last letter, as if Adams endorsed Jefferson's interpretation of the enduring truths of the Revolution.[12] This may not be sound history; rather, it is another example of the "usable past" that a nation and a people develop to reassure themselves of the continuing value of their basic principles.

What might be called the Adams-Jefferson myth of 1826 finds a place in David Hackett Fischer's acerbic monograph *Historians' Fallacies*,[13] which lavishes witty scorn on the present-mindedness of many historians. In particular, Fischer derides the tendency to produce reflexively patriotic, flag-waving commemorative essays on the theme "Thomas Jefferson Still Lives." Although Fischer is right about the essays themselves, his discussion misses a crucial point about the actual past that prompts the writing of such presentist tracts.

As noted above, Adams and Jefferson were deeply aware of their symbolic roles as Revolutionary patriarchs. They and their contemporaries knew the power of gestures—for example, the spectacular embrace of Franklin and Voltaire in Paris in the 1770s and the equally histrionic encounter of the aged Jefferson and Lafayette in 1824. Indeed, as John McManners has shown in his study *Death and the Enlightenment*, Voltaire stage-managed his death in 1778 as the culmination of his fame

---

[12] This view is made explicit in the radio play in verse by Archibald MacLeish, *The Great Fourth of July Bicentennial Parade* (Pittsburgh, 1977), in which the spirits of Adams and Jefferson contemplate the United States of 1976. The climax of the play is Jefferson's recital of the text of his last letter to a representative sampling of Americans of the 1970s; John Adams has the last words: "Thomas Jefferson still survives."

[13] David Hackett Fischer, *Historians' Fallacies* (New York, 1970).

and a final vindication of his ideas.[14] So, too, Adams and Jefferson strove to live to the fiftieth anniversary of the Declaration, each man knowing that his death on that day would be invested with extraordinary symbolic significance by his countrymen.

No one—least of all Adams and Jefferson themselves—could have expected that they both would die on the Fourth of July; some envious Federalists growled their suspicions that Jefferson had taken poison to ensure that he would die on the Fourth. The coincidence seemed a powerful statement of divine favor of the American experiment; although later generations did not share the religious fervor of the generation of President John Quincy Adams, they too marveled at the event.[15]

* * * *

This essay was written during a time of unparalleled worldwide political and social change—a time when, it seems, human beings have seen and acted on Jefferson's "Signal . . . to burst the chains, under which Monkish ignorance and superstition [have] persuaded [human beings] to bind themselves, and to assume the blessings & security of self-government." It is not clear at this writing whether the promise of the revolutions in Eastern Europe will be realized, whether the peoples of the Soviet Union will follow the examples of the other Warsaw Pact nations in seeking pluralist democracy, whether South Africa will manage a peaceful and democratic abolition of apartheid and racial oppression, or whether the Chinese people will get the chance to redeem the horrors and sacrifices of Tienanmen Square. What is clear is that now, as at few times in the more than two centuries of American independence, the example of the American Revolution may be bearing fruit throughout the world. In this sense, the message of Thomas Jefferson's valedictory letter still survives.[16]

[14] John McManners, *Death and the Enlightenment* (Oxford, England, 1981).

[15] On the symbolism of the deaths of Adams and Jefferson, as well as the story of "what history has made of Thomas Jefferson," see Merrill D. Peterson, *The Jefferson Image in the American Mind* (New York, 1960).

[16] See also Richard B. Morris, *The Emerging Nations and the American Revolution* (New York, 1970). It is a source of abiding regret for all those who knew Professor Morris that he did not live to see the vindication of his views in 1989 and 1990.

Appendix

Catalog of American Founding Documents

COMPILED BY DONALD S. LUTZ

A List of Constitution-Like Documents Written by American Colonists Before 1722

Articles, Laws, and Orders, Divine, Politic, and Martial for the Colony in Virginia—1610–1611.

Laws Enacted by the First General Assembly of Virginia—Aug. 2–4, 1619.

Plymouth Combination (also known as the Mayflower Compact, and as the Agreement Between the Settlers at New Plymouth)—Nov. 11, 1620.

Plymouth Oath of Allegiance and Fidelity—1625.

Salem "Civil" Covenant—1629.

Agreement of the Massachusetts Bay Company at Cambridge, England—August 26, 1629.

Watertown Covenant (Massachusetts)—July 30, 1630.

Massachusetts Election Agreement—Oct. 19, 1630.

Massachusetts Agreement on a Legislature—May 9, 1632.

Reprinted from Donald S. Lutz, "From Covenant to Constitution in American Political Thought," *Publius* 10 (Fall 1980), 129–33.

Cambridge Agreement (Massachusetts)—Dec. 24, 1632.

Dorchester Agreement (Massachusetts)—Oct. 8, 1633.

Cambridge Agreement on a Town Council—Feb. 3, 1634.

Cambridge Oath of a Freeman—1634.

Massachusetts Agreement on the Legislature—May 14, 1634.

1st Salem Oath (Massachusetts)—April 1, 1634.

2nd Salem Oath—May 14, 1634.

Watertown Agreement (Massachusetts)—Aug. 23, 1634.

Charlestown Agreement on, and Election of, a Board of Selectmen—
Feb. 10, 1635.

Salem's "Enlarged Covenant"—1636.

Plymouth Agreement (attached to the Pilgrim Code of Law)—Nov. 15, 1636.

Pilgrim Code of Law (also known as the Structure of the Government
of New Plymouth)—Nov. 15, 1636.

Providence Agreement (Rhode Island)—Aug. 20, 1637.

New Haven Plantation Covenant—1638.

Act for Establishing the House of Assembly and the Laws to be Made
Therein (Maryland)—March 12, 1638.

Government of Pocasset (Portsmouth, Rhode Island)—April 7, 1638.

Act for Swearing Allegiance (Maryland)—1638.

An Act What Persons Shall be Called to Every General Assembly and
An Act Concerning the Calling of General Assemblies (Maryland)—
1638.

Act for the Liberties of the People (Maryland)—1638.

Fundamental Orders of Connecticut—Jan. 14, 1639.

Government of Portsmouth (Rhode Island)—April 30, 1639.

Newport Agreement (Rhode Island, also known as Government of Newport)—May 28, 1639.

Guilford Covenant (Connecticut)—June 1, 1939. Structure of Town Governments (Windsor, Hartford, Wethersfield)—Oct. 10, 1639.

Fundamental Articles of New Haven—June 4-14, 1639.

Agreement of Settlers at Exeter (New Hampshire)—Nov. 4, 1639.

Dover Combination (New Hampshire)—1639.

Connecticut Oaths of Fidelity (Hartford)—1640.

Plantation Agreement at Providence (Rhode Island)—Aug. 27, 1640.

Connecticut Oath of Agreement—1640.

Massachusetts Body of Liberties—December, 1641.

The Combination of the Inhabitants Upon the Piscataqua River for
Government (New Hampshire)—Oct. 22, 1641.

Organization of the Government of Rhode Island—March 16-19, 1641.

Laws Regulating Church Government (Virginia)—March, 1642.

Capital Laws of Connecticut—Dec. 1, 1642.

New Haven Fundamentals (also known as Government of New Haven Colony)—Oct. 27, 1643.

New Haven Oaths of Fidelitie—July, 1644.

Massachusetts Bicameral Ordinance—March 7, 1644.

Massachusetts Ordinance on the Legislature—Nov. 14, 1644.

"Charter" of Providence (Rhode Island)—March 14, 1644.

Majority Vote of Deputies and Magistrates Required for the Passage of Laws in Connecticut—Feb. 3, 1644.

Warwick Agreement (Rhode Island)—Aug. 8, 1647.

Acts and Orders of 1647 (Agreement Among Providence, Warwick, Portsmouth, and Newport to form a Common Assembly)—May 19–21, 1647.

Laws and Liberties of Massachusetts—1647.

Massachusetts Ordinance on Legislative Procedure—Oct. 18, 1648.

The Cambridge Platform (Massachusetts)—Aug., 1648.

Maryland Toleration Act—April 21, 1649.

Duties and Privileges of New Plymouth Townships—1649.

Towns of Wells, Gorgiana, and Piscataqua Form an Independent Government (Maine)—July, 1649.

Connecticut Code of Laws—1650.

The Government of Virginia During the Commonwealth Period (A series of acts for governing)—April 30, 1652–March, 1659.

Puritan Laws and Liberties—Sept. 29, 1658.

Charter of Connecticut—April 23–May 25, 1662.

Charter of Rhode Island and Providence Plantations—July 8–18, 1663.

Concessions and Agreement of New Jersey (Nova Caesarea)—1664.

Concessions and Agreement of the Proprietors of Carolina with the Prospective Settlers—1665.

General Assembly of Rhode Island is divided into two houses—March 27, 1666.

A Declaration of the True Intent and Meaning of the Lords Proprietors, and Explanation of Their Concessions Made to the Adventurers and Planters of New Caeserea or New Jersey—1672.

Preface to the General Laws and Liberties of Connecticut Revised and Published by Order of the General Court at Hartford—Oct., 1672.

Charter of Fundamentals of West New Jersey (also known as the Concessions of West New Jersey)—1676.

Freedom of Conscience in West New Jersey—March 3, 1679.

General Laws and Liberties of New Hampshire—March 16, 1679.

Fundamentals of West New Jersey—1681.

Concessions to the Province of Pennsylvania—1681.

Act for Freedom of Conscience in Pennsylvania—Dec. 7, 1682.

Penn's Charter of Liberties—1682.

Frame of Government of Pennsylvania—1682.

Frame of Government of Pennsylvania—1683.

Laws on Personal Freedom (Pennsylvania)—1683.

Fundamental Constitutions for the Province of East New Jersey—Nov. 23, 1683.

The Charter of Liberties and Privileges (New York)—Oct. 30, 1683.

Articles of Agreement Between the Members of the Frankfort Company, for the Settlement of Germantown, Pennsylvania—Nov. 12, 1686.

New York Charter and Privileges of His Majesty's Subjects—1691.

Frame of Government of Pennsylvania—Nov. 7, 1696.

Division of the Connecticut General Assembly into two houses—Oct. 13, 1698.

Charter of Privileges Granted by William Penn to the Inhabitants of Pennsylvania and Territories—Oct. 28, 1701.

Act to Ascertain the Manner and Form of Electing Members to Represent the Inhabitants of this Province (South Carolina) in the Commons House of Assembly—1721.

A List of Constitution-Like Documents Written in England for the Colonists Before 1735

Letters Patent to Sir Humphrey Gilbert—June 11, 1578.

Charter to Sir Walter Raleigh—March 25, 1584.

Charter of Acadia Granted by Henry IV of France to Pierre du Gast; Sieur de Monts—Dec. 18, 1603.

First Charter of Virginia—April 10, 1606.

Instructions for the Governing of Virginia—Nov. 20, 1606.

Instructions from the Virginia Council to Sir Thomas Gates—May, 1609.

Second Charter of Virginia—May 23–June 2, 1609.

Third Charter of Virginia—March 12–22, 1611–12.

The Charter of New England—Nov. 3, 1620.

Ordinance of 1621: Establishment of Representative Government in Virginia (supposedly much the same as the now missing Great Charter of 1618 which called the first Virginia Assembly in 1619).

Constitution for the Council and Assembly in Virginia (also known as Ordinance for Virginia)—July 24, 1621.

Charter, Dutch West India Company—June 3, 1621.

Grant of New Hampshire to Capt. John Mason—Nov. 7, 1629.

Charter of the Colony of New Plymouth Granted to William Bradford and his Associates—Jan. 10, 1629.

The Charter of Massachusetts Bay—March 4, 1629.

The Form of Government for the Colony (Massachusetts Bay)—April 30, 1629.

Dutch Charter of Privileges to Patroons—1629.

The Charter of Maryland—June 20, 1632.

Grant of the Province of New Hampshire to John Wallaston, Esq.—April 11, 1635.

Grant of the Province of New Hampshire from Mr. Wollaston to Mr. Mason—June 11, 1635.

Grant of the Province of New Hampshire to Mr. Mason—April 22, 1635.

Grant of the Province of Maine—April 3–13, 1639.

Commission from Sir Ferdinando Gorges for Governing Maine—March 10, 1639.

Bradford's Surrender of His Patent of Plymouth Colony to the Freemen—March 2, 1640.

Patent for Providence Plantations (Rhode Island)—Nov. 2, 1643.

First Charter of Carolina—March 24–April 3, 1663.

Grant to the Duke of York—March 12–22, 1664.

The Duke of York's Release to John Lord Berkeley and Sir George Carteret—June 24, 1664.

Charter of Carolina—June 30, 1665.

Order for the Submission of the Province of Maine to Massachusetts—May 27, 1668.

The Fundamental Constitutions of Carolina (only partially put into effect)—1669.

Temporary Laws of Carolina—1671–1672.

His Royal Highness's Grant to the Lords Proprietors, Sir George Carteret—July 29, 1674.

Commission of John Cutt—1680.

Proposals for the Future Settlement of the Affairs of Maine—Oct. 15, 1681.

Charter for the Province of Pennsylvania—Feb. 20, 1681.

Commission of Sir Edmund Andros for the Dominion of New England—April 7, 1688.

The Charter of Massachusetts Bay—1691.

Instructions for Colonel Philip Ludwell, Governor of Carolina—Nov. 8, 1691.

Surrender From the Proprietors of East and West New Jersey of their Pretended Right of Government of Her Majesty—April 15, 1702.

Charles II's Grant of New England to the Duke of York 1676—Exemplified by Queen Anne—1712.
Charter of Georgia—1732.

Early State Constitutions

1725 Massachusetts
1776 New Hampshire
1776 South Carolina
1776 Virginia
1776 Maryland
1776 Delaware
1776 Rhode Island Constitution (actually, the 1663 Charter readopted)
1776 Connecticut Constitution (the 1662 Charter readopted)
1776 Pennsylvania
1776 North Carolina
1777 Georgia
1777 New York
1777 Vermont
1778 South Carolina
1780 Massachusetts
1784 New Hampshire
1786 Vermont
1789 Georgia

Index

Adams, Henry, 4
Adams, John, 9, 12, 119, 121, 190, 191, 192–93, 194, 442, 444, 445; death of, 447–48; *Defence of the Constitutions*, 399
—*Thoughts on Government*, 5; text of, 129–37, 167; commentary on, 118–28
Adams, Samuel, 191, 193
Adamson v. *California*, 429
Agreements: defined, 6
Albany Plan of Union, 7, 11–12, 228
—text of, 114–17; commentary on, 106–13
Alien and Sedition Acts, 446
Amendments: to Articles of Confederation, 245–46; to Constitution, 289, 329; and federalism, 268–69
Andros, Edmund, 52–54, 57–58, 59–60, 86
Ann-Hoock, 36
Antifederalists: areas of strength, 292, 294–95, 382–83; and Bill of Rights, 425, 425–26; commentaries on the Constitution, 14–15; and federal principle, 304; oppose James Madison's amendments to Constitution, 427; principles of, 297–98, 382, 383–87

—Essays and Speeches: texts of, 391–422; commentary on, 381–90
Appropriations, 214–15
Arms, Right to Bear, 200, 431
Articles of Confederation, 7, 12, 13, 269, 270, 381, 388, 427; amendment procedure, 229, 232; Article II limits Congress, 436; based on Albany Plan of Union, 112; binding on new states, 263–64; compared with Constitution, 10; and confederacy versus republic, 271; as political compact, 138, 153; defects of, 228–29, 337, 339, 340–41, 346, 356–63, 401, 424; praised, 384, 393; signers of, 227, 247–48
—text of, 235–48; commentary on, 227–34
Assembly, Right of, 200, 430
Atkinson, Theodore, 108
Attainder, Bill of, 283, 349, 374–75

Bail, 71, 80, 156, 263, 435
Barron v. *Mayor and City Council of Baltimore*, 428–29
Bayard, Nicholas, 87, 96
Beccaria, Marquis de, 407, 418
Beekman, William, 85
Berkeley, John Lord, 49–50, 53

Bicameralism, 125, 126, 132–33
Bill of Rights, 14, 15, 143, 144, 389, 427–28
—text of, 430–36; commentary on,
    423–40
Black, Hugo L., 429
Blacks, 4, 189. *See also* Slavery
Blackstone, Sir William, 344
Bland, Richard, 151
Bowdoin, James, 191, 226
Bradford, William, 89
Brockholls, Anthony, 54
Broome, John, 169
"Brutus," 15, 382, 384, 385, 386; quoted,
    388, 389; texts of, 401–10, 411–16
Bryan, Samuel: as "Centinel," 397–401
Burnet, Salisbury Gilbert, 130

"Cæsar" (Alexander Hamilton?), 293,
    296
Calvinism, 51–52, 57
Canada, 233, 245, 252
Carteret, Sir George, 49–50, 53
Catholicism, 51–52, 58–59; first mass in
    America, 84
"Cato" (George Clinton?), 293, 296, 298,
    382
Census, 177, 277–78
"Centinel" (Samuel Bryan), 15, 382, 385,
    386; quoted, 388; text of, 397–401
Charles I, 68n, 70n
Charles II, 37, 48, 51, 53, 57
Charter: defined, 6–7
Checks and Balances, 126; in
    Constitution, 272–76, 330–32, 336,
    388, 393–94; in Albany Plan of
    Union, 113; Constitution lacks, 384,
    395, 399–400
Clinton, George, 292, 344, 369n. *See also*
    "Cato"
Coercive Power: lacking under Articles
    of Confederation, 340–41, 359–62
Commerce, 116, 143–44, 228–29, 264, 281,
    405
Common Law, 4, 28, 143, 144, 184, 187,
    433, 434
Common Sense (Thomas Paine), 124
Concessions and Agreements of
    February 1665 (New Jersey), 50
Confucius, 130

Congress, Confederation, 231; creation
    of, 236–37; powers of, 243–45. *See
    also* Articles of Confederation
Congress, Continental, 118–19;
    appointment of delegates to, 183;
    and Articles of Confederation, 227;
    resolution calling for state
    constitutions, 167; resolution for
    creation of state governments, 120,
    173, 174; weakness of, 340–41. *See
    also* Articles of Confederation
Congress under Constitution: election of,
    162; state representation in, 228;
    creation of, 277–84
Connecticut: government of, 134; federal
    system of, 25; ratifies Constitution,
    382; state constitution of, 150–51;
    terms of office for elected officials in,
    26–28; governor of, 27, 30;
    legislature of, 26–30, 33, 34. *See also*
    Fundamental Orders of Connecticut
Conscientious Objection, 186
Conservatism: and constitutions, 169–70
Constitution, U.S., 12, 13–14, 227, 385;
    amendments to, 303, 426; as
    national compact, 234; based on
    Albany Plan of Union, 112–13;
    compared with Articles of
    Confederation, 10; as political
    compact, 138, 153; origins of, 2;
    influence of New York and
    Massachusetts constitutions, 193;
    Preamble of, 267, 277, 391;
    ratification by nine states required,
    232–33; relationship to Northwest
    Ordinance, 250–51; signers of, 290
—text of, 277–90; commentary on,
    266–67
Constitutional Convention, 292, 424–25
Constitutions: amendment of, 9, 245–46,
    289, 329; benefits of, 136–37; and
    conservatism, 169–70; creation of,
    7–9; defined, 122; ratification, 9;
    signatures on, 19; state, 342–43, 422
Contracts, 263
Coote, Richard, 64
Council of Revision (New York), 175–76,
    365n
Covenants, 19, 144

Cruel and Unusual Punishment, 156, 201, 263, 435
Cutler, Manasseh, 249, 254

Dane, Nathan, 250–51, 254, 255
Debt, Public, 245, 289, 357
Declaration of Independence, 6, 13, 118, 121, 227, 389, 423; as covenant, 144; drafting of, 150; fiftieth anniversary of, 442; as national compact, 234; as political compact, 153; right of revolution, 377n; signers of, 19, 139, 141, 149
—text of, 146–49; commentary on, 138–45
DeLancey, John, 107, 110
Delaware, 292, 382
Delegated Powers: Constitution provides, 436
De Witt, Charles, 169
De Witt, Cornelius, 50–51
De Witt, Jan, 50–51
Dickinson, John, 119, 120
Dinwiddie, Robert, 111
Division of Power, 321, 336
Dominion of New England, 107–8
Dongan, Thomas, 11, 55, 56, 57, 58, 61, 83–86, 91, 92
Dual Officeholding: prohibited, 223–24
Duane, James, 119, 169, 352
Due Process of Law, 199, 263, 432–33. See also Law of the land
Duer, William, 169–70
Duke's Laws, 48, 54, 55

Education, 43, 136, 192, 219–21, 263
Eminent Domain, 198–99, 433
Executive Power: and The Federalist, 341–46, 363–72. See also Governor; President, U.S.
Ex Post Facto Laws, 201, 283, 349, 375
Extradition, 236, 288

"The Federal Farmer," 382
Federalism, 271, 334; in Articles of Confederation, 230, 233–34; and constitutionalism, 169; defined, 381–82; elements of, 267–69; and The Federalist, 291–334; first instituted in America, 24, 25; and New York Constitution, 166; traditions

embodied in Constitution, 168; versus nationalism, 326–29
The Federalist, 9, 14–15, 15, 231, 382, 386, 387–89; and energetic government, 335–80; and executive power, 341–46, 363–72; and judicial review, 346–52; and judiciary, 372–80
—text of, 305–34, 355–63, 355–80, 363–72, 372–80; commentary on, 291–304, 335–54
Federalists, 292, 298–99, 425, 427. See also Antifederalists; The Federalist
Fines, 201, 263, 435
Fourteenth Amendment, 428–29
Frankfurter, Felix, 429
Franklin, Benjamin, 190, 228, 399, 443, 447–48; and Albany Plan of Union, 108–9, 112, 113; in Constitutional Convention, 342
Fugitive Slave Clause, 288
Full Faith and Credit, 236, 288
Fundamental Orders of Connecticut, 7, 11, 19, 21, 38, 152
—text of, 29–35; commentary on, 24–28

Gallaway, Joseph, 112
Georgia, 167, 228, 382
Gitlow v. New York, 429
Gladstone, William E., 1
God: as the great creator and preserver of the universe, 196; as Great Governor of the World, 246; as Great Legislator of the Universe, 193, 195; as party to agreement among individuals, 6, 18, 19, 22, 40, 42, 43, 45, 145, 146, 149; importance of worship, 197
Governor, 171; creation of, 27, 66–67, 77, 125, 133–34, 161, 180, 211–12; election of, 30; state, 151; strong, 169; term of office, 181; territorial, 260, powers of, 260–61
Great Britain, 393; commercial policy toward U.S., 229; Constitution praised, 399–400; Declaration of Rights, 58; Glorious Revolution, 47, 108; insurrections and civil wars in, 422; judiciary of, 411–12, 414; limitations on standing army, 408; Magna Carta, 434; monarchy of, 369–70, 391

Habeas Corpus, 225, 263, 282
Half Way Covenant, 38–40
Hamilton, Alexander, 348–52, 388, 443;
    as possible author of "Cæsar," 293;
    in Constitutional Convention, 343
—as author of *The Federalist*, 15, 293–94,
    295–96, 336–37, 338, 340–41, 341–46;
    quoted, 3–4, 339, 341–42, 342, 346;
    texts of, 305–9, 355–63, 363–72,
    372–80
Hancock, John, 344
Happiness, 423; as end of government,
    154–55, 195, 196, 198, 377, 401–2; way
    to achieve, 384
Harrington, John, 130
Harvey, Thomas, 84
Henry, Patrick, 15, 151, 377n, 383, 384,
    386, 387–88
—texts of speeches to Virginia ratifying
    convention, 391–94, 394–96
Hoadley, Benjamin, 130
Hobart, John Sloss, 169
Holland, 391, 393
Hooper, William, 123
Hopkins, Stephen, 108
Human Nature, 5
Hume, David, 233
Hutchinson, Anne, 38
Hutchinson, Thomas, 108, 109

Impeachment, 163–64, 184, 208, 209, 273,
    278, 279, 286, 326, 348, 350, 373n, 413
Indians, 106–13, 115, 158, 165, 186, 231, 277,
    281; and Confederation Congress,
    242; excluded from political
    participation, 4, 189; and Northwest
    Ordinance, 261, 263; incited by King
    George, 148
Iroquois Confederacy, 231

Jackson, James, 428
James II, 37, 48, 51, 52, 54, 57, 58, 59, 83–
    85, 89, 91, 107–8
Jay, John, 119, 120, 169, 170; and *The
    Federalist*, 293–94, 336–37, 339–40
Jefferson, Thomas, 121, 132n, 138–39, 144,
    150, 249, 253, 254–55; death of, 447–
    48; letter from, 15–16
—text of letter to Mayor Weightman,
    444–45; commentary on, 441–48

Johnson, William, 112
Judicial Review, 272, 337, 375–77, 389,
    414; and *The Federalist*, 346–52
Judiciary, 182–83; appointment of, 152,
    372; creation of, 70–71, 79–80, 103,
    125, 135, 162–63, 184, 203–4, 260, 286;
    criticism of Constitution's provisions
    regarding, 404–5, 411–15; declared
    weakest branch of federal
    government, 349; and *The Federalist*,
    372–80; independence of, 135, 147,
    202, 351, 377–80, 389, 412, 413;
    jurisdiction of, 218; powers of, 286–
    87; term of office, 373, 377–80; under
    Articles of Confederation, 230, 240–
    42; weakness of, 373–74
"Junius," 370
Jury Trials, 69, 70, 79–80, 144, 147, 156,
    158, 172, 187, 199, 200, 263, 287, 397,
    433–34, 434–35; endangered by
    Constitution, 391, 392, 398; safe
    under Constitution, 348

Kennedy, Archibald, 108
Kent, James, 83, 87, 89

Lafayette, Marquis de, 447
Land: inheritance of, 259–60; regulations
    regarding, 43, 46, 72, 79, 93–94, 102,
    115–16, 185–86, 249–65. *See also*
    Eminent domain
Lansing, John, Jr., 343
Law of the Land, 69, 79, 384. *See also*
    Due process of law
Lee, Henry, 138
Lee, Richard Henry, 123
Legislative Privilege, 210, 238
Legislature: creation of, 26–27, 29–30,
    66–68, 77–78, 92–93, 114, 131–32,
    159–60, 175, 202–3, 256, 277–84;
    dominant in republican form of
    government, 345; powers of, 26–28,
    34, 281–82; representation in, 33, 67,
    77–78, 114–15, 176–77, 179, 205, 208–
    9, 416–21, 421–22; supremacy of, 151;
    term of office, 159–60, 179, 261–62.
    See also Congress
Leisler, Jacob, 47, 57–58, 59–60, 60–64,
    108

Liberty: endangered by Constitution, 392, 398; importance of to Puritans, 18
Limited Government, 267–68, 336
Lincoln, Abraham, 445
Livingston, Robert R., 169–70
Locke, John, 21, 28, 130, 141–42
Ludlow, Roger, 37–38

McCulloch v. *Maryland*, 436
McKean, Thomas, 141
Madison, James, 15, 151, 168; and amendments to Constitution, 426–28; argues for large republican government, 299–303; and federal principle, 304; and Virginia Plan, 342; at Virginia ratifying convention, 383
—as author of *The Federalist*, 10, 231, 233–34, 293–94, 298–99, 336–37, 339–40, 381–82; texts of, 309–16, 317–23, 324–29, 330–34; quoted, 345
Mahomet, 130
Majority Tyranny, 270, 275, 313, 333
Manvielle, Gabriel, 85
Marbury v. *Madison*, 347
Marshall, John, 347, 428–29, 436
Martin, Luther, 377n
Mary II, 58, 77
Maryland, 48, 227, 383
Mason, George, 151, 383
Massachusetts, 430; governor of, 211–12; judiciary of, 203–4, 218; legislature of, 202–3; ratifies Constitution, 232, 382, 426; and Shays's Rebellion, 422
—Constitution of 1780, 127, 150, 152, 193, 266, 276, 343; text of, 195–226; commentary on, 188–94
Mayflower Compact, 6, 11, 24, 152, 227
—text of, 22–23; commentary on, 17–21
Mecklenburg Resolutions, 139
Milborne, Jacob, 63
Military, 71–72, 80, 116, 135, 136, 157, 162, 186–87, 201, 212–14, 238–39, 282, 404, 405; subordinate to civil, 143; under Articles of Confederation, 228, 243–44
Milton, John, 130, 137
Mississippi River, 264, 357
Monarchy, 343, 395

Money Bills, 280
Monroe, James, 255
Montesquieu, Charles, Baron de, 272, 298, 374n, 406–7
Morris, Gouverneur, 169, 170

Nationalism versus Federalism, 326–29
Necessary and Proper Clause, 384, 388; attacked, 402–3, 405, 425
Nedham, Marchamont, 130
Neville, Henry, 130
New England Confederation, 11, 38, 107–8
New Hampshire, 150, 167, 343, 383
New Jersey, 167, 365, 382
New Jersey Plan, 343
Newton, Isaac, 274
New York: governor of, 66–67, 77, 180; judiciary of, 70–71, 79–80, 184; legislature of, 66–68, 77–78, 175; ratifies Constitution, 232, 292, 383, 383, 426; speeches in ratifying convention, 416–22; Antifederalists in, 382–83
—Charter of Liberties, 7, 11; text of, 66–82; commentary on, 47–65
—Constitution of 1777, 193, 276, 343, 351, 365, 430; Council of Appointment, 369–71; Council of Revision, 175–76, 365n; significance of, 171–72; text of, 173–87; commentary on, 166–72
New York City: judiciary of, 103; legislature, 92–93; mayor of, 95–96
—City Charter: text of, 91–105; commentary on, 83–90
Nicholson, Francis, 58, 59
Nicolls, Matthias, 55
Nicolls, Richard, 48–49, 85
North Carolina, 383, 426
Northwest Ordinance, 12, 13, 112; defects of, 257–58; First Federal Congress reenacts, 250, 252; relationship to Constitution, 250–51
—text of, 259–65; commentary on, 249–58
Northwest Territory, 144, 357
Noyes, John Humphrey, 40, 41

Oaths, 30, 35, 81, 221–23, 262, 285, 289; used as political weapons, 4
Ohio Company of New England, 251, 254

Ordinance of 1784, 249, 254, 255
Ordinance of 1785, 251, 252, 255

Paine, Thomas, 125; *Common Sense,* 124
Paper Money, 378n–79n, 404
Pardoning Power, 161, 181, 213, 285
Parsons, Theophilus, 190
Pell, Thomas, 36–37
Pendleton, Edmund, 151
Penn, John, 123
Penn, William, 53, 53–55
Pennsylvania: Antifederalists in, 377n;
    ratifies Constitution, 232, 382;
    Constitution of 1776, 151, 170, 343,
    397, 400
Peters, Richard, 109
Petition, Right of, 200, 430, 431
Pilgrims and Puritans, 18
Pitkin, William, 108
Plowman, Matthew, 60
Pope, Alexander, 5, 124–25, 129
Preamble, U.S., 267, 277, 391
President, U.S.: accused of having too
    much power, 396; creation of, 114,
    284; election of, 344; debate over
    plural, 345, 363–72; powers of, 285–
    86, 337, 344; term of office, 284, 344
Press, Freedom of, 156, 200, 397, 430,
    430–31; endangered by
    Constitution, 391, 392, 398
Privileges and Immunities, 229–30, 236,
    288
Privy Council, 161–62, 346, 365n
Property Rights, 156. *See also* Eminent
    domain; Land
Puritans, 17, 18, 40, 50

Quakers, 53–55
Quartering Soldiers, 71, 80, 143, 147, 158,
    201, 431–32

Randolph, Edmund, 151, 342, 383
Religion, 51–52, 57; and Puritans, 17–18;
    and Ten Farms Covenant, 39–40,
    43, 44, 45; and Declaration of
    Independence, 141–42; freedom of,
    73–74, 81–82, 84, 157, 172, 186, 196–
    97, 197, 263, 430; endangered by
    Constitution, 391. *See also* God
Religious Tests, 81, 289

Representation, 28, 159–60, 270; criticism
    of Constitution's provisions
    regarding, 416–21, 421–22;
    proportional, 112, 277–78
Republican Form of Government, 8, 125,
    402–10; benefits of, 332–34; can exist
    in large territory, 231–33, 269–71,
    299–303; cannot exist in large
    territory, 298, 339–40, 388, 393;
    constitutional theory of, 168, 170;
    defined, 324–25; described, 400; and
    direct election by the people, 270;
    Constitution guarantees to states,
    288; legislature dominates in, 345;
    limited, 4; praised, 131, 400; popular
    consent to, 4; representation in, 8
Revolution, Right of, 146, 198, 377, 377n
Rhode Island: colonial government of, 25;
    paper money policies of, 378n–79n,
    422; hostility to Constitution, 232,
    383; ratifies Constitution, 383, 426;
    state constitution of, 150, 167
Rights: retained by people, 435;
    unalienable, 146, 154, 196, 389, 423
Roe v. *Wade,* 435
Rotation in Office, 134–35, 198, 228;
    praised in Pennsylvania, 400; under
    Articles of Confederation, 237;
    Virginia governor, 161
Rudyard, Thomas, 55–56
Rumbold, Richard, 446
Rush, Benjamin, 12, 126
Rutgers v. *Waddington,* 351–52, 378n–79n
Rutledge, John, 347

Sargeant, Jonathan Dickinson, 123
Scott, John Morin, 169, 170
Search and Seizure, 199, 397, 432
Separate Confederacies, 339–40
Separation of Powers, 155, 159, 202, 271–
    72, 330–32, 373; in Massachusetts
    Constitution, 192; necessity of,
    132–33
Shakespeare, William, 445
Shays's Rebellion, 422, 424
Sherman, Roger, 428
Shirley, William, 111
Sidney, Algernon, 130, 142
Slavery, 446; fugitive clause, 265, 288;
    prohibited in Northwest Ordinance,

254, 256, 265; three-fifths clause, 277; trade, 144, 158, 282, 289. *See also* Blacks

Sloughter, Henry, 63

Smith, Melancton, 15, 385, 386, 388–89
—texts of speeches to New York ratifying convention, 416–21, 421–22

Smith, William, 108, 169

Social Compact, 146, 191, 195, 255–56

Socrates, 130

South Carolina, 150, 167, 383

Sovereignty, 28; popular, 154, 174, 197–98, 267, 336, 350, 376, 401, 414; of states, 228, 235, 391, 424

Spain, 229, 357

Speech, Freedom of, 201, 397, 430, 430–31

Standing Army, 143, 157, 158, 200, 408–9

State Constitutions: attempts to make, 2–3; drafting and adoption of, 12–13; have weak governors in, 342–43, 423–24; have strong legislatures, 423–24. *See also* Massachusetts; New York; Virginia

States: admission of new, 249, 264–65, 270, 288; fear that Constitution will abolish governments of, 414–15; Constitution will remove power from, 405–6; limitation of powers, 283–84; linked by federalism, 271; retention of powers, 436; and U.S. Bill of Rights, 428–29

Stuyvesant, Peter, 48, 51, 84, 85

Suffrage, 67, 77, 155, 161, 171, 177–78, 189, 190, 205–7, 209, 261

Supremacy Clause, 28, 289, 303, 388; of Articles of Confederation, 245–46; criticism of Constitution's, 403, 405, 425

Taney, Roger B., 250, 257

Tasker, Benjamin, 108

Taxation, 35, 136, 143; by consent, 84, 147, 155–56, 158; Articles of Confederation's provisions criticized, 228; Constitution's provisions criticized, 394–95, 403–4, 405, 416; money bills originate in House, 210; power of, 26–28, 34, 69–70, 79, 116, 201, 204, 238, 239–40, 264, 281

Ten Farms Covenant, 2, 6, 11
—text of, 43–46; commentary on, 36–42

Titles of Nobility: prohibited, 198, 238, 283

Townsend, Samuel, 169

Treason, 201, 287–88, 413

Treaties, 238, 240, 244, 285, 359–60; flaws in Articles of Confederation regarding, 228–29

Trumbull, John, 443

Unicameralism, 231

Veto Power, 125, 133, 152, 171, 175–76, 192, 203, 274, 280–81, 344

Vice President, U.S., 273, 279, 284

Virginia: Antifederalists in, 382–83; governor of, 161; judiciary of, 162–63; land cessions to Congress, 251, 252; legislature of, 159–60; ratifies Constitution, 232, 383, 426; ratifies U.S. Bill of Rights, 428; and religious toleration, 430
—Speeches in ratifying convention, 391–96
—Declaration of Rights, 139, 423; text of, 154–57; commentary on, 150–53
—Constitution of 1776, 121, 167, 276; text of, 157–65; commentary on, 150–53

Virginia Plan, 342, 343

Voltaire, 447–48

War, Declaration of, 240, 244, 281

Warren, James, 123

Washington, George, 167, 340–41, 399, 424, 443; and amendments to Constitution, 426; and French and Indian War, 106; letter from, 353; sends amendments to states, 428

Weightman, Roger D.
—letter to from Jefferson, 15–16; text of, 444–45; commentary on, 441–43

Western Lands: policy under Confederation, 251–53. *See also* Northwest Ordinance

Whigs, 168; philosophy of government, 170

Willet, Thomas, 85

William of Orange, 51, 52, 54, 58, 59, 60, 63, 77

Wilson, James, 15, 342, 382
Wilson, Woodrow, 1
Winthrop, Fitz-John, 63
Wisconsin Organic Act, 256
Wisner, Henry, 169
Women: did not sign Mayflower
    Compact, 20; rights of, 72, 73, 80–81

Wythe, George, 121, 123, 150, 443

Yates, Abraham, Jr., 169
Yates, Robert, 169, 343

Zoroaster, 130

Contributors

RICHARD B. BERNSTEIN served as research director of the New York State Commission on the Bicentennial of the United States Constitution from 1989 to 1990. His books and articles on American constitutional history include: *Are We to Be a Nation?* (with Kym S. Rice, 1987); *Well Begun: Chronicles of the Early National Period* (co-edited, with Stephen L. Schechter, 1989); and *Contexts of the Bill of Rights* (co-edited with Stephen L. Schechter, 1990). He is completing *"Conven'd in Firm Debate": The First Congress as an Institution of Government, 1789–1791.*

THOMAS E. BURKE was research director of the New York State Commission on the Bicentennial of the United States Constitution from 1986 to 1989. He has also worked for the Colonial Albany Social History Project at the New York State Museum, and written on colonial Albany. He has contributed to *Contexts of the Bill of Rights* (1990) and *New York and the Union* (1990).

LEO HERSHKOWITZ is Professor of History at Queens College of the City University of New York. His works on New York's political and legal history include *Courts and Law in Early New York* (co-edited, with Milton M. Klein, 1978); and contributions to *American Journal of Legal History, New York History*, and *World of the Founders: New York Communities in the Federal Period* (1990).

JOHN P. KAMINSKI, director of the Center for the Study of the American Constitution at the University of Wisconsin-Madison, is co-editor of *The Documentary History of the Ratification of the Constitution and the Bill of Rights*. His books and articles on the making of the Constitution and the early national period include: *The Constitution and the States* (co-edited, with Patrick T. Conley, 1988); *A Great and Good Man* (co-edited, with Jill Adair McCaughan, 1989); *George Clinton: Yeoman Politician of the New Republic* (1990); Madison House's *Constitutional Heritage Series*; and contributions to *The Reluctant Pillar* (1985), *Ratifying the Constitution* (1989), *Contexts of the Bill of Rights* (1990), and *New York and the Union* (1990).

RALPH KETCHAM is Professor of History, Political Science, and Public Affairs in the Maxwell School of Syracuse University. He is the editor of *The Antifederalist Papers and the Constitutional Debates* (1986). He also has written *Presidents Above Party: The First American Presidency,*

1789–1829 (1984) and the biographies *Ben Franklin* (1965) and *James Madison* (1971; reprinted 1990), nominated in 1972 for a National Book Award.

DONALD S. LUTZ, Professor of Political Science at the University of Houston, has written or edited several books on American political thought, including *Popular Consent and Popular Control* (1980); *American Political Writings during the Founding Era, 1760–1805* (co-edited, with Charles S. Hyneman, 1983); *Documents of Political Foundation Written by Colonial Americans* (1986); *The Origins of American Constitutionalism* (1988); and contributions to *Ratifying the Constitution* (1989) and *Contexts of the Bill of Rights* (1990).

JOHN M. MURRIN is Professor of History at Princeton University. He has written an essay on the New York Charter of Liberties in *Authority and Resistance in Early New York* (1988). His other books and articles on colonial America include *Colonial America: Essays in Politics and Social Development*, 3rd edition (co-edited with Stanley N. Katz, 1983); *Saints and Revolutionaries: Essays in Early American History* (co-edited with David D. Hall and Thad W. Tate, 1984); and contributions to *Three British Revolutions: 1641, 1688, and 1776* (1980) and *Colonial British America: Essays in the New History of the Early Modern Era* (1984).

PETER S. ONUF is Thomas Jefferson Professor of History at The University of Virginia. He has written *The Origins of the Federal Republic* (1983); *Statehood and Union* (1987); *The Midwest and the Nation* (with Andrew R. L. Cayton, 1989); *A Union of Interests* (with Cathy D. Matson, 1990); as well as many articles and essays in scholarly journals and books.

STEPHEN L. SCHECHTER served as director of the New York State Commission on the Bicentennial of the United States Constitution from 1986 to 1990. He is currently Professor of Political Science and director of the Council for Citizenship Education at Russell Sage College. He has edited or co-edited several books on the making of the Constitution and the early national period, among them *The Reluctant Pillar* (1985); *Well Begun: Chronicles of the Early National Period* (co-edited, with Richard B. Bernstein, 1989); *Contexts of the Bill of Rights* (co-edited, with Richard B. Bernstein, 1990); *New York and the Union* (co-edited, with Richard B. Bernstein, 1990); and *World of the Founders: New York Communities in the Federal Period* (co-edited, with Wendell Tripp, 1990).